Europa-Institut of Saarland University (ed.)

European Law
Selected Documents

Third revised and extended Edition

Europa-Institut of Saarland University
Selected legal documents

Edited by
Europa-Institut of Saarland University
Law Department

Volume II

EUROPEAN LAW
SELECTED DOCUMENTS

Third revised and extended Edition

EUROPA-INSTITUT OF SAARLAND UNIVERSITY (ED.)

Verlag Alma Mater, Saarbrücken

Die Deutsche Bibliothek verzeichnet diese Veröffentlichung in der
Deutschen Nationalbibliographie. Die bibliographischen Daten
im Detail finden Sie im Internet unter http://dnb.ddb.de

© Verlag Alma Mater. 2015
www.verlag-alma-mater.de

Druck: Faber, Mandelbachtal
ISBN 978-3-935009-91-1
EAN 9783935009911

Preface

The Europa-Institut, as the editor, is the second eldest institution of its kind in Europe. More than 5.000 students from all over the world have been educated in the fields of European and International Law at the Europa-Institut since its foundation in 1951. Each year students from over 30 countries come to the one-year postgraduate master's program "European and International Law" to study the legal, political, economic and cultural foundations of the European Union. The program is characterized by five special study units – European Integration, European Economic Law, Foreign Trade and Investment, International Dispute Resolution and European Protection of Human Rights. It provides students with great freedom of choice regarding the courses they wish to attend and offers a high degree of specialization. The program can be completed entirely in English, entirely in German or in a combination of these and results in the award of the title Master of Laws (LL.M.) to its successful participants.

We decided to assemble our own collection series compiling key documents for each respective field of our LL.M. program after recognizing that existing collections do not comply with the specific requirements necessary for the successful performance of our students. In attempting to fill the gap we have published five volumes so far – "International Dispute Resolution" as volume I, "European Law" as volume II, "International Trade Law" as volume III, "Public International Law" as volume IV and "International Human Rights Law" as volume V.

The first two editions of this collection of European Law were compiled with three main considerations in mind: Firstly, to publish an up-to-date selection of the primary legislation as the supreme source of law of the European Union (EU) based on the newest consolidated versions of the Treaties and Protocols published in October 2012. Secondly, to include recent important developments related to the financial crisis in the form of the Treaty establishing the European Stability Mechanism as well as the Treaty on Stability, Coordination and Governance in the Economic and Monetary Union. Thirdly, to include the Charter of Fundamental Rights of the European Union, the official explanations relating to the Charter of Fundamental Rights of the EU as well as the Convention for the Protection of Human Rights and Fundamental Freedoms (ECHR) with Protocols as the decisive documents on the protection of human rights in Europe. In addition the second edition comprised the European Council Decision concerning the number of Members of the European Commission, the European Council Decision establishing the composition of the European Parliament as well as tables of equivalences.

This updated third edition includes now several new documents, e.g. the Act concerning the Elections of the Members of the European Parliament by Direct Universal Suffrage, the Framework Agreement on Relations between the European Parliament and the European Commission, Regulation (EU) No 182/2011 laying down the Rules and General Principles concerning Mechanisms for Control by Member States of the Commission's Exercise of Implementing Powers and Regulation (EU) No 211/2011 on the Citizens' Initiative. Moreover, it publishes updated versions of the TEU and TFEU, as amended in the course of the Croatian accession. We therefore decided to delete the Treaty and Act of Accession of Croatia. In consequence of the Opinion 2/13 of the Court of Justice of 18 December 2014, we also eliminated the draft revised agreement on the accession of the EU to the ECHR.

This new edition comprises a comprehensive yet handy collection of relevant European Law documents from both the EU and the Council of Europe. It is addressed not only to the students in our LL.M. program but to universities in general, practitioners, policy makers and European lawyers.

We thank Akad. Dir. Julia Legleitner LL.M. (program director), Ass. iur. Anja Trautmann LL.M. (managing editor), and Uwe Loebens (art editor) who have made this book possible by designing the layout, formatting and proofreading the texts. Thanks must also go to the Alumni Association of the Europa-Institut's Law Section (EVER e.V.) for its financial support.

Finally, all documents are presented in their official version. Most of the materials have been taken from the online EUR-Lex website. According to Article 1(2) of the Council Regulation (EU) No 216/2013 only the Official Journal published in electronic form shall be authentic and shall produce legal effects. Furthermore, we acknowledge with thanks the permission granted by the Council of Europe to reproduce their materials.

We hope that this selection of documents will prove a useful roadmap through the system of European Law for the students in our LL.M. program and beyond.

Professor Dr. Marc Bungenberg LL.M. (Lausanne)
Professor Dr. Thomas Giegerich LL.M. (University of Virginia)
Saarbrücken, August 2015

Contents

I	**Treaty on European Union**	11
II	**Treaty on the Functioning of the European Union**	41
III	**Protocols**	

Protocol (No 1) on the Role of national Parliaments in the European Union — 173

Protocol (No 2) on the Application of the Principles of Subsidiarity and Proportionality — 176

Protocol (No 3) on the Statute of the Court of Justice of the European Union — 179

Protocol (No 4) on the Statute of the European System of Central Banks and of the European Central Bank — 199

Protocol (No 5) on the Statute of the European Investment Bank — 217

Protocol (No 6) on the Location of the Seats of the Institutions and of certain Bodies, Offices, Agencies and Departments of the European Union — 229

Protocol (No 7) on the Privileges and Immunities of the European Union — 230

Protocol (No 8) relating to Article 6(2) of the Treaty on European Union on the Accession of the Union to the European Convention on the Protection of Human Rights and Fundamental Freedoms — 236

Protocol (No 9) on the Decision of the Council relating to the Implementation of Article 16(4) of the Treaty on European Union and Article 238(2) of the Treaty on the Functioning of the European Union between 1 November 2014 and 31 March 2017 on the one hand, and as from 1 April 2017 on the other — 237

Protocol (No 10) on Permanent Structured Cooperation established by Article 42 of the Treaty on European Union — 238

Protocol (No 11) on Article 42 of the Treaty on European Union — 241

Protocol (No 12) on the Excessive Deficit Procedure — 242

Protocol (No 13) on the Convergence Criteria — 243

Protocol (No 14) on the Euro Group — 245

Protocol (No 15) on certain Provisions relating to the United Kingdom of Great Britain and Northern Ireland — 246

Protocol (No 16) on certain Provisions relating to Denmark — 248

Protocol (No 17) on Denmark — 249

	Protocol (No 18) on France	250
	Protocol (No 19) on the Schengen Acquis integrated into the Framework of the European Union	251
	Protocol (No 20) on the Application of certain Aspects of Article 26 of the Treaty on the Functioning of the European Union to the United Kingdom and to Ireland	254
	Protocol (No 21) on the Position of the United Kingdom and Ireland in respect of the Area of Freedom, Security and Justice	256
	Protocol (No 22) on the Position of Denmark	259
	Protocol (No 23) on External Relations of the Member States with regard to the Crossing of External Borders	265
	Protocol (No 24) on Asylum for Nationals of Member States of the European Union	266
	Protocol (No 25) on the Exercise of Shared Competence	268
	Protocol (No 26) on Services of General Interest	269
	Protocol (No 27) on the Internal Market and Competition	270
	Protocol (No 28) on Economic, Social and Territorial Cohesion	271
	Protocol (No 29) on the System of Public Broadcasting in the Member States	273
	Protocol (No 30) on the Application of the Charter of Fundamental Rights of the European Union to Poland and to the United Kingdom	274
	Protocol (No 31) concerning Imports into the European Union of Petroleum Products refined in the Netherlands Antilles	276
	Protocol (No 32) on the Acquisition of Property in Denmark	279
	Protocol (No 33) concerning Article 157 of the Treaty on the Functioning of the European Union	280
	Protocol (No 34) on Special Arrangements for Greenland	281
	Protocol (No 35) on Article 40.3.3 of the Constitution of Ireland	282
	Protocol (No 36) on Transitional Provisions	283
	Protocol (No 37) on the Financial Consequences of the Expiry of the ECSC Treaty and on the Research Fund for Coal and Steel	289
IV	**Declarations**	291
V	**Tables of Equivalences**	
	Treaty on European Union	311
	Treaty on the Functioning of the European Union	317
VI	**Protocol on the concerns of the Irish people on the Treaty of Lisbon**	339
VII	**Rules of Procedure of the Court of Justice**	343
VIII	**Charter of Fundamental Rights of the European Union**	403
	Explanations relating to the Charter of Fundamental Rights	414
IX	**Convention for the Protection of Human Rights and Fundamental Freedoms**	437
	Protocol to the Convention for the Protection of Human Rights and Fundamental Freedoms	452

	Protocol No. 4 to the Convention for the Protection of Human Rights and Fundamental Freedoms securing certain rights and freedoms other than those already included in the Convention and in the First Protocol thereto	454
	Protocol No. 6 to the Convention for the Protection of Human Rights and Fundamental Freedoms concerning the Abolition of the Death Penalty	457
	Protocol No. 7 to the Convention for the Protection of Human Rights and Fundamental Freedoms	460
	Protocol No. 12 to the Convention for the Protection of Human Rights and Fundamental Freedoms	464
	Protocol No. 13 to the Convention for the Protection of Human Rights and Fundamental Freedoms concerning the Abolition of the Death Penalty in all circumstances	467
	Protocol No. 15 amending the Convention for the Protection of Human Rights and Fundamental Freedoms	470
	Protocol No. 16 to the Convention for the Protection of Human Rights and Fundamental Freedoms	473
X	**Act concerning the Elections of the Members of the European Parliament by Direct Universal Suffrage**	477
XI	**Council Decision of 13 December 2007 relating to the Implementation of Article 9c(4) of the Treaty on European Union and Article 205(2) of the Treaty on the Functioning of the European Union between 1 November 2014 and 31 March 2017 on the one hand, and as from 1 April 2017 on the other (2009/857/EC)**	483
XII	**Framework Agreement on Relations between the European Parliament and the European Commission**	487
	Council Statement – Framework Agreement on Relations between the European Parliament and the Commission	510
XIII	**European Council Decision of 22 May 2013 concerning the Number of Members of the European Commission (2013/272/EU)**	511
XIV	**European Council Decision of 28 June 2013 establishing the Composition of the European Parliament (2013/312/EU)**	513
XV	**Regulation (EU) No 182/2011 of the European Parliament and of the Council of 16 February 2011 laying down the Rules and General Principles concerning Mechanisms for Control by Member States of the Commission's Exercise of Implementing Powers**	517
XVI	**Regulation (EU) No 211/2011 of the European Parliament and of the Council of 16 February 2011 on the Citizens' Initiative**	529
XVII	**Treaty establishing the European Stability Mechanism**	545
XVIII	**Treaty on Stability, Coordination and Governance in the Economic and Monetary Union**	569

Treaty on European Union

Source   consolidated Version OJ C 326 of 26 October 2012, p. 13
last amended by the Act concerning the conditions of accession of the Republic of Croatia and the adjustments to the Treaty on European Union, the Treaty on the Functioning of the European Union and the Treaty establishing the European Atomic Energy Community, OJ L 112 of 24 April 2012, p. 21

Preamble

His Majesty the King of Belgians, her Majesty the Queen of Denmark, the President of the Federal Republic of Germany, the President of Ireland, the President of the Hellenic Republic, his Majesty the King of Spain, the President of the Frensh Republic, the President of the Italian Republic, his Royal Highness the Grand Duke of Luxembourg, her Majesty the Queen of the Netherlands, the President of the Portuguese Republic, her Majesty the Queen of the United Kingdom of Great Britain and Northern Ireland[1],

Resolved to mark a new stage in the process of European integration undertaken with the establishment of the European Communities,

Drawing inspiration from the cultural, religious and humanist inheritance of Europe, from which have developed the universal values of the inviolable and inalienable rights of the human person, freedom, democracy, equality and the rule of law,

Recalling the historic importance of the ending of the division of the European continent and the need to create firm bases for the construction of the future Europe,

---

1   The Republic of Bulgaria, the Czech Republic, the Republic of Estonia, the Republic of Cyprus, the Republic of Latvia, the Republic of Lithuania, the Republic of Hungary, the Republic of Malta, the Republic of Austria, the Republic of Poland, Romania, the Republic of Slovenia, the Slovak Republic, the Republic of Finland and the Kingdom of Sweden have since become members of the European Union.

©   European Union, http://eur-lex.europa.eu/, 1998-2015.

Confirming their attachment to the principles of liberty, democracy and respect for human rights and fundamental freedoms and of the rule of law,

Confirming their attachment to fundamental social rights as defined in the European Social Charter signed at Turin on 18 October 1961 and in the 1989 Community Charter of the Fundamental Social Rights of Workers,

Desiring to deepen the solidarity between their peoples while respecting their history, their culture and their traditions,

Desiring to enhance further the democratic and efficient functioning of the institutions so as to enable them better to carry out, within a single institutional framework, the tasks entrusted to them,

Resolved to achieve the strengthening and the convergence of their economies and to establish an economic and monetary union including, in accordance with the provisions of this Treaty and of the Treaty on the Functioning of the European Union, a single and stable currency,

Determined to promote economic and social progress for their peoples, taking into account the principle of sustainable development and within the context of the accomplishment of the internal market and of reinforced cohesion and environmental protection, and to implement policies ensuring that advances in economic integration are accompanied by parallel progress in other fields,

Resolved to establish a citizenship common to nationals of their countries,

Resolved to implement a common foreign and security policy including the progressive framing of a common defence policy, which might lead to a common defence in accordance with the provisions of Article 42, thereby reinforcing the European identity and its independence in order to promote peace, security and progress in Europe and in the world,

Resolved to facilitate the free movement of persons, while ensuring the safety and security of their peoples, by establishing an area of freedom, security and justice, in accordance with the provisions of this Treaty and of the Treaty on the Functioning of the European Union,

Resolved to continue the process of creating an ever closer union among the peoples of Europe, in which decisions are taken as closely as possible to the citizen in accordance with the principle of subsidiarity,

In view of further steps to be taken in order to advance European integration,

Have decided to establish a European Union and to this end have designated as their Plenipotentiaries:

[List of plenipotentiaries not reproduced]

Who, having exchanged their full powers, found in good and due form, have agreed as follows:

Title I
Common Provisions

Article 1 (ex Article 1 TEU)[2]
By this Treaty, the HIGH CONTRACTING PARTIES establish among themselves a EUROPEAN UNION, hereinafter called 'the Union', on which the Member States confer competences to attain objectives they have in common.
This Treaty marks a new stage in the process of creating an ever closer union among the peoples of Europe, in which decisions are taken as openly as possible and as closely as possible to the citizen.
The Union shall be founded on the present Treaty and on the Treaty on the Functioning of the European Union (hereinafter referred to as 'the Treaties'). Those two Treaties shall have the same legal value. The Union shall replace and succeed the European Community.

Article 2
The Union is founded on the values of respect for human dignity, freedom, democracy, equality, the rule of law and respect for human rights, including the rights of persons belonging to minorities. These values are common to the Member States in a society in which pluralism, non-discrimination, tolerance, justice, solidarity and equality between women and men prevail.

Article 3 (ex Article 2 TEU)
1. The Union's aim is to promote peace, its values and the well-being of its peoples.
2. The Union shall offer its citizens an area of freedom, security and justice without internal frontiers, in which the free movement of persons is ensured in conjunction with appropriate measures with respect to external border controls, asylum, immigration and the prevention and combating of crime.
3. The Union shall establish an internal market. It shall work for the sustainable development of Europe based on balanced economic growth and price stability, a highly competitive social market economy, aiming at full employment and social progress, and a high level of protection and improvement of the quality of the environment. It shall promote scientific and technological advance.
It shall combat social exclusion and discrimination, and shall promote social justice and protection, equality between women and men, solidarity between generations and protection of the rights of the child.
It shall promote economic, social and territorial cohesion, and solidarity among Member States.

---

2 These references are merely indicative. For more ample information, please refer to the tables of equivalences between the old and the new numbering of the Treaties.

It shall respect its rich cultural and linguistic diversity, and shall ensure that Europe's cultural heritage is safeguarded and enhanced.

4. The Union shall establish an economic and monetary union whose currency is the euro.

5. In its relations with the wider world, the Union shall uphold and promote its values and interests and contribute to the protection of its citizens. It shall contribute to peace, security, the sustainable development of the Earth, solidarity and mutual respect among peoples, free and fair trade, eradication of poverty and the protection of human rights, in particular the rights of the child, as well as to the strict observance and the development of international law, including respect for the principles of the United Nations Charter.

6. The Union shall pursue its objectives by appropriate means commensurate with the competences which are conferred upon it in the Treaties.

Article 4

1. In accordance with Article 5, competences not conferred upon the Union in the Treaties remain with the Member States.

2. The Union shall respect the equality of Member States before the Treaties as well as their national identities, inherent in their fundamental structures, political and constitutional, inclusive of regional and local self-government. It shall respect their essential State functions, including ensuring the territorial integrity of the State, maintaining law and order and safeguarding national security. In particular, national security remains the sole responsibility of each Member State.

3. Pursuant to the principle of sincere cooperation, the Union and the Member States shall, in full mutual respect, assist each other in carrying out tasks which flow from the Treaties.

The Member States shall take any appropriate measure, general or particular, to ensure fulfilment of the obligations arising out of the Treaties or resulting from the acts of the institutions of the Union.

The Member States shall facilitate the achievement of the Union's tasks and refrain from any measure which could jeopardise the attainment of the Union's objectives.

Article 5 (ex Article 5 TEC)

1. The limits of Union competences are governed by the principle of conferral. The use of Union competences is governed by the principles of subsidiarity and proportionality.

2. Under the principle of conferral, the Union shall act only within the limits of the competences conferred upon it by the Member States in the Treaties to attain the objectives set out therein. Competences not conferred upon the Union in the Treaties remain with the Member States.

3. Under the principle of subsidiarity, in areas which do not fall within its exclusive competence, the Union shall act only if and in so far as the objectives of the proposed action cannot be sufficiently achieved by the Member States, either at central level or at regional and local level, but can rather, by reason of the scale or effects of the proposed action, be better achieved at Union level.

The institutions of the Union shall apply the principle of subsidiarity as laid down in the Protocol on the application of the principles of subsidiarity and proportionality. National Parliaments ensure compliance with the principle of subsidiarity in accordance with the procedure set out in that Protocol.

4. Under the principle of proportionality, the content and form of Union action shall not exceed what is necessary to achieve the objectives of the Treaties.

The institutions of the Union shall apply the principle of proportionality as laid down in the Protocol on the application of the principles of subsidiarity and proportionality.

Article 6 (ex Article 6 TEU)

1. The Union recognises the rights, freedoms and principles set out in the Charter of Fundamental Rights of the European Union of 7 December 2000, as adapted at Strasbourg, on 12 December 2007, which shall have the same legal value as the Treaties.

The provisions of the Charter shall not extend in any way the competences of the Union as defined in the Treaties.

The rights, freedoms and principles in the Charter shall be interpreted in accordance with the general provisions in Title VII of the Charter governing its interpretation and application and with due regard to the explanations referred to in the Charter, that set out the sources of those provisions.

2. The Union shall accede to the European Convention for the Protection of Human Rights and Fundamental Freedoms. Such accession shall not affect the Union's competences as defined in the Treaties.

3. Fundamental rights, as guaranteed by the European Convention for the Protection of Human Rights and Fundamental Freedoms and as they result from the constitutional traditions common to the Member States, shall constitute general principles of the Union's law.

Article 7 (ex Article 7 TEU)

1. On a reasoned proposal by one third of the Member States, by the European Parliament or by the European Commission, the Council, acting by a majority of four fifths of its members after obtaining the consent of the European Parliament, may determine that there is a clear risk of a serious breach by a Member State of the values referred to in Article 2. Before making such a determination, the Council shall hear the Member State in question and may address recommendations to it, acting in accordance with the same procedure.

The Council shall regularly verify that the grounds on which such a determination was made continue to apply.

2. The European Council, acting by unanimity on a proposal by one third of the Member States or by the Commission and after obtaining the consent of the European Parliament, may determine the existence of a serious and persistent breach by a Member State of the values referred to in Article 2, after inviting the Member State in question to submit its observations.

3. Where a determination under paragraph 2 has been made, the Council, acting by a qualified majority, may decide to suspend certain of the rights deriving from the application of the Treaties to the Member State in question, including the voting rights of the representative of the government of that Member State in the Council. In doing so, the Council shall take into account the possible consequences of such a suspension on the rights and obligations of natural and legal persons.

The obligations of the Member State in question under the Treaties shall in any case continue to be binding on that State.

4. The Council, acting by a qualified majority, may decide subsequently to vary or revoke measures taken under paragraph 3 in response to changes in the situation which led to their being imposed.

5. The voting arrangements applying to the European Parliament, the European Council and the Council for the purposes of this Article are laid down in Article 354 of the Treaty on the Functioning of the European Union.

Article 8

1. The Union shall develop a special relationship with neighbouring countries, aiming to establish an area of prosperity and good neighbourliness, founded on the values of the Union and characterised by close and peaceful relations based on cooperation.

2. For the purposes of paragraph 1, the Union may conclude specific agreements with the countries concerned. These agreements may contain reciprocal rights and obligations as well as the possibility of undertaking activities jointly. Their implementation shall be the subject of periodic consultation.

Title II
Provisions on Democratic Principles

Article 9

In all its activities, the Union shall observe the principle of the equality of its citizens, who shall receive equal attention from its institutions, bodies, offices and agencies. Every national of a Member State shall be a citizen of the Union. Citizenship of the Union shall be additional to and not replace national citizenship.

Article 10

1. The functioning of the Union shall be founded on representative democracy.

2. Citizens are directly represented at Union level in the European Parliament.

Member States are represented in the European Council by their Heads of State or Government and in the Council by their governments, themselves democratically accountable either to their national Parliaments, or to their citizens.

3. Every citizen shall have the right to participate in the democratic life of the Union. Decisions shall be taken as openly and as closely as possible to the citizen.

4. Political parties at European level contribute to forming European political awareness and to expressing the will of citizens of the Union.

Article 11

1. The institutions shall, by appropriate means, give citizens and representative associations the opportunity to make known and publicly exchange their views in all areas of Union action.

2. The institutions shall maintain an open, transparent and regular dialogue with representative associations and civil society.

3. The European Commission shall carry out broad consultations with parties concerned in order to ensure that the Union's actions are coherent and transparent.

4. Not less than one million citizens who are nationals of a significant number of Member States may take the initiative of inviting the European Commission, within the framework of its powers, to submit any appropriate proposal on matters where citizens consider that a legal act of the Union is required for the purpose of implementing the Treaties.

The procedures and conditions required for such a citizens' initiative shall be determined in accordance with the first paragraph of Article 24 of the Treaty on the Functioning of the European Union.

Article 12

National Parliaments contribute actively to the good functioning of the Union:

(a) through being informed by the institutions of the Union and having draft legislative acts of the Union forwarded to them in accordance with the Protocol on the role of national Parliaments in the European Union;

(b) by seeing to it that the principle of subsidiarity is respected in accordance with the procedures provided for in the Protocol on the application of the principles of subsidiarity and proportionality;

(c) by taking part, within the framework of the area of freedom, security and justice, in the evaluation mechanisms for the implementation of the Union policies in that area, in accordance with Article 70 of the Treaty on the Functioning of the European Union, and through being involved in the political monitoring of Europol and the evaluation of Eurojust's activities in accordance with Articles 88 and 85 of that Treaty;

(d) by taking part in the revision procedures of the Treaties, in accordance with Article 48 of this Treaty;

(e) by being notified of applications for accession to the Union, in accordance with Article 49 of this Treaty;

(f) by taking part in the inter-parliamentary cooperation between national Parliaments and with the European Parliament, in accordance with the Protocol on the role of national Parliaments in the European Union.

Title III
Provisions on the Institutions

Article 13
1. The Union shall have an institutional framework which shall aim to promote its values, advance its objectives, serve its interests, those of its citizens and those of the Member States, and ensure the consistency, effectiveness and continuity of its policies and actions.
The Union's institutions shall be:
- the European Parliament,
- the European Council,
- the Council,
- the European Commission (hereinafter referred to as 'the Commission'),
- the Court of Justice of the European Union,
- the European Central Bank,
- the Court of Auditors.

2. Each institution shall act within the limits of the powers conferred on it in the Treaties, and in conformity with the procedures, conditions and objectives set out in them. The institutions shall practice mutual sincere cooperation.
3. The provisions relating to the European Central Bank and the Court of Auditors and detailed provisions on the other institutions are set out in the Treaty on the Functioning of the European Union.
4. The European Parliament, the Council and the Commission shall be assisted by an Economic and Social Committee and a Committee of the Regions acting in an advisory capacity.

Article 14
1. The European Parliament shall, jointly with the Council, exercise legislative and budgetary functions. It shall exercise functions of political control and consultation as laid down in the Treaties. It shall elect the President of the Commission.
2. The European Parliament shall be composed of representatives of the Union's citizens. They shall not exceed seven hundred and fifty in number, plus the President. Representation of citizens shall be degressively proportional, with a minimum threshold of six members per Member State. No Member State shall be allocated more than ninety-six seats.
The European Council shall adopt by unanimity, on the initiative of the European Parliament and with its consent, a decision establishing the composition of the European Parliament, respecting the principles referred to in the first subparagraph.
3. The members of the European Parliament shall be elected for a term of five years by direct universal suffrage in a free and secret ballot.
4. The European Parliament shall elect its President and its officers from among its members.

Article 15

1. The European Council shall provide the Union with the necessary impetus for its development and shall define the general political directions and priorities thereof. It shall not exercise legislative functions.

2. The European Council shall consist of the Heads of State or Government of the Member States, together with its President and the President of the Commission. The High Representative of the Union for Foreign Affairs and Security Policy shall take part in its work.

3. The European Council shall meet twice every six months, convened by its President. When the agenda so requires, the members of the European Council may decide each to be assisted by a minister and, in the case of the President of the Commission, by a member of the Commission. When the situation so requires, the President shall convene a special meeting of the European Council.

4. Except where the Treaties provide otherwise, decisions of the European Council shall be taken by consensus.

5. The European Council shall elect its President, by a qualified majority, for a term of two and a half years, renewable once. In the event of an impediment or serious misconduct, the European Council can end the President's term of office in accordance with the same procedure.

6. The President of the European Council:
   (a) shall chair it and drive forward its work;
   (b) shall ensure the preparation and continuity of the work of the European Council in cooperation with the President of the Commission, and on the basis of the work of the General Affairs Council;
   (c) shall endeavour to facilitate cohesion and consensus within the European Council;
   (d) shall present a report to the European Parliament after each of the meetings of the European Council.

The President of the European Council shall, at his level and in that capacity, ensure the external representation of the Union on issues concerning its common foreign and security policy, without prejudice to the powers of the High Representative of the Union for Foreign Affairs and Security Policy.

The President of the European Council shall not hold a national office.

Article 16

1. The Council shall, jointly with the European Parliament, exercise legislative and budgetary functions. It shall carry out policy-making and coordinating functions as laid down in the Treaties.

2. The Council shall consist of a representative of each Member State at ministerial level, who may commit the government of the Member State in question and cast its vote.

3. The Council shall act by a qualified majority except where the Treaties provide otherwise.

4. As from 1 November 2014, a qualified majority shall be defined as at least 55 % of the members of the Council, comprising at least fifteen of them and representing Member States comprising at least 65 % of the population of the Union.

A blocking minority must include at least four Council members, failing which the qualified majority shall be deemed attained.

The other arrangements governing the qualified majority are laid down in Article 238(2) of the Treaty on the Functioning of the European Union.

5. The transitional provisions relating to the definition of the qualified majority which shall be applicable until 31 October 2014 and those which shall be applicable from 1 November 2014 to 31 March 2017 are laid down in the Protocol on transitional provisions.

6. The Council shall meet in different configurations, the list of which shall be adopted in accordance with Article 236 of the Treaty on the Functioning of the European Union.

The General Affairs Council shall ensure consistency in the work of the different Council configurations. It shall prepare and ensure the follow-up to meetings of the European Council, in liaison with the President of the European Council and the Commission.

The Foreign Affairs Council shall elaborate the Union's external action on the basis of strategic guidelines laid down by the European Council and ensure that the Union's action is consistent.

7. A Committee of Permanent Representatives of the Governments of the Member States shall be responsible for preparing the work of the Council.

8. The Council shall meet in public when it deliberates and votes on a draft legislative act. To this end, each Council meeting shall be divided into two parts, dealing respectively with deliberations on Union legislative acts and non-legislative activities.

9. The Presidency of Council configurations, other than that of Foreign Affairs, shall be held by Member State representatives in the Council on the basis of equal rotation, in accordance with the conditions established in accordance with Article 236 of the Treaty on the Functioning of the European Union.

Article 17

1. The Commission shall promote the general interest of the Union and take appropriate initiatives to that end. It shall ensure the application of the Treaties, and of measures adopted by the institutions pursuant to them. It shall oversee the application of Union law under the control of the Court of Justice of the European Union. It shall execute the budget and manage programmes. It shall exercise coordinating, executive and management functions, as laid down in the Treaties. With the exception of the common foreign and security policy, and other cases provided for in the Treaties, it shall ensure the Union's external representation. It shall initiate the Union's annual and multiannual programming with a view to achieving interinstitutional agreements.

2. Union legislative acts may only be adopted on the basis of a Commission proposal, except where the Treaties provide otherwise. Other acts shall be adopted on the basis of a Commission proposal where the Treaties so provide.

3. The Commission's term of office shall be five years.

The members of the Commission shall be chosen on the ground of their general competence and European commitment from persons whose independence is beyond doubt.

In carrying out its responsibilities, the Commission shall be completely independent. Without prejudice to Article 18(2), the members of the Commission shall neither seek nor take instructions from any Government or other institution, body, office or entity. They shall refrain from any action incompatible with their duties or the performance of their tasks.

4. The Commission appointed between the date of entry into force of the Treaty of Lisbon and 31 October 2014, shall consist of one national of each Member State, including its President and the High Representative of the Union for Foreign Affairs and Security Policy who shall be one of its Vice-Presidents.

5. As from 1 November 2014, the Commission shall consist of a number of members, including its President and the High Representative of the Union for Foreign Affairs and Security Policy, corresponding to two thirds of the number of Member States, unless the European Council, acting unanimously, decides to alter this number.

The members of the Commission shall be chosen from among the nationals of the Member States on the basis of a system of strictly equal rotation between the Member States, reflecting the demographic and geographical range of all the Member States. This system shall be established unanimously by the European Council in accordance with Article 244 of the Treaty on the Functioning of the European Union.

6. The President of the Commission shall:
   (a) lay down guidelines within which the Commission is to work;
   (b) decide on the internal organisation of the Commission, ensuring that it acts consistently, efficiently and as a collegiate body;
   (c) appoint Vice-Presidents, other than the High Representative of the Union for Foreign Affairs and Security Policy, from among the members of the Commission.

A member of the Commission shall resign if the President so requests. The High Representative of the Union for Foreign Affairs and Security Policy shall resign, in accordance with the procedure set out in Article 18(1), if the President so requests.

7. Taking into account the elections to the European Parliament and after having held the appropriate consultations, the European Council, acting by a qualified majority, shall propose to the European Parliament a candidate for President of the Commission. This candidate shall be elected by the European Parliament by a majority of its component members. If he does not obtain the required majority, the European Council, acting by a qualified majority, shall within one month propose a new candidate who shall be elected by the European Parliament following the same procedure.

The Council, by common accord with the President-elect, shall adopt the list of the other persons whom it proposes for appointment as members of the Commission. They shall be selected, on the basis of the suggestions made by Member States, in accordance with the criteria set out in paragraph 3, second subparagraph, and paragraph 5, second subparagraph.

The President, the High Representative of the Union for Foreign Affairs and Security Policy and the other members of the Commission shall be subject as a body to a vote of consent by the European Parliament. On the basis of this consent the Commission shall be appointed by the European Council, acting by a qualified majority.

8. The Commission, as a body, shall be responsible to the European Parliament. In accordance with Article 234 of the Treaty on the Functioning of the European Union, the European Parliament may vote on a motion of censure of the Commission. If such a motion is carried, the members of the Commission shall resign as a body and the High Representative of the Union for Foreign Affairs and Security Policy shall resign from the duties that he carries out in the Commission.

Article 18

1. The European Council, acting by a qualified majority, with the agreement of the President of the Commission, shall appoint the High Representative of the Union for Foreign Affairs and Security Policy. The European Council may end his term of office by the same procedure.
2. The High Representative shall conduct the Union's common foreign and security policy. He shall contribute by his proposals to the development of that policy, which he shall carry out as mandated by the Council. The same shall apply to the common security and defence policy.
3. The High Representative shall preside over the Foreign Affairs Council.
4. The High Representative shall be one of the Vice-Presidents of the Commission. He shall ensure the consistency of the Union's external action. He shall be responsible within the Commission for responsibilities incumbent on it in external relations and for coordinating other aspects of the Union's external action. In exercising these responsibilities within the Commission, and only for these responsibilities, the High Representative shall be bound by Commission procedures to the extent that this is consistent with paragraphs 2 and 3.

Article 19

1. The Court of Justice of the European Union shall include the Court of Justice, the General Court and specialised courts. It shall ensure that in the interpretation and application of the Treaties the law is observed.
Member States shall provide remedies sufficient to ensure effective legal protection in the fields covered by Union law.
2. The Court of Justice shall consist of one judge from each Member State. It shall be assisted by Advocates-General.
The General Court shall include at least one judge per Member State.
The Judges and the Advocates-General of the Court of Justice and the Judges of the General Court shall be chosen from persons whose independence is beyond doubt and who satisfy the conditions set out in Articles 253 and 254 of the Treaty on the Functioning of the European Union. They shall be appointed by common accord of the governments of the Member States for six years. Retiring Judges and Advocates-General may be reappointed.

3. The Court of Justice of the European Union shall, in accordance with the Treaties:
(a) rule on actions brought by a Member State, an institution or a natural or legal person;
(b) give preliminary rulings, at the request of courts or tribunals of the Member States, on the interpretation of Union law or the validity of acts adopted by the institutions;
(c) rule in other cases provided for in the Treaties.

Title IV
Provisions on Enhanced Cooperation

Article 20
(ex Articles 27a to 27e, 40 to 40b and 43 to 45 TEU and ex Articles 11 and 11a TEC)

1. Member States which wish to establish enhanced cooperation between themselves within the framework of the Union's non-exclusive competences may make use of its institutions and exercise those competences by applying the relevant provisions of the Treaties, subject to the limits and in accordance with the detailed arrangements laid down in this Article and in Articles 326 to 334 of the Treaty on the Functioning of the European Union.

Enhanced cooperation shall aim to further the objectives of the Union, protect its interests and reinforce its integration process. Such cooperation shall be open at any time to all Member States, in accordance with Article 328 of the Treaty on the Functioning of the European Union.

2. The decision authorising enhanced cooperation shall be adopted by the Council as a last resort, when it has established that the objectives of such cooperation cannot be attained within a reasonable period by the Union as a whole, and provided that at least nine Member States participate in it. The Council shall act in accordance with the procedure laid down in Article 329 of the Treaty on the Functioning of the European Union.

3. All members of the Council may participate in its deliberations, but only members of the Council representing the Member States participating in enhanced cooperation shall take part in the vote. The voting rules are set out in Article 330 of the Treaty on the Functioning of the European Union.

4. Acts adopted in the framework of enhanced cooperation shall bind only participating Member States. They shall not be regarded as part of the acquis which has to be accepted by candidate States for accession to the Union.

Title V
General Provisions on the Union's External Action and Specific Provisions on the Common Foreign and Security Policy

Chapter 1
General Provisions on the Union's External Action

Article 21
1. The Union's action on the international scene shall be guided by the principles which have inspired its own creation, development and enlargement, and which it seeks to advance in the wider world: democracy, the rule of law, the universality and indivisibility of human rights and fundamental freedoms, respect for human dignity, the principles of equality and solidarity, and respect for the principles of the United Nations Charter and international law. The Union shall seek to develop relations and build partnerships with third countries, and international, regional or global organisations which share the principles referred to in the first subparagraph. It shall promote multilateral solutions to common problems, in particular in the framework of the United Nations.
2. The Union shall define and pursue common policies and actions, and shall work for a high degree of cooperation in all fields of international relations, in order to:
    (a) safeguard its values, fundamental interests, security, independence and integrity;
    (b) consolidate and support democracy, the rule of law, human rights and the principles of international law;
    (c) preserve peace, prevent conflicts and strengthen international security, in accordance with the purposes and principles of the United Nations Charter, with the principles of the Helsinki Final Act and with the aims of the Charter of Paris, including those relating to external borders;
    (d) foster the sustainable economic, social and environmental development of developing countries, with the primary aim of eradicating poverty;
    (e) encourage the integration of all countries into the world economy, including through the progressive abolition of restrictions on international trade;
    (f) help develop international measures to preserve and improve the quality of the environment and the sustainable management of global natural resources, in order to ensure sustainable development;
    (g) assist populations, countries and regions confronting natural or man-made disasters; and
    (h) promote an international system based on stronger multilateral cooperation and good global governance.
3. The Union shall respect the principles and pursue the objectives set out in paragraphs 1 and 2 in the development and implementation of the different areas of the Union's external action covered by this Title and by Part Five of the Treaty on the Functioning of the European Union, and of the external aspects of its other policies.

The Union shall ensure consistency between the different areas of its external action and between these and its other policies. The Council and the Commission, assisted by the High Representative of the Union for Foreign Affairs and Security Policy, shall ensure that consistency and shall cooperate to that effect.

Article 22

1. On the basis of the principles and objectives set out in Article 21, the European Council shall identify the strategic interests and objectives of the Union.

Decisions of the European Council on the strategic interests and objectives of the Union shall relate to the common foreign and security policy and to other areas of the external action of the Union. Such decisions may concern the relations of the Union with a specific country or region or may be thematic in approach. They shall define their duration, and the means to be made available by the Union and the Member States.

The European Council shall act unanimously on a recommendation from the Council, adopted by the latter under the arrangements laid down for each area. Decisions of the European Council shall be implemented in accordance with the procedures provided for in the Treaties.

2. The High Representative of the Union for Foreign Affairs and Security Policy, for the area of common foreign and security policy, and the Commission, for other areas of external action, may submit joint proposals to the Council.

Chapter 2
Specific Provisions on the Common Foreign and Security Policy

Section 1
Common Provisions

Article 23

The Union's action on the international scene, pursuant to this Chapter, shall be guided by the principles, shall pursue the objectives of, and be conducted in accordance with, the general provisions laid down in Chapter 1.

Article 24 (ex Article 11 TEU)

1. The Union's competence in matters of common foreign and security policy shall cover all areas of foreign policy and all questions relating to the Union's security, including the progressive framing of a common defence policy that might lead to a common defence.

The common foreign and security policy is subject to specific rules and procedures. It shall be defined and implemented by the European Council and the Council acting unanimously, except where the Treaties provide otherwise. The adoption of legislative acts shall be excluded. The common foreign and security policy shall be put into effect by the High Representative of the Union for Foreign Affairs and Security Policy and by Member States, in accordance with the Treaties. The specific role of the European Parliament and of the Commission in this area is defined by the Treaties. The Court of Justice of the European Union shall not have jurisdiction with respect to these provisions, with the exception of its jurisdiction to monitor compliance with Article 40 of this Treaty and to review the legality of certain decisions as provided for by the second paragraph of Article 275 of the Treaty on the Functioning of the European Union.

2. Within the framework of the principles and objectives of its external action, the Union shall conduct, define and implement a common foreign and security policy, based on the development of mutual political solidarity among Member States, the identification of questions of general interest and the achievement of an ever-increasing degree of convergence of Member States' actions.

3. The Member States shall support the Union's external and security policy actively and unreservedly in a spirit of loyalty and mutual solidarity and shall comply with the Union's action in this area.

The Member States shall work together to enhance and develop their mutual political solidarity. They shall refrain from any action which is contrary to the interests of the Union or likely to impair its effectiveness as a cohesive force in international relations.

The Council and the High Representative shall ensure compliance with these principles.

Article 25 (ex Article 12 TEU)

The Union shall conduct the common foreign and security policy by:

(a) defining the general guidelines;

(b) adopting decisions defining:

   (i) actions to be undertaken by the Union;

   (ii) positions to be taken by the Union;

   (iii) arrangements for the implementation of the decisions referred to in points (i) and (ii); and by

(c) strengthening systematic cooperation between Member States in the conduct of policy.

Article 26 (ex Article 13 TEU)

1. The European Council shall identify the Union's strategic interests, determine the objectives of and define general guidelines for the common foreign and security policy, including for matters with defence implications. It shall adopt the necessary decisions.

If international developments so require, the President of the European Council shall convene an extraordinary meeting of the European Council in order to define the strategic lines of the Union's policy in the face of such developments.

2. The Council shall frame the common foreign and security policy and take the decisions necessary for defining and implementing it on the basis of the general guidelines and strategic lines defined by the European Council.

The Council and the High Representative of the Union for Foreign Affairs and Security Policy shall ensure the unity, consistency and effectiveness of action by the Union.

3. The common foreign and security policy shall be put into effect by the High Representative and by the Member States, using national and Union resources.

Article 27

1. The High Representative of the Union for Foreign Affairs and Security Policy, who shall chair the Foreign Affairs Council, shall contribute through his proposals to the development of the common foreign and security policy and shall ensure implementation of the decisions adopted by the European Council and the Council.
2. The High Representative shall represent the Union for matters relating to the common foreign and security policy. He shall conduct political dialogue with third parties on the Union's behalf and shall express the Union's position in international organisations and at international conferences.
3. In fulfilling his mandate, the High Representative shall be assisted by a European External Action Service. This service shall work in cooperation with the diplomatic services of the Member States and shall comprise officials from relevant departments of the General Secretariat of the Council and of the Commission as well as staff seconded from national diplomatic services of the Member States. The organisation and functioning of the European External Action Service shall be established by a decision of the Council. The Council shall act on a proposal from the High Representative after consulting the European Parliament and after obtaining the consent of the Commission.

Article 28 (ex Article 14 TEU)

1. Where the international situation requires operational action by the Union, the Council shall adopt the necessary decisions. They shall lay down their objectives, scope, the means to be made available to the Union, if necessary their duration, and the conditions for their implementation.
    If there is a change in circumstances having a substantial effect on a question subject to such a decision, the Council shall review the principles and objectives of that decision and take the necessary decisions.
2. Decisions referred to in paragraph 1 shall commit the Member States in the positions they adopt and in the conduct of their activity.
3. Whenever there is any plan to adopt a national position or take national action pursuant to a decision as referred to in paragraph 1, information shall be provided by the Member State concerned in time to allow, if necessary, for prior consultations within the Council. The obligation to provide prior information shall not apply to measures which are merely a national transposition of Council decisions.
4. In cases of imperative need arising from changes in the situation and failing a review of the Council decision as referred to in paragraph 1, Member States may take the necessary measures as a matter of urgency having regard to the general objectives of that decision. The Member State concerned shall inform the Council immediately of any such measures.
5. Should there be any major difficulties in implementing a decision as referred to in this Article, a Member State shall refer them to the Council which shall discuss them and seek

appropriate solutions. Such solutions shall not run counter to the objectives of the decision referred to in paragraph 1 or impair its effectiveness.

Article 29 (ex Article 15 TEU)
The Council shall adopt decisions which shall define the approach of the Union to a particular matter of a geographical or thematic nature. Member States shall ensure that their national policies conform to the Union positions.

Article 30 (ex Article 22 TEU)
1. Any Member State, the High Representative of the Union for Foreign Affairs and Security Policy, or the High Representative with the Commission's support, may refer any question relating to the common foreign and security policy to the Council and may submit to it, respectively, initiatives or proposals.
2. In cases requiring a rapid decision, the High Representative, of his own motion, or at the request of a Member State, shall convene an extraordinary Council meeting within 48 hours or, in an emergency, within a shorter period.

Article 31 (ex Article 23 TEU)
1. Decisions under this Chapter shall be taken by the European Council and the Council acting unanimously, except where this Chapter provides otherwise. The adoption of legislative acts shall be excluded.
When abstaining in a vote, any member of the Council may qualify its abstention by making a formal declaration under the present subparagraph. In that case, it shall not be obliged to apply the decision, but shall accept that the decision commits the Union. In a spirit of mutual solidarity, the Member State concerned shall refrain from any action likely to conflict with or impede Union action based on that decision and the other Member States shall respect its position. If the members of the Council qualifying their abstention in this way represent at least one third of the Member States comprising at least one third of the population of the Union, the decision shall not be adopted.
2. By derogation from the provisions of paragraph 1, the Council shall act by qualified majority:
   – when adopting a decision defining a Union action or position on the basis of a decision of the European Council relating to the Union's strategic interests and objectives, as referred to in Article 22(1),
   – when adopting a decision defining a Union action or position, on a proposal which the High Representative of the Union for Foreign Affairs and Security Policy has presented following a specific request from the European Council, made on its own initiative or that of the High Representative,
   – when adopting any decision implementing a decision defining a Union action or position,
   – when appointing a special representative in accordance with Article 33.

If a member of the Council declares that, for vital and stated reasons of national policy, it intends to oppose the adoption of a decision to be taken by qualified majority, a vote shall not be taken. The High Representative will, in close consultation with the Member State involved, search for a solution acceptable to it. If he does not succeed, the Council may, acting by a qualified majority, request that the matter be referred to the European Council for a decision by unanimity.

3. The European Council may unanimously adopt a decision stipulating that the Council shall act by a qualified majority in cases other than those referred to in paragraph 2.

4. Paragraphs 2 and 3 shall not apply to decisions having military or defence implications.

5. For procedural questions, the Council shall act by a majority of its members.

Article 32 (ex Article 16 TEU)

Member States shall consult one another within the European Council and the Council on any matter of foreign and security policy of general interest in order to determine a common approach. Before undertaking any action on the international scene or entering into any commitment which could affect the Union's interests, each Member State shall consult the others within the European Council or the Council. Member States shall ensure, through the convergence of their actions, that the Union is able to assert its interests and values on the international scene. Member States shall show mutual solidarity.

When the European Council or the Council has defined a common approach of the Union within the meaning of the first paragraph, the High Representative of the Union for Foreign Affairs and Security Policy and the Ministers for Foreign Affairs of the Member States shall coordinate their activities within the Council.

The diplomatic missions of the Member States and the Union delegations in third countries and at international organisations shall cooperate and shall contribute to formulating and implementing the common approach.

Article 33 (ex Article 18 TEU)

The Council may, on a proposal from the High Representative of the Union for Foreign Affairs and Security Policy, appoint a special representative with a mandate in relation to particular policy issues. The special representative shall carry out his mandate under the authority of the High Representative.

Article 34 (ex Article 19 TEU)

1. Member States shall coordinate their action in international organisations and at international conferences. They shall uphold the Union's positions in such forums. The High Representative of the Union for Foreign Affairs and Security Policy shall organise this coordination.

In international organisations and at international conferences where not all the Member States participate, those which do take part shall uphold the Union's positions.

2. In accordance with Article 24(3), Member States represented in international organisations or international conferences where not all the Member States participate shall keep

the other Member States and the High Representative informed of any matter of common interest.

Member States which are also members of the United Nations Security Council will concert and keep the other Member States and the High Representative fully informed. Member States which are members of the Security Council will, in the execution of their functions, defend the positions and the interests of the Union, without prejudice to their responsibilities under the provisions of the United Nations Charter.

When the Union has defined a position on a subject which is on the United Nations Security Council agenda, those Member States which sit on the Security Council shall request that the High Representative be invited to present the Union's position.

Article 35 (ex Article 20 TEU)

The diplomatic and consular missions of the Member States and the Union delegations in third countries and international conferences, and their representations to international organisations, shall cooperate in ensuring that decisions defining Union positions and actions adopted pursuant to this Chapter are complied with and implemented.

They shall step up cooperation by exchanging information and carrying out joint assessments.

They shall contribute to the implementation of the right of citizens of the Union to protection in the territory of third countries as referred to in Article 20(2)(c) of the Treaty on the Functioning of the European Union and of the measures adopted pursuant to Article 23 of that Treaty.

Article 36 (ex Article 21 TEU)

The High Representative of the Union for Foreign Affairs and Security Policy shall regularly consult the European Parliament on the main aspects and the basic choices of the common foreign and security policy and the common security and defence policy and inform it of how those policies evolve. He shall ensure that the views of the European Parliament are duly taken into consideration. Special representatives may be involved in briefing the European Parliament.

The European Parliament may address questions or make recommendations to the Council or the High Representative. Twice a year it shall hold a debate on progress in implementing the common foreign and security policy, including the common security and defence policy.

Article 37 (ex Article 24 TEU)

The Union may conclude agreements with one or more States or international organisations in areas covered by this Chapter.

Article 38 (ex Article 25 TEU)

Without prejudice to Article 240 of the Treaty on the Functioning of the European Union, a Political and Security Committee shall monitor the international situation in the areas covered by the common foreign and security policy and contribute to the definition of policies by delivering opinions to the Council at the request of the Council or of the High Representative of the Union for Foreign Affairs and Security Policy or on its own initiative. It shall also monitor the implementation of agreed policies, without prejudice to the powers of the High Representative.

Within the scope of this Chapter, the Political and Security Committee shall exercise, under the responsibility of the Council and of the High Representative, the political control and strategic direction of the crisis management operations referred to in Article 43.

The Council may authorise the Committee, for the purpose and for the duration of a crisis management operation, as determined by the Council, to take the relevant decisions concerning the political control and strategic direction of the operation.

Article 39

In accordance with Article 16 of the Treaty on the Functioning of the European Union and by way of derogation from paragraph 2 thereof, the Council shall adopt a decision laying down the rules relating to the protection of individuals with regard to the processing of personal data by the Member States when carrying out activities which fall within the scope of this Chapter, and the rules relating to the free movement of such data. Compliance with these rules shall be subject to the control of independent authorities.

Article 40 (ex Article 47 TEU)

The implementation of the common foreign and security policy shall not affect the application of the procedures and the extent of the powers of the institutions laid down by the Treaties for the exercise of the Union competences referred to in Articles 3 to 6 of the Treaty on the Functioning of the European Union.

Similarly, the implementation of the policies listed in those Articles shall not affect the application of the procedures and the extent of the powers of the institutions laid down by the Treaties for the exercise of the Union competences under this Chapter.

Article 41 (ex Article 28 TEU)

1. Administrative expenditure to which the implementation of this Chapter gives rise for the institutions shall be charged to the Union budget.

2. Operating expenditure to which the implementation of this Chapter gives rise shall also be charged to the Union budget, except for such expenditure arising from operations having military or defence implications and cases where the Council acting unanimously decides otherwise.

In cases where expenditure is not charged to the Union budget, it shall be charged to the Member States in accordance with the gross national product scale, unless the Council acting unanimously decides otherwise. As for expenditure arising from operations having military or defence implications, Member States whose representatives in the Council have made a formal declaration under Article 31(1), second subparagraph, shall not be obliged to contribute to the financing thereof.

3. The Council shall adopt a decision establishing the specific procedures for guaranteeing rapid access to appropriations in the Union budget for urgent financing of initiatives in the framework of the common foreign and security policy, and in particular for preparatory activities for the tasks referred to in Article 42(1) and Article 43. It shall act after consulting the European Parliament.

Preparatory activities for the tasks referred to in Article 42(1) and Article 43 which are not charged to the Union budget shall be financed by a start-up fund made up of Member States' contributions.

The Council shall adopt by a qualified majority, on a proposal from the High Representative of the Union for Foreign Affairs and Security Policy, decisions establishing:

    (a) the procedures for setting up and financing the start-up fund, in particular the amounts allocated to the fund;

    (b) the procedures for administering the start-up fund;

    (c) the financial control procedures.

When the task planned in accordance with Article 42(1) and Article 43 cannot be charged to the Union budget, the Council shall authorise the High Representative to use the fund. The High Representative shall report to the Council on the implementation of this remit.

Section 2
Provisions on the Common Security and Defence Policy

Article 42 (ex Article 17 TEU)

1. The common security and defence policy shall be an integral part of the common foreign and security policy. It shall provide the Union with an operational capacity drawing on civilian and military assets. The Union may use them on missions outside the Union for peace-keeping, conflict prevention and strengthening international security in accordance with the principles of the United Nations Charter. The performance of these tasks shall be undertaken using capabilities provided by the Member States.

2. The common security and defence policy shall include the progressive framing of a common Union defence policy. This will lead to a common defence, when the European Council, acting unanimously, so decides. It shall in that case recommend to the Member States the adoption of such a decision in accordance with their respective constitutional requirements.

The policy of the Union in accordance with this Section shall not prejudice the specific character of the security and defence policy of certain Member States and shall respect the obligations of certain Member States, which see their common defence realised in the North Atlantic Treaty Organisation (NATO), under the North Atlantic Treaty and be compatible with the common security and defence policy established within that framework.

3. Member States shall make civilian and military capabilities available to the Union for the implementation of the common security and defence policy, to contribute to the objectives defined by the Council. Those Member States which together establish multinational forces may also make them available to the common security and defence policy.

Member States shall undertake progressively to improve their military capabilities. The Agency in the field of defence capabilities development, research, acquisition and armaments (hereinafter referred to as 'the European Defence Agency') shall identify operational requirements, shall promote measures to satisfy those requirements, shall contribute to identifying and, where appropriate, implementing any measure needed to strengthen the industrial and technological base of the defence sector, shall participate in defining a European capabilities and armaments policy, and shall assist the Council in evaluating the improvement of military capabilities.

4. Decisions relating to the common security and defence policy, including those initiating a mission as referred to in this Article, shall be adopted by the Council acting unanimously on a proposal from the High Representative of the Union for Foreign Affairs and Security Policy or an initiative from a Member State. The High Representative may propose the use of both national resources and Union instruments, together with the Commission where appropriate.

5. The Council may entrust the execution of a task, within the Union framework, to a group of Member States in order to protect the Union's values and serve its interests. The execution of such a task shall be governed by Article 44.

6. Those Member States whose military capabilities fulfil higher criteria and which have made more binding commitments to one another in this area with a view to the most demanding missions shall establish permanent structured cooperation within the Union framework. Such cooperation shall be governed by Article 46. It shall not affect the provisions of Article 43.

7. If a Member State is the victim of armed aggression on its territory, the other Member States shall have towards it an obligation of aid and assistance by all the means in their power, in accordance with Article 51 of the United Nations Charter. This shall not prejudice the specific character of the security and defence policy of certain Member States.

Commitments and cooperation in this area shall be consistent with commitments under the North Atlantic Treaty Organisation, which, for those States which are members of it, remains the foundation of their collective defence and the forum for its implementation.

Article 43

1. The tasks referred to in Article 42(1), in the course of which the Union may use civilian and military means, shall include joint disarmament operations, humanitarian and rescue tasks, military advice and assistance tasks, conflict prevention and peace-keeping tasks, tasks of combat forces in crisis management, including peace-making and post-conflict stabilisation. All these tasks may contribute to the fight against terrorism, including by supporting third countries in combating terrorism in their territories.

2. The Council shall adopt decisions relating to the tasks referred to in paragraph 1, defining their objectives and scope and the general conditions for their implementation. The High Representative of the Union for Foreign Affairs and Security Policy, acting under the authority of the Council and in close and constant contact with the Political and Security Committee, shall ensure coordination of the civilian and military aspects of such tasks.

Article 44

1. Within the framework of the decisions adopted in accordance with Article 43, the Council may entrust the implementation of a task to a group of Member States which are willing and have the necessary capability for such a task. Those Member States, in association with the High Representative of the Union for Foreign Affairs and Security Policy, shall agree among themselves on the management of the task.

2. Member States participating in the task shall keep the Council regularly informed of its progress on their own initiative or at the request of another Member State. Those States shall inform the Council immediately should the completion of the task entail major consequences or require amendment of the objective, scope and conditions determined for the task in the decisions referred to in paragraph 1. In such cases, the Council shall adopt the necessary decisions.

Article 45

1. The European Defence Agency referred to in Article 42(3), subject to the authority of the Council, shall have as its task to:

   (a) contribute to identifying the Member States' military capability objectives and evaluating observance of the capability commitments given by the Member States;

   (b) promote harmonisation of operational needs and adoption of effective, compatible procurement methods;

   (c) propose multilateral projects to fulfil the objectives in terms of military capabilities, ensure coordination of the programmes implemented by the Member States and management of specific cooperation programmes;

   (d) support defence technology research, and coordinate and plan joint research activities and the study of technical solutions meeting future operational needs;

   (e) contribute to identifying and, if necessary, implementing any useful measure for strengthening the industrial and technological base of the defence sector and for improving the effectiveness of military expenditure.

2. The European Defence Agency shall be open to all Member States wishing to be part of it. The Council, acting by a qualified majority, shall adopt a decision defining the Agency's statute, seat and operational rules. That decision should take account of the level of effective participation in the Agency's activities. Specific groups shall be set up within the Agency bringing together Member States engaged in joint projects. The Agency shall carry out its tasks in liaison with the Commission where necessary.

Article 46

1. Those Member States which wish to participate in the permanent structured cooperation referred to in Article 42(6), which fulfil the criteria and have made the commitments on military capabilities set out in the Protocol on permanent structured cooperation, shall notify their intention to the Council and to the High Representative of the Union for Foreign Affairs and Security Policy.

2. Within three months following the notification referred to in paragraph 1 the Council shall adopt a decision establishing permanent structured cooperation and determining the list of participating Member States. The Council shall act by a qualified majority after consulting the High Representative.

3. Any Member State which, at a later stage, wishes to participate in the permanent structured cooperation shall notify its intention to the Council and to the High Representative. The Council shall adopt a decision confirming the participation of the Member State concerned which fulfils the criteria and makes the commitments referred to in Articles 1 and 2 of the Protocol on permanent structured cooperation. The Council shall act by a qualified majority after consulting the High Representative. Only members of the Council representing the participating Member States shall take part in the vote.

A qualified majority shall be defined in accordance with Article 238(3)(a) of the Treaty on the Functioning of the European Union.

4. If a participating Member State no longer fulfils the criteria or is no longer able to meet the commitments referred to in Articles 1 and 2 of the Protocol on permanent structured cooperation, the Council may adopt a decision suspending the participation of the Member State concerned.

The Council shall act by a qualified majority. Only members of the Council representing the participating Member States, with the exception of the Member State in question, shall take part in the vote.

A qualified majority shall be defined in accordance with Article 238(3)(a) of the Treaty on the Functioning of the European Union.

5. Any participating Member State which wishes to withdraw from permanent structured cooperation shall notify its intention to the Council, which shall take note that the Member State in question has ceased to participate.

6. The decisions and recommendations of the Council within the framework of permanent structured cooperation, other than those provided for in paragraphs 2 to 5, shall be adopted by unanimity. For the purposes of this paragraph, unanimity shall be constituted by the votes of the representatives of the participating Member States only.

Title VI
Final Provisions

Article 47
The Union shall have legal personality.

Article 48 (ex Article 48 TEU)
1. The Treaties may be amended in accordance with an ordinary revision procedure. They may also be amended in accordance with simplified revision procedures.

Ordinary revision procedure

2. The Government of any Member State, the European Parliament or the Commission may submit to the Council proposals for the amendment of the Treaties. These proposals may, inter alia, serve either to increase or to reduce the competences conferred on the Union in the Treaties. These proposals shall be submitted to the European Council by the Council and the national Parliaments shall be notified.

3. If the European Council, after consulting the European Parliament and the Commission, adopts by a simple majority a decision in favour of examining the proposed amendments, the President of the European Council shall convene a Convention composed of representatives of the national Parliaments, of the Heads of State or Government of the Member States, of the European Parliament and of the Commission. The European Central Bank shall also be consulted in the case of institutional changes in the monetary area. The Convention shall examine the proposals for amendments and shall adopt by consensus a recommendation to a conference of representatives of the governments of the Member States as provided for in paragraph 4.

The European Council may decide by a simple majority, after obtaining the consent of the European Parliament, not to convene a Convention should this not be justified by the extent of the proposed amendments. In the latter case, the European Council shall define the terms of reference for a conference of representatives of the governments of the Member States.

4. A conference of representatives of the governments of the Member States shall be convened by the President of the Council for the purpose of determining by common accord the amendments to be made to the Treaties.

The amendments shall enter into force after being ratified by all the Member States in accordance with their respective constitutional requirements.

5. If, two years after the signature of a treaty amending the Treaties, four fifths of the Member States have ratified it and one or more Member States have encountered difficulties in proceeding with ratification, the matter shall be referred to the European Council.

Simplified revision procedures

6. The Government of any Member State, the European Parliament or the Commission may submit to the European Council proposals for revising all or part of the provisions of Part Three of the Treaty on the Functioning of the European Union relating to the internal policies and action of the Union.

The European Council may adopt a decision amending all or part of the provisions of Part Three of the Treaty on the Functioning of the European Union. The European Council shall act by unanimity after consulting the European Parliament and the Commission, and the European Central Bank in the case of institutional changes in the monetary area. That decision shall not enter into force until it is approved by the Member States in accordance with their respective constitutional requirements.

The decision referred to in the second subparagraph shall not increase the competences conferred on the Union in the Treaties.

7. Where the Treaty on the Functioning of the European Union or Title V of this Treaty provides for the Council to act by unanimity in a given area or case, the European Council

may adopt a decision authorising the Council to act by a qualified majority in that area or in that case. This subparagraph shall not apply to decisions with military implications or those in the area of defence.

Where the Treaty on the Functioning of the European Union provides for legislative acts to be adopted by the Council in accordance with a special legislative procedure, the European Council may adopt a decision allowing for the adoption of such acts in accordance with the ordinary legislative procedure.

Any initiative taken by the European Council on the basis of the first or the second subparagraph shall be notified to the national Parliaments. If a national Parliament makes known its opposition within six months of the date of such notification, the decision referred to in the first or the second subparagraph shall not be adopted. In the absence of opposition, the European Council may adopt the decision.

For the adoption of the decisions referred to in the first and second subparagraphs, the European Council shall act by unanimity after obtaining the consent of the European Parliament, which shall be given by a majority of its component members.

Article 49 (ex Article 49 TEU)

Any European State which respects the values referred to in Article 2 and is committed to promoting them may apply to become a member of the Union. The European Parliament and national Parliaments shall be notified of this application. The applicant State shall address its application to the Council, which shall act unanimously after consulting the Commission and after receiving the consent of the European Parliament, which shall act by a majority of its component members. The conditions of eligibility agreed upon by the European Council shall be taken into account.

The conditions of admission and the adjustments to the Treaties on which the Union is founded, which such admission entails, shall be the subject of an agreement between the Member States and the applicant State. This agreement shall be submitted for ratification by all the contracting States in accordance with their respective constitutional requirements.

Article 50

1. Any Member State may decide to withdraw from the Union in accordance with its own constitutional requirements.

2. A Member State which decides to withdraw shall notify the European Council of its intention. In the light of the guidelines provided by the European Council, the Union shall negotiate and conclude an agreement with that State, setting out the arrangements for its withdrawal, taking account of the framework for its future relationship with the Union. That agreement shall be negotiated in accordance with Article 218(3) of the Treaty on the Functioning of the European Union. It shall be concluded on behalf of the Union by the Council, acting by a qualified majority, after obtaining the consent of the European Parliament.

3. The Treaties shall cease to apply to the State in question from the date of entry into force of the withdrawal agreement or, failing that, two years after the notification referred to in

paragraph 2, unless the European Council, in agreement with the Member State concerned, unanimously decides to extend this period.

4. For the purposes of paragraphs 2 and 3, the member of the European Council or of the Council representing the withdrawing Member State shall not participate in the discussions of the European Council or Council or in decisions concerning it.

A qualified majority shall be defined in accordance with Article 238(3)(b) of the Treaty on the Functioning of the European Union.

5. If a State which has withdrawn from the Union asks to rejoin, its request shall be subject to the procedure referred to in Article 49.

Article 51

The Protocols and Annexes to the Treaties shall form an integral part thereof.

Article 52

1. The Treaties shall apply to the Kingdom of Belgium, the Republic of Bulgaria, the Czech Republic, the Kingdom of Denmark, the Federal Republic of Germany, the Republic of Estonia, Ireland, the Hellenic Republic, the Kingdom of Spain, the French Republic, the Republic of Croatia, the Italian Republic, the Republic of Cyprus, the Republic of Latvia, the Republic of Lithuania, the Grand Duchy of Luxembourg, the Republic of Hungary, the Republic of Malta, the Kingdom of the Netherlands, the Republic of Austria, the Republic of Poland, the Portuguese Republic, Romania, the Republic of Slovenia, the Slovak Republic, the Republic of Finland, the Kingdom of Sweden and the United Kingdom of Great Britain and Northern Ireland.

2. The territorial scope of the Treaties is specified in Article 355 of the Treaty on the Functioning of the European Union.

Article 53 (ex Article 51 TEU)

This Treaty is concluded for an unlimited period.

Article 54 (ex Article 52 TEU)

1. This Treaty shall be ratified by the High Contracting Parties in accordance with their respective constitutional requirements. The instruments of ratification shall be deposited with the Government of the Italian Republic.

2. This Treaty shall enter into force on 1 January 1993, provided that all the Instruments of ratification have been deposited, or, failing that, on the first day of the month following the deposit of the Instrument of ratification by the last signatory State to take this step.

Article 55 (ex Article 53 TEU)

1. This Treaty, drawn up in a single original in the Bulgarian, Croatian, Czech, Danish, Dutch, English, Estonian, Finnish, French, German, Greek, Hungarian, Irish, Italian, Latvian, Lithuanian, Maltese, Polish, Portuguese, Romanian, Slovak, Slovenian, Spanish and Swedish

languages, the texts in each of these languages being equally authentic, shall be deposited in the archives of the Government of the Italian Republic, which will transmit a certified copy to each of the Governments of the other signatory States.

2. This Treaty may also be translated into any other languages as determined by Member States among those which, in accordance with their constitutional order, enjoy official status in all or part of their territory. A certified copy of such translations shall be provided by the Member States concerned to be deposited in the archives of the Council.

In witness whereof the undersigned Plenipotentiaries have signed this Treaty.
Done at Maastricht on the seventh day of February in the year one thousand nine hundred and ninety-two.
[List of signatories not reproduced.]

Treaty on the Functioning of the European Union

Source consolidated Version OJ C 326 of 26 October 2012, p. 47
last amended by the Act concerning the conditions of accession of the Republic of Croatia and the adjustments to the Treaty on European Union, the Treaty on the Functioning of the European Union and the Treaty establishing the European Atomic Energy Community, OJ L 112 of 24 April 2012, p. 21

Preamble

His Majesty the King of the Belgians, the President of the Federal Republic of Germany, the President of the French Republic, the President of the Italian Republic, her Royal Highness the Grand Duchess of Luxembourg, her Majesty the Queen of the Netherlands,[1]
Determined to lay the foundations of an ever closer union among the peoples of Europe,
Resolved to ensure the economic and social progress of their States by common action to eliminate the barriers which divide Europe,
Affirming as the essential objective of their efforts the constant improvements of the living and working conditions of their peoples,
Recognising that the removal of existing obstacles calls for concerted action in order to guarantee steady expansion, balanced trade and fair competition,
Anxious to strengthen the unity of their economies and to ensure their harmonious development by reducing the differences existing between the various regions and the backwardness of the less favoured regions,

---

1   The Republic of Bulgaria, the Czech Republic, the Kingdom of Denmark, the Republic of Estonia, Ireland, the Hellenic Republic, the Kingdom of Spain, the Republic of Cyprus, the Republic of Latvia, the Republic of Lithuania, the Republic of Hungary, the Republic of Malta, the Republic of Austria, the Republic of Poland, the Portuguese Republic, Romania, the Republic of Slovenia, the Slovak Republic, the Republic of Finland, the Kingdom of Sweden and the United Kingdom of Great Britain and Northern Ireland have since become members of the European Union.

©   European Union, http://eur-lex.europa.eu/, 1998-2015.

Desiring to contribute, by means of a common commercial policy, to the progressive abolition of restrictions on international trade,
Intending to confirm the solidarity which binds Europe and the overseas countries and desiring to ensure the development of their prosperity, in accordance with the principles of the Charter of the United Nations,
Resolved by thus pooling their resources to preserve and strengthen peace and liberty, and calling upon the other peoples of Europe who share their ideal to join in their efforts,
Determined to promote the development of the highest possible level of knowledge for their peoples through a wide access to education and through its continuous updating,
and to this end **have designated** as their Plenipotentiaries:
[List of plenipotentiaries not reproduced]
Who, having exchanged their full powers, found in good and due form, have agreed as follows.

Part One
Principles

Article 1
1. This Treaty organises the functioning of the Union and determines the areas of, delimitation of, and arrangements for exercising its competences.
2. This Treaty and the Treaty on European Union constitute the Treaties on which the Union is founded. These two Treaties, which have the same legal value, shall be referred to as 'the Treaties'.

Title I
Categories and Areas of Union Competence

Article 2
1. When the Treaties confer on the Union exclusive competence in a specific area, only the Union may legislate and adopt legally binding acts, the Member States being able to do so themselves only if so empowered by the Union or for the implementation of Union acts.
2. When the Treaties confer on the Union a competence shared with the Member States in a specific area, the Union and the Member States may legislate and adopt legally binding acts in that area. The Member States shall exercise their competence to the extent that the Union has not exercised its competence. The Member States shall again exercise their competence to the extent that the Union has decided to cease exercising its competence.
3. The Member States shall coordinate their economic and employment policies within arrangements as determined by this Treaty, which the Union shall have competence to provide.

4. The Union shall have competence, in accordance with the provisions of the Treaty on European Union, to define and implement a common foreign and security policy, including the progressive framing of a common defence policy.

5. In certain areas and under the conditions laid down in the Treaties, the Union shall have competence to carry out actions to support, coordinate or supplement the actions of the Member States, without thereby superseding their competence in these areas.

Legally binding acts of the Union adopted on the basis of the provisions of the Treaties relating to these areas shall not entail harmonisation of Member States' laws or regulations.

6. The scope of and arrangements for exercising the Union's competences shall be determined by the provisions of the Treaties relating to each area.

Article 3

1. The Union shall have exclusive competence in the following areas:

   (a) customs union;

   (b) the establishing of the competition rules necessary for the functioning of the internal market;

   (c) monetary policy for the Member States whose currency is the euro;

   (d) the conservation of marine biological resources under the common fisheries policy;

   (e) common commercial policy.

2. The Union shall also have exclusive competence for the conclusion of an international agreement when its conclusion is provided for in a legislative act of the Union or is necessary to enable the Union to exercise its internal competence, or in so far as its conclusion may affect common rules or alter their scope.

Article 4

1. The Union shall share competence with the Member States where the Treaties confer on it a competence which does not relate to the areas referred to in Articles 3 and 6.

2. Shared competence between the Union and the Member States applies in the following principal areas:

   (a) internal market;

   (b) social policy, for the aspects defined in this Treaty;

   (c) economic, social and territorial cohesion;

   (d) agriculture and fisheries, excluding the conservation of marine biological resources;

   (e) environment;

   (f) consumer protection;

   (g) transport;

   (h) trans-European networks;

   (i) energy;

   (j) area of freedom, security and justice;

   (k) common safety concerns in public health matters, for the aspects defined in this Treaty.

3. In the areas of research, technological development and space, the Union shall have competence to carry out activities, in particular to define and implement programmes; however, the exercise of that competence shall not result in Member States being prevented from exercising theirs.

4. In the areas of development cooperation and humanitarian aid, the Union shall have competence to carry out activities and conduct a common policy; however, the exercise of that competence shall not result in Member States being prevented from exercising theirs.

Article 5

1. The Member States shall coordinate their economic policies within the Union. To this end, the Council shall adopt measures, in particular broad guidelines for these policies. Specific provisions shall apply to those Member States whose currency is the euro.

2. The Union shall take measures to ensure coordination of the employment policies of the Member States, in particular by defining guidelines for these policies.

3. The Union may take initiatives to ensure coordination of Member States' social policies.

Article 6

The Union shall have competence to carry out actions to support, coordinate or supplement the actions of the Member States. The areas of such action shall, at European level, be:

   (a) protection and improvement of human health;
   (b) industry;
   (c) culture;
   (d) tourism;
   (e) education, vocational training, youth and sport;
   (f) civil protection;
   (g) administrative cooperation.

Title II
Provisions having General Application

Article 7

The Union shall ensure consistency between its policies and activities, taking all of its objectives into account and in accordance with the principle of conferral of powers.

Article 8 (ex Article 3(2) TEC)[2]

In all its activities, the Union shall aim to eliminate inequalities, and to promote equality, between men and women.

---

2   These references are merely indicative. For more ample information, please refer to the tables of equivalences between the old and the new numbering of the Treaties.

Article 9
In defining and implementing its policies and activities, the Union shall take into account requirements linked to the promotion of a high level of employment, the guarantee of adequate social protection, the fight against social exclusion, and a high level of education, training and protection of human health.

Article 10
In defining and implementing its policies and activities, the Union shall aim to combat discrimination based on sex, racial or ethnic origin, religion or belief, disability, age or sexual orientation.

Article 11 (ex Article 6 TEC)
Environmental protection requirements must be integrated into the definition and implementation of the Union's policies and activities, in particular with a view to promoting sustainable development.

Article 12 (ex Article 153(2) TEC)
Consumer protection requirements shall be taken into account in defining and implementing other Union policies and activities.

Article 13
In formulating and implementing the Union's agriculture, fisheries, transport, internal market, research and technological development and space policies, the Union and the Member States shall, since animals are sentient beings, pay full regard to the welfare requirements of animals, while respecting the legislative or administrative provisions and customs of the Member States relating in particular to religious rites, cultural traditions and regional heritage.

Article 14 (ex Article 16 TEC)
Without prejudice to Article 4 of the Treaty on European Union or to Articles 93, 106 and 107 of this Treaty, and given the place occupied by services of general economic interest in the shared values of the Union as well as their role in promoting social and territorial cohesion, the Union and the Member States, each within their respective powers and within the scope of application of the Treaties, shall take care that such services operate on the basis of principles and conditions, particularly economic and financial conditions, which enable them to fulfil their missions. The European Parliament and the Council, acting by means of regulations in accordance with the ordinary legislative procedure, shall establish these principles and set these conditions without prejudice to the competence of Member States, in compliance with the Treaties, to provide, to commission and to fund such services.

Article 15 (ex Article 255 TEC)

1. In order to promote good governance and ensure the participation of civil society, the Union's institutions, bodies, offices and agencies shall conduct their work as openly as possible.
2. The European Parliament shall meet in public, as shall the Council when considering and voting on a draft legislative act.
3. Any citizen of the Union, and any natural or legal person residing or having its registered office in a Member State, shall have a right of access to documents of the Union's institutions, bodies, offices and agencies, whatever their medium, subject to the principles and the conditions to be defined in accordance with this paragraph.

General principles and limits on grounds of public or private interest governing this right of access to documents shall be determined by the European Parliament and the Council, by means of regulations, acting in accordance with the ordinary legislative procedure.

Each institution, body, office or agency shall ensure that its proceedings are transparent and shall elaborate in its own Rules of Procedure specific provisions regarding access to its documents, in accordance with the regulations referred to in the second subparagraph.

The Court of Justice of the European Union, the European Central Bank and the European Investment Bank shall be subject to this paragraph only when exercising their administrative tasks.

The European Parliament and the Council shall ensure publication of the documents relating to the legislative procedures under the terms laid down by the regulations referred to in the second subparagraph.

Article 16 (ex Article 286 TEC)

1. Everyone has the right to the protection of personal data concerning them.
2. The European Parliament and the Council, acting in accordance with the ordinary legislative procedure, shall lay down the rules relating to the protection of individuals with regard to the processing of personal data by Union institutions, bodies, offices and agencies, and by the Member States when carrying out activities which fall within the scope of Union law, and the rules relating to the free movement of such data. Compliance with these rules shall be subject to the control of independent authorities.

The rules adopted on the basis of this Article shall be without prejudice to the specific rules laid down in Article 39 of the Treaty on European Union.

Article 17

1. The Union respects and does not prejudice the status under national law of churches and religious associations or communities in the Member States.
2. The Union equally respects the status under national law of philosophical and non-confessional organisations.
3. Recognising their identity and their specific contribution, the Union shall maintain an open, transparent and regular dialogue with these churches and organisations.

Part Two
Non-Discrimination and Citizenship of the Union

Article 18 (ex Article 12 TEC)
Within the scope of application of the Treaties, and without prejudice to any special provisions contained therein, any discrimination on grounds of nationality shall be prohibited.
The European Parliament and the Council, acting in accordance with the ordinary legislative procedure, may adopt rules designed to prohibit such discrimination.

Article 19 (ex Article 13 TEC)
1. Without prejudice to the other provisions of the Treaties and within the limits of the powers conferred by them upon the Union, the Council, acting unanimously in accordance with a special legislative procedure and after obtaining the consent of the European Parliament, may take appropriate action to combat discrimination based on sex, racial or ethnic origin, religion or belief, disability, age or sexual orientation.
2. By way of derogation from paragraph 1, the European Parliament and the Council, acting in accordance with the ordinary legislative procedure, may adopt the basic principles of Union incentive measures, excluding any harmonisation of the laws and regulations of the Member States, to support action taken by the Member States in order to contribute to the achievement of the objectives referred to in paragraph 1.

Article 20 (ex Article 17 TEC)
1. Citizenship of the Union is hereby established. Every person holding the nationality of a Member State shall be a citizen of the Union. Citizenship of the Union shall be additional to and not replace national citizenship.
2. Citizens of the Union shall enjoy the rights and be subject to the duties provided for in the Treaties. They shall have, inter alia:
   (a) the right to move and reside freely within the territory of the Member States;
   (b) the right to vote and to stand as candidates in elections to the European Parliament and in municipal elections in their Member State of residence, under the same conditions as nationals of that State;
   (c) the right to enjoy, in the territory of a third country in which the Member State of which they are nationals is not represented, the protection of the diplomatic and consular authorities of any Member State on the same conditions as the nationals of that State;
   (d) the right to petition the European Parliament, to apply to the European Ombudsman, and to address the institutions and advisory bodies of the Union in any of the Treaty languages and to obtain a reply in the same language.
These rights shall be exercised in accordance with the conditions and limits defined by the Treaties and by the measures adopted thereunder.

Article 21 (ex Article 18 TEC)
1. Every citizen of the Union shall have the right to move and reside freely within the territory of the Member States, subject to the limitations and conditions laid down in the Treaties and by the measures adopted to give them effect.
2. If action by the Union should prove necessary to attain this objective and the Treaties have not provided the necessary powers, the European Parliament and the Council, acting in accordance with the ordinary legislative procedure, may adopt provisions with a view to facilitating the exercise of the rights referred to in paragraph 1.
3. For the same purposes as those referred to in paragraph 1 and if the Treaties have not provided the necessary powers, the Council, acting in accordance with a special legislative procedure, may adopt measures concerning social security or social protection. The Council shall act unanimously after consulting the European Parliament.

Article 22 (ex Article 19 TEC)
1. Every citizen of the Union residing in a Member State of which he is not a national shall have the right to vote and to stand as a candidate at municipal elections in the Member State in which he resides, under the same conditions as nationals of that State. This right shall be exercised subject to detailed arrangements adopted by the Council, acting unanimously in accordance with a special legislative procedure and after consulting the European Parliament; these arrangements may provide for derogations where warranted by problems specific to a Member State.
2. Without prejudice to Article 223(1) and to the provisions adopted for its implementation, every citizen of the Union residing in a Member State of which he is not a national shall have the right to vote and to stand as a candidate in elections to the European Parliament in the Member State in which he resides, under the same conditions as nationals of that State. This right shall be exercised subject to detailed arrangements adopted by the Council, acting unanimously in accordance with a special legislative procedure and after consulting the European Parliament; these arrangements may provide for derogations where warranted by problems specific to a Member State.

Article 23 (ex Article 20 TEC)
Every citizen of the Union shall, in the territory of a third country in which the Member State of which he is a national is not represented, be entitled to protection by the diplomatic or consular authorities of any Member State, on the same conditions as the nationals of that State. Member States shall adopt the necessary provisions and start the international negotiations required to secure this protection.
The Council, acting in accordance with a special legislative procedure and after consulting the European Parliament, may adopt directives establishing the coordination and cooperation measures necessary to facilitate such protection.

Article 24 (ex Article 21 TEC)

The European Parliament and the Council, acting by means of regulations in accordance with the ordinary legislative procedure, shall adopt the provisions for the procedures and conditions required for a citizens' initiative within the meaning of Article 11 of the Treaty on European Union, including the minimum number of Member States from which such citizens must come.

Every citizen of the Union shall have the right to petition the European Parliament in accordance with Article 227.

Every citizen of the Union may apply to the Ombudsman established in accordance with Article 228.

Every citizen of the Union may write to any of the institutions or bodies referred to in this Article or in Article 13 of the Treaty on European Union in one of the languages mentioned in Article 55(1) of the Treaty on European Union and have an answer in the same language.

Article 25 (ex Article 22 TEC)

The Commission shall report to the European Parliament, to the Council and to the Economic and Social Committee every three years on the application of the provisions of this Part. This report shall take account of the development of the Union.

On this basis, and without prejudice to the other provisions of the Treaties, the Council, acting unanimously in accordance with a special legislative procedure and after obtaining the consent of the European Parliament, may adopt provisions to strengthen or to add to the rights listed in Article 20(2). These provisions shall enter into force after their approval by the Member States in accordance with their respective constitutional requirements.

Part Three
Union Policies and Internal Actions

Title I
The Internal Market

Article 26 (ex Article 14 TEC)

1. The Union shall adopt measures with the aim of establishing or ensuring the functioning of the internal market, in accordance with the relevant provisions of the Treaties.
2. The internal market shall comprise an area without internal frontiers in which the free movement of goods, persons, services and capital is ensured in accordance with the provisions of the Treaties.
3. The Council, on a proposal from the Commission, shall determine the guidelines and conditions necessary to ensure balanced progress in all the sectors concerned.

Article 27 (ex Article 15 TEC)

When drawing up its proposals with a view to achieving the objectives set out in Article 26, the Commission shall take into account the extent of the effort that certain economies showing differences in development will have to sustain for the establishment of the internal market and it may propose appropriate provisions.

If these provisions take the form of derogations, they must be of a temporary nature and must cause the least possible disturbance to the functioning of the internal market.

Title II
Free Movement of Goods

Article 28 (ex Article 23 TEC)

1. The Union shall comprise a customs union which shall cover all trade in goods and which shall involve the prohibition between Member States of customs duties on imports and exports and of all charges having equivalent effect, and the adoption of a common customs tariff in their relations with third countries.

2. The provisions of Article 30 and of Chapter 3 of this Title shall apply to products originating in Member States and to products coming from third countries which are in free circulation in Member States.

Article 29 (ex Article 24 TEC)

Products coming from a third country shall be considered to be in free circulation in a Member State if the import formalities have been complied with and any customs duties or charges having equivalent effect which are payable have been levied in that Member State, and if they have not benefited from a total or partial drawback of such duties or charges.

Chapter 1
The Customs Union

Article 30 (ex Article 25 TEC)

Customs duties on imports and exports and charges having equivalent effect shall be prohibited between Member States. This prohibition shall also apply to customs duties of a fiscal nature.

Article 31 (ex Article 26 TEC)

Common Customs Tariff duties shall be fixed by the Council on a proposal from the Commission.

Article 32 (ex Article 27 TEC)

In carrying out the tasks entrusted to it under this Chapter the Commission shall be guided by:
    (a) the need to promote trade between Member States and third countries;

(b) developments in conditions of competition within the Union in so far as they lead to an improvement in the competitive capacity of undertakings;

(c) the requirements of the Union as regards the supply of raw materials and semi-finished goods; in this connection the Commission shall take care to avoid distorting conditions of competition between Member States in respect of finished goods;

(d) the need to avoid serious disturbances in the economies of Member States and to ensure rational development of production and an expansion of consumption within the Union.

Chapter 2
Customs Cooperation

Article 33 (ex Article 135 TEC)

Within the scope of application of the Treaties, the European Parliament and the Council, acting in accordance with the ordinary legislative procedure, shall take measures in order to strengthen customs cooperation between Member States and between the latter and the Commission.

Chapter 3
Prohibition of Quantitative Restrictions between Member States

Article 34 (ex Article 28 TEC)

Quantitative restrictions on imports and all measures having equivalent effect shall be prohibited between Member States.

Article 35 (ex Article 29 TEC)

Quantitative restrictions on exports, and all measures having equivalent effect, shall be prohibited between Member States.

Article 36 (ex Article 30 TEC)

The provisions of Articles 34 and 35 shall not preclude prohibitions or restrictions on imports, exports or goods in transit justified on grounds of public morality, public policy or public security; the protection of health and life of humans, animals or plants; the protection of national treasures possessing artistic, historic or archaeological value; or the protection of industrial and commercial property. Such prohibitions or restrictions shall not, however, constitute a means of arbitrary discrimination or a disguised restriction on trade between Member States.

Article 37 (ex Article 31 TEC)

1. Member States shall adjust any State monopolies of a commercial character so as to ensure that no discrimination regarding the conditions under which goods are procured and marketed exists between nationals of Member States.

The provisions of this Article shall apply to any body through which a Member State, in law or in fact, either directly or indirectly supervises, determines or appreciably influences imports or exports between Member States. These provisions shall likewise apply to monopolies delegated by the State to others.

2. Member States shall refrain from introducing any new measure which is contrary to the principles laid down in paragraph 1 or which restricts the scope of the articles dealing with the prohibition of customs duties and quantitative restrictions between Member States.

3. If a State monopoly of a commercial character has rules which are designed to make it easier to dispose of agricultural products or obtain for them the best return, steps should be taken in applying the rules contained in this Article to ensure equivalent safeguards for the employment and standard of living of the producers concerned.

Title III
Agriculture and Fisheries

Article 38 (ex Article 32 TEC)
1. The Union shall define and implement a common agriculture and fisheries policy.
The internal market shall extend to agriculture, fisheries and trade in agricultural products. 'Agricultural products' means the products of the soil, of stockfarming and of fisheries and products of first-stage processing directly related to these products. References to the common agricultural policy or to agriculture, and the use of the term 'agricultural', shall be understood as also referring to fisheries, having regard to the specific characteristics of this sector.

2. Save as otherwise provided in Articles 39 to 44, the rules laid down for the establishment and functioning of the internal market shall apply to agricultural products.

3. The products subject to the provisions of Articles 39 to 44 are listed in Annex I.

4. The operation and development of the internal market for agricultural products must be accompanied by the establishment of a common agricultural policy.

Article 39 (ex Article 33 TEC)
1. The objectives of the common agricultural policy shall be:

(a) to increase agricultural productivity by promoting technical progress and by ensuring the rational development of agricultural production and the optimum utilisation of the factors of production, in particular labour;

(b) thus to ensure a fair standard of living for the agricultural community, in particular by increasing the individual earnings of persons engaged in agriculture;

(c) to stabilise markets;

(d) to assure the availability of supplies;

(e) to ensure that supplies reach consumers at reasonable prices.

2. In working out the common agricultural policy and the special methods for its application, account shall be taken of:

(a) the particular nature of agricultural activity, which results from the social structure of agriculture and from structural and natural disparities between the various agricultural regions;
(b) the need to effect the appropriate adjustments by degrees;
(c) the fact that in the Member States agriculture constitutes a sector closely linked with the economy as a whole.

Article 40 (ex Article 34 TEC)

1. In order to attain the objectives set out in Article 39, a common organisation of agricultural markets shall be established.
This organisation shall take one of the following forms, depending on the product concerned:
   (a) common rules on competition;
   (b) compulsory coordination of the various national market organisations;
   (c) a European market organisation.
2. The common organisation established in accordance with paragraph 1 may include all measures required to attain the objectives set out in Article 39, in particular regulation of prices, aids for the production and marketing of the various products, storage and carryover arrangements and common machinery for stabilising imports or exports.
The common organisation shall be limited to pursuit of the objectives set out in Article 39 and shall exclude any discrimination between producers or consumers within the Union.
Any common price policy shall be based on common criteria and uniform methods of calculation.
3. In order to enable the common organisation referred to in paragraph 1 to attain its objectives, one or more agricultural guidance and guarantee funds may be set up.

Article 41 (ex Article 35 TEC)

To enable the objectives set out in Article 39 to be attained, provision may be made within the framework of the common agricultural policy for measures such as:
   (a) an effective coordination of efforts in the spheres of vocational training, of research and of the dissemination of agricultural knowledge; this may include joint financing of projects or institutions;
   (b) joint measures to promote consumption of certain products.

Article 42 (ex Article 36 TEC)

The provisions of the Chapter relating to rules on competition shall apply to production of and trade in agricultural products only to the extent determined by the European Parliament and the Council within the framework of Article 43(2) and in accordance with the procedure laid down therein, account being taken of the objectives set out in Article 39.
The Council, on a proposal from the Commission, may authorise the granting of aid:
   (a) for the protection of enterprises handicapped by structural or natural conditions;
   (b) within the framework of economic development programmes.

Article 43 (ex Article 37 TEC)

1. The Commission shall submit proposals for working out and implementing the common agricultural policy, including the replacement of the national organisations by one of the forms of common organisation provided for in Article 40(1), and for implementing the measures specified in this Title.

These proposals shall take account of the interdependence of the agricultural matters mentioned in this Title.

2. The European Parliament and the Council, acting in accordance with the ordinary legislative procedure and after consulting the Economic and Social Committee, shall establish the common organisation of agricultural markets provided for in Article 40(1) and the other provisions necessary for the pursuit of the objectives of the common agricultural policy and the common fisheries policy.

3. The Council, on a proposal from the Commission, shall adopt measures on fixing prices, levies, aid and quantitative limitations and on the fixing and allocation of fishing opportunities.

4. In accordance with paragraph 2, the national market organisations may be replaced by the common organisation provided for in Article 40(1) if:

(a) the common organisation offers Member States which are opposed to this measure and which have an organisation of their own for the production in question equivalent safeguards for the employment and standard of living of the producers concerned, account being taken of the adjustments that will be possible and the specialisation that will be needed with the passage of time;

(b) such an organisation ensures conditions for trade within the Union similar to those existing in a national market.

5. If a common organisation for certain raw materials is established before a common organisation exists for the corresponding processed products, such raw materials as are used for processed products intended for export to third countries may be imported from outside the Union.

Article 44 (ex Article 38 TEC)

Where in a Member State a product is subject to a national market organisation or to internal rules having equivalent effect which affect the competitive position of similar production in another Member State, a countervailing charge shall be applied by Member States to imports of this product coming from the Member State where such organisation or rules exist, unless that State applies a countervailing charge on export.

The Commission shall fix the amount of these charges at the level required to redress the balance; it may also authorise other measures, the conditions and details of which it shall determine.

Title IV
Free Movement of Persons, Services and Capital

Chapter 1
Workers

Article 45 (ex Article 39 TEC)
1. Freedom of movement for workers shall be secured within the Union.
2. Such freedom of movement shall entail the abolition of any discrimination based on nationality between workers of the Member States as regards employment, remuneration and other conditions of work and employment.
3. It shall entail the right, subject to limitations justified on grounds of public policy, public security or public health:
    (a) to accept offers of employment actually made;
    (b) to move freely within the territory of Member States for this purpose;
    (c) to stay in a Member State for the purpose of employment in accordance with the provisions governing the employment of nationals of that State laid down by law, regulation or administrative action;
    (d) to remain in the territory of a Member State after having been employed in that State, subject to conditions which shall be embodied in regulations to be drawn up by the Commission.
4. The provisions of this Article shall not apply to employment in the public service.

Article 46 (ex Article 40 TEC)
The European Parliament and the Council shall, acting in accordance with the ordinary legislative procedure and after consulting the Economic and Social Committee, issue directives or make regulations setting out the measures required to bring about freedom of movement for workers, as defined in Article 45, in particular:
    (a) by ensuring close cooperation between national employment services;
    (b) by abolishing those administrative procedures and practices and those qualifying periods in respect of eligibility for available employment, whether resulting from national legislation or from agreements previously concluded between Member States, the maintenance of which would form an obstacle to liberalisation of the movement of workers;
    (c) by abolishing all such qualifying periods and other restrictions provided for either under national legislation or under agreements previously concluded between Member States as imposed on workers of other Member States conditions regarding the free choice of employment other than those imposed on workers of the State concerned;
    (d) by setting up appropriate machinery to bring offers of employment into touch with applications for employment and to facilitate the achievement of a balance between supply and demand in the employment market in such a way as to avoid serious threats to the standard of living and level of employment in the various regions and industries.

Article 47 (ex Article 41 TEC)

Member States shall, within the framework of a joint programme, encourage the exchange of young workers.

Article 48 (ex Article 42 TEC)

The European Parliament and the Council shall, acting in accordance with the ordinary legislative procedure, adopt such measures in the field of social security as are necessary to provide freedom of movement for workers; to this end, they shall make arrangements to secure for employed and self-employed migrant workers and their dependants:

(a) aggregation, for the purpose of acquiring and retaining the right to benefit and of calculating the amount of benefit, of all periods taken into account under the laws of the several countries;

(b) payment of benefits to persons resident in the territories of Member States.

Where a member of the Council declares that a draft legislative act referred to in the first subparagraph would affect important aspects of its social security system, including its scope, cost or financial structure, or would affect the financial balance of that system, it may request that the matter be referred to the European Council. In that case, the ordinary legislative procedure shall be suspended. After discussion, the European Council shall, within four months of this suspension, either:

(a) refer the draft back to the Council, which shall terminate the suspension of the ordinary legislative procedure; or

(b) take no action or request the Commission to submit a new proposal; in that case, the act originally proposed shall be deemed not to have been adopted.

Chapter 2
Right of Establishment

Article 49 (ex Article 43 TEC)

Within the framework of the provisions set out below, restrictions on the freedom of establishment of nationals of a Member State in the territory of another Member State shall be prohibited. Such prohibition shall also apply to restrictions on the setting-up of agencies, branches or subsidiaries by nationals of any Member State established in the territory of any Member State.

Freedom of establishment shall include the right to take up and pursue activities as self-employed persons and to set up and manage undertakings, in particular companies or firms within the meaning of the second paragraph of Article 54, under the conditions laid down for its own nationals by the law of the country where such establishment is effected, subject to the provisions of the Chapter relating to capital.

Article 50 (ex Article 44 TEC)

1. In order to attain freedom of establishment as regards a particular activity, the European Parliament and the Council, acting in accordance with the ordinary legislative procedure and after consulting the Economic and Social Committee, shall act by means of directives.

2. The European Parliament, the Council and the Commission shall carry out the duties devolving upon them under the preceding provisions, in particular:

(a) by according, as a general rule, priority treatment to activities where freedom of establishment makes a particularly valuable contribution to the development of production and trade;

(b) by ensuring close cooperation between the competent authorities in the Member States in order to ascertain the particular situation within the Union of the various activities concerned;

(c) by abolishing those administrative procedures and practices, whether resulting from national legislation or from agreements previously concluded between Member States, the maintenance of which would form an obstacle to freedom of establishment;

(d) by ensuring that workers of one Member State employed in the territory of another Member State may remain in that territory for the purpose of taking up activities therein as self-employed persons, where they satisfy the conditions which they would be required to satisfy if they were entering that State at the time when they intended to take up such activities;

(e) by enabling a national of one Member State to acquire and use land and buildings situated in the territory of another Member State, in so far as this does not conflict with the principles laid down in Article 39(2);

(f) by effecting the progressive abolition of restrictions on freedom of establishment in every branch of activity under consideration, both as regards the conditions for setting up agencies, branches or subsidiaries in the territory of a Member State and as regards the subsidiaries in the territory of a Member State and as regards the conditions governing the entry of personnel belonging to the main establishment into managerial or supervisory posts in such agencies, branches or subsidiaries;

(g) by coordinating to the necessary extent the safeguards which, for the protection of the interests of members and others, are required by Member States of companies or firms within the meaning of the second paragraph of Article 54 with a view to making such safeguards equivalent throughout the Union;

(h) by satisfying themselves that the conditions of establishment are not distorted by aids granted by Member States.

Article 51 (ex Article 45 TEC)

The provisions of this Chapter shall not apply, so far as any given Member State is concerned, to activities which in that State are connected, even occasionally, with the exercise of official authority.

The European Parliament and the Council, acting in accordance with the ordinary legislative procedure, may rule that the provisions of this Chapter shall not apply to certain activities.

Article 52 (ex Article 46 TEC)

1. The provisions of this Chapter and measures taken in pursuance thereof shall not prejudice the applicability of provisions laid down by law, regulation or administrative action

providing for special treatment for foreign nationals on grounds of public policy, public security or public health.

2. The European Parliament and the Council shall, acting in accordance with the ordinary legislative procedure, issue directives for the coordination of the abovementioned provisions.

Article 53 (ex Article 47 TEC)

1. In order to make it easier for persons to take up and pursue activities as self-employed persons, the European Parliament and the Council shall, acting in accordance with the ordinary legislative procedure, issue directives for the mutual recognition of diplomas, certificates and other evidence of formal qualifications and for the coordination of the provisions laid down by law, regulation or administrative action in Member States concerning the taking-up and pursuit of activities as self-employed persons.

2. In the case of the medical and allied and pharmaceutical professions, the progressive abolition of restrictions shall be dependent upon coordination of the conditions for their exercise in the various Member States.

Article 54 (ex Article 48 TEC)

Companies or firms formed in accordance with the law of a Member State and having their registered office, central administration or principal place of business within the Union shall, for the purposes of this Chapter, be treated in the same way as natural persons who are nationals of Member States.

'Companies or firms' means companies or firms constituted under civil or commercial law, including cooperative societies, and other legal persons governed by public or private law, save for those which are non-profit-making.

Article 55 (ex Article 294 TEC)

Member States shall accord nationals of the other Member States the same treatment as their own nationals as regards participation in the capital of companies or firms within the meaning of Article 54, without prejudice to the application of the other provisions of the Treaties.

Chapter 3
Services

Article 56 (ex Article 49 TEC)

Within the framework of the provisions set out below, restrictions on freedom to provide services within the Union shall be prohibited in respect of nationals of Member States who are established in a Member State other than that of the person for whom the services are intended.

The European Parliament and the Council, acting in accordance with the ordinary legislative procedure, may extend the provisions of the Chapter to nationals of a third country who provide services and who are established within the Union.

Article 57 (ex Article 50 TEC)
Services shall be considered to be 'services' within the meaning of the Treaties where they are normally provided for remuneration, in so far as they are not governed by the provisions relating to freedom of movement for goods, capital and persons.

'Services' shall in particular include:
- (a) activities of an industrial character;
- (b) activities of a commercial character;
- (c) activities of craftsmen;
- (d) activities of the professions.

Without prejudice to the provisions of the Chapter relating to the right of establishment, the person providing a service may, in order to do so, temporarily pursue his activity in the Member State where the service is provided, under the same conditions as are imposed by that State on its own nationals.

Article 58 (ex Article 51 TEC)
1. Freedom to provide services in the field of transport shall be governed by the provisions of the Title relating to transport.
2. The liberalisation of banking and insurance services connected with movements of capital shall be effected in step with the liberalisation of movement of capital.

Article 59 (ex Article 52 TEC)
1. In order to achieve the liberalisation of a specific service, the European Parliament and the Council, acting in accordance with the ordinary legislative procedure and after consulting the Economic and Social Committee, shall issue directives.
2. As regards the directives referred to in paragraph 1, priority shall as a general rule be given to those services which directly affect production costs or the liberalisation of which helps to promote trade in goods.

Article 60 (ex Article 53 TEC)
The Member States shall endeavour to undertake the liberalisation of services beyond the extent required by the directives issued pursuant to Article 59(1), if their general economic situation and the situation of the economic sector concerned so permit.

To this end, the Commission shall make recommendations to the Member States concerned.

Article 61 (ex Article 54 TEC)
As long as restrictions on freedom to provide services have not been abolished, each Member State shall apply such restrictions without distinction on grounds of nationality or residence to all persons providing services within the meaning of the first paragraph of Article 56.

Article 62 (ex Article 55 TEC)
The provisions of Articles 51 to 54 shall apply to the matters covered by this Chapter.

Chapter 4
Capital and Payments

Article 63 (ex Article 56 TEC)
1. Within the framework of the provisions set out in this Chapter, all restrictions on the movement of capital between Member States and between Member States and third countries shall be prohibited.
2. Within the framework of the provisions set out in this Chapter, all restrictions on payments between Member States and between Member States and third countries shall be prohibited.

Article 64 (ex Article 57 TEC)
1. The provisions of Article 63 shall be without prejudice to the application to third countries of any restrictions which exist on 31 December 1993 under national or Union law adopted in respect of the movement of capital to or from third countries involving direct investment – including in real estate – establishment, the provision of financial services or the admission of securities to capital markets. In respect of restrictions existing under national law in Bulgaria, Estonia and Hungary, the relevant date shall be 31 December 1999. In respect of restrictions existing under national law in Croatia, the relevant date shall be 31 December 2002.
2. Whilst endeavouring to achieve the objective of free movement of capital between Member States and third countries to the greatest extent possible and without prejudice to the other Chapters of the Treaties, the European Parliament and the Council, acting in accordance with the ordinary legislative procedure, shall adopt the measures on the movement of capital to or from third countries involving direct investment – including investment in real estate – establishment, the provision of financial services or the admission of securities to capital markets.
3. Notwithstanding paragraph 2, only the Council, acting in accordance with a special legislative procedure, may unanimously, and after consulting the European Parliament, adopt measures which constitute a step backwards in Union law as regards the liberalisation of the movement of capital to or from third countries.

Article 65 (ex Article 58 TEC)
1. The provisions of Article 63 shall be without prejudice to the right of Member States:
    (a) to apply the relevant provisions of their tax law which distinguish between taxpayers who are not in the same situation with regard to their place of residence or with regard to the place where their capital is invested;
    (b) to take all requisite measures to prevent infringements of national law and regulations, in particular in the field of taxation and the prudential supervision of financial institutions, or to lay down procedures for the declaration of capital movements for purposes of administrative or statistical information, or to take measures which are justified on grounds of public policy or public security.

2. The provisions of this Chapter shall be without prejudice to the applicability of restrictions on the right of establishment which are compatible with the Treaties.
3. The measures and procedures referred to in paragraphs 1 and 2 shall not constitute a means of arbitrary discrimination or a disguised restriction on the free movement of capital and payments as defined in Article 63.
4. In the absence of measures pursuant to Article 64(3), the Commission or, in the absence of a Commission decision within three months from the request of the Member State concerned, the Council, may adopt a decision stating that restrictive tax measures adopted by a Member State concerning one or more third countries are to be considered compatible with the Treaties in so far as they are justified by one of the objectives of the Union and compatible with the proper functioning of the internal market. The Council shall act unanimously on application by a Member State.

Article 66 (ex Article 59 TEC)
Where, in exceptional circumstances, movements of capital to or from third countries cause, or threaten to cause, serious difficulties for the operation of economic and monetary union, the Council, on a proposal from the Commission and after consulting the European Central Bank, may take safeguard measures with regard to third countries for a period not exceeding six months if such measures are strictly necessary.

Title V
Area of Freedom, Security and Justice

Chapter 1
General Provisions

Article 67 (ex Article 61 TEC and ex Article 29 TEU)
1. The Union shall constitute an area of freedom, security and justice with respect for fundamental rights and the different legal systems and traditions of the Member States.
2. It shall ensure the absence of internal border controls for persons and shall frame a common policy on asylum, immigration and external border control, based on solidarity between Member States, which is fair towards third-country nationals. For the purpose of this Title, stateless persons shall be treated as third-country nationals.
3. The Union shall endeavour to ensure a high level of security through measures to prevent and combat crime, racism and xenophobia, and through measures for coordination and cooperation between police and judicial authorities and other competent authorities, as well as through the mutual recognition of judgments in criminal matters and, if necessary, through the approximation of criminal laws.
4. The Union shall facilitate access to justice, in particular through the principle of mutual recognition of judicial and extrajudicial decisions in civil matters.

Article 68
The European Council shall define the strategic guidelines for legislative and operational planning within the area of freedom, security and justice.

Article 69
National Parliaments ensure that the proposals and legislative initiatives submitted under Chapters 4 and 5 comply with the principle of subsidiarity, in accordance with the arrangements laid down by the Protocol on the application of the principles of subsidiarity and proportionality.

Article 70
Without prejudice to Articles 258, 259 and 260, the Council may, on a proposal from the Commission, adopt measures laying down the arrangements whereby Member States, in collaboration with the Commission, conduct objective and impartial evaluation of the implementation of the Union policies referred to in this Title by Member States' authorities, in particular in order to facilitate full application of the principle of mutual recognition. The European Parliament and national Parliaments shall be informed of the content and results of the evaluation.

Article 71 (ex Article 36 TEU)
A standing committee shall be set up within the Council in order to ensure that operational cooperation on internal security is promoted and strengthened within the Union. Without prejudice to Article 240, it shall facilitate coordination of the action of Member States' competent authorities. Representatives of the Union bodies, offices and agencies concerned may be involved in the proceedings of this committee. The European Parliament and national Parliaments shall be kept informed of the proceedings.

Article 72 (ex Article 64(1) TEC and ex Article 33 TEU)
This Title shall not affect the exercise of the responsibilities incumbent upon Member States with regard to the maintenance of law and order and the safeguarding of internal security.

Article 73
It shall be open to Member States to organise between themselves and under their responsibility such forms of cooperation and coordination as they deem appropriate between the competent departments of their administrations responsible for safeguarding national security.

Article 74 (ex Article 66 TEC)
The Council shall adopt measures to ensure administrative cooperation between the relevant departments of the Member States in the areas covered by this Title, as well as between those departments and the Commission. It shall act on a Commission proposal, subject to Article 76, and after consulting the European Parliament.

Article 75 (ex Article 60 TEC)
Where necessary to achieve the objectives set out in Article 67, as regards preventing and combating terrorism and related activities, the European Parliament and the Council, acting by means of regulations in accordance with the ordinary legislative procedure, shall define a framework for administrative measures with regard to capital movements and payments, such as the freezing of funds, financial assets or economic gains belonging to, or owned or held by, natural or legal persons, groups or non-State entities.

The Council, on a proposal from the Commission, shall adopt measures to implement the framework referred to in the first paragraph.

The acts referred to in this Article shall include necessary provisions on legal safeguards.

Article 76
The acts referred to in Chapters 4 and 5, together with the measures referred to in Article 74 which ensure administrative cooperation in the areas covered by these Chapters, shall be adopted:

    (a) on a proposal from the Commission, or

    (b) on the initiative of a quarter of the Member States.

Chapter 2
Policies on Border Checks, Asylum and Immigration

Article 77 (ex Article 62 TEC)
1. The Union shall develop a policy with a view to:

    (a) ensuring the absence of any controls on persons, whatever their nationality, when crossing internal borders;

    (b) carrying out checks on persons and efficient monitoring of the crossing of external borders;

    (c) the gradual introduction of an integrated management system for external borders.

2. For the purposes of paragraph 1, the European Parliament and the Council, acting in accordance with the ordinary legislative procedure, shall adopt measures concerning:

    (a) the common policy on visas and other short-stay residence permits;

    (b) the checks to which persons crossing external borders are subject;

    (c) the conditions under which nationals of third countries shall have the freedom to travel within the Union for a short period;

    (d) any measure necessary for the gradual establishment of an integrated management system for external borders;

    (e) the absence of any controls on persons, whatever their nationality, when crossing internal borders.

3. If action by the Union should prove necessary to facilitate the exercise of the right referred to in Article 20(2)(a), and if the Treaties have not provided the necessary powers, the Council, acting in accordance with a special legislative procedure, may adopt provisions

concerning passports, identity cards, residence permits or any other such document. The Council shall act unanimously after consulting the European Parliament.

4. This Article shall not affect the competence of the Member States concerning the geographical demarcation of their borders, in accordance with international law.

Article 78 (ex Articles 63, points 1 and 2, and 64(2) TEC)

1. The Union shall develop a common policy on asylum, subsidiary protection and temporary protection with a view to offering appropriate status to any third-country national requiring inter national protection and ensuring compliance with the principle of non-refoulement. This policy must be in accordance with the Geneva Convention of 28 July 1951 and the Protocol of 31 January 1967 relating to the status of refugees, and other relevant treaties.

2. For the purposes of paragraph 1, the European Parliament and the Council, acting in accordance with the ordinary legislative procedure, shall adopt measures for a common European asylum system comprising:

(a) a uniform status of asylum for nationals of third countries, valid throughout the Union;

(b) a uniform status of subsidiary protection for nationals of third countries who, without obtaining European asylum, are in need of international protection;

(c) a common system of temporary protection for displaced persons in the event of a massive inflow;

(d) common procedures for the granting and withdrawing of uniform asylum or subsidiary protection status;

(e) criteria and mechanisms for determining which Member State is responsible for considering an application for asylum or subsidiary protection;

(f) standards concerning the conditions for the reception of applicants for asylum or subsidiary protection;

(g) partnership and cooperation with third countries for the purpose of managing inflows of people applying for asylum or subsidiary or temporary protection.

3. In the event of one or more Member States being confronted by an emergency situation characterised by a sudden inflow of nationals of third countries, the Council, on a proposal from the Commission, may adopt provisional measures for the benefit of the Member State(s) concerned. It shall act after consulting the European Parliament.

Article 79 (ex Article 63, points 3 and 4, TEC)

1. The Union shall develop a common immigration policy aimed at ensuring, at all stages, the efficient management of migration flows, fair treatment of third-country nationals residing legally in Member States, and the prevention of, and enhanced measures to combat, illegal immigration and trafficking in human beings.

2. For the purposes of paragraph 1, the European Parliament and the Council, acting in accordance with the ordinary legislative procedure, shall adopt measures in the following areas:

(a) the conditions of entry and residence, and standards on the issue by Member States of long-term visas and residence permits, including those for the purpose of family reunification;
(b) the definition of the rights of third-country nationals residing legally in a Member State, including the conditions governing freedom of movement and of residence in other Member States;
(c) illegal immigration and unauthorised residence, including removal and repatriation of persons residing without authorisation;
(d) combating trafficking in persons, in particular women and children.

3. The Union may conclude agreements with third countries for the readmission to their countries of origin or provenance of third-country nationals who do not or who no longer fulfil the conditions for entry, presence or residence in the territory of one of the Member States.

4. The European Parliament and the Council, acting in accordance with the ordinary legislative procedure, may establish measures to provide incentives and support for the action of Member States with a view to promoting the integration of third-country nationals residing legally in their territories, excluding any harmonisation of the laws and regulations of the Member States.

5. This Article shall not affect the right of Member States to determine volumes of admission of third-country nationals coming from third countries to their territory in order to seek work, whether employed or self-employed.

Article 80

The policies of the Union set out in this Chapter and their implementation shall be governed by the principle of solidarity and fair sharing of responsibility, including its financial implications, between the Member States. Whenever necessary, the Union acts adopted pursuant to this Chapter shall contain appropriate measures to give effect to this principle.

Chapter 3
Judicial Cooperation in Civil Matters

Article 81 (ex Article 65 TEC)

1. The Union shall develop judicial cooperation in civil matters having cross-border implications, based on the principle of mutual recognition of judgments and of decisions in extrajudicial cases. Such cooperation may include the adoption of measures for the approximation of the laws and regulations of the Member States.

2. For the purposes of paragraph 1, the European Parliament and the Council, acting in accordance with the ordinary legislative procedure, shall adopt measures, particularly when necessary for the proper functioning of the internal market, aimed at ensuring:
(a) the mutual recognition and enforcement between Member States of judgments and of decisions in extrajudicial cases;
(b) the cross-border service of judicial and extrajudicial documents;

(c) the compatibility of the rules applicable in the Member States concerning conflict of laws and of jurisdiction;

(d) cooperation in the taking of evidence;

(e) effective access to justice;

(f) the elimination of obstacles to the proper functioning of civil proceedings, if necessary by promoting the compatibility of the rules on civil procedure applicable in the Member States;

(g) the development of alternative methods of dispute settlement;

(h) support for the training of the judiciary and judicial staff.

3. Notwithstanding paragraph 2, measures concerning family law with cross-border implications shall be established by the Council, acting in accordance with a special legislative procedure. The Council shall act unanimously after consulting the European Parliament.

The Council, on a proposal from the Commission, may adopt a decision determining those aspects of family law with cross-border implications which may be the subject of acts adopted by the ordinary legislative procedure. The Council shall act unanimously after consulting the European Parliament.

The proposal referred to in the second subparagraph shall be notified to the national Parliaments. If a national Parliament makes known its opposition within six months of the date of such notification, the decision shall not be adopted. In the absence of opposition, the Council may adopt the decision.

Chapter 4
Judicial Cooperation in Criminal Matters

Article 82 (ex Article 31 TEU)

1. Judicial cooperation in criminal matters in the Union shall be based on the principle of mutual recognition of judgments and judicial decisions and shall include the approximation of the laws and regulations of the Member States in the areas referred to in paragraph 2 and in Article 83.

The European Parliament and the Council, acting in accordance with the ordinary legislative procedure, shall adopt measures to:

(a) lay down rules and procedures for ensuring recognition throughout the Union of all forms of judgments and judicial decisions;

(b) prevent and settle conflicts of jurisdiction between Member States;

(c) support the training of the judiciary and judicial staff;

(d) facilitate cooperation between judicial or equivalent authorities of the Member States in relation to proceedings in criminal matters and the enforcement of decisions.

2. To the extent necessary to facilitate mutual recognition of judgments and judicial decisions and police and judicial cooperation in criminal matters having a cross-border dimension, the European Parliament and the Council may, by means of directives adopted

in accordance with the ordinary legislative procedure, establish minimum rules. Such rules shall take into account the differences between the legal traditions and systems of the Member States.

They shall concern:

(a) mutual admissibility of evidence between Member States;
(b) the rights of individuals in criminal procedure;
(c) the rights of victims of crime;
(d) any other specific aspects of criminal procedure which the Council has identified in advance by a decision; for the adoption of such a decision, the Council shall act unanimously after obtaining the consent of the European Parliament.

Adoption of the minimum rules referred to in this paragraph shall not prevent Member States from maintaining or introducing a higher level of protection for individuals.

3. Where a member of the Council considers that a draft directive as referred to in paragraph 2 would affect fundamental aspects of its criminal justice system, it may request that the draft directive be referred to the European Council. In that case, the ordinary legislative procedure shall be suspended. After discussion, and in case of a consensus, the European Council shall, within four months of this suspension, refer the draft back to the Council, which shall terminate the suspension of the ordinary legislative procedure.

Within the same timeframe, in case of disagreement, and if at least nine Member States wish to establish enhanced cooperation on the basis of the draft directive concerned, they shall notify the European Parliament, the Council and the Commission accordingly. In such a case, the authorisation to proceed with enhanced cooperation referred to in Article 20(2) of the Treaty on European Union and Article 329(1) of this Treaty shall be deemed to be granted and the provisions on enhanced cooperation shall apply.

Article 83 (ex Article 31 TEU)

1. The European Parliament and the Council may, by means of directives adopted in accordance with the ordinary legislative procedure, establish minimum rules concerning the definition of criminal offences and sanctions in the areas of particularly serious crime with a cross-border dimension resulting from the nature or impact of such offences or from a special need to combat them on a common basis.

These areas of crime are the following: terrorism, trafficking in human beings and sexual exploitation of women and children, illicit drug trafficking, illicit arms trafficking, money laundering, corruption, counterfeiting of means of payment, computer crime and organised crime.

On the basis of developments in crime, the Council may adopt a decision identifying other areas of crime that meet the criteria specified in this paragraph. It shall act unanimously after obtaining the consent of the European Parliament.

2. If the approximation of criminal laws and regulations of the Member States proves essential to ensure the effective implementation of a Union policy in an area which has been subject to harmonisation measures, directives may establish minimum rules with regard to

the definition of criminal offences and sanctions in the area concerned. Such directives shall be adopted by the same ordinary or special legislative procedure as was followed for the adoption of the harmonisation measures in question, without prejudice to Article 76.

3. Where a member of the Council considers that a draft directive as referred to in paragraph 1 or 2 would affect fundamental aspects of its criminal justice system, it may request that the draft directive be referred to the European Council. In that case, the ordinary legislative procedure shall be suspended. After discussion, and in case of a consensus, the European Council shall, within four months of this suspension, refer the draft back to the Council, which shall terminate the suspension of the ordinary legislative procedure.

Within the same timeframe, in case of disagreement, and if at least nine Member States wish to establish enhanced cooperation on the basis of the draft directive concerned, they shall notify the European Parliament, the Council and the Commission accordingly. In such a case, the authorisation to proceed with enhanced cooperation referred to in Article 20(2) of the Treaty on European Union and Article 329(1) of this Treaty shall be deemed to be granted and the provisions on enhanced cooperation shall apply.

Article 84

The European Parliament and the Council, acting in accordance with the ordinary legislative procedure, may establish measures to promote and support the action of Member States in the field of crime prevention, excluding any harmonisation of the laws and regulations of the Member States.

Article 85 (ex Article 31 TEU)

1. Eurojust's mission shall be to support and strengthen coordination and cooperation between national investigating and prosecuting authorities in relation to serious crime affecting two or more Member States or requiring a prosecution on common bases, on the basis of operations conducted and information supplied by the Member States' authorities and by Europol.

In this context, the European Parliament and the Council, by means of regulations adopted in accordance with the ordinary legislative procedure, shall determine Eurojust's structure, operation, field of action and tasks. These tasks may include:

(a) the initiation of criminal investigations, as well as proposing the initiation of prosecutions conducted by competent national authorities, particularly those relating to offences against the financial interests of the Union;

(b) the coordination of investigations and prosecutions referred to in point (a);

(c) the strengthening of judicial cooperation, including by resolution of conflicts of jurisdiction and by close cooperation with the European Judicial Network.

These regulations shall also determine arrangements for involving the European Parliament and national Parliaments in the evaluation of Eurojust's activities.

2. In the prosecutions referred to in paragraph 1, and without prejudice to Article 86, formal acts of judicial procedure shall be carried out by the competent national officials.

Article 86

1. In order to combat crimes affecting the financial interests of the Union, the Council, by means of regulations adopted in accordance with a special legislative procedure, may establish a European Public Prosecutor's Office from Eurojust. The Council shall act unanimously after obtaining the consent of the European Parliament.

In the absence of unanimity in the Council, a group of at least nine Member States may request that the draft regulation be referred to the European Council. In that case, the procedure in the Council shall be suspended. After discussion, and in case of a consensus, the European Council shall, within four months of this suspension, refer the draft back to the Council for adoption.

Within the same timeframe, in case of disagreement, and if at least nine Member States wish to establish enhanced cooperation on the basis of the draft regulation concerned, they shall notify the European Parliament, the Council and the Commission accordingly. In such a case, the authorisation to proceed with enhanced cooperation referred to in Article 20(2) of the Treaty on European Union and Article 329(1) of this Treaty shall be deemed to be granted and the provisions on enhanced cooperation shall apply.

2. The European Public Prosecutor's Office shall be responsible for investigating, prosecuting and bringing to judgment, where appropriate in liaison with Europol, the perpetrators of, and accomplices in, offences against the Union's financial interests, as determined by the regulation provided for in paragraph 1. It shall exercise the functions of prosecutor in the competent courts of the Member States in relation to such offences.

3. The regulations referred to in paragraph 1 shall determine the general rules applicable to the European Public Prosecutor's Office, the conditions governing the performance of its functions, the rules of procedure applicable to its activities, as well as those governing the admissibility of evidence, and the rules applicable to the judicial review of procedural measures taken by it in the performance of its functions.

4. The European Council may, at the same time or subsequently, adopt a decision amending paragraph 1 in order to extend the powers of the European Public Prosecutor's Office to include serious crime having a cross-border dimension and amending accordingly paragraph 2 as regards the perpetrators of, and accomplices in, serious crimes affecting more than one Member State. The European Council shall act unanimously after obtaining the consent of the European Parliament and after consulting the Commission.

Chapter 5
Police Cooperation

Article 87 (ex Article 30 TEU)

1. The Union shall establish police cooperation involving all the Member States' competent authorities, including police, customs and other specialised law enforcement services in relation to the prevention, detection and investigation of criminal offences.

2. For the purposes of paragraph 1, the European Parliament and the Council, acting in accordance with the ordinary legislative procedure, may establish measures concerning:

(a) the collection, storage, processing, analysis and exchange of relevant information;
(b) support for the training of staff, and cooperation on the exchange of staff, on equipment and on research into crime-detection;
(c) common investigative techniques in relation to the detection of serious forms of organised crime.

3. The Council, acting in accordance with a special legislative procedure, may establish measures concerning operational cooperation between the authorities referred to in this Article. The Council shall act unanimously after consulting the European Parliament.

In case of the absence of unanimity in the Council, a group of at least nine Member States may request that the draft measures be referred to the European Council. In that case, the procedure in the Council shall be suspended. After discussion, and in case of a consensus, the European Council shall, within four months of this suspension, refer the draft back to the Council for adoption.

Within the same timeframe, in case of disagreement, and if at least nine Member States wish to establish enhanced cooperation on the basis of the draft measures concerned, they shall notify the European Parliament, the Council and the Commission accordingly. In such a case, the authorisation to proceed with enhanced cooperation referred to in Article 20(2) of the Treaty on European Union and Article 329(1) of this Treaty shall be deemed to be granted and the provisions on enhanced cooperation shall apply.

The specific procedure provided for in the second and third subparagraphs shall not apply to acts which constitute a development of the Schengen acquis.

Article 88 (ex Article 30 TEU)

1. Europol's mission shall be to support and strengthen action by the Member States' police authorities and other law enforcement services and their mutual cooperation in preventing and combating serious crime affecting two or more Member States, terrorism and forms of crime which affect a common interest covered by a Union policy.

2. The European Parliament and the Council, by means of regulations adopted in accordance with the ordinary legislative procedure, shall determine Europol's structure, operation, field of action and tasks. These tasks may include:

(a) the collection, storage, processing, analysis and exchange of information, in particular that forwarded by the authorities of the Member States or third countries or bodies;

(b) the coordination, organisation and implementation of investigative and operational action carried out jointly with the Member States' competent authorities or in the context of joint investigative teams, where appropriate in liaison with Eurojust.

These regulations shall also lay down the procedures for scrutiny of Europol's activities by the European Parliament, together with national Parliaments.

3. Any operational action by Europol must be carried out in liaison and in agreement with the authorities of the Member State or States whose territory is concerned. The application of coercive measures shall be the exclusive responsibility of the competent national authorities.

Article 89 (ex Article 32 TEU)

The Council, acting in accordance with a special legislative procedure, shall lay down the conditions and limitations under which the competent authorities of the Member States referred to in Articles 82 and 87 may operate in the territory of another Member State in liaison and in agreement with the authorities of that State. The Council shall act unanimously after consulting the European Parliament.

Title VI
Transport

Article 90 (ex Article 70 TEC)

The objectives of the Treaties shall, in matters governed by this Title, be pursued within the framework of a common transport policy.

Article 91 (ex Article 71 TEC)

1. For the purpose of implementing Article 90, and taking into account the distinctive features of transport, the European Parliament and the Council shall, acting in accordance with the ordinary legislative procedure and after consulting the Economic and Social Committee and the Committee of the Regions, lay down:

(a) common rules applicable to international transport to or from the territory of a Member State or passing across the territory of one or more Member States;

(b) the conditions under which non-resident carriers may operate transport services within a Member State;

(c) measures to improve transport safety;

(d) any other appropriate provisions.

2. When the measures referred to in paragraph 1 are adopted, account shall be taken of cases where their application might seriously affect the standard of living and level of employment in certain regions, and the operation of transport facilities.

Article 92 (ex Article 72 TEC)

Until the provisions referred to in Article 91(1) have been laid down, no Member State may, unless the Council has unanimously adopted a measure granting a derogation, make the various provisions governing the subject on 1 January 1958 or, for acceding States, the date of their accession less favourable in their direct or indirect effect on carriers of other Member States as compared with carriers who are nationals of that State.

Article 93 (ex Article 73 TEC)

Aids shall be compatible with the Treaties if they meet the needs of coordination of transport or if they represent reimbursement for the discharge of certain obligations inherent in the concept of a public service.

Article 94 (ex Article 74 TEC)
Any measures taken within the framework of the Treaties in respect of transport rates and conditions shall take account of the economic circumstances of carriers.

Article 95 (ex Article 75 TEC)
1. In the case of transport within the Union, discrimination which takes the form of carriers charging different rates and imposing different conditions for the carriage of the same goods over the same transport links on grounds of the country of origin or of destination of the goods in question shall be prohibited.
2. Paragraph 1 shall not prevent the European Parliament and the Council from adopting other measures pursuant to Article 91(1).
3. The Council shall, on a proposal from the Commission and after consulting the European Parliament and the Economic and Social Committee, lay down rules for implementing the provisions of paragraph 1.
The Council may in particular lay down the provisions needed to enable the institutions of the Union to secure compliance with the rule laid down in paragraph 1 and to ensure that users benefit from it to the full.
4. The Commission shall, acting on its own initiative or on application by a Member State, investigate any cases of discrimination falling within paragraph 1 and, after consulting any Member State concerned, shall take the necessary decisions within the framework of the rules laid down in accordance with the provisions of paragraph 3.

Article 96 (ex Article 76 TEC)
1. The imposition by a Member State, in respect of transport operations carried out within the Union, of rates and conditions involving any element of support or protection in the interest of one or more particular undertakings or industries shall be prohibited, unless authorised by the Commission.
2. The Commission shall, acting on its own initiative or on application by a Member State, examine the rates and conditions referred to in paragraph 1, taking account in particular of the requirements of an appropriate regional economic policy, the needs of underdeveloped areas and the problems of areas seriously affected by political circumstances on the one hand, and of the effects of such rates and conditions on competition between the different modes of transport on the other.
After consulting each Member State concerned, the Commission shall take the necessary decisions.
3. The prohibition provided for in paragraph 1 shall not apply to tariffs fixed to meet competition.

Article 97 (ex Article 77 TEC)
Charges or dues in respect of the crossing of frontiers which are charged by a carrier in addition to the transport rates shall not exceed a reasonable level after taking the costs actually incurred thereby into account.

Member States shall endeavour to reduce these costs progressively.

The Commission may make recommendations to Member States for the application of this Article.

Article 98 (ex Article 78 TEC)

The provisions of this Title shall not form an obstacle to the application of measures taken in the Federal Republic of Germany to the extent that such measures are required in order to compensate for the economic disadvantages caused by the division of Germany to the economy of certain areas of the Federal Republic affected by that division. Five years after the entry into force of the Treaty of Lisbon, the Council, acting on a proposal from the Commission, may adopt a decision repealing this Article.

Article 99 (ex Article 79 TEC)

An Advisory Committee consisting of experts designated by the governments of Member States shall be attached to the Commission. The Commission, whenever it considers it desirable, shall consult the Committee on transport matters.

Article 100 (ex Article 80 TEC)

1. The provisions of this Title shall apply to transport by rail, road and inland waterway.

2. The European Parliament and the Council, acting in accordance with the ordinary legislative procedure, may lay down appropriate provisions for sea and air transport. They shall act after consulting the Economic and Social Committee and the Committee of the Regions.

Title VII
Common Rules on Competition, Taxation and Approximation of Laws

Chapter 1
Rules on Competition

Section 1
Rules Applying to Undertakings

Article 101 (ex Article 81 TEC)

1. The following shall be prohibited as incompatible with the internal market: all agreements between undertakings, decisions by associations of undertakings and concerted practices which may affect trade between Member States and which have as their object or effect the prevention, restriction or distortion of competition within the internal market, and in particular those which:

    (a) directly or indirectly fix purchase or selling prices or any other trading conditions;

    (b) limit or control production, markets, technical development, or investment;

    (c) share markets or sources of supply;

(d) apply dissimilar conditions to equivalent transactions with other trading parties, thereby placing them at a competitive disadvantage;
(e) make the conclusion of contracts subject to acceptance by the other parties of supplementary obligations which, by their nature or according to commercial usage, have no connection with the subject of such contracts.
2. Any agreements or decisions prohibited pursuant to this Article shall be automatically void.
3. The provisions of paragraph 1 may, however, be declared inapplicable in the case of:
   – any agreement or category of agreements between undertakings,
   – any decision or category of decisions by associations of undertakings,
   – any concerted practice or category of concerted practices,

which contributes to improving the production or distribution of goods or to promoting technical or economic progress, while allowing consumers a fair share of the resulting benefit, and which does not:
   (a) impose on the undertakings concerned restrictions which are not indispensable to the attainment of these objectives;
   (b) afford such undertakings the possibility of eliminating competition in respect of a substantial part of the products in question.

Article 102 (ex Article 82 TEC)

Any abuse by one or more undertakings of a dominant position within the internal market or in a substantial part of it shall be prohibited as incompatible with the internal market in so far as it may affect trade between Member States.
Such abuse may, in particular, consist in:
   (a) directly or indirectly imposing unfair purchase or selling prices or other unfair trading conditions;
   (b) limiting production, markets or technical development to the prejudice of consumers;
   (c) applying dissimilar conditions to equivalent transactions with other trading parties, thereby placing them at a competitive disadvantage;
   (d) making the conclusion of contracts subject to acceptance by the other parties of supplementary obligations which, by their nature or according to commercial usage, have no connection with the subject of such contracts.

Article 103 (ex Article 83 TEC)

1. The appropriate regulations or directives to give effect to the principles set out in Articles 101 and 102 shall be laid down by the Council, on a proposal from the Commission and after consulting the European Parliament.
2. The regulations or directives referred to in paragraph 1 shall be designed in particular:
   (a) to ensure compliance with the prohibitions laid down in Article 101(1) and in Article 102 by making provision for fines and periodic penalty payments;

(b) to lay down detailed rules for the application of Article 101(3), taking into account the need to ensure effective supervision on the one hand, and to simplify administration to the greatest possible extent on the other;

(c) to define, if need be, in the various branches of the economy, the scope of the provisions of Articles 101 and 102;

(d) to define the respective functions of the Commission and of the Court of Justice of the European Union in applying the provisions laid down in this paragraph;

(e) to determine the relationship between national laws and the provisions contained in this Section or adopted pursuant to this Article.

Article 104 (ex Article 84 TEC)

Until the entry into force of the provisions adopted in pursuance of Article 103, the authorities in Member States shall rule on the admissibility of agreements, decisions and concerted practices and on abuse of a dominant position in the internal market in accordance with the law of their country and with the provisions of Article 101, in particular paragraph 3, and of Article 102.

Article 105 (ex Article 85 TEC)

1. Without prejudice to Article 104, the Commission shall ensure the application of the principles laid down in Articles 101 and 102. On application by a Member State or on its own initiative, and in cooperation with the competent authorities in the Member States, which shall give it their assistance, the Commission shall investigate cases of suspected infringement of these principles. If it finds that there has been an infringement, it shall propose appropriate measures to bring it to an end.

2. If the infringement is not brought to an end, the Commission shall record such infringement of the principles in a reasoned decision. The Commission may publish its decision and authorise Member States to take the measures, the conditions and details of which it shall determine, needed to remedy the situation.

3. The Commission may adopt regulations relating to the categories of agreement in respect of which the Council has adopted a regulation or a directive pursuant to Article 103(2)(b).

Article 106 (ex Article 86 TEC)

1. In the case of public undertakings and undertakings to which Member States grant special or exclusive rights, Member States shall neither enact nor maintain in force any measure contrary to the rules contained in the Treaties, in particular to those rules provided for in Article 18 and Articles 101 to 109.

2. Undertakings entrusted with the operation of services of general economic interest or having the character of a revenue-producing monopoly shall be subject to the rules contained in the Treaties, in particular to the rules on competition, in so far as the application of such rules does not obstruct the performance, in law or in fact, of the particular tasks assigned

to them. The development of trade must not be affected to such an extent as would be contrary to the interests of the Union.

3. The Commission shall ensure the application of the provisions of this Article and shall, where necessary, address appropriate directives or decisions to Member States.

Section 2
Aids Granted by States

Article 107 (ex Article 87 TEC)

1. Save as otherwise provided in the Treaties, any aid granted by a Member State or through State resources in any form whatsoever which distorts or threatens to distort competition by favouring certain undertakings or the production of certain goods shall, in so far as it affects trade between Member States, be incompatible with the internal market.

2. The following shall be compatible with the internal market:

(a) aid having a social character, granted to individual consumers, provided that such aid is granted without discrimination related to the origin of the products concerned;

(b) aid to make good the damage caused by natural disasters or exceptional occurrences;

(c) aid granted to the economy of certain areas of the Federal Republic of Germany affected by the division of Germany, in so far as such aid is required in order to compensate for the economic disadvantages caused by that division. Five years after the entry into force of the Treaty of Lisbon, the Council, acting on a proposal from the Commission, may adopt a decision repealing this point.

3. The following may be considered to be compatible with the internal market:

(a) aid to promote the economic development of areas where the standard of living is abnormally low or where there is serious underemployment, and of the regions referred to in Article 349, in view of their structural, economic and social situation;

(b) aid to promote the execution of an important project of common European interest or to remedy a serious disturbance in the economy of a Member State;

(c) aid to facilitate the development of certain economic activities or of certain economic areas, where such aid does not adversely affect trading conditions to an extent contrary to the common interest;

(d) aid to promote culture and heritage conservation where such aid does not affect trading conditions and competition in the Union to an extent that is contrary to the common interest;

(e) such other categories of aid as may be specified by decision of the Council on a proposal from the Commission.

Article 108 (ex Article 88 TEC)

1. The Commission shall, in cooperation with Member States, keep under constant review all systems of aid existing in those States. It shall propose to the latter any appropriate measures required by the progressive development or by the functioning of the internal market.

2. If, after giving notice to the parties concerned to submit their comments, the Commission finds that aid granted by a State or through State resources is not compatible with the internal market having regard to Article 107, or that such aid is being misused, it shall decide that the State concerned shall abolish or alter such aid within a period of time to be determined by the Commission.

If the State concerned does not comply with this decision within the prescribed time, the Commission or any other interested State may, in derogation from the provisions of Articles 258 and 259, refer the matter to the Court of Justice of the European Union direct.

On application by a Member State, the Council may, acting unanimously, decide that aid which that State is granting or intends to grant shall be considered to be compatible with the internal market, in derogation from the provisions of Article 107 or from the regulations provided for in Article 109, if such a decision is justified by exceptional circumstances. If, as regards the aid in question, the Commission has already initiated the procedure provided for in the first subparagraph of this paragraph, the fact that the State concerned has made its application to the Council shall have the effect of suspending that procedure until the Council has made its attitude known.

If, however, the Council has not made its attitude known within three months of the said application being made, the Commission shall give its decision on the case.

3. The Commission shall be informed, in sufficient time to enable it to submit its comments, of any plans to grant or alter aid. If it considers that any such plan is not compatible with the internal market having regard to Article 107, it shall without delay initiate the procedure provided for in paragraph 2. The Member State concerned shall not put its proposed measures into effect until this procedure has resulted in a final decision.

4. The Commission may adopt regulations relating to the categories of State aid that the Council has, pursuant to Article 109, determined may be exempted from the procedure provided for by paragraph 3 of this Article.

Article 109 (ex Article 89 TEC)

The Council, on a proposal from the Commission and after consulting the European Parliament, may make any appropriate regulations for the application of Articles 107 and 108 and may in particular determine the conditions in which Article 108(3) shall apply and the categories of aid exempted from this procedure.

Chapter 2
Tax Provisions

Article 110 (ex Article 90 TEC)

No Member State shall impose, directly or indirectly, on the products of other Member States any internal taxation of any kind in excess of that imposed directly or indirectly on similar domestic products.

Furthermore, no Member State shall impose on the products of other Member States any internal taxation of such a nature as to afford indirect protection to other products.

Article 111 (ex Article 91 TEC)
Where products are exported to the territory of any Member State, any repayment of internal taxation shall not exceed the internal taxation imposed on them whether directly or indirectly.

Article 112 (ex Article 92 TEC)
In the case of charges other than turnover taxes, excise duties and other forms of indirect taxation, remissions and repayments in respect of exports to other Member States may not be granted and countervailing charges in respect of imports from Member States may not be imposed unless the measures contemplated have been previously approved for a limited period by the Council on a proposal from the Commission.

Article 113 (ex Article 93 TEC)
The Council shall, acting unanimously in accordance with a special legislative procedure and after consulting the European Parliament and the Economic and Social Committee, adopt provisions for the harmonisation of legislation concerning turnover taxes, excise duties and other forms of indirect taxation to the extent that such harmonisation is necessary to ensure the establishment and the functioning of the internal market and to avoid distortion of competition.

Chapter 3
Approximation of Laws

Article 114 (ex Article 95 TEC)
1. Save where otherwise provided in the Treaties, the following provisions shall apply for the achievement of the objectives set out in Article 26. The European Parliament and the Council shall, acting in accordance with the ordinary legislative procedure and after consulting the Economic and Social Committee, adopt the measures for the approximation of the provisions laid down by law, regulation or administrative action in Member States which have as their object the establishment and functioning of the internal market.
2. Paragraph 1 shall not apply to fiscal provisions, to those relating to the free movement of persons nor to those relating to the rights and interests of employed persons.
3. The Commission, in its proposals envisaged in paragraph 1 concerning health, safety, environ mental protection and consumer protection, will take as a base a high level of protection, taking account in particular of any new development based on scientific facts. Within their respective powers, the European Parliament and the Council will also seek to achieve this objective.
4. If, after the adoption of a harmonisation measure by the European Parliament and the Council, by the Council or by the Commission, a Member State deems it necessary to maintain national provisions on grounds of major needs referred to in Article 36, or relating to the protection of the environment or the working environment, it shall notify the Commission of these provisions as well as the grounds for maintaining them.

5. Moreover, without prejudice to paragraph 4, if, after the adoption of a harmonisation measure by the European Parliament and the Council, by the Council or by the Commission, a Member State deems it necessary to introduce national provisions based on new scientific evidence relating to the protection of the environment or the working environment on grounds of a problem specific to that Member State arising after the adoption of the harmonisation measure, it shall notify the Commission of the envisaged provisions as well as the grounds for introducing them.

6. The Commission shall, within six months of the notifications as referred to in paragraphs 4 and 5, approve or reject the national provisions involved after having verified whether or not they are a means of arbitrary discrimination or a disguised restriction on trade between Member States and whether or not they shall constitute an obstacle to the functioning of the internal market.

In the absence of a decision by the Commission within this period the national provisions referred to in paragraphs 4 and 5 shall be deemed to have been approved.

When justified by the complexity of the matter and in the absence of danger for human health, the Commission may notify the Member State concerned that the period referred to in this paragraph may be extended for a further period of up to six months.

7. When, pursuant to paragraph 6, a Member State is authorised to maintain or introduce national provisions derogating from a harmonisation measure, the Commission shall immediately examine whether to propose an adaptation to that measure.

8. When a Member State raises a specific problem on public health in a field which has been the subject of prior harmonisation measures, it shall bring it to the attention of the Commission which shall immediately examine whether to propose appropriate measures to the Council.

9. By way of derogation from the procedure laid down in Articles 258 and 259, the Commission and any Member State may bring the matter directly before the Court of Justice of the European Union if it considers that another Member State is making improper use of the powers provided for in this Article.

10. The harmonisation measures referred to above shall, in appropriate cases, include a safeguard clause authorising the Member States to take, for one or more of the non-economic reasons referred to in Article 36, provisional measures subject to a Union control procedure.

Article 115 (ex Article 94 TEC)

Without prejudice to Article 114, the Council shall, acting unanimously in accordance with a special legislative procedure and after consulting the European Parliament and the Economic and Social Committee, issue directives for the approximation of such laws, regulations or administrative provisions of the Member States as directly affect the establishment or functioning of the internal market.

Article 116 (ex Article 96 TEC)

Where the Commission finds that a difference between the provisions laid down by law, regulation or administrative action in Member States is distorting the conditions of competition in the internal market and that the resultant distortion needs to be eliminated, it shall consult the Member States concerned.

If such consultation does not result in an agreement eliminating the distortion in question, the European, Parliament and the Council, acting in accordance with the ordinary legislative procedure, shall issue the necessary directives. Any other appropriate measures provided for in the Treaties may be adopted.

Article 117 (ex Article 97 TEC)

1. Where there is a reason to fear that the adoption or amendment of a provision laid down by law, regulation or administrative action may cause distortion within the meaning of Article 116, a Member State desiring to proceed therewith shall consult the Commission. After consulting the Member States, the Commission shall recommend to the States concerned such measures as may be appropriate to avoid the distortion in question.

2. If a State desiring to introduce or amend its own provisions does not comply with the recommendation addressed to it by the Commission, other Member States shall not be required, pursuant to Article 116, to amend their own provisions in order to eliminate such distortion. If the Member State which has ignored the recommendation of the Commission causes distortion detrimental only to itself, the provisions of Article 116 shall not apply.

Article 118

In the context of the establishment and functioning of the internal market, the European Parliament and the Council, acting in accordance with the ordinary legislative procedure, shall establish measures for the creation of European intellectual property rights to provide uniform protection of intellectual property rights throughout the Union and for the setting up of centralised Union-wide authorisation, coordination and supervision arrangements.

The Council, acting in accordance with a special legislative procedure, shall by means of regulations establish language arrangements for the European intellectual property rights. The Council shall act unanimously after consulting the European Parliament.

Title VIII
Economic and Monetary Policy

Article 119 (ex Article 4 TEC)

1. For the purposes set out in Article 3 of the Treaty on European Union, the activities of the Member States and the Union shall include, as provided in the Treaties, the adoption of an economic policy which is based on the close coordination of Member States' economic policies, on the internal market and on the definition of common objectives, and conducted in accordance with the principle of an open market economy with free competition.

2. Concurrently with the foregoing, and as provided in the Treaties and in accordance with the procedures set out therein, these activities shall include a single currency, the euro, and the definition and conduct of a single monetary policy and exchange-rate policy the primary

objective of both of which shall be to maintain price stability and, without prejudice to this objective, to support the general economic policies in the Union, in accordance with the principle of an open market economy with free competition.

3. These activities of the Member States and the Union shall entail compliance with the following guiding principles: stable prices, sound public finances and monetary conditions and a sustainable balance of payments.

Chapter 1
Economic Policy

Article 120 (ex Article 98 TEC)

Member States shall conduct their economic policies with a view to contributing to the achievement of the objectives of the Union, as defined in Article 3 of the Treaty on European Union, and in the context of the broad guidelines referred to in Article 121(2). The Member States and the Union shall act in accordance with the principle of an open market economy with free competition, favouring an efficient allocation of resources, and in compliance with the principles set out in Article 119.

Article 121 (ex Article 99 TEC)

1. Member States shall regard their economic policies as a matter of common concern and shall coordinate them within the Council, in accordance with the provisions of Article 120.
2. The Council shall, on a recommendation from the Commission, formulate a draft for the broad guidelines of the economic policies of the Member States and of the Union, and shall report its findings to the European Council.
The European Council shall, acting on the basis of the report from the Council, discuss a conclusion on the broad guidelines of the economic policies of the Member States and of the Union.
On the basis of this conclusion, the Council shall adopt a recommendation setting out these broad guidelines. The Council shall inform the European Parliament of its recommendation.
3. In order to ensure closer coordination of economic policies and sustained convergence of the economic performances of the Member States, the Council shall, on the basis of reports submitted by the Commission, monitor economic developments in each of the Member States and in the Union as well as the consistency of economic policies with the broad guidelines referred to in paragraph 2, and regularly carry out an overall assessment.
For the purpose of this multilateral surveillance, Member States shall forward information to the Commission about important measures taken by them in the field of their economic policy and such other information as they deem necessary.
4. Where it is established, under the procedure referred to in paragraph 3, that the economic policies of a Member State are not consistent with the broad guidelines referred to in paragraph 2 or that they risk jeopardising the proper functioning of economic and monetary union, the Commission may address a warning to the Member State concerned. The Council, on a recommendation from the Commission, may address the necessary

recommendations to the Member State concerned. The Council may, on a proposal from the Commission, decide to make its recommendations public.
Within the scope of this paragraph, the Council shall act without taking into account the vote of the member of the Council representing the Member State concerned.
A qualified majority of the other members of the Council shall be defined in accordance with Article 238(3)(a).
5. The President of the Council and the Commission shall report to the European Parliament on the results of multilateral surveillance. The President of the Council may be invited to appear before the competent committee of the European Parliament if the Council has made its recommendations public.
6. The European Parliament and the Council, acting by means of regulations in accordance with the ordinary legislative procedure, may adopt detailed rules for the multilateral surveillance procedure referred to in paragraphs 3 and 4.

Article 122 (ex Article 100 TEC)
1. Without prejudice to any other procedures provided for in the Treaties, the Council, on a proposal from the Commission, may decide, in a spirit of solidarity between Member States, upon the measures appropriate to the economic situation, in particular if severe difficulties arise in the supply of certain products, notably in the area of energy.
2. Where a Member State is in difficulties or is seriously threatened with severe difficulties caused by natural disasters or exceptional occurrences beyond its control, the Council, on a proposal from the Commission, may grant, under certain conditions, Union financial assistance to the Member State concerned. The President of the Council shall inform the European Parliament of the decision taken.

Article 123 (ex Article 101 TEC)
1. Overdraft facilities or any other type of credit facility with the European Central Bank or with the central banks of the Member States (hereinafter referred to as 'national central banks') in favour of Union institutions, bodies, offices or agencies, central governments, regional, local or other public authorities, other bodies governed by public law, or public undertakings of Member States shall be prohibited, as shall the purchase directly from them by the European Central Bank or national central banks of debt instruments.
2. Paragraph 1 shall not apply to publicly owned credit institutions which, in the context of the supply of reserves by central banks, shall be given the same treatment by national central banks and the European Central Bank as private credit institutions.

Article 124 (ex Article 102 TEC)
Any measure, not based on prudential considerations, establishing privileged access by Union institutions, bodies, offices or agencies, central governments, regional, local or other public authorities, other bodies governed by public law, or public undertakings of Member States to financial institutions, shall be prohibited.

Article 125 (ex Article 103 TEC)
1. The Union shall not be liable for or assume the commitments of central governments, regional, local or other public authorities, other bodies governed by public law, or public undertakings of any Member State, without prejudice to mutual financial guarantees for the joint execution of a specific project. A Member State shall not be liable for or assume the commitments of central governments, regional, local or other public authorities, other bodies governed by public law, or public under takings of another Member State, without prejudice to mutual financial guarantees for the joint execution of a specific project.
2. The Council, on a proposal from the Commission and after consulting the European Parliament, may, as required, specify definitions for the application of the prohibitions referred to in Articles 123 and 124 and in this Article.

Article 126 (ex Article 104 TEC)
1. Member States shall avoid excessive government deficits.
2. The Commission shall monitor the development of the budgetary situation and of the stock of government debt in the Member States with a view to identifying gross errors. In particular it shall examine compliance with budgetary discipline on the basis of the following two criteria:
> (a) whether the ratio of the planned or actual government deficit to gross domestic product exceeds a reference value, unless:
>> – either the ratio has declined substantially and continuously and reached a level that comes close to the reference value,
>> – or, alternatively, the excess over the reference value is only exceptional and temporary and the ratio remains close to the reference value;
>
> (b) whether the ratio of government debt to gross domestic product exceeds a reference value, unless the ratio is sufficiently diminishing and approaching the reference value at a satisfactory pace.

The reference values are specified in the Protocol on the excessive deficit procedure annexed to the Treaties.

3. If a Member State does not fulfil the requirements under one or both of these criteria, the Commission shall prepare a report. The report of the Commission shall also take into account whether the government deficit exceeds government investment expenditure and take into account all other relevant factors, including the medium-term economic and budgetary position of the Member State.

The Commission may also prepare a report if, notwithstanding the fulfilment of the requirements under the criteria, it is of the opinion that there is a risk of an excessive deficit in a Member State.

4. The Economic and Financial Committee shall formulate an opinion on the report of the Commission.
5. If the Commission considers that an excessive deficit in a Member State exists or may occur, it shall address an opinion to the Member State concerned and shall inform the Council accordingly.

6. The Council shall, on a proposal from the Commission, and having considered any observations which the Member State concerned may wish to make, decide after an overall assessment whether an excessive deficit exists.

7. Where the Council decides, in accordance with paragraph 6, that an excessive deficit exists, it shall adopt, without undue delay, on a recommendation from the Commission, recommendations addressed to the Member State concerned with a view to bringing that situation to an end within a given period. Subject to the provisions of paragraph 8, these recommendations shall not be made public.

8. Where it establishes that there has been no effective action in response to its recommendations within the period laid down, the Council may make its recommendations public.

9. If a Member State persists in failing to put into practice the recommendations of the Council, the Council may decide to give notice to the Member State to take, within a specified time limit, measures for the deficit reduction which is judged necessary by the Council in order to remedy the situation.

In such a case, the Council may request the Member State concerned to submit reports in accordance with a specific timetable in order to examine the adjustment efforts of that Member State.

10. The rights to bring actions provided for in Articles 258 and 259 may not be exercised within the framework of paragraphs 1 to 9 of this Article.

11. As long as a Member State fails to comply with a decision taken in accordance with paragraph 9, the Council may decide to apply or, as the case may be, intensify one or more of the following measures:

– to require the Member State concerned to publish additional information, to be specified by the Council, before issuing bonds and securities,

– to invite the European Investment Bank to reconsider its lending policy towards the Member State concerned,

– to require the Member State concerned to make a non-interest-bearing deposit of an appropriate size with the Union until the excessive deficit has, in the view of the Council, been corrected,

– to impose fines of an appropriate size.

The President of the Council shall inform the European Parliament of the decisions taken.

12. The Council shall abrogate some or all of its decisions or recommendations referred to in paragraphs 6 to 9 and 11 to the extent that the excessive deficit in the Member State concerned has, in the view of the Council, been corrected. If the Council has previously made public recommendations, it shall, as soon as the decision under paragraph 8 has been abrogated, make a public statement that an excessive deficit in the Member State concerned no longer exists.

13. When taking the decisions or recommendations referred to in paragraphs 8, 9, 11 and 12, the Council shall act on a recommendation from the Commission.

When the Council adopts the measures referred to in paragraphs 6 to 9, 11 and 12, it shall act without taking into account the vote of the member of the Council representing the Member State concerned.

A qualified majority of the other members of the Council shall be defined in accordance with Article 238(3)(a).

14. Further provisions relating to the implementation of the procedure described in this Article are set out in the Protocol on the excessive deficit procedure annexed to the Treaties.

The Council shall, acting unanimously in accordance with a special legislative procedure and after consulting the European Parliament and the European Central Bank, adopt the appropriate provisions which shall then replace the said Protocol.

Subject to the other provisions of this paragraph, the Council shall, on a proposal from the Commission and after consulting the European Parliament, lay down detailed rules and definitions for the application of the provisions of the said Protocol.

Chapter 2
Monetary Policy

Article 127 (ex Article 105 TEC)

1. The primary objective of the European System of Central Banks (hereinafter referred to as 'the ESCB') shall be to maintain price stability. Without prejudice to the objective of price stability, the ESCB shall support the general economic policies in the Union with a view to contributing to the achievement of the objectives of the Union as laid down in Article 3 of the Treaty on European Union. The ESCB shall act in accordance with the principle of an open market economy with free competition, favouring an efficient allocation of resources, and in compliance with the principles set out in Article 119.
2. The basic tasks to be carried out through the ESCB shall be:
    – to define and implement the monetary policy of the Union,
    – to conduct foreign-exchange operations consistent with the provisions of Article 219,
    – to hold and manage the official foreign reserves of the Member States,
    – to promote the smooth operation of payment systems.
3. The third indent of paragraph 2 shall be without prejudice to the holding and management by the governments of Member States of foreign-exchange working balances.
4. The European Central Bank shall be consulted:
    – on any proposed Union act in its fields of competence,
    – by national authorities regarding any draft legislative provision in its fields of competence, but within the limits and under the conditions set out by the Council in accordance with the procedure laid down in Article 129(4).

The European Central Bank may submit opinions to the appropriate Union institutions, bodies, offices or agencies or to national authorities on matters in its fields of competence.

5. The ESCB shall contribute to the smooth conduct of policies pursued by the competent authorities relating to the prudential supervision of credit institutions and the stability of the financial system.
6. The Council, acting by means of regulations in accordance with a special legislative procedure, may unanimously, and after consulting the European Parliament and the

European Central Bank, confer specific tasks upon the European Central Bank concerning policies relating to the prudential supervision of credit institutions and other financial institutions with the exception of insurance undertakings.

Article 128 (ex Article 106 TEC)
1. The European Central Bank shall have the exclusive right to authorise the issue of euro banknotes within the Union. The European Central Bank and the national central banks may issue such notes. The banknotes issued by the European Central Bank and the national central banks shall be the only such notes to have the status of legal tender within the Union.
2. Member States may issue euro coins subject to approval by the European Central Bank of the volume of the issue. The Council, on a proposal from the Commission and after consulting the European Parliament and the European Central Bank, may adopt measures to harmonise the denominations and technical specifications of all coins intended for circulation to the extent necessary to permit their smooth circulation within the Union.

Article 129 (ex Article 107 TEC)
1. The ESCB shall be governed by the decision-making bodies of the European Central Bank which shall be the Governing Council and the Executive Board.
2. The Statute of the European System of Central Banks and of the European Central Bank (hereinafter referred to as 'the Statute of the ESCB and of the ECB') is laid down in a Protocol annexed to the Treaties.
3. Articles 5.1, 5.2, 5.3, 17, 18, 19.1, 22, 23, 24, 26, 32.2, 32.3, 32.4, 32.6, 33.1(a) and 36 of the Statute of the ESCB and of the ECB may be amended by the European Parliament and the Council, acting in accordance with the ordinary legislative procedure. They shall act either on a recommendation from the European Central Bank and after consulting the Commission or on a proposal from the Commission and after consulting the European Central Bank.
4. The Council, either on a proposal from the Commission and after consulting the European Parliament and the European Central Bank or on a recommendation from the European Central Bank and after consulting the European Parliament and the Commission, shall adopt the provisions referred to in Articles 4, 5.4, 19.2, 20, 28.1, 29.2, 30.4 and 34.3 of the Statute of the ESCB and of the ECB.

Article 130 (ex Article 108 TEC)
When exercising the powers and carrying out the tasks and duties conferred upon them by the Treaties and the Statute of the ESCB and of the ECB, neither the European Central Bank, nor a national central bank, nor any member of their decision-making bodies shall seek or take instructions from Union institutions, bodies, offices or agencies, from any government of a Member State or from any other body. The Union institutions, bodies, offices or agencies and the governments of the Member States undertake to respect this principle and not to seek to influence the members of the decision-making bodies of the European Central Bank or of the national central banks in the performance of their tasks.

Article 131 (ex Article 109 TEC)
Each Member State shall ensure that its national legislation including the statutes of its national central bank is compatible with the Treaties and the Statute of the ESCB and of the ECB.

Article 132 (ex Article 110 TEC)
1. In order to carry out the tasks entrusted to the ESCB, the European Central Bank shall, in accordance with the provisions of the Treaties and under the conditions laid down in the Statute of the ESCB and of the ECB:
 - make regulations to the extent necessary to implement the tasks defined in Article 3.1, first indent, Articles 19.1, 22 and 25.2 of the Statute of the ESCB and of the ECB in cases which shall be laid down in the acts of the Council referred to in Article 129(4),
 - take decisions necessary for carrying out the tasks entrusted to the ESCB under the Treaties and the Statute of the ESCB and of the ECB,
 - make recommendations and deliver opinions.
2. The European Central Bank may decide to publish its decisions, recommendations and opinions.
3. Within the limits and under the conditions adopted by the Council under the procedure laid down in Article 129(4), the European Central Bank shall be entitled to impose fines or periodic penalty payments on undertakings for failure to comply with obligations under its regulations and decisions.

Article 133
Without prejudice to the powers of the European Central Bank, the European Parliament and the Council, acting in accordance with the ordinary legislative procedure, shall lay down the measures necessary for the use of the euro as the single currency. Such measures shall be adopted after consultation of the European Central Bank.

Chapter 3
Institutional Provisions

Article 134 (ex Article 114 TEC)
1. In order to promote coordination of the policies of Member States to the full extent needed for the functioning of the internal market, an Economic and Financial Committee is hereby set up.
2. The Economic and Financial Committee shall have the following tasks:
 - to deliver opinions at the request of the Council or of the Commission, or on its own initiative for submission to those institutions,
 - to keep under review the economic and financial situation of the Member States and of the Union and to report regularly thereon to the Council and to the Commission, in particular on financial relations with third countries and international institutions,

- without prejudice to Article 240, to contribute to the preparation of the work of the Council referred to in Articles 66, 75, 121(2), (3), (4) and (6), 122, 124, 125, 126, 127(6), 128(2), 129(3) and (4), 138, 140(2) and (3), 143, 144(2) and (3), and in Article 219, and to carry out other advisory and preparatory tasks assigned to it by the Council,

- to examine, at least once a year, the situation regarding the movement of capital and the freedom of payments, as they result from the application of the Treaties and of measures adopted by the Council; the examination shall cover all measures relating to capital movements and payments; the Committee shall report to the Commission and to the Council on the outcome of this examination.

The Member States, the Commission and the European Central Bank shall each appoint no more than two members of the Committee.

3. The Council shall, on a proposal from the Commission and after consulting the European Central Bank and the Committee referred to in this Article, lay down detailed provisions concerning the composition of the Economic and Financial Committee. The President of the Council shall inform the European Parliament of such a decision.

4. In addition to the tasks set out in paragraph 2, if and as long as there are Member States with a derogation as referred to in Article 139, the Committee shall keep under review the monetary and financial situation and the general payments system of those Member States and report regularly thereon to the Council and to the Commission.

Article 135 (ex Article 115 TEC)

For matters within the scope of Articles 121(4), 126 with the exception of paragraph 14, 138, 140(1), 140(2), first subparagraph, 140(3) and 219, the Council or a Member State may request the Commission to make a recommendation or a proposal, as appropriate. The Commission shall examine this request and submit its conclusions to the Council without delay.

Chapter 4
Provisions Specific to Member States whose Currency is the Euro

Article 136

1. In order to ensure the proper functioning of economic and monetary union, and in accordance with the relevant provisions of the Treaties, the Council shall, in accordance with the relevant procedure from among those referred to in Articles 121 and 126, with the exception of the procedure set out in Article 126(14), adopt measures specific to those Member States whose currency is the euro:

(a) to strengthen the coordination and surveillance of their budgetary discipline;

(b) to set out economic policy guidelines for them, while ensuring that they are compatible with those adopted for the whole of the Union and are kept under surveillance.

2. For those measures set out in paragraph 1, only members of the Council representing Member States whose currency is the euro shall take part in the vote.

A qualified majority of the said members shall be defined in accordance with Article 238(3)(a).

3. The Member States whose currency is the euro may establish a stability mechanism to be activated if indispensable to safeguard the stability of the euro area as a whole. The granting of any required financial assistance under the mechanism will be made subject to strict conditionality.*

Article 137

Arrangements for meetings between ministers of those Member States whose currency is the euro are laid down by the Protocol on the Euro Group.

Article 138 (ex Article 111(4), TEC)

1. In order to secure the euro's place in the international monetary system, the Council, on a proposal from the Commission, shall adopt a decision establishing common positions on matters of particular interest for economic and monetary union within the competent international financial institutions and conferences. The Council shall act after consulting the European Central Bank.

2. The Council, on a proposal from the Commission, may adopt appropriate measures to ensure unified representation within the international financial institutions and conferences. The Council shall act after consulting the European Central Bank.

3. For the measures referred to in paragraphs 1 and 2, only members of the Council representing Member States whose currency is the euro shall take part in the vote.

A qualified majority of the said members shall be defined in accordance with Article 238(3)(a).

Chapter 5
Transitional Provisions

Article 139

1. Member States in respect of which the Council has not decided that they fulfil the necessary conditions for the adoption of the euro shall hereinafter be referred to as 'Member States with a derogation'.

2. The following provisions of the Treaties shall not apply to Member States with a derogation:

(a) adoption of the parts of the broad economic policy guidelines which concern the euro area generally (Article 121(2));

(b) coercive means of remedying excessive deficits (Article 126(9) and (11));

---

* Editor's Note: Art. 136 TFEU was amended by decision 2011/199/EU adopted by the European Council on 25 March 2011, OJ L 91 of 6 April 2011, p. 1.

(c) the objectives and tasks of the ESCB (Article 127(1) to (3) and (5));

(d) issue of the euro (Article 128);

(e) acts of the European Central Bank (Article 132);

(f) measures governing the use of the euro (Article 133);

(g) monetary agreements and other measures relating to exchange-rate policy (Article 219);

(h) appointment of members of the Executive Board of the European Central Bank (Article 283(2));

(i) decisions establishing common positions on issues of particular relevance for economic and monetary union within the competent international financial institutions and conferences (Article 138(1));

(j) measures to ensure unified representation within the international financial institutions and conferences (Article 138(2)).

In the Articles referred to in points (a) to (j), 'Member States' shall therefore mean Member States whose currency is the euro.

3. Under Chapter IX of the Statute of the ESCB and of the ECB, Member States with a derogation and their national central banks are excluded from rights and obligations within the ESCB.

4. The voting rights of members of the Council representing Member States with a derogation shall be suspended for the adoption by the Council of the measures referred to in the Articles listed in paragraph 2, and in the following instances:

(a) recommendations made to those Member States whose currency is the euro in the framework of multilateral surveillance, including on stability programmes and warnings (Article 121(4));

(b) measures relating to excessive deficits concerning those Member States whose currency is the euro (Article 126(6), (7), (8), (12) and (13)).

A qualified majority of the other members of the Council shall be defined in accordance with Article 238(3)(a).

Article 140 (ex Articles 121(1), 122(2), second sentence, and 123(5) TEC)

1. At least once every two years, or at the request of a Member State with a derogation, the Commission and the European Central Bank shall report to the Council on the progress made by the Member States with a derogation in fulfilling their obligations regarding the achievement of economic and monetary union. These reports shall include an examination of the compatibility between the national legislation of each of these Member States, including the statutes of its national central bank, and Articles 130 and 131 and the Statute of the ESCB and of the ECB. The reports shall also examine the achievement of a high degree of sustainable convergence by reference to the fulfilment by each Member State of the following criteria:

– the achievement of a high degree of price stability; this will be apparent from a rate of inflation which is close to that of, at most, the three best performing Member States in terms of price stability,

- the sustainability of the government financial position; this will be apparent from having achieved a government budgetary position without a deficit that is excessive as determined in accordance with Article 126(6),
- the observance of the normal fluctuation margins provided for by the exchange-rate mechanism of the European Monetary System, for at least two years, without devaluing against the euro,
- the durability of convergence achieved by the Member State with a derogation and of its participation in the exchange-rate mechanism being reflected in the long-term interest-rate levels.

The four criteria mentioned in this paragraph and the relevant periods over which they are to be respected are developed further in a Protocol annexed to the Treaties. The reports of the Commission and the European Central Bank shall also take account of the results of the integration of markets, the situation and development of the balances of payments on current account and an examination of the development of unit labour costs and other price indices.

2. After consulting the European Parliament and after discussion in the European Council, the Council shall, on a proposal from the Commission, decide which Member States with a derogation fulfil the necessary conditions on the basis of the criteria set out in paragraph 1, and abrogate the derogations of the Member States concerned.

The Council shall act having received a recommendation of a qualified majority of those among its members representing Member States whose currency is the euro. These members shall act within six months of the Council receiving the Commission's proposal.

The qualified majority of the said members, as referred to in the second subparagraph, shall be defined in accordance with Article 238(3)(a).

3. If it is decided, in accordance with the procedure set out in paragraph 2, to abrogate a derogation, the Council shall, acting with the unanimity of the Member States whose currency is the euro and the Member State concerned, on a proposal from the Commission and after consulting the European Central Bank, irrevocably fix the rate at which the euro shall be substituted for the currency of the Member State concerned, and take the other measures necessary for the introduction of the euro as the single currency in the Member State concerned.

Article 141 (ex Articles 123(3) and 117(2) first five indents, TEC)

1. If and as long as there are Member States with a derogation, and without prejudice to Article 129(1), the General Council of the European Central Bank referred to in Article 44 of the Statute of the ESCB and of the ECB shall be constituted as a third decision-making body of the European Central Bank.

2. If and as long as there are Member States with a derogation, the European Central Bank shall, as regards those Member States:
- strengthen cooperation between the national central banks,
- strengthen the coordination of the monetary policies of the Member States, with the aim of ensuring price stability,

- monitor the functioning of the exchange-rate mechanism,
- hold consultations concerning issues falling within the competence of the national central banks and affecting the stability of financial institutions and markets,
- carry out the former tasks of the European Monetary Cooperation Fund which had subsequently been taken over by the European Monetary Institute.

Article 142 (ex Article 124(1) TEC)
Each Member State with a derogation shall treat its exchange-rate policy as a matter of common interest. In so doing, Member States shall take account of the experience acquired in cooperation within the framework of the exchange-rate mechanism.

Article 143 (ex Article 119 TEC)
1. Where a Member State with a derogation is in difficulties or is seriously threatened with difficulties as regards its balance of payments either as a result of an overall disequilibrium in its balance of payments, or as a result of the type of currency at its disposal, and where such difficulties are liable in particular to jeopardise the functioning of the internal market or the implementation of the common commercial policy, the Commission shall immediately investigate the position of the State in question and the action which, making use of all the means at its disposal, that State has taken or may take in accordance with the provisions of the Treaties. The Commission shall state what measures it recommends the State concerned to take.
If the action taken by a Member State with a derogation and the measures suggested by the Commission do not prove sufficient to overcome the difficulties which have arisen or which threaten, the Commission shall, after consulting the Economic and Financial Committee, recommend to the Council the granting of mutual assistance and appropriate methods therefor.
The Commission shall keep the Council regularly informed of the situation and of how it is developing.
2. The Council shall grant such mutual assistance; it shall adopt directives or decisions laying down the conditions and details of such assistance, which may take such forms as:
   (a) a concerted approach to or within any other international organisations to which Member States with a derogation may have recourse;
   (b) measures needed to avoid deflection of trade where the Member State with a derogation which is in difficulties maintains or reintroduces quantitative restrictions against third countries;
   (c) the granting of limited credits by other Member States, subject to their agreement.
3. If the mutual assistance recommended by the Commission is not granted by the Council or if the mutual assistance granted and the measures taken are insufficient, the Commission shall authorise the Member State with a derogation which is in difficulties to take protective measures, the conditions and details of which the Commission shall determine.
Such authorisation may be revoked and such conditions and details may be changed by the Council.

Article 144 (ex Article 120 TEC)
1. Where a sudden crisis in the balance of payments occurs and a decision within the meaning of Article 143(2) is not immediately taken, a Member State with a derogation may, as a precaution, take the necessary protective measures. Such measures must cause the least possible disturbance in the functioning of the internal market and must not be wider in scope than is strictly necessary to remedy the sudden difficulties which have arisen.
2. The Commission and the other Member States shall be informed of such protective measures not later than when they enter into force. The Commission may recommend to the Council the granting of mutual assistance under Article 143.
3. After the Commission has delivered a recommendation and the Economic and Financial Committee has been consulted, the Council may decide that the Member State concerned shall amend, suspend or abolish the protective measures referred to above.

Title IX
Employment

Article 145 (ex Article 125 TEC)
Member States and the Union shall, in accordance with this Title, work towards developing a coordinated strategy for employment and particularly for promoting a skilled, trained and adaptable workforce and labour markets responsive to economic change with a view to achieving the objectives defined in Article 3 of the Treaty on European Union.

Article 146 (ex Article 126 TEC)
1. Member States, through their employment policies, shall contribute to the achievement of the objectives referred to in Article 145 in a way consistent with the broad guidelines of the economic policies of the Member States and of the Union adopted pursuant to Article 121(2).
2. Member States, having regard to national practices related to the responsibilities of management and labour, shall regard promoting employment as a matter of common concern and shall coordinate their action in this respect within the Council, in accordance with the provisions of Article 148.

Article 147 (ex Article 127 TEC)
1. The Union shall contribute to a high level of employment by encouraging cooperation between Member States and by supporting and, if necessary, complementing their action. In doing so, the competences of the Member States shall be respected.
2. The objective of a high level of employment shall be taken into consideration in the formulation and implementation of Union policies and activities.

Article 148 (ex Article 128 TEC)

1. The European Council shall each year consider the employment situation in the Union and adopt conclusions thereon, on the basis of a joint annual report by the Council and the Commission.

2. On the basis of the conclusions of the European Council, the Council, on a proposal from the Commission and after consulting the European Parliament, the Economic and Social Committee, the Committee of the Regions and the Employment Committee referred to in Article 150, shall each year draw up guidelines which the Member States shall take into account in their employment policies. These guidelines shall be consistent with the broad guidelines adopted pursuant to Article 121(2).

3. Each Member State shall provide the Council and the Commission with an annual report on the principal measures taken to implement its employment policy in the light of the guidelines for employment as referred to in paragraph 2.

4. The Council, on the basis of the reports referred to in paragraph 3 and having received the views of the Employment Committee, shall each year carry out an examination of the implementation of the employment policies of the Member States in the light of the guidelines for employment. The Council, on a recommendation from the Commission, may, if it considers it appropriate in the light of that examination, make recommendations to Member States.

5. On the basis of the results of that examination, the Council and the Commission shall make a joint annual report to the European Council on the employment situation in the Union and on the implementation of the guidelines for employment.

Article 149 (ex Article 129 TEC)

The European Parliament and the Council, acting in accordance with the ordinary legislative procedure and after consulting the Economic and Social Committee and the Committee of the Regions, may adopt incentive measures designed to encourage cooperation between Member States and to support their action in the field of employment through initiatives aimed at developing exchanges of information and best practices, providing comparative analysis and advice as well as promoting innovative approaches and evaluating experiences, in particular by recourse to pilot projects.

Those measures shall not include harmonisation of the laws and regulations of the Member States.

Article 150 (ex Article 130 TEC)

The Council, acting by a simple majority after consulting the European Parliament, shall establish an Employment Committee with advisory status to promote coordination between Member States on employment and labour market policies. The tasks of the Committee shall be:

– to monitor the employment situation and employment policies in the Member States and the Union,

- without prejudice to Article 240, to formulate opinions at the request of either the Council or the Commission or on its own initiative, and to contribute to the preparation of the Council proceedings referred to in Article 148.

In fulfilling its mandate, the Committee shall consult management and labour.

Each Member State and the Commission shall appoint two members of the Committee.

Title X
Social Policy

Article 151 (ex Article 136 TEC)

The Union and the Member States, having in mind fundamental social rights such as those set out in the European Social Charter signed at Turin on 18 October 1961 and in the 1989 Community Charter of the Fundamental Social Rights of Workers, shall have as their objectives the promotion of employment, improved living and working conditions, so as to make possible their harmonisation while the improvement is being maintained, proper social protection, dialogue between management and labour, the development of human resources with a view to lasting high employment and the combating of exclusion.

To this end the Union and the Member States shall implement measures which take account of the diverse forms of national practices, in particular in the field of contractual relations, and the need to maintain the competitiveness of the Union economy.

They believe that such a development will ensue not only from the functioning of the internal market, which will favour the harmonisation of social systems, but also from the procedures provided for in the Treaties and from the approximation of provisions laid down by law, regulation or administrative action.

Article 152

The Union recognises and promotes the role of the social partners at its level, taking into account the diversity of national systems. It shall facilitate dialogue between the social partners, respecting their autonomy.

The Tripartite Social Summit for Growth and Employment shall contribute to social dialogue.

Article 153 (ex Article 137 TEC)

1. With a view to achieving the objectives of Article 151, the Union shall support and complement the activities of the Member States in the following fields:

    (a) improvement in particular of the working environment to protect workers' health and safety;

    (b) working conditions;

    (c) social security and social protection of workers;

    (d) protection of workers where their employment contract is terminated;

    (e) the information and consultation of workers;

(f) representation and collective defence of the interests of workers and employers, including co-determination, subject to paragraph 5;

(g) conditions of employment for third-country nationals legally residing in Union territory;

(h) the integration of persons excluded from the labour market, without prejudice to Article 166;

(i) equality between men and women with regard to labour market opportunities and treatment at work;

(j) the combating of social exclusion;

(k) the modernisation of social protection systems without prejudice to point (c).

2. To this end, the European Parliament and the Council:

(a) may adopt measures designed to encourage cooperation between Member States through initiatives aimed at improving knowledge, developing exchanges of information and best practices, promoting innovative approaches and evaluating experiences, excluding any harmonisation of the laws and regulations of the Member States;

(b) may adopt, in the fields referred to in paragraph 1(a) to (i), by means of directives, minimum requirements for gradual implementation, having regard to the conditions and technical rules obtaining in each of the Member States. Such directives shall avoid imposing administrative, financial and legal constraints in a way which would hold back the creation and development of small and medium-sized undertakings.

The European Parliament and the Council shall act in accordance with the ordinary legislative procedure after consulting the Economic and Social Committee and the Committee of the Regions.

In the fields referred to in paragraph 1(c), (d), (f) and (g), the Council shall act unanimously, in accordance with a special legislative procedure, after consulting the European Parliament and the said Committees.

The Council, acting unanimously on a proposal from the Commission, after consulting the European Parliament, may decide to render the ordinary legislative procedure applicable to paragraph 1(d), (f) and (g).

3. A Member State may entrust management and labour, at their joint request, with the implementation of directives adopted pursuant to paragraph 2, or, where appropriate, with the implementation of a Council decision adopted in accordance with Article 155.

In this case, it shall ensure that, no later than the date on which a directive or a decision must be transposed or implemented, management and labour have introduced the necessary measures by agreement, the Member State concerned being required to take any necessary measure enabling it at any time to be in a position to guarantee the results imposed by that directive or that decision.

4. The provisions adopted pursuant to this Article:

– shall not affect the right of Member States to define the fundamental principles of their social security systems and must not significantly affect the financial equilibrium thereof,

- shall not prevent any Member State from maintaining or introducing more stringent protective measures compatible with the Treaties.
5. The provisions of this Article shall not apply to pay, the right of association, the right to strike or the right to impose lock-outs.

Article 154 (ex Article 138 TEC)
1. The Commission shall have the task of promoting the consultation of management and labour at Union level and shall take any relevant measure to facilitate their dialogue by ensuring balanced support for the parties.
2. To this end, before submitting proposals in the social policy field, the Commission shall consult management and labour on the possible direction of Union action.
3. If, after such consultation, the Commission considers Union action advisable, it shall consult management and labour on the content of the envisaged proposal. Management and labour shall forward to the Commission an opinion or, where appropriate, a recommendation.
4. On the occasion of the consultation referred to in paragraphs 2 and 3, management and labour may inform the Commission of their wish to initiate the process provided for in Article 155. The duration of this process shall not exceed nine months, unless the management and labour concerned and the Commission decide jointly to extend it.

Article 155 (ex Article 139 TEC)
1. Should management and labour so desire, the dialogue between them at Union level may lead to contractual relations, including agreements.
2. Agreements concluded at Union level shall be implemented either in accordance with the procedures and practices specific to management and labour and the Member States or, in matters covered by Article 153, at the joint request of the signatory parties, by a Council decision on a proposal from the Commission. The European Parliament shall be informed.
The Council shall act unanimously where the agreement in question contains one or more provisions relating to one of the areas for which unanimity is required pursuant to Article 153(2).

Article 156 (ex Article 140 TEC)
With a view to achieving the objectives of Article 151 and without prejudice to the other provisions of the Treaties, the Commission shall encourage cooperation between the Member States and facilitate the coordination of their action in all social policy fields under this Chapter, particularly in matters relating to:
- employment,
- labour law and working conditions,
- basic and advanced vocational training,
- social security,
- prevention of occupational accidents and diseases,

- occupational hygiene,
- the right of association and collective bargaining between employers and workers.

To this end, the Commission shall act in close contact with Member States by making studies, delivering opinions and arranging consultations both on problems arising at national level and on those of concern to international organisations, in particular initiatives aiming at the establishment of guidelines and indicators, the organisation of exchange of best practice, and the preparation of the necessary elements for periodic monitoring and evaluation. The European Parliament shall be kept fully informed.

Before delivering the opinions provided for in this Article, the Commission shall consult the Economic and Social Committee.

Article 157 (ex Article 141 TEC)

1. Each Member State shall ensure that the principle of equal pay for male and female workers for equal work or work of equal value is applied.

2. For the purpose of this Article, 'pay' means the ordinary basic or minimum wage or salary and any other consideration, whether in cash or in kind, which the worker receives directly or indirectly, in respect of his employment, from his employer.

Equal pay without discrimination based on sex means:

(a) that pay for the same work at piece rates shall be calculated on the basis of the same unit of measurement;

(b) that pay for work at time rates shall be the same for the same job.

3. The European Parliament and the Council, acting in accordance with the ordinary legislative procedure, and after consulting the Economic and Social Committee, shall adopt measures to ensure the application of the principle of equal opportunities and equal treatment of men and women in matters of employment and occupation, including the principle of equal pay for equal work or work of equal value.

4. With a view to ensuring full equality in practice between men and women in working life, the principle of equal treatment shall not prevent any Member State from maintaining or adopting measures providing for specific advantages in order to make it easier for the underrepresented sex to pursue a vocational activity or to prevent or compensate for disadvantages in professional careers.

Article 158 (ex Article 142 TEC)

Member States shall endeavour to maintain the existing equivalence between paid holiday schemes.

Article 159 (ex Article 143 TEC)

The Commission shall draw up a report each year on progress in achieving the objectives of Article 151, including the demographic situation in the Union. It shall forward the report to the European Parliament, the Council and the Economic and Social Committee.

Article 160 (ex Article 144 TEC)

The Council, acting by a simple majority after consulting the European Parliament, shall establish a Social Protection Committee with advisory status to promote cooperation on social protection policies between Member States and with the Commission. The tasks of the Committee shall be:
- to monitor the social situation and the development of social protection policies in the Member States and the Union,
- to promote exchanges of information, experience and good practice between Member States and with the Commission,
- without prejudice to Article 240, to prepare reports, formulate opinions or undertake other work within its fields of competence, at the request of either the Council or the Commission or on its own initiative.

In fulfilling its mandate, the Committee shall establish appropriate contacts with management and labour.

Each Member State and the Commission shall appoint two members of the Committee.

Article 161 (ex Article 145 TEC)

The Commission shall include a separate chapter on social developments within the Union in its annual report to the European Parliament.

The European Parliament may invite the Commission to draw up reports on any particular problems concerning social conditions.

Title XI
The European Social Fund

Article 162 (ex Article 146 TEC)

In order to improve employment opportunities for workers in the internal market and to contribute thereby to raising the standard of living, a European Social Fund is hereby established in accordance with the provisions set out below; it shall aim to render the employment of workers easier and to increase their geographical and occupational mobility within the Union, and to facilitate their adaptation to industrial changes and to changes in production systems, in particular through vocational training and retraining.

Article 163 (ex Article 147 TEC)

The Fund shall be administered by the Commission.

The Commission shall be assisted in this task by a Committee presided over by a Member of the Commission and composed of representatives of governments, trade unions and employers' organisations.

Article 164 (ex Article 148 TEC)
The European Parliament and the Council, acting in accordance with the ordinary legislative procedure and after consulting the Economic and Social Committee and the Committee of the Regions, shall adopt implementing regulations relating to the European Social Fund.

Title XII
Education, Vocational Training, Youth and Sport

Article 165 (ex Article 149 TEC)
1. The Union shall contribute to the development of quality education by encouraging cooperation between Member States and, if necessary, by supporting and supplementing their action, while fully respecting the responsibility of the Member States for the content of teaching and the organisation of education systems and their cultural and linguistic diversity.
The Union shall contribute to the promotion of European sporting issues, while taking account of the specific nature of sport, its structures based on voluntary activity and its social and educational function.
2. Union action shall be aimed at:
    - developing the European dimension in education, particularly through the teaching and dissemination of the languages of the Member States,
    - encouraging mobility of students and teachers, by encouraging inter alia, the academic recognition of diplomas and periods of study,
    - promoting cooperation between educational establishments,
    - developing exchanges of information and experience on issues common to the education systems of the Member States,
    - encouraging the development of youth exchanges and of exchanges of socio-educational instructors, and encouraging the participation of young people in democratic life in Europe,
    - encouraging the development of distance education,
    - developing the European dimension in sport, by promoting fairness and openness in sporting competitions and cooperation between bodies responsible for sports, and by protecting the physical and moral integrity of sportsmen and sportswomen, especially the youngest sportsmen and sportswomen.
3. The Union and the Member States shall foster cooperation with third countries and the competent international organisations in the field of education and sport, in particular the Council of Europe.
4. In order to contribute to the achievement of the objectives referred to in this Article:
    - the European Parliament and the Council, acting in accordance with the ordinary legislative procedure, after consulting the Economic and Social Committee and the Committee of the Regions, shall adopt incentive measures, excluding any harmonisation of the laws and regulations of the Member States,
    - the Council, on a proposal from the Commission, shall adopt recommendations.

Article 166 (ex Article 150 TEC)
1. The Union shall implement a vocational training policy which shall support and supplement the action of the Member States, while fully respecting the responsibility of the Member States for the content and organisation of vocational training.
2. Union action shall aim to:
- facilitate adaptation to industrial changes, in particular through vocational training and retraining,
- improve initial and continuing vocational training in order to facilitate vocational integration and reintegration into the labour market,
- facilitate access to vocational training and encourage mobility of instructors and trainees and particularly young people,
- stimulate cooperation on training between educational or training establishments and firms,
- develop exchanges of information and experience on issues common to the training systems of the Member States.
3. The Union and the Member States shall foster cooperation with third countries and the competent international organisations in the sphere of vocational training.
4. The European Parliament and the Council, acting in accordance with the ordinary legislative procedure and after consulting the Economic and Social Committee and the Committee of the Regions, shall adopt measures to contribute to the achievement of the objectives referred to in this Article, excluding any harmonisation of the laws and regulations of the Member States, and the Council, on a proposal from the Commission, shall adopt recommendations.

Title XIII
Culture

Article 167 (ex Article 151 TEC)
1. The Union shall contribute to the flowering of the cultures of the Member States, while respecting their national and regional diversity and at the same time bringing the common cultural heritage to the fore.
2. Action by the Union shall be aimed at encouraging cooperation between Member States and, if necessary, supporting and supplementing their action in the following areas:
- improvement of the knowledge and dissemination of the culture and history of the European peoples,
- conservation and safeguarding of cultural heritage of European significance,
- non-commercial cultural exchanges,
- artistic and literary creation, including in the audiovisual sector.
3. The Union and the Member States shall foster cooperation with third countries and the competent international organisations in the sphere of culture, in particular the Council of Europe.

4. The Union shall take cultural aspects into account in its action under other provisions of the Treaties, in particular in order to respect and to promote the diversity of its cultures.
5. In order to contribute to the achievement of the objectives referred to in this Article:
   – the European Parliament and the Council acting in accordance with the ordinary legislative procedure and after consulting the Committee of the Regions, shall adopt incentive measures, excluding any harmonisation of the laws and regulations of the Member States,
   – the Council, on a proposal from the Commission, shall adopt recommendations.

Title XIV
Public Health

Article 168 (ex Article 152 TEC)
1. A high level of human health protection shall be ensured in the definition and implementation of all Union policies and activities.

Union action, which shall complement national policies, shall be directed towards improving public health, preventing physical and mental illness and diseases, and obviating sources of danger to physical and mental health. Such action shall cover the fight against the major health scourges, by promoting research into their causes, their transmission and their prevention, as well as health information and education, and monitoring, early warning of and combating serious cross-border threats to health.

The Union shall complement the Member States' action in reducing drugs-related health damage, including information and prevention.

2. The Union shall encourage cooperation between the Member States in the areas referred to in this Article and, if necessary, lend support to their action. It shall in particular encourage cooperation between the Member States to improve the complementarity of their health services in cross-border areas.

Member States shall, in liaison with the Commission, coordinate among themselves their policies and programmes in the areas referred to in paragraph 1. The Commission may, in close contact with the Member States, take any useful initiative to promote such coordination, in particular initiatives aiming at the establishment of guidelines and indicators, the organisation of exchange of best practice, and the preparation of the necessary elements for periodic monitoring and evaluation. The European Parliament shall be kept fully informed.

3. The Union and the Member States shall foster cooperation with third countries and the competent international organisations in the sphere of public health.

4. By way of derogation from Article 2(5) and Article 6(a) and in accordance with Article 4(2)(k) the European Parliament and the Council, acting in accordance with the ordinary legislative procedure and after consulting the Economic and Social Committee and the Committee of the Regions, shall contribute to the achievement of the objectives referred to in this Article through adopting in order to meet common safety concerns:

(a) measures setting high standards of quality and safety of organs and substances of human origin, blood and blood derivatives; these measures shall not prevent any Member State from maintaining or introducing more stringent protective measures;

(b) measures in the veterinary and phytosanitary fields which have as their direct objective the protection of public health;

(c) measures setting high standards of quality and safety for medicinal products and devices for medical use.

5. The European Parliament and the Council, acting in accordance with the ordinary legislative procedure and after consulting the Economic and Social Committee and the Committee of the Regions, may also adopt incentive measures designed to protect and improve human health and in particular to combat the major cross-border health scourges, measures concerning monitoring, early warning of and combating serious cross-border threats to health, and measures which have as their direct objective the protection of public health regarding tobacco and the abuse of alcohol, excluding any harmonisation of the laws and regulations of the Member States.

6. The Council, on a proposal from the Commission, may also adopt recommendations for the purposes set out in this Article.

7. Union action shall respect the responsibilities of the Member States for the definition of their health policy and for the organisation and delivery of health services and medical care. The responsibilities of the Member States shall include the management of health services and medical care and the allocation of the resources assigned to them. The measures referred to in paragraph 4(a) shall not affect national provisions on the donation or medical use of organs and blood.

Title XV
Consumer Protection

Article 169 (ex Article 153 TEC)

1. In order to promote the interests of consumers and to ensure a high level of consumer protection, the Union shall contribute to protecting the health, safety and economic interests of consumers, as well as to promoting their right to information, education and to organise themselves in order to safeguard their interests.

2. The Union shall contribute to the attainment of the objectives referred to in paragraph 1 through:

(a) measures adopted pursuant to Article 114 in the context of the completion of the internal market;

(b) measures which support, supplement and monitor the policy pursued by the Member States.

3. The European Parliament and the Council, acting in accordance with the ordinary legislative procedure and after consulting the Economic and Social Committee, shall adopt the measures referred to in paragraph 2(b).

4. Measures adopted pursuant to paragraph 3 shall not prevent any Member State from maintaining or introducing more stringent protective measures. Such measures must be compatible with the Treaties. The Commission shall be notified of them.

Title XVI
Trans-European Networks

Article 170 (ex Article 154 TEC)
1. To help achieve the objectives referred to in Articles 26 and 174 and to enable citizens of the Union, economic operators and regional and local communities to derive full benefit from the setting-up of an area without internal frontiers, the Union shall contribute to the establishment and development of trans-European networks in the areas of transport, telecommunications and energy infrastructures.
2. Within the framework of a system of open and competitive markets, action by the Union shall aim at promoting the interconnection and interoperability of national networks as well as access to such networks. It shall take account in particular of the need to link island, landlocked and peripheral regions with the central regions of the Union.

Article 171 (ex Article 155 TEC)
1. In order to achieve the objectives referred to in Article 170, the Union:
   – shall establish a series of guidelines covering the objectives, priorities and broad lines of measures envisaged in the sphere of trans-European networks; these guidelines shall identify projects of common interest,
   – shall implement any measures that may prove necessary to ensure the interoperability of the networks, in particular in the field of technical standardisation,
   – may support projects of common interest supported by Member States, which are identified in the framework of the guidelines referred to in the first indent, particularly through feasibility studies, loan guarantees or interest-rate subsidies; the Union may also contribute, through the Cohesion Fund set up pursuant to Article 177, to the financing of specific projects in Member States in the area of transport infrastructure.
The Union's activities shall take into account the potential economic viability of the projects.
2. Member States shall, in liaison with the Commission, coordinate among themselves the policies pursued at national level which may have a significant impact on the achievement of the objectives referred to in Article 170. The Commission may, in close cooperation with the Member State, take any useful initiative to promote such coordination.
3. The Union may decide to cooperate with third countries to promote projects of mutual interest and to ensure the interoperability of networks.

Article 172 (ex Article 156 TEC)

The guidelines and other measures referred to in Article 171(1) shall be adopted by the European Parliament and the Council, acting in accordance with the ordinary legislative procedure and after consulting the Economic and Social Committee and the Committee of the Regions.

Guidelines and projects of common interest which relate to the territory of a Member State shall require the approval of the Member State concerned.

Title XVII
Industry

Article 173 (ex Article 157 TEC)

1. The Union and the Member States shall ensure that the conditions necessary for the competitiveness of the Union's industry exist.

For that purpose, in accordance with a system of open and competitive markets, their action shall be aimed at:
- speeding up the adjustment of industry to structural changes,
- encouraging an environment favourable to initiative and to the development of undertakings throughout the Union, particularly small and medium-sized undertakings,
- encouraging an environment favourable to cooperation between undertakings,
- fostering better exploitation of the industrial potential of policies of innovation, research and technological development.

2. The Member States shall consult each other in liaison with the Commission and, where necessary, shall coordinate their action. The Commission may take any useful initiative to promote such coordination, in particular initiatives aiming at the establishment of guidelines and indicators, the organisation of exchange of best practice, and the preparation of the necessary elements for periodic monitoring and evaluation. The European Parliament shall be kept fully informed.

3. The Union shall contribute to the achievement of the objectives set out in paragraph 1 through the policies and activities it pursues under other provisions of the Treaties. The European Parliament and the Council, acting in accordance with the ordinary legislative procedure and after consulting the Economic and Social Committee, may decide on specific measures in support of action taken in the Member States to achieve the objectives set out in paragraph 1, excluding any harmonisation of the laws and regulations of the Member States.

This Title shall not provide a basis for the introduction by the Union of any measure which could lead to a distortion of competition or contains tax provisions or provisions relating to the rights and interests of employed persons.

Title XVIII
Economic, Social and Territorial Cohesion

Article 174 (ex Article 158 TEC)
In order to promote its overall harmonious development, the Union shall develop and pursue its actions leading to the strengthening of its economic, social and territorial cohesion.
In particular, the Union shall aim at reducing disparities between the levels of development of the various regions and the backwardness of the least favoured regions.
Among the regions concerned, particular attention shall be paid to rural areas, areas affected by industrial transition, and regions which suffer from severe and permanent natural or demographic handicaps such as the northernmost regions with very low population density and island, cross-border and mountain regions.

Article 175 (ex Article 159 TEC)
Member States shall conduct their economic policies and shall coordinate them in such a way as, in addition, to attain the objectives set out in Article 174. The formulation and implementation of the Union's policies and actions and the implementation of the internal market shall take into account the objectives set out in Article 174 and shall contribute to their achievement. The Union shall also support the achievement of these objectives by the action it takes through the Structural Funds (European Agricultural Guidance and Guarantee Fund, Guidance Section; European Social Fund; European Regional Development Fund), the European Investment Bank and the other existing Financial Instruments.
The Commission shall submit a report to the European Parliament, the Council, the Economic and Social Committee and the Committee of the Regions every three years on the progress made towards achieving economic, social and territorial cohesion and on the manner in which the various means provided for in this Article have contributed to it. This report shall, if necessary, be accompanied by appropriate proposals.
If specific actions prove necessary outside the Funds and without prejudice to the measures decided upon within the framework of the other Union policies, such actions may be adopted by the European Parliament and the Council acting in accordance with the ordinary legislative procedure and after consulting the Economic and Social Committee and the Committee of the Regions.

Article 176 (ex Article 160 TEC)
The European Regional Development Fund is intended to help to redress the main regional imbalances in the Union through participation in the development and structural adjustment of regions whose development is lagging behind and in the conversion of declining industrial regions.

Article 177 (ex Article 161 TEC)
Without prejudice to Article 178, the European Parliament and the Council, acting by means of regulations in accordance with the ordinary legislative procedure and consulting the

Economic and Social Committee and the Committee of the Regions, shall define the tasks, priority objectives and the organisation of the Structural Funds, which may involve grouping the Funds. The general rules applicable to them and the provisions necessary to ensure their effectiveness and the coordination of the Funds with one another and with the other existing Financial Instruments shall also be defined by the same procedure.

A Cohesion Fund set up in accordance with the same procedure shall provide a financial contribution to projects in the fields of environment and trans-European networks in the area of transport infrastructure.

Article 178 (ex Article 162 TEC)

Implementing regulations relating to the European Regional Development Fund shall be taken by the European Parliament and the Council, acting in accordance with the ordinary legislative procedure and after consulting the Economic and Social Committee and the Committee of the Regions.

With regard to the European Agricultural Guidance and Guarantee Fund, Guidance Section, and the European Social Fund, Articles 43 and 164 respectively shall continue to apply.

Title XIX
Research and Technological Development and Space

Article 179 (ex Article 163 TEC)

1. The Union shall have the objective of strengthening its scientific and technological bases by achieving a European research area in which researchers, scientific knowledge and technology circulate freely, and encouraging it to become more competitive, including in its industry, while promoting all the research activities deemed necessary by virtue of other Chapters of the Treaties.

2. For this purpose the Union shall, throughout the Union, encourage undertakings, including small and medium-sized undertakings, research centres and universities in their research and technological development activities of high quality; it shall support their efforts to cooperate with one another, aiming, notably, at permitting researchers to cooperate freely across borders and at enabling undertakings to exploit the internal market potential to the full, in particular through the opening-up of national public contracts, the definition of common standards and the removal of legal and fiscal obstacles to that cooperation.

3. All Union activities under the Treaties in the area of research and technological development, including demonstration projects, shall be decided on and implemented in accordance with the provisions of this Title.

Article 180 (ex Article 164 TEC)

In pursuing these objectives, the Union shall carry out the following activities, complementing the activities carried out in the Member States:

(a) implementation of research, technological development and demonstration programmes, by promoting cooperation with and between undertakings, research centres and universities;

(b) promotion of cooperation in the field of Union research, technological development and demonstration with third countries and international organisations;

(c) dissemination and optimisation of the results of activities in Union research, technological development and demonstration;

(d) stimulation of the training and mobility of researchers in the Union.

Article 181 (ex Article 165 TEC)

1. The Union and the Member States shall coordinate their research and technological development activities so as to ensure that national policies and Union policy are mutually consistent.

2. In close cooperation with the Member State, the Commission may take any useful initiative to promote the coordination referred to in paragraph 1, in particular initiatives aiming at the establishment of guidelines and indicators, the organisation of exchange of best practice, and the preparation of the necessary elements for periodic monitoring and evaluation. The European Parliament shall be kept fully informed.

Article 182 (ex Article 166 TEC)

1. A multiannual framework programme, setting out all the activities of the Union, shall be adopted by the European Parliament and the Council, acting in accordance with the ordinary legislative procedure after consulting the Economic and Social Committee.

The framework programme shall:

- establish the scientific and technological objectives to be achieved by the activities provided for in Article 180 and fix the relevant priorities,
- indicate the broad lines of such activities,
- fix the maximum overall amount and the detailed rules for Union financial participation in the framework programme and the respective shares in each of the activities provided for.

2. The framework programme shall be adapted or supplemented as the situation changes.

3. The framework programme shall be implemented through specific programmes developed within each activity. Each specific programme shall define the detailed rules for implementing it, fix its duration and provide for the means deemed necessary. The sum of the amounts deemed necessary, fixed in the specific programmes, may not exceed the overall maximum amount fixed for the framework programme and each activity.

4. The Council, acting in accordance with a special legislative procedure and after consulting the European Parliament and the Economic and Social Committee, shall adopt the specific programmes.

5. As a complement to the activities planned in the multiannual framework programme, the European Parliament and the Council, acting in accordance with the ordinary legislative

procedure and after consulting the Economic and Social Committee, shall establish the measures necessary for the implementation of the European research area.

Article 183 (ex Article 167 TEC)
For the implementation of the multiannual framework programme the Union shall:
- determine the rules for the participation of undertakings, research centres and universities,
- lay down the rules governing the dissemination of research results.

Article 184 (ex Article 168 TEC)
In implementing the multiannual framework programme, supplementary programmes may be decided on involving the participation of certain Member States only, which shall finance them subject to possible Union participation.

The Union shall adopt the rules applicable to supplementary programmes, particularly as regards the dissemination of knowledge and access by other Member States.

Article 185 (ex Article 169 TEC)
In implementing the multiannual framework programme, the Union may make provision, in agreement with the Member States concerned, for participation in research and development programmes undertaken by several Member States, including participation in the structures created for the execution of those programmes.

Article 186 (ex Article 170 TEC)
In implementing the multiannual framework programme the Union may make provision for cooperation in Union research, technological development and demonstration with third countries or international organisations.

The detailed arrangements for such cooperation may be the subject of agreements between the Union and the third parties concerned.

Article 187 (ex Article 171 TEC)
The Union may set up joint undertakings or any other structure necessary for the efficient execution of Union research, technological development and demonstration programmes.

Article 188 (ex Article 172 TEC)
The Council, on a proposal from the Commission and after consulting the European Parliament and the Economic and Social Committee, shall adopt the provisions referred to in Article 187.

The European Parliament and the Council, acting in accordance with the ordinary legislative procedure and after consulting the Economic and Social Committee, shall adopt the provisions referred to in Articles 183, 184 and 185. Adoption of the supplementary programmes shall require the agreement of the Member States concerned.

Article 189

1. To promote scientific and technical progress, industrial competitiveness and the implementation of its policies, the Union shall draw up a European space policy. To this end, it may promote joint initiatives, support research and technological development and coordinate the efforts needed for the exploration and exploitation of space.

2. To contribute to attaining the objectives referred to in paragraph 1, the European Parliament and the Council, acting in accordance with the ordinary legislative procedure, shall establish the necessary measures, which may take the form of a European space programme, excluding any harmonisation of the laws and regulations of the Member States.

3. The Union shall establish any appropriate relations with the European Space Agency.

4. This Article shall be without prejudice to the other provisions of this Title.

Article 190 (ex Article 173 TEC)

At the beginning of each year the Commission shall send a report to the European Parliament and to the Council. The report shall include information on research and technological development activities and the dissemination of results during the previous year, and the work programme for the current year.

Title XX
Environment

Article 191 (ex Article 174 TEC)

1. Union policy on the environment shall contribute to pursuit of the following objectives:
   - preserving, protecting and improving the quality of the environment,
   - protecting human health,
   - prudent and rational utilisation of natural resources,
   - promoting measures at international level to deal with regional or worldwide environmental problems, and in particular combating climate change.

2. Union policy on the environment shall aim at a high level of protection taking into account the diversity of situations in the various regions of the Union. It shall be based on the precautionary principle and on the principles that preventive action should be taken, that environmental damage should as a priority be rectified at source and that the polluter should pay.

In this context, harmonisation measures answering environmental protection requirements shall include, where appropriate, a safeguard clause allowing Member States to take provisional measures, for non-economic environmental reasons, subject to a procedure of inspection by the Union.

3. In preparing its policy on the environment, the Union shall take account of:
   - available scientific and technical data,
   - environmental conditions in the various regions of the Union,
   - the potential benefits and costs of action or lack of action,

- the economic and social development of the Union as a whole and the balanced development of its regions.

4. Within their respective spheres of competence, the Union and the Member States shall cooperate with third countries and with the competent international organisations. The arrangements for Union cooperation may be the subject of agreements between the Union and the third parties concerned.

The previous subparagraph shall be without prejudice to Member States' competence to negotiate in international bodies and to conclude international agreements.

Article 192 (ex Article 175 TEC)

1. The European Parliament and the Council, acting in accordance with the ordinary legislative procedure and after consulting the Economic and Social Committee and the Committee of the Regions, shall decide what action is to be taken by the Union in order to achieve the objectives referred to in Article 191.

2. By way of derogation from the decision-making procedure provided for in paragraph 1 and without prejudice to Article 114, the Council acting unanimously in accordance with a special legislative procedure and after consulting the European Parliament, the Economic and Social Committee and the Committee of the Regions, shall adopt:

    (a) provisions primarily of a fiscal nature;
    (b) measures affecting:
        - town and country planning,
        - quantitative management of water resources or affecting, directly or indirectly, the availability of those resources,
        - land use, with the exception of waste management;
    (c) measures significantly affecting a Member State's choice between different energy sources and the general structure of its energy supply.

The Council, acting unanimously on a proposal from the Commission and after consulting the European Parliament, the Economic and Social Committee and the Committee of the Regions, may make the ordinary legislative procedure applicable to the matters referred to in the first subparagraph.

3. General action programmes setting out priority objectives to be attained shall be adopted by the European Parliament and the Council, acting in accordance with the ordinary legislative procedure and after consulting the Economic and Social Committee and the Committee of the Regions.

The measures necessary for the implementation of these programmes shall be adopted under the terms of paragraph 1 or 2, as the case may be.

4. Without prejudice to certain measures adopted by the Union, the Member States shall finance and implement the environment policy.

5. Without prejudice to the principle that the polluter should pay, if a measure based on the provisions of paragraph 1 involves costs deemed disproportionate for the public authorities of a Member State, such measure shall lay down appropriate provisions in the form of:

- temporary derogations, and/or
- financial support from the Cohesion Fund set up pursuant to Article 177.

Article 193 (ex Article 176 TEC)
The protective measures adopted pursuant to Article 192 shall not prevent any Member State from maintaining or introducing more stringent protective measures. Such measures must be compatible with the Treaties. They shall be notified to the Commission.

Title XXI
Energy

Article 194
1. In the context of the establishment and functioning of the internal market and with regard for the need to preserve and improve the environment, Union policy on energy shall aim, in a spirit of solidarity between Member States, to:
    (a) ensure the functioning of the energy market;
    (b) ensure security of energy supply in the Union;
    (c) promote energy efficiency and energy saving and the development of new and renewable forms of energy; and
    (d) promote the interconnection of energy networks.
2. Without prejudice to the application of other provisions of the Treaties, the European Parliament and the Council, acting in accordance with the ordinary legislative procedure, shall establish the measures necessary to achieve the objectives in paragraph 1. Such measures shall be adopted after consultation of the Economic and Social Committee and the Committee of the Regions.

Such measures shall not affect a Member State's right to determine the conditions for exploiting its energy resources, its choice between different energy sources and the general structure of its energy supply, without prejudice to Article 192(2)(c).

3. By way of derogation from paragraph 2, the Council, acting in accordance with a special legislative procedure, shall unanimously and after consulting the European Parliament, establish the measures referred to therein when they are primarily of a fiscal nature.

Title XXII
Tourism

Article 195
1. The Union shall complement the action of the Member States in the tourism sector, in particular by promoting the competitiveness of Union undertakings in that sector.
To that end, Union action shall be aimed at:

(a) encouraging the creation of a favourable environment for the development of undertakings in this sector;

(b) promoting cooperation between the Member States, particularly by the exchange of good practice.

2. The European Parliament and the Council, acting in accordance with the ordinary legislative procedure, shall establish specific measures to complement actions within the Member States to achieve the objectives referred to in this Article, excluding any harmonisation of the laws and regulations of the Member States.

Title XXIII
Civil Protection

Article 196

1. The Union shall encourage cooperation between Member States in order to improve the effectiveness of systems for preventing and protecting against natural or man-made disasters.

Union action shall aim to:

(a) support and complement Member States' action at national, regional and local level in risk prevention, in preparing their civil-protection personnel and in responding to natural or man-made disasters within the Union;

(b) promote swift, effective operational cooperation within the Union between national civil-protection services;

(c) promote consistency in international civil-protection work.

2. The European Parliament and the Council, acting in accordance with the ordinary legislative procedure shall establish the measures necessary to help achieve the objectives referred to in paragraph 1, excluding any harmonisation of the laws and regulations of the Member States.

Title XXIV
Administrative Cooperation

Article 197

1. Effective implementation of Union law by the Member States, which is essential for the proper functioning of the Union, shall be regarded as a matter of common interest.

2. The Union may support the efforts of Member States to improve their administrative capacity to implement Union law. Such action may include facilitating the exchange of information and of civil servants as well as supporting training schemes. No Member State shall be obliged to avail itself of such support. The European Parliament and the Council, acting by means of regulations in accordance with the ordinary legislative procedure, shall

establish the necessary measures to this end, excluding any harmonisation of the laws and regulations of the Member States.

3. This Article shall be without prejudice to the obligations of the Member States to implement Union law or to the prerogatives and duties of the Commission. It shall also be without prejudice to other provisions of the Treaties providing for administrative cooperation among the Member States and between them and the Union.

Part Four
Association of the Overseas Countries and Territories

Article 198 (ex Article 182 TEC)

The Member States agree to associate with the Union the non-European countries and territories which have special relations with Denmark, France, the Netherlands and the United Kingdom. These countries and territories (hereinafter called the 'countries and territories') are listed in Annex II.

The purpose of association shall be to promote the economic and social development of the countries and territories and to establish close economic relations between them and the Union as a whole.

In accordance with the principles set out in the preamble to this Treaty, association shall serve primarily to further the interests and prosperity of the inhabitants of these countries and territories in order to lead them to the economic, social and cultural development to which they aspire.

Article 199 (ex Article 183 TEC)

Association shall have the following objectives.

1. Member States shall apply to their trade with the countries and territories the same treatment as they accord each other pursuant to the Treaties.

2. Each country or territory shall apply to its trade with Member States and with the other countries and territories the same treatment as that which it applies to the European State with which is has special relations.

3. The Member States shall contribute to the investments required for the progressive development of these countries and territories.

4. For investments financed by the Union, participation in tenders and supplies shall be open on equal terms to all natural and legal persons who are nationals of a Member State or of one of the countries and territories.

5. In relations between Member States and the countries and territories the right of establishment of nationals and companies or firms shall be regulated in accordance with the provisions and procedures laid down in the Chapter relating to the right of establishment and on a non-discriminatory basis, subject to any special provisions laid down pursuant to Article 203.

Article 200 (ex Article 184 TEC)
1. Customs duties on imports into the Member States of goods originating in the countries and territories shall be prohibited in conformity with the prohibition of customs duties between Member States in accordance with the provisions of the Treaties.
2. Customs duties on imports into each country or territory from Member States or from the other countries or territories shall be prohibited in accordance with the provisions of Article 30.
3. The countries and territories may, however, levy customs duties which meet the needs of their development and industrialisation or produce revenue for their budgets.
The duties referred to in the preceding subparagraph may not exceed the level of those imposed on imports of products from the Member State with which each country or territory has special relations.
4. Paragraph 2 shall not apply to countries and territories which, by reason of the particular international obligations by which they are bound, already apply a non-discriminatory customs tariff.
5. The introduction of or any change in customs duties imposed on goods imported into the countries and territories shall not, either in law or in fact, give rise to any direct or indirect discrimination between imports from the various Member States.

Article 201 (ex Article 185 TEC)
If the level of the duties applicable to goods from a third country on entry into a country or territory is liable, when the provisions of Article 200(1) have been applied, to cause deflections of trade to the detriment of any Member State, the latter may request the Commission to propose to the other Member States the measures needed to remedy the situation.

Article 202 (ex Article 186 TEC)
Subject to the provisions relating to public health, public security or public policy, freedom of movement within Member States for workers from the countries and territories, and within the countries and territories for workers from Member States, shall be regulated by acts adopted in accordance with Article 203.

Article 203 (ex Article 187 TEC)
The Council, acting unanimously on a proposal from the Commission, shall, on the basis of the experience acquired under the association of the countries and territories with the Union and of the principles set out in the Treaties, lay down provisions as regards the detailed rules and the procedure for the association of the countries and territories with the Union. Where the provisions in question are adopted by the Council in accordance with a special legislative procedure, it shall act unanimously on a proposal from the Commission and after consulting the European Parliament.

Article 204 (ex Article 188 TEC)
The provisions of Articles 198 to 203 shall apply to Greenland, subject to the specific provisions for Greenland set out in the Protocol on special arrangements for Greenland, annexed to the Treaties.

Part Five
The Union's External Action

Title I
General Provisions on the Union's External Action

Article 205
The Union's action on the international scene, pursuant to this Part, shall be guided by the principles, pursue the objectives and be conducted in accordance with the general provisions laid down in Chapter 1 of Title V of the Treaty on European Union.

Title II
Common Commercial Policy

Article 206 (ex Article 131 TEC)
By establishing a customs union in accordance with Articles 28 to 32, the Union shall contribute, in the common interest, to the harmonious development of world trade, the progressive abolition of restrictions on international trade and on foreign direct investment, and the lowering of customs and other barriers.

Article 207 (ex Article 133 TEC)
1. The common commercial policy shall be based on uniform principles, particularly with regard to changes in tariff rates, the conclusion of tariff and trade agreements relating to trade in goods and services, and the commercial aspects of intellectual property, foreign direct investment, the achievement of uniformity in measures of liberalisation, export policy and measures to protect trade such as those to be taken in the event of dumping or subsidies. The common commercial policy shall be conducted in the context of the principles and objectives of the Union's external action.
2. The European Parliament and the Council, acting by means of regulations in accordance with the ordinary legislative procedure, shall adopt the measures defining the framework for implementing the common commercial policy.
3. Where agreements with one or more third countries or international organisations need to be negotiated and concluded, Article 218 shall apply, subject to the special provisions of this Article.

The Commission shall make recommendations to the Council, which shall authorise it to open the necessary negotiations. The Council and the Commission shall be responsible for ensuring that the agreements negotiated are compatible with internal Union policies and rules.

The Commission shall conduct these negotiations in consultation with a special committee appointed by the Council to assist the Commission in this task and within the framework of such directives as the Council may issue to it. The Commission shall report regularly to the special committee and to the European Parliament on the progress of negotiations.

4. For the negotiation and conclusion of the agreements referred to in paragraph 3, the Council shall act by a qualified majority.

For the negotiation and conclusion of agreements in the fields of trade in services and the commercial aspects of intellectual property, as well as foreign direct investment, the Council shall act unanimously where such agreements include provisions for which unanimity is required for the adoption of internal rules.

The Council shall also act unanimously for the negotiation and conclusion of agreements:

(a) in the field of trade in cultural and audiovisual services, where these agreements risk prejudicing the Union's cultural and linguistic diversity;

(b) in the field of trade in social, education and health services, where these agreements risk seriously disturbing the national organisation of such services and prejudicing the responsibility of Member States to deliver them.

5. The negotiation and conclusion of international agreements in the field of transport shall be subject to Title VI of Part Three and to Article 218.

6. The exercise of the competences conferred by this Article in the field of the common commercial policy shall not affect the delimitation of competences between the Union and the Member States, and shall not lead to harmonisation of legislative or regulatory provisions of the Member States in so far as the Treaties exclude such harmonisation.

Title III
Cooperation with Third Countries and Humanitarian Aid

Chapter 1
Development Cooperation

Article 208 (ex Article 177 TEC)

1. Union policy in the field of development cooperation shall be conducted within the framework of the principles and objectives of the Union's external action. The Union's development cooperation policy and that of the Member States complement and reinforce each other.

Union development cooperation policy shall have as its primary objective the reduction and, in the long term, the eradication of poverty. The Union shall take account of the objectives of development cooperation in the policies that it implements which are likely to affect developing countries.

2. The Union and the Member States shall comply with the commitments and take account of the objectives they have approved in the context of the United Nations and other competent international organisations.

Article 209 (ex Article 179 TEC)
1. The European Parliament and the Council, acting in accordance with the ordinary legislative procedure, shall adopt the measures necessary for the implementation of development cooperation policy, which may relate to multiannual cooperation programmes with developing countries or programmes with a thematic approach.
2. The Union may conclude with third countries and competent international organisations any agreement helping to achieve the objectives referred to in Article 21 of the Treaty on European Union and in Article 208 of this Treaty.
The first subparagraph shall be without prejudice to Member States' competence to negotiate in international bodies and to conclude agreements.
3. The European Investment Bank shall contribute, under the terms laid down in its Statute, to the implementation of the measures referred to in paragraph 1.

Article 210 (ex Article 180 TEC)
1. In order to promote the complementarity and efficiency of their action, the Union and the Member States shall coordinate their policies on development cooperation and shall consult each other on their aid programmes, including in international organisations and during international conferences. They may undertake joint action. Member States shall contribute if necessary to the implementation of Union aid programmes.
2. The Commission may take any useful initiative to promote the coordination referred to in paragraph 1.

Article 211 (ex Article 181 TEC)
Within their respective spheres of competence, the Union and the Member States shall cooperate with third countries and with the competent international organisations.

Chapter 2
Economic, Financial and Technical Cooperation with Third Countries

Article 212 (ex Article 181a TEC)
1. Without prejudice to the other provisions of the Treaties, and in particular Articles 208 to 211, the Union shall carry out economic, financial and technical cooperation measures, including assistance, in particular financial assistance, with third countries other than developing countries. Such measures shall be consistent with the development policy of the Union and shall be carried out within the framework of the principles and objectives of its external action. The Union's operations and those of the Member States shall complement and reinforce each other.

2. The European Parliament and the Council, acting in accordance with the ordinary legislative procedure, shall adopt the measures necessary for the implementation of paragraph 1.

3. Within their respective spheres of competence, the Union and the Member States shall cooperate with third countries and the competent international organisations. The arrangements for Union cooperation may be the subject of agreements between the Union and the third parties concerned.

The first subparagraph shall be without prejudice to the Member States' competence to negotiate in international bodies and to conclude international agreements.

Article 213

When the situation in a third country requires urgent financial assistance from the Union, the Council shall adopt the necessary decisions on a proposal from the Commission.

Chapter 3
Humanitarian Aid

Article 214

1. The Union's operations in the field of humanitarian aid shall be conducted within the framework of the principles and objectives of the external action of the Union. Such operations shall be intended to provide ad hoc assistance and relief and protection for people in third countries who are victims of natural or man-made disasters, in order to meet the humanitarian needs resulting from these different situations. The Union's measures and those of the Member States shall complement and reinforce each other.

2. Humanitarian aid operations shall be conducted in compliance with the principles of international law and with the principles of impartiality, neutrality and non-discrimination.

3. The European Parliament and the Council, acting in accordance with the ordinary legislative procedure, shall establish the measures defining the framework within which the Union's humanitarian aid operations shall be implemented.

4. The Union may conclude with third countries and competent international organisations any agreement helping to achieve the objectives referred to in paragraph 1 and in Article 21 of the Treaty on European Union.

The first subparagraph shall be without prejudice to Member States' competence to negotiate in international bodies and to conclude agreements.

5. In order to establish a framework for joint contributions from young Europeans to the humanitarian aid operations of the Union, a European Voluntary Humanitarian Aid Corps shall be set up. The European Parliament and the Council, acting by means of regulations in accordance with the ordinary legislative procedure, shall determine the rules and procedures for the operation of the Corps.

6. The Commission may take any useful initiative to promote coordination between actions of the Union and those of the Member States, in order to enhance the efficiency and complementarity of Union and national humanitarian aid measures.

7. The Union shall ensure that its humanitarian aid operations are coordinated and consistent with those of international organisations and bodies, in particular those forming part of the United Nations system.

Title IV
Restrictive Measures

Article 215 (ex Article 301 TEC)
1. Where a decision, adopted in accordance with Chapter 2 of Title V of the Treaty on European Union, provides for the interruption or reduction, in part or completely, of economic and financial relations with one or more third countries, the Council, acting by a qualified majority on a joint proposal from the High Representative of the Union for Foreign Affairs and Security Policy and the Commission, shall adopt the necessary measures. It shall inform the European Parliament thereof.
2. Where a decision adopted in accordance with Chapter 2 of Title V of the Treaty on European Union so provides, the Council may adopt restrictive measures under the procedure referred to in paragraph 1 against natural or legal persons and groups or non-State entities.
3. The acts referred to in this Article shall include necessary provisions on legal safeguards.

Title V
International Agreements

Article 216
1. The Union may conclude an agreement with one or more third countries or international organisations where the Treaties so provide or where the conclusion of an agreement is necessary in order to achieve, within the framework of the Union's policies, one of the objectives referred to in the Treaties, or is provided for in a legally binding Union act or is likely to affect common rules or alter their scope.
2. Agreements concluded by the Union are binding upon the institutions of the Union and on its Member States.

Article 217 (ex Article 310 TEC)
The Union may conclude with one or more third countries or international organisations agreements establishing an association involving reciprocal rights and obligations, common action and special procedure.

Article 218 (ex Article 300 TEC)
1. Without prejudice to the specific provisions laid down in Article 207, agreements between the Union and third countries or international organisations shall be negotiated and concluded in accordance with the following procedure.
2. The Council shall authorise the opening of negotiations, adopt negotiating directives, authorise the signing of agreements and conclude them.
3. The Commission, or the High Representative of the Union for Foreign Affairs and Security Policy where the agreement envisaged relates exclusively or principally to the common foreign and security policy, shall submit recommendations to the Council, which shall adopt a decision authorising the opening of negotiations and, depending on the subject of the agreement envisaged, nominating the Union negotiator or the head of the Union's negotiating team.
4. The Council may address directives to the negotiator and designate a special committee in consultation with which the negotiations must be conducted.
5. The Council, on a proposal by the negotiator, shall adopt a decision authorising the signing of the agreement and, if necessary, its provisional application before entry into force.
6. The Council, on a proposal by the negotiator, shall adopt a decision concluding the agreement.
Except where agreements relate exclusively to the common foreign and security policy, the Council shall adopt the decision concluding the agreement:
    (a) after obtaining the consent of the European Parliament in the following cases:
        (i) association agreements;
        (ii) agreement on Union accession to the European Convention for the Protection of Human Rights and Fundamental Freedoms;
        (iii) agreements establishing a specific institutional framework by organising cooperation procedures;
        (iv) agreements with important budgetary implications for the Union;
        (v) agreements covering fields to which either the ordinary legislative procedure applies, or the special legislative procedure where consent by the European Parliament is required.
The European Parliament and the Council may, in an urgent situation, agree upon a time-limit for consent.
    (b) after consulting the European Parliament in other cases. The European Parliament shall deliver its opinion within a time-limit which the Council may set depending on the urgency of the matter. In the absence of an opinion within that time-limit, the Council may act.
7. When concluding an agreement, the Council may, by way of derogation from paragraphs 5, 6 and 9, authorise the negotiator to approve on the Union's behalf modifications to the agreement where it provides for them to be adopted by a simplified procedure or by a body set up by the agreement. The Council may attach specific conditions to such authorisation.

8. The Council shall act by a qualified majority throughout the procedure.

However, it shall act unanimously when the agreement covers a field for which unanimity is required for the adoption of a Union act as well as for association agreements and the agreements referred to in Article 212 with the States which are candidates for accession. The Council shall also act unanimously for the agreement on accession of the Union to the European Convention for the Protection of Human Rights and Fundamental Freedoms; the decision concluding this agreement shall enter into force after it has been approved by the Member States in accordance with their respective constitutional requirements.

9. The Council, on a proposal from the Commission or the High Representative of the Union for Foreign Affairs and Security Policy, shall adopt a decision suspending application of an agreement and establishing the positions to be adopted on the Union's behalf in a body set up by an agreement, when that body is called upon to adopt acts having legal effects, with the exception of acts supplementing or amending the institutional framework of the agreement.

10. The European Parliament shall be immediately and fully informed at all stages of the procedure.

11. A Member State, the European Parliament, the Council or the Commission may obtain the opinion of the Court of Justice as to whether an agreement envisaged is compatible with the Treaties. Where the opinion of the Court is adverse, the agreement envisaged may not enter into force unless it is amended or the Treaties are revised.

Article 219 (ex Article 111(1) to (3) and (5) TEC)

1. By way of derogation from Article 218, the Council, either on a recommendation from the European Central Bank or on a recommendation from the Commission and after consulting the European Central Bank, in an endeavour to reach a consensus consistent with the objective of price stability, may conclude formal agreements on an exchange-rate system for the euro in relation to the currencies of third States. The Council shall act unanimously after consulting the European Parliament and in accordance with the procedure provided for in paragraph 3.

The Council may, either on a recommendation from the European Central Bank or on a recommendation from the Commission, and after consulting the European Central Bank, in an endeavour to reach a consensus consistent with the objective of price stability, adopt, adjust or abandon the central rates of the euro within the exchange-rate system. The President of the Council shall inform the European Parliament of the adoption, adjustment or abandonment of the euro central rates.

2. In the absence of an exchange-rate system in relation to one or more currencies of third States as referred to in paragraph 1, the Council, either on a recommendation from the Commission and after consulting the European Central Bank or on a recommendation from the European Central Bank, may formulate general orientations for exchange-rate policy in relation to these currencies. These general orientations shall be without prejudice to the primary objective of the ESCB to maintain price stability.

3. By way of derogation from Article 218, where agreements concerning monetary or foreign exchange regime matters need to be negotiated by the Union with one or more third States or international organisations, the Council, on a recommendation from the Commission and after consulting the European Central Bank, shall decide the arrangements for the negotiation and for the conclusion of such agreements. These arrangements shall ensure that the Union expresses a single position. The Commission shall be fully associated with the negotiations.

4. Without prejudice to Union competence and Union agreements as regards economic and monetary union, Member States may negotiate in international bodies and conclude international agreements.

Title VI
The Union's Relations with International Organisations and Third Countries and Union Delegations

Article 220 (ex Articles 302 to 304 TEC)
1. The Union shall establish all appropriate forms of cooperation with the organs of the United Nations and its specialised agencies, the Council of Europe, the Organisation for Security and Cooperation in Europe and the Organisation for Economic Cooperation and Development.

The Union shall also maintain such relations as are appropriate with other international organisations.

2. The High Representative of the Union for Foreign Affairs and Security Policy and the Commission shall implement this Article.

Article 221
1. Union delegations in third countries and at international organisations shall represent the Union.

2. Union delegations shall be placed under the authority of the High Representative of the Union for Foreign Affairs and Security Policy. They shall act in close cooperation with Member States' diplomatic and consular missions.

Title VII
Solidarity Clause

Article 222
1. The Union and its Member States shall act jointly in a spirit of solidarity if a Member State is the object of a terrorist attack or the victim of a natural or man-made disaster. The Union shall mobilise all the instruments at its disposal, including the military resources made available by the Member States, to:

(a) – prevent the terrorist threat in the territory of the Member States;
– protect democratic institutions and the civilian population from any terrorist attack;
– assist a Member State in its territory, at the request of its political authorities, in the event of a terrorist attack;
(b) assist a Member State in its territory, at the request of its political authorities, in the event of a natural or man-made disaster.
2. Should a Member State be the object of a terrorist attack or the victim of a natural or man-made disaster, the other Member States shall assist it at the request of its political authorities. To that end, the Member States shall coordinate between themselves in the Council.
3. The arrangements for the implementation by the Union of the solidarity clause shall be defined by a decision adopted by the Council acting on a joint proposal by the Commission and the High Representative of the Union for Foreign Affairs and Security Policy. The Council shall act in accordance with Article 31(1) of the Treaty on European Union where this decision has defence implications. The European Parliament shall be informed.
For the purposes of this paragraph and without prejudice to Article 240, the Council shall be assisted by the Political and Security Committee with the support of the structures developed in the context of the common security and defence policy and by the Committee referred to in Article 71; the two committees shall, if necessary, submit joint opinions.
4. The European Council shall regularly assess the threats facing the Union in order to enable the Union and its Member States to take effective action.

Part Six
Institutional and Financial Provisions

Title I
Institutional Provisions

Chapter 1
The Institutions

Section 1
The European Parliament

Article 223 (ex Article 190(4) and (5) TEC)
1. The European Parliament shall draw up a proposal to lay down the provisions necessary for the election of its Members by direct universal suffrage in accordance with a uniform procedure in all Member States or in accordance with principles common to all Member States.

The Council, acting unanimously in accordance with a special legislative procedure and after obtaining the consent of the European Parliament, which shall act by a majority of its component Members, shall lay down the necessary provisions. These provisions shall enter into force following their approval by the Member States in accordance with their respective constitutional requirements.

2. The European Parliament, acting by means of regulations on its own initiative in accordance with a special legislative procedure after seeking an opinion from the Commission and with the consent of the Council, shall lay down the regulations and general conditions governing the performance of the duties of its Members. All rules or conditions relating to the taxation of Members or former Members shall require unanimity within the Council.

Article 224 (ex Article 191, second subparagraph, TEC)

The European Parliament and the Council, acting in accordance with the ordinary legislative procedure, by means of regulations, shall lay down the regulations governing political parties at European level referred to in Article 10(4) of the Treaty on European Union and in particular the rules regarding their funding.

Article 225 (ex Article 192, second subparagraph, TEC)

The European Parliament may, acting by a majority of its component Members, request the Commission to submit any appropriate proposal on matters on which it considers that a Union act is required for the purpose of implementing the Treaties. If the Commission does not submit a proposal, it shall inform the European Parliament of the reasons.

Article 226 (ex Article 193 TEC)

In the course of its duties, the European Parliament may, at the request of a quarter of its component Members, set up a temporary Committee of Inquiry to investigate, without prejudice to the powers conferred by the Treaties on other institutions or bodies, alleged contraventions or maladministration in the implementation of Union law, except where the alleged facts are being examined before a court and while the case is still subject to legal proceedings.

The temporary Committee of Inquiry shall cease to exist on the submission of its report.

The detailed provisions governing the exercise of the right of inquiry shall be determined by the European Parliament, acting by means of regulations on its own initiative in accordance with a special legislative procedure, after obtaining the consent of the Council and the Commission.

Article 227 (ex Article 194 TEC)

Any citizen of the Union, and any natural or legal person residing or having its registered office in a Member State, shall have the right to address, individually or in association with other citizens or persons, a petition to the European Parliament on a matter which comes within the Union's fields of activity and which affects him, her or it directly.

Article 228 (ex Article 195 TEC)

1. A European Ombudsman, elected by the European Parliament, shall be empowered to receive complaints from any citizen of the Union or any natural or legal person residing or having its registered office in a Member State concerning instances of maladministration in the activities of the Union institutions, bodies, offices or agencies, with the exception of the Court of Justice of the European Union acting in its judicial role. He or she shall examine such complaints and report on them.

In accordance with his duties, the Ombudsman shall conduct inquiries for which he finds grounds, either on his own initiative or on the basis of complaints submitted to him direct or through a Member of the European Parliament, except where the alleged facts are or have been the subject of legal proceedings. Where the Ombudsman establishes an instance of maladministration, he shall refer the matter to the institution, body, office or agency concerned, which shall have a period of three months in which to inform him of its views. The Ombudsman shall then forward a report to the European Parliament and the institution, body, office or agency concerned. The person lodging the complaint shall be informed of the outcome of such inquiries.

The Ombudsman shall submit an annual report to the European Parliament on the outcome of his inquiries.

2. The Ombudsman shall be elected after each election of the European Parliament for the duration of its term of office. The Ombudsman shall be eligible for reappointment.

The Ombudsman may be dismissed by the Court of Justice at the request of the European Parliament if he no longer fulfils the conditions required for the performance of his duties or if he is guilty of serious misconduct.

3. The Ombudsman shall be completely independent in the performance of his duties. In the performance of those duties he shall neither seek nor take instructions from any Government, institution, body, office or entity. The Ombudsman may not, during his term of office, engage in any other occupation, whether gainful or not.

4. The European Parliament acting by means of regulations on its own initiative in accordance with a special legislative procedure shall, after seeking an opinion from the Commission and with the consent of the Council, lay down the regulations and general conditions governing the performance of the Ombudsman's duties.

Article 229 (ex Article 196 TEC)

The European Parliament shall hold an annual session. It shall meet, without requiring to be convened, on the second Tuesday in March.

The European Parliament may meet in extraordinary part-session at the request of a majority of its component Members or at the request of the Council or of the Commission.

Article 230 (ex Article 197, second, third and fourth paragraph, TEC)

The Commission may attend all the meetings and shall, at its request, be heard.

The Commission shall reply orally or in writing to questions put to it by the European Parliament or by its Members.

The European Council and the Council shall be heard by the European Parliament in accordance with the conditions laid down in the Rules of Procedure of the European Council and those of the Council.

Article 231 (ex Article 198 TEC)
Save as otherwise provided in the Treaties, the European Parliament shall act by a majority of the votes cast.

The Rules of Procedure shall determine the quorum.

Article 232 (ex Article 199 TEC)
The European Parliament shall adopt its Rules of Procedure, acting by a majority of its Members.

The proceedings of the European Parliament shall be published in the manner laid down in the Treaties and in its Rules of Procedure.

Article 233 (ex Article 200 TEC)
The European Parliament shall discuss in open session the annual general report submitted to it by the Commission.

Article 234 (ex Article 201 TEC)
If a motion of censure on the activities of the Commission is tabled before it, the European Parliament shall not vote thereon until at least three days after the motion has been tabled and only by open vote.

If the motion of censure is carried by a two-thirds majority of the votes cast, representing a majority of the component Members of the European Parliament, the members of the Commission shall resign as a body and the High Representative of the Union for Foreign Affairs and Security Policy shall resign from duties that he or she carries out in the Commission. They shall remain in office and continue to deal with current business until they are replaced in accordance with Article 17 of the Treaty on European Union. In this case, the term of office of the members of the Commission appointed to replace them shall expire on the date on which the term of office of the members of the Commission obliged to resign as a body would have expired.

Section 2
The European Council

Article 235
1. Where a vote is taken, any member of the European Council may also act on behalf of not more than one other member.

Article 16(4) of the Treaty on European Union and Article 238(2) of this Treaty shall apply to the European Council when it is acting by a qualified majority. Where the European

Council decides by vote, its President and the President of the Commission shall not take part in the vote.

Abstentions by members present in person or represented shall not prevent the adoption by the European Council of acts which require unanimity.

2. The President of the European Parliament may be invited to be heard by the European Council.

3. The European Council shall act by a simple majority for procedural questions and for the adoption of its Rules of Procedure.

4. The European Council shall be assisted by the General Secretariat of the Council.

Article 236

The European Council shall adopt by a qualified majority:

(a) a decision establishing the list of Council configurations, other than those of the General Affairs Council and of the Foreign Affairs Council, in accordance with Article 16(6) of the Treaty on European Union;

(b) a decision on the Presidency of Council configurations, other than that of Foreign Affairs, in accordance with Article 16(9) of the Treaty on European Union.

Section 3
The Council

Article 237 (ex Article 204 TEC)

The Council shall meet when convened by its President on his own initiative or at the request of one of its Members or of the Commission.

Article 238 (ex Article 205(1) and (2), TEC)

1. Where it is required to act by a simple majority, the Council shall act by a majority of its component members.

2. By way of derogation from Article 16(4) of the Treaty on European Union, as from 1 November 2014 and subject to the provisions laid down in the Protocol on transitional provisions, where the Council does not act on a proposal from the Commission or from the High Representative of the Union for Foreign Affairs and Security Policy, the qualified majority shall be defined as at least 72 % of the members of the Council, representing Member States comprising at least 65 % of the population of the Union.

3. As from 1 November 2014 and subject to the provisions laid down in the Protocol on transitional provisions, in cases where, under the Treaties, not all the members of the Council participate in voting, a qualified majority shall be defined as follows:

(a) A qualified majority shall be defined as at least 55 % of the members of the Council representing the participating Member States, comprising at least 65 % of the population of these States.

A blocking minority must include at least the minimum number of Council members representing more than 35 % of the population of the participating Member States, plus one member, failing which the qualified majority shall be deemed attained;

(b) By way of derogation from point (a), where the Council does not act on a proposal from the Commission or from the High Representative of the Union for Foreign Affairs and Security Policy, the qualified majority shall be defined as at least 72 % of the members of the Council representing the participating Member States, comprising at least 65 % of the population of these States.
4. Abstentions by Members present in person or represented shall not prevent the adoption by the Council of acts which require unanimity.

Article 239 (ex Article 206 TEC)
Where a vote is taken, any Member of the Council may also act on behalf of not more than one other member.

Article 240 (ex Article 207 TEC)
1. A committee consisting of the Permanent Representatives of the Governments of the Member States shall be responsible for preparing the work of the Council and for carrying out the tasks assigned to it by the latter. The Committee may adopt procedural decisions in cases provided for in the Council's Rules of Procedure.
2. The Council shall be assisted by a General Secretariat, under the responsibility of a Secretary-General appointed by the Council.
The Council shall decide on the organisation of the General Secretariat by a simple majority.
3. The Council shall act by a simple majority regarding procedural matters and for the adoption of its Rules of Procedure.

Article 241 (ex Article 208 TEC)
The Council, acting by a simple majority, may request the Commission to undertake any studies the Council considers desirable for the attainment of the common objectives, and to submit to it any appropriate proposals. If the Commission does not submit a proposal, it shall inform the Council of the reasons.

Article 242 (ex Article 209 TEC)
The Council, acting by a simple majority shall, after consulting the Commission, determine the rules governing the committees provided for in the Treaties.

Article 243 (ex Article 210 TEC)
The Council shall determine the salaries, allowances and pensions of the President of the European Council, the President of the Commission, the High Representative of the Union for Foreign Affairs and Security Policy, the Members of the Commission, the Presidents, Members and Registrars of the Court of Justice of the European Union, and the Secretary-General of the Council. It shall also determine any payment to be made instead of remuneration.

Section 4
The Commission

Article 244
In accordance with Article 17(5) of the Treaty on European Union, the Members of the Commission shall be chosen on the basis of a system of rotation established unanimously by the European Council and on the basis of the following principles:

(a) Member States shall be treated on a strictly equal footing as regards determination of the sequence of, and the time spent by, their nationals as members of the Commission; consequently, the difference between the total number of terms of office held by nationals of any given pair of Member States may never be more than one;

(b) subject to point (a), each successive Commission shall be so composed as to reflect satisfactorily the demographic and geographical range of all the Member States.

Article 245 (ex Article 213 TEC)
The Members of the Commission shall refrain from any action incompatible with their duties. Member States shall respect their independence and shall not seek to influence them in the performance of their tasks.

The Members of the Commission may not, during their term of office, engage in any other occupation, whether gainful or not. When entering upon their duties they shall give a solemn undertaking that, both during and after their term of office, they will respect the obligations arising therefrom and in particular their duty to behave with integrity and discretion as regards the acceptance, after they have ceased to hold office, of certain appointments or benefits. In the event of any breach of these obligations, the Court of Justice may, on application by the Council acting by a simple majority or the Commission, rule that the Member concerned be, according to the circumstances, either compulsorily retired in accordance with Article 247 or deprived of his right to a pension or other benefits in its stead.

Article 246 (ex Article 215 TEC)
Apart from normal replacement, or death, the duties of a Member of the Commission shall end when he resigns or is compulsorily retired.

A vacancy caused by resignation, compulsory retirement or death shall be filled for the remainder of the Member's term of office by a new Member of the same nationality appointed by the Council, by common accord with the President of the Commission, after consulting the European Parliament and in accordance with the criteria set out in the second subparagraph of Article 17(3) of the Treaty on European Union.

The Council may, acting unanimously on a proposal from the President of the Commission, decide that such a vacancy need not be filled, in particular when the remainder of the Member's term of office is short.

In the event of resignation, compulsory retirement or death, the President shall be replaced for the remainder of his term of office. The procedure laid down in the first subparagraph of Article 17(7) of the Treaty on European Union shall be applicable for the replacement of the President.

In the event of resignation, compulsory retirement or death, the High Representative of the Union for Foreign Affairs and Security Policy shall be replaced, for the remainder of his or her term of office, in accordance with Article 18(1) of the Treaty on European Union.

In the case of the resignation of all the Members of the Commission, they shall remain in office and continue to deal with current business until they have been replaced, for the remainder of their term of office, in accordance with Article 17 of the Treaty on European Union.

Article 247 (ex Article 216 TEC)

If any Member of the Commission no longer fulfils the conditions required for the performance of his duties or if he has been guilty of serious misconduct, the Court of Justice may, on application by the Council acting by a simple majority or the Commission, compulsorily retire him.

Article 248 (ex Article 217(2) TEC)

Without prejudice to Article 18(4) of the Treaty on European Union, the responsibilities incumbent upon the Commission shall be structured and allocated among its members by its President, in accordance with Article 17(6) of that Treaty. The President may reshuffle the allocation of those responsibilities during the Commission's term of office. The Members of the Commission shall carry out the duties devolved upon them by the President under his authority.

Article 249 (ex Articles 218(2) and 212 TEC)

1. The Commission shall adopt its Rules of Procedure so as to ensure that both it and its departments operate. It shall ensure that these Rules are published.
2. The Commission shall publish annually, not later than one month before the opening of the session of the European Parliament, a general report on the activities of the Union.

Article 250 (ex Article 219 TEC)

The Commission shall act by a majority of its Members. Its Rules of Procedure shall determine the quorum.

Section 5
The Court of Justice of the European Union

Article 251 (ex Article 221 TEC)

The Court of Justice shall sit in chambers or in a Grand Chamber, in accordance with the rules laid down for that purpose in the Statute of the Court of Justice of the European Union. When provided for in the Statute, the Court of Justice may also sit as a full Court.

Article 252 (ex Article 222 TEC)

The Court of Justice shall be assisted by eight Advocates-General. Should the Court of Justice so request, the Council, acting unanimously, may increase the number of Advocates-General.

It shall be the duty of the Advocate-General, acting with complete impartiality and independence, to make, in open court, reasoned submissions on cases which, in accordance with the Statute of the Court of Justice of the European Union, require his involvement.

Article 253 (ex Article 223 TEC)

The Judges and Advocates-General of the Court of Justice shall be chosen from persons whose independence is beyond doubt and who possess the qualifications required for appointment to the highest judicial offices in their respective countries or who are jurisconsults of recognised competence; they shall be appointed by common accord of the governments of the Member States for a term of six years, after consultation of the panel provided for in Article 255.

Every three years there shall be a partial replacement of the Judges and Advocates-General, in accordance with the conditions laid down in the Statute of the Court of Justice of the European Union.

The Judges shall elect the President of the Court of Justice from among their number for a term of three years. He may be re-elected.

Retiring Judges and Advocates-General may be reappointed.

The Court of Justice shall appoint its Registrar and lay down the rules governing his service.

The Court of Justice shall establish its Rules of Procedure. Those Rules shall require the approval of the Council.

Article 254 (ex Article 224 TEC)

The number of Judges of the General Court shall be determined by the Statute of the Court of Justice of the European Union. The Statute may provide for the General Court to be assisted by Advocates-General.

The members of the General Court shall be chosen from persons whose independence is beyond doubt and who possess the ability required for appointment to high judicial office. They shall be appointed by common accord of the governments of the Member States for a term of six years, after consultation of the panel provided for in Article 255. The membership shall be partially renewed every three years. Retiring members shall be eligible for reappointment.

The Judges shall elect the President of the General Court from among their number for a term of three years. He may be re-elected.

The General Court shall appoint its Registrar and lay down the rules governing his service. The General Court shall establish its Rules of Procedure in agreement with the Court of Justice. Those Rules shall require the approval of the Council.

Unless the Statute of the Court of Justice of the European Union provides otherwise, the provisions of the Treaties relating to the Court of Justice shall apply to the General Court.

Article 255

A panel shall be set up in order to give an opinion on candidates' suitability to perform the duties of Judge and Advocate-General of the Court of Justice and the General Court before the governments of the Member States make the appointments referred to in Articles 253 and 254.

The panel shall comprise seven persons chosen from among former members of the Court of Justice and the General Court, members of national supreme courts and lawyers of recognised competence, one of whom shall be proposed by the European Parliament. The Council shall adopt a decision establishing the panel's operating rules and a decision appointing its members. It shall act on the initiative of the President of the Court of Justice.

Article 256 (ex Article 225 TEC)

1. The General Court shall have jurisdiction to hear and determine at first instance actions or proceedings referred to in Articles 263, 265, 268, 270 and 272, with the exception of those assigned to a specialised court set up under Article 257 and those reserved in the Statute for the Court of Justice. The Statute may provide for the General Court to have jurisdiction for other classes of action or proceeding.

Decisions given by the General Court under this paragraph may be subject to a right of appeal to the Court of Justice on points of law only, under the conditions and within the limits laid down by the Statute.

2. The General Court shall have jurisdiction to hear and determine actions or proceedings brought against decisions of the specialised courts.

Decisions given by the General Court under this paragraph may exceptionally be subject to review by the Court of Justice, under the conditions and within the limits laid down by the Statute, where there is a serious risk of the unity or consistency of Union law being affected.

3. The General Court shall have jurisdiction to hear and determine questions referred for a preliminary ruling under Article 267, in specific areas laid down by the Statute.

Where the General Court considers that the case requires a decision of principle likely to affect the unity or consistency of Union law, it may refer the case to the Court of Justice for a ruling.

Decisions given by the General Court on questions referred for a preliminary ruling may exceptionally be subject to review by the Court of Justice, under the conditions and within the limits laid down by the Statute, where there is a serious risk of the unity or consistency of Union law being affected.

Article 257 (ex Article 225a TEC)

The European Parliament and the Council, acting in accordance with the ordinary legislative procedure, may establish specialised courts attached to the General Court to hear and determine at first instance certain classes of action or proceeding brought in specific areas. The European Parliament and the Council shall act by means of regulations either on a proposal from the Commission after consultation of the Court of Justice or at the request of the Court of Justice after consultation of the Commission.

The regulation establishing a specialised court shall lay down the rules on the organisation of the court and the extent of the jurisdiction conferred upon it.

Decisions given by specialised courts may be subject to a right of appeal on points of law only or, when provided for in the regulation establishing the specialised court, a right of appeal also on matters of fact, before the General Court.

The members of the specialised courts shall be chosen from persons whose independence is beyond doubt and who possess the ability required for appointment to judicial office. They shall be appointed by the Council, acting unanimously.

The specialised courts shall establish their Rules of Procedure in agreement with the Court of Justice. Those Rules shall require the approval of the Council.

Unless the regulation establishing the specialised court provides otherwise, the provisions of the Treaties relating to the Court of Justice of the European Union and the provisions of the Statute of the Court of Justice of the European Union shall apply to the specialised courts. Title I of the Statute and Article 64 thereof shall in any case apply to the specialised courts.

Article 258 (ex Article 226 TEC)

If the Commission considers that a Member State has failed to fulfil an obligation under the Treaties, it shall deliver a reasoned opinion on the matter after giving the State concerned the opportunity to submit its observations.

If the State concerned does not comply with the opinion within the period laid down by the Commission, the latter may bring the matter before the Court of Justice of the European Union.

Article 259 (ex Article 227 TEC)

A Member State which considers that another Member State has failed to fulfil an obligation under the Treaties may bring the matter before the Court of Justice of the European Union.

Before a Member State brings an action against another Member State for an alleged infringement of an obligation under the Treaties, it shall bring the matter before the Commission.

The Commission shall deliver a reasoned opinion after each of the States concerned has been given the opportunity to submit its own case and its observations on the other party's case both orally and in writing.

If the Commission has not delivered an opinion within three months of the date on which the matter was brought before it, the absence of such opinion shall not prevent the matter from being brought before the Court.

Article 260 (ex Article 228 TEC)

1. If the Court of Justice of the European Union finds that a Member State has failed to fulfil an obligation under the Treaties, the State shall be required to take the necessary measures to comply with the judgment of the Court.

2. If the Commission considers that the Member State concerned has not taken the necessary measures to comply with the judgment of the Court, it may bring the case before

the Court after giving that State the opportunity to submit its observations. It shall specify the amount of the lump sum or penalty payment to be paid by the Member State concerned which it considers appropriate in the circumstances.

If the Court finds that the Member State concerned has not complied with its judgment it may impose a lump sum or penalty payment on it.

This procedure shall be without prejudice to Article 259.

3. When the Commission brings a case before the Court pursuant to Article 258 on the grounds that the Member State concerned has failed to fulfil its obligation to notify measures transposing a directive adopted under a legislative procedure, it may, when it deems appropriate, specify the amount of the lump sum or penalty payment to be paid by the Member State concerned which it considers appropriate in the circumstances.

If the Court finds that there is an infringement it may impose a lump sum or penalty payment on the Member State concerned not exceeding the amount specified by the Commission. The payment obligation shall take effect on the date set by the Court in its judgment.

Article 261 (ex Article 229 TEC)

Regulations adopted jointly by the European Parliament and the Council, and by the Council, pursuant to the provisions of the Treaties, may give the Court of Justice of the European Union unlimited jurisdiction with regard to the penalties provided for in such regulations.

Article 262 (ex Article 229a TEC)

Without prejudice to the other provisions of the Treaties, the Council, acting unanimously in accordance with a special legislative procedure and after consulting the European Parliament, may adopt provisions to confer jurisdiction, to the extent that it shall determine, on the Court of Justice of the European Union in disputes relating to the application of acts adopted on the basis of the Treaties which create European intellectual property rights. These provisions shall enter into force after their approval by the Member States in accordance with their respective constitutional requirements.

Article 263 (ex Article 230 TEC)

The Court of Justice of the European Union shall review the legality of legislative acts, of acts of the Council, of the Commission and of the European Central Bank, other than recommendations and opinions, and of acts of the European Parliament and of the European Council intended to produce legal effects vis-à-vis third parties. It shall also review the legality of acts of bodies, offices or agencies of the Union intended to produce legal effects vis-à-vis third parties.

It shall for this purpose have jurisdiction in actions brought by a Member State, the European Parliament, the Council or the Commission on grounds of lack of competence, infringement of an essential procedural requirement, infringement of the Treaties or of any rule of law relating to their application, or misuse of powers.

The Court shall have jurisdiction under the same conditions in actions brought by the Court of Auditors, by the European Central Bank and by the Committee of the Regions for the purpose of protecting their prerogatives.

Any natural or legal person may, under the conditions laid down in the first and second paragraphs, institute proceedings against an act addressed to that person or which is of direct and individual concern to them, and against a regulatory act which is of direct concern to them and does not entail implementing measures.

Acts setting up bodies, offices and agencies of the Union may lay down specific conditions and arrangements concerning actions brought by natural or legal persons against acts of these bodies, offices or agencies intended to produce legal effects in relation to them.

The proceedings provided for in this Article shall be instituted within two months of the publication of the measure, or of its notification to the plaintiff, or, in the absence thereof, of the day on which it came to the knowledge of the latter, as the case may be.

Article 264 (ex Article 231 TEC)

If the action is well founded, the Court of Justice of the European Union shall declare the act concerned to be void.

However, the Court shall, if it considers this necessary, state which of the effects of the act which it has declared void shall be considered as definitive.

Article 265 (ex Article 232 TEC)

Should the European Parliament, the European Council, the Council, the Commission or the European Central Bank, in infringement of the Treaties, fail to act, the Member States and the other institutions of the Union may bring an action before the Court of Justice of the European Union to have the infringement established. This Article shall apply, under the same conditions, to bodies, offices and agencies of the Union which fail to act.

The action shall be admissible only if the institution, body, office or agency concerned has first been called upon to act. If, within two months of being so called upon, the institution, body, office or agency concerned has not defined its position, the action may be brought within a further period of two months.

Any natural or legal person may, under the conditions laid down in the preceding paragraphs, complain to the Court that an institution, body, office or agency of the Union has failed to address to that person any act other than a recommendation or an opinion.

Article 266 (ex Article 233 TEC)

The institution whose act has been declared void or whose failure to act has been declared contrary to the Treaties shall be required to take the necessary measures to comply with the judgment of the Court of Justice of the European Union.

This obligation shall not affect any obligation which may result from the application of the second paragraph of Article 340.

Article 267 (ex Article 234 TEC)

The Court of Justice of the European Union shall have jurisdiction to give preliminary rulings concerning:

    (a) the interpretation of the Treaties;

(b) the validity and interpretation of acts of the institutions, bodies, offices or agencies of the Union;

Where such a question is raised before any court or tribunal of a Member State, that court or tribunal may, if it considers that a decision on the question is necessary to enable it to give judgment, request the Court to give a ruling thereon.

Where any such question is raised in a case pending before a court or tribunal of a Member State against whose decisions there is no judicial remedy under national law, that court or tribunal shall bring the matter before the Court.

If such a question is raised in a case pending before a court or tribunal of a Member State with regard to a person in custody, the Court of Justice of the European Union shall act with the minimum of delay.

Article 268 (ex Article 235 TEC)

The Court of Justice of the European Union shall have jurisdiction in disputes relating to compensation for damage provided for in the second and third paragraphs of Article 340.

Article 269

The Court of Justice shall have jurisdiction to decide on the legality of an act adopted by the European Council or by the Council pursuant to Article 7 of the Treaty on European Union solely at the request of the Member State concerned by a determination of the European Council or of the Council and in respect solely of the procedural stipulations contained in that Article.

Such a request must be made within one month from the date of such determination. The Court shall rule within one month from the date of the request.

Article 270 (ex Article 236 TEC)

The Court of Justice of the European Union shall have jurisdiction in any dispute between the Union and its servants within the limits and under the conditions laid down in the Staff Regulations of Officials and the Conditions of Employment of other servants of the Union.

Article 271 (ex Article 237 TEC)

The Court of Justice of the European Union shall, within the limits hereinafter laid down, have jurisdiction in disputes concerning:

(a) the fulfilment by Member States of obligations under the Statute of the European Investment Bank. In this connection, the Board of Directors of the Bank shall enjoy the powers conferred upon the Commission by Article 258;

(b) measures adopted by the Board of Governors of the European Investment Bank. In this connection, any Member State, the Commission or the Board of Directors of the Bank may institute proceedings under the conditions laid down in Article 263;

(c) measures adopted by the Board of Directors of the European Investment Bank. Proceedings against such measures may be instituted only by Member States or by the Commission, under the conditions laid down in Article 263, and solely on the grounds of non-compliance with the procedure provided for in Article 19(2), (5), (6) and (7) of the Statute of the Bank;

(d) the fulfilment by national central banks of obligations under the Treaties and the Statute of the ESCB and of the ECB. In this connection the powers of the Governing Council of the European Central Bank in respect of national central banks shall be the same as those conferred upon the Commission in respect of Member States by Article 258. If the Court finds that a national central bank has failed to fulfil an obligation under the Treaties, that bank shall be required to take the necessary measures to comply with the judgment of the Court.

Article 272 (ex Article 238 TEC)
The Court of Justice of the European Union shall have jurisdiction to give judgment pursuant to any arbitration clause contained in a contract concluded by or on behalf of the Union, whether that contract be governed by public or private law.

Article 273 (ex Article 239 TEC)
The Court of Justice shall have jurisdiction in any dispute between Member States which relates to the subject matter of the Treaties if the dispute is submitted to it under a special agreement between the parties.

Article 274 (ex Article 240 TEC)
Save where jurisdiction is conferred on the Court of Justice of the European Union by the Treaties, disputes to which the Union is a party shall not on that ground be excluded from the jurisdiction of the courts or tribunals of the Member States.

Article 275
The Court of Justice of the European Union shall not have jurisdiction with respect to the provisions relating to the common foreign and security policy nor with respect to acts adopted on the basis of those provisions.

However, the Court shall have jurisdiction to monitor compliance with Article 40 of the Treaty on European Union and to rule on proceedings, brought in accordance with the conditions laid down in the fourth paragraph of Article 263 of this Treaty, reviewing the legality of decisions providing for restrictive measures against natural or legal persons adopted by the Council on the basis of Chapter 2 of Title V of the Treaty on European Union.

Article 276
In exercising its powers regarding the provisions of Chapters 4 and 5 of Title V of Part Three relating to the area of freedom, security and justice, the Court of Justice of the European Union shall have no jurisdiction to review the validity or proportionality of operations carried out by the police or other law-enforcement services of a Member State or the exercise of the responsibilities incumbent upon Member States with regard to the maintenance of law and order and the safeguarding of internal security.

Article 277 (ex Article 241 TEC)
Notwithstanding the expiry of the period laid down in Article 263, sixth paragraph, any party may, in proceedings in which an act of general application adopted by an institution, body, office or agency of the Union is at issue, plead the grounds specified in Article 263, second paragraph, in order to invoke before the Court of Justice of the European Union the inapplicability of that act.

Article 278 (ex Article 242 TEC)
Actions brought before the Court of Justice of the European Union shall not have suspensory effect. The Court may, however, if it considers that circumstances so require, order that application of the contested act be suspended.

Article 279 (ex Article 243 TEC)
The Court of Justice of the European Union may in any cases before it prescribe any necessary interim measures.

Article 280 (ex Article 244 TEC)
The judgments of the Court of Justice of the European Union shall be enforceable under the conditions laid down in Article 299.

Article 281 (ex Article 245 TEC)
The Statute of the Court of Justice of the European Union shall be laid down in a separate Protocol.

The European Parliament and the Council, acting in accordance with the ordinary legislative procedure, may amend the provisions of the Statute, with the exception of Title I and Article 64. The European Parliament and the Council shall act either at the request of the Court of Justice and after consultation of the Commission, or on a proposal from the Commission and after consultation of the Court of Justice.

Section 6
The European Central Bank

Article 282
1. The European Central Bank, together with the national central banks, shall constitute the European System of Central Banks (ESCB). The European Central Bank, together with the national central banks of the Member States whose currency is the euro, which constitute the Eurosystem, shall conduct the monetary policy of the Union.
2. The ESCB shall be governed by the decision-making bodies of the European Central Bank. The primary objective of the ESCB shall be to maintain price stability. Without prejudice to that objective, it shall support the general economic policies in the Union in order to contribute to the achievement of the latter's objectives.

3. The European Central Bank shall have legal personality. It alone may authorise the issue of the euro. It shall be independent in the exercise of its powers and in the management of its finances. Union institutions, bodies, offices and agencies and the governments of the Member States shall respect that independence.

4. The European Central Bank shall adopt such measures as are necessary to carry out its tasks in accordance with Articles 127 to 133, with Article 138, and with the conditions laid down in the Statute of the ESCB and of the ECB. In accordance with these same Articles, those Member States whose currency is not the euro, and their central banks, shall retain their powers in monetary matters.

5. Within the areas falling within its responsibilities, the European Central Bank shall be consulted on all proposed Union acts, and all proposals for regulation at national level, and may give an opinion.

Article 283 (ex Article 112 TEC)

1. The Governing Council of the European Central Bank shall comprise the members of the Executive Board of the European Central Bank and the Governors of the national central banks of the Member States whose currency is the euro.

2. The Executive Board shall comprise the President, the Vice-President and four other members. The President, the Vice-President and the other members of the Executive Board shall be appointed by the European Council, acting by a qualified majority, from among persons of recognised standing and professional experience in monetary or banking matters, on a recommendation from the Council, after it has consulted the European Parliament and the Governing Council of the European Central Bank.

Their term of office shall be eight years and shall not be renewable.

Only nationals of Member States may be members of the Executive Board.

Article 284 (ex Article 113 TEC)

1. The President of the Council and a Member of the Commission may participate, without having the right to vote, in meetings of the Governing Council of the European Central Bank. The President of the Council may submit a motion for deliberation to the Governing Council of the European Central Bank.

2. The President of the European Central Bank shall be invited to participate in Council meetings when the Council is discussing matters relating to the objectives and tasks of the ESCB.

3. The European Central Bank shall address an annual report on the activities of the ESCB and on the monetary policy of both the previous and current year to the European Parliament, the Council and the Commission, and also to the European Council. The President of the European Central Bank shall present this report to the Council and to the European Parliament, which may hold a general debate on that basis.

The President of the European Central Bank and the other members of the Executive Board may, at the request of the European Parliament or on their own initiative, be heard by the competent committees of the European Parliament.

Section 7
The Court of Auditors

Article 285 (ex Article 246 TEC)
The Court of Auditors shall carry out the Union's audit.
It shall consist of one national of each Member State. Its Members shall be completely independent in the performance of their duties, in the Union's general interest.

Article 286 (ex Article 247 TEC)
1. The Members of the Court of Auditors shall be chosen from among persons who belong or have belonged in their respective States to external audit bodies or who are especially qualified for this office. Their independence must be beyond doubt.
2. The Members of the Court of Auditors shall be appointed for a term of six years. The Council, after consulting the European Parliament, shall adopt the list of Members drawn up in accordance with the proposals made by each Member State. The term of office of the Members of the Court of Auditors shall be renewable.
They shall elect the President of the Court of Auditors from among their number for a term of three years. The President may be re-elected.
3. In the performance of these duties, the Members of the Court of Auditors shall neither seek nor take instructions from any government or from any other body. The Members of the Court of Auditors shall refrain from any action incompatible with their duties.
4. The Members of the Court of Auditors may not, during their term of office, engage in any other occupation, whether gainful or not. When entering upon their duties they shall give a solemn undertaking that, both during and after their term of office, they will respect the obligations arising therefrom and in particular their duty to behave with integrity and discretion as regards the acceptance, after they have ceased to hold office, of certain appointments or benefits.
5. Apart from normal replacement, or death, the duties of a Member of the Court of Auditors shall end when he resigns, or is compulsorily retired by a ruling of the Court of Justice pursuant to paragraph 6.
The vacancy thus caused shall be filled for the remainder of the Member's term of office.
Save in the case of compulsory retirement, Members of the Court of Auditors shall remain in office until they have been replaced.
6. A Member of the Court of Auditors may be deprived of his office or of his right to a pension or other benefits in its stead only if the Court of Justice, at the request of the Court of Auditors, finds that he no longer fulfils the requisite conditions or meets the obligations arising from his office.
7. The Council shall determine the conditions of employment of the President and the Members of the Court of Auditors and in particular their salaries, allowances and pensions. It shall also determine any payment to be made instead of remuneration.
8. The provisions of the Protocol on the privileges and immunities of the European Union applicable to the Judges of the Court of Justice of the European Union shall also apply to the Members of the Court of Auditors.

Article 287 (ex Article 248 TEC)

1. The Court of Auditors shall examine the accounts of all revenue and expenditure of the Union. It shall also examine the accounts of all revenue and expenditure of all bodies, offices or agencies set up by the Union in so far as the relevant constituent instrument does not preclude such examination.

The Court of Auditors shall provide the European Parliament and the Council with a statement of assurance as to the reliability of the accounts and the legality and regularity of the underlying transactions which shall be published in the Official Journal of the European Union. This statement may be supplemented by specific assessments for each major area of Union activity.

2. The Court of Auditors shall examine whether all revenue has been received and all expenditure incurred in a lawful and regular manner and whether the financial management has been sound. In doing so, it shall report in particular on any cases of irregularity.

The audit of revenue shall be carried out on the basis both of the amounts established as due and the amounts actually paid to the Union.

The audit of expenditure shall be carried out on the basis both of commitments undertaken and payments made.

These audits may be carried out before the closure of accounts for the financial year in question.

3. The audit shall be based on records and, if necessary, performed on the spot in the other institutions of the Union, on the premises of any body, office or agency which manages revenue or expenditure on behalf of the Union and in the Member States, including on the premises of any natural or legal person in receipt of payments from the budget. In the Member States the audit shall be carried out in liaison with national audit bodies or, if these do not have the necessary powers, with the competent national departments. The Court of Auditors and the national audit bodies of the Member States shall cooperate in a spirit of trust while maintaining their independence. These bodies or departments shall inform the Court of Auditors whether they intend to take part in the audit.

The other institutions of the Union, any bodies, offices or agencies managing revenue or expenditure on behalf of the Union, any natural or legal person in receipt of payments from the budget, and the national audit bodies or, if these do not have the necessary powers, the competent national departments, shall forward to the Court of Auditors, at its request, any document or information necessary to carry out its task.

In respect of the European Investment Bank's activity in managing Union expenditure and revenue, the Court's rights of access to information held by the Bank shall be governed by an agreement between the Court, the Bank and the Commission. In the absence of an agreement, the Court shall nevertheless have access to information necessary for the audit of Union expenditure and revenue managed by the Bank.

4. The Court of Auditors shall draw up an annual report after the close of each financial year. It shall be forwarded to the other institutions of the Union and shall be published, together with the replies of these institutions to the observations of the Court of Auditors, in the Official Journal of the European Union.

The Court of Auditors may also, at any time, submit observations, particularly in the form of special reports, on specific questions and deliver opinions at the request of one of the other institutions of the Union.

It shall adopt its annual reports, special reports or opinions by a majority of its Members. However, it may establish internal chambers in order to adopt certain categories of reports or opinions under the conditions laid down by its Rules of Procedure.

It shall assist the European Parliament and the Council in exercising their powers of control over the implementation of the budget.

The Court of Auditors shall draw up its Rules of Procedure. Those rules shall require the approval of the Council.

Chapter 2
Legal Acts of the Union, Adoption Procedures and Other Provisions

Section 1
The Legal Acts of the Union

Article 288 (ex Article 249 TEC)

To exercise the Union's competences, the institutions shall adopt regulations, directives, decisions, recommendations and opinions.

A regulation shall have general application. It shall be binding in its entirety and directly applicable in all Member States.

A directive shall be binding, as to the result to be achieved, upon each Member State to which it is addressed, but shall leave to the national authorities the choice of form and methods.

A decision shall be binding in its entirety. A decision which specifies those to whom it is addressed shall be binding only on them.

Recommendations and opinions shall have no binding force.

Article 289

1. The ordinary legislative procedure shall consist in the joint adoption by the European Parliament and the Council of a regulation, directive or decision on a proposal from the Commission. This procedure is defined in Article 294.
2. In the specific cases provided for by the Treaties, the adoption of a regulation, directive or decision by the European Parliament with the participation of the Council, or by the latter with the participation of the European Parliament, shall constitute a special legislative procedure.
3. Legal acts adopted by legislative procedure shall constitute legislative acts.
4. In the specific cases provided for by the Treaties, legislative acts may be adopted on the initiative of a group of Member States or of the European Parliament, on a recommendation from the European Central Bank or at the request of the Court of Justice or the European Investment Bank.

Article 290

1. A legislative act may delegate to the Commission the power to adopt non-legislative acts of general application to supplement or amend certain non-essential elements of the legislative act.

The objectives, content, scope and duration of the delegation of power shall be explicitly defined in the legislative acts. The essential elements of an area shall be reserved for the legislative act and accordingly shall not be the subject of a delegation of power.

2. Legislative acts shall explicitly lay down the conditions to which the delegation is subject; these conditions may be as follows:

(a) the European Parliament or the Council may decide to revoke the delegation;

(b) the delegated act may enter into force only if no objection has been expressed by the European Parliament or the Council within a period set by the legislative act.

For the purposes of (a) and (b), the European Parliament shall act by a majority of its component members, and the Council by a qualified majority.

3. The adjective 'delegated' shall be inserted in the title of delegated acts.

Article 291

1. Member States shall adopt all measures of national law necessary to implement legally binding Union acts.

2. Where uniform conditions for implementing legally binding Union acts are needed, those acts shall confer implementing powers on the Commission, or, in duly justified specific cases and in the cases provided for in Articles 24 and 26 of the Treaty on European Union, on the Council.

3. For the purposes of paragraph 2, the European Parliament and the Council, acting by means of regulations in accordance with the ordinary legislative procedure, shall lay down in advance the rules and general principles concerning mechanisms for control by Member States of the Commission's exercise of implementing powers.

4. The word 'implementing' shall be inserted in the title of implementing acts.

Article 292

The Council shall adopt recommendations. It shall act on a proposal from the Commission in all cases where the Treaties provide that it shall adopt acts on a proposal from the Commission. It shall act unanimously in those areas in which unanimity is required for the adoption of a Union act. The Commission, and the European Central Bank in the specific cases provided for in the Treaties, shall adopt recommendations.

Section 2
Procedures for the Adaption of Acts and other Provisions

Article 293 (ex Article 250 TEC)
1. Where, pursuant to the Treaties, the Council acts on a proposal from the Commission, it may amend that proposal only by acting unanimously, except in the cases referred to in paragraphs 10 and 13 of Article 294, in Articles 310, 312 and 314 and in the second paragraph of Article 315.
2. As long as the Council has not acted, the Commission may alter its proposal at any time during the procedures leading to the adoption of a Union act.

Article 294 (ex Article 251 TEC)
1. Where reference is made in the Treaties to the ordinary legislative procedure for the adoption of an act, the following procedure shall apply.
2. The Commission shall submit a proposal to the European Parliament and the Council.
First reading
3. The European Parliament shall adopt its position at first reading and communicate it to the Council.
4. If the Council approves the European Parliament's position, the act concerned shall be adopted in the wording which corresponds to the position of the European Parliament.
5. If the Council does not approve the European Parliament's position, it shall adopt its position at first reading and communicate it to the European Parliament.
6. The Council shall inform the European Parliament fully of the reasons which led it to adopt its position at first reading. The Commission shall inform the European Parliament fully of its position.
Second reading
7. If, within three months of such communication, the European Parliament:

   (a) approves the Council's position at first reading or has not taken a decision, the act concerned shall be deemed to have been adopted in the wording which corresponds to the position of the Council;

   (b) rejects, by a majority of its component members, the Council's position at first reading, the proposed act shall be deemed not to have been adopted;

   (c) proposes, by a majority of its component members, amendments to the Council's position at first reading, the text thus amended shall be forwarded to the Council and to the Commission, which shall deliver an opinion on those amendments.
8. If, within three months of receiving the European Parliament's amendments, the Council, acting by a qualified majority:

   (a) approves all those amendments, the act in question shall be deemed to have been adopted;

   (b) does not approve all the amendments, the President of the Council, in agreement with the President of the European Parliament, shall within six weeks convene a meeting of the Conciliation Committee.

9. The Council shall act unanimously on the amendments on which the Commission has delivered a negative opinion.

Conciliation

10. The Conciliation Committee, which shall be composed of the members of the Council or their representatives and an equal number of members representing the European Parliament, shall have the task of reaching agreement on a joint text, by a qualified majority of the members of the Council or their representatives and by a majority of the members representing the European Parliament within six weeks of its being convened, on the basis of the positions of the European Parliament and the Council at second reading.

11. The Commission shall take part in the Conciliation Committee's proceedings and shall take all necessary initiatives with a view to reconciling the positions of the European Parliament and the Council.

12. If, within six weeks of its being convened, the Conciliation Committee does not approve the joint text, the proposed act shall be deemed not to have been adopted.

Third reading

13. If, within that period, the Conciliation Committee approves a joint text, the European Parliament, acting by a majority of the votes cast, and the Council, acting by a qualified majority, shall each have a period of six weeks from that approval in which to adopt the act in question in accordance with the joint text. If they fail to do so, the proposed act shall be deemed not to have been adopted.

14. The periods of three months and six weeks referred to in this Article shall be extended by a maximum of one month and two weeks respectively at the initiative of the European Parliament or the Council.

Special provisions

15. Where, in the cases provided for in the Treaties, a legislative act is submitted to the ordinary legislative procedure on the initiative of a group of Member States, on a recommendation by the European Central Bank, or at the request of the Court of Justice, paragraph 2, the second sentence of paragraph 6, and paragraph 9 shall not apply.

In such cases, the European Parliament and the Council shall communicate the proposed act to the Commission with their positions at first and second readings. The European Parliament or the Council may request the opinion of the Commission throughout the procedure, which the Commission may also deliver on its own initiative. It may also, if it deems it necessary, take part in the Conciliation Committee in accordance with paragraph 11.

Article 295

The European Parliament, the Council and the Commission shall consult each other and by common agreement make arrangements for their cooperation. To that end, they may, in compliance with the Treaties, conclude interinstitutional agreements which may be of a binding nature.

Article 296 (ex Article 253 TEC)
Where the Treaties do not specify the type of act to be adopted, the institutions shall select it on a case-by-case basis, in compliance with the applicable procedures and with the principle of proportionality.

Legal acts shall state the reasons on which they are based and shall refer to any proposals, initiatives, recommendations, requests or opinions required by the Treaties.

When considering draft legislative acts, the European Parliament and the Council shall refrain from adopting acts not provided for by the relevant legislative procedure in the area in question.

Article 297 (ex Article 254 TEC)
1. Legislative acts adopted under the ordinary legislative procedure shall be signed by the President of the European Parliament and by the President of the Council.

Legislative acts adopted under a special legislative procedure shall be signed by the President of the institution which adopted them.

Legislative acts shall be published in the Official Journal of the European Union. They shall enter into force on the date specified in them or, in the absence thereof, on the twentieth day following that of their publication.

2. Non-legislative acts adopted in the form of regulations, directives or decisions, when the latter do not specify to whom they are addressed, shall be signed by the President of the institution which adopted them.

Regulations and directives which are addressed to all Member States, as well as decisions which do not specify to whom they are addressed, shall be published in the Official Journal of the European Union. They shall enter into force on the date specified in them or, in the absence thereof, on the twentieth day following that of their publication.

Other directives, and decisions which specify to whom they are addressed, shall be notified to those to whom they are addressed and shall take effect upon such notification.

Article 298
1. In carrying out their missions, the institutions, bodies, offices and agencies of the Union shall have the support of an open, efficient and independent European administration.

2. In compliance with the Staff Regulations and the Conditions of Employment adopted on the basis of Article 336, the European Parliament and the Council, acting by means of regulations in accordance with the ordinary legislative procedure, shall establish provisions to that end.

Article 299 (ex Article 256 TEC)
Acts of the Council, the Commission or the European Central Bank which impose a pecuniary obligation on persons other than States, shall be enforceable.

Enforcement shall be governed by the rules of civil procedure in force in the State in the territory of which it is carried out. The order for its enforcement shall be appended to the decision, without other formality than verification of the authenticity of the decision, by the national authority which the government of each Member State shall designate for this purpose and shall make known to the Commission and to the Court of Justice of the European Union.

When these formalities have been completed on application by the party concerned, the latter may proceed to enforcement in accordance with the national law, by bringing the matter directly before the competent authority.

Enforcement may be suspended only by a decision of the Court. However, the courts of the country concerned shall have jurisdiction over complaints that enforcement is being carried out in an irregular manner.

Chapter 3
The Union's Advisory Bodies

Article 300

1. The European Parliament, the Council and the Commission shall be assisted by an Economic and Social Committee and a Committee of the Regions, exercising advisory functions.
2. The Economic and Social Committee shall consist of representatives of organisations of employers, of the employed, and of other parties representative of civil society, notably in socio-economic, civic, professional and cultural areas.
3. The Committee of the Regions shall consist of representatives of regional and local bodies who either hold a regional or local authority electoral mandate or are politically accountable to an elected assembly.
4. The members of the Economic and Social Committee and of the Committee of the Regions shall not be bound by any mandatory instructions. They shall be completely independent in the performance of their duties, in the Union's general interest.
5. The rules referred to in paragraphs 2 and 3 governing the nature of the composition of the Committees shall be reviewed at regular intervals by the Council to take account of economic, social and demographic developments within the Union. The Council, on a proposal from the Commission, shall adopt decisions to that end.

Section 1
The Economic and Social Committee

Article 301 (ex Article 258 TEC)

The number of members of the Economic and Social Committee shall not exceed 350.
The Council, acting unanimously on a proposal from the Commission, shall adopt a decision determining the Committee's composition.
The Council shall determine the allowances of members of the Committee.

Article 302 (ex Article 259 TEC)
1. The members of the Committee shall be appointed for five years The Council shall adopt the list of members drawn up in accordance with the proposals made by each Member State. The term of office of the members of the Committee shall be renewable.
2. The Council shall act after consulting the Commission. It may obtain the opinion of European bodies which are representative of the various economic and social sectors and of civil society to which the Union's activities are of concern.

Article 303 (ex Article 260 TEC)
The Committee shall elect its chairman and officers from among its members for a term of two and a half years.
It shall adopt its Rules of Procedure.
The Committee shall be convened by its chairman at the request of the European Parliament, the Council or of the Commission. It may also meet on its own initiative.

Article 304 (ex Article 262 TEC)
The Committee shall be consulted by the European Parliament, by the Council or by the Commission where the Treaties so provide. The Committee may be consulted by these institutions in all cases in which they consider it appropriate. It may issue an opinion on its own initiative in cases in which it considers such action appropriate.
The European Parliament, the Council or the Commission shall, if it considers it necessary, set the Committee, for the submission of its opinion, a time limit which may not be less than one month from the date on which the chairman receives notification to this effect. Upon expiry of the time limit, the absence of an opinion shall not prevent further action.
The opinion of the Committee, together with a record of the proceedings, shall be forwarded to the European Parliament, to the Council and to the Commission.

Section 2
The Committee of the Regions

Article 305 (ex Article 263, second, third and fourth paragraphs, TEC)
The number of members of the Committee of the Regions shall not exceed 350.
The Council, acting unanimously on a proposal from the Commission, shall adopt a decision determining the Committee's composition.
The members of the Committee and an equal number of alternate members shall be appointed for five years. Their term of office shall be renewable. The Council shall adopt the list of members and alternate members drawn up in accordance with the proposals made by each Member State. When the mandate referred to in Article 300(3) on the basis of which they were proposed comes to an end, the term of office of members of the Committee shall terminate automatically and they shall then be replaced for the remainder of the said term of office in accordance with the same procedure. No member of the Committee shall at the same time be a Member of the European Parliament.

Article 306 (ex Article 264 TEC)

The Committee of the Regions shall elect its chairman and officers from among its members for a term of two and a half years.

It shall adopt its Rules of Procedure.

The Committee shall be convened by its chairman at the request of the European Parliament, the Council or of the Commission. It may also meet on its own initiative.

Article 307 (ex Article 265 TEC)

The Committee of the Regions shall be consulted by the European Parliament, by the Council or by the Commission where the Treaties so provide and in all other cases, in particular those which concern cross-border cooperation, in which one of these institutions considers it appropriate.

The European Parliament, the Council or the Commission shall, if it considers it necessary, set the Committee, for the submission of its opinion, a time limit which may not be less than one month from the date on which the chairman receives notification to this effect. Upon expiry of the time limit, the absence of an opinion shall not prevent further action.

Where the Economic and Social Committee is consulted pursuant to Article 304, the Committee of the Regions shall be informed by the European Parliament, the Council or the Commission of the request for an opinion. Where it considers that specific regional interests are involved, the Committee of the Regions may issue an opinion on the matter.

It may issue an opinion on its own initiative in cases in which it considers such action appropriate. The opinion of the Committee, together with a record of the proceedings, shall be forwarded to the European Parliament, to the Council and to the Commission.

Chapter 4
The European Investment Bank

Article 308 (ex Article 266 TEC)

The European Investment Bank shall have legal personality.

The members of the European Investment Bank shall be the Member States.

The Statute of the European Investment Bank is laid down in a Protocol annexed to the Treaties. The Council acting unanimously in accordance with a special legislative procedure, at the request of the European Investment Bank and after consulting the European Parliament and the Commission, or on a proposal from the Commission and after consulting the European Parliament and the European Investment Bank, may amend the Statute of the Bank.

Article 309 (ex Article 267 TEC)

The task of the European Investment Bank shall be to contribute, by having recourse to the capital market and utilising its own resources, to the balanced and steady development of the internal market in the interest of the Union. For this purpose the Bank shall, operating on a non-profit-making basis, grant loans and give guarantees which facilitate the financing of the following projects in all sectors of the economy:

(a) projects for developing less-developed regions;
(b) projects for modernising or converting undertakings or for developing fresh activities called for by the establishment or functioning of the internal market, where these projects are of such a size or nature that they cannot be entirely financed by the various means available in the individual Member States;
(c) projects of common interest to several Member States which are of such a size or nature that they cannot be entirely financed by the various means available in the individual Member States.

In carrying out its task, the Bank shall facilitate the financing of investment programmes in conjunction with assistance from the Structural Funds and other Union Financial Instruments.

Title II
Financial Provisions

Article 310 (ex Article 268 TEC)

1. All items of revenue and expenditure of the Union shall be included in estimates to be drawn up for each financial year and shall be shown in the budget.
The Union's annual budget shall be established by the European Parliament and the Council in accordance with Article 314.
The revenue and expenditure shown in the budget shall be in balance.
2. The expenditure shown in the budget shall be authorised for the annual budgetary period in accordance with the regulation referred to in Article 322.
3. The implementation of expenditure shown in the budget shall require the prior adoption of a legally binding Union act providing a legal basis for its action and for the implementation of the corresponding expenditure in accordance with the regulation referred to in Article 322, except in cases for which that law provides.
4. With a view to maintaining budgetary discipline, the Union shall not adopt any act which is likely to have appreciable implications for the budget without providing an assurance that the expenditure arising from such an act is capable of being financed within the limit of the Union's own resources and in compliance with the multiannual financial framework referred to in Article 312.
5. The budget shall be implemented in accordance with the principle of sound financial management. Member States shall cooperate with the Union to ensure that the appropriations entered in the budget are used in accordance with this principle.
6. The Union and the Member States, in accordance with Article 325, shall counter fraud and any other illegal activities affecting the financial interests of the Union.

Chapter 1
The Union's own Resources

Article 311 (ex Article 269 TEC)

The Union shall provide itself with the means necessary to attain its objectives and carry through its policies.

Without prejudice to other revenue, the budget shall be financed wholly from own resources.

The Council, acting in accordance with a special legislative procedure, shall unanimously and after consulting the European Parliament adopt a decision laying down the provisions relating to the system of own resources of the Union. In this context it may establish new categories of own resources or abolish an existing category. That decision shall not enter into force until it is approved by the Member States in accordance with their respective constitutional requirements.

The Council, acting by means of regulations in accordance with a special legislative procedure, shall lay down implementing measures for the Union's own resources system in so far as this is provided for in the decision adopted on the basis of the third paragraph. The Council shall act after obtaining the consent of the European Parliament.

Chapter 2
The Multiannual Financial Framework

Article 312

1. The multiannual financial framework shall ensure that Union expenditure develops in an orderly manner and within the limits of its own resources.

It shall be established for a period of at least five years.

The annual budget of the Union shall comply with the multiannual financial framework.

2. The Council, acting in accordance with a special legislative procedure, shall adopt a regulation laying down the multiannual financial framework. The Council shall act unanimously after obtaining the consent of the European Parliament, which shall be given by a majority of its component members.

The European Council may, unanimously, adopt a decision authorising the Council to act by a qualified majority when adopting the regulation referred to in the first subparagraph.

3. The financial framework shall determine the amounts of the annual ceilings on commitment appropriations by category of expenditure and of the annual ceiling on payment appropriations. The categories of expenditure, limited in number, shall correspond to the Union's major sectors of activity.

The financial framework shall lay down any other provisions required for the annual budgetary procedure to run smoothly.

4. Where no Council regulation determining a new financial framework has been adopted by the end of the previous financial framework, the ceilings and other provisions

corresponding to the last year of that framework shall be extended until such time as that act is adopted.

5. Throughout the procedure leading to the adoption of the financial framework, the European Parliament, the Council and the Commission shall take any measure necessary to facilitate its adoption.

Chapter 3
The Union's Annual Budget

Article 313 (ex Article 272(1), TEC)

The financial year shall run from 1 January to 31 December.

Article 314 (ex Article 272(2) to (10), TEC)

The European Parliament and the Council, acting in accordance with a special legislative procedure, shall establish the Union's annual budget in accordance with the following provisions.

1. With the exception of the European Central Bank, each institution shall, before 1 July, draw up estimates of its expenditure for the following financial year. The Commission shall consolidate these estimates in a draft budget. which may contain different estimates.

The draft budget shall contain an estimate of revenue and an estimate of expenditure.

2. The Commission shall submit a proposal containing the draft budget to the European Parliament and to the Council not later than 1 September of the year preceding that in which the budget is to be implemented.

The Commission may amend the draft budget during the procedure until such time as the Conciliation Committee, referred to in paragraph 5, is convened.

3. The Council shall adopt its position on the draft budget and forward it to the European Parliament not later than 1 October of the year preceding that in which the budget is to be implemented. The Council shall inform the European Parliament in full of the reasons which led it to adopt its position.

4. If, within forty-two days of such communication, the European Parliament:

(a) approves the position of the Council, the budget shall be adopted;

(b) has not taken a decision, the budget shall be deemed to have been adopted;

(c) adopts amendments by a majority of its component members, the amended draft shall be forwarded to the Council and to the Commission. The President of the European Parliament, in agreement with the President of the Council, shall immediately convene a meeting of the Conciliation Committee. However, if within ten days of the draft being forwarded the Council informs the European Parliament that it has approved all its amendments, the Conciliation Committee shall not meet.

5. The Conciliation Committee, which shall be composed of the members of the Council or their representatives and an equal number of members representing the European Parliament, shall have the task of reaching agreement on a joint text, by a qualified majority of the members of the Council or their representatives and by a majority of the

representatives of the European Parliament within twenty-one days of its being convened, on the basis of the positions of the European Parliament and the Council.

The Commission shall take part in the Conciliation Committee's proceedings and shall take all the necessary initiatives with a view to reconciling the positions of the European Parliament and the Council.

6. If, within the twenty-one days referred to in paragraph 5, the Conciliation Committee agrees on a joint text, the European Parliament and the Council shall each have a period of fourteen days from the date of that agreement in which to approve the joint text.

7. If, within the period of fourteen days referred to in paragraph 6:

(a) the European Parliament and the Council both approve the joint text or fail to take a decision, or if one of these institutions approves the joint text while the other one fails to take a decision, the budget shall be deemed to be definitively adopted in accordance with the joint text; or

(b) the European Parliament, acting by a majority of its component members, and the Council both reject the joint text, or if one of these institutions rejects the joint text while the other one fails to take a decision, a new draft budget shall be submitted by the Commission; or

(c) the European Parliament, acting by a majority of its component members, rejects the joint text while the Council approves it, a new draft budget shall be submitted by the Commission; or

(d) the European Parliament approves the joint text whilst the Council rejects it, the European Parliament may, within fourteen days from the date of the rejection by the Council and acting by a majority of its component members and three-fifths of the votes cast, decide to confirm all or some of the amendments referred to in paragraph 4(c). Where a European Parliament amendment is not confirmed, the position agreed in the Conciliation Committee on the budget heading which is the subject of the amendment shall be retained. The budget shall be deemed to be definitively adopted on this basis.

8. If, within the twenty-one days referred to in paragraph 5, the Conciliation Committee does not agree on a joint text, a new draft budget shall be submitted by the Commission.

9. When the procedure provided for in this Article has been completed, the President of the European Parliament shall declare that the budget has been definitively adopted.

10. Each institution shall exercise the powers conferred upon it under this Article in compliance with the Treaties and the acts adopted thereunder, with particular regard to the Union's own resources and the balance between revenue and expenditure.

Article 315 (ex Article 273 TEC)

If, at the beginning of a financial year, the budget has not yet been definitively adopted, a sum equivalent to not more than one twelfth of the budget appropriations for the preceding financial year may be spent each month in respect of any chapter of the budget in accordance with the provisions of the Regulations made pursuant to Article 322; that sum shall not, however, exceed one twelfth of the appropriations provided for in the same chapter of the draft budget.

The Council on a proposal by the Commission, may, provided that the other conditions laid down in the first paragraph are observed, authorise expenditure in excess of one twelfth in accordance with the regulations made pursuant to Article 322. The Council shall forward the decision immediately to the European Parliament.

The decision referred to in the second paragraph shall lay down the necessary measures relating to resources to ensure application of this Article, in accordance with the acts referred to in Article 311.

It shall enter into force thirty days following its adoption if the European Parliament, acting by a majority of its component Members, has not decided to reduce this expenditure within that time-limit.

Article 316 (ex Article 271 TEC)

In accordance with conditions to be laid down pursuant to Article 322, any appropriations, other than those relating to staff expenditure, that are unexpended at the end of the financial year may be carried forward to the next financial year only.

Appropriations shall be classified under different chapters grouping items of expenditure according to their nature or purpose and subdivided in accordance with the regulations made pursuant to Article 322.

The expenditure of the European Parliament, the European Council and the Council, the Commission and the Court of Justice of the European Union shall be set out in separate parts of the budget, without prejudice to special arrangements for certain common items of expenditure.

Chapter 4
Implementation of the Budget and Discharge

Article 317 (ex Article 274 TEC)

The Commission shall implement the budget in cooperation with the Member States, in accordance with the provisions of the regulations made pursuant to Article 322, on its own responsibility and within the limits of the appropriations, having regard to the principles of sound financial management. Member States shall cooperate with the Commission to ensure that the appropriations are used in accordance with the principles of sound financial management.

The regulations shall lay down the control and audit obligations of the Member States in the implementation of the budget and the resulting responsibilities. They shall also lay down the responsibilities and detailed rules for each institution concerning its part in effecting its own expenditure.

Within the budget, the Commission may, subject to the limits and conditions laid down in the regulations made pursuant to Article 322, transfer appropriations from one chapter to another or from one subdivision to another.

Article 318 (ex Article 275 TEC)
The Commission shall submit annually to the European Parliament and to the Council the accounts of the preceding financial year relating to the implementation of the budget. The Commission shall also forward to them a financial statement of the assets and liabilities of the Union.

The Commission shall also submit to the European Parliament and to the Council an evaluation report on the Union's finances based on the results achieved, in particular in relation to the indications given by the European Parliament and the Council pursuant to Article 319.

Article 319 (ex Article 276 TEC)
1. The European Parliament, acting on a recommendation from the Council, shall give a discharge to the Commission in respect of the implementation of the budget. To this end, the Council and the European Parliament in turn shall examine the accounts, the financial statement and the evaluation report referred to in Article 318, the annual report by the Court of Auditors together with the replies of the institutions under audit to the observations of the Court of Auditors, the statement of assurance referred to in Article 287(1), second subparagraph and any relevant special reports by the Court of Auditors.

2. Before giving a discharge to the Commission, or for any other purpose in connection with the exercise of its powers over the implementation of the budget, the European Parliament may ask to hear the Commission give evidence with regard to the execution of expenditure or the operation of financial control systems. The Commission shall submit any necessary information to the European Parliament at the latter's request.

3. The Commission shall take all appropriate steps to act on the observations in the decisions giving discharge and on other observations by the European Parliament relating to the execution of expenditure, as well as on comments accompanying the recommendations on discharge adopted by the Council.

At the request of the European Parliament or the Council, the Commission shall report on the measures taken in the light of these observations and comments and in particular on the instructions given to the departments which are responsible for the implementation of the budget. These reports shall also be forwarded to the Court of Auditors.

Chapter 5
Common Provisions

Article 320 (ex Article 277 TEC)
The multiannual financial framework and the annual budget shall be drawn up in euro.

Article 321 (ex Article 278 TEC)
The Commission may, provided it notifies the competent authorities of the Member States concerned, transfer into the currency of one of the Member States its holdings in the currency of another Member State, to the extent necessary to enable them to be used for purposes

which come within the scope of the Treaties. The Commission shall as far as possible avoid making such transfers if it possesses cash or liquid assets in the currencies which it needs. The Commission shall deal with each Member State through the authority designated by the State concerned. In carrying out financial operations the Commission shall employ the services of the bank of issue of the Member State concerned or of any other financial institution approved by that State.

Article 322 (ex Article 279 TEC)
1. The European Parliament and the Council, acting in accordance with the ordinary legislative procedure, and after consulting the Court of Auditors, shall adopt by means of regulations:
   (a) the financial rules which determine in particular the procedure to be adopted for establishing and implementing the budget and for presenting and auditing accounts;
   (b) rules providing for checks on the responsibility of financial actors, in particular authorising officers and accounting officers.
2. The Council, acting on a proposal from the Commission and after consulting the European Parliament and the Court of Auditors, shall determine the methods and procedure whereby the budget revenue provided under the arrangements relating to the Union's own resources shall be made available to the Commission, and determine the measures to be applied, if need be, to meet cash requirements.

Article 323
The European Parliament, the Council and the Commission shall ensure that the financial means are made available to allow the Union to fulfil its legal obligations in respect of third parties.

Article 324
Regular meetings between the Presidents of the European Parliament, the Council and the Commission shall be convened, on the initiative of the Commission, under the budgetary procedures referred to in this Title. The Presidents shall take all the necessary steps to promote consultation and the reconciliation of the positions of the institutions over which they preside in order to facilitate the implementation of this Title.

Chapter 6
Combatting Fraud

Article 325 (ex Article 280 TEC)
1. The Union and the Member States shall counter fraud and any other illegal activities affecting the financial interests of the Union through measures to be taken in accordance with this Article, which shall act as a deterrent and be such as to afford effective protection in the Member States, and in all the Union's institutions, bodies, offices and agencies.

2. Member States shall take the same measures to counter fraud affecting the financial interests of the Union as they take to counter fraud affecting their own financial interests.

3. Without prejudice to other provisions of the Treaties, the Member States shall coordinate their action aimed at protecting the financial interests of the Union against fraud. To this end they shall organise, together with the Commission, close and regular cooperation between the competent authorities.

4. The European Parliament and the Council, acting in accordance with the ordinary legislative procedure, after consulting the Court of Auditors, shall adopt the necessary measures in the fields of the prevention of and fight against fraud affecting the financial interests of the Union with a view to affording effective and equivalent protection in the Member States and in all the Union's institutions, bodies, offices and agencies.

5. The Commission, in cooperation with Member States, shall each year submit to the European Parliament and to the Council a report on the measures taken for the implementation of this Article.

Title III
Enhanced Cooperation

Article 326
(ex Articles 27a to 27e, 40 to 40b and 43 to 45 TEU and ex Articles 11 and 11a TEC)

Any enhanced cooperation shall comply with the Treaties and Union law.

Such cooperation shall not undermine the internal market or economic, social and territorial cohesion. It shall not constitute a barrier to or discrimination in trade between Member States, nor shall it distort competition between them.

Article 327
(ex Articles 27a to 27e, 40 to 40b and 43 to 45 TEU and ex Articles 11 and 11a TEC)

Any enhanced cooperation shall respect the competences, rights and obligations of those Member States which do not participate in it. Those Member States shall not impede its implementation by the participating Member States.

Article 328
(ex Articles 27a to 27e, 40 to 40b and 43 to 45 TEU and ex Articles 11 and 11a TEC)

1. When enhanced cooperation is being established, it shall be open to all Member States, subject to compliance with any conditions of participation laid down by the authorising decision. It shall also be open to them at any other time, subject to compliance with the acts already adopted within that framework, in addition to those conditions.

The Commission and the Member States participating in enhanced cooperation shall ensure that they promote participation by as many Member States as possible.

2. The Commission and, where appropriate, the High Representative of the Union for Foreign Affairs and Security Policy shall keep the European Parliament and the Council regularly informed regarding developments in enhanced cooperation.

Article 329
(ex Articles 27a to 27e, 40 to 40b and 43 to 45 TEU and ex Articles 11 and 11a TEC)

1. Member States which wish to establish enhanced cooperation between themselves in one of the areas covered by the Treaties, with the exception of fields of exclusive competence and the common foreign and security policy, shall address a request to the Commission, specifying the scope and objectives of the enhanced cooperation proposed. The Commission may submit a proposal to the Council to that effect. In the event of the Commission not submitting a proposal, it shall inform the Member States concerned of the reasons for not doing so.

Authorisation to proceed with the enhanced cooperation referred to in the first subparagraph shall be granted by the Council, on a proposal from the Commission and after obtaining the consent of the European Parliament.

2. The request of the Member States which wish to establish enhanced cooperation between themselves within the framework of the common foreign and security policy shall be addressed to the Council. It shall be forwarded to the High Representative of the Union for Foreign Affairs and Security Policy, who shall give an opinion on whether the enhanced cooperation proposed is consistent with the Union's common foreign and security policy, and to the Commission, which shall give its opinion in particular on whether the enhanced cooperation proposed is consistent with other Union policies. It shall also be forwarded to the European Parliament for information.

Authorisation to proceed with enhanced cooperation shall be granted by a decision of the Council acting unanimously.

Article 330
(ex Articles 27a to 27e, 40 to 40b and 43 to 45 TEU and ex Articles 11 and 11a TEC)

All members of the Council may participate in its deliberations, but only members of the Council representing the Member States participating in enhanced cooperation shall take part in the vote.

Unanimity shall be constituted by the votes of the representatives of the participating Member States only.

A qualified majority shall be defined in accordance with Article 238(3).

Article 331
(ex Articles 27a to 27e, 40 to 40b and 43 to 45 TEU and ex Articles 11 and 11a TEC)

1. Any Member State which wishes to participate in enhanced cooperation in progress in one of the areas referred to in Article 329(1) shall notify its intention to the Council and the Commission.

The Commission shall, within four months of the date of receipt of the notification, confirm the participation of the Member State concerned. It shall note where necessary that the conditions of participation have been fulfilled and shall adopt any transitional measures necessary with regard to the application of the acts already adopted within the framework of enhanced cooperation.

However, if the Commission considers that the conditions of participation have not been fulfilled, it shall indicate the arrangements to be adopted to fulfil those conditions and shall set a deadline for re-examining the request. On the expiry of that deadline, it shall re-examine the request, in accordance with the procedure set out in the second subparagraph. If the Commission considers that the conditions of participation have still not been met, the Member State concerned may refer the matter to the Council, which shall decide on the request. The Council shall act in accordance with Article 330. It may also adopt the transitional measures referred to in the second subparagraph on a proposal from the Commission.

2. Any Member State which wishes to participate in enhanced cooperation in progress in the framework of the common foreign and security policy shall notify its intention to the Council, the High Representative of the Union for Foreign Affairs and Security Policy and the Commission.

The Council shall confirm the participation of the Member State concerned, after consulting the High Representative of the Union for Foreign Affairs and Security Policy and after noting, where necessary, that the conditions of participation have been fulfilled. The Council, on a proposal from the High Representative, may also adopt any transitional measures necessary with regard to the application of the acts already adopted within the framework of enhanced cooperation. However, if the Council considers that the conditions of participation have not been fulfilled, it shall indicate the arrangements to be adopted to fulfil those conditions and shall set a deadline for re-examining the request for participation.

For the purposes of this paragraph, the Council shall act unanimously and in accordance with Article 330.

Article 332
(ex Articles 27a to 27e, 40 to 40b and 43 to 45 TEU and ex Articles 11 and 11a TEC)

Expenditure resulting from implementation of enhanced cooperation, other than administrative costs entailed for the institutions, shall be borne by the participating Member States, unless all members of the Council, acting unanimously after consulting the European Parliament, decide otherwise.

Article 333
(ex Articles 27a to 27e, 40 to 40b and 43 to 45 TEU and ex Articles 11 and 11a TEC)
1. Where a provision of the Treaties which may be applied in the context of enhanced cooperation stipulates that the Council shall act unanimously, the Council, acting unanimously in accordance with the arrangements laid down in Article 330, may adopt a decision stipulating that it will act by a qualified majority.
2. Where a provision of the Treaties which may be applied in the context of enhanced cooperation stipulates that the Council shall adopt acts under a special legislative procedure, the Council, acting unanimously in accordance with the arrangements laid down in Article 330, may adopt a decision stipulating that it will act under the ordinary legislative procedure. The Council shall act after consulting the European Parliament.
3. Paragraphs 1 and 2 shall not apply to decisions having military or defence implications.

Article 334
(ex Articles 27a to 27e, 40 to 40b and 43 to 45 TEU and ex Articles 11 and 11a TEC)
The Council and the Commission shall ensure the consistency of activities undertaken in the context of enhanced cooperation and the consistency of such activities with the policies of the Union, and shall cooperate to that end.

Part Seven
General and Final Provisions

Article 335 (ex Article 282 TEC)
In each of the Member States, the Union shall enjoy the most extensive legal capacity accorded to legal persons under their laws; it may, in particular, acquire or dispose of movable and immovable property and may be a party to legal proceedings. To this end, the Union shall be represented by the Commission. However, the Union shall be represented by each of the institutions, by virtue of their administrative autonomy, in matters relating to their respective operation.

Article 336 (ex Article 283 TEC)
The European Parliament and the Council shall, acting by means of regulations in accordance with the ordinary legislative procedure and after consulting the other institutions concerned, lay down the Staff Regulations of Officials of the European Union and the Conditions of Employment of other servants of the Union.

Article 337 (ex Article 284 TEC)
The Commission may, within the limits and under conditions laid down by the Council acting by a simple majority in accordance with the provisions of the Treaties, collect any information and carry out any checks required for the performance of the tasks entrusted to it.

Article 338 (ex Article 285 TEC)
1. Without prejudice to Article 5 of the Protocol on the Statute of the European System of Central Banks and of the European Central Bank, the European Parliament and the Council, acting in accordance with the ordinary legislative procedure, shall adopt measures for the production of statistics where necessary for the performance of the activities of the Union.
2. The production of Union statistics shall conform to impartiality, reliability, objectivity, scientific independence, cost-effectiveness and statistical confidentiality; it shall not entail excessive burdens on economic operators.

Article 339 (ex Article 287 TEC)
The members of the institutions of the Union, the members of committees, and the officials and other servants of the Union shall be required, even after their duties have ceased, not to disclose information of the kind covered by the obligation of professional secrecy, in particular information about undertakings, their business relations or their cost components.

Article 340 (ex Article 288 TEC)
The contractual liability of the Union shall be governed by the law applicable to the contract in question.
In the case of non-contractual liability, the Union shall, in accordance with the general principles common to the laws of the Member States, make good any damage caused by its institutions or by its servants in the performance of their duties.
Notwithstanding the second paragraph, the European Central Bank shall, in accordance with the general principles common to the laws of the Member States, make good any damage caused by it or by its servants in the performance of their duties.
The personal liability of its servants towards the Union shall be governed by the provisions laid down in their Staff Regulations or in the Conditions of Employment applicable to them.

Article 341 (ex Article 289 TEC)
The seat of the institutions of the Union shall be determined by common accord of the governments of the Member States.

Article 342 (ex Article 290 TEC)
The rules governing the languages of the institutions of the Union shall, without prejudice to the provisions contained in the Statute of the Court of Justice of the European Union, be determined by the Council, acting unanimously by means of regulations.

Article 343 (ex Article 291 TEC)
The Union shall enjoy in the territories of the Member States such privileges and immunities as are necessary for the performance of its tasks, under the conditions laid down in the Protocol of 8 April 1965 on the privileges and immunities of the European Union. The same shall apply to the European Central Bank and the European Investment Bank.

Article 344 (ex Article 292 TEC)
Member States undertake not to submit a dispute concerning the interpretation or application of the Treaties to any method of settlement other than those provided for therein.

Article 345 (ex Article 295 TEC)
The Treaties shall in no way prejudice the rules in Member States governing the system of property ownership.

Article 346 (ex Article 296 TEC)
1. The provisions of the Treaties shall not preclude the application of the following rules:
   (a) no Member State shall be obliged to supply information the disclosure of which it considers contrary to the essential interests of its security;
   (b) any Member State may take such measures as it considers necessary for the protection of the essential interests of its security which are connected with the production of or trade in arms, munitions and war material; such measures shall not adversely affect the conditions of competition in the internal market regarding products which are not intended for specifically military purposes.
2. The Council may, acting unanimously on a proposal from the Commission, make changes to the list, which it drew up on 15 April 1958, of the products to which the provisions of paragraph 1(b) apply.

Article 347 (ex Article 297 TEC)
Member States shall consult each other with a view to taking together the steps needed to prevent the functioning of the internal market being affected by measures which a Member State may be called upon to take in the event of serious internal disturbances affecting the maintenance of law and order, in the event of war, serious international tension constituting a threat of war, or in order to carry out obligations it has accepted for the purpose of maintaining peace and international security.

Article 348 (ex Article 298 TEC)
If measures taken in the circumstances referred to in Articles 346 and 347 have the effect of distorting the conditions of competition in the internal market, the Commission shall, together with the State concerned, examine how these measures can be adjusted to the rules laid down in the Treaties.

By way of derogation from the procedure laid down in Articles 258 and 259, the Commission or any Member State may bring the matter directly before the Court of Justice if it considers that another Member State is making improper use of the powers provided for in Articles 346 and 347. The Court of Justice shall give its ruling in camera.

Article 349 (ex Article 299(2), second, third and fourth subparagraphs, TEC)
Taking account of the structural social and economic situation of Guadeloupe, French Guiana, Martinique, Réunion, Saint-Barthélemy, Saint-Martin, the Azores, Madeira and the Canary Islands, which is compounded by their remoteness, insularity, small size, difficult topography and climate, economic dependence on a few products, the permanence and combination of which severely restrain their development, the Council, on a proposal from the Commission and after consulting the European Parliament, shall adopt specific measures aimed, in particular, at laying down the conditions of application of the Treaties to those regions, including common policies. Where the specific measures in question are adopted by the Council in accordance with a special legislative procedure, it shall also act on a proposal from the Commission and after consulting the European Parliament.

The measures referred to in the first paragraph concern in particular areas such as customs and trade policies, fiscal policy, free zones, agriculture and fisheries policies, conditions for supply of raw materials and essential consumer goods, State aids and conditions of access to structural funds and to horizontal Union programmes.

The Council shall adopt the measures referred to in the first paragraph taking into account the special characteristics and constraints of the outermost regions without undermining the integrity and the coherence of the Union legal order, including the internal market and common policies.

Article 350 (ex Article 306 TEC)
The provisions of the Treaties shall not preclude the existence or completion of regional unions between Belgium and Luxembourg, or between Belgium, Luxembourg and the Netherlands, to the extent that the objectives of these regional unions are not attained by application of the Treaties.

Article 351 (ex Article 307 TEC)
The rights and obligations arising from agreements concluded before 1 January 1958 or, for acceding States, before the date of their accession, between one or more Member States on the one hand, and one or more third countries on the other, shall not be affected by the provisions of the Treaties.

To the extent that such agreements are not compatible with the Treaties, the Member State or States concerned shall take all appropriate steps to eliminate the incompatibilities established. Member States shall, where necessary, assist each other to this end and shall, where appropriate, adopt a common attitude.

In applying the agreements referred to in the first paragraph, Member States shall take into account the fact that the advantages accorded under the Treaties by each Member State form an integral part of the establishment of the Union and are thereby inseparably linked with the creation of common institutions, the conferring of powers upon them and the granting of the same advantages by all the other Member States.

Article 352 (ex Article 308 TEC)
1. If action by the Union should prove necessary, within the framework of the policies defined in the Treaties, to attain one of the objectives set out in the Treaties, and the Treaties have not provided the necessary powers, the Council, acting unanimously on a proposal from the Commission and after obtaining the consent of the European Parliament, shall adopt the appropriate measures. Where the measures in question are adopted by the Council in accordance with a special legislative procedure, it shall also act unanimously on a proposal from the Commission and after obtaining the consent of the European Parliament.
2. Using the procedure for monitoring the subsidiarity principle referred to in Article 5(3) of the Treaty on European Union, the Commission shall draw national Parliaments' attention to proposals based on this Article.
3. Measures based on this Article shall not entail harmonisation of Member States' laws or regulations in cases where the Treaties exclude such harmonisation.
4. This Article cannot serve as a basis for attaining objectives pertaining to the common foreign and security policy and any acts adopted pursuant to this Article shall respect the limits set out in Article 40, second paragraph, of the Treaty on European Union.

Article 353
Article 48(7) of the Treaty on European Union shall not apply to the following Articles:
- Article 311, third and fourth paragraphs,
- Article 312(2), first subparagraph,
- Article 352, and
- Article 354.

Article 354 (ex Article 309 TEC)
For the purposes of Article 7 of the Treaty on European Union on the suspension of certain rights resulting from Union membership, the member of the European Council or of the Council representing the Member State in question shall not take part in the vote and the Member State in question shall not be counted in the calculation of the one third or four fifths of Member States referred to in paragraphs 1 and 2 of that Article. Abstentions by members present in person or represented shall not prevent the adoption of decisions referred to in paragraph 2 of that Article.

For the adoption of the decisions referred to in paragraphs 3 and 4 of Article 7 of the Treaty on European Union, a qualified majority shall be defined in accordance with Article 238(3)(b) of this Treaty.

Where, following a decision to suspend voting rights adopted pursuant to paragraph 3 of Article 7 of the Treaty on European Union, the Council acts by a qualified majority on the basis of a provision of the Treaties, that qualified majority shall be defined in accordance with Article 238(3)(b) of this Treaty, or, where the Council acts on a proposal from the Commission or from the High Representative of the Union for Foreign Affairs and Security Policy, in accordance with Article 238(3)(a).

For the purposes of Article 7 of the Treaty on European Union, the European Parliament shall act by a two-thirds majority of the votes cast, representing the majority of its component Members.

Article 355
(ex Article 299(2), first subparagraph, and Article 299(3) to (6) TEC)

In addition to the provisions of Article 52 of the Treaty on European Union relating to the territorial scope of the Treaties, the following provisions shall apply:

1. The provisions of the Treaties shall apply to Guadeloupe, French Guiana, Martinique, Réunion, Saint-Barthélemy, Saint-Martin, the Azores, Madeira and the Canary Islands in accordance with Article 349.

2. The special arrangements for association set out in Part Four shall apply to the overseas countries and territories listed in Annex II.

The Treaties shall not apply to those overseas countries and territories having special relations with the United Kingdom of Great Britain and Northern Ireland which are not included in the aforementioned list.

3. The provisions of the Treaties shall apply to the European territories for whose external relations a Member State is responsible.

4. The provisions of the Treaties shall apply to the Åland Islands in accordance with the provisions set out in Protocol 2 to the Act concerning the conditions of accession of the Republic of Austria, the Republic of Finland and the Kingdom of Sweden.

5. Notwithstanding Article 52 of the Treaty on European Union and paragraphs 1 to 4 of this Article:

  (a) the Treaties shall not apply to the Faeroe Islands;

  (b) the Treaties shall not apply to the United Kingdom Sovereign Base Areas of Akrotiri and Dhekelia in Cyprus except to the extent necessary to ensure the implementation of the arrangements set out in the Protocol on the Sovereign Base Areas of the United Kingdom of Great Britain and Northern Ireland in Cyprus annexed to the Act concerning the conditions of accession of the Czech Republic, the Republic of Estonia, the Republic of Cyprus, the Republic of Latvia, the Republic of Lithuania, the Republic of Hungary, the Republic of Malta, the Republic of Poland, the Republic of Slovenia and the Slovak Republic to the European Union and in accordance with the terms of that Protocol;

  (c) the Treaties shall apply to the Channel Islands and the Isle of Man only to the extent necessary to ensure the implementation of the arrangements for those islands set out in the Treaty concerning the accession of new Member States to the European Economic Community and to the European Atomic Energy Community signed on 22 January 1972.

6. The European Council may, on the initiative of the Member State concerned, adopt a decision amending the status, with regard to the Union, of a Danish, French or Netherlands

country or territory referred to in paragraphs 1 and 2. The European Council shall act unanimously after consulting the Commission.

Article 356 (ex Article 312 TEC)
This Treaty is concluded for an unlimited period.

Article 357 (ex Article 313 TEC)
This Treaty shall be ratified by the High Contracting Parties in accordance with their respective constitutional requirements. The Instruments of ratification shall be deposited with the Government of the Italian Republic.

This Treaty shall enter into force on the first day of the month following the deposit of the Instrument of ratification by the last signatory State to take this step. If, however, such deposit is made less than 15 days before the beginning of the following month, this Treaty shall not enter into force until the first day of the second month after the date of such deposit.

Article 358
The provisions of Article 55 of the Treaty on European Union shall apply to this Treaty.

In witness whereof, the undersigned Plenipotentiaries have signed this Treaty.
Done at Rome this twenty-fifth day of March in the year one thousand nine hundred and fifty-seven.
[List of signatories not reproduced.]

Annex I
List referred to in Article 38 of the Treaty on the Functioning of the European Union

(1) No in the Brussels nomenclature	(2) No in the Brussels Description of products
Chapter 1	Live animals
Chapter 2	Meat and edible meat offal
Chapter 3	Fish, crustaceans and molluscs
Chapter 4	Dairy produce; birds' eggs; natural honey
Chapter 5	
05.04	Guts, bladders and stomachs of animals (other than fish), whole and pieces thereof
05.15	Animal products not elsewhere specified or included; dead animals of Chapter 1 or Chapter 3, unfit for human consumption
Chapter 6	Live trees and other plants; bulbs, roots and the like; cut flowers and ornamental foliage
Chapter 7	Edible vegetables and certain roots and tubers
Chapter 8	Edible fruit and nuts; peel of melons or citrus fruit
Chapter 9	Coffee, tea and spices, excluding maté (heading No 09.03)
Chapter 10	Cereals
Chapter 11	Products of the milling industry; malt and starches; gluten; inulin
Chapter 12	Oil seeds and oleaginous fruit; miscellaneous grains, seeds and fruit; industrial and medical plants; straw and fodder
Chapter 13	
ex 13.03	Pectin

Chapter 15	
15.01	Lard and other rendered pig fat; rendered poultry fat
15.02	Unrendered fats of bovine cattle, sheep or goats; tallow (including 'premier jus') produced from those fats
15.03	Lard stearin, oleostearin and tallow stearin; lard oil, oleo-oil and tallow oil, not emulsified or mixed or prepared in any way
15.04	Fats and oil, of fish and marine mammals, whether or not refined
15.07	Fixed vegetable oils, fluid or solid, crude, refined or purified
15.12	Animal or vegetable fats and oils, hydrogenated, whether or not refined, but not further prepared
15.13	Margarine, imitation lard and other prepared edible fats
15.17	Residues resulting from the treatment of fatty substances or animal or vegetable waxes
Chapter 16	Preparations of meat, of fish, of crustaceans or molluscs
Chapter 17	
17.01	Beet sugar and cane sugar, solid
17.02	Other sugars; sugar syrups; artificial honey (whether or not mixed with natural honey); caramel
17.03	Molasses, whether or not decolourised
17.05 (*)	Flavoured or coloured sugars, syrups and molasses (including vanilla sugar or vanillin), with the exception of fruit juice containing added sugar in any proportion

(*) Entry added by Article 1 of Regulation No 7a of the Council of the European Economic Community of 18 December 1959 (OJ No 7, 30.1.1961, p. 71/61).

Chapter 18	
18.01	Cocoa beans, whole or broken, raw or roasted
18.02	Cocoa shells, husks, skins and waste
Chapter 20	Preparations of vegetables, fruit or other parts of plants
Chapter 22	
22.04	Grape must, in fermentation or with fermentation arrested otherwise than by the addition of alcohol
22.05	Wine of fresh grapes; grape must with fermentation arrested by the addition of alcohol
22.07	Other fermented beverages (for example, cider, perry and mead)
ex 22.08 (*) ex 22.09 (*)	Ethyl alcohol or neutral spirits, whether or not denatured, of any strength, obtained from agricultural products listed in Annex I, excluding liqueurs and other spirituous beverages and compound alcoholic preparations (known as 'concentrated extracts') for the manufacture of beverages
22.10 (*)	Vinegar and substitutes for vinegar
Chapter 23	Residues and waste from the food industries; prepared animal fodder
Chapter 24	
24.01	Unmanufactured tobacco, tobacco refuse
Chapter 45	
45.01	Natural cork, unworked, crushed, granulated or ground; waste cork

(*) Entry added by Article 1 of Regulation No 7a of the Council of the European Economic Community of 18 December 1959 (OJ No 7, 30.1.1961, p. 71/61).

Chapter 54	
54.01	Flax, raw or processed but not spun; flax tow and waste (including pulled or garnetted rags)
Chapter 57	
57.01	True hemp (Cannabis sativa), raw or processed but not spun; tow and waste of true hemp (including pulled or garnetted rags or ropes)

Annex II
Overseas Countries and Territories to which the Provisions of Part Four of the Treaty on the Functioning of the European Union apply

- Greenland,
- New Caledonia and Dependencies,
- French Polynesia,
- French Southern and Antarctic Territories,
- Wallis and Futuna Islands,
- Mayotte,
- Saint Pierre and Miquelon,
- Aruba,
- Netherlands Antilles:
    - Bonaire,
    - Curaçao,
    - Saba,
    - Sint Eustatius,
    - Sint Maarten,
- Anguilla,
- Cayman Islands,
- Falkland Islands,
- South Georgia and the South Sandwich Islands,
- Montserrat,
- Pitcairn,
- Saint Helena and Dependencies,
- British Antarctic Territory,
- British Indian Ocean Territory,
- Turks and Caicos Islands,
- British Virgin Islands,
- Bermuda.

Protocol (No 1)
on the Role of national Parliaments
in the European Union

The High Contracting Parties,
Recalling that the way in which national Parliaments scrutinise their governments in relation to the activities of the Union is a matter for the particular constitutional organisation and practice of each Member State,
Desiring to encourage greater involvement of national Parliaments in the activities of the European Union and to enhance their ability to express their views on draft legislative acts of the Union as well as on other matters which may be of particular interest to them,
Have agreed upon the following provisions, which shall be annexed to the Treaty on European Union, to the Treaty on the Functioning of the European Union and to the Treaty establishing the European Atomic Energy Community:

Title I
Information for national Parliaments

Article 1
Commission consultation documents (green and white papers and communications) shall be forwarded directly by the Commission to national Parliaments upon publication. The Commission shall also forward the annual legislative programme as well as any other instrument of legislative planning or policy to national Parliaments, at the same time as to the European Parliament and the Council.

© European Union, http://eur-lex.europa.eu/, 1998-2015.

Article 2

Draft legislative acts sent to the European Parliament and to the Council shall be forwarded to national Parliaments.

For the purposes of this Protocol, 'draft legislative acts' shall mean proposals from the Commission, initiatives from a group of Member States, initiatives from the European Parliament, requests from the Court of Justice, recommendations from the European Central Bank and requests from the European Investment Bank, for the adoption of a legislative act.

Draft legislative acts originating from the Commission shall be forwarded to national Parliaments directly by the Commission, at the same time as to the European Parliament and the Council.

Draft legislative acts originating from the European Parliament shall be forwarded to national Parliaments directly by the European Parliament.

Draft legislative acts originating from a group of Member States, the Court of Justice, the European Central Bank or the European Investment Bank shall be forwarded to national Parliaments by the Council.

Article 3

National Parliaments may send to the Presidents of the European Parliament, the Council and the Commission a reasoned opinion on whether a draft legislative act complies with the principle of subsidiarity, in accordance with the procedure laid down in the Protocol on the application of the principles of subsidiarity and proportionality.

If the draft legislative act originates from a group of Member States, the President of the Council shall forward the reasoned opinion or opinions to the governments of those Member States.

If the draft legislative act originates from the Court of Justice, the European Central Bank or the European Investment Bank, the President of the Council shall forward the reasoned opinion or opinions to the institution or body concerned.

Article 4

An eight-week period shall elapse between a draft legislative act being made available to national Parliaments in the official languages of the Union and the date when it is placed on a provisional agenda for the Council for its adoption or for adoption of a position under a legislative procedure. Exceptions shall be possible in cases of urgency, the reasons for which shall be stated in the act or position of the Council. Save in urgent cases for which due reasons have been given, no agreement may be reached on a draft legislative act during those eight weeks. Save in urgent cases for which due reasons have been given, a ten-day period shall elapse between the placing of a draft legislative act on the provisional agenda for the Council and the adoption of a position.

Article 5

The agendas for and the outcome of meetings of the Council, including the minutes of meetings where the Council is deliberating on draft legislative acts, shall be forwarded directly to national Parliaments, at the same time as to Member States' governments.

Article 6
When the European Council intends to make use of the first or second subparagraphs of Article 48(7) of the Treaty on European Union, national Parliaments shall be informed of the initiative of the European Council at least six months before any decision is adopted.

Article 7
The Court of Auditors shall forward its annual report to national Parliaments, for information, at the same time as to the European Parliament and to the Council.

Article 8
Where the national Parliamentary system is not unicameral, Articles 1 to 7 shall apply to the component chambers.

Title II
Interparliamentary cooperation

Article 9
The European Parliament and national Parliaments shall together determine the organisation and promotion of effective and regular interparliamentary cooperation within the Union.

Article 10
A conference of Parliamentary Committees for Union Affairs may submit any contribution it deems appropriate for the attention of the European Parliament, the Council and the Commission. That conference shall in addition promote the exchange of information and best practice between national Parliaments and the European Parliament, including their special committees. It may also organise interparliamentary conferences on specific topics, in particular to debate matters of common foreign and security policy, including common security and defence policy. Contributions from the conference shall not bind national Parliaments and shall not prejudge their positions.

Protocol (No 2) on the Application of the Principles of Subsidiarity and Proportionality

The High Contracting Parties,

Wishing to ensure that decisions are taken as closely as possible to the citizens of the Union,

Resolved to establish the conditions for the application of the principles of subsidiarity and proportionality, as laid down in Article 5 of the Treaty on European Union, and to establish a system for monitoring the application of those principles,

Have agreed upon the following provisions, which shall be annexed to the Treaty on European Union and to the Treaty on the Functioning of the European Union:

Article 1

Each institution shall ensure constant respect for the principles of subsidiarity and proportionality, as laid down in Article 5 of the Treaty on European Union.

Article 2

Before proposing legislative acts, the Commission shall consult widely. Such consultations shall, where appropriate, take into account the regional and local dimension of the action envisaged. In cases of exceptional urgency, the Commission shall not conduct such consultations. It shall give reasons for its decision in its proposal.

Article 3

For the purposes of this Protocol, "draft legislative acts" shall mean proposals from the Commission, initiatives from a group of Member States, initiatives from the European Parliament, requests from the Court of Justice, recommendations from the European Central Bank and requests from the European Investment Bank, for the adoption of a legislative act.

Article 4

The Commission shall forward its draft legislative acts and its amended drafts to national Parliaments at the same time as to the Union legislator.

The European Parliament shall forward its draft legislative acts and its amended drafts to national Parliaments.

The Council shall forward draft legislative acts originating from a group of Member States, the Court of Justice, the European Central Bank or the European Investment Bank and amended drafts to national Parliaments.

Upon adoption, legislative resolutions of the European Parliament and positions of the Council shall be forwarded by them to national Parliaments.

Article 5
Draft legislative acts shall be justified with regard to the principles of subsidiarity and proportionality. Any draft legislative act should contain a detailed statement making it possible to appraise compliance with the principles of subsidiarity and proportionality. This statement should contain some assessment of the proposal's financial impact and, in the case of a directive, of its implications for the rules to be put in place by Member States, including, where necessary, the regional legislation. The reasons for concluding that a Union objective can be better achieved at Union level shall be substantiated by qualitative and, wherever possible, quantitative indicators. Draft legislative acts shall take account of the need for any burden, whether financial or administrative, falling upon the Union, national governments, regional or local authorities, economic operators and citizens, to be minimised and commensurate with the objective to be achieved.

Article 6
Any national Parliament or any chamber of a national Parliament may, within eight weeks from the date of transmission of a draft legislative act, in the official languages of the Union, send to the Presidents of the European Parliament, the Council and the Commission a reasoned opinion stating why it considers that the draft in question does not comply with the principle of subsidiarity. It will be for each national Parliament or each chamber of a national Parliament to consult, where appropriate, regional parliaments with legislative powers.
If the draft legislative act originates from a group of Member States, the President of the Council shall forward the opinion to the governments of those Member States.
If the draft legislative act originates from the Court of Justice, the European Central Bank or the European Investment Bank, the President of the Council shall forward the opinion to the institution or body concerned.

Article 7
1. The European Parliament, the Council and the Commission, and, where appropriate, the group of Member States, the Court of Justice, the European Central Bank or the European Investment Bank, if the draft legislative act originates from them, shall take account of the reasoned opinions issued by national Parliaments or by a chamber of a national Parliament.
Each national Parliament shall have two votes, shared out on the basis of the national Parliamentary system. In the case of a bicameral Parliamentary system, each of the two chambers shall have one vote.
2. Where reasoned opinions on a draft legislative act's non-compliance with the principle of subsidiarity represent at least one third of all the votes allocated to the national Parliaments in accordance with the second subparagraph of paragraph 1, the draft must be reviewed. This threshold shall be a quarter in the case of a draft legislative act submitted on the basis of Article 76 of the Treaty on the Functioning of the European Union on the area of freedom, security and justice.

After such review, the Commission or, where appropriate, the group of Member States, the European Parliament, the Court of Justice, the European Central Bank or the European Investment Bank, if the draft legislative act originates from them, may decide to maintain, amend or withdraw the draft. Reasons must be given for this decision.

3. Furthermore, under the ordinary legislative procedure, where reasoned opinions on the non-compliance of a proposal for a legislative act with the principle of subsidiarity represent at least a simple majority of the votes allocated to the national Parliaments in accordance with the second subparagraph of paragraph 1, the proposal must be reviewed. After such review, the Commission may decide to maintain, amend or withdraw the proposal.

If it chooses to maintain the proposal, the Commission will have, in a reasoned opinion, to justify why it considers that the proposal complies with the principle of subsidiarity. This reasoned opinion, as well as the reasoned opinions of the national Parliaments, will have to be submitted to the Union legislator, for consideration in the procedure:

(a) before concluding the first reading, the legislator (the European Parliament and the Council) shall consider whether the legislative proposal is compatible with the principle of subsidiarity, taking particular account of the reasons expressed and shared by the majority of national Parliaments as well as the reasoned opinion of the Commission;

(b) if, by a majority of 55 % of the members of the Council or a majority of the votes cast in the European Parliament, the legislator is of the opinion that the proposal is not compatible with the principle of subsidiarity, the legislative proposal shall not be given further consideration.

Article 8

The Court of Justice of the European Union shall have jurisdiction in actions on grounds of infringement of the principle of subsidiarity by a legislative act, brought in accordance with the rules laid down in Article 263 of the Treaty on the Functioning of the European Union by Member States, or notified by them in accordance with their legal order on behalf of their national Parliament or a chamber thereof.

In accordance with the rules laid down in the said Article, the Committee of the Regions may also bring such actions against legislative acts for the adoption of which the Treaty on the Functioning of the European Union provides that it be consulted.

Article 9

The Commission shall submit each year to the European Council, the European Parliament, the Council and national Parliaments a report on the application of Article 5 of the Treaty on European Union, This annual report shall also be forwarded to the Economic and Social Committee and the Committee of the Regions.

Protocol (No 3)
on the Statute of the Court of Justice
of the European Union

The High Contracting Parties,
Desiring to lay down the Statute of the Court of Justice of the European Union provided for in Article 281 of the Treaty on the Functioning of the European Union,
Have agreed upon the following provisions, which shall be annexed to the Treaty on European Union, the Treaty on the Functioning of the European Union and the Treaty establishing the European Atomic Energy Community:

Article 1
The Court of Justice of the European Union shall be constituted and shall function in accordance with the provisions of the Treaties, of the Treaty establishing the European Atomic Energy Community (the EAEC Treaty) and of this Statute.

Title I
Judges and Advocates-General

Article 2
Before taking up his duties each Judge shall, before the Court of Justice sitting in open court, take an oath to perform his duties impartially and conscientiously and to preserve the secrecy of the deliberations of the Court.

Article 3
The Judges shall be immune from legal proceedings. After they have ceased to hold office, they shall continue to enjoy immunity in respect of acts performed by them in their official capacity, including words spoken or written.

The Court of Justice, sitting as a full Court, may waive the immunity. If the decision concerns a member of the General Court or of a specialised court, the Court shall decide after consulting the court concerned.

Where immunity has been waived and criminal proceedings are instituted against a Judge, he shall be tried, in any of the Member States, only by the court competent to judge the members of the highest national judiciary.

Articles 11 to 14 and Article 17 of the Protocol on the privileges and immunities of the European Union shall apply to the Judges, Advocates-General, Registrar and Assistant Rapporteurs of the Court of Justice of the European Union, without prejudice to the provisions relating to immunity from legal proceedings of Judges which are set out in the preceding paragraphs.

Article 4

The Judges may not hold any political or administrative office.

They may not engage in any occupation, whether gainful or not, unless exemption is exceptionally granted by the Council, acting by a simple majority.

When taking up their duties, they shall give a solemn undertaking that, both during and after their term of office, they will respect the obligations arising therefrom, in particular the duty to behave with integrity and discretion as regards the acceptance, after they have ceased to hold office, of certain appointments or benefits.

Any doubt on this point shall be settled by decision of the Court of Justice. If the decision concerns a member of the General Court or of a specialised court, the Court shall decide after consulting the court concerned.

Article 5

Apart from normal replacement, or death, the duties of a Judge shall end when he resigns.

Where a Judge resigns, his letter of resignation shall be addressed to the President of the Court of Justice for transmission to the President of the Council. Upon this notification a vacancy shall arise on the bench.

Save where Article 6 applies, a Judge shall continue to hold office until his successor takes up his duties.

Article 6

A Judge may be deprived of his office or of his right to a pension or other benefits in its stead only if, in the unanimous opinion of the Judges and Advocates-General of the Court of Justice, he no longer fulfils the requisite conditions or meets the obligations arising from his office. The Judge concerned shall not take part in any such deliberations. If the person concerned is a member of the General Court or of a specialised court, the Court shall decide after consulting the court concerned.

The Registrar of the Court shall communicate the decision of the Court to the President of the European Parliament and to the President of the Commission and shall notify it to the President of the Council.

In the case of a decision depriving a Judge of his office, a vacancy shall arise on the bench upon this latter notification.

Article 7
A Judge who is to replace a member of the Court whose term of office has not expired shall be appointed for the remainder of his predecessor's term.

Article 8
The provisions of Articles 2 to 7 shall apply to the Advocates-General.

Title II
Organisation of the Court of Justice

Article 9
When, every three years, the Judges are partially replaced, 14 Judges shall be replaced. When, every three years, the Advocates-General are partially replaced, four Advocates-General shall be replaced on each occasion.

Article 10
The Registrar shall take an oath before the Court of Justice to perform his duties impartially and conscientiously and to preserve the secrecy of the deliberations of the Court of Justice.

Article 11
The Court of Justice shall arrange for replacement of the Registrar on occasions when he is prevented from attending the Court of Justice.

Article 12
Officials and other servants shall be attached to the Court of Justice to enable it to function. They shall be responsible to the Registrar under the authority of the President.

Article 13
At the request of the Court of Justice, the European Parliament and the Council may, acting in accordance with the ordinary legislative procedure, provide for the appointment of Assistant Rapporteurs and lay down the rules governing their service. The Assistant Rapporteurs may be required, under conditions laid down in the Rules of Procedure, to participate in preparatory inquiries in cases pending before the Court and to cooperate with the Judge who acts as Rapporteur.

The Assistant Rapporteurs shall be chosen from persons whose independence is beyond doubt and who possess the necessary legal qualifications; they shall be appointed by the Council, acting by a simple majority. They shall take an oath before the Court to perform their duties impartially and conscientiously and to preserve the secrecy of the deliberations of the Court.

Article 14
The Judges, the Advocates-General and the Registrar shall be required to reside at the place where the Court of Justice has its seat.

Article 15
The Court of Justice shall remain permanently in session. The duration of the judicial vacations shall be determined by the Court with due regard to the needs of its business.

Article 16
The Court of Justice shall form chambers consisting of three and five Judges. The Judges shall elect the Presidents of the chambers from among their number. The Presidents of the chambers of five Judges shall be elected for three years. They may be re-elected once.

The Grand Chamber shall consist of 13 Judges. It shall be presided over by the President of the Court. The Presidents of the chambers of five Judges and other Judges appointed in accordance with the conditions laid down in the Rules of Procedure shall also form part of the Grand Chamber.

The Court shall sit in a Grand Chamber when a Member State or an institution of the Union that is party to the proceedings so requests.

The Court shall sit as a full Court where cases are brought before it pursuant to Article 228(2), Article 245(2), Article 247 or Article 286(6) of the Treaty on the Functioning of the European Union.

Moreover, where it considers that a case before it is of exceptional importance, the Court may decide, after hearing the Advocate-General, to refer the case to the full Court.

Article 17
Decisions of the Court of Justice shall be valid only when an uneven number of its members is sitting in the deliberations.

Decisions of the chambers consisting of either three or five Judges shall be valid only if they are taken by three Judges.

Decisions of the Grand Chamber shall be valid only if nine Judges are sitting. Decisions of the full Court shall be valid only if 15 Judges are sitting.

In the event of one of the Judges of a chamber being prevented from attending, a Judge of another chamber may be called upon to sit in accordance with conditions laid down in the Rules of Procedure.

Article 18
No Judge or Advocate-General may take part in the disposal of any case in which he has previously taken part as agent or adviser or has acted for one of the parties, or in which he

has been called upon to pronounce as a member of a court or tribunal, of a commission of inquiry or in any other capacity.

If, for some special reason, any Judge or Advocate-General considers that he should not take part in the judgment or examination of a particular case, he shall so inform the President. If, for some special reason, the President considers that any Judge or Advocate-General should not sit or make submissions in a particular case, he shall notify him accordingly.

Any difficulty arising as to the application of this Article shall be settled by decision of the Court of Justice.

A party may not apply for a change in the composition of the Court or of one of its chambers on the grounds of either the nationality of a Judge or the absence from the Court or from the chamber of a Judge of the nationality of that party.

Title III
Procedure before the Court of Justice

Article 19

The Member States and the institutions of the Union shall be represented before the Court of Justice by an agent appointed for each case; the agent may be assisted by an adviser or by a lawyer.

The States, other than the Member States, which are parties to the Agreement on the European Economic Area and also the EFTA Surveillance Authority referred to in that Agreement shall be represented in same manner.

Other parties must be represented by a lawyer.

Only a lawyer authorised to practise before a court of a Member State or of another State which is a party to the Agreement on the European Economic Area may represent or assist a party before the Court.

Such agents, advisers and lawyers shall, when they appear before the Court, enjoy the rights and immunities necessary to the independent exercise of their duties, under conditions laid down in the Rules of Procedure.

As regards such advisers and lawyers who appear before it, the Court shall have the powers normally accorded to courts of law, under conditions laid down in the Rules of Procedure.

University teachers being nationals of a Member State whose law accords them a right of audience shall have the same rights before the Court as are accorded by this Article to lawyers.

Article 20

The procedure before the Court of Justice shall consist of two parts: written and oral.

The written procedure shall consist of the communication to the parties and to the institutions of the Union whose decisions are in dispute, of applications, statements of case, defences and observations, and of replies, if any, as well as of all papers and documents in support or of certified copies of them.

Communications shall be made by the Registrar in the order and within the time laid down in the Rules of Procedure.

The oral procedure shall consist of the reading of the report presented by a Judge acting as Rapporteur, the hearing by the Court of agents, advisers and lawyers and of the submissions of the Advocate-General, as well as the hearing, if any, of witnesses and experts.

Where it considers that the case raises no new point of law, the Court may decide, after hearing the Advocate-General, that the case shall be determined without a submission from the Advocate-General.

Article 21

A case shall be brought before the Court of Justice by a written application addressed to the Registrar. The application shall contain the applicant's name and permanent address and the description of the signatory, the name of the party or names of the parties against whom the application is made, the subject-matter of the dispute, the form of order sought and a brief statement of the pleas in law on which the application is based.

The application shall be accompanied, where appropriate, by the measure the annulment of which is sought or, in the circumstances referred to in Article 265 of the Treaty on the Functioning of the European Union, by documentary evidence of the date on which an institution was, in accordance with those Articles, requested to act. If the documents are not submitted with the application, the Registrar shall ask the party concerned to produce them within a reasonable period, but in that event the rights of the party shall not lapse even if such documents are produced after the time limit for bringing proceedings.

Article 22

A case governed by Article 18 of the EAEC Treaty shall be brought before the Court of Justice by an appeal addressed to the Registrar. The appeal shall contain the name and permanent address of the applicant and the description of the signatory, a reference to the decision against which the appeal is brought, the names of the respondents, the subject-matter of the dispute, the submissions and a brief statement of the grounds on which the appeal is based. The appeal shall be accompanied by a certified copy of the decision of the Arbitration Committee which is contested.

If the Court rejects the appeal, the decision of the Arbitration Committee shall become final. If the Court annuls the decision of the Arbitration Committee, the matter may be re-opened, where appropriate, on the initiative of one of the parties in the case, before the Arbitration Committee. The latter shall conform to any decisions on points of law given by the Court.

Article 23

In the cases governed by Article 267 of the Treaty on the Functioning of the European Union, the decision of the court or tribunal of a Member State which suspends its proceedings and refers a case to the Court of Justice shall be notified to the Court by the court or tribunal concerned. The decision shall then be notified by the Registrar of the Court to the parties, to the Member States and to the Commission, and to the institution, body, office or agency of the Union which adopted the act the validity or interpretation of which is in dispute.

Within two months of this notification, the parties, the Member States, the Commission and, where appropriate, the institution, body, office or agency which adopted the act the validity or interpretation of which is in dispute, shall be entitled to submit statements of case or written observations to the Court.

In the cases governed by Article 267 of the Treaty on the Functioning of the European Union, the decision of the national court or tribunal shall, moreover, be notified by the Registrar of the Court to the States, other than the Member States, which are parties to the Agreement on the European Economic Area and also to the EFTA Surveillance Authority referred to in that Agreement which may, within two months of notification, where one of the fields of application of that Agreement is concerned, submit statements of case or written observations to the Court.

Where an agreement relating to a specific subject matter, concluded by the Council and one or more non-member States, provides that those States are to be entitled to submit statements of case or written observations where a court or tribunal of a Member State refers to the Court of Justice for a preliminary ruling a question falling within the scope of the agreement, the decision of the national court or tribunal containing that question shall also be notified to the non-member States concerned. Within two months from such notification, those States may lodge at the Court statements of case or written observations.

Article 23a*

The Rules of Procedure may provide for an expedited or accelerated procedure and, for references for a preliminary ruling relating to the area of freedom, security and justice, an urgent procedure.

Those procedures may provide, in respect of the submission of statements of case or written observations, for a shorter period than that provided for by Article 23, and, in derogation from the fourth paragraph of Article 20, for the case to be determined without a submission from the Advocate General.

In addition, the urgent procedure may provide for restriction of the parties and other interested persons mentioned in Article 23, authorised to submit statements of case or written observations and, in cases of extreme urgency, for the written stage of the procedure to be omitted.

Article 24

The Court of Justice may require the parties to produce all documents and to supply all information which the Court considers desirable. Formal note shall be taken of any refusal.

The Court may also require the Member States and institutions, bodies, offices and agencies not being parties to the case to supply all information which the Court considers necessary for the proceedings.

---

*   Article inserted by Decision 2008/79/EC, Euratom (OJ L 24, 29.1.2008, p. 42).

Article 25
The Court of Justice may at any time entrust any individual, body, authority, committee or other organisation it chooses with the task of giving an expert opinion.

Article 26
Witnesses may be heard under conditions laid down in the Rules of Procedure.

Article 27
With respect to defaulting witnesses the Court of Justice shall have the powers generally granted to courts and tribunals and may impose pecuniary penalties under conditions laid down in the Rules of Procedure.

Article 28
Witnesses and experts may be heard on oath taken in the form laid down in the Rules of Procedure or in the manner laid down by the law of the country of the witness or expert.

Article 29
The Court of Justice may order that a witness or expert be heard by the judicial authority of his place of permanent residence.

The order shall be sent for implementation to the competent judicial authority under conditions laid down in the Rules of Procedure. The documents drawn up in compliance with the letters rogatory shall be returned to the Court under the same conditions.

The Court shall defray the expenses, without prejudice to the right to charge them, where appropriate, to the parties.

Article 30
A Member State shall treat any violation of an oath by a witness or expert in the same manner as if the offence had been committed before one of its courts with jurisdiction in civil proceedings. At the instance of the Court of Justice, the Member State concerned shall prosecute the offender before its competent court.

Article 31
The hearing in court shall be public, unless the Court of Justice, of its own motion or on application by the parties, decides otherwise for serious reasons.

Article 32
During the hearings the Court of Justice may examine the experts, the witnesses and the parties themselves. The latter, however, may address the Court of Justice only through their representatives.

Article 33
Minutes shall be made of each hearing and signed by the President and the Registrar.

Article 34
The case list shall be established by the President.

Article 35
The deliberations of the Court of Justice shall be and shall remain secret.

Article 36
Judgments shall state the reasons on which they are based. They shall contain the names of the Judges who took part in the deliberations.

Article 37
Judgments shall be signed by the President and the Registrar. They shall be read in open court.

Article 38
The Court of Justice shall adjudicate upon costs.

Article 39
The President of the Court of Justice may, by way of summary procedure, which may, in so far as necessary, differ from some of the rules contained in this Statute and which shall be laid down in the Rules of Procedure, adjudicate upon applications to suspend execution, as provided for in Article 278 of the Treaty on the Functioning of the European Union and Article 157 of the EAEC Treaty, or to prescribe interim measures pursuant to Article 279 of the Treaty on the Functioning of the European Union, or to suspend enforcement in accordance with the fourth paragraph of Article 299 of the Treaty on the Functioning of the European Union or the third paragraph of Article 164 of the EAEC Treaty.
Should the President be prevented from attending, his place shall be taken by another Judge under conditions laid down in the Rules of Procedure.
The ruling of the President or of the Judge replacing him shall be provisional and shall in no way prejudice the decision of the Court on the substance of the case.

Article 40
Member States and institutions of the Union may intervene in cases before the Court of Justice.
The same right shall be open to the bodies, offices and agencies of the Union and to any other person which can establish an interest in the result of a case submitted to the Court. Natural or legal persons shall not intervene in cases between Member States, between institutions of the Union or between Member States and institutions of the Union.
Without prejudice to the second paragraph, the States, other than the Member States, which are parties to the Agreement on the European Economic Area, and also the EFTA Surveillance Authority referred to in that Agreement, may intervene in cases before the Court where one of the fields of application of that Agreement is concerned.

An application to intervene shall be limited to supporting the form of order sought by one of the parties.

Article 41
Where the defending party, after having been duly summoned, fails to file written submissions in defence, judgment shall be given against that party by default. An objection may be lodged against the judgment within one month of it being notified. The objection shall not have the effect of staying enforcement of the judgment by default unless the Court of Justice decides otherwise.

Article 42
Member States, institutions, bodies, offices and agencies of the Union and any other natural or legal persons may, in cases and under conditions to be determined by the Rules of Procedure, institute third-party proceedings to contest a judgment rendered without their being heard, where the judgment is prejudicial to their rights.

Article 43
If the meaning or scope of a judgment is in doubt, the Court of Justice shall construe it on application by any party or any institution of the Union establishing an interest therein.

Article 44
An application for revision of a judgment may be made to the Court of Justice only on discovery of a fact which is of such a nature as to be a decisive factor, and which, when the judgment was given, was unknown to the Court and to the party claiming the revision.
The revision shall be opened by a judgment of the Court expressly recording the existence of a new fact, recognising that it is of such a character as to lay the case open to revision and declaring the application admissible on this ground.
No application for revision may be made after the lapse of 10 years from the date of the judgment.

Article 45
Periods of grace based on considerations of distance shall be determined by the Rules of Procedure.
No right shall be prejudiced in consequence of the expiry of a time limit if the party concerned proves the existence of unforeseeable circumstances or of force majeure.

Article 46
Proceedings against the Union in matters arising from non-contractual liability shall be barred after a period of five years from the occurrence of the event giving rise thereto. The period of limitation shall be interrupted if proceedings are instituted before the Court of Justice or if prior to such proceedings an application is made by the aggrieved party to the

relevant institution of the Union. In the latter event the proceedings must be instituted within the period of two months provided for in Article 263 of the Treaty on the Functioning of the European Union; the provisions of the second paragraph of Article 265 of the Treaty on the Functioning of the European Union shall apply where appropriate.

This Article shall also apply to proceedings against the European Central Bank regarding non-contractual liability.

Title IV
General Court

Article 47

The first paragraph of Article 9, Articles 14 and 15, the first, second, fourth and fifth paragraphs of Article 17 and Article 18 shall apply to the General Court and its members. The fourth paragraph of Article 3 and Articles 10, 11 and 14 shall apply to the Registrar of the General Court mutatis mutandis.

Article 48

The General Court shall consist of 28 Judges.

Article 49

The Members of the General Court may be called upon to perform the task of an Advocate-General.

It shall be the duty of the Advocate-General, acting with complete impartiality and independence, to make, in open court, reasoned submissions on certain cases brought before the General Court in order to assist the General Court in the performance of its task.

The criteria for selecting such cases, as well as the procedures for designating the Advocates-General, shall be laid down in the Rules of Procedure of the General Court.

A Member called upon to perform the task of Advocate-General in a case may not take part in the judgment of the case.

Article 50

The General Court shall sit in chambers of three or five Judges. The Judges shall elect the Presidents of the chambers from among their number. The Presidents of the chambers of five Judges shall be elected for three years. They may be re-elected once.

The composition of the chambers and the assignment of cases to them shall be governed by the Rules of Procedure. In certain cases governed by the Rules of Procedure, the General Court may sit as a full court or be constituted by a single Judge.

The Rules of Procedure may also provide that the General Court may sit in a Grand Chamber in cases and under the conditions specified therein.

Article 51

By way of derogation from the rule laid down in Article 256(1) of the Treaty on the Functioning of the European Union, jurisdiction shall be reserved to the Court of Justice in the actions referred to in Articles 263 and 265 of the Treaty on the Functioning of the European Union when they are brought by a Member State against:

(a) an act of or failure to act by the European Parliament or the Council, or by those institutions acting jointly, except for:

– decisions taken by the Council under the third subparagraph of Article 108(2) of the Treaty on the Functioning of the European Union;

– acts of the Council adopted pursuant to a Council regulation concerning measures to protect trade within the meaning of Article 207 of the Treaty on the Functioning of the European Union;

– acts of the Council by which the Council exercises implementing powers in accordance with the second paragraph of Article 291 of the Treaty on the Functioning of the European Union;

(b) against an act of or failure to act by the Commission under the first paragraph of Article 331 of the Treaty on the Functioning of the European Union.

Jurisdiction shall also be reserved to the Court of Justice in the actions referred to in the same Articles when they are brought by an institution of the Union against an act of or failure to act by the European Parliament, the Council, both those institutions acting jointly, or the Commission, or brought by an institution of the Union against an act of or failure to act by the European Central Bank.

Article 52

The President of the Court of Justice and the President of the General Court shall determine, by common accord, the conditions under which officials and other servants attached to the Court of Justice shall render their services to the General Court to enable it to function. Certain officials or other servants shall be responsible to the Registrar of the General Court under the authority of the President of the General Court.

Article 53

The procedure before the General Court shall be governed by Title III.

Such further and more detailed provisions as may be necessary shall be laid down in its Rules of Procedure. The Rules of Procedure may derogate from the fourth paragraph of Article 40 and from Article 41 in order to take account of the specific features of litigation in the field of intellectual property.

Notwithstanding the fourth paragraph of Article 20, the Advocate-General may make his reasoned submissions in writing.

Article 54

Where an application or other procedural document addressed to the General Court is lodged by mistake with the Registrar of the Court of Justice, it shall be transmitted immediately by that Registrar to the Registrar of the General Court; likewise, where an application or other procedural document addressed to the Court of Justice is lodged by mistake with the Registrar of the General Court, it shall be transmitted immediately by that Registrar to the Registrar of the Court of Justice.

Where the General Court finds that it does not have jurisdiction to hear and determine an action in respect of which the Court of Justice has jurisdiction, it shall refer that action to the Court of Justice; likewise, where the Court of Justice finds that an action falls within the jurisdiction of the General Court, it shall refer that action to the General Court, whereupon that Court may not decline jurisdiction.

Where the Court of Justice and the General Court are seised of cases in which the same relief is sought, the same issue of interpretation is raised or the validity of the same act is called in question, the General Court may, after hearing the parties, stay the proceedings before it until such time as the Court of Justice has delivered judgment or, where the action is one brought pursuant to Article 263 of the Treaty on the Functioning of the European Union, may decline jurisdiction so as to allow the Court of Justice to rule on such actions. In the same circumstances, the Court of Justice may also decide to stay the proceedings before it; in that event, the proceedings before the General Court shall continue.

Where a Member State and an institution of the Union are challenging the same act, the General Court shall decline jurisdiction so that the Court of Justice may rule on those applications.

Article 55

Final decisions of the General Court, decisions disposing of the substantive issues in part only or disposing of a procedural issue concerning a plea of lack of competence or inadmissibility, shall be notified by the Registrar of the General Court to all parties as well as all Member States and the institutions of the Union even if they did not intervene in the case before the General Court.

Article 56

An appeal may be brought before the Court of Justice, within two months of the notification of the decision appealed against, against final decisions of the General Court and decisions of that Court disposing of the substantive issues in part only or disposing of a procedural issue concerning a plea of lack of competence or inadmissibility.

Such an appeal may be brought by any party which has been unsuccessful, in whole or in part, in its submissions. However, interveners other than the Member States and the institutions of the Union may bring such an appeal only where the decision of the General Court directly affects them.

With the exception of cases relating to disputes between the Union and its servants, an appeal may also be brought by Member States and institutions of the Union which did not intervene in the proceedings before the General Court. Such Member States and institutions shall be in the same position as Member States or institutions which intervened at first instance.

Article 57

Any person whose application to intervene has been dismissed by the General Court may appeal to the Court of Justice within two weeks from the notification of the decision dismissing the application.

The parties to the proceedings may appeal to the Court of Justice against any decision of the General Court made pursuant to Article 278 or Article 279 or the fourth paragraph of Article 299 of the Treaty on the Functioning of the European Union or Article 157 or the third paragraph of Article 164 of the EAEC Treaty within two months from their notification.

The appeal referred to in the first two paragraphs of this Article shall be heard and determined under the procedure referred to in Article 39.

Article 58

An appeal to the Court of Justice shall be limited to points of law. It shall lie on the grounds of lack of competence of the General Court, a breach of procedure before it which adversely affects the interests of the appellant as well as the infringement of Union law by the General Court.

No appeal shall lie regarding only the amount of the costs or the party ordered to pay them.

Article 59

Where an appeal is brought against a decision of the General Court, the procedure before the Court of Justice shall consist of a written part and an oral part. In accordance with conditions laid down in the Rules of Procedure, the Court of Justice, having heard the Advocate-General and the parties, may dispense with the oral procedure.

Article 60

Without prejudice to Articles 278 and 279 of the Treaty on the Functioning of the European Union or Article 157 of the EAEC Treaty, an appeal shall not have suspensory effect.

By way of derogation from Article 280 of the Treaty on the Functioning of the European Union, decisions of the General Court declaring a regulation to be void shall take effect only as from the date of expiry of the period referred to in the first paragraph of Article 56 of this Statute or, if an appeal shall have been brought within that period, as from the date of dismissal of the appeal, without prejudice, however, to the right of a party to apply to the Court of Justice, pursuant to Articles 278 and 279 of the Treaty on the Functioning of the European Union or Article 157 of the EAEC Treaty, for the suspension of the effects of the regulation which has been declared void or for the prescription of any other interim measure.

Article 61

If the appeal is well founded, the Court of Justice shall quash the decision of the General Court. It may itself give final judgment in the matter, where the state of the proceedings so permits, or refer the case back to the General Court for judgment.

Where a case is referred back to the General Court, that Court shall be bound by the decision of the Court of Justice on points of law.

When an appeal brought by a Member State or an institution of the Union, which did not intervene in the proceedings before the General Court, is well founded, the Court of Justice may, if it considers this necessary, state which of the effects of the decision of the General Court which has been quashed shall be considered as definitive in respect of the parties to the litigation.

Article 62

In the cases provided for in Article 256(2) and (3) of the Treaty on the Functioning of the European Union, where the First Advocate-General considers that there is a serious risk of the unity or consistency of Union law being affected, he may propose that the Court of Justice review the decision of the General Court.

The proposal must be made within one month of delivery of the decision by the General Court. Within one month of receiving the proposal made by the First Advocate-General, the Court of Justice shall decide whether or not the decision should be reviewed.

Article 62a

The Court of Justice shall give a ruling on the questions which are subject to review by means of an urgent procedure on the basis of the file forwarded to it by the General Court.

Those referred to in Article 23 of this Statute and, in the cases provided for in Article 256(2) of the EC Treaty, the parties to the proceedings before the General Court shall be entitled to lodge statements or written observations with the Court of Justice relating to questions which are subject to review within a period prescribed for that purpose.

The Court of Justice may decide to open the oral procedure before giving a ruling.

Article 62b

In the cases provided for in Article 256(2) of the Treaty on the Functioning of the European Union, without prejudice to Articles 278 and 279 of the Treaty on the Functioning of the European Union, proposals for review and decisions to open the review procedure shall not have suspensory effect. If the Court of Justice finds that the decision of the General Court affects the unity or consistency of Union law, it shall refer the case back to the General Court which shall be bound by the points of law decided by the Court of Justice; the Court of Justice may state which of the effects of the decision of the General Court are to be considered as definitive in respect of the parties to the litigation. If, however, having regard to the result of the review, the outcome of the proceedings flows from the findings of fact on which the decision of the General Court was based, the Court of Justice shall give final judgment.

In the cases provided for in Article 256(3) of the Treaty on the Functioning of the European Union, in the absence of proposals for review or decisions to open the review procedure, the answer(s) given by the General Court to the questions submitted to it shall take effect upon expiry of the periods prescribed for that purpose in the second paragraph of Article 62. Should a review procedure be opened, the answer(s) subject to review shall take effect following that procedure, unless the Court of Justice decides otherwise. If the Court of Justice finds that the decision of the General Court affects the unity or consistency of Union law, the answer given by the Court of Justice to the questions subject to review shall be substituted for that given by the General Court.

Title IVa
Specialised courts

Article 62c
The provisions relating to the jurisdiction, composition, organisation and procedure of the specialised courts established under Article 257 of the Treaty on the Functioning of the European Union are set out in an Annex to this Statute.

Title V
Final provisions

Article 63
The Rules of Procedure of the Court of Justice and of the General Court shall contain any provisions necessary for applying and, where required, supplementing this Statute.

Article 64
The rules governing the language arrangements applicable at the Court of Justice of the European Union shall be laid down by a regulation of the Council acting unanimously. This regulation shall be adopted either at the request of the Court of Justice and after consultation of the Commission and the European Parliament, or on a proposal from the Commission and after consultation of the Court of Justice and of the European Parliament.

Until those rules have been adopted, the provisions of the Rules of Procedure of the Court of Justice and of the Rules of Procedure of the General Court governing language arrangements shall continue to apply. By way of derogation from Articles 253 and 254 of the Treaty on the Functioning of the European Union, those provisions may only be amended or repealed with the unanimous consent of the Council.

Annex
The European Union Civil Service Tribunal

Article 1
The European Union Civil Service Tribunal (hereafter 'the Civil Service Tribunal') shall exercise at first instance jurisdiction in disputes between the Union and its servants referred to in Article 270 of the Treaty on the Functioning of the European Union, including disputes

between all bodies or agencies and their servants in respect of which jurisdiction is conferred on the Court of Justice of the European Union.

Article 2
The Civil Service Tribunal shall consist of seven judges. Should the Court of Justice so request, the Council, acting by a qualified majority, may increase the number of judges.
The judges shall be appointed for a period of six years. Retiring judges may be reappointed. Any vacancy shall be filled by the appointment of a new judge for a period of six years.

Article 3
1. The judges shall be appointed by the Council, acting in accordance with the fourth paragraph of Article 257 of the Treaty on the Functioning of the European Union, after consulting the committee provided for by this Article. When appointing judges, the Council shall ensure a balanced composition of the Civil Service Tribunal on as broad a geographical basis as possible from among nationals of the Member States and with respect to the national legal systems represented.
2. Any person who is a Union citizen and fulfils the conditions laid down in the fourth paragraph of Article 257 of the Treaty on the Functioning of the European Union may submit an application. The Council, acting on a recommendation from the Court of Justice, shall determine the conditions and the arrangements governing the submission and processing of such applications.
3. A committee shall be set up comprising seven persons chosen from among former members of the Court of Justice and the General Court and lawyers of recognised competence. The committee's membership and operating rules shall be determined by the Council, acting on a recommendation by the President of the Court of Justice.
4. The committee shall give an opinion on candidates' suitability to perform the duties of judge at the Civil Service Tribunal. The committee shall append to its opinion a list of candidates having the most suitable high-level experience. Such list shall contain the names of at least twice as many candidates as there are judges to be appointed by the Council.

Article 4
1. The judges shall elect the President of the Civil Service Tribunal from among their number for a term of three years. He may be re-elected.
2. The Civil Service Tribunal shall sit in chambers of three judges. It may, in certain cases determined by its rules of procedure, sit in full court or in a chamber of five judges or of a single judge.
3. The President of the Civil Service Tribunal shall preside over the full court and the chamber of five judges. The Presidents of the chambers of three judges shall be designated as provided in paragraph 1. If the President of the Civil Service Tribunal is assigned to a chamber of three judges, he shall preside over that chamber.
4. The jurisdiction of and quorum for the full court as well as the composition of the chambers and the assignment of cases to them shall be governed by the Rules of Procedure.

Article 5

Articles 2 to 6, 14, 15, the first, second and fifth paragraphs of Article 17, and Article 18 of the Statute of the Court of Justice of the European Union shall apply to the Civil Service Tribunal and its members.

The oath referred to in Article 2 of the Statute shall be taken before the Court of Justice, and the decisions referred to in Articles 3, 4 and 6 thereof shall be adopted by the Court of Justice after consulting the Civil Service Tribunal.

Article 6

1. The Civil Service Tribunal shall be supported by the departments of the Court of Justice and of the General Court. The President of the Court of Justice or, in appropriate cases, the President of the General Court, shall determine by common accord with the President of the Civil Service Tribunal the conditions under which officials and other servants attached to the Court of Justice or the General Court shall render their services to the Civil Service Tribunal to enable it to function. Certain officials or other servants shall be responsible to the Registrar of the Civil Service Tribunal under the authority of the President of that Tribunal.

2. The Civil Service Tribunal shall appoint its Registrar and lay down the rules governing his service. The fourth paragraph of Article 3 and Articles 10, 11 and 14 of the Statute of the Court of Justice of the European Union shall apply to the Registrar of the Tribunal.

Article 7

1. The procedure before the Civil Service Tribunal shall be governed by Title III of the Statute of the Court of Justice of the European Union, with the exception of Articles 22 and 23. Such further and more detailed provisions as may be necessary shall be laid down in the Rules of Procedure.

2. The provisions concerning the General Court's language arrangements shall apply to the Civil Service Tribunal.

3. The written stage of the procedure shall comprise the presentation of the application and of the statement of defence, unless the Civil Service Tribunal decides that a second exchange of written pleadings is necessary. Where there is such second exchange, the Civil Service Tribunal may, with the agreement of the parties, decide to proceed to judgment without an oral procedure.

4. At all stages of the procedure, including the time when the application is filed, the Civil Service Tribunal may examine the possibilities of an amicable settlement of the dispute and may try to facilitate such settlement.

5. The Civil Service Tribunal shall rule on the costs of a case. Subject to the specific provisions of the Rules of Procedure, the unsuccessful party shall be ordered to pay the costs should the court so decide.

Article 8

1. Where an application or other procedural document addressed to the Civil Service Tribunal is lodged by mistake with the Registrar of the Court of Justice or General Court, it shall be transmitted immediately by that Registrar to the Registrar of the Civil Service Tribunal. Likewise, where an application or other procedural document addressed to the Court of Justice or to the General Court is lodged by mistake with the Registrar of the Civil Service Tribunal, it shall be transmitted immediately by that Registrar to the Registrar of the Court of Justice or General Court.

2. Where the Civil Service Tribunal finds that it does not have jurisdiction to hear and determine an action in respect of which the Court of Justice or the General Court has jurisdiction, it shall refer that action to the Court of Justice or to the General Court. Likewise, where the Court of Justice or the General Court finds that an action falls within the jurisdiction of the Civil Service Tribunal, the Court seised shall refer that action to the Civil Service Tribunal, whereupon that Tribunal may not decline jurisdiction.

3. Where the Civil Service Tribunal and the General Court are seised of cases in which the same issue of interpretation is raised or the validity of the same act is called in question, the Civil Service Tribunal, after hearing the parties, may stay the proceedings until the judgment of the General Court has been delivered.

Where the Civil Service Tribunal and the General Court are seised of cases in which the same relief is sought, the Civil Service Tribunal shall decline jurisdiction so that the General Court may act on those cases.

Article 9

An appeal may be brought before the General Court, within two months of notification of the decision appealed against, against final decisions of the Civil Service Tribunal and decisions of that Tribunal disposing of the substantive issues in part only or disposing of a procedural issue concerning a plea of lack of jurisdiction or inadmissibility.

Such an appeal may be brought by any party which has been unsuccessful, in whole or in part, in its submissions. However, interveners other than the Member States and the institutions of the Union may bring such an appeal only where the decision of the Civil Service Tribunal directly affects them.

Article 10

1. Any person whose application to intervene has been dismissed by the Civil Service Tribunal may appeal to the General Court within two weeks of notification of the decision dismissing the application.

2. The parties to the proceedings may appeal to the General Court against any decision of the Civil Service Tribunal made pursuant to Article 278 or Article 279 or the fourth paragraph of Article 299 of the Treaty on the Functioning of the European Union or Article 157 or the third paragraph of Article 164 of the EAEC Treaty within two months of its notification.

3. The President of the General Court may, by way of summary procedure, which may, in so far as necessary, differ from some of the rules contained in this Annex and which shall be laid down in the rules of procedure of the General Court, adjudicate upon appeals brought in accordance with paragraphs 1 and 2.

Article 11
1. An appeal to the General Court shall be limited to points of law. It shall lie on the grounds of lack of jurisdiction of the Civil Service Tribunal, a breach of procedure before it which adversely affects the interests of the appellant, as well as the infringement of Union law by the Tribunal.
2. No appeal shall lie regarding only the amount of the costs or the party ordered to pay them.

Article 12
1. Without prejudice to Articles 278 and 279 of the Treaty on the Functioning of the European Union or Article 157 of the EAEC Treaty, an appeal before the General Court shall not have suspensory effect.
2. Where an appeal is brought against a decision of the Civil Service Tribunal, the procedure before the General Court shall consist of a written part and an oral part. In accordance with conditions laid down in the rules of procedure, the General Court, having heard the parties, may dispense with the oral procedure.

Article 13
1. If the appeal is well founded, the General Court shall quash the decision of the Civil Service Tribunal and itself give judgment in the matter. It shall refer the case back to the Civil Service Tribunal for judgment where the state of the proceedings does not permit a decision by the Court.
2. Where a case is referred back to the Civil Service Tribunal, the Tribunal shall be bound by the decision of the General Court on points of law.

Protocol (No 4) on the Statute of the European System of Central Banks and of the European Central Bank

The High Contracting Parties,
Desiring to lay down the Statute of the European System of Central Banks and of the European Central Bank provided for in the second paragraph of Article 129 of the Treaty on the Functioning of the European Union,
Have agreed upon the following provisions, which shall be annexed to the Treaty on European Union and to the Treaty on the Functioning of the European Union:

Chapter 1
The European System of Central Banks

Article 1 The European System of Central Banks
In accordance with Article 282(1) of the Treaty on the Functioning of the European Union, the European Central Bank (ECB) and the national central banks shall constitute the European System of Central Banks (ESCB). The ECB and the national central banks of those Member States whose currency is the euro shall constitute the Eurosystem.
The ESCB and the ECB shall perform their tasks and carry on their activities in accordance with the provisions of the Treaties and of this Statute.

Chapter II
Objectives and tasks of the ESCB

Article 2 Objectives

In accordance with Article 127(1) and Article 282(2) of the Treaty on the Functioning of the European Union, the primary objective of the ESCB shall be to maintain price stability. Without prejudice to the objective of price stability, it shall support the general economic policies in the Union with a view to contributing to the achievement of the objectives of the Union as laid down in Article 3 of the Treaty on European Union. The ESCB shall act in accordance with the principle of an open market economy with free competition, favouring an efficient allocation of resources, and in compliance with the principles set out in Article 119 of the Treaty on the Functioning of the European Union.

Article 3 Tasks

3.1. In accordance with Article 127(2) of the Treaty on the Functioning of the European Union, the basic tasks to be carried out through the ESCB shall be:
 – to define and implement the monetary policy of the Union;
 – to conduct foreign-exchange operations consistent with the provisions of Article 219 of that Treaty;
 – to hold and manage the official foreign reserves of the Member States;
 – to promote the smooth operation of payment systems.

3.2. In accordance with Article 127(3) of the Treaty on the Functioning of the European Union, the third indent of Article 3.1 shall be without prejudice to the holding and management by the governments of Member States of foreign-exchange working balances.

3.3. In accordance with Article 127(5) of the Treaty on the Functioning of the European Union, the ESCB shall contribute to the smooth conduct of policies pursued by the competent authorities relating to the prudential supervision of credit institutions and the stability of the financial system.

Article 4 Advisory functions

In accordance with Article 127(4) of the Treaty on the Functioning of the European Union:
 (a) the ECB shall be consulted:
  – on any proposed Union act in its fields of competence;
  – by national authorities regarding any draft legislative provision in its fields of competence, but within the limits and under the conditions set out by the Council in accordance with the procedure laid down in Article 41;
 (b) the ECB may submit opinions to the Union institutions, bodies, offices or agencies or to national authorities on matters in its fields of competence.

Article 5 Collection of statistical information

5.1. In order to undertake the tasks of the ESCB, the ECB, assisted by the national central banks, shall collect the necessary statistical information either from the competent national authorities or directly from economic agents. For these purposes it shall cooperate with the Union institutions, bodies, offices or agencies and with the competent authorities of the Member States or third countries and with international organisations.

5.2. The national central banks shall carry out, to the extent possible, the tasks described in Article 5.1.

5.3. The ECB shall contribute to the harmonisation, where necessary, of the rules and practices governing the collection, compilation and distribution of statistics in the areas within its fields of competence.

5.4. The Council, in accordance with the procedure laid down in Article 41, shall define the natural and legal persons subject to reporting requirements, the confidentiality regime and the appropriate provisions for enforcement.

Article 6 International cooperation

6.1. In the field of international cooperation involving the tasks entrusted to the ESCB, the ECB shall decide how the ESCB shall be represented.

6.2. The ECB and, subject to its approval, the national central banks may participate in international monetary institutions.

6.3. Articles 6.1 and 6.2 shall be without prejudice to Article 138 of the Treaty on the Functioning of the European Union.

Chapter III
Organisation of the ESCB

Article 7 Independence

In accordance with Article 130 of the Treaty on the Functioning of the European Union, when exercising the powers and carrying out the tasks and duties conferred upon them by the Treaties and this Statute, neither the ECB, nor a national central bank, nor any member of their decision-making bodies shall seek or take instructions from Union institutions, bodies, offices or agencies, from any government of a Member State or from any other body. The Union institutions, bodies, offices or agencies and the governments of the Member States undertake to respect this principle and not to seek to influence the members of the decision-making bodies of the ECB or of the national central banks in the performance of their tasks.

Article 8 General principle

The ESCB shall be governed by the decision-making bodies of the ECB.

Article 9 The European Central Bank

9.1. The ECB which, in accordance with Article 282(3) of the Treaty on the Functioning of the European Union, shall have legal personality, shall enjoy in each of the Member States the most extensive legal capacity accorded to legal persons under its law; it may, in particular, acquire or dispose of movable and immovable property and may be a party to legal proceedings.

9.2. The ECB shall ensure that the tasks conferred upon the ESCB under Article 127(2), (3) and (5) of the Treaty on the Functioning of the European Union are implemented either by its own activities pursuant to this Statute or through the national central banks pursuant to Articles 12.1 and 14.

9.3. In accordance with Article 129(1) of the Treaty on the Functioning of the European Union, the decision making bodies of the ECB shall be the Governing Council and the Executive Board.

Article 10 The Governing Council

10.1. In accordance with Article 283(1) of the Treaty on the Functioning of the European Union, the Governing Council shall comprise the members of the Executive Board of the ECB and the governors of the national central banks of the Member States whose currency is the euro.

10.2. Each member of the Governing Council shall have one vote. As from the date on which the number of members of the Governing Council exceeds 21, each member of the Executive Board shall have one vote and the number of governors with a voting right shall be 15. The latter voting rights shall be assigned and shall rotate as follows:

- as from the date on which the number of governors exceeds 15, until it reaches 22, the governors shall be allocated to two groups, according to a ranking of the size of the share of their national central bank's Member State in the aggregate gross domestic product at market prices and in the total aggregated balance sheet of the monetary financial institutions of the Member States whose currency is the euro. The shares in the aggregate gross domestic product at market prices and in the total aggregated balance sheet of the monetary financial institutions shall be assigned weights of 5/6 and 1/6, respectively. The first group shall be composed of five governors and the second group of the remaining governors. The frequency of voting rights of the governors allocated to the first group shall not be lower than the frequency of voting rights of those of the second group. Subject to the previous sentence, the first group shall be assigned four voting rights and the second group eleven voting rights,

- as from the date on which the number of governors reaches 22, the governors shall be allocated to three groups according to a ranking based on the above criteria. The first group shall be composed of five governors and shall be assigned four voting rights. The second group shall be composed of half of the total number of governors, with any fraction rounded up to the nearest integer, and shall be assigned eight voting rights. The third group shall be composed of the remaining governors and shall be assigned three voting rights,

- within each group, the governors shall have their voting rights for equal amounts of time,

- for the calculation of the shares in the aggregate gross domestic product at market prices Article 29.2 shall apply. The total aggregated balance sheet of the monetary financial institutions shall be calculated in accordance with the statistical framework applying in the Union at the time of the calculation,

- whenever the aggregate gross domestic product at market prices is adjusted in accordance with Article 29.3, or whenever the number of governors increases, the size and/or composition of the groups shall be adjusted in accordance with the above principles,

- the Governing Council, acting by a two-thirds majority of all its members, with and without a voting right, shall take all measures necessary for the implementation of the above principles and may decide to postpone the start of the rotation system until the date on which the number of governors exceeds 18.

The right to vote shall be exercised in person. By way of derogation from this rule, the Rules of Procedure referred to in Article 12.3 may lay down that members of the Governing Council may cast their vote by means of teleconferencing. These rules shall also provide that a member of the Governing Council who is prevented from attending meetings of the Governing Council for a prolonged period may appoint an alternate as a member of the Governing Council.

The provisions of the previous paragraphs are without prejudice to the voting rights of all members of the Governing Council, with and without a voting right, under Articles 10.3, 40.2 and 40.3.

Save as otherwise provided for in this Statute, the Governing Council shall act by a simple majority of the members having a voting right. In the event of a tie, the President shall have the casting vote.

In order for the Governing Council to vote, there shall be a quorum of two-thirds of the members having a voting right. If the quorum is not met, the President may convene an extraordinary meeting at which decisions may be taken without regard to the quorum.

10.3. For any decisions to be taken under Articles 28, 29, 30, 32 and 33, the votes in the Governing Council shall be weighted according to the national central banks' shares in the subscribed capital of the ECB. The weights of the votes of the members of the Executive Board shall be zero. A decision requiring a qualified majority shall be adopted if the votes cast in favour represent at least two thirds of the subscribed capital of the ECB and represent at least half of the shareholders. If a Governor is unable to be present, he may nominate an alternate to cast his weighted vote.

10.4. The proceedings of the meetings shall be confidential. The Governing Council may decide to make the outcome of its deliberations public.

10.5. The Governing Council shall meet at least 10 times a year.

Article 11 The Executive Board

11.1. In accordance with the first subparagraph of Article 283(2) of the Treaty on the Functioning of the European Union, the Executive Board shall comprise the President, the Vice-President and four other members.

The members shall perform their duties on a full-time basis. No member shall engage in any occupation, whether gainful or not, unless exemption is exceptionally granted by the Governing Council.

11.2. In accordance with the second subparagraph of Article 283(2) of the Treaty on the Functioning of the European Union, the President, the Vice-President and the other members of the Executive Board shall be appointed by the European Council, acting by a qualified majority, from among persons of recognised standing and professional experience in monetary or banking matters, on a recommendation from the Council after it has consulted the European Parliament and the Governing Council.

Their term of office shall be eight years and shall not be renewable.

Only nationals of Member States may be members of the Executive Board.

11.3. The terms and conditions of employment of the members of the Executive Board, in particular their salaries, pensions and other social security benefits shall be the subject of contracts with the ECB and shall be fixed by the Governing Council on a proposal from a Committee comprising three members appointed by the Governing Council and three members appointed by the Council. The members of the Executive Board shall not have the right to vote on matters referred to in this paragraph.

11.4. If a member of the Executive Board no longer fulfils the conditions required for the performance of his duties or if he has been guilty of serious misconduct, the Court of Justice may, on application by the Governing Council or the Executive Board, compulsorily retire him.

11.5. Each member of the Executive Board present in person shall have the right to vote and shall have, for that purpose, one vote. Save as otherwise provided, the Executive Board shall act by a simple majority of the votes cast. In the event of a tie, the President shall have the casting vote. The voting arrangements shall be specified in the Rules of Procedure referred to in Article 12.3.

11.6. The Executive Board shall be responsible for the current business of the ECB.

11.7. Any vacancy on the Executive Board shall be filled by the appointment of a new member in accordance with Article 11.2.

Article 12 Responsibilities of the decision-making bodies

12.1. The Governing Council shall adopt the guidelines and take the decisions necessary to ensure the performance of the tasks entrusted to the ESCB under these Treaties and this Statute. The Governing Council shall formulate the monetary policy of the Union including, as appropriate, decisions relating to intermediate monetary objectives, key interest rates and the supply of reserves in the ESCB, and shall establish the necessary guidelines for their implementation.

The Executive Board shall implement monetary policy in accordance with the guidelines and decisions laid down by the Governing Council. In doing so the Executive Board shall give the necessary instructions to national central banks. In addition the Executive Board may have certain powers delegated to it where the Governing Council so decides.

To the extent deemed possible and appropriate and without prejudice to the provisions of this Article, the ECB shall have recourse to the national central banks to carry out operations which form part of the tasks of the ESCB.

12.2. The Executive Board shall have responsibility for the preparation of meetings of the Governing Council.

12.3. The Governing Council shall adopt Rules of Procedure which determine the internal organisation of the ECB and its decision-making bodies.

12.4. The Governing Council shall exercise the advisory functions referred to in Article 4.

12.5. The Governing Council shall take the decisions referred to in Article 6.

Article 13 The President

13.1. The President or, in his absence, the Vice-President shall chair the Governing Council and the Executive Board of the ECB.

13.2. Without prejudice to Article 38, the President or his nominee shall represent the ECB externally.

Article 14 National central banks

14.1. In accordance with Article 131 of the Treaty on the Functioning of the European Union, each Member State shall ensure that its national legislation, including the statutes of its national central bank, is compatible with these Treaties and this Statute.

14.2. The statutes of the national central banks shall, in particular, provide that the term of office of a Governor of a national central bank shall be no less than five years.

A Governor may be relieved from office only if he no longer fulfils the conditions required for the performance of his duties or if he has been guilty of serious misconduct. A decision to this effect may be referred to the Court of Justice by the Governor concerned or the Governing Council on grounds of infringement of these Treaties or of any rule of law relating to their application. Such proceedings shall be instituted within two months of the publication of the decision or of its notification to the plaintiff or, in the absence thereof, of the day on which it came to the knowledge of the latter, as the case may be.

14.3. The national central banks are an integral part of the ESCB and shall act in accordance with the guidelines and instructions of the ECB. The Governing Council shall take the necessary steps to ensure compliance with the guidelines and instructions of the ECB, and shall require that any necessary information be given to it.

14.4. National central banks may perform functions other than those specified in this Statute unless the Governing Council finds, by a majority of two thirds of the votes cast, that these interfere with the objectives and tasks of the ESCB. Such functions shall be performed on the responsibility and liability of national central banks and shall not be regarded as being part of the functions of the ESCB.

Article 15 Reporting commitments

15.1. The ECB shall draw up and publish reports on the activities of the ESCB at least quarterly.

15.2. A consolidated financial statement of the ESCB shall be published each week.

15.3. In accordance with Article 284(3) of the Treaty on the Functioning of the European Union, the ECB shall address an annual report on the activities of the ESCB and on the monetary policy of both the previous and the current year to the European Parliament, the Council and the Commission, and also to the European Council.

15.4. The reports and statements referred to in this Article shall be made available to interested parties free of charge.

Article 16 Banknotes

In accordance with Article 128(1) of the Treaty on the Functioning of the European Union, the Governing Council shall have the exclusive right to authorise the issue of euro banknotes within the Union. The ECB and the national central banks may issue such notes. The banknotes issued by the ECB and the national central banks shall be the only such notes to have the status of legal tender within the Union.

The ECB shall respect as far as possible existing practices regarding the issue and design of banknotes.

Chapter IV
Monetary functions and operations of the ESCB

Article 17 Accounts with the ECB and the national central banks

In order to conduct their operations, the ECB and the national central banks may open accounts for credit institutions, public entities and other market participants and accept assets, including book entry securities, as collateral.

Article 18 Open market and credit operations

18.1. In order to achieve the objectives of the ESCB and to carry out its tasks, the ECB and the national central banks may:
- operate in the financial markets by buying and selling outright (spot and forward) or under repurchase agreement and by lending or borrowing claims and marketable instruments, whether in euro or other currencies, as well as precious metals;
- conduct credit operations with credit institutions and other market participants, with lending being based on adequate collateral.

18.2. The ECB shall establish general principles for open market and credit operations carried out by itself or the national central banks, including for the announcement of conditions under which they stand ready to enter into such transactions.

Article 19 Minimum reserves

19.1. Subject to Article 2, the ECB may require credit institutions established in Member States to hold minimum reserve on accounts with the ECB and national central banks in pursuance of monetary policy objectives. Regulations concerning the calculation and determination of the required minimum reserves may be established by the Governing Council. In cases of non-compliance the ECB shall be entitled to levy penalty interest and to impose other sanctions with comparable effect.

19.2. For the application of this Article, the Council shall, in accordance with the procedure laid down in Article 41, define the basis for minimum reserves and the maximum permissible ratios between those reserves and their basis, as well as the appropriate sanctions in cases of non-compliance.

Article 20 Other instruments of monetary control

The Governing Council may, by a majority of two thirds of the votes cast, decide upon the use of such other operational methods of monetary control as it sees fit, respecting Article 2.

The Council shall, in accordance with the procedure laid down in Article 41, define the scope of such methods if they impose obligations on third parties.

Article 21 Operations with public entities

21.1. In accordance with Article 123 of the Treaty on the Functioning of the European Union, overdrafts or any other type of credit facility with the ECB or with the national central banks in favour of Union institutions, bodies, offices or agencies, central governments, regional, local or other public authorities, other bodies governed by public law, or public undertakings of Member States shall be prohibited, as shall the purchase directly from them by the ECB or national central banks of debt instruments.

21.2. The ECB and national central banks may act as fiscal agents for the entities referred to in Article 21.1.

21.3. The provisions of this Article shall not apply to publicly owned credit institutions which, in the context of the supply of reserves by central banks, shall be given the same treatment by national central banks and the ECB as private credit institutions.

Article 22 Clearing and payment systems

The ECB and national central banks may provide facilities, and the ECB may make regulations, to ensure efficient and sound clearing and payment systems within the Union and with other countries.

Article 23 External operations

The ECB and national central banks may:
- establish relations with central banks and financial institutions in other countries and, where appropriate, with international organisations;
- acquire and sell spot and forward all types of foreign exchange assets and precious metals; the term 'foreign exchange asset' shall include securities and all other assets in the currency of any country or units of account and in whatever form held;
- hold and manage the assets referred to in this Article;
- conduct all types of banking transactions in relations with third countries and international organisations, including borrowing and lending operations.

Article 24 Other operations

In addition to operations arising from their tasks, the ECB and national central banks may enter into operations for their administrative purposes or for their staff.

Chapter V
Prudential supervision

Article 25 Prudential supervision

25.1. The ECB may offer advice to and be consulted by the Council, the Commission and the competent authorities of the Member States on the scope and implementation of Union legislation relating to the prudential supervision of credit institutions and to the stability of the financial system.

25.2. In accordance with any regulation of the Council under Article 127(6) of the Treaty on the Functioning of the European Union, the ECB may perform specific tasks concerning policies relating to the prudential supervision of credit institutions and other financial institutions with the exception of insurance undertakings.

Chapter VI
Financial provisions of the ESCB

Article 26 Financial accounts

26.1. The financial year of the ECB and national central banks shall begin on the first day of January and end on the last day of December.

26.2. The annual accounts of the ECB shall be drawn up by the Executive Board, in accordance with the principles established by the Governing Council. The accounts shall be approved by the Governing Council and shall thereafter be published.

26.3. For analytical and operational purposes, the Executive Board shall draw up a consolidated balance sheet of the ESCB, comprising those assets and liabilities of the national central banks that fall within the ESCB.

26.4. For the application of this Article, the Governing Council shall establish the necessary rules for standardising the accounting and reporting of operations undertaken by the national central banks.

Article 27 Auditing

27.1. The accounts of the ECB and national central banks shall be audited by independent external auditors recommended by the Governing Council and approved by the Council. The auditors shall have full power to examine all books and accounts of the ECB and national central banks and obtain full information about their transactions.

27.2. The provisions of Article 287 of the Treaty on the Functioning of the European Union shall only apply to an examination of the operational efficiency of the management of the ECB.

Article 28 Capital of the ECB

28.1. The capital of the ECB shall be euro 5 000 million. The capital may be increased by such amounts as may be decided by the Governing Council acting by the qualified majority provided for in Article 10.3, within the limits and under the conditions set by the Council under the procedure laid down in Article 41.

28.2. The national central banks shall be the sole subscribers to and holders of the capital of the ECB. The subscription of capital shall be according to the key established in accordance with Article 29.

28.3. The Governing Council, acting by the qualified majority provided for in Article 10.3, shall determine the extent to which and the form in which the capital shall be paid up.

28.4. Subject to Article 28.5, the shares of the national central banks in the subscribed capital of the ECB may not be transferred, pledged or attached.

28.5. If the key referred to in Article 29 is adjusted, the national central banks shall transfer among themselves capital shares to the extent necessary to ensure that the distribution of capital shares corresponds to the adjusted key. The Governing Council shall determine the terms and conditions of such transfers.

Article 29 Key for capital subscription

29.1. The key for subscription of the ECB's capital, fixed for the first time in 1998 when the ESCB was established, shall be determined by assigning to each national central bank a weighting in this key equal to the sum of:
- 50 % of the share of its respective Member State in the population of the Union in the penultimate year preceding the establishment of the ESCB;
- 50 % of the share of its respective Member State in the gross domestic product at market prices of the Union as recorded in the last five years preceding the penultimate year before the establishment of the ESCB.

The percentages shall be rounded up or down to the nearest multiple of 0,0001 percentage points.

29.2. The statistical data to be used for the application of this Article shall be provided by the Commission in accordance with the rules adopted by the Council under the procedure provided for in Article 41.

29.3. The weightings assigned to the national central banks shall be adjusted every five years after the establishment of the ESCB by analogy with the provisions laid down in Article 29.1. The adjusted key shall apply with effect from the first day of the following year.

29.4. The Governing Council shall take all other measures necessary for the application of this Article.

Article 30 Transfer of foreign reserve assets to the ECB

30.1. Without prejudice to Article 28, the ECB shall be provided by the national central banks with foreign reserve assets, other than Member States' currencies, euro, IMF reserve positions and SDRs, up to an amount equivalent to euro 50 000 million. The Governing Council shall decide upon the proportion to be called up by the ECB following its establishment and the amounts called up at later dates. The ECB shall have the full right to hold and manage the foreign reserves that are transferred to it and to use them for the purposes set out in this Statute.

30.2. The contributions of each national central bank shall be fixed in proportion to its share in the subscribed capital of the ECB.

30.3. Each national central bank shall be credited by the ECB with a claim equivalent to its contribution. The Governing Council shall determine the denomination and remuneration of such claims.

30.4. Further calls of foreign reserve assets beyond the limit set in Article 30.1 may be effected by the ECB, in accordance with Article 30.2, within the limits and under the conditions set by the Council in accordance with the procedure laid down in Article 41.

30.5. The ECB may hold and manage IMF reserve positions and SDRs and provide for the pooling of such assets.

30.6. The Governing Council shall take all other measures necessary for the application of this Article.

Article 31 Foreign reserve assets held by national central banks

31.1. The national central banks shall be allowed to perform transactions in fulfilment of their obligations towards international organisations in accordance with Article 23.

31.2. All other operations in foreign reserve assets remaining with the national central banks after the transfers referred to in Article 30, and Member States' transactions with their foreign exchange working balances shall, above a certain limit to be established within the framework of Article 31.3, be subject to approval by the ECB in order to ensure consistency with the exchange rate and monetary policies of the Union.

31.3. The Governing Council shall issue guidelines with a view to facilitating such operations.

Article 32 Allocation of monetary income of national central banks

32.1. The income accruing to the national central banks in the performance of the ESCB's monetary policy function (hereinafter referred to as 'monetary income') shall be allocated at the end of each financial year in accordance with the provisions of this Article.

32.2. The amount of each national central bank's monetary income shall be equal to its annual income derived from its assets held against notes in circulation and deposit liabilities to credit institutions. These assets shall be earmarked by national central banks in accordance with guidelines to be established by the Governing Council.

32.3. If, after the introduction of the euro, the balance sheet structures of the national central banks do not, in the judgment of the Governing Council, permit the application of Article 32.2. the Governing Council, acting by a qualified majority, may decide that, by way of derogation from Article 32.2, monetary income shall be measured according to an alternative method for a period of not more than five years.

32.4. The amount of each national central bank's monetary income shall be reduced by an amount equivalent to any interest paid by that central bank on its deposit liabilities to credit institutions in accordance with Article 19.

The Governing Council may decide that national central banks shall be indemnified against costs incurred in connection with the issue of banknotes or in exceptional circumstances for specific losses arising from monetary policy operations undertaken for the ESCB. Indemnification shall be in a form deemed appropriate in the judgment of the Governing Council; these amounts may be offset against the national central banks' monetary income.

32.5. The sum of the national central banks' monetary income shall be allocated to the national central banks in proportion to their paid up shares in the capital of the ECB, subject to any decision taken by the Governing Council pursuant to Article 33.2.

32.6. The clearing and settlement of the balances arising from the allocation of monetary income shall be carried out by the ECB in accordance with guidelines established by the Governing Council.

32.7. The Governing Council shall take all other measures necessary for the application of this Article.

Article 33 Allocation of net profits and losses of the ECB

33.1. The net profit of the ECB shall be transferred in the following order:

(a) an amount to be determined by the Governing Council, which may not exceed 20 % of the net profit, shall be transferred to the general reserve fund subject to a limit equal to 100 % of the capital;

(b) the remaining net profit shall be distributed to the shareholders of the ECB in proportion to their paid-up shares.

33.2. In the event of a loss incurred by the ECB, the shortfall may be offset against the general reserve fund of the ECB and, if necessary, following a decision by the Governing Council, against the monetary income of the relevant financial year in proportion and up to the amounts allocated to the national central banks in accordance with Article 32.5.

Chapter VII
General provisions

Article 34 Legal acts

34.1. In accordance with Article 132 of the Treaty on the Functioning of the European Union, the ECB shall:

– make regulations to the extent necessary to implement the tasks defined in Article 3.1, first indent, Articles 19.1, 22 or 25.2 and in cases which shall be laid down in the acts of the Council referred to in Article 41;

– take decisions necessary for carrying out the tasks entrusted to the ESCB under these Treaties and this Statute;

– make recommendations and deliver opinions.

34.2. The ECB may decide to publish its decisions, recommendations and opinions.

34.3. Within the limits and under the conditions adopted by the Council under the procedure laid down in Article 41, the ECB shall be entitled to impose fines or periodic penalty payments on undertakings for failure to comply with obligations under its regulations and decisions.

Article 35 Judicial control and related matters

35.1. The acts or omissions of the ECB shall be open to review or interpretation by the Court of Justice of the European Union in the cases and under the conditions laid down in the Treaty on the Functioning of the European Union. The ECB may institute proceedings in the cases and under the conditions laid down in the Treaties.

35.2. Disputes between the ECB, on the one hand, and its creditors, debtors or any other person, on the other, shall be decided by the competent national courts, save where jurisdiction has been conferred upon the Court of Justice of the European Union.

35.3. The ECB shall be subject to the liability regime provided for in Article 340 of the Treaty on the Functioning of the European Union. The national central banks shall be liable according to their respective national laws.

35.4. The Court of Justice of the European Union shall have jurisdiction to give judgment pursuant to any arbitration clause contained in a contract concluded by or on behalf of the ECB, whether that contract be governed by public or private law.

35.5. A decision of the ECB to bring an action before the Court of Justice of the European Union shall be taken by the Governing Council.

35.6. The Court of Justice of the European Union shall have jurisdiction in disputes concerning the fulfilment by a national central bank of obligations under the Treaties and this Statute. If the ECB considers that a national central bank has failed to fulfil an obligation under the Treaties and this Statute, it shall deliver a reasoned opinion on the matter after giving the national central bank concerned the opportunity to submit its observations. If the national central bank concerned does not comply with the opinion within the period laid down by the ECB, the latter may bring the matter before the Court of Justice of the European Union.

Article 36 Staff

36.1. The Governing Council, on a proposal from the Executive Board, shall lay down the conditions of employment of the staff of the ECB.

36.2. The Court of Justice of the European Union shall have jurisdiction in any dispute between the ECB and its servants within the limits and under the conditions laid down in the conditions of employment.

Article 37 (ex Article 38) Professional secrecy

37.1. Members of the governing bodies and the staff of the ECB and the national central banks shall be required, even after their duties have ceased, not to disclose information of the kind covered by the obligation of professional secrecy.

37.2. Persons having access to data covered by Union legislation imposing an obligation of secrecy shall be subject to such legislation.

Article 38 (ex Article 39) Signatories
The ECB shall be legally committed to third parties by the President or by two members of the Executive Board or by the signatures of two members of the staff of the ECB who have been duly authorised by the President to sign on behalf of the ECB.

Article 39 (ex Article 40) Privileges and immunities
The ECB shall enjoy in the territories of the Member States such privileges and immunities as are necessary for the performance of its tasks, under the conditions laid down in the Protocol on the privileges and immunities of the European Union.

Chapter VIII
Amendment of the Statute and complementary legislation

Article 40 (ex Article 41) Simplified amendment procedure
40.1. In accordance with Article 129(3) of the Treaty on the Functioning of the European Union, Articles 5.1, 5.2, 5.3, 17, 18, 19.1, 22, 23, 24, 26, 32.2, 32.3, 32.4, 32.6, 33.1(a) and 36 of this Statute may be amended by the European Parliament and the Council, acting in accordance with the ordinary legislative procedure either on a recommendation from the ECB and after consulting the Commission, or on a proposal from the Commission and after consulting the ECB.
40.2. Article 10.2 may be amended by a decision of the European Council, acting unanimously, either on a recommendation from the European Central Bank and after consulting the European Parliament and the Commission, or on a recommendation from the Commission and after consulting the European Parliament and the European Central Bank. These amendments shall not enter into force until they are approved by the Member States in accordance with their respective constitutional requirements.
40.3. A recommendation made by the ECB under this Article shall require a unanimous decision by the Governing Council.

Article 41 (ex Article 42) Complementary legislation
In accordance with Article 129(4) of the Treaty on the Functioning of the European Union, the Council, either on a proposal from the Commission and after consulting the European Parliament and the ECB or on a recommendation from the ECB and after consulting the European Parliament and the Commission, shall adopt the provisions referred to in Articles 4, 5.4, 19.2, 20, 28.1, 29.2, 30.4 and 34.3 of this Statute.

Chapter IX
Transitional and other provisions for the ESCB

Article 42 (ex Article 43) General provisions
42.1. A derogation as referred to in Article 139 of the Treaty on the Functioning of the European Union shall entail that the following Articles of this Statute shall not confer any rights or impose any obligations on the Member State concerned: 3, 6, 9.2, 12.1, 14.3, 16, 18, 19, 20, 22, 23, 26.2, 27, 30, 31, 32, 33, 34, and 49.

42.2. The central banks of Member States with a derogation as specified in Article 139(1) of the Treaty on the Functioning of the European Union shall retain their powers in the field of monetary policy according to national law.

42.3. In accordance with Article 139 of the Treaty on the Functioning of the European Union, 'Member States' shall be read as 'Member States whose currency is the euro' in the following Articles of this Statute: 3, 11.2 and 19.

42.4. 'National central banks' shall be read as 'central banks of Member States whose currency is the euro' in the following Articles of this Statute: 9.2, 10.2, 10.3, 12.1, 16, 17, 18, 22, 23, 27, 30, 31, 32, 33.2 and 49.

42.5. 'Shareholders' shall be read as 'central banks of Member States whose currency is the euro' in Articles 10.3 and 33.1.

42.6. 'Subscribed capital of the ECB' shall be read as 'capital of the ECB subscribed by the central banks of Member States whose currency is the euro' in Articles 10.3 and 30.2.

Article 43 (ex Article 44) Transitional tasks of the ECB
The ECB shall take over the former tasks of the EMI referred to in Article 141(2) of the Treaty on the Functioning of the European Union which, because of the derogations of one or more Member States, still have to be performed after the introduction of the euro.

The ECB shall give advice in the preparations for the abrogation of the derogations specified in Article 140 of the Treaty on the Functioning of the European Union.

Article 44 (ex Article 45) The General Council of the ECB
44.1. Without prejudice to Article 129(1) of the Treaty on the Functioning of the European Union, the General Council shall be constituted as a third decision-making body of the ECB.

44.2. The General Council shall comprise the President and Vice-President of the ECB and the Governors of the national central banks. The other members of the Executive Board may participate, without having the right to vote, in meetings of the General Council.

44.3. The responsibilities of the General Council are listed in full in Article 46 of this Statute.

Article 45 (ex Article 46) Rules of Procedure of the General Council
45.1. The President or, in his absence, the Vice-President of the ECB shall chair the General Council of the ECB.

45.2. The President of the Council and a Member of the Commission may participate, without having the right to vote, in meetings of the General Council.

45.3. The President shall prepare the meetings of the General Council.

45.4. By way of derogation from Article 12.3, the General Council shall adopt its Rules of Procedure.

45.5. The Secretariat of the General Council shall be provided by the ECB.

Article 46 (ex Article 47) Responsibilities of the General Council

46.1. The General Council shall:
- perform the tasks referred to in Article 43;
- contribute to the advisory functions referred to in Articles 4 and 25.1.

46.2. The General Council shall contribute to:
- the collection of statistical information as referred to in Article 5;
- the reporting activities of the ECB as referred to in Article 15;
- the establishment of the necessary rules for the application of Article 26 as referred to in Article 26.4;
- the taking of all other measures necessary for the application of Article 29 as referred to in Article 29.4;
- the laying down of the conditions of employment of the staff of the ECB as referred to in Article 36.

46.3. The General Council shall contribute to the necessary preparations for irrevocably fixing the exchange rates of the currencies of Member States with a derogation against the euro as referred to in Article 140(3) of the Treaty on the Functioning of the European Union.

46.4. The General Council shall be informed by the President of the ECB of decisions of the Governing Council.

Article 47 (ex Article 48) Transitional provisions for the capital of the ECB

In accordance with Article 29.1, each national central bank shall be assigned a weighting in the key for subscription of the ECB's capital. By way of derogation from Article 28.3, central banks of Member States with a derogation shall not pay up their subscribed capital unless the General Council, acting by a majority representing at least two thirds of the subscribed capital of the ECB and at least half of the shareholders, decides that a minimal percentage has to be paid up as a contribution to the operational costs of the ECB.

Article 48 (ex Article 49) Deferred payment of capital, reserves and provisions of the ECB

48.1. The central bank of a Member State whose derogation has been abrogated shall pay up its subscribed share of the capital of the ECB to the same extent as the central banks of other Member States whose currency is the euro, and shall transfer to the ECB foreign reserve assets in accordance with Article 30.1. The sum to be transferred shall be determined by multiplying the euro value at current exchange rates of the foreign reserve assets which have already been transferred to the ECB in accordance with Article 30.1, by the ratio between the number of shares subscribed by the national central bank concerned and the number of shares already paid up by the other national central banks.

48.2. In addition to the payment to be made in accordance with Article 48.1, the central bank concerned shall contribute to the reserves of the ECB, to those provisions equivalent to reserves, and to the amount still to be appropriated to the reserves and provisions corresponding to the balance of the profit and loss account as at 31 December of the year prior to the abrogation of the derogation.

The sum to be contributed shall be determined by multiplying the amount of the reserves, as defined above and as stated in the approved balance sheet of the ECB, by the ratio between the number of shares subscribed by the central bank concerned and the number of shares already paid up by the other central banks.

48.3. Upon one or more countries becoming Member States and their respective national central banks becoming part of the ESCB, the subscribed capital of the ECB and the limit on the amount of foreign reserve assets that may be transferred to the ECB shall be automatically increased. The increase shall be determined by multiplying the respective amounts then prevailing by the ratio, within the expanded capital key, between the weighting of the entering national central banks concerned and the weighting of the national central banks already members of the ESCB. Each national central bank's weighting in the capital key shall be calculated by analogy with Article 29.1 and in compliance with Article 29.2. The reference periods to be used for the statistical data shall be identical to those applied for the latest quinquennial adjustment of the weightings under Article 29.3.

Article 49 (ex Article 52) Exchange of banknotes in the currencies of the Member States

Following the irrevocable fixing of exchange rates in accordance with Article 140 of the Treaty on the Functioning of the European Union, the Governing Council shall take the necessary measures to ensure that banknotes denominated in currencies with irrevocably fixed exchange rates are exchanged by the national central banks at their respective par values.

Article 50 (ex Article 53) Applicability of the transitional provisions

If and as long as there are Member States with a derogation, Articles 42 to 47 shall be applicable.

Protocol (No 5)
on the Statute of the European Investment Bank

The High Contracting Parties,

Desiring to lay down the Statute of the European Investment Bank provided for in Article 308 of the Treaty on the Functioning of the European Union,

Have agreed upon the following provisions, which shall be annexed to the Treaty on European Union and to the Treaty on the Functioning of the European Union:

Article 1
The European Investment Bank established by Article 308 of the Treaty on the Functioning of the European Union (hereinafter called the 'Bank') is hereby constituted; it shall perform its functions and carry on its activities in accordance with the provisions of the Treaties and of this Statute.

Article 2
The task of the Bank shall be that defined in Article 309 of the Treaty on the Functioning of the European Union.

Article 3
In accordance with Article 308 of the Treaty on the Functioning of the European Union, the Bank's members shall be the Member States.

Article 4

1. The capital of the Bank shall be EUR 233 247 390 000, subscribed by the Member States as follows:

Germany	37 578 019 000
France	37 578 019 000
Italy	37 578 019 000
United Kingdom	37 578 019 000
Spain	22 546 811 500
Belgium	10 416 365 500
Netherlands	10 416 365 500
Sweden	6 910 226 000
Denmark	5 274 105 000
Austria	5 170 732 500
Poland	4 810 160 500
Finland	2 970 783 000
Greece	2 825 416 500
Portugal	1 820 820 000
Czech Republic	1 774 990 500
Hungary	1 679 222 000
Ireland	1 318 525 000
Romania	1 217 626 000
Croatia	854 400 000
Slovakia	604 206 500
Slovenia	560 951 500
Bulgaria	410 217 500
Lithuania	351 981 000
Luxembourg	263 707 000
Cyprus	258 583 500
Latvia	214 805 000
Estonia	165 882 000
Malta	98 429 500

The Member States shall be liable only up to the amount of their share of the capital subscribed and not paid up.

2. The admission of a new member shall entail an increase in the subscribed capital corresponding to the capital brought in by the new member.

3. The Board of Governors may, acting unanimously, decide to increase the subscribed capital.

4. The share of a member in the subscribed capital may not be transferred, pledged or attached.

Article 5

1. The subscribed capital shall be paid in by Member States to the extent of 5 % on average of the amounts laid down in Article 4(1).

2. In the event of an increase in the subscribed capital, the Board of Governors, acting unanimously, shall fix the percentage to be paid up and the arrangements for payment. Cash payments shall be made exclusively in euro.

3. The Board of Directors may require payment of the balance of the subscribed capital, to such extent as may be required for the Bank to meet its obligations.

Each Member State shall make this payment in proportion to its share of the subscribed capital.

Article 6 (ex Article 8)

The Bank shall be directed and managed by a Board of Governors, a Board of Directors and a Management Committee.

Article 7 (ex Article 9)

1. The Board of Governors shall consist of the ministers designated by the Member States.

2. The Board of Governors shall lay down general directives for the credit policy of the Bank, in accordance with the Union's objectives. The Board of Governors shall ensure that these directives are implemented.

3. The Board of Governors shall in addition:

    (a) decide whether to increase the subscribed capital in accordance with Article 4(3) and Article 5(2);

    (b) for the purposes of Article 9(1), determine the principles applicable to financing operations undertaken within the framework of the Bank's task;

    (c) exercise the powers provided in Articles 9 and 11 in respect of the appointment and the compulsory retirement of the members of the Board of Directors and of the Management Committee, and those powers provided in the second subparagraph of Article 11(1);

    (d) take decisions in respect of the granting of finance for investment operations to be carried out, in whole or in part, outside the territories of the Member States in accordance with Article 16(1);

    (e) approve the annual report of the Board of Directors;

    (f) approve the annual balance sheet and profit and loss account;

    (g) exercise the other powers and functions conferred by this Statute;

    (h) approve the rules of procedure of the Bank.

4. Within the framework of the Treaty and this Statute, the Board of Governors shall be competent to take, acting unanimously, any decisions concerning the suspension of the operations of the Bank and, should the event arise, its liquidation.

Article 8 (ex Article 10)

Save as otherwise provided in this Statute, decisions of the Board of Governors shall be taken by a majority of its members. This majority must represent at least 50 % of the subscribed capital.

A qualified majority shall require eighteen votes in favour and 68 % of the subscribed capital.

Abstentions by members present in person or represented shall not prevent the adoption of decisions requiring unanimity.

Article 9 (ex Article 11)

1. The Board of Directors shall take decisions in respect of granting finance, in particular in the form of loans and guarantees, and raising loans; it shall fix the interest rates on loans granted and the commission and other charges. It may, on the basis of a decision taken by a qualified majority, delegate some of its functions to the Management Committee. It shall determine the terms and conditions for such delegation and shall supervise its execution.

The Board of Directors shall see that the Bank is properly run; it shall ensure that the Bank is managed in accordance with the provisions of the Treaties and of this Statute and with the general directives laid down by the Board of Governors.

At the end of the financial year the Board of Directors shall submit a report to the Board of Governors and shall publish it when approved.

2. The Board of Directors shall consist of twenty-nine directors and nineteen alternate directors.

The directors shall be appointed by the Board of Governors for five years, one nominated by each Member State, and one nominated by the Commission.

The alternate directors shall be appointed by the Board of Governors for five years as shown below:

- two alternates nominated by the Federal Republic of Germany,
- two alternates nominated by the French Republic,
- two alternates nominated by the Italian Republic,
- two alternates nominated by the United Kingdom of Great Britain and Northern Ireland,
- one alternate nominated by common accord of the Kingdom of Spain and the Portuguese Republic,
- one alternate nominated by common accord of the Kingdom of Belgium, the Grand Duchy of Luxembourg and the Kingdom of the Netherlands,
- two alternates nominated by common accord of the Kingdom of Denmark, the Hellenic Republic, Ireland and Romania,
- two alternates nominated by common accord of the Republic of Estonia, the Republic of Latvia, the Republic of Lithuania, the Republic of Austria, the Republic of Finland and the Kingdom of Sweden,
- four alternates nominated by common accord of the Republic of Bulgaria, the Czech Republic, the Republic of Croatia, the Republic of Cyprus, the Republic of Hungary, the Republic of Malta, the Republic of Poland, the Republic of Slovenia and the Slovak Republic,
- one alternate nominated by the Commission.

The Board of Directors shall co-opt six non-voting experts: three as members and three as alternates.

The appointments of the directors and the alternates shall be renewable.

The Rules of Procedure shall lay down arrangements for participating in the meetings of the Board of Directors and the provisions applicable to alternates and co-opted experts.

The President of the Management Committee or, in his absence, one of the Vice-Presidents, shall preside over meetings of the Board of Directors but shall not vote.

Members of the Board of Directors shall be chosen from persons whose independence and competence are beyond doubt; they shall be responsible only to the Bank.

3. A director may be compulsorily retired by the Board of Governors only if he no longer fulfils the conditions required for the performance of his duties; the Board must act by a qualified majority.

If the annual report is not approved, the Board of Directors shall resign.

4. Any vacancy arising as a result of death, voluntary resignation, compulsory retirement or collective resignation shall be filled in accordance with paragraph 2. A member shall be replaced for the remainder of his term of office, save where the entire Board of Directors is being replaced.

5. The Board of Governors shall determine the remuneration of members of the Board of Directors. The Board of Governors shall lay down what activities are incompatible with the duties of a director or an alternate.

Article 10 (ex Article 12)

1. Each director shall have one vote on the Board of Directors. He may delegate his vote in all cases, according to procedures to be laid down in the Rules of Procedure of the Bank.

2. Save as otherwise provided in this Statute, decisions of the Board of Directors shall be taken by at least one third of the members entitled to vote representing at least fifty per cent of the subscribed capital. A qualified majority shall require eighteen votes in favour and sixty-eight per cent of the subscribed capital. The rules of procedure of the Bank shall lay down the quorum required for the decisions of the Board of Directors to be valid.

Article 11 (ex Article 13)

1. The Management Committee shall consist of a President and eight Vice-Presidents appointed for a period of six years by the Board of Governors on a proposal from the Board of Directors.

Their appointments shall be renewable. The Board of Governors, acting unanimously, may vary the number of members on the Management Committee.

2. On a proposal from the Board of Directors adopted by a qualified majority, the Board of Governors may, acting in its turn by a qualified majority, compulsorily retire a member of the Management Committee.

3. The Management Committee shall be responsible for the current business of the Bank, under the authority of the President and the supervision of the Board of Directors.

It shall prepare the decisions of the Board of Directors, in particular decisions on the raising of loans and the granting of finance, in particular in the form of loans and guarantees; it shall ensure that these decisions are implemented.

4. The Management Committee shall act by a majority when delivering opinions on proposals for raising loans or granting of finance, in particular in the form of loans and guarantees.

5. The Board of Governors shall determine the remuneration of members of the Management Committee and shall lay down what activities are incompatible with their duties.

6. The President or, if he is prevented, a Vice-President shall represent the Bank in judicial and other matters.

7. The staff of the Bank shall be under the authority of the President. They shall be engaged and discharged by him. In the selection of staff, account shall be taken not only of personal ability and qualifications but also of an equitable representation of nationals of Member States. The Rules of Procedure shall determine which organ is competent to adopt the provisions applicable to staff.

8. The Management Committee and the staff of the Bank shall be responsible only to the Bank and shall be completely independent in the performance of their duties.

Article 12 (ex Article 14)

1. A Committee consisting of six members, appointed on the grounds of their competence by the Board of Governors, shall verify that the activities of the Bank conform to best banking practice and shall be responsible for the auditing of its accounts.

2. The Committee referred to in paragraph 1 shall annually ascertain that the operations of the Bank have been conducted and its books kept in a proper manner. To this end, it shall verify that the Bank's operations have been carried out in compliance with the formalities and procedures laid down by this Statute and the Rules of Procedure.

3. The Committee referred to in paragraph 1 shall confirm that the financial statements, as well as any other financial information contained in the annual accounts drawn up by the Board of Directors, give a true and fair view of the financial position of the Bank in respect of its assets and liabilities, and of the results of its operations and its cash flows for the financial year under review.

4. The Rules of Procedure shall specify the qualifications required of the members of the Committee and lay down the terms and conditions for the Committee's activity.

Article 13 (ex Article 15)

The Bank shall deal with each Member State through the authority designated by that State. In the conduct of financial operations the Bank shall have recourse to the national central bank of the Member State concerned or to other financial institutions approved by that State.

Article 14 (ex Article 16)

1. The Bank shall cooperate with all international organisations active in fields similar to its own.

2. The Bank shall seek to establish all appropriate contacts in the interests of cooperation with banking and financial institutions in the countries to which its operations extend.

Article 15 (ex Article 17)

At the request of a Member State or of the Commission, or on its own initiative, the Board of Governors shall, in accordance with the same provisions as governed their adoption, interpret or supplement the directives laid down by it under Article 7 of this Statute.

Article 16 (ex Article 18)

1. Within the framework of the task set out in Article 309 of the Treaty on the Functioning of the European Union, the Bank shall grant finance, in particular in the form of loans and guarantees to its members or to private or public undertakings for investments to be carried out in the territories of Member States, to the extent that funds are not available from other sources on reasonable terms.

However, by decision of the Board of Governors, acting by a qualified majority on a proposal from the Board of Directors, the Bank may grant financing for investment to be carried out, in whole or in part, outside the territories of Member States.

2. As far as possible, loans shall be granted only on condition that other sources of finance are also used.

3. When granting a loan to an undertaking or to a body other than a Member State, the Bank shall make the loan conditional either on a guarantee from the Member State in whose territory the investment will be carried out or on other adequate guarantees, or on the financial strength of the debtor.

Furthermore, in accordance with the principles established by the Board of Governors pursuant to Article 7(3)(b), and where the implementation of projects provided for in Article 309 of the Treaty on the Functioning of the European Union so requires, the Board of Directors shall, acting by a qualified majority, lay down the terms and conditions of any financing operation presenting a specific risk profile and thus considered to be a special activity.

4. The Bank may guarantee loans contracted by public or private undertakings or other bodies for the purpose of carrying out projects provided for in Article 309 of the Treaty on the Functioning of the European Union.

5. The aggregate amount outstanding at any time of loans and guarantees granted by the Bank shall not exceed 250 % of its subscribed capital, reserves, non-allocated provisions and profit and loss account surplus. The latter aggregate amount shall be reduced by an amount equal to the amount subscribed (whether or not paid in) for any equity participation of the Bank.

The amount of the Bank's disbursed equity participations shall not exceed at any time an amount corresponding to the total of its paid-in subscribed capital, reserves, non-allocated provisions and profit and loss account surplus.

By way of exception, the special activities of the Bank, as decided by the Board of Governors and the Board of Directors in accordance with paragraph 3, will have a specific allocation of reserve.

This paragraph shall also apply to the consolidated accounts of the Bank.

6. The Bank shall protect itself against exchange risks by including in contracts for loans and guarantees such clauses as it considers appropriate.

Article 17 (ex Article 19)
1. Interest rates on loans to be granted by the Bank and commission and other charges shall be adjusted to conditions prevailing on the capital market and shall be calculated in such a way that the income therefrom shall enable the Bank to meet its obligations, to cover its expenses and risks and to build up a reserve fund as provided for in Article 22.
2. The Bank shall not grant any reduction in interest rates. Where a reduction in the interest rate appears desirable in view of the nature of the investment to be financed, the Member State concerned or some other agency may grant aid towards the payment of interest to the extent that this is compatible with Article 107 of the Treaty on the Functioning of the European Union.

Article 18 (ex Article 20)
In its financing operations, the Bank shall observe the following principles:
1. It shall ensure that its funds are employed as rationally as possible in the interests of the Union. It may grant loans or guarantees only:
 (a) where, in the case of investments by undertakings in the production sector, interest and amortisation payments are covered out of operating profits or, in the case of other investments, either by a commitment entered into by the State in which the investment is made or by some other means; and
 (b) where the execution of the investment contributes to an increase in economic productivity in general and promotes the attainment of the internal market.
2. It shall neither acquire any interest in an undertaking nor assume any responsibility in its management unless this is required to safeguard the rights of the Bank in ensuring recovery of funds lent.
However, in accordance with the principles determined by the Board of Governors pursuant to Article 7(3)(b), and where the implementation of operations provided for in Article 309 of the Treaty on the Functioning of the European Union so requires, the Board of Directors shall, acting by a qualified majority, lay down the terms and conditions for taking an equity participation in a commercial undertaking, normally as a complement to a loan or a guarantee, in so far as this is required to finance an investment or programme.
3. It may dispose of its claims on the capital market and may, to this end, require its debtors to issue bonds or other securities.
4. Neither the Bank nor the Member States shall impose conditions requiring funds lent by the Bank to be spent within a specified Member State.
5. The Bank may make its loans conditional on international invitations to tender being arranged.
6. The Bank shall not finance, in whole or in part, any investment opposed by the Member State in whose territory it is to be carried out.

7. As a complement to its lending activity, the Bank may provide technical assistance services in accordance with the terms and conditions laid down by the Board of Governors, acting by a qualified majority, and in compliance with this Statute.

Article 19 (ex Article 21)
1. Any undertaking or public or private entity may apply directly to the Bank for financing. Applications to the Bank may also be made either through the Commission or through the Member State on whose territory the investment will be carried out.
2. Applications made through the Commission shall be submitted for an opinion to the Member State in whose territory the investment will be carried out. Applications made through a Member State shall be submitted to the Commission for an opinion. Applications made direct by an under taking shall be submitted to the Member State concerned and to the Commission.
The Member State concerned and the Commission shall deliver their opinions within two months. If no reply is received within this period, the Bank may assume that there is no objection to the investment in question.
3. The Board of Directors shall rule on financing operations submitted to it by the Management Committee.
4. The Management Committee shall examine whether financing operations submitted to it comply with the provisions of this Statute, in particular with Articles 16 and 18. Where the Management Committee is in favour of the financing operation, it shall submit the corresponding proposal to the Board of Directors; the Committee may make its favourable opinion subject to such conditions, as it considers essential. Where the Management Committee is against granting the finance, it shall submit the relevant documents together with its opinion to the Board of Directors.
5. Where the Management Committee delivers an unfavourable opinion, the Board of Directors may not grant the finance concerned unless its decision is unanimous.
6. Where the Commission delivers an unfavourable opinion, the Board of Directors may not grant the finance concerned unless its decision is unanimous, the director nominated by the Commission abstaining.
7. Where both the Management Committee and the Commission deliver an unfavourable opinion, the Board of Directors may not grant the finance.
8. In the event that a financing operation relating to an approved investment has to be restructured in order to safeguard the Bank's rights and interests, the Management Committee shall take without delay the emergency measures which it deems necessary, subject to immediate reporting thereon to the Board of Directors.

Article 20 (ex Article 22)
1. The Bank shall borrow on the capital markets the funds necessary for the performance of its tasks.
2. The Bank may borrow on the capital markets of the Member States in accordance with the legal provisions applying to those markets.

The competent authorities of a Member State with a derogation within the meaning of Article 139(1) of the Treaty on the Functioning of the European Union may oppose this only if there is reason to fear serious disturbances on the capital market of that State.

Article 21 (ex Article 23)

1. The Bank may employ any available funds which it does not immediately require to meet its obligations in the following ways:

   (a) it may invest on the money markets;

   (b) it may, subject to the provisions of Article 18(2), buy and sell securities;

   (c) it may carry out any other financial operation linked with its objectives.

2. Without prejudice to the provisions of Article 23, the Bank shall not, in managing its investments, engage in any currency arbitrage not directly required to carry out its lending operations or fulfil commitments arising out of loans raised or guarantees granted by it.

3. The Bank shall, in the fields covered by this Article, act in agreement with the competent authorities or with the national central bank of the Member State concerned.

Article 22 (ex Article 24)

1. A reserve fund of up to 10 % of the subscribed capital shall be built up progressively. If the state of the liabilities of the Bank should so justify, the Board of Directors may decide to set aside additional reserves. Until such time as the reserve fund has been fully built up, it shall be fed by:

   (a) interest received on loans granted by the Bank out of sums to be paid up by the Member States pursuant to Article 5;

   (b) interest received on loans granted by the Bank out of funds derived from repayment of the loans referred to in (a);

to the extent that this income is not required to meet the obligations of the Bank or to cover its expenses.

2. The resources of the reserve fund shall be so invested as to be available at any time to meet the purpose of the fund.

Article 23 (ex Article 25)

1. The Bank shall at all times be entitled to transfer its assets in the currency of a Member State whose currency is not the euro in order to carry out financial operations corresponding to the task set out in Article 309 of the Treaty on the Functioning of the European Union, taking into account the provisions of Article 21 of this Statute. The Bank shall, as far as possible, avoid making such transfers if it has cash or liquid assets in the currency required.

2. The Bank may not convert its assets in the currency of a Member State whose currency is not the euro into the currency of a third country without the agreement of the Member State concerned.

3. The Bank may freely dispose of that part of its capital which is paid up and of any currency borrowed on markets outside the Union.

4. The Member States undertake to make available to the debtors of the Bank the currency needed to repay the capital and pay the interest on loans or commission on guarantees granted by the Bank for investments to be carried out in their territory.

Article 24 (ex Article 26)
If a Member State fails to meet the obligations of membership arising from this Statute, in particular the obligation to pay its share of the subscribed capital or to service its borrowings, the granting of loans or guarantees to that Member State or its nationals may be suspended by a decision of the Board of Governors, acting by a qualified majority.
Such decision shall not release either the State or its nationals from their obligations towards the Bank.

Article 25 (ex Article 27)
1. If the Board of Governors decides to suspend the operations of the Bank, all its activities shall cease forthwith, except those required to ensure the due realisation, protection and preservation of its assets and the settlement of its liabilities.
2. In the event of liquidation, the Board of Governors shall appoint the liquidators and give them instructions for carrying out the liquidation. It shall ensure that the rights of the members of staff are safeguarded.

Article 26 (ex Article 28)
1. In each of the Member States, the Bank shall enjoy the most extensive legal capacity accorded to legal persons under their laws; it may, in particular, acquire or dispose of movable or immovable property and may be a party to legal proceedings.
2. The property of the Bank shall be exempt from all forms of requisition or expropriation.

Article 27 (ex Article 29)
Disputes between the Bank on the one hand, and its creditors, debtors or any other person on the other, shall be decided by the competent national courts, save where jurisdiction has been conferred on the Court of Justice of the European Union. The Bank may provide for arbitration in any contract.
The Bank shall have an address for service in each Member State. It may, however, in any contract, specify a particular address for service.
The property and assets of the Bank shall not be liable to attachment or to seizure by way of execution except by decision of a court.

Article 28 (ex Article 30)
1. The Board of Governors may, acting unanimously, decide to establish subsidiaries or other entities, which shall have legal personality and financial autonomy.
2. The Board of Governors shall establish the Statutes of the bodies referred to in paragraph 1. The Statutes shall define, in particular, their objectives, structure, capital,

membership, the location of their seat, their financial resources, means of intervention and auditing arrangements, as well as their relationship with the organs of the Bank.

3. The Bank shall be entitled to participate in the management of these bodies and contribute to their subscribed capital up to the amount determined by the Board of Governors, acting unanimously.

4. The Protocol on the privileges and immunities of the European Union shall apply to the bodies referred to in paragraph 1 in so far as they are incorporated under the law of the Union, to the members of their organs in the performance of their duties as such and to their staff, under the same terms and conditions as those applicable to the Bank.

Those dividends, capital gains or other forms of revenue stemming from such bodies to which the members, other than the European Union and the Bank, are entitled, shall however remain subject to the fiscal provisions of the applicable legislation.

5. The Court of Justice of the European Union shall, within the limits hereinafter laid down, have jurisdiction in disputes concerning measures adopted by organs of a body incorporated under Union law. Proceedings against such measures may be instituted by any member of such a body in its capacity as such or by Member States under the conditions laid down in Article 263 of the Treaty on the Functioning of the European Union.

6. The Board of Governors may, acting unanimously, decide to admit the staff of bodies incorporated under Union law to joint schemes with the Bank, in compliance with the respective internal procedures.

Protocol (No 6) on the Location of the Seats of the Institutions and of certain Bodies, Offices, Agencies and Departments of the European Union

The Representatives of the Governments of the Member States,
Having regard to Article 341 of the Treaty on the Functioning of the European Union and Article 189 of the Treaty establishing the European Atomic Energy Community,
Recalling and confirming the Decision of 8 April 1965, and without prejudice to the decisions concerning the seat of future institutions, bodies, offices, agencies and departments,
Have agreed upon the following provisions, which shall be annexed to the Treaty on European Union and to the Treaty on the Functioning of the European Union, and to the Treaty establishing the European Atomic Energy Community:

Sole Article
(a) The European Parliament shall have its seat in Strasbourg where the 12 periods of monthly plenary sessions, including the budget session, shall be held. The periods of additional plenary sessions shall be held in Brussels. The committees of the European Parliament shall meet in Brussels. The General Secretariat of the European Parliament and its departments shall remain in Luxembourg.
(b) The Council shall have its seat in Brussels. During the months of April, June and October, the Council shall hold its meetings in Luxembourg.
(c) The Commission shall have its seat in Brussels. The departments listed in Articles 7, 8 and 9 of the Decision of 8 April 1965 shall be established in Luxembourg.
(d) The Court of Justice of the European Union shall have its seat in Luxembourg.
(e) The Court of Auditors shall have its seat in Luxembourg.
(f) The Economic and Social Committee shall have its seat in Brussels.
(g) The Committee of the Regions shall have its seat in Brussels.
(h) The European Investment Bank shall have its seat in Luxembourg.
(i) The European Central Bank shall have its seat in Frankfurt.
(j) The European Police Office (Europol) shall have its seat in The Hague.

Protocol (No 7) on the Privileges and Immunities of the European Union

The High Contracting parties,

Considering that, in accordance with Article 343 of the Treaty on the Functioning of the European Union and Article 191 of the Treaty establishing the European Atomic Energy Community ('EAEC'), the European Union and the EAEC shall enjoy in the territories of the Member States such privileges and immunities as are necessary for the performance of their tasks,

Have agreed upon the following provisions, which shall be annexed to the Treaty on European Union, the Treaty on the Functioning of the European Union and the Treaty establishing the European Atomic Energy Community:

Chapter I
Property, funds, assets and operations of the European Union

Article 1
The premises and buildings of the Union shall be inviolable. They shall be exempt from search, requisition, confiscation or expropriation. The property and assets of the Union shall not be the subject of any administrative or legal measure of constraint without the authorisation of the Court of Justice.

Article 2
The archives of the Union shall be inviolable.

Article 3
The Union, its assets, revenues and other property shall be exempt from all direct taxes.
The governments of the Member States shall, wherever possible, take the appropriate measures to remit or refund the amount of indirect taxes or sales taxes included in the price of movable or immovable property, where the Union makes, for its official use, substantial purchases the price of which includes taxes of this kind. These provisions shall not be applied, however, so as to have the effect of distorting competition within the Union.
No exemption shall be granted in respect of taxes and dues which amount merely to charges for public utility services.

Article 4

The Union shall be exempt from all customs duties, prohibitions and restrictions on imports and exports in respect of articles intended for its official use: articles so imported shall not be disposed of, whether or not in return for payment, in the territory of the country into which they have been imported, except under conditions approved by the government of that country.

The Union shall also be exempt from any customs duties and any prohibitions and restrictions on import and exports in respect of its publications.

Chapter II
Communications and laissez-passer

Article 5 (ex Article 6)

For their official communications and the transmission of all their documents, the institutions of the Union shall enjoy in the territory of each Member State the treatment accorded by that State to diplomatic missions.

Official correspondence and other official communications of the institutions of the Union shall not be subject to censorship.

Article 6 (ex Article 7)

Laissez-passer in a form to be prescribed by the Council, acting by a simple majority, which shall be recognised as valid travel documents by the authorities of the Member States, may be issued to members and servants of the institutions of the Union by the Presidents of these institutions. These laissez-passer shall be issued to officials and other servants under conditions laid down in the Staff Regulations of Officials and the Conditions of Employment of other servants of the Union.

The Commission may conclude agreements for these laissez-passer to be recognised as valid travel documents within the territory of third countries.

Chapter III
Members of the European Parliament

Article 7 (ex Article 8)

No administrative or other restriction shall be imposed on the free movement of Members of the European Parliament travelling to or from the place of meeting of the European Parliament.

Members of the European Parliament shall, in respect of customs and exchange control, be accorded:

    (a) by their own government, the same facilities as those accorded to senior officials travelling abroad on temporary official missions;

(b) by the government of other Member States, the same facilities as those accorded to representatives of foreign governments on temporary official missions.

Article 8 (ex Article 9)
Members of the European Parliament shall not be subject to any form of inquiry, detention or legal proceedings in respect of opinions expressed or votes cast by them in the performance of their duties.

Article 9 (ex Article 10)
During the sessions of the European Parliament, its Members shall enjoy:
> (a) in the territory of their own State, the immunities accorded to members of their parliament;
>
> (b) in the territory of any other Member State, immunity from any measure of detention and from legal proceedings.

Immunity shall likewise apply to Members while they are travelling to and from the place of meeting of the European Parliament.

Immunity cannot be claimed when a Member is found in the act of committing an offence and shall not prevent the European Parliament from exercising its right to waive the immunity of one of its Members.

Chapter IV
Representatives of Member States taking part in the work of the institutions of the European Union

Article 10 (ex Article 11)
Representatives of Member States taking part in the work of the institutions of the Union, their advisers and technical experts shall, in the performance of their duties and during their travel to and from the place of meeting, enjoy the customary privileges, immunities and facilities.

This Article shall also apply to members of the advisory bodies of the Union.

Chapter V
Officials and other servants of the European Union

Article 11 (ex Article 12)
In the territory of each Member State and whatever their nationality, officials and other servants of the Union shall:
> (a) subject to the provisions of the Treaties relating, on the one hand, to the rules on the liability of officials and other servants towards the Union and, on the other hand, to the jurisdiction of the Court of Justice of the European Union in disputes between the

Union and its officials and other servants, be immune from legal proceedings in respect of acts performed by them in their official capacity, including their words spoken or written. They shall continue to enjoy this immunity after they have ceased to hold office;

(b) together with their spouses and dependent members of their families, not be subject to immigration restrictions or to formalities for the registration of aliens;

(c) in respect of currency or exchange regulations, be accorded the same facilities as are customarily accorded to officials of international organisations;

(d) enjoy the right to import free of duty their furniture and effects at the time of first taking up their post in the country concerned, and the right to re-export free of duty their furniture and effects, on termination of their duties in that country, subject in either case to the conditions considered to be necessary by the government of the country in which this right is exercised;

(e) have the right to import free of duty a motor car for their personal use, acquired either in the country of their last residence or in the country of which they are nationals on the terms ruling in the home market in that country, and to re-export it free of duty, subject in either case to the conditions considered to be necessary by the government of the country concerned.

Article 12 (ex Article 13)

Officials and other servants of the Union shall be liable to a tax for the benefit of the Union on salaries, wages and emoluments paid to them by the Union, in accordance with the conditions and procedure laid down by the European Parliament and the Council, acting by means of regulations in accordance with the ordinary legislative procedure and after consultation of the institutions concerned.

They shall be exempt from national taxes on salaries, wages and emoluments paid by the Union.

Article 13 (ex Article 14)

In the application of income tax, wealth tax and death duties and in the application of conventions on the avoidance of double taxation concluded between Member States of the Union, officials and other servants of the Union who, solely by reason of the performance of their duties in the service of the Union, establish their residence in the territory of a Member State other than their country of domicile for tax purposes at the time of entering the service of the Union, shall be considered, both in the country of their actual residence and in the country of domicile for tax purposes, as having maintained their domicile in the latter country provided that it is a member of the Union. This provision shall also apply to a spouse, to the extent that the latter is not separately engaged in a gainful occupation, and to children dependent on and in the care of the persons referred to in this Article.

Movable property belonging to persons referred to in the preceding paragraph and situated in the territory of the country where they are staying shall be exempt from death duties in that country; such property shall, for the assessment of such duty, be considered as being in the country of domicile for tax purposes, subject to the rights of third countries and to the possible application of provisions of international conventions on double taxation.

Any domicile acquired solely by reason of the performance of duties in the service of other international organisations shall not be taken into consideration in applying the provisions of this Article.

Article 14 (ex Article 15)

The European Parliament and the Council, acting by means of regulations in accordance with the ordinary legislative procedure and after consultation of the institutions concerned, shall lay down the scheme of social security benefits for officials and other servants of the Union.

Article 15 (ex Article 16)

The European Parliament and the Council, acting by means of regulations in accordance with the ordinary legislative procedure, and after consulting the other institutions concerned, shall determine the categories of officials and other servants of the Union to whom the provisions of Article 11, the second paragraph of Article 12, and Article 13 shall apply, in whole or in part.

The names, grades and addresses of officials and other servants included in such categories shall be communicated periodically to the governments of the Member States.

Chapter VI
Privileges and immunities of missions of third countries accredited to the European Union

Article 16 (ex Article 17)

The Member State in whose territory the Union has its seat shall accord the customary diplomatic immunities and privileges to missions of third countries accredited to the Union.

Chapter VII
General provisions

Article 17 (ex Article 18)

Privileges, immunities and facilities shall be accorded to officials and other servants of the Union solely in the interests of the Union.

Each institution of the Union shall be required to waive the immunity accorded to an official or other servant wherever that institution considers that the waiver of such immunity is not contrary to the interests of the Union.

Article 18 (ex Article 19)
The institutions of the Union shall, for the purpose of applying this Protocol, cooperate with the responsible authorities of the Member States concerned.

Article 19 (ex Article 20)
Articles 11 to 14 and Article 17 shall apply to the President of the European Council.
They shall also apply to Members of the Commission.

Article 20 (ex Article 21)
Articles 11 to 14 and Article 17 shall apply to the Judges, the Advocates-General, the Registrars and the Assistant Rapporteurs of the Court of Justice of the European Union, without prejudice to the provisions of Article 3 of the Protocol on the Statute of the Court of Justice of the European Union relating to immunity from legal proceedings of Judges and Advocates-General.

Article 21 (ex Article 22)
This Protocol shall also apply to the European Investment Bank, to the members of its organs, to its staff and to the representatives of the Member States taking part in its activities, without prejudice to the provisions of the Protocol on the Statute of the Bank.
The European Investment Bank shall in addition be exempt from any form of taxation or imposition of a like nature on the occasion of any increase in its capital and from the various formalities which may be connected therewith in the State where the Bank has its seat. Similarly, its dissolution or liquidation shall not give rise to any imposition. Finally, the activities of the Bank and of its organs carried on in accordance with its Statute shall not be subject to any turnover tax.

Article 22 (ex Article 23)
This Protocol shall also apply to the European Central Bank, to the members of its organs and to its staff, without prejudice to the provisions of the Protocol on the Statute of the European System of Central Banks and the European Central Bank.
The European Central Bank shall, in addition, be exempt from any form of taxation or imposition of a like nature on the occasion of any increase in its capital and from the various formalities which may be connected therewith in the State where the bank has its seat. The activities of the Bank and of its organs carried on in accordance with the Statute of the European System of Central Banks and of the European Central Bank shall not be subject to any turnover tax.

Protocol (No 8)
relating to Article 6(2) of the Treaty on European Union on the Accession of the Union to the European Convention on the Protection of Human Rights and Fundamental Freedoms

The High Contracting Parties,

Have agreed upon the following provisions, which shall be annexed to the Treaty on European Union and to the Treaty on the Functioning of the European Union:

Article 1
The agreement relating to the accession of the Union to the European Convention on the Protection of Human Rights and Fundamental Freedoms (hereinafter referred to as the 'European Convention') provided for in Article 6(2) of the Treaty on European Union shall make provision for preserving the specific characteristics of the Union and Union law, in particular with regard to:

(a) the specific arrangements for the Union's possible participation in the control bodies of the European Convention;

(b) the mechanisms necessary to ensure that proceedings by non-Member States and individual applications are correctly addressed to Member States and/or the Union as appropriate.

Article 2
The agreement referred to in Article 1 shall ensure that accession of the Union shall not affect the competences of the Union or the powers of its institutions. It shall ensure that nothing therein affects the situation of Member States in relation to the European Convention, in particular in relation to the Protocols thereto, measures taken by Member States derogating from the European Convention in accordance with Article 15 thereof and reservations to the European Convention made by Member States in accordance with Article 57 thereof.

Article 3
Nothing in the agreement referred to in Article 1 shall affect Article 344 of the Treaty on the Functioning of the European Union.

Protocol (No 9)
on the Decision of the Council relating to the Implementation of Article 16(4) of the Treaty on European Union and Article 238(2) of the Treaty on the Functioning of the European Union between 1 November 2014 and 31 March 2017 on the one hand, and as from 1 April 2017 on the other

The High Contracting Parties,

Taking into account the fundamental importance that agreeing on the Decision of the Council relating to the implementation of Article 16(4) of the Treaty on European Union and Article 238(2) of the Treaty on the Functioning of the European Union between 1 November 2014 and 31 March 2017 on the one hand, and as from 1 April 2017 on the other (hereinafter 'the Decision'), had when approving the Treaty of Lisbon,

Have agreed upon the following provisions, which shall be annexed to the Treaty on European Union and to the Treaty on the Functioning of the European Union:

Sole Article

Before the examination by the Council of any draft which would aim either at amending or abrogating the Decision or any of its provisions, or at modifying indirectly its scope or its meaning through the modification of another legal act of the Union, the European Council shall hold a preliminary deliberation on the said draft, acting by consensus in accordance with Article 15(4) of the Treaty on European Union.

Protocol (No 10) on Permanent Structured Cooperation established by Article 42 of the Treaty on European Union

The High Contracting Parties,

Having regard to Article 42(6) and Article 46 of the Treaty on European Union,

Recalling that the Union is pursuing a common foreign and security policy based on the achievement of growing convergence of action by Member States,

Recalling that the common security and defence policy is an integral part of the common foreign and security policy; that it provides the Union with operational capacity drawing on civil and military assets; that the Union may use such assets in the tasks referred to in Article 43 of the Treaty on European Union outside the Union for peace-keeping, conflict prevention and strengthening inter national security in accordance with the principles of the United Nations Charter; that the performance of these tasks is to be undertaken using capabilities provided by the Member States in accordance with the principle of a single set of forces,

Recalling that the common security and defence policy of the Union does not prejudice the specific character of the security and defence policy of certain Member States,

Recalling that the common security and defence policy of the Union respects the obligations under the North Atlantic Treaty of those Member States which see their common defence realised in the North Atlantic Treaty Organisation, which remains the foundation of the collective defence of its members, and is compatible with the common security and defence policy established within that framework,

Convinced that a more assertive Union role in security and defence matters will contribute to the vitality of a renewed Atlantic Alliance, in accordance with the Berlin Plus arrangements,

Determined to ensure that the Union is capable of fully assuming its responsibilities within the international community,

Recognising that the United Nations Organisation may request the Union's assistance for the urgent implementation of missions undertaken under Chapters VI and VII of the United Nations Charter,

Recognising that the strengthening of the security and defence policy will require efforts by Member States in the area of capabilities,

Conscious that embarking on a new stage in the development of the European security and defence policy involves a determined effort by the Member States concerned,

Recalling the importance of the High Representative of the Union for Foreign Affairs and Security Policy being fully involved in proceedings relating to permanent structured cooperation,

Have agreed upon the following provisions, which shall be annexed to the Treaty on European Union and to the Treaty on the Functioning of the European Union:

Article 1

The permanent structured cooperation referred to in Article 42(6) of the Treaty on European Union shall be open to any Member State which undertakes, from the date of entry into force of the Treaty of Lisbon, to:

(a) proceed more intensively to develop its defence capacities through the development of its national contributions and participation, where appropriate, in multinational forces, in the main European equipment programmes, and in the activity of the Agency in the field of defence capabilities development, research, acquisition and armaments (European Defence Agency), and

(b) have the capacity to supply by 2010 at the latest, either at national level or as a component of multinational force groups, targeted combat units for the missions planned, structured at a tactical level as a battle group, with support elements including transport and logistics, capable of carrying out the tasks referred to in Article 43 of the Treaty on European Union, within a period of five to 30 days, in particular in response to requests from the United Nations Organisation, and which can be sustained for an initial period of 30 days and be extended up to at least 120 days.

Article 2

To achieve the objectives laid down in Article 1, Member States participating in permanent structured cooperation shall undertake to:

(a) cooperate, as from the entry into force of the Treaty of Lisbon, with a view to achieving approved objectives concerning the level of investment expenditure on defence equipment, and regularly review these objectives, in the light of the security environment and of the Union's international responsibilities;

(b) bring their defence apparatus into line with each other as far as possible, particularly by harmonising the identification of their military needs, by pooling and, where appropriate, specialising their defence means and capabilities, and by encouraging cooperation in the fields of training and logistics;

(c) take concrete measures to enhance the availability, interoperability, flexibility and deployability of their forces, in particular by identifying common objectives regarding the commitment of forces, including possibly reviewing their national decision-making procedures;

(d) work together to ensure that they take the necessary measures to make good, including through multinational approaches, and without prejudice to undertakings in this regard within the North Atlantic Treaty Organisation, the shortfalls perceived in the framework of the 'Capability Development Mechanism';

(e) take part, where appropriate, in the development of major joint or European equipment programmes in the framework of the European Defence Agency.

Article 3

The European Defence Agency shall contribute to the regular assessment of participating Member States' contributions with regard to capabilities, in particular contributions made in accordance with the criteria to be established, inter alia, on the basis of Article 2, and shall report thereon at least once a year. The assessment may serve as a basis for Council recommendations and decisions adopted in accordance with Article 46 of the Treaty on European Union.

Protocol (No 11)
on Article 42 of the Treaty on European Union

The High Contracting Parties,

Bearing in mind the need to implement fully the provisions of Article 42(2) of the Treaty on European Union,

Bearing in mind that the policy of the Union in accordance with Article 42 shall not prejudice the specific character of the security and defence policy of certain Member States and shall respect the obligations of certain Member States, which see their common defence realised in NATO, under the North Atlantic Treaty and be compatible with the common security and defence policy established within that framework,

Have agreed upon the following provision, which shall be annexed to the Treaty on European Union and to the Treaty on the Functioning of the European Union:

The European Union shall draw up, together with the Western European Union, arrangements for enhanced cooperation between them.

Protocol (No 12)
on the Excessive Deficit Procedure

The High Contracting Parties,

Desiring to lay down the details of the excessive deficit procedure referred to in Article 126 of the Treaty on the Functioning of the European Union,

Have agreed upon the following provisions, which shall be annexed to the Treaty on European Union and to the Treaty on the Functioning of the European Union:

Article 1
The reference values referred to in Article 126(2) of the Treaty on the Functioning of the European Union are:
- 3 % for the ratio of the planned or actual government deficit to gross domestic product at market prices;
- 60 % for the ratio of government debt to gross domestic product at market prices.

Article 2
In Article 126 of the said Treaty and in this Protocol:
- 'government' means general government, that is central government, regional or local government and social security funds, to the exclusion of commercial operations, as defined in the European System of Integrated Economic Accounts;
- 'deficit' means net borrowing as defined in the European System of Integrated Economic Accounts;
- 'investment' means gross fixed capital formation as defined in the European System of Integrated Economic Accounts;
- 'debt' means total gross debt at nominal value outstanding at the end of the year and consolidated between and within the sectors of general government as defined in the first indent.

Article 3
In order to ensure the effectiveness of the excessive deficit procedure, the governments of the Member States shall be responsible under this procedure for the deficits of general government as defined in the first indent of Article 2. The Member States shall ensure that national procedures in the budgetary area enable them to meet their obligations in this area deriving from these Treaties. The Member States shall report their planned and actual deficits and the levels of their debt promptly and regularly to the Commission.

Article 4
The statistical data to be used for the application of this Protocol shall be provided by the Commission.

Protocol (No 13)
on the Convergence Criteria

The High Contracting Parties,

Desiring to lay down the details of the convergence criteria which shall guide the Union in taking decisions to end the derogations of those Member States with a derogation, referred to in Article 140 of the Treaty on the Functioning of the European Union,

Have agreed upon the following provisions, which shall be annexed to the Treaty on European Union and to the Treaty on the Functioning of the European Union:

Article 1

The criterion on price stability referred to in the first indent of Article 140(1) of the Treaty on the Functioning of the European Union shall mean that a Member State has a price performance that is sustainable and an average rate of inflation, observed over a period of one year before the examination, that does not exceed by more than 1 ½ percentage points that of, at most, the three best performing Member States in terms of price stability. Inflation shall be measured by means of the consumer price index on a comparable basis taking into account differences in national definitions.

Article 2

The criterion on the government budgetary position referred to in the second indent of Article 140(1) of the said Treaty shall mean that at the time of the examination the Member State is not the subject of a Council decision under Article 126(6) of the said Treaty that an excessive deficit exists.

Article 3

The criterion on participation in the Exchange Rate mechanism of the European Monetary System referred to in the third indent of Article 140(1) of the said Treaty shall mean that a Member State has respected the normal fluctuation margins provided for by the exchange-rate mechanism on the European Monetary System without severe tensions for at least the last two years before the examination. In particular, the Member State shall not have devalued its currency's bilateral central rate against the euro on its own initiative for the same period.

Article 4

The criterion on the convergence of interest rates referred to in the fourth indent of Article 140(1) of the said Treaty shall mean that, observed over a period of one year before the examination, a Member State has had an average nominal long-term interest rate that does not exceed by more than two percentage points that of, at most, the three best performing Member States in terms of price stability. Interest rates shall be measured on the basis of long-term government bonds or comparable securities, taking into account differences in national definitions.

Article 5

The statistical data to be used for the application of this Protocol shall be provided by the Commission.

Article 6

The Council shall, acting unanimously on a proposal from the Commission and after consulting the European Parliament, the ECB and the Economic and Financial Committee, adopt appropriate provisions to lay down the details of the convergence criteria referred to in Article 140(1) of the said Treaty, which shall then replace this Protocol.

Protocol (No 14)
on the Euro Group

The High Contracting Parties,
Desiring to promote conditions for stronger economic growth in the European Union and, to that end, to develop ever-closer coordination of economic policies within the euro area,
Conscious of the need to lay down special provisions for enhanced dialogue between the Member States whose currency is the euro, pending the euro becoming the currency of all Member States of the Union,
Have agreed upon the following provisions, which shall be annexed to the Treaty on European Union and to the Treaty on the Functioning of the European Union:

Article 1
The Ministers of the Member States whose currency is the euro shall meet informally. Such meetings shall take place, when necessary, to discuss questions related to the specific responsibilities they share with regard to the single currency. The Commission shall take part in the meetings. The European Central Bank shall be invited to take part in such meetings, which shall be prepared by the representatives of the Ministers with responsibility for finance of the Member States whose currency is the euro and of the Commission.

Article 2
The Ministers of the Member States whose currency is the euro shall elect a president for two and a half years, by a majority of those Member States.

Protocol (No 15) on certain Provisions relating to the United Kingdom of Great Britain and Northern Ireland

The High Contracting Parties,

Recognising that the United Kingdom shall not be obliged or committed to adopt the euro without a separate decision to do so by its government and parliament,

Given that on 16 October 1996 and 30 October 1997 the United Kingdom government notified the Council of its intention not to participate in the third stage of economic and monetary union,

Noting the practice of the government of the United Kingdom to fund its borrowing requirement by the sale of debt to the private sector,

Have agreed upon the following provisions, which shall be annexed to the Treaty on European Union and to the Treaty on the Functioning of the European Union:

1. Unless the United Kingdom notifies the Council that it intends to adopt the euro, it shall be under no obligation to do so.
2. In view of the notice given to the Council by the United Kingdom government on 16 October 1996 and 30 October 1997, paragraphs 3 to 8 and 10 shall apply to the United Kingdom.
3. The United Kingdom shall retain its powers in the field of monetary policy according to national law.
4. Articles 119, second paragraph, 126(1), (9) and (11), 127(1) to (5), 128, 130, 131, 132, 133, 138, 140(3), 219, 282(2), with the exception of the first and last sentences thereof, 282(5), and 283 of the Treaty on the Functioning of the European Union shall not apply to the United Kingdom. The same applies to Article 121(2) of this Treaty as regards the adoption of the parts of the broad economic policy guidelines which concern the euro area generally. In these provisions references to the Union or the Member States shall not include the United Kingdom and references to national central banks shall not include the Bank of England.
5. The United Kingdom shall endeavour to avoid an excessive government deficit.

Articles 143 and 144 of the Treaty on the Functioning of the European Union shall continue to apply to the United Kingdom. Articles 134(4) and 142 shall apply to the United Kingdom as if it had a derogation.

6. The voting rights of the United Kingdom shall be suspended in respect of acts of the Council referred to in the Articles listed in paragraph 4 and in the instances referred to in the first subparagraph of Article 139(4) of the Treaty on the Functioning of the European Union. For this purpose the second subparagraph of Article 139(4) of the Treaty shall apply.

The United Kingdom shall also have no right to participate in the appointment of the President, the Vice-President and the other members of the Executive Board of the ECB under the second subparagraph of Article 283(2) of the said Treaty.

7. Articles 3, 4, 6, 7, 9.2, 10.1, 10.3, 11.2, 12.1, 14, 16, 18 to 20, 22, 23, 26, 27, 30 to 34 and 49 of the Protocol on the Statute of the European System of Central Banks and of the European Central Bank ('the Statute') shall not apply to the United Kingdom.

In those Articles, references to the Union or the Member States shall not include the United Kingdom and references to national central banks or shareholders shall not include the Bank of England.

References in Articles 10.3 and 30.2 of the Statute to 'subscribed capital of the ECB' shall not include capital subscribed by the Bank of England.

8. Article 141(1) of the Treaty on the Functioning of the European Union and Articles 43 to 47 of the Statute shall have effect, whether or not there is any Member State with a derogation, subject to the following amendments:

(a) References in Article 43 to the tasks of the ECB and the EMI shall include those tasks that still need to be performed in the third stage owing to any decision of the United Kingdom not to adopt the euro.

(b) In addition to the tasks referred to in Article 46, the ECB shall also give advice in relation to and contribute to the preparation of any decision of the Council with regard to the United Kingdom taken in accordance with paragraphs 9(a) and 9(c).

(c) The Bank of England shall pay up its subscription to the capital of the ECB as a contribution to its operational costs on the same basis as national central banks of Member States with a derogation.

9. The United Kingdom may notify the Council at any time of its intention to adopt the euro. In that event:

(a) The United Kingdom shall have the right to adopt the euro provided only that it satisfies the necessary conditions. The Council, acting at the request of the United Kingdom and under the conditions and in accordance with the procedure laid down in Article 140(1) and (2) of the Treaty on the Functioning of the European Union, shall decide whether it fulfils the necessary conditions.

(b) The Bank of England shall pay up its subscribed capital, transfer to the ECB foreign reserve assets and contribute to its reserves on the same basis as the national central bank of a Member State whose derogation has been abrogated.

(c) The Council, acting under the conditions and in accordance with the procedure laid down in Article 140(3) of the said Treaty, shall take all other necessary decisions to enable the United Kingdom to adopt the euro.

If the United Kingdom adopts the euro pursuant to the provisions of this Protocol, paragraphs 3 to 8 shall cease to have effect.

10. Notwithstanding Article 123 of the Treaty on the Functioning of the European Union and Article 21.1 of the Statute, the Government of the United Kingdom may maintain its 'ways and means' facility with the Bank of England if and so long as the United Kingdom does not adopt the euro.

Protocol (No 16)
on certain Provisions relating to Denmark

The High Contracting Parties,

Taking into account that the Danish Constitution contains provisions which may imply a referendum in Denmark prior to Denmark renouncing its exemption,

Given that, on 3 November 1993, the Danish Government notified the Council of its intention not to participate in the third stage of economic and monetary union,

Have agreed upon the following provisions, which shall be annexed to the Treaty on European Union and to the Treaty on the Functioning of the European Union:

1. In view of the notice given to the Council by the Danish Government on 3 November 1993, Denmark shall have an exemption. The effect of the exemption shall be that all Articles and provisions of the Treaties and the Statute of the ESCB referring to a derogation shall be applicable to Denmark.
2. As for the abrogation of the exemption, the procedure referred to in Article 140 shall only be initiated at the request of Denmark.
3. In the event of abrogation of the exemption status, the provisions of this Protocol shall cease to apply.

Protocol (No 17) on Denmark

The High Contracting Parties,
Desiring to settle certain particular problems relating to Denmark,
Have agreed upon the following provisions, which shall be annexed to the Treaty on European Union and the Treaty on the Functioning of the European Union:

The provisions of Article 14 of the Protocol on the Statute of the European System of Central Banks and of the European Central Bank shall not affect the right of the National Bank of Denmark to carry out its existing tasks concerning those parts of the Kingdom of Denmark which are not part of the Union.

Protocol (No 18) on France

The High Contracting Parties,
Desiring to take into account a particular point relating to France,
Have agreed upon the following provisions, which shall be annexed to the Treaty on European Union and to the Treaty on the Functioning of the European Union:

France will keep the privilege of monetary emission in New Caledonia, French Polynesia and Wallis and Futuna under the terms established by its national laws, and will be solely entitled to determine the parity of the CFP franc.

Protocol (No 19) on the Schengen Acquis integrated into the Framework of the European Union

The High Contracting Parties,

Noting that the Agreements on the gradual abolition of checks at common borders signed by some Member States of the European Union in Schengen on 14 June 1985 and on 19 June 1990, as well as related agreements and the rules adopted on the basis of these agreements, have been integrated into the framework of the European Union by the Treaty of Amsterdam of 2 October 1997,

Desiring to preserve the Schengen acquis, as developed since the entry into force of the Treaty of Amsterdam, and to develop this acquis in order to contribute towards achieving the objective of offering citizens of the Union an area of freedom, security and justice without internal borders,

Taking into account the special position of Denmark,

Taking into account the fact that Ireland and the United Kingdom of Great Britain and Northern Ireland do not participate in all the provisions of the Schengen acquis; that provision should, however, be made to allow those Member States to accept other provisions of this acquis in full or in part,

Recognising that, as a consequence, it is necessary to make use of the provisions of the Treaties concerning closer cooperation between some Member States,

Taking into account the need to maintain a special relationship with the Republic of Iceland and the Kingdom of Norway, both States being bound by the provisions of the Nordic passport union, together with the Nordic States which are members of the European Union,

Have agreed upon the following provisions, which shall be annexed to the Treaty on European Union and to the Treaty on the Functioning of the European Union:

Article 1

The Kingdom of Belgium, the Republic of Bulgaria, the Czech Republic, the Kingdom of Denmark, the Federal Republic of Germany, the Republic of Estonia, the Hellenic Republic, the Kingdom of Spain, the French Republic, the Italian Republic, the Republic of Cyprus, the Republic of Latvia, the Republic of Lithuania, the Grand Duchy of Luxembourg, the Republic of Hungary, Malta, the Kingdom of the Netherlands, the Republic of Austria, the Republic of Poland, the Portuguese Republic, Romania, the Republic of Slovenia, the Slovak Republic, the Republic of Finland and the Kingdom of Sweden shall be authorised to establish closer cooperation among themselves in areas covered by provisions defined by the Council which constitute the Schengen acquis. This cooperation shall be conducted within the institutional and legal framework of the European Union and with respect for the relevant provisions of the Treaties.

Article 2
The Schengen acquis shall apply to the Member States referred to in Article 1, without prejudice to Article 3 of the Act of Accession of 16 April 2003 or to Article 4 of the Act of Accession of 25 April 2005. The Council will substitute itself for the Executive Committee established by the Schengen agreements.

Article 3
The participation of Denmark in the adoption of measures constituting a development of the Schengen acquis, as well as the implementation of these measures and their application to Denmark, shall be governed by the relevant provisions of the Protocol on the position of Denmark.

Article 4
Ireland and the United Kingdom of Great Britain and Northern Ireland may at any time request to take part in some or all of the provisions of the Schengen acquis.
The Council shall decide on the request with the unanimity of its members referred to in Article 1 and of the representative of the Government of the State concerned.

Article 5
1. Proposals and initiatives to build upon the Schengen acquis shall be subject to the relevant provisions of the Treaties.
In this context, where either Ireland or the United Kingdom has not notified the Council in writing within a reasonable period that it wishes to take part, the authorisation referred to in Article 329 of the Treaty on the Functioning of the European Union shall be deemed to have been granted to the Member States referred to in Article 1 and to Ireland or the United Kingdom where either of them wishes to take part in the areas of cooperation in question.
2. Where either Ireland or the United Kingdom is deemed to have given notification pursuant to a decision under Article 4, it may nevertheless notify the Council in writing, within three months, that it does not wish to take part in such a proposal or initiative. In that case, Ireland or the United Kingdom shall not take part in its adoption. As from the latter notification, the procedure for adopting the measure building upon the Schengen acquis shall be suspended until the end of the procedure set out in paragraphs 3 or 4 or until the notification is withdrawn at any moment during that procedure.
3. For the Member State having made the notification referred to in paragraph 2, any

decision taken by the Council pursuant to Article 4 shall, as from the date of entry into force of the proposed measure, cease to apply to the extent considered necessary by the Council and under the conditions to be determined in a decision of the Council acting by a qualified majority on a proposal from the Commission. That decision shall be taken in accordance with the following criteria: the Council shall seek to retain the widest possible measure of participation of the Member State concerned without seriously affecting the practical operability of the various parts of the Schengen acquis, while respecting their coherence. The Commission shall submit its proposal as soon as possible after the notification referred to in paragraph 2. The Council shall, if needed after convening two successive meetings, act within four months of the Commission proposal.

4. If, by the end of the period of four months, the Council has not adopted a decision, a Member State may, without delay, request that the matter be referred to the European Council. In that case, the European Council shall, at its next meeting, acting by a qualified majority on a proposal from the Commission, take a decision in accordance with the criteria referred to in paragraph 3.

5. If, by the end of the procedure set out in paragraphs 3 or 4, the Council or, as the case may be, the European Council has not adopted its decision, the suspension of the procedure for adopting the measure building upon the Schengen acquis shall be terminated. If the said measure is subsequently adopted any decision taken by the Council pursuant to Article 4 shall, as from the date of entry into force of that measure, cease to apply for the Member State concerned to the extent and under the conditions decided by the Commission, unless the said Member State has withdrawn its notification referred to in paragraph 2 before the adoption of the measure. The Commission shall act by the date of this adoption. When taking its decision, the Commission shall respect the criteria referred to in paragraph 3.

Article 6

The Republic of Iceland and the Kingdom of Norway shall be associated with the implementation of the Schengen acquis and its further development. Appropriate procedures shall be agreed to that effect in an Agreement to be concluded with those States by the Council, acting by the unanimity of its Members mentioned in Article 1. Such Agreement shall include provisions on the contribution of Iceland and Norway to any financial consequences resulting from the implementation of this Protocol.

A separate Agreement shall be concluded with Iceland and Norway by the Council, acting unanimously, for the establishment of rights and obligations between Ireland and the United Kingdom of Great Britain and Northern Ireland on the one hand, and Iceland and Norway on the other, in domains of the Schengen acquis which apply to these States.

Article 7

For the purposes of the negotiations for the admission of new Member States into the European Union, the Schengen acquis and further measures taken by the institutions within its scope shall be regarded as an acquis which must be accepted in full by all States candidates for admission.

Protocol (No 20) on the Application of certain Aspects of Article 26 of the Treaty on the Functioning of the European Union to the United Kingdom and to Ireland

The High Contracting Parties,
Desiring to settle certain questions relating to the United Kingdom and Ireland,
Having regard to the existence for many years of special travel arrangements between the United Kingdom and Ireland,
Have agreed upon the following provisions, which shall be annexed to the Treaty on European Union and the Treaty on the Functioning of the European Union:

Article 1
The United Kingdom shall be entitled, notwithstanding Articles 26 and 77 of the Treaty on the Functioning of the European Union, any other provision of that Treaty or of the Treaty on European Union, any measure adopted under those Treaties, or any international agreement concluded by the Union or by the Union and its Member States with one or more third States, to exercise at its frontiers with other Member States such controls on persons seeking to enter the United Kingdom as it may consider necessary for the purpose:

(a) of verifying the right to enter the United Kingdom of citizens of Member States and of their dependants exercising rights conferred by Union law, as well as citizens of other States on whom such rights have been conferred by an agreement by which the United Kingdom is bound; and

(b) of determining whether or not to grant other persons permission to enter the United Kingdom.

Nothing in Articles 26 and 77 of the Treaty on the Functioning of the European Union or in any other provision of that Treaty or of the Treaty on European Union or in any measure adopted under them shall prejudice the right of the United Kingdom to adopt or exercise any such controls. References to the United Kingdom in this Article shall include territories for whose external relations the United Kingdom is responsible.

Article 2

The United Kingdom and Ireland may continue to make arrangements between themselves relating to the movement of persons between their territories ("the Common Travel Area"), while fully respecting the rights of persons referred to in Article 1, first paragraph, point (a) of this Protocol.

Accordingly, as long as they maintain such arrangements, the provisions of Article 1 of this Protocol shall apply to Ireland under the same terms and conditions as for the United Kingdom. Nothing in Articles 26 and 77 of the Treaty on the Functioning of the European Union, in any other provision of that Treaty or of the Treaty on European Union or in any measure adopted under them, shall affect any such arrangements.

Article 3

The other Member States shall be entitled to exercise at their frontiers or at any point of entry into their territory such controls on persons seeking to enter their territory from the United Kingdom or any territories whose external relations are under its responsibility for the same purposes stated in Article 1 of this Protocol, or from Ireland as long as the provisions of Article 1 of this Protocol apply to Ireland.

Nothing in Articles 26 and 77 of the Treaty on the Functioning of the European Union or in any other provision of that Treaty or of the Treaty on European Union or in any measure adopted under them shall prejudice the right of the other Member States to adopt or exercise any such controls.

Protocol (No 21) on the Position of the United Kingdom and Ireland in respect of the Area of Freedom, Security and Justice

The High Contracting Parties,
Desiring to settle certain questions relating to the United Kingdom and Ireland,
Having regard to the Protocol on the application of certain aspects of Article 26 of the Treaty on the Functioning of the European Union to the United Kingdom and to Ireland,
Have agreed upon the following provisions, which shall be annexed to the Treaty on European Union and the Treaty on the Functioning of the European Union:

Article 1
Subject to Article 3, the United Kingdom and Ireland shall not take part in the adoption by the Council of proposed measures pursuant to Title V of Part Three of the Treaty on the Functioning of the European Union. The unanimity of the members of the Council, with the exception of the representatives of the governments of the United Kingdom and Ireland, shall be necessary for decisions of the Council which must be adopted unanimously.
For the purposes of this Article, a qualified majority shall be defined in accordance with Article 238(3) of the Treaty on the Functioning of the European Union.

Article 2
In consequence of Article 1 and subject to Articles 3, 4 and 6, none of the provisions of Title V of Part Three of the Treaty on the Functioning of the European Union, no measure adopted pursuant to that Title, no provision of any international agreement concluded by the Union pursuant to that Title, and no decision of the Court of Justice interpreting any such provision or measure shall be binding upon or applicable in the United Kingdom or Ireland; and no such provision, measure or decision shall in any way affect the competences, rights and obligations of those States; and no such provision, measure or decision shall in any way affect the Community or Union acquis nor form part of Union law as they apply to the United Kingdom or Ireland.

Article 3
1. The United Kingdom or Ireland may notify the President of the Council in writing, within three months after a proposal or initiative has been presented to the Council pursuant to

Title V of Part Three of the Treaty on the Functioning of the European Union, that it wishes to take part in the adoption and application of any such proposed measure, whereupon that State shall be entitled to do so.

The unanimity of the members of the Council, with the exception of a member which has not made such a notification, shall be necessary for decisions of the Council which must be adopted unanimously. A measure adopted under this paragraph shall be binding upon all Member States which took part in its adoption.

Measures adopted pursuant to Article 70 of the Treaty on the Functioning of the European Union shall lay down the conditions for the participation of the United Kingdom and Ireland in the evaluations concerning the areas covered by Title V of Part Three of that Treaty.

For the purposes of this Article, a qualified majority shall be defined in accordance with Article 238(3) of the Treaty on the Functioning of the European Union.

2. If after a reasonable period of time a measure referred to in paragraph 1 cannot be adopted with the United Kingdom or Ireland taking part, the Council may adopt such measure in accordance with Article 1 without the participation of the United Kingdom or Ireland. In that case Article 2 applies.

Article 4

The United Kingdom or Ireland may at any time after the adoption of a measure by the Council pursuant to Title V of Part Three of the Treaty on the Functioning of the European Union notify its intention to the Council and to the Commission that it wishes to accept that measure. In that case, the procedure provided for in Article 331(1) of the Treaty on the Functioning of the European Union shall apply mutatis mutandis.

Article 4a

1. The provisions of this Protocol apply for the United Kingdom and Ireland also to measures proposed or adopted pursuant to Title V of Part Three of the Treaty on the Functioning of the European Union amending an existing measure by which they are bound.

2. However, in cases where the Council, acting on a proposal from the Commission, determines that the non-participation of the United Kingdom or Ireland in the amended version of an existing measure makes the application of that measure inoperable for other Member States or the Union, it may urge them to make a notification under Article 3 or 4. For the purposes of Article 3, a further period of two months starts to run as from the date of such determination by the Council.

If at the expiry of that period of two months from the Council's determination the United Kingdom or Ireland has not made a notification under Article 3 or Article 4, the existing measure shall no longer be binding upon or applicable to it, unless the Member State concerned has made a notification under Article 4 before the entry into force of the amending measure. This shall take effect from the date of entry into force of the amending measure or of expiry of the period of two months, whichever is the later.

For the purpose of this paragraph, the Council shall, after a full discussion of the matter, act by a qualified majority of its members representing the Member States participating or having participated in the adoption of the amending measure. A qualified majority of the Council shall be defined in accordance with Article 238(3)(a) of the Treaty on the Functioning of the European Union.

3. The Council, acting by a qualified majority on a proposal from the Commission, may determine that the United Kingdom or Ireland shall bear the direct financial consequences, if any, necessarily and unavoidably incurred as a result of the cessation of its participation in the existing measure.

4. This Article shall be without prejudice to Article 4.

Article 5

A Member State which is not bound by a measure adopted pursuant to Title V of Part Three of the Treaty on the Functioning of the European Union shall bear no financial consequences of that measure other than administrative costs entailed for the institutions, unless all members of the Council, acting unanimously after consulting the European Parliament, decide otherwise.

Article 6

Where, in cases referred to in this Protocol, the United Kingdom or Ireland is bound by a measure adopted by the Council pursuant to Title V of Part Three of the Treaty on the Functioning of the European Union, the relevant provisions of the Treaties shall apply to that State in relation to that measure.

Article 6a

The United Kingdom and Ireland shall not be bound by the rules laid down on the basis of Article 16 of the Treaty on the Functioning of the European Union which relate to the processing of personal data by the Member States when carrying out activities which fall within the scope of Chapter 4 or Chapter 5 of Title V of Part Three of that Treaty where the United Kingdom and Ireland are not bound by the rules governing the forms of judicial cooperation in criminal matters or police cooperation which require compliance with the provisions laid down on the basis of Article 16.

Article 7

Articles 3, 4 and 4a shall be without prejudice to the Protocol on the Schengen acquis integrated into the framework of the European Union.

Article 8

Ireland may notify the Council in writing that it no longer wishes to be covered by the terms of this Protocol. In that case, the normal treaty provisions will apply to Ireland.

Article 9

With regard to Ireland, this Protocol shall not apply to Article 75 of the Treaty on the Functioning of the European Union.

Protocol (No 22)
on the Position of Denmark

The High Contracting Parties,

Recalling the Decision of the Heads of State or Government, meeting within the European Council at Edinburgh on 12 December 1992, concerning certain problems raised by Denmark on the Treaty on European Union,

Having noted the position of Denmark with regard to Citizenship, Economic and Monetary Union, Defence Policy and Justice and Home Affairs as laid down in the Edinburgh Decision,

Conscious of the fact that a continuation under the Treaties of the legal regime originating in the Edinburgh decision will significantly limit Denmark's participation in important areas of cooperation of the Union, and that it would be in the best interest of the Union to ensure the integrity of the acquis in the area of freedom, security and justice,

Wishing therefore to establish a legal framework that will provide an option for Denmark to participate in the adoption of measures proposed on the basis of Title V of Part Three of the Treaty on the Functioning of the European Union and welcoming the intention of Denmark to avail itself of this option when possible in accordance with its constitutional requirements,

Noting that Denmark will not prevent the other Member States from further developing their cooperation with respect to measures not binding on Denmark,

Bearing in mind Article 3 of the Protocol on the Schengen acquis integrated into the framework of the European Union,

Have agreed upon the following provisions, which shall be annexed to the Treaty on European Union and the Treaty on the Functioning of the European Union:

Part I

Article 1
Denmark shall not take part in the adoption by the Council of proposed measures pursuant to Title V of Part Three of the Treaty on the Functioning of the European Union. The unanimity of the members of the Council, with the exception of the representative of the government of Denmark, shall be necessary for the decisions of the Council which must be adopted unanimously.

For the purposes of this Article, a qualified majority shall be defined in accordance with Article 238(3) of the Treaty on the Functioning of the European Union.

Article 2
None of the provisions of Title V of Part Three of the Treaty on the Functioning of the European Union, no measure adopted pursuant to that Title, no provision of any international agreement concluded by the Union pursuant to that Title, and no decision of the Court of Justice of the European Union interpreting any such provision or measure or any measure amended or amendable pursuant to that Title shall be binding upon or applicable in Denmark; and no such provision, measure or decision shall in any way affect the competences, rights and obligations of Denmark; and no such provision, measure or decision shall in any way affect the Community or Union acquis nor form part of Union law as they apply to Denmark. In particular, acts of the Union in the field of police cooperation and judicial cooperation in criminal matters adopted before the entry into force of the Treaty of Lisbon which are amended shall continue to be binding upon and applicable to Denmark unchanged.

Article 2a
Article 2 of this Protocol shall also apply in respect of those rules laid down on the basis of Article 16 of the Treaty on the Functioning of the European Union which relate to the processing of personal data by the Member States when carrying out activities which fall within the scope of Chapter 4 or Chapter 5 of Title V of Part Three of that Treaty.

Article 3
Denmark shall bear no financial consequences of measures referred to in Article 1, other than administrative costs entailed for the institutions.

Article 4
1. Denmark shall decide within a period of six months after the Council has decided on a proposal or initiative to build upon the Schengen acquis covered by this Part, whether it will implement this measure in its national law. If it decides to do so, this measure will create an obligation under international law between Denmark and the other Member States bound by the measure.

2. If Denmark decides not to implement a measure of the Council as referred to in paragraph 1, the Member States bound by that measure and Denmark will consider appropriate measures to be taken.

Part II

Article 5

With regard to measures adopted by the Council pursuant to Article 26(1), Article 42 and Articles 43 to 46 of the Treaty on European Union, Denmark does not participate in the elaboration and the implementation of decisions and actions of the Union which have defence implications. Therefore Denmark shall not participate in their adoption. Denmark will not prevent the other Member States from further developing their cooperation in this area. Denmark shall not be obliged to contribute to the financing of operational expenditure arising from such measures, nor to make military capabilities available to the Union.

The unanimity of the members of the Council, with the exception of the representative of the government of Denmark, shall be necessary for the acts of the Council which must be adopted unanimously.

For the purposes of this Article, a qualified majority shall be defined in accordance with Article 238(3) of the Treaty on the Functioning of the European Union.

Part III

Article 6

Articles 1, 2 and 3 shall not apply to measures determining the third countries whose nationals must be in possession of a visa when crossing the external borders of the Member States, or measures relating to a uniform format for visas.

Part IV

Article 7

At any time Denmark may, in accordance with its constitutional requirements, inform the other Member States that it no longer wishes to avail itself of all or part of this Protocol. In that event, Denmark will apply in full all relevant measures then in force taken within the framework of the European Union.

Article 8

1. At any time and without prejudice to Article 7, Denmark may, in accordance with its constitutional requirements, notify the other Member States that, with effect from the first day of the month following the notification, Part I shall consist of the provisions in the Annex. In that case Articles 5 to 8 shall be renumbered in consequence.

2. Six months after the date on which the notification referred to in paragraph 1 takes effect all Schengen acquis and measures adopted to build upon this acquis, which until then have been binding on Denmark as obligations under international law, shall be binding upon Denmark as Union law.

Annex

Article 1

Subject to Article 3, Denmark shall not take part in the adoption by the Council of measures proposed pursuant to Title V of Part Three of the Treaty on the Functioning of the European Union. The unanimity of the members of the Council, with the exception of the representative of the government of Denmark, shall be necessary for the acts of the Council which must be adopted unanimously.

For the purposes of this Article, a qualified majority shall be defined in accordance with Article 238(3) of the Treaty on the Functioning of the European Union.

Article 2

Pursuant to Article 1 and subject to Articles 3, 4 and 8, none of the provisions in Title V of Part Three of the Treaty on the Functioning of the European Union, no measure adopted pursuant to that Title, no provision of any international agreements concluded by the Union pursuant to that Title, no decision of the Court of Justice of the European Union interpreting any such provision or measure shall be binding upon or applicable in Denmark; and no such provision, measure or decision shall in any way affect the competences, rights and obligations of Denmark; and no such provision, measure or decision shall in any way affect the Community or Union acquis nor form part of Union law as they apply to Denmark.

Article 3

1. Denmark may notify the President of the Council in writing, within three months after a proposal or initiative has been presented to the Council pursuant to Title V of Part Three of the Treaty on the Functioning of the European Union, that it wishes to take part in the adoption and application of any such proposed measure, whereupon Denmark shall be entitled to do so.

2. If after a reasonable period of time a measure referred to in paragraph 1 cannot be adopted with Denmark taking part, the Council may adopt that measure referred to in paragraph 1 in accordance with Article 1 without the participation of Denmark. In that case Article 2 applies.

Article 4

Denmark may at any time after the adoption of a measure pursuant to Title V of Part Three of the Treaty on the Functioning of the European Union notify its intention to the Council and the Commission that it wishes to accept that measure. In that case, the procedure provided for in Article 331(1) of that Treaty shall apply mutatis mutandis.

Article 5

1. The provisions of this Protocol apply for Denmark also to measures proposed or adopted pursuant to Title V of Part Three of the Treaty on the Functioning of the European Union amending an existing measure by which it is bound.

2. However, in cases where the Council, acting on a proposal from the Commission, determines that the non-participation of Denmark in the amended version of an existing measure makes the application of that measure inoperable for other Member States or the Union, it may urge it to make a notification under Article 3 or 4. For the purposes of Article 3 a further period of two months starts to run as from the date of such determination by the Council.

If, at the expiry of that period of two months from the Council's determination, Denmark has not made a notification under Article 3 or Article 4, the existing measure shall no longer be binding upon or applicable to it, unless it has made a notification under Article 4 before the entry into force of the amending measure. This shall take effect from the date of entry into force of the amending measure or of expiry of the period of two months, whichever is the later.

For the purpose of this paragraph, the Council shall, after a full discussion of the matter, act by a qualified majority of its members representing the Member States participating or having participated in the adoption of the amending measure. A qualified majority of the Council shall be defined in accordance with Article 238(3)(a) of the Treaty on the Functioning of the European Union.

3. The Council, acting by a qualified majority on a proposal from the Commission, may determine that Denmark shall bear the direct financial consequences, if any, necessarily and unavoidably incurred as a result of the cessation of its participation in the existing measure.

4. This Article shall be without prejudice to Article 4.

Article 6

1. Notification pursuant to Article 4 shall be submitted no later than six months after the final adoption of a measure if this measure builds upon the Schengen acquis.

If Denmark does not submit a notification in accordance with Articles 3 or 4 regarding a measure building upon the Schengen acquis, the Member States bound by that measure and Denmark will consider appropriate measures to be taken.

2. A notification pursuant to Article 3 with respect to a measure building upon the Schengen acquis shall be deemed irrevocably to be a notification pursuant to Article 3 with respect to any further proposal or initiative aiming to build upon that measure to the extent that such proposal or initiative builds upon the Schengen acquis.

Article 7

Denmark shall not be bound by the rules laid down on the basis of Article 16 of the Treaty on the Functioning of the European Union which relate to the processing of personal data by the Member States when carrying out activities which fall within the scope of Chapter 4 or Chapter 5 of Title V of Part Three of that Treaty where Denmark is not bound by the rules governing the forms of judicial cooperation in criminal matters or police cooperation which require compliance with the provisions laid down on the basis of Article 16.

Article 8

Where, in cases referred to in this Part, Denmark is bound by a measure adopted by the Council pursuant to Title V of Part Three of the Treaty on the Functioning of the European Union, the relevant provisions of the Treaties shall apply to Denmark in relation to that measure.

Article 9

Where Denmark is not bound by a measure adopted pursuant to Title V of Part Three of the Treaty on the Functioning of the European Union, it shall bear no financial consequences of that measure other than administrative costs entailed for the institutions unless the Council, with all its Members acting unanimously after consulting the European Parliament, decides otherwise.

Protocol (No 23)
on External Relations of the Member States with regard to the Crossing of External Borders

The High Contracting Parties,

Taking into account the need of the Member States to ensure effective controls at their external borders, in cooperation with third countries where appropriate,

Have agreed upon the following provisions, which shall be annexed to the Treaty on European Union and to the Treaty on the Functioning of the European Union:

The provisions on the measures on the crossing of external borders included in Article 77(2)(b) of the Treaty on the Functioning of the European Union shall be without prejudice to the competence of Member States to negotiate or conclude agreements with third countries as long as they respect Union law and other relevant international agreements.

Protocol (No 24) on Asylum for Nationals of Member States of the European Union

The High Contracting Parties,

Whereas, in accordance with Article 6(1) of the Treaty on European Union, the Union recognises the rights, freedoms and principles set out in the Charter of Fundamental Rights,

Whereas pursuant to Article 6(3) of the Treaty on European Union, fundamental rights, as guar anteed by the European Convention for the Protection of Human Rights and Fundamental Freedoms, constitute part of the Union's law as general principles,

Whereas the Court of Justice of the European Union has jurisdiction to ensure that in the interpretation and application of Article 6, paragraphs (1) and (3) of the Treaty on European Union the law is observed by the European Union,

Whereas pursuant to Article 49 of the Treaty on European Union any European State, when applying to become a Member of the Union, must respect the values set out in Article 2 of the Treaty on European Union,

Bearing in mind that Article 7 of the Treaty on European Union establishes a mechanism for the suspension of certain rights in the event of a serious and persistent breach by a Member State of those values,

Recalling that each national of a Member State, as a citizen of the Union, enjoys a special status and protection which shall be guaranteed by the Member States in accordance with the provisions of Part Two of the Treaty on the Functioning of the European Union,

Bearing in mind that the Treaties establish an area without internal frontiers and grant every citizen of the Union the right to move and reside freely within the territory of the Member States,

Wishing to prevent the institution of asylum being resorted to for purposes alien to those for which it is intended,

Whereas this Protocol respects the finality and the objectives of the Geneva Convention of 28 July 1951 relating to the status of refugees,

Have agreed upon the following provisions, which shall be annexed to the Treaty on European Union and to the Treaty on the Functioning of the European Union:

Sole Article

Given the level of protection of fundamental rights and freedoms by the Member States of the European Union, Member States shall be regarded as constituting safe countries of origin in respect of each other for all legal and practical purposes in relation to asylum matters. Accordingly, any application for asylum made by a national of a Member State may be taken into consideration or declared admissible for processing by another Member State only in the following cases:

(a) if the Member State of which the applicant is a national proceeds after the entry into force of the Treaty of Amsterdam, availing itself of the provisions of Article 15 of the European Convention for the Protection of Human Rights and Fundamental Freedoms, to take measures derogating in its territory from its obligations under that Convention;

(b) if the procedure referred to Article 7(1) of the Treaty on European Union has been initiated and until the Council, or, where appropriate, the European Council, takes a decision in respect thereof with regard to the Member State of which the applicant is a national;

(c) if the Council has adopted a decision in accordance with Article 7(1) of the Treaty on European Union in respect of the Member State of which the applicant is a national or if the European Council has adopted a decision in accordance with Article 7(2) of that Treaty in respect of the Member State of which the applicant is a national;

(d) if a Member State should so decide unilaterally in respect of the application of a national of another Member State; in that case the Council shall be immediately informed; the application shall be dealt with on the basis of the presumption that it is manifestly unfounded without affecting in any way, whatever the cases may be, the decision-making power of the Member State.

Protocol (No 25) on the Exercise of Shared Competence

The High Contracting Parties,

Have agreed upon the following provisions, which shall be annexed to the Treaty on European Union and to the Treaty on the Functioning of the European Union:

Sole Article

With reference to Article 2(2) of the Treaty on the Functioning of the European Union on shared competence, when the Union has taken action in a certain area, the scope of this exercise of competence only covers those elements governed by the Union act in question and therefore does not cover the whole area.

Protocol (No 26)
on Services of General Interest

The High Contracting Parties,
Wishing to emphasise the importance of services of general interest,
Have agreed upon the following interpretative provisions, which shall be annexed to the Treaty on European Union and to the Treaty on the Functioning of the European Union:

Article 1
The shared values of the Union in respect of services of general economic interest within the meaning of Article 14 of the Treaty on the Functioning of the European Union include in particular:
- the essential role and the wide discretion of national, regional and local authorities in providing, commissioning and organising services of general economic interest as closely as possible to the needs of the users;
- the diversity between various services of general economic interest and the differences in the needs and preferences of users that may result from different geographical, social or cultural situations;
- a high level of quality, safety and affordability, equal treatment and the promotion of universal access and of user rights.

Article 2
The provisions of the Treaties do not affect in any way the competence of Member States to provide, commission and organise non-economic services of general interest.

Protocol (No 27)
on the Internal Market and Competition

The High Contracting Parties,
Considering that the internal market as set out in Article 3 of the Treaty on European Union includes a system ensuring that competition is not distorted,
Have agreed that:

To this end, the Union shall, if necessary, take action under the provisions of the Treaties, including under Article 352 of the Treaty on the Functioning of the European Union.
This protocol shall be annexed to the Treaty on European Union and to the Treaty on the Functioning of the European Union.

Protocol (No 28)
on Economic, Social and Territorial Cohesion

The High Contracting Parties,

Recalling that Article 3 of the Treaty on European Union includes the objective of promoting economic, social and territorial cohesion and solidarity between Member States and that the said cohesion figures among the areas of shared competence of the Union listed in Article 4(2)(c) of the Treaty on the Functioning of the European Union,

Recalling that the provisions of Part Three, Title XVIII, on economic, social and territorial cohesion as a whole provide the legal basis for consolidating and further developing the Union's action in the field of economic, social and territorial cohesion, including the creation of a new fund,

Recalling that the provisions of Article 177 of the Treaty on the Functioning of the European Union envisage setting up a Cohesion Fund,

Noting that the European Investment Bank is lending large and increasing amounts for the benefit of the poorer regions,

Noting the desire for greater flexibility in the arrangements for allocations from the Structural Funds,

Noting the desire for modulation of the levels of Union participation in programmes and projects in certain countries,

Noting the proposal to take greater account of the relative prosperity of Member States in the system of own resources,

Reaffirm that the promotion of economic, social and territorial cohesion is vital to the full development and enduring success of the Union,

Reaffirm their conviction that the Structural Funds should continue to play a considerable part in the achievement of Union objectives in the field of cohesion,

Reaffirm their conviction that the European Investment Bank should continue to devote the majority of its resources to the promotion of economic, social and territorial cohesion, and declare their willingness to review the capital needs of the European Investment Bank as soon as this is necessary for that purpose,

Agree that the Cohesion Fund will provide Union financial contributions to projects in the fields of environment and trans-European networks in Member States with a per capita GNP of less than 90 % of the Union average which have a programme leading to the fulfilment of the conditions of economic convergence as set out in Article 126,

Declare their intention of allowing a greater margin of flexibility in allocating financing from the Structural Funds to specific needs not covered under the present Structural Funds regulations,

Declare their willingness to modulate the levels of Union participation in the context of programmes and projects of the Structural Funds, with a view to avoiding excessive increases in budgetary expenditure in the less prosperous Member States,

Recognise the need to monitor regularly the progress made towards achieving economic, social and territorial cohesion and state their willingness to study all necessary measures in this respect,

Declare their intention of taking greater account of the contributive capacity of individual Member States in the system of own resources, and of examining means of correcting, for the less prosperous Member States, regressive elements existing in the present own resources system,

Agree to annex this Protocol to the Treaty on European Union and the Treaty on the Functioning of the European Union.

Protocol (No 29)
on the System of Public Broadcasting
in the Member States

The High Contracting Parties,

Considering that the system of public broadcasting in the Member States is directly related to the democratic, social and cultural needs of each society and to the need to preserve media pluralism,

Have agreed upon the following interpretive provisions, which shall be annexed to the Treaty on European Union and to the Treaty on the Functioning of the European Union:

The provisions of the Treaties shall be without prejudice to the competence of Member States to provide for the funding of public service broadcasting and in so far as such funding is granted to broadcasting organisations for the fulfilment of the public service remit as conferred, defined and organised by each Member State, and in so far as such funding does not affect trading conditions and competition in the Union to an extent which would be contrary to the common interest, while the realisation of the remit of that public service shall be taken into account.

Protocol (No 30) on the Application of the Charter of Fundamental Rights of the European Union to Poland and to the United Kingdom

The High Contracting Parties,

Whereas in Article 6 of the Treaty on European Union, the Union recognises the rights, freedoms and principles set out in the Charter of Fundamental Rights of the European Union,

Whereas the Charter is to be applied in strict accordance with the provisions of the aforementioned Article 6 and Title VII of the Charter itself,

Whereas the aforementioned Article 6 requires the Charter to be applied and interpreted by the courts of Poland and of the United Kingdom strictly in accordance with the explanations referred to in that Article,

Whereas the Charter contains both rights and principles,

Whereas the Charter contains both provisions which are civil and political in character and those which are economic and social in character,

Whereas the Charter reaffirms the rights, freedoms and principles recognised in the Union and makes those rights more visible, but does not create new rights or principles,

Recalling the obligations devolving upon Poland and the United Kingdom under the Treaty on European Union, the Treaty on the Functioning of the European Union, and Union law generally,

Noting the wish of Poland and the United Kingdom to clarify certain aspects of the application of the Charter,

Desirous therefore of clarifying the application of the Charter in relation to the laws and administrative action of Poland and of the United Kingdom and of its justiciability within Poland and within the United Kingdom,

Reaffirming that references in this Protocol to the operation of specific provisions of the Charter are strictly without prejudice to the operation of other provisions of the Charter,
Reaffirming that this Protocol is without prejudice to the application of the Charter to other Member States,
Reaffirming that this Protocol is without prejudice to other obligations devolving upon Poland and the United Kingdom under the Treaty on European Union, the Treaty on the Functioning of the European Union, and Union law generally,
Have agreed upon the following provisions, which shall be annexed to the Treaty on European Union and to the Treaty on the Functioning of the European Union:

Article 1

1. The Charter does not extend the ability of the Court of Justice of the European Union, or any court or tribunal of Poland or of the United Kingdom, to find that the laws, regulations or administrative provisions, practices or action of Poland or of the United Kingdom are inconsistent with the fundamental rights, freedoms and principles that it reaffirms.
2. In particular, and for the avoidance of doubt, nothing in Title IV of the Charter creates justiciable rights applicable to Poland or the United Kingdom except in so far as Poland or the United Kingdom has provided for such rights in its national law.

Article 2

To the extent that a provision of the Charter refers to national laws and practices, it shall only apply to Poland or the United Kingdom to the extent that the rights or principles that it contains are recognised in the law or practices of Poland or of the United Kingdom.

Protocol (No 31) concerning Imports into the European Union of Petroleum Products refined in the Netherlands Antilles

The High Contracting Parties,

Being desirous of giving fuller details about the system of trade applicable to imports into the European Union of petroleum products refined in the Netherlands Antilles,

Have agreed upon the following provisions, which shall be annexed to the Treaty on European Union and to the Treaty on the Functioning of the European Union:

Article 1

This Protocol is applicable to petroleum products coming under the Brussels Nomenclature numbers 27.10, 27.11, 27.12, ex 27.13 (paraffin wax, petroleum or shale wax and paraffin residues) and 27.14, imported for use in Member States.

Article 2

Member States shall undertake to grant to petroleum products refined in the Netherlands Antilles the tariff preferences resulting from the association of the latter with the Union, under the conditions provided for in this Protocol. These provisions shall hold good whatever may be the rules of origin applied by the Member States.

Article 3

1. When the Commission, at the request of a Member State or on its own initiative, establishes that imports into the Union of petroleum products refined in the Netherlands Antilles under the system provided for in Article 2 above are giving rise to real difficulties on the market of one or more Member States, it shall decide that customs duties on the said imports shall be introduced, increased or re-introduced by the Member States in question, to such an extent and for such a period as may be necessary to meet that situation. The rates of the customs duties thus introduced, increased or re-introduced may not exceed the customs duties applicable to third countries for these same products.

2. The provisions of paragraph 1 can in any case be applied when imports into the Union of petroleum products refined in the Netherlands Antilles reach two million metric tons a year.

3. The Council shall be informed of decisions taken by the Commission in pursuance of paragraphs 1 and 2, including those directed at rejecting the request of a Member State. The Council shall, at the request of any Member State, assume responsibility for the matter and may at any time amend or revoke them.

Article 4

1. If a Member State considers that imports of petroleum products refined in the Netherlands Antilles, made either directly or through another Member State under the system provided for in Article 2 above, are giving rise to real difficulties on its market and that immediate action is necessary to meet them, it may on its own initiative decide to apply customs duties to such imports, the rate of which may not exceed those of the customs duties applicable to third countries in respect of the same products. It shall notify its decision to the Commission which shall decide within one month whether the measures taken by the State should be maintained or must be amended or cancelled. The provisions of Article 3(3) shall be applicable to such decision of the Commission.

2. When the quantities of petroleum products refined in the Netherlands Antilles imported either directly or through another Member State, under the system provided for in Article 2 above, into a Member State or States of the European Union exceed during a calendar year the tonnage shown in the Annex to this Protocol, the measures taken in pursuance of paragraph 1 by that or those Member States for the current year shall be considered to be justified; the Commission shall, after assuring itself that the tonnage fixed has been reached, formally record the measures taken. In such a case the other Member States shall abstain from formally placing the matter before the Council.

Article 5

If the Union decides to apply quantitative restrictions to petroleum products, no matter whence they are imported, these restrictions may also be applied to imports of such products from the Netherlands Antilles. In such a case preferential treatment shall be granted to the Netherlands Antilles as compared with third countries.

Article 6

1. The provisions of Articles 2 to 5 shall be reviewed by the Council, by unanimous decision, after consulting the European Parliament and the Commission, when a common definition of origin for petroleum products from third countries and associated countries is adopted, or when decisions are taken within the framework of a common commercial policy for the products in question or when a common energy policy is established.

2. When such revision is made, however, equivalent preferences must in any case be maintained in favour of the Netherlands Antilles in a suitable form and for a minimum quantity of 21½ million metric tons of petroleum products.

3. The Union's commitments in regard to equivalent preferences as mentioned in paragraph 2 of this Article may, if necessary, be broken down country by country taking into account the tonnage indicated in the Annex to this Protocol.

Article 7
For the implementation of this Protocol, the Commission is responsible for following the pattern of imports into the Member States of petroleum products refined in the Netherlands Antilles. Member States shall communicate to the Commission, which shall see that it is circulated, all useful information to that end in accordance with the administrative conditions recommended by it.

Annex to the Protocol

For the implementation of Article 4(2) of the Protocol concerning imports into the European Union of petroleum products refined in the Netherlands Antilles, the High Contracting Parties have decided that the quantity of 2 million metric tons of petroleum products from the Antilles shall be allocated among the Member States as follows:

Germany	625 000 metric tons
Belgo-Luxembourg Economic Union	200 000 metric tons
France	75 000 metric tons
Italy	100 000 metric tons
Netherlands	1 000 000 metric tons

Protocol (No 32)
on the Acquisition of Property in Denmark

The High Contracting Parties,
Desiring to settle certain particular problems relating to Denmark,
Have agreed upon the following provisions, which shall be annexed to the Treaty on European Union and to the Treaty on the Functioning of the European Union:

Notwithstanding the provisions of the Treaties, Denmark may maintain the existing legislation on the acquisition of second homes.

Protocol (No 33) concerning Article 157 of the Treaty on the Functioning of the European Union

The High Contracting Parties,

Have agreed upon the following provision, which shall be annexed to the Treaty on European Union and to the Treaty on the Functioning of the European Union:

For the purposes of Article 157 of the Treaty on the Functioning of the European Union, benefits under occupational social security schemes shall not be considered as remuneration if and in so far as they are attributable to periods of employment prior to 17 May 1990, except in the case of workers or those claiming under them who have before that date initiated legal proceedings or introduced an equivalent claim under the applicable national law.

Protocol (No 34)
on Special Arrangements for Greenland

Sole Article

1. The treatment on import into the Union of products subject to the common organisation of the market in fishery products, originating in Greenland, shall, while complying with the mechanisms of the internal market organisation, involve exemption from customs duties and charges having equivalent effect and the absence of quantitative restrictions or measures having equivalent effect if the possibilities for access to Greenland fishing zones granted to the Union pursuant to an agreement between the Union and the authority responsible for Greenland are satisfactory to the Union.

2. All measures relating to the import arrangements for such products, including those relating to the adoption of such measures, shall be adopted in accordance with the procedure laid down in Article 43 of the Treaty establishing the European Union.

Protocol (No 35)
on Article 40.3.3 of the Constitution of Ireland

The High Contracting Parties,

Have agreed upon the following provision, which shall be annexed to the Treaty on European Union and to the Treaty on the Functioning of the European Union and to the Treaty establishing the European Atomic Energy Community:

Nothing in the Treaties, or in the Treaty establishing the European Atomic Energy Community, or in the Treaties or Acts modifying or supplementing those Treaties, shall affect the application in Ireland of Article 40.3.3 of the Constitution of Ireland.

Protocol (No 36) on Transitional Provisions

The High Contracting Parties,

Whereas, in order to organise the transition from the institutional provisions of the Treaties applicable prior to the entry into force of the Treaty of Lisbon to the provisions contained in that Treaty, it is necessary to lay down transitional provisions,

Have agreed upon the following provisions, which shall be annexed to the Treaty on European Union, to the Treaty on the Functioning of the European Union and to the Treaty establishing the European Atomic Energy Community:

Article 1

In this Protocol, the words 'the Treaties' shall mean the Treaty on European Union, the Treaty on the Functioning of the European Union and the Treaty establishing the European Atomic Energy Community.

Title I
Provisions concerning the European Parliament

Article 2

1. For the period of the 2009-2014 parliamentary term remaining at the date of entry into force of this Article, and by way of derogation from Articles 189, second paragraph, and 190(2) of the Treaty establishing the European Community and Articles 107, second paragraph, and 108(2) of the Treaty establishing the European Atomic Energy Community, which were in force at the time of the European Parliament elections in June 2009, and by way of derogation from the number of seats provided for in the first subparagraph of Article 14(2) of the Treaty on European Union, the following 18 seats shall be added to the existing 736 seats, thus provisionally bringing the total number of members of the European Parliament to 754 until the end of the 2009-2014 parliamentary term:

Bulgaria	1	Netherlands	1
Spain	4	Austria	2
France	2	Poland	1
Italy	1	Slovenia	1
Latvia	1	Sweden	2
Malta	1	United Kingdom	1

2. By way of derogation from Article 14(3) of the Treaty on European Union, the Member States concerned shall designate the persons who will fill the additional seats referred to in paragraph 1, in accordance with the legislation of the Member States concerned and provided that the persons in question have been elected by direct universal suffrage:

(a) in ad hoc elections by direct universal suffrage in the Member State concerned, in accordance with the provisions applicable for elections to the European Parliament;

(b) by reference to the results of the European Parliament elections from 4 to 7 June 2009; or

(c) by designation, by the national parliament of the Member State concerned from among its members, of the requisite number of members, according to the procedure determined by each of those Member States.

3. In accordance with the second subparagraph of Article 14(2) of the Treaty on European Union, the European Council shall adopt a decision determining the composition of the European Parliament in good time before the 2014 European Parliament elections.

Title II
Provisions concerning the qualified majority

Article 3

1. In accordance with Article 16(4) of the Treaty on European Union, the provisions of that paragraph and of Article 238(2) of the Treaty on the Functioning of the European Union relating to the definition of the qualified majority in the European Council and the Council shall take effect on1 November 2014.

2. Between 1 November 2014 and 31 March 2017, when an act is to be adopted by qualified majority, a member of the Council may request that it be adopted in accordance with the qualified majority as defined in paragraph 3. In that case, paragraphs 3 and 4 shall apply.

3. Until 31 October 2014, the following provisions shall remain in force, without prejudice to the second subparagraph of Article 235(1) of the Treaty on the Functioning of the European Union.

For acts of the European Council and of the Council requiring a qualified majority, members' votes shall be weighted as follows:

Country	Votes	Country	Votes
Belgium	12	Lithuania	7
Bulgaria	10	Luxembourg	4
Czech Republic	12	Hungary	12
Denmark	7	Malta	3
Germany	29	Netherlands	13
Estonia	4	Austria	10
Ireland	7	Poland	27
Greece	12	Portugal	12
Spain	27	Romania	14
France	29	Slovenia	4

Croatia	7	Slovakia	7
Italy	29	Finland	7
Cyprus	4	Sweden	10
Latvia	4	United Kingdom	29

Acts shall be adopted if there are at least 260 votes in favour representing a majority of the members where, under the Treaties, they must be adopted on a proposal from the Commission. In other cases decisions shall be adopted if there are at least 260 votes in favour representing at least two thirds of the members.

A member of the European Council or the Council may request that, where an act is adopted by the European Council or the Council by a qualified majority, a check is made to ensure that the Member States comprising the qualified majority represent at least 62 % of the total population of the Union. If that proves not to be the case, the act shall not be adopted.

4. Until 31 October 2014, the qualified majority shall, in cases where, under the Treaties, not all the members of the Council participate in voting, namely in the cases where reference is made to the qualified majority as defined in Article 238(3) of the Treaty on the Functioning of the European Union, be defined as the same proportion of the weighted votes and the same proportion of the number of the Council members and, if appropriate, the same percentage of the population of the Member States concerned as laid down in paragraph 3 of this Article.

Title III
Provisions concerning the configurations of the Council

Article 4
Until the entry into force of the decision referred to in the first subparagraph of Article 16(6) of the Treaty on European Union, the Council may meet in the configurations laid down in the second and third subparagraphs of that paragraph and in the other configurations on the list established by a decision of the General Affairs Council, acting by a simple majority.

Title IV
Provisions concerning the Commission, including the High Representative of the Union for Foreign Affairs and Security Policy

Article 5
The members of the Commission in office on the date of entry into force of the Treaty of Lisbon shall remain in office until the end of their term of office. However, on the day of the appointment of the High Representative of the Union for Foreign Affairs and Security Policy, the term of office of the member having the same nationality as the High Representative shall end.

Title V
Provisions concerning the Secretary-General of the Council, High Representative for the Common Foreign and Security Policy, and the Deputy Secretary-General of the Council

Article 6
The terms of office of the Secretary-General of the Council, High Representative for the common foreign and security policy, and the Deputy Secretary-General of the Council shall end on the date of entry into force of the Treaty of Lisbon. The Council shall appoint a Secretary-General in conformity with Article 240(2) of the Treaty on the Functioning of the European Union.

Title VI
Provisions concerning Advisory Bodies

Article 7
Until the entry into force of the decision referred to in Article 301 of the Treaty on the Functioning of the European Union, the allocation of members of the Economic and Social Committee shall be as follows:

Belgium	12	Lithuania	9
Bulgaria	12	Luxembourg	6
Czech Republic	12	Hungary	12
Denmark	9	Malta	5
Germany	24	Netherlands	12
Estonia	7	Austria	12
Ireland	9	Poland	21
Greece	12	Portugal	12
Spain	21	Romania	15
France	24	Slovenia	7
Croatia	9	Slovakia	9
Italy	24	Finland	9
Cyprus	6	Sweden	12
Latvia	7	United Kingdom	24

Article 8
Until the entry into force of the decision referred to in Article 305 of the Treaty on the Functioning of the European Union, the allocation of members of the Committee of the Regions shall be as follows:

Belgium	12	Lithuania	9
Bulgaria	12	Luxembourg	6

Czech Republic	12	Hungary	12
Denmark	9	Malta	5
Germany	24	Netherlands	12
Estonia	7	Austria	12
Ireland	9	Poland	21
Greece	12	Portugal	12
Spain	21	Romania	15
France	24	Slovenia	7
Croatia	9	Slovakia	9
Italy	24	Finland	9
Cyprus	6	Sweden	12
Latvia	7	United Kingdom	24

Title VII
Transitional provisions concerning acts adopted on the basis of Titles V and VI of the Treaty on European Union prior to the entry into force of the Treaty of Lisbon

Article 9
The legal effects of the acts of the institutions, bodies, offices and agencies of the Union adopted on the basis of the Treaty on European Union prior to the entry into force of the Treaty of Lisbon shall be preserved until those acts are repealed, annulled or amended in implementation of the Treaties. The same shall apply to agreements concluded between Member States on the basis of the Treaty on European Union.

Article 10
1. As a transitional measure, and with respect to acts of the Union in the field of police cooperation and judicial cooperation in criminal matters which have been adopted before the entry into force of the Treaty of Lisbon, the powers of the institutions shall be the following at the date of entry into force of that Treaty: the powers of the Commission under Article 258 of the Treaty on the Functioning of the European Union shall not be applicable and the powers of the Court of Justice of the European Union under Title VI of the Treaty on European Union, in the version in force before the entry into force of the Treaty of Lisbon, shall remain the same, including where they have been accepted under Article 35(2) of the said Treaty on European Union.
2. The amendment of an act referred to in paragraph 1 shall entail the applicability of the powers of the institutions referred to in that paragraph as set out in the Treaties with respect to the amended act for those Member States to which that amended act shall apply.
3. In any case, the transitional measure mentioned in paragraph 1 shall cease to have effect five years after the date of entry into force of the Treaty of Lisbon.

4. At the latest six months before the expiry of the transitional period referred to in paragraph 3, the United Kingdom may notify to the Council that it does not accept, with respect to the acts referred to in paragraph 1, the powers of the institutions referred to in paragraph 1 as set out in the Treaties. In case the United Kingdom has made that notification, all acts referred to in paragraph 1 shall cease to apply to it as from the date of expiry of the transitional period referred to in paragraph 3. This subparagraph shall not apply with respect to the amended acts which are applicable to the United Kingdom as referred to in paragraph 2.

The Council, acting by a qualified majority on a proposal from the Commission, shall determine the necessary consequential and transitional arrangements. The United Kingdom shall not participate in the adoption of this decision. A qualified majority of the Council shall be defined in accordance with Article 238(3)(a) of the Treaty on the Functioning of the European Union.

The Council, acting by a qualified majority on a proposal from the Commission, may also adopt a decision determining that the United Kingdom shall bear the direct financial consequences, if any, necessarily and unavoidably incurred as a result of the cessation of its participation in those acts.

5. The United Kingdom may, at any time afterwards, notify the Council of its wish to participate in acts which have ceased to apply to it pursuant to paragraph 4, first subparagraph. In that case, the relevant provisions of the Protocol on the Schengen acquis integrated into the framework of the European Union or of the Protocol on the position of the United Kingdom and Ireland in respect of the area of freedom, security and justice, as the case may be, shall apply. The powers of the institutions with regard to those acts shall be those set out in the Treaties. When acting under the relevant Protocols, the Union institutions and the United Kingdom shall seek to re-establish the widest possible measure of participation of the United Kingdom in the acquis of the Union in the area of freedom, security and justice without seriously affecting the practical operability of the various parts thereof, while respecting their coherence.

Protocol (No 37) on the Financial Consequences of the Expiry of the ECSC Treaty and on the Research Fund for Coal and Steel

The High Contracting Parties,

Recalling that all assets and liabilities of the European Coal and Steel Community, as they existed on 23 July 2002, were transferred to the European Community on 24 July 2002,

Taking account of the desire to use these funds for research in sectors related to the coal and steel industry and therefore the necessity to provide for certain special rules in this regard,

Have agreed upon the following provisions, which shall be annexed to the Treaty on European Union and to the Treaty on the Functioning of the European Union:

Article 1

1. The net worth of these assets and liabilities, as they appear in the balance sheet of the ECSC of 23 July 2002, subject to any increase or decrease which may occur as a result of the liquidation operations, shall be considered as assets intended for research in the sectors related to the coal and steel industry, referred to as the 'ECSC in liquidation'. On completion of the liquidation they shall be referred to as the 'assets of the Research Fund for Coal and Steel'.

2. The revenue from these assets, referred to as the 'Research Fund for Coal and Steel', shall be used exclusively for research, outside the research framework programme, in the sectors related to the coal and steel industry in accordance with the provisions of this Protocol and of acts adopted on the basis hereof.

Article 2

The Council, acting in accordance with a special legislative procedure and after obtaining the consent of the European Parliament, shall adopt all the necessary provisions for the implementation of this Protocol, including essential principles.

The Council shall adopt, on a proposal from the Commission and after consulting the European Parliament, measures establishing multiannual financial guidelines for managing the assets of the Research Fund for Coal and Steel and technical guidelines for the research programme of the Research Fund for Coal and Steel.

Article 3

Except as otherwise provided in this Protocol and in the acts adopted on the basis hereof, the provisions of the Treaties shall apply.

Declarations annexed to the Final Act of the Intergovernmental Conference which adopted the Treaty of Lisbon

Date signed on 13 December 2007
Source consolidated Version OJ C 326 of 26 October 2012, p. 337

A. Declarations concerning Provisions of the Treaties

1. Declaration concerning the Charter of Fundamental Rights of the European Union

The Charter of Fundamental Rights of the European Union, which has legally binding force, confirms the fundamental rights guaranteed by the European Convention for the Protection of Human Rights and Fundamental Freedoms and as they result from the constitutional traditions common to the Member States.

The Charter does not extend the field of application of Union law beyond the powers of the Union or establish any new power or task for the Union, or modify powers and tasks as defined by the Treaties.

2. Declaration on Article 6(2) of the Treaty on European Union

The Conference agrees that the Union's accession to the European Convention for the Protection of Human Rights and Fundamental Freedoms should be arranged in such a way as to preserve the specific features of Union law. In this connection, the Conference notes the existence of a regular dialogue between the Court of Justice of the European Union and the European Court of Human Rights; such dialogue could be reinforced when the Union accedes to that Convention.

© European Union, http://eur-lex.europa.eu/, 1998-2015.

3. Declaration on Article 8 of the Treaty on European Union

The Union will take into account the particular situation of small-sized countries which maintain specific relations of proximity with it.

4. Declaration on the composition of the European Parliament

The additional seat in the European Parliament will be attributed to Italy.

5. Declaration on the political agreement by the European Council concerning the draft Decision on the composition of the European Parliament

The European Council will give its political agreement on the revised draft Decision on the composition of the European Parliament for the legislative period 2009-2014, based on the proposal from the European Parliament.

6. Declaration on Article 15(5) and (6), Article 17(6) and (7) and Article 18 of the Treaty on European Union

In choosing the persons called upon to hold the offices of President of the European Council, President of the Commission and High Representative of the Union for Foreign Affairs and Security Policy, due account is to be taken of the need to respect the geographical and demographic diversity of the Union and its Member States.

7. Declaration on Article 16(4) of the Treaty on European Union and Article 238(2) of the Treaty on the Functioning of the European Union*

The Conference declares that the decision relating to the implementation of Article 16(4) of the Treaty on European Union and Article 238(2) of the Treaty on the Functioning of the European Union will be adopted by the Council on the date of the signature of the Treaty of Lisbon and will enter into force on the day that Treaty enters into force. The draft decision is set out below:

Draft Decision of the Council
relating to the implementation of Article 16(4) of the Treaty on European Union and Article 238(2) of the Treaty on the Functioning of the European Union between 1 November 2014 and 31 March 2017 on the one hand, and as from 1 April 2017 on the other

The Council of the European Union,
Whereas:

(1) Provisions should be adopted allowing for a smooth transition from the system for decision-making in the Council by a qualified majority as defined in Article 3(3) of the

---

* Editor's Note: Council Decision of 13 December 2007 relating to the implementation of Article 9C(4) of the Treaty on European Union and Article 205(2) of the Treaty on the Functioning of the European Union between 1 November 2014 and 31 March 2017 on the one hand, and as from 1 April 2017 on the other, OJ L 314 of 1 September 2009, p. 73.

Protocol on the transitional provisions, which will continue to apply until 31 October 2014, to the voting system provided for in Article 16(4) of the Treaty on European Union and Article 238(2) of the Treaty on the Functioning of the European Union, which will apply with effect from 1 November 2014, including, during a transitional period until 31 March 2017, specific provisions laid down in Article 3(2) of that Protocol.

(2) It is recalled that it is the practice of the Council to devote every effort to strengthening the democratic legitimacy of decisions taken by a qualified majority,

Has decided as follows:

Section 1
Provisions to be applied from 1 November 2014 to 31 March 2017

Article 1

From 1 November 2014 to 31 March 2017, if members of the Council, representing:

(a) at least three quarters of the population, or

(b) at least three quarters of the number of Member States

necessary to constitute a blocking minority resulting from the application of Article 16(4), first subparagraph, of the Treaty on European Union or Article 238(2) of the Treaty on the Functioning of the European Union, indicate their opposition to the Council adopting an act by a qualified majority, the Council shall discuss the issue.

Article 2

The Council shall, in the course of these discussions, do all in its power to reach, within a reasonable time and without prejudicing obligatory time limits laid down by Union law, a satisfactory solution to address concerns raised by the members of the Council referred to in Article 1.

Article 3

To this end, the President of the Council, with the assistance of the Commission and in compliance with the Rules of Procedure of the Council, shall undertake any initiative necessary to facilitate a wider basis of agreement in the Council. The members of the Council shall lend him or her their assistance.

Section 2
Provisions to be applied as from 1 April 2017

Article 4

As from 1 April 2017, if members of the Council, representing:

(a) at least 55 % of the population, or

(b) at least 55 % of the number of Member States

necessary to constitute a blocking minority resulting from the application of Article 16(4), first subparagraph, of the Treaty on European Union or Article 238(2) of the Treaty on the

Functioning of the European Union, indicate their opposition to the Council adopting an act by a qualified majority, the Council shall discuss the issue.

Article 5
The Council shall, in the course of these discussions, do all in its power to reach, within a reasonable time and without prejudicing obligatory time limits laid down by Union law, a satisfactory solution to address concerns raised by the members of the Council referred to in Article 4.

Article 6
To this end, the President of the Council, with the assistance of the Commission and in compliance with the Rules of Procedure of the Council, shall undertake any initiative necessary to facilitate a wider basis of agreement in the Council. The members of the Council shall lend him or her their assistance.

Section 3
Entry into force

Article 7
This Decision shall enter into force on the date of the entry into force of the Treaty of Lisbon.

8. Declaration on practical measures to be taken upon the entry into force of the Treaty of Lisbon as regards the Presidency of the European Council and of the Foreign Affairs Council

In the event that the Treaty of Lisbon enters into force later than 1 January 2009, the Conference requests the competent authorities of the Member State holding the six-monthly Presidency of the Council at that time, on the one hand, and the person elected President of the European Council and the person appointed High Representative of the Union for Foreign Affairs and Security Policy, on the other hand, to take the necessary specific measures, in consultation with the following six-monthly Presidency, to allow an efficient handover of the material and organisational aspects of the Presidency of the European Council and of the Foreign Affairs Council.

9. Declaration on Article 16(9) of the Treaty on European Union concerning the European Council decision on the exercise of the Presidency of the Council

The Conference declares that the Council should begin preparing the decision establishing the procedures for implementing the decision on the exercise of the Presidency of the Council as soon as the Treaty of Lisbon is signed, and should give its political approval within six months. A draft decision of the European Council, which will be adopted on the date of entry into force of the said Treaty, is set out below:

Draft decision of the European Council
on the exercise of the Presidency of the Council

Article 1
1. The Presidency of the Council, with the exception of the Foreign Affairs configuration, shall be held by pre-established groups of three Member States for a period of 18 months. The groups shall be made up on a basis of equal rotation among the Member States, taking into account their diversity and geographical balance within the Union.
2. Each member of the group shall in turn chair for a six-month period all configurations of the Council, with the exception of the Foreign Affairs configuration. The other members of the group shall assist the Chair in all its responsibilities on the basis of a common programme. Members of the team may decide alternative arrangements among themselves.

Article 2
The Committee of Permanent Representatives of the Governments of the Member States shall be chaired by a representative of the Member State chairing the General Affairs Council.
The Chair of the Political and Security Committee shall be held by a representative of the High Representative of the Union for Foreign Affairs and Security Policy.
The chair of the preparatory bodies of the various Council configurations, with the exception of the Foreign Affairs configuration, shall fall to the member of the group chairing the relevant configuration, unless decided otherwise in accordance with Article 4.

Article 3
The General Affairs Council shall ensure consistency and continuity in the work of the different Council configurations in the framework of multiannual programmes in cooperation with the Commission. The Member States holding the Presidency shall take all necessary measures for the organisation and smooth operation of the Council's work, with the assistance of the General Secretariat of the Council.

Article 4
The Council shall adopt a decision establishing the measures for the implementation of this decision.

10. Declaration on Article 17 of the Treaty on European Union
The Conference considers that when the Commission no longer includes nationals of all Member States, the Commission should pay particular attention to the need to ensure full transparency in relations with all Member States. Accordingly, the Commission should liaise closely with all Member States, whether or not they have a national serving as member of the Commission, and in this context pay special attention to the need to share information and consult with all Member States.

The Conference also considers that the Commission should take all the necessary measures to ensure that political, social and economic realities in all Member States, including those which have no national serving as member of the Commission, are fully taken into account. These measures should include ensuring that the position of those Member States is addressed by appropriate organisational arrangements.

11. Declaration on Article 17(6) and (7) of the Treaty on European Union

The Conference considers that, in accordance with the provisions of the Treaties, the European Parliament and the European Council are jointly responsible for the smooth running of the process leading to the election of the President of the European Commission. Prior to the decision of the European Council, representatives of the European Parliament and of the European Council will thus conduct the necessary consultations in the framework deemed the most appropriate. These consultations will focus on the backgrounds of the candidates for President of the Commission, taking account of the elections to the European Parliament, in accordance with the first subparagraph of Article 17(7). The arrangements for such consultations may be determined, in due course, by common accord between the European Parliament and the European Council.

12. Declaration on Article 18 of the Treaty on European Union

1. The Conference declares that, in the course of the preparatory work preceding the appointment of the High Representative of the Union for Foreign Affairs and Security Policy which is due to take place on the date of entry into force of the Treaty of Lisbon in accordance with Article 18 of the Treaty on European Union and Article 5 of the Protocol on transitional provisions and whose term of office will be from that date until the end of the term of office of the Commission in office on that date, appropriate contacts will be made with the European Parliament.
2. Furthermore, the Conference recalls that, as regards the High Representative of the Union for Foreign Affairs and Security Policy whose term of office will start in November 2009 at the same time and for the same duration as the next Commission, he or she will be appointed in accordance with the provisions of Articles 17 and 18 of the Treaty on European Union.

13. Declaration concerning the common foreign and security policy

The Conference underlines that the provisions in the Treaty on European Union covering the Common Foreign and Security Policy, including the creation of the office of High Representative of the Union for Foreign Affairs and Security Policy and the establishment of an External Action Service, do not affect the responsibilities of the Member States, as they currently exist, for the formulation and conduct of their foreign policy nor of their national representation in third countries and international organisations.

The Conference also recalls that the provisions governing the Common Security and Defence Policy do not prejudice the specific character of the security and defence policy of the Member States.

It stresses that the European Union and its Member States will remain bound by the provisions of the Charter of the United Nations and, in particular, by the primary responsibility of the Security Council and of its Members for the maintenance of international peace and security.

14. Declaration concerning the common foreign and security policy

In addition to the specific rules and procedures referred to in paragraph 1 of Article 24 of the Treaty on European Union, the Conference underlines that the provisions covering the Common Foreign and Security Policy including in relation to the High Representative of the Union for Foreign Affairs and Security Policy and the External Action Service will not affect the existing legal basis, responsibilities, and powers of each Member State in relation to the formulation and conduct of its foreign policy, its national diplomatic service, relations with third countries and participation in international organisations, including a Member State's membership of the Security Council of the United Nations.

The Conference also notes that the provisions covering the Common Foreign and Security Policy do not give new powers to the Commission to initiate decisions nor do they increase the role of the European Parliament.

The Conference also recalls that the provisions governing the Common Security and Defence Policy do not prejudice the specific character of the security and defence policy of the Member States.

15. Declaration on Article 27 of the Treaty on European Union

The Conference declares that, as soon as the Treaty of Lisbon is signed, the Secretary-General of the Council, High Representative for the common foreign and security policy, the Commission and the Member States should begin preparatory work on the European External Action Service.

16. Declaration on Article 55(2) of the Treaty on European Union

The Conference considers that the possibility of producing translations of the Treaties in the languages mentioned in Article 55(2) contributes to fulfilling the objective of respecting the Union's rich cultural and linguistic diversity as set forth in the fourth subparagraph of Article 3(3). In this context, the Conference confirms the attachment of the Union to the cultural diversity of Europe and the special attention it will continue to pay to these and other languages.

The Conference recommends that those Member States wishing to avail themselves of the possibility recognised in Article 55(2) communicate to the Council, within six months from the date of the signature of the Treaty of Lisbon, the language or languages into which translations of the Treaties will be made.

17. Declaration concerning primacy

The Conference recalls that, in accordance with well settled case law of the Court of Justice of the European Union, the Treaties and the law adopted by the Union on the basis of the

Treaties have primacy over the law of Member States, under the conditions laid down by the said case law.

The Conference has also decided to attach as an Annex to this Final Act the Opinion of the Council Legal Service on the primacy of EC law as set out in 11197/07 (JUR 260):

'Opinion of the Council Legal Service of 22 June 2007

It results from the case-law of the Court of Justice that primacy of EC law is a cornerstone principle of Community law. According to the Court, this principle is inherent to the specific nature of the European Community. At the time of the first judgment of this established case law (Costa/ENEL, 15 July 1964, Case 6/641[1]) there was no mention of primacy in the treaty. It is still the case today. The fact that the principle of primacy will not be included in the future treaty shall not in any way change the existence of the principle and the existing case-law of the Court of Justice.

18. Declaration in relation to the delimitation of competences

The Conference underlines that, in accordance with the system of division of competences between the Union and the Member States as provided for in the Treaty on European Union and the Treaty on the Functioning of the European Union, competences not conferred upon the Union in the Treaties remain with the Member States.

When the Treaties confer on the Union a competence shared with the Member States in a specific area, the Member States shall exercise their competence to the extent that the Union has not exercised, or has decided to cease exercising, its competence. The latter situation arises when the relevant EU institutions decide to repeal a legislative act, in particular better to ensure constant respect for the principles of subsidiarity and proportionality. The Council may, at the initiative of one or several of its members (representatives of Member States) and in accordance with Article 241 of the Treaty on the Functioning of the European Union, request the Commission to submit proposals for repealing a legislative act. The Conference welcomes the Commission's declaration that it will devote particular attention to these requests.

Equally, the representatives of the governments of the Member States, meeting in an Intergovernmental Conference, in accordance with the ordinary revision procedure provided for in Article 48(2) to (5) of the Treaty on European Union, may decide to amend the Treaties upon which the Union is founded, including either to increase or to reduce the competences conferred on the Union in the said Treaties.

19. Declaration on Article 8 of the Treaty on the Functioning of the European Union

The Conference agrees that, in its general efforts to eliminate inequalities between women and men, the Union will aim in its different policies to combat all kinds of domestic violence.

---

1 "It follows (...) that the law stemming from the treaty, an independent source of law, could not, because of its special and original nature, be overridden by domestic legal provisions, however framed, without being deprived of its character as Community law and without the legal basis of the Community itself being called into question."'

The Member States should take all necessary measures to prevent and punish these criminal acts and to support and protect the victims.

20. Declaration on Article 16 of the Treaty on the Functioning of the European Union

The Conference declares that, whenever rules on protection of personal data to be adopted on the basis of Article 16 could have direct implications for national security, due account will have to be taken of the specific characteristics of the matter. It recalls that the legislation presently applicable (see in particular Directive 95/46/EC) includes specific derogations in this regard.

21. Declaration on the protection of personal data in the fields of judicial cooperation in criminal matters and police cooperation

The Conference acknowledges that specific rules on the protection of personal data and the free movement of such data in the fields of judicial cooperation in criminal matters and police cooperation based on Article 16 of the Treaty on the Functioning of the European Union may prove necessary because of the specific nature of these fields.

22. Declaration on Articles 48 and 79 of the Treaty on the Functioning of the European Union

The Conference considers that in the event that a draft legislative act based on Article 79(2) would affect important aspects of the social security system of a Member State, including its scope, cost or financial structure, or would affect the financial balance of that system as set out in the second paragraph of Article 48, the interests of that Member State will be duly taken into account.

23. Declaration on the second paragraph of Article 48 of the Treaty on the Functioning of the European Union

The Conference recalls that in that case, in accordance with Article 15(4) of the Treaty on European Union, the European Council acts by consensus.

24. Declaration concerning the legal personality of the European Union

The Conference confirms that the fact that the European Union has a legal personality will not in any way authorise the Union to legislate or to act beyond the competences conferred upon it by the Member States in the Treaties.

25. Declaration on Articles 75 and 215 of the Treaty on the Functioning of the European Union

The Conference recalls that the respect for fundamental rights and freedoms implies, in particular, that proper attention is given to the protection and observance of the due process rights of the individuals or entities concerned. For this purpose and in order to guarantee a thorough judicial review of decisions subjecting an individual or entity to restrictive measures, such decisions must be based on clear and distinct criteria. These criteria should be tailored to the specifics of each restrictive measure.

26. Declaration on non-participation by a Member State in a measure based on Title V of Part Three of the Treaty on the Functioning of the European Union

The Conference declares that, where a Member State opts not to participate in a measure based on Title V of Part Three of the Treaty on the Functioning of the European Union, the Council will hold a full discussion on the possible implications and effects of that Member State's non-participation in the measure.

In addition, any Member State may ask the Commission to examine the situation on the basis of Article 116 of the Treaty on the Functioning of the European Union.

The above paragraphs are without prejudice to the entitlement of a Member State to refer the matter to the European Council.

27. Declaration on Article 85(1), second subparagraph, of the Treaty on the Functioning of the European Union

The Conference considers that the regulations referred to in the second subparagraph of Article 85(1) of the Treaty on the Functioning of the European Union should take into account national rules and practices relating to the initiation of criminal investigations.

28. Declaration on Article 98 of the Treaty on the Functioning of the European Union

The Conference notes that the provisions of Article 98 shall be applied in accordance with the current practice. The terms 'such measures are required in order to compensate for the economic disadvantages caused by the division of Germany to the economy of certain areas of the Federal Republic affected by that division' shall be interpreted in accordance with the existing case law of the Court of Justice of the European Union.

29. Declaration on Article 107(2)(c) of the Treaty on the Functioning of the European Union

The Conference notes that Article 107(2)(c) shall be interpreted in accordance with the existing case law of the Court of Justice of the European Union regarding the applicability of the provisions to aid granted to certain areas of the Federal Republic of Germany affected by the former division of Germany.

30. Declaration on Article 126 of the Treaty on the Functioning of the European Union

With regard to Article 126, the Conference confirms that raising growth potential and securing sound budgetary positions are the two pillars of the economic and fiscal policy of the Union and the Member States. The Stability and Growth Pact is an important tool to achieve these goals.

The Conference reaffirms its commitment to the provisions concerning the Stability and Growth Pact as the framework for the coordination of budgetary policies in the Member States.

The Conference confirms that a rule-based system is the best guarantee for commitments to be enforced and for all Member States to be treated equally.

Within this framework, the Conference also reaffirms its commitment to the goals of the Lisbon Strategy: job creation, structural reforms, and social cohesion.

The Union aims at achieving balanced economic growth and price stability. Economic and budgetary policies thus need to set the right priorities towards economic reforms, innovation, competitiveness and strengthening of private investment and consumption in phases of weak economic growth. This should be reflected in the orientations of budgetary decisions at the national and Union level in particular through restructuring of public revenue and expenditure while respecting budgetary discipline in accordance with the Treaties and the Stability and Growth Pact.

Budgetary and economic challenges facing the Member States underline the importance of sound budgetary policy throughout the economic cycle.

The Conference agrees that Member States should use periods of economic recovery actively to consolidate public finances and improve their budgetary positions. The objective is to gradually achieve a budgetary surplus in good times which creates the necessary room to accommodate economic downturns and thus contribute to the long-term sustainability of public finances.

The Member States look forward to possible proposals of the Commission as well as further contributions of Member States with regard to strengthening and clarifying the implementation of the Stability and Growth Pact. The Member States will take all necessary measures to raise the growth potential of their economies. Improved economic policy coordination could support this objective. This Declaration does not prejudge the future debate on the Stability and Growth Pact.

31. Declaration on Article 156 of the Treaty on the Functioning of the European Union

The Conference confirms that the policies described in Article 156 fall essentially within the competence of the Member States. Measures to provide encouragement and promote coordination to be taken at Union level in accordance with this Article shall be of a complementary nature. They shall serve to strengthen cooperation between Member States and not to harmonise national systems. The guarantees and practices existing in each Member State as regards the responsibility of the social partners will not be affected.

This Declaration is without prejudice to the provisions of the Treaties conferring competence on the Union, including in social matters.

32. Declaration on Article 168(4)(c) of the Treaty on the Functioning of the European Union

The Conference declares that the measures to be adopted pursuant to Article 168(4)(c) must meet common safety concerns and aim to set high standards of quality and safety where national standards affecting the internal market would otherwise prevent a high level of human health protection being achieved.

33. Declaration on Article 174 of the Treaty on the Functioning of the European Union

The Conference considers that the reference in Article 174 to island regions can include island States in their entirety, subject to the necessary criteria being met.

34. Declaration on Article 179 of the Treaty on the Functioning of the European Union

The Conference agrees that the Union's action in the area of research and technological development will pay due respect to the fundamental orientations and choices of the research policies of the Member States.

35. Declaration on Article 194 of the Treaty on the Functioning of the European Union

The Conference believes that Article 194 does not affect the right of the Member States to take the necessary measures to ensure their energy supply under the conditions provided for in Article 347.

36. Declaration on Article 218 of the Treaty on the Functioning of the European Union concerning the negotiation and conclusion of international agreements by Member States relating to the area of freedom, security and justice

The Conference confirms that Member States may negotiate and conclude agreements with third countries or international organisations in the areas covered by Chapters 3, 4 and 5 of Title V of Part Three in so far as such agreements comply with Union law.

37. Declaration on Article 222 of the Treaty on the Functioning of the European Union

Without prejudice to the measures adopted by the Union to comply with its solidarity obligation towards a Member State which is the object of a terrorist attack or the victim of natural or man-made disaster, none of the provisions of Article 222 is intended to affect the right of another Member State to choose the most appropriate means to comply with its own solidarity obligation towards that Member State.

38. Declaration on Article 252 of the Treaty on the Functioning of the European Union regarding the number of Advocates-General in the Court of Justice

The Conference declares that if, in accordance with Article 252, first paragraph, of the Treaty on the Functioning of the European Union, the Court of Justice requests that the number of

Advocates-General be increased by three (eleven instead of eight), the Council will, acting unanimously, agree on such an increase.

In that case, the Conference agrees that Poland will, as is already the case for Germany, France, Italy, Spain and the United Kingdom, have a permanent Advocate-General and no longer take part in the rotation system, while the existing rotation system will involve the rotation of five Advocates-General instead of three.

39. Declaration on Article 290 of the Treaty on the Functioning of the European Union

The Conference takes note of the Commission's intention to continue to consult experts appointed by the Member States in the preparation of draft delegated acts in the financial services area, in accordance with its established practice.

40. Declaration on Article 329 of the Treaty on the Functioning of the European Union

The Conference declares that Member States may indicate, when they make a request to establish enhanced cooperation, if they intend already at that stage to make use of Article 333 providing for the extension of qualified majority voting or to have recourse to the ordinary legislative procedure.

41. Declaration on Article 352 of the Treaty on the Functioning of the European Union

The Conference declares that the reference in Article 352(1) of the Treaty on the Functioning of the European Union to objectives of the Union refers to the objectives as set out in Article 3(2) and (3) of the Treaty on European Union and to the objectives of Article 3(5) of the said Treaty with respect to external action under Part Five of the Treaty on the Functioning of the European Union. It is therefore excluded that an action based on Article 352 of the Treaty on the Functioning of the European Union would only pursue objectives set out in Article 3(1) of the Treaty on European Union. In this connection, the Conference notes that in accordance with Article 31(1) of the Treaty on European Union, legislative acts may not be adopted in the area of the Common Foreign and Security Policy.

42. Declaration on Article 352 of the Treaty on the Functioning of the European Union

The Conference underlines that, in accordance with the settled case law of the Court of Justice of the European Union, Article 352 of the Treaty on the Functioning of the European Union, being an integral part of an institutional system based on the principle of conferred powers, cannot serve as a basis for widening the scope of Union powers beyond the general framework created by the provisions of the Treaties as a whole and, in particular, by those that define the tasks and the activities of the Union. In any event, this Article cannot be used as a basis for the adoption of provisions whose effect would, in substance, be to amend the Treaties without following the procedure which they provide for that purpose.

43. Declaration on Article 355(6) of the Treaty on the Functioning of the European Union

The High Contracting Parties agree that the European Council, pursuant to Article 355(6), will take a decision leading to the modification of the status of Mayotte with regard to the Union in order to make this territory an outermost region within the meaning of Article 355(1) and Article 349, when the French authorities notify the European Council and the Commission that the evolution currently under way in the internal status of the island so allows.

B. Declarations concerning Protocols annexed to the Treaties

44. Declaration on Article 5 of the Protocol on the Schengen acquis integrated into the framework of the European Union

The Conference notes that where a Member State has made a notification under Article 5(2) of the Protocol on the Schengen acquis integrated into the framework of the European Union that it does not wish to take part in a proposal or initiative, that notification may be withdrawn at any moment before the adoption of the measure building upon the Schengen acquis.

45. Declaration on Article 5(2) of the Protocol on the Schengen acquis integrated into the framework of the European Union

The Conference declares that whenever the United Kingdom or Ireland indicates to the Council its intention not to participate in a measure building upon a part of the Schengen acquis in which it participates, the Council will have a full discussion on the possible implications of the non-participation of that Member State in that measure. The discussion within the Council should be conducted in the light of the indications given by the Commission concerning the relationship between the proposal and the Schengen acquis.

46. Declaration on Article 5(3) of the Protocol on the Schengen acquis integrated into the framework of the European Union

The Conference recalls that if the Council does not take a decision after a first substantive discussion of the matter, the Commission may present an amended proposal for a further substantive re-examination by the Council within the deadline of 4 months.

47. Declaration on Article 5(3), (4) and (5) of the Protocol on the Schengen acquis integrated into the framework of the European Union

The Conference notes that the conditions to be determined in the decision referred to in paragraphs 3, 4 or 5 of Article 5 of the Protocol on the Schengen acquis integrated into the framework of the European Union may determine that the Member State concerned shall bear the direct financial consequences, if any, necessarily and unavoidably incurred as a result of the cessation of its participation in some or all of the acquis referred to in any decision taken by the Council pursuant to Article 4 of the said Protocol.

48. Declaration concerning the Protocol on the position of Denmark

The Conference notes that with respect to legal acts to be adopted by the Council acting alone or jointly with the European Parliament and containing provisions applicable to Denmark as well as provisions not applicable to Denmark because they have a legal basis to which Part I of the Protocol on the position of Denmark applies, Denmark declares that it will not use its voting right to prevent the adoption of the provisions which are not applicable to Denmark.

Furthermore, the Conference notes that on the basis of the Declaration by the Conference on Article 222, Denmark declares that Danish participation in actions or legal acts pursuant to Article 222 will take place in accordance with Part I and Part II of the Protocol on the position of Denmark.

49. Declaration concerning Italy

The Conference notes that the Protocol on Italy annexed in 1957 to the Treaty establishing the European Economic Community, as amended upon adoption of the Treaty on European Union, stated that:

'The High Contracting Parties,
Desiring to settle certain particular problems relating to Italy,
Have agreed upon the following provisions, which shall be annexed to this Treaty:

The Member States of the Community
Take note of the fact that the Italian Government is carrying out a ten-year programme of economic expansion designed to rectify the disequilibria in the structure of the Italian economy, in particular by providing an infrastructure for the less developed areas in Southern Italy and in the Italian islands and by creating new jobs in order to eliminate unemployment;
Recall that the principles and objectives of this programme of the Italian Government have been considered and approved by organisations for international cooperation of which the Member States are members;
Recognise that it is in their common interest that the objectives of the Italian programme should be attained;
Agree, in order to facilitate the accomplishment of this task by the Italian Government, to recommend to the institutions of the Community that they should employ all the methods and procedures provided in this Treaty and, in particular, make appropriate use of the resources of the European Investment Bank and the European Social Fund;
Are the opinion that the institutions of the Community should, in applying this Treaty, take account of the sustained effort to be made by the Italian economy in the coming years and

of the desirability of avoiding dangerous stresses in particular within the balance of payments or the level of employment, which might jeopardise the application of this Treaty in Italy;
Recognise that in the event of Articles 109 H and 109 I being applied it will be necessary to take care that any measures required of the Italian Government do not prejudice the completion of its programme for economic expansion and for raising the standard of living of the population.'

50. Declaration concerning Article 10 of the Protocol on transitional provisions
The Conference invites the European Parliament, the Council and the Commission, within their respective powers, to seek to adopt, in appropriate cases and as far as possible within the five-year period referred to in Article 10(3) of the Protocol on transitional provisions, legal acts amending or replacing the acts referred to in Article 10(1) of that Protocol.

C. Declarations by Member States

51. Declaration by the Kingdom of Belgium on national Parliaments
Belgium wishes to make clear that, in accordance with its constitutional law, not only the Chamber of Representatives and Senate of the Federal Parliament but also the parliamentary assemblies of the Communities and the Regions act, in terms of the competences exercised by the Union, as components of the national parliamentary system or chambers of the national Parliament.

52. Declaration by the Kingdom of Belgium, the Republic of Bulgaria, the Federal Republic of Germany, the Hellenic Republic, the Kingdom of Spain, the Italian Republic, the Republic of Cyprus, the Republic of Lithuania, the Grand-Duchy of Luxembourg, the Republic of Hungary, the Republic of Malta, the Republic of Austria, the Portuguese Republic, Romania, the Republic of Slovenia and the Slovak Republic on the symbols of the European Union
Belgium, Bulgaria, Germany, Greece, Spain, Italy, Cyprus, Lithuania, Luxemburg, Hungary, Malta, Austria, Portugal, Romania, Slovenia and the Slovak Republic declare that the flag with a circle of twelve golden stars on a blue background, the anthem based on the 'Ode to Joy' from the Ninth Symphony by Ludwig van Beethoven, the motto 'United in diversity', the euro as the currency of the European Union and Europe Day on 9 May will for them continue as symbols to express the sense of community of the people in the European Union and their allegiance to it.

53. Declaration by the Czech Republic on the Charter of Fundamental Rights of the European Union
1. The Czech Republic recalls that the provisions of the Charter of Fundamental Rights of the European Union are addressed to the institutions and bodies of the European Union with

due regard for the principle of subsidiarity and division of competences between the European Union and its Member States, as reaffirmed in Declaration (No 18) in relation to the delimitation of competences. The Czech Republic stresses that its provisions are addressed to the Member States only when they are implementing Union law, and not when they are adopting and implementing national law independently from Union law.

2. The Czech Republic also emphasises that the Charter does not extend the field of application of Union law and does not establish any new power for the Union. It does not diminish the field of application of national law and does not restrain any current powers of the national authorities in this field.

3. The Czech Republic stresses that, in so far as the Charter recognises fundamental rights and principles as they result from constitutional traditions common to the Member States, those rights and principles are to be interpreted in harmony with those traditions.

4. The Czech Republic further stresses that nothing in the Charter may be interpreted as restricting or adversely affecting human rights and fundamental freedoms as recognised, in their respective field of application, by Union law and by international agreements to which the Union or all the Member States are party, including the European Convention for the Protection of Human Rights and Fundamental Freedoms, and by the Member States' Constitutions.

54. Declaration by the Federal Republic of Germany, Ireland, the Republic of Hungary, the Republic of Austria and the Kingdom of Sweden

Germany, Ireland, Hungary, Austria and Sweden note that the core provisions of the Treaty establishing the European Atomic Energy Community have not been substantially amended since its entry into force and need to be brought up to date. They therefore support the idea of a Conference of the Representatives of the Governments of the Member States, which should be convened as soon as possible.

55. Declaration by the Kingdom of Spain and the United Kingdom of Great Britain and Northern Ireland

The Treaties apply to Gibraltar as a European territory for whose external relations a Member State is responsible. This shall not imply changes in the respective positions of the Member States concerned.

56. Declaration by Ireland on Article 3 of the Protocol on the position of the United Kingdom and Ireland in respect of the area of freedom, security and justice

Ireland affirms its commitment to the Union as an area of freedom, security and justice respecting fundamental rights and the different legal systems and traditions of the Member States within which citizens are provided with a high level of safety.

Accordingly, Ireland declares its firm intention to exercise its right under Article 3 of the Protocol on the position of the United Kingdom and Ireland in respect of the area of freedom, security and justice to take part in the adoption of measures pursuant to Title V of Part Three of the Treaty on the Functioning of the European Union to the maximum extent it deems possible.

Ireland will, in particular, participate to the maximum possible extent in measures in the field of police cooperation.

Furthermore, Ireland recalls that in accordance with Article 8 of the Protocol it may notify the Council in writing that it no longer wishes to be covered by the terms of the Protocol. Ireland intends to review the operation of these arrangements within three years of the entry into force of the Treaty of Lisbon.

57. Declaration by the Italian Republic on the composition of the European Parliament

Italy notes that, pursuant to Articles 10 and 14 of the Treaty on European Union, the European Parliament is to be composed of representatives of the Union's citizens; this representation is to be degressively proportional.

Italy likewise notes that on the basis of Article 9 of the Treaty on European Union and Article 20 of the Treaty on the Functioning of the European Union, every national of a Member State is a citizen of the Union.

Italy therefore considers that, without prejudice to the decision on the 2009-2014 legislative period, any decision adopted by the European Council, at the initiative of the European Parliament and with its consent, establishing the composition of the European Parliament, must abide by the principles laid down out in the first subparagraph of Article 14.

58. Declaration by the Republic of Latvia, the Republic of Hungary and the Republic of Malta on the spelling of the name of the single currency in the Treaties

Without prejudice to the unified spelling of the name of the single currency of the European Union referred to in the Treaties as displayed on the banknotes and on the coins, Latvia, Hungary and Malta declare that the spelling of the name of the single currency, including its derivatives as applied throughout the Latvian, Hungarian and Maltese text of the Treaties, has no effect on the existing rules of the Latvian, Hungarian or Maltese languages.

59. Declaration by the Kingdom of the Netherlands on Article 312 of the Treaty on the Functioning of the European Union

The Kingdom of the Netherlands will agree to a decision as referred to in the second subparagraph of Article 312(2) of the Treaty on the Functioning of the European Union once a revision of the decision referred to in the third paragraph of Article 311 of that Treaty has provided the Netherlands with a satisfactory solution for its excessive negative net payment position vis-à-vis the Union budget.

60. Declaration by the Kingdom of the Netherlands on Article 355 of the Treaty on the Functioning of the European Union

The Kingdom of the Netherlands declares that an initiative for a decision, as referred to in Article 355(6) aimed at amending the status of the Netherlands Antilles and/or Aruba with regard to the Union, will be submitted only on the basis of a decision taken in conformity with the Charter for the Kingdom of the Netherlands.

61. Declaration by the Republic of Poland on the Charter of Fundamental Rights of the European Union

The Charter does not affect in any way the right of Member States to legislate in the sphere of public morality, family law, as well as the protection of human dignity and respect for human physical and moral integrity.

62. Declaration by the Republic of Poland concerning the Protocol on the application of the Charter of Fundamental Rights of the European Union in relation to Poland and the United Kingdom

Poland declares that, having regard to the tradition of social movement of 'Solidarity' and its significant contribution to the struggle for social and labour rights, it fully respects social and labour rights, as established by European Union law, and in particular those reaffirmed in Title IV of the Charter of Fundamental Rights of the European Union.

63. Declaration by the United Kingdom of Great Britain and Northern Ireland on the definition of the term "nationals"

In respect of the Treaties and the Treaty establishing the European Atomic Energy Community, and in any of the acts deriving from those Treaties or continued in force by those Treaties, the United Kingdom reiterates the Declaration it made on 31 December 1982 on the definition of the term 'nationals' with the exception that the reference to 'British Dependent Territories Citizens' shall be read as meaning 'British overseas territories citizens'.

64. Declaration by the United Kingdom of Great Britain and Northern Ireland on the franchise for elections to the European Parliament

The United Kingdom notes that Article 14 of the Treaty on European Union and other provisions of the Treaties are not intended to change the basis for the franchise for elections to the European Parliament.

65. Declaration by the United Kingdom of Great Britain and Northern Ireland on Article 75 of the Treaty on the Functioning of the European Union

The United Kingdom fully supports robust action with regard to adopting financial sanctions designed to prevent and combat terrorism and related activities. Therefore, the United Kingdom declares that it intends to exercise its right under Article 3 of the Protocol on the position of the United Kingdom and Ireland in respect of the area of freedom, security and justice to take part in the adoption of all proposals made under Article 75 of the Treaty on the Functioning of the European Union.

Tables of Equivalences*

Source OJ C 326 of 26 October 2012, p. 363

Treaty on European Union

Old numbering of the Treaty on European Union	New numbering of the Treaty on European Union
Title I – Common provisions	Title I – Common provisions
Article 1	Article 1
	Article 2
Article 2	Article 3
Article 3 (repealed)[1]	
	Article 4
	Article 5[2]
Article 4 (repealed)[3]	
Article 5 (repealed)[4]	
Article 6	Article 6

---

*   Tables of equivalences as referred to in Article 5 of the Treaty of Lisbon. The original centre column, which set out the intermediate numbering as used in that Treaty, has been omitted.
1   Replaced, in substance, by Article 7 of the Treaty on the Functioning of the European Union ('TFEU') and by Articles 13(1) and 21, paragraph 3, second subparagraph of the Treaty on European Union ('TEU').
2   Replaces Article 5 of the Treaty establishing the European Community ('TEC').
3   Replaced, in substance, by Article 15.
4   Replaced, in substance, by Article 13, paragraph 2.
©   European Union, http://eur-lex.europa.eu/, 1998-2015.

Article 7	Article 7
	Article 8
Title II - Provisions amending the Treaty establishing the European Economic Community with a view to establishing the European Community	Title II - Provisions on democratic principles
Article 8 (repealed)[5]	Article 9
	Article 10[6]
	Article 11
	Article 12
Title III - Provisions amending the Treaty establishing the European Coal and Steel Community	Title III - Provisions on the institutions
Article 9 (repealed)[7]	Article 13
	Article 14[8]
	Article 15[9]
	Article 16[10]
	Article 17[11]

5   Article 8 TEU, which was in force until the entry into force of the Treaty of Lisbon (hereinafter 'current'), amended the TEC. Those amendments are incorporated into the latter Treaty and Article 8 is repealed. Its number is used to insert a new provision.

6   Paragraph 4 replaces, in substance, the first subparagraph of Article 191 TEC.

7   The current Article 9 TEU amended the Treaty establishing the European Coal and Steel Community. This latter expired on 23 July 2002. Article 9 is repealed and the number thereof is used to insert another provision.

8   - Paragraphs 1 and 2 replace, in substance, Article 189 TEC;
      - paragraphs 1 to 3 replace, in substance, paragraphs 1 to 3 of Article 190 TEC;
      - paragraph 1 replaces, in substance, the first subparagraph of Article 192 TEC;
      - paragraph 4 replaces, in substance, the first subparagraph of Article 197 TEC.

9   Replaces, in substance, Article 4.

10   - Paragraph 1 replaces, in substance, the first and second indents of Article 202 TEC;
      - paragraphs 2 and 9 replace, in substance, Article 203 TEC;
      - paragraphs 4 and 5 replace, in substance, paragraphs 2 and 4 of Article 205 TEC.

11   - Paragraph 1 replaces, in substance, Article 211 TEC;
      - paragraphs 3 and 7 replace, in substance, Article 214 TEC.
      - paragraph 6 replaces, in substance, paragraphs 1, 3 and 4 of Article 217 TEC.

	Article 18
	Article 19[12]
Title IV – Provisions amending the Treaty establishing the European Atomic Energy Community	Title IV – Provisions on enhanced cooperation
Article 10 (repealed)[13] Articles 27a to 27e (replaced) Articles 40 to 40b (replaced) Articles 43 to 45 (replaced)	Article 20[14]
Title V – Provisions on a common foreign and security policy	Title V – General provisions on the Union's external action and specific provisions on the common foreign and security policy
	Chapter 1 – General provisions on the Union's external action
	Article 21
	Article 22
	Chapter 2 – Specific provisions on the common foreign and security policy
	Section 1 – Common provisions
	Article 23
Article 11	Article 24
Article 12	Article 25
Article 13	Article 26
	Article 27
Article 14	Article 28
Article 15	Article 29
Article 22 (moved)	Article 30

12 – Replaces, in substance, Article 220 TEC.
   – the first subparagraph of paragraph 2 replaces, in substance, the first subparagraph of Article 221 TEC.
13 The current Article 10 TEU amended the Treaty establishing the European Atomic Energy Community. Those amendments are incorporated into the Treaty of Lisbon. Article 10 is repealed and the number thereof is used to insert another provision.
14 Also replaces Articles 11 and 11a TEC.

Article 23 (moved)	Article 31
Article 16	Article 32
Article 17 (moved)	Article 42
Article 18	Article 33
Article 19	Article 34
Article 20	Article 35
Article 21	Article 36
Article 22 (moved)	Article 30
Article 23 (moved)	Article 31
Article 24	Article 37
Article 25	Article 38
	Article 39
Article 47 (moved)	Article 40
Article 26 (repealed)	
Article 27 (repealed)	
Article 27a (replaced)[15]	Article 20
Article 27b (replaced)[15]	Article 20
Article 27c (replaced)[15]	Article 20
Article 27d (replaced)[15]	Article 20
Article 27e (replaced)[15]	Article 20
Article 28	Article 41
	Section 2 – Provisions on the common security and defence policy
Article 17 (moved)	Article 42
	Article 43
	Article 44
	Article 45
	Article 46

15 The current Articles 27a to 27e, on enhanced cooperation, are also replaced by Articles 326 to 334 TFEU.

Title VI – Provisions on policy and judicial cooperation in criminal matters (repealed)[16]	
Article 29 (replaced)[17]	
Article 30 (replaced)[18]	
Article 31 (replaced)[19]	
Article 32 (replaced)[20]	
Article 33 (replaced)[21]	
Article 34 (repealed)	
Article 35 (repealed)	
Article 36 (replaced)[22]	
Article 37 (repealed)	
Article 38 (repealed)	
Article 39 (repealed)	
Article 40 (replaced)[23]	Article 20
Article 40 A (replaced)[23]	Article 20
Article 40 B (replaced)[23]	Article 20
Article 41 (repealed)	
Article 42 (repealed)	

[16] The current provisions of Title VI of the TEU, on police and judicial cooperation in criminal matters, are replaced by the provisions of Chapters 1, 4 and 5 of Title IV (renumbered V) of Part Three of the TFEU.
[17] Replaced by Article 67 TFEU.
[18] Replaced by Articles 87 and 88 TFEU.
[19] Replaced by Articles 82, 83 and 85 TFEU.
[20] Replaced by Article 89 TFEU.
[21] Replaced by Article 72 TFEU.
[22] Replaced by Article 71 TFEU.
[23] The current Articles 40 to 40 B TEU, on enhanced cooperation, are also replaced by Articles 326 to 334 TFEU.

V-Tables of Equivalences

Title VII – Provisions on enhanced cooperation (replaced)[24]	Title IV – Provisions on enhanced cooperation
Article 43 (replaced)[24]	Article 20
Article 43 A (replaced)[24]	Article 20
Article 43 B (replaced)[24]	Article 20
Article 44 (replaced)[24]	Article 20
Article 44 A (replaced)[24]	Article 20
Article 45 (replaced)[24]	Article 20
Title VIII – Final provisions	Title VI – Final provisions
Article 46 (repealed)	
	Article 47
Article 47 (replaced)	Article 40
Article 48	Article 48
Article 49	Article 49
	Article 50
	Article 51
	Article 52
Article 50 (repealed)	
Article 51	Article 53
Article 52	Article 54
Article 53	Article 55

---

24   The current Articles 43 to 45 and Title VII of the TEU, on enhanced cooperation, are also replaced by Articles 326 to 334 TFEU.

Treaty on the Functioning of the European Union

Old numbering of the Treaty establishing the European Community	New numbering of the Treaty on the Functioning of the European Union
Part One – Principles	Part One – Principles
Article 1 (repealed)	
	Article 1
Article 2 (repealed)[25]	
	Title I – Categories and areas of union competence
	Article 2
	Article 3
	Article 4
	Article 5
	Article 6
	Title II – Provisions having general application
	Article 7
Article 3, paragraph 1 (repealed)[26]	
Article 3, paragraph 2	Article 8
Article 4 (moved)	Article 119
Article 5 (replaced)[27]	
	Article 9
	Article 10
Article 6	Article 11
Article 153, paragraph 2 (moved)	Article 12
	Article 13[28]

25 Replaced, in substance, by Article 3 TEU.
26 Replaced, in substance, by Articles 3 to 6 TFEU.
27 Replaced by Article 5 TEU.
28 Insertion of the operative part of the protocol on protection and welfare of animals.

Article 7 (repealed)[29]	
Article 8 (repealed)[30]	
Article 9 (repealed)	
Article 10 (repealed)[31]	
Article 11 (replaced)[32]	Articles 326 to 334
Article 11a (replaced)[32]	Articles 326 to 334
Article 12 (moved)	Article 18
Article 13 (moved)	Article 19
Article 14 (moved)	Article 26
Article 15 (moved)	Article 27
Article 16	Article 14
Article 255 (moved)	Article 15
Article 286 (moved)	Article 16
	Article 17
Part Two – Citizenship of the Union	Part Two – Nondiscrimination and citizenship of the Union
Article 12 (moved)	Article 18
Article 13 (moved)	Article 19
Article 17	Article 20
Article 18	Article 21
Article 19	Article 22
Article 20	Article 23
Article 21	Article 24
Article 22	Article 25
Part Three – Community policies	Part Three – Policies and internal actions of the Union

29 Replaced, in substance, by Article 13 TEU.
30 Replaced, in substance, by Article 13 TEU and Article 282, paragraph 1, TFEU.
31 Replaced, in substance, by Article 4, paragraph 3, TEU.
32 Also replaced by Article 20 TEU.

	Title I - The internal market
Article 14 (moved)	Article 26
Article 15 (moved)	Article 27
Title I - Free movement of goods	Title II - Free movement of goods
Article 23	Article 28
Article 24	Article 29
Chapter 1 - The customs union	Chapter 1 - The customs union
Article 25	Article 30
Article 26	Article 31
Article 27	Article 32
Part Three, Title X, Customs cooperation (moved)	Chapter 2 - Customs cooperation
Article 135 (moved)	Article 33
Chapter 2 - Prohibition of quantitative restrictions between Member States	Chapter 3 - Prohibition of quantitative restrictions between Member States
Article 28	Article 34
Article 29	Article 35
Article 30	Article 36
Article 31	Article 37
Title II - Agriculture	Title III - Agriculture and fisheries
Article 32	Article 38
Article 33	Article 39
Article 34	Article 40
Article 35	Article 41
Article 36	Article 42
Article 37	Article 43
Article 38	Article 44
Title III - Free movement of persons, services and capital	Title IV - Free movement of persons, services and capital
Chapter 1 - Workers	Chapter 1 - Workers

V-Tables of Equivalences

Article 39	Article 45
Article 40	Article 46
Article 41	Article 47
Article 42	Article 48
Chapter 2 – Right of establishment	Chapter 2 – Right of establishment
Article 43	Article 49
Article 44	Article 50
Article 45	Article 51
Article 46	Article 52
Article 47	Article 53
Article 48	Article 54
Article 294 (moved)	Article 55
Chapter 3 – Services	Chapter 3 – Services
Article 49	Article 56
Article 50	Article 57
Article 51	Article 58
Article 52	Article 59
Article 53	Article 60
Article 54	Article 61
Article 55	Article 62
Chapter 4 – Capital and payments	Chapter 4 – Capital and payments
Article 56	Article 63
Article 57	Article 64
Article 58	Article 65
Article 59	Article 66
Article 60 (moved)	Article 75
Title IV – Visas, asylum, immigration and other policies related to free movement of persons	Title V – Area of freedom, security and justice
	Chapter 1 – General provisions

Article 61	Article 67[33]
	Article 68
	Article 69
	Article 70
	Article 71[34]
Article 64, paragraph 1 (replaced)	Article 72[35]
	Article 73
Article 66 (replaced)	Article 74
Article 60 (moved)	Article 75
	Article 76
	Chapter 2 – Policies on border checks, asylum and immigration
Article 62	Article 77
Article 63, points 1 et 2, and Article 64, paragraph 2[36]	Article 78
Article 63, points 3 and 4	Article 79
	Article 80
Article 64, paragraph 1 (replaced)	Article 72
	Chapter 3 – Judicial cooperation in civil matters
Article 65	Article 81
Article 66 (replaced)	Article 74
Article 67 (repealed)	
Article 68 (repealed)	
Article 69 (repealed)	
	Chapter 4 – Judicial cooperation in criminal matters

33 Also replaces the current Article 29 TEU.
34 Replaces the current Article 36 TEU.
35 Also replaces the current Article 33 TEU.
36 Points 1 and 2 of Article 63 EC are replaced by paragraphs 1 and 2 of Article 78 TFEU, and paragraph 2 of Article 64 is replaced by paragraph 3 of Article 78 TFEU.

	Article 82[37]
	Article 83[37]
	Article 84
	Article 85[37]
	Article 86
	Chapter 5 – Police cooperation
	Article 87[38]
	Article 88[38]
	Article 89[39]
Title V – Transport	Title VI – Transport
Article 70	Article 90
Article 71	Article 91
Article 72	Article 92
Article 73	Article 93
Article 74	Article 94
Article 75	Article 95
Article 76	Article 96
Article 77	Article 97
Article 78	Article 98
Article 79	Article 99
Article 80	Article 100
Title VI – Common rules on competition, taxation and approximation of laws	Title VII – Common rules on competition, taxation and approximation of laws
Chapter 1 – Rules on competition	Chapter 1 – Rules on competition
Section 1 – Rules applying to undertakings	Section 1 – Rules applying to undertakings
Article 81	Article 101
Article 82	Article 102

37   Replaces the current Article 31 TEU.
38   Replaces the current Article 30 TEU.
39   Replaces the current Article 32 TEU.

Article 83	Article 103
Article 84	Article 104
Article 85	Article 105
Article 86	Article 106
Section 2 – Aids granted by States	Section 2 – Aids granted by States
Article 87	Article 107
Article 88	Article 108
Article 89	Article 109
Chapter 2 – Tax provisions	Chapter 2 – Tax provisions
Article 90	Article 110
Article 91	Article 111
Article 92	Article 112
Article 93	Article 113
Chapter 3 – Approximation of laws	Chapter 3 – Approximation of laws
Article 95 (moved)	Article 114
Article 94 (moved)	Article 115
Article 96	Article 116
Article 97	Article 117
	Article 118
Title VII – Economic and monetary policy	Title VIII – Economic and monetary policy
Article 4 (moved)	Article 2
Chapter 1 – Economic policy	Chapter 1 – Economic policy
Article 98	Article 120
Article 99	Article 121
Article 100	Article 122
Article 101	Article 123
Article 102	Article 124
Article 103	Article 125
Article 104	Article 126

Chapter 2 – monetary policy	Chapter 2 – monetary policy
Article 105	Article 127
Article 106	Article 128
Article 107	Article 129
Article 108	Article 130
Article 109	Article 131
Article 110	Article 132
Article 111, paragraphs 1 to 3 and 5 (moved)	Article 219
Article 111, paragraph 4 (moved)	Article 138
	Article 133
Chapter 3 – Institutional provisions	Chapter 3 – Institutional provisions
Article 112 (moved)	Article 283
Article 113 (moved)	Article 284
Article 114	Article 134
Article 115	Article 135
	Chapter 4 – Provisions specific to Member States whose currency is the euro
	Article 136
	Article 137
Article 111, paragraph 4 (moved)	Article 138
Chapter 4 – Transitional provisions	Chapter 5 – Transitional provisions
Article 116 (repealed)	
	Article 139
Article 117, paragraphs 1, 2, sixth indent, and 3 to 9 (repealed)	
Article 117, paragraph 2, first five indents (moved)	Article 141, paragraph 2

Article 121, paragraph 1 (moved) Article 122, paragraph 2, second sentence (moved) Article 123, paragraph 5 (moved)	Article 140[40]
Article 118 (repealed)	
Article 123, paragraph 3 (moved) Article 117, paragraph 2, first five indents (moved)	Article 141[41]
Article 124, paragraph 1 (moved)	Article 142
Article 119	Article 143
Article 120	Article 144
Article 121, paragraph 1 (moved)	Article 140, paragraph 1
Article 121, paragraphs 2 to 4 (repealed)	
Article 122, paragraphs 1, 2, first sentence, 3, 4, 5 and 6 (repealed)	
Article 122, paragraph 2, second sentence (moved)	Article 140, paragraph 2, first subparagraph
Article 123, paragraphs 1, 2 and 4 (repealed)	
Article 123, paragraph 3 (moved)	Article 141, paragraph 1
Article 123, paragraph 5 (moved)	Article 140, paragraph 3
Article 124, paragraph 1 (moved)	Article 142
Article 124, paragraph 2 (repealed)	
Title VIII – Employment	Title IX – Employment
Article 125	Article 145
Article 126	Article 146
Article 127	Article 147
Article 128	Article 148

40 - Article 140, paragraph 1 takes over the wording of paragraph 1 of Article 121.
    - Article 140, paragraph 2 takes over the second sentence of paragraph 2 of Article 122.
    - Article 140, paragraph 3 takes over paragraph 5 of Article 123.
41 - Article 141, paragraph 1 takes over paragraph 3 of Article 123.
    - Article 141, paragraph 2 takes over the first five indents of paragraph 2 of Article 117.

Article 129	Article 149
Article 130	Article 150
Title IX – Common commercial policy (moved)	Part Five, Title II – Common commercial policy
Article 131 (moved)	Article 206
Article 132 (repealed)	
Article 133 (moved)	Article 207
Article 134 (repealed)	
Title X – Customs cooperation (moved)	Part Three, Title II, Chapter 2 – Customs cooperation
Article 135 (moved)	Article 33
Title XI – Social policy, education, vocational training and youth	Title X – Social policy
Chapter 1 – Social provisions (repealed)	
Article 136	Article 151
	Article 152
Article 137	Article 153
Article 138	Article 154
Article 139	Article 155
Article 140	Article 156
Article 141	Article 157
Article 142	Article 158
Article 143	Article 159
Article 144	Article 160
Article 145	Article 161
Chapter 2 – The European Social Fund	Title XI – The European Social Fund
Article 146	Article 162
Article 147	Article 163
Article 148	Article 164

Chapter 3 – Education, vocational training and youth	Title XII – Education, vocational training, youth and sport
Article 149	Article 165
Article 150	Article 166
Title XII – Culture	Title XIII – Culture
Article 151	Article 167
Title XIII – Public health	Title XIV – Public health
Article 152	Article 168
Title XIV – Consumer protection	Title XV – Consumer protection
Article 153, paragraphs 1, 3, 4 and 5	Article 169
Article 153, paragraph 2 (moved)	Article 12
Title XV – Trans-European networks	Title XVI – Trans-European networks
Article 154	Article 170
Article 155	Article 171
Article 156	Article 172
Title XVI – Industry	Title XVII – Industry
Article 157	Article 173
Title XVII – Economic and social cohesion	Title XVIII – Economic, social and territorial cohesion
Article 158	Article 174
Article 159	Article 175
Article 160	Article 176
Article 161	Article 177
Article 162	Article 178
Title XVIII – Research and technological development	Title XIX – Research and technological development and space
Article 163	Article 179
Article 164	Article 180
Article 165	Article 181

Article 166	Article 182
Article 167	Article 183
Article 168	Article 184
Article 169	Article 185
Article 170	Article 186
Article 171	Article 187
Article 172	Article 188
	Article 189
Article 173	Article 190
Title XIX – Environment	Title XX – Environment
Article 174	Article 191
Article 175	Article 192
Article 176	Article 193
	Titre XXI – Energy
	Article 194
	Title XXII – Tourism
	Article 195
	Title XXIII – Civil protection
	Article 196
	Title XXIV – Administrative cooperation
	Article 197
Title XX – Development cooperation (moved)	Part Five, Title III, Chapter 1 – Development cooperation
Article 177 (moved)	Article 208
Article 178 (repealed)[42]	
Article 179 (moved)	Article 209
Article 180 (moved)	Article 210
Article 181 (moved)	Article 211

42 Replaced, in substance, by the second sentence of the second subparagraph of paragraph 1 of Article 208 TFEU.

Title XXI – Economic, financial and technical cooperation with third countries (moved)	Part Five, Title III, Chapter 2 – Economic, financial and technical cooperation with third countries
Article 181a (moved)	Article 212
Part Four – Association of the overseas countries and territories	Part Four – Association of the overseas countries and territories
Article 182	Article 198
Article 183	Article 199
Article 184	Article 200
Article 185	Article 201
Article 186	Article 202
Article 187	Article 203
Article 188	Article 204
	Part Five – The Union's external action
	Title I – General provisions on the Union's external action
	Article 205
Part Three, Title IX, Common commercial policy (moved)	Title II – Common commercial policy
Article 131 (moved)	Article 206
Article 133 (moved)	Article 207
	Title III – Cooperation with third countries and humanitarian aid
Part Three, Title XX, Development cooperation (moved)	Chapter 1 – development cooperation
Article 177 (moved)	Article 208[43]
Article 179 (moved)	Article 209
Article 180 (moved)	Article 210
Article 181 (moved)	Article 211

43 The second sentence of the second subparagraph of paragraph 1 replaces, in substance, Article 178 TEC.

Part Three, Title XXI, Economic, financial and technical cooperation with third countries (moved)	Chapter 2 – Economic, financial and technical cooperation with third countries
Article 181a (moved)	Article 212
	Article 213
	Chapter 3 – Humanitarian aid
	Article 214
	Title IV – Restrictive measures
Article 301 (replaced)	Article 215
	Title V – International agreements
	Article 216
Article 310 (moved)	Article 217
Article 300 (replaced)	Article 218
Article 111, paragraphs 1 to 3 and 5 (moved)	Article 219
	Title VI – The Union's relations with international organisations and third countries and the Union delegations
Articles 302 to 304 (replaced)	Article 220
	Article 221
	Title VII – Solidarity clause
	Article 222
Part Five – Institutions of the Community	Part Six – Institutional and financial provisions
Title I – Institutional provisions	Title I – Institutional provisions
Chapter 1 – The institutions	Chapter 1 – The institutions
Section 1 – The European Parliament	Section 1 – The European Parliament
Article 189 (repealed)[44]	
Article 190, paragraphs 1 to 3 (repealed)[45]	

[44] Replaced, in substance, by Article 14, paragraphs 1 and 2, TEU.
[45] Replaced, in substance, by Article 14, paragraphs 1 to 3, TEU.

Article 190, paragraphs 4 and 5	Article 223
Article 191, first paragraph (repealed)[46]	
Article 191, second paragraph	Article 224
Article 192, first paragraph (repealed)[47]	
Article 192, second paragraph	Article 225
Article 193	Article 226
Article 194	Article 227
Article 195	Article 228
Article 196	Article 229
Article 197, first paragraph (repealed)[48]	
Article 197, second, third and fourth paragraphs	Article 230
Article 198	Article 231
Article 199	Article 232
Article 200	Article 233
Article 201	Article 234
	Section 2 – The European Council
	Article 235
	Article 236
Section 2 – The Council	Section 3 – The Council
Article 202 (repealed)[49]	
Article 203 (repealed)[50]	
Article 204	Article 237
Article 205, paragraphs 2 and 4 (repealed)[51]	

[46] Replaced, in substance, by Article 11, paragraph 4, TEU.
[47] Replaced, in substance, by Article 14, paragraph 1, TEU.
[48] Replaced, in substance, by Article 14, paragraph 4, TEU.
[49] Replaced, in substance, by Article 16, paragraph 1, TEU and by Articles 290 and 291 TFEU.
[50] Replaced, in substance, by Article 16, paragraphs 2 and 9 TEU.
[51] Replaced, in substance, by Article 16, paragraphs 4 and 5 TEU.

Article 205, paragraphs 1 and 3	Article 238
Article 206	Article 239
Article 207	Article 240
Article 208	Article 241
Article 209	Article 242
Article 210	Article 243
Section 3 - The Commission	Section 4 - The Commission
Article 211 (repealed)[52]	
	Article 244
Article 212 (moved)	Article 249, paragraph 2
Article 213	Article 245
Article 214 (repealed)[53]	
Article 215	Article 246
Article 216	Article 247
Article 217, paragraphs 1, 3 and 4 (repealed)[54]	
Article 217, paragraph 2	Article 248
Article 218, paragraph 1 (repealed)[55]	
Article 218, paragraph 2	Article 249
Article 219	Article 250
Section 4 - The Court of Justice	Section 5 - The Court of Justice of the European Union
Article 220 (repealed)[56]	
Article 221, first paragraph (repealed)[57]	
Article 221, second and third paragraphs	Article 251

[52] Replaced, in substance, by Article 17, paragraph 1 TEU.
[53] Replaced, in substance, by Article 17, paragraphs 3 and 7 TEU.
[54] Replaced, in substance, by Article 17, paragraph 6, TEU.
[55] Replaced, in substance, by Article 295 TFEU.
[56] Replaced, in substance, by Article 19 TEU.
[57] Replaced, in substance, by Article 19, paragraph 2, first subparagraph, of the TEU.

Article 222	Article 252
Article 223	Article 253
Article 224[58]	Article 254
	Article 255
Article 225	Article 256
Article 225a	Article 257
Article 226	Article 258
Article 227	Article 259
Article 228	Article 260
Article 229	Article 261
Article 229a	Article 262
Article 230	Article 263
Article 231	Article 264
Article 232	Article 265
Article 233	Article 266
Article 234	Article 267
Article 235	Article 268
	Article 269
Article 236	Article 270
Article 237	Article 271
Article 238	Article 272
Article 239	Article 273
Article 240	Article 274
	Article 275
	Article 276
Article 241	Article 277
Article 242	Article 278

58   The first sentence of the first subparagraph is replaced, in substance, by Article 19, paragraph 2, second subparagraph of the TEU.

Article 243	Article 279
Article 244	Article 280
Article 245	Article 281
	Section 6 – The European Central Bank
	Article 282
Article 112 (moved)	Article 283
Article 113 (moved)	Article 284
Section 5 – The Court of Auditors	Section 7 – The Court of Auditors
Article 246	Article 285
Article 247	Article 286
Article 248	Article 287
Chapter 2 – Provisions common to several institutions	Chapter 2 – Legal acts of the Union, adoption procedures and other provisions
	Section 1 – The legal acts of the Union
Article 249	Article 288
	Article 289
	Article 290[59]
	Article 291[59]
	Article 292
	Section 2 – Procedures for the adoption of acts and other provisions
Article 250	Article 293
Article 251	Article 294
Article 252 (repealed)	
	Article 295
Article 253	Article 296
Article 254	Article 297
	Article 298

[59] Replaces, in substance, the third indent of Article 202 TEC.

Article 255 (moved)	Article 15
Article 256	Article 299
	Chapter 3 - The Union's advisory bodies
	Article 300
Chapter 3 - The Economic and Social Committee	Section 1 - The Economic and Social Committee
Article 257 (repealed)[60]	
Article 258, first, second and fourth paragraphs	Article 301
Article 258, third paragraph (repealed)[61]	
Article 259	Article 302
Article 260	Article 303
Article 261 (repealed)	
Article 262	Article 304
Chapter 4 - The Committee of the Regions	Section 2 - The Committee of the Regions
Article 263, first and fifth paragraphs (repealed)[62]	
Article 263, second to fourth paragraphs	Article 305
Article 264	Article 306
Article 265	Article 307
Chapter 5 - The European Investment Bank	Chapter 4 - The European Investment Bank
Article 266	Article 308
Article 267	Article 309
Title II - Financial provisions	Title II - Financial provisions
Article 268	Article 310
	Chapter 1 - The Union's own resources
Article 269	Article 311

60 Replaced, in substance, by Article 300, paragraph 2 of the TFEU.
61 Replaced, in substance, by Article 300, paragraph 4 of the TFEU.
62 Replaced, in substance, by Article 300, paragraphs 3 and 4, TFEU.

V-Tables of Equivalences

Article 270 (repealed)[63]	
	Chapter 2 - The multiannual financial framework
	Article 312
	Chapter 3 - The Union's annual budget
Article 272, paragraph 1 (moved)	Article 313
Article 271 (moved)	Article 316
Article 272, paragraph 1 (moved)	Article 313
Article 272, paragraphs 2 to 10	Article 314
Article 273	Article 315
Article 271 (moved)	Article 316
	Chapter 4 - Implementation of the budget and discharge
Article 274	Article 317
Article 275	Article 318
Article 276	Article 319
	Chapter 5 - Common provisions
Article 277	Article 320
Article 278	Article 321
Article 279	Article 322
	Article 323
	Article 324
	Chapter 6 - Combating fraud
Article 280	Article 325
	Title III - Enhanced cooperation
Articles 11 and 11a (replaced)	Article 326[64]
Articles 11 and 11a (replaced)	Article 327[64]
Articles 11 and 11a (replaced)	Article 328[64]

63 Replaced, in substance, by Article 310, paragraph 4, TFEU.
64 Also replaces the current Articles 27a to 27e, 40 to 40b, and 43 to 45 TEU.

Articles 11 and 11a (replaced)	Article 329[64]
Articles 11 and 11a (replaced)	Article 330[64]
Articles 11 and 11a (replaced)	Article 331[64]
Articles 11 and 11a (replaced)	Article 332[64]
Articles 11 and 11a (replaced)	Article 333[64]
Articles 11 and 11a (replaced)	Article 334[64]
Part Six – General and final provisions	Part Seven – General and final provisions
Article 281 (repealed)[65]	
Article 282	Article 335
Article 283	Article 336
Article 284	Article 337
Article 285	Article 338
Article 286 (replaced)	Article 16
Article 287	Article 339
Article 288	Article 340
Article 289	Article 341
Article 290	Article 342
Article 291	Article 343
Article 292	Article 344
Article 293 (repealed)	
Article 294 (moved)	Article 55
Article 295	Article 345
Article 296	Article 346
Article 297	Article 347
Article 298	Article 348
Article 299, paragraph 1 (repealed)[66]	
Article 299, paragraph 2, second, third and fourth subparagraphs	Article 349

65 Replaced, in substance, by Article 47 TEU.
66 Replaced, in substance by Article 52 TEU.

Article 299, paragraph 2, first subparagraph, and paragraphs 3 to 6 (moved)	Article 355
Article 300 (replaced)	Article 218
Article 301 (replaced)	Article 215
Article 302 (replaced)	Article 220
Article 303 (replaced)	Article 220
Article 304 (replaced)	Article 220
Article 305 (repealed)	
Article 306	Article 350
Article 307	Article 351
Article 308	Article 352
	Article 353
Article 309	Article 354
Article 310 (moved)	Article 217
Article 311 (repealed)[68]	
Article 299, paragraph 2, first subparagraph, and paragraphs 3 to 6 (moved)	Article 355
Article 312	Article 356
Final Provisions	
Article 313	Article 357
	Article 358
Article 314 (repealed)[68]	

[67] Replaced, in substance by Article 51 TEU.
[68] Replaced, in substance by Article 55 TEU.

Protocol on the concerns of the Irish people on the Treaty of Lisbon*

Date 13 June 2012
Source OJ L 60 of 2.3.2013, p. 131

The Kingdom of Belgium, the Republic of Bulgaria, the Czech Republic, the Kingdom of Denmark, the Federal Republic of Germany, the Republic of Estonia, Ireland, the Hellenic Republic, the Kingdom of Spain, the French Republic, the Italian Republic, the Republic of Cyprus, the Republic of Latvia, the Republic of Lithuania, the Grand Duchy of Luxembourg, Hungary, Malta, the Kingdom of the Netherlands, the Republic of Austria, the Republic of Poland, the Portuguese Republic, Romania, the Republic of Slovenia, the Slovak Republic, the Republic of Finland, the Kingdom of Sweden, the United Kingdom of Great Britain and Northern Ireland,
hereinafter referred to as 'the High Contracting Parties',
Recalling the Decision of the Heads of State or Government of the 27 Member States of the European Union, meeting within the European Council, on 18-19 June 2009, on the concerns of the Irish people on the Treaty of Lisbon;
Recalling the declaration of the Heads of State or Government, meeting within the European Council, on 18-19 June 2009, that they would, at the time of the conclusion of the next Accession Treaty, set out the provisions of that Decision in a Protocol to be attached, in accordance with their respective constitutional requirements, to the Treaty on European Union and the Treaty on the Functioning of the European Union;
Noting the signature by the High Contracting Parties of the Treaty between the High Contracting Parties and the Republic of Croatia concerning the accession of the Republic of Croatia to the European Union;
Have agreed upon the following provisions, which shall be annexed to the Treaty on European Union and to the Treaty on the Functioning of the European Union:

---

* See the press release of the European Council of 22 May 2013, The European Council decides on the number of members of the European Commission, EUCO 119/13, PRESSE 210.
© European Union, http://eur-lex.europa.eu/, 1998-2015.

Title I
Right to Life, Family and Education

Article 1
Nothing in the Treaty of Lisbon attributing legal status to the Charter of Fundamental Rights of the European Union, or in the provisions of that Treaty in the area of Freedom, Security and Justice affects in any way the scope and applicability of the protection of the right to life in Article 40.3.1, 40.3.2 and 40.3.3, the protection of the family in Article 41 and the protection of the rights in respect of education in Articles 42 and 44.2.4 and 44.2.5 provided by the Constitution of Ireland.

Title II
Taxation

Article 2
Nothing in the Treaty of Lisbon makes any change of any kind, for any Member State, to the extent or operation of the competence of the European Union in relation to taxation.

Title III
Security and Defence

Article 3
The Union's action on the international scene is guided by the principles of democracy, the rule of law, the universality and indivisibility of human rights and fundamental freedoms, respect for human dignity, the principles of equality and solidarity, and respect for the principles of the United Nations Charter and international law.

The Union's common security and defence policy is an integral part of the common foreign and security policy and provides the Union with an operational capacity to undertake missions outside the Union for peace-keeping, conflict prevention and strengthening international security in accordance with the principles of the United Nations Charter.

It does not prejudice the security and defence policy of each Member State, including Ireland, or the obligations of any Member State.

The Treaty of Lisbon does not affect or prejudice Ireland's traditional policy of military neutrality.

It will be for Member States – including Ireland, acting in a spirit of solidarity and without prejudice to its traditional policy of military neutrality – to determine the nature of aid or assistance to be provided to a Member State which is the object of a terrorist attack or the victim of armed aggression on its territory.

Any decision to move to a common defence will require a unanimous decision of the European Council. It would be a matter for the Member States, including Ireland, to decide, in accordance with the provisions of the Treaty of Lisbon and with their respective constitutional requirements, whether or not to adopt a common defence.

Nothing in this Title affects or prejudices the position or policy of any other Member State on security and defence.

It is also a matter for each Member State to decide, in accordance with the provisions of the Treaty of Lisbon and any domestic legal requirements, whether to participate in permanent structured cooperation or the European Defence Agency.

The Treaty of Lisbon does not provide for the creation of a European army or for conscription to any military formation.

It does not affect the right of Ireland or any other Member State to determine the nature and volume of its defence and security expenditure and the nature of its defence capabilities.

It will be a matter for Ireland or any other Member State, to decide, in accordance with any domestic legal requirements, whether or not to participate in any military operation.

Title IV
Final Provisions

Article 4

This Protocol shall remain open for signature by the High Contracting Parties until 30 June 2012.

This Protocol shall be ratified by the High Contracting Parties, and by the Republic of Croatia in the event that this Protocol has not entered into force by the date of accession of the Republic of Croatia to the European Union, in accordance with their respective constitutional requirements. The instruments of ratification shall be deposited with the Government of the Italian Republic.

This Protocol shall enter into force if possible on 30 June 2013, provided that all the instruments of ratification have been deposited, or, failing that, on the first day of the month following the deposit of the instrument of ratification by the last Member State to take this step.

Article 5

This Protocol, drawn up in a single original in the Bulgarian, Czech, Danish, Dutch, English, Estonian, Finnish, French, German, Greek, Hungarian, Irish, Italian, Latvian, Lithuanian, Maltese, Polish, Portuguese, Romanian, Slovak, Slovenian, Spanish and Swedish languages, each text being equally authentic, shall be deposited in the archives of the Government of the Italian Republic, which shall transmit a certified copy to each of the governments of the other Member States.

Once the Republic of Croatia has become bound by this Protocol pursuant to Article 2 of the Act concerning the conditions of accession of the Republic of Croatia, the Croatian text of this Protocol, which shall be equally authentic to the texts referred to in the first paragraph, shall also be deposited in the archives of the Government of the Italian Republic, which shall transmit a certified copy to each of the governments of the other Member States.

In witness whereof, the undersigned Plenipotentiaries have signed this Protocol.
Done at Brussels on the thirteenth day of June in the year two thousand and twelve.
[List of signatories not reproduced.]

Rules of Procedure of the Court of Justice

Date   25 September 2012
In force 1 November 2012
Source   OJ L 265 of 29 September 2012, p. 1
         last amended by OJ L 173 of 26 June 2013, p. 65

The Court of Justice
Having regard to the Treaty on European Union, and in particular Article 19 thereof,
Having regard to the Treaty on the Functioning of the European Union, and in particular the sixth paragraph of Article 253 thereof,
Having regard to the Treaty establishing the European Atomic Energy Community, and in particular Article 106a(1) thereof,
Having regard to the Protocol on the Statute of the Court of Justice of the European Union, and in particular Article 63 and the second paragraph of Article 64 thereof,

Whereas:
(1) Despite having been amended on several occasions over the years, the Rules of Procedure of the Court of Justice have remained fundamentally unchanged in structure since their original adoption on 4 March 1953. The Rules of Procedure of 19 June 1991, which are currently in force, still reflect the initial preponderance of direct actions, whereas in fact the majority of such actions now fall within the jurisdiction of the General Court, and references for a preliminary ruling from the courts and tribunals of the Member States represent, quantitatively, the primary category of cases brought before the Court. That fact should be taken into account and the structure and content of the Rules of Procedure of the Court adapted, in consequence, to changes in its caseload.
(2) While references for a preliminary ruling should be given their proper place in the Rules of Procedure, it is also appropriate to draw a clearer distinction between the rules that apply to all types of action and those that are specific to each type, to be contained in separate titles. In the interests of clarification, procedural provisions common to all cases brought before the Court should, therefore, all be contained in an initial title.
(3) In the light of experience gained in the course of implementing the various procedures, it is also necessary to supplement or to clarify, for the benefit of litigants as well as of national courts and tribunals, the rules that apply to each procedure. The rules in question concern, in particular, the concepts of party to the main proceedings, intervener and party to the proceedings before the General Court, or, in preliminary rulings, the rules governing the

© European Union, http://eur-lex.europa.eu/, 1998-2015.

bringing of matters before the Court and the content of the order for reference. With regard to appeals against decisions of the General Court, a clearer distinction must also be drawn between appeals and cross-appeals in consequence of the service of an appeal on the cross-appellant.

(4) Conversely, the excessive complexity of certain procedures, such as the review procedure, has come to light on their implementation. Accordingly, they should be simplified by providing, inter alia, for a Chamber of five Judges to be designated for a period of one year to be responsible for ruling both on the First Advocate General's proposal to review and on the questions to be reviewed.

(5) Similarly, the procedural arrangements for dealing with requests for Opinions should be eased by aligning them with those that apply to other cases and by providing, in consequence, for a single Advocate General to be involved in dealing with the request for an Opinion. In the interests of making the Rules easier to understand, all the particular procedures currently to be found in a number of separate titles and chapters of the Rules of Procedure should also be brought together in a single title.

(6) In order to maintain the Court's capacity, in the face of an ever-increasing caseload, to dispose within a reasonable period of time of the cases brought before it, it is also necessary to continue the efforts made to reduce the duration of proceedings before the Court, in particular by extending the opportunities for the Court to rule by reasoned order, simplifying the rules relating to the intervention of the States and institutions referred to in the first and third paragraphs of Article 40 of the Statute and providing for the Court to be able to rule without a hearing if it considers that it has sufficient information on the basis of all the written observations lodged in a case.

(7) In the interests of making the Rules applied by the Court easier to understand, lastly, certain rules which are outdated or not applied should be deleted, every paragraph of the present Rules numbered, each article given a specific heading summarising its content and the terminology harmonised.

With the Council's approval given on 24 September 2012.

Has adopted these Rules of Procedure:

Introductory provisions

Article 1 Definitions

1. In these Rules:

    (a) provisions of the Treaty on European Union are referred to by the number of the article concerned followed by 'TEU',

    (b) provisions of the Treaty on the Functioning of the European Union are referred to by the number of the article concerned followed by 'TFEU',

    (c) provisions of the Treaty establishing the European Atomic Energy Community are referred to by the number of the article concerned followed by 'TEAEC',

(d) 'Statute' means the Protocol on the Statute of the Court of Justice of the European Union,
(e) 'EEA Agreement' means the Agreement on the European Economic Area,[1]
(f) 'Council Regulation No 1' means Council Regulation No 1 of 15 April 1958 determining the languages to be used by the European Economic Community.[2]
2. For the purposes of these Rules:
(a) 'institutions' means the institutions of the European Union referred to in Article 13(1) TEU and bodies, offices and agencies established by the Treaties, or by an act adopted in implementation thereof, which may be parties before the Court,
(b) 'EFTA Surveillance Authority' means the surveillance authority referred to in the EEA Agreement,
(c) 'interested persons referred to in Article 23 of the Statute' means all the parties, States, institutions, bodies, offices and agencies authorised, pursuant to that Article, to submit statements of case or observations in the context of a reference for a preliminary ruling.

Article 2 Purport of these Rules
These Rules implement and supplement, so far as necessary, the relevant provisions of the EU, FEU and EAEC Treaties, and the Statute.

Title I
Organisation of the Court

Chapter 1
Judges and Advocates General

Article 3 Commencement of the term of office of Judges and Advocates General
The term of office of a Judge or Advocate General shall begin on the date fixed for that purpose in the instrument of appointment. In the absence of any provisions in that instrument regarding the date of commencement of the term of office, that term shall begin on the date of publication of the instrument in the Official Journal of the European Union.

Article 4 Taking of the oath
Before taking up his duties, a Judge or Advocate General shall, at the first public sitting of the Court which he attends after his appointment, take the following oath provided for in Article 2 of the Statute:
'I swear that I will perform my duties impartially and conscientiously; I swear that I will preserve the secrecy of the deliberations of the Court.'

---

1 OJ L 1, 3.1.1994, p. 27.
2 OJ, English Special Edition 1952-1958 (I), p. 59.

Article 5 Solemn undertaking

Immediately after taking the oath, a Judge or Advocate General shall sign a declaration by which he gives the solemn undertaking provided for in the third paragraph of Article 4 of the Statute.

Article 6 Depriving a Judge or Advocate General of his office

1. Where the Court is called upon, pursuant to Article 6 of the Statute, to decide whether a Judge or Advocate General no longer fulfils the requisite conditions or no longer meets the obligations arising from his office, the President shall invite the Judge or Advocate General concerned to make representations.
2. The Court shall give a decision in the absence of the Registrar.

Article 7 Order of seniority

1. The seniority of Judges and Advocates General shall be calculated without distinction according to the date on which they took up their duties.
2. Where there is equal seniority on that basis, the order of seniority shall be determined by age.
3. Judges and Advocates General whose terms of office are renewed shall retain their former seniority.

Chapter 2
Presidency of the Court, constitution of the Chambers and designation of the First Advocate General

Article 8 Election of the President and of the Vice-President of the Court

1. The Judges shall, immediately after the partial replacement provided for in the second paragraph of Article 253 TFEU, elect one of their number as President of the Court for a term of three years.
2. If the office of the President falls vacant before the normal date of expiry of the term thereof, the Court shall elect a successor for the remainder of the term.
3. The elections provided for in this Article shall be by secret ballot. The Judge obtaining the votes of more than half the Judges of the Court shall be elected. If no Judge obtains that majority, further ballots shall be held until that majority is attained.
4. The Judges shall then elect one of their number as Vice-President of the Court for a term of three years, in accordance with the procedures laid down in the preceding paragraph. Paragraph 2 shall apply if the office of the Vice-President of the Court falls vacant before the normal date of expiry of the term thereof.
5. The names of the President and Vice-President elected in accordance with this Article shall be published in the Official Journal of the European Union.

Article 9 Responsibilities of the President of the Court
1. The President shall represent the Court.
2. The President shall direct the judicial business of the Court. He shall preside at general meetings of the Members of the Court and at hearings before and deliberations of the full Court and the Grand Chamber.
3. The President shall ensure the proper functioning of the services of the Court.

Article 10 Responsibilities of the Vice-President of the Court
1. The Vice-President shall assist the President of the Court in the performance of his duties and shall take the President's place when the latter is prevented from acting.
2. He shall take the President's place, at his request, in performing the duties referred to in Article 9(1) and (3) of these Rules.
3. The Court shall, by decision, specify the conditions under which the Vice-President shall take the place of the President of the Court in the performance of his judicial duties. That decision shall be published in the Official Journal of the European Union.

Article 11 Constitution of Chambers
1. The Court shall set up Chambers of five and three Judges in accordance with Article 16 of the Statute and shall decide which Judges shall be attached to them.
2. The Court shall designate the Chambers of five Judges which, for a period of one year, shall be responsible for cases of the kind referred to in Article 107 and Articles 193 and 194.
3. In respect of cases assigned to a formation of the Court in accordance with Article 60, the word 'Court' in these Rules shall mean that formation.
4. In respect of cases assigned to a Chamber of five or three Judges, the powers of the President of the Court shall be exercised by the President of the Chamber.
5. The composition of the Chambers and the designation of the Chambers responsible for cases of the kind referred to in Article 107 and Articles 193 and 194 shall be published in the Official Journal of the European Union.

Article 12 Election of Presidents of Chambers
1. The Judges shall, immediately after the election of the President and Vice-President of the Court, elect the Presidents of the Chambers of five Judges for a term of three years.
2. The Judges shall then elect the Presidents of the Chambers of three Judges for a term of one year.
3. The provisions of Article 8(2) and (3) shall apply.
4. The names of the Presidents of Chambers elected in accordance with this Article shall be published in the Official Journal of the European Union.

Article 13
Where the President and Vice-President of the Court are prevented from acting
When the President and the Vice-President of the Court are prevented from acting, the functions of President shall be exercised by one of the Presidents of the Chambers of five

Judges or, failing that, by one of the Presidents of the Chambers of three Judges or, failing that, by one of the other Judges, according to the order of seniority laid down in Article 7.

Article 14 Designation of the First Advocate General

1. The Court shall, after hearing the Advocates General, designate a First Advocate General for a period of one year.
2. If the office of the First Advocate General falls vacant before the normal date of expiry of the term thereof, the Court shall designate a successor for the remainder of the term.
3. The name of the First Advocate General designated in accordance with this Article shall be published in the Official Journal of the European Union.

Chapter 3
Assignment of cases to Judge-Rapporteurs and Advocates General

Article 15 Designation of the Judge-Rapporteur

1. As soon as possible after the document initiating proceedings has been lodged, the President of the Court shall designate a Judge to act as Rapporteur in the case.
2. For cases of the kind referred to in Article 107 and Articles 193 and 194, the Judge-Rapporteur shall be selected from among the Judges of the Chamber designated in accordance with Article 11(2), on a proposal from the President of that Chamber. If, pursuant to Article 109, the Chamber decides that the reference is not to be dealt with under the urgent procedure, the President of the Court may reassign the case to a Judge-Rapporteur attached to another Chamber.
3. The President of the Court shall take the necessary steps if a Judge-Rapporteur is prevented from acting.

Article 16 Designation of the Advocate General

1. The First Advocate General shall assign each case to an Advocate General.
2. The First Advocate General shall take the necessary steps if an Advocate General is prevented from acting.

Chapter 4
Assistant Rapporteurs

Article 17 Assistant Rapporteurs

1. Where the Court is of the opinion that the consideration of and preparatory inquiries in cases before it so require, it shall, pursuant to Article 13 of the Statute, propose the appointment of Assistant Rapporteurs.

2. Assistant Rapporteurs shall in particular:
   (a) assist the President of the Court in interim proceedings and
   (b) assist the Judge-Rapporteurs in their work.
3. In the performance of their duties the Assistant Rapporteurs shall be responsible to the President of the Court, the President of a Chamber or a Judge-Rapporteur, as the case may be.
4. Before taking up his duties, an Assistant Rapporteur shall take before the Court the oath set out in Article 4 of these Rules.

Chapter 5
Registry

Article 18 Appointment of the Registrar
1. The Court shall appoint the Registrar.
2. When the post of Registrar is vacant, an advertisement shall be published in the Official Journal of the European Union. Interested persons shall be invited to submit their applications within a time-limit of not less than three weeks, accompanied by full details of their nationality, university degrees, knowledge of languages, present and past occupations, and experience, if any, in judicial and international fields.
3. The vote, in which the Judges and the Advocates General shall take part, shall take place in accordance with the procedure laid down in Article 8(3) of these Rules.
4. The Registrar shall be appointed for a term of six years. He may be reappointed. The Court may decide to renew the term of office of the incumbent Registrar without availing itself of the procedure laid down in paragraph 2 of this Article.
5. The Registrar shall take the oath set out in Article 4 and sign the declaration provided for in Article 5.
6. The Registrar may be deprived of his office only if he no longer fulfils the requisite conditions or no longer meets the obligations arising from his office. The Court shall take its decision after giving the Registrar an opportunity to make representations.
7. If the office of Registrar falls vacant before the normal date of expiry of the term thereof, the Court shall appoint a new Registrar for a term of six years.
8. The name of the Registrar elected in accordance with this Article shall be published in the Official Journal of the European Union.

Article 19 Deputy Registrar
The Court may, in accordance with the procedure laid down in respect of the Registrar, appoint a Deputy Registrar to assist the Registrar and to take his place if he is prevented from acting.

Article 20 Responsibilities of the Registrar

1. The Registrar shall be responsible, under the authority of the President of the Court, for the acceptance, transmission and custody of all documents and for effecting service as provided for by these Rules.
2. The Registrar shall assist the Members of the Court in all their official functions.
3. The Registrar shall have custody of the seals and shall be responsible for the records. He shall be in charge of the publications of the Court and, in particular, the European Court Reports.
4. The Registrar shall direct the services of the Court under the authority of the President of the Court. He shall be responsible for the management of the staff and the administration, and for the preparation and implementation of the budget.

Article 21 Keeping of the register

1. There shall be kept in the Registry, under the responsibility of the Registrar, a register in which all procedural documents and supporting items and documents lodged shall be entered in the order in which they are submitted.
2. When a document has been registered, the Registrar shall make a note to that effect on the original and, if a party so requests, on any copy submitted for the purpose.
3. Entries in the register and the notes provided for in the preceding paragraph shall be authentic.
4. A notice shall be published in the Official Journal of the European Union indicating the date of registration of an application initiating proceedings, the names of the parties, the form of order sought by the applicant and a summary of the pleas in law and of the main supporting arguments or, as the case may be, the date of lodging of a request for a preliminary ruling, the identity of the referring court or tribunal and the parties to the main proceedings, and the questions referred to the Court.

Article 22 Consultation of the register and of judgments and orders

1. Anyone may consult the register at the Registry and may obtain copies or extracts on payment of a charge on a scale fixed by the Court on a proposal from the Registrar.
2. The parties to a case may, on payment of the appropriate charge, obtain certified copies of procedural documents.
3. Anyone may, on payment of the appropriate charge, also obtain certified copies of judgments and orders.

Chapter 6
The working of the Court

Article 23 Location of the sittings of the Court

The Court may choose to hold one or more specific sittings in a place other than that in which it has its seat.

Article 24 Calendar of the Court's judicial business
1. The judicial year shall begin on 7 October of each calendar year and end on 6 October of the following year.
2. The judicial vacations shall be determined by the Court.
3. In a case of urgency, the President may convene the Judges and the Advocates General during the judicial vacations.
4. The Court shall observe the official holidays of the place in which it has its seat.
5. The Court may, in proper circumstances, grant leave of absence to any Judge or Advocate General.
6. The dates of the judicial vacations and the list of official holidays shall be published annually in the Official Journal of the European Union.

Article 25 General meeting
Decisions concerning administrative issues or the action to be taken upon the proposals contained in the preliminary report referred to in Article 59 of these Rules shall be taken by the Court at the general meeting in which all the Judges and Advocates General shall take part and have a vote. The Registrar shall be present, unless the Court decides to the contrary.

Article 26 Drawing-up of minutes
Where the Court sits without the Registrar being present it shall, if necessary, instruct the most junior Judge for the purposes of Article 7 of these Rules to draw up minutes, which shall be signed by that Judge and by the President.

Chapter 7
Formations of the Court

Section 1
Composition of the formations of the Court

Article 27 Composition of the Grand Chamber
1. The Grand Chamber shall, for each case, be composed of the President and the Vice-President of the Court, three Presidents of Chambers of five Judges, the Judge-Rapporteur and the number of Judges necessary to reach 15. The last-mentioned Judges and the three Presidents of Chambers of five Judges shall be designated from the lists referred to in paragraphs 3 and 4 of this Article, following the order laid down therein. The starting-point on each of those lists, in every case assigned to the Grand Chamber, shall be the name of the Judge immediately following the last Judge designated from the list concerned for the preceding case assigned to that formation of the Court.
2. After the election of the President and the Vice-President of the Court, and then of the Presidents of the Chambers of five Judges, a list of the Presidents of Chambers of five Judges

and a list of the other Judges shall be drawn up for the purposes of determining the composition of the Grand Chamber.

3. The list of the Presidents of Chambers of five Judges shall be drawn up according to the order laid down in Article 7 of these Rules.

4. The list of the other Judges shall be drawn up according to the order laid down in Article 7 of these Rules, alternating with the reverse order: the first Judge on that list shall be the first according to the order laid down in that Article, the second Judge shall be the last according to that order, the third Judge shall be the second according to that order, the fourth Judge the penultimate according to that order, and so on.

5. The lists referred to in paragraphs 3 and 4 shall be published in the Official Journal of the European Union.

6. In cases which are assigned to the Grand Chamber between the beginning of a calendar year in which there is a partial replacement of Judges and the moment when that replacement has taken place, two substitute Judges may be designated to complete the formation of the Court for so long as the attainment of the quorum referred to in the third paragraph of Article 17 of the Statute is in doubt. Those substitute Judges shall be the two Judges appearing on the list referred to in paragraph 4 immediately after the last Judge designated for the composition of the Grand Chamber in the case.

7. The substitute Judges shall replace, in the order of the list referred to in paragraph 4, such Judges as are unable to take part in the determination of the case.

Article 28 Composition of the Chambers of five and of three Judges

1. The Chambers of five Judges and of three Judges shall, for each case, be composed of the President of the Chamber, the Judge-Rapporteur and the number of Judges required to attain the number of five and three Judges respectively. Those last-mentioned Judges shall be designated from the lists referred to in paragraphs 2 and 3, following the order laid down therein. The starting-point on those lists, in every case assigned to a Chamber, shall be the name of the Judge immediately following the last Judge designated from the list for the preceding case assigned to the Chamber concerned.

2. For the composition of the Chambers of five Judges, after the election of the Presidents of those Chambers lists shall be drawn up including all the Judges attached to the Chamber concerned, with the exception of its President. The lists shall be drawn up in the same way as the list referred to in Article 27(4).

3. For the composition of the Chambers of three Judges, after the election of the Presidents of those Chambers lists shall be drawn up including all the Judges attached to the Chamber concerned, with the exception of its President. The lists shall be drawn up according to the order laid down in Article 7.

4. The lists referred to in paragraphs 2 and 3 shall be published in the Official Journal of the European Union.

Article 29 Composition of Chambers where cases are related or referred back

1. Where the Court considers that a number of cases must be heard and determined to-

gether by one and the same formation of the Court, the composition of that formation shall be that fixed for the case in respect of which the preliminary report was examined first.

2. Where a Chamber to which a case has been assigned requests the Court, pursuant to Article 60(3) of these Rules, to assign the case to a formation composed of a greater number of Judges, that formation shall include the members of the Chamber which has referred the case back.

Article 30 Where a President of a Chamber is prevented from acting

1. When the President of a Chamber of five Judges is prevented from acting, the functions of President of the Chamber shall be exercised by a President of a Chamber of three Judges, where necessary according to the order laid down in Article 7 of these Rules, or, if that formation of the Court does not include a President of a Chamber of three Judges, by one of the other Judges according to the order laid down in Article 7.

2. When the President of a Chamber of three Judges is prevented from acting, the functions of President of the Chamber shall be exercised by a Judge of that formation of the Court according to the order laid down in Article 7.

Article 31
Where a member of the formation of the Court is prevented from acting

1. When a member of the Grand Chamber is prevented from acting, he shall be replaced by another Judge according to the order of the list referred to in Article 27(4).

2. When a member of a Chamber of five Judges is prevented from acting, he shall be replaced by another Judge of that Chamber, according to the order of the list referred to in Article 28(2). If it is not possible to replace the Judge prevented from acting by a Judge of the same Chamber, the President of that Chamber shall so inform the President of the Court who may designate another Judge to complete the Chamber.

3. When a member of a Chamber of three Judges is prevented from acting, he shall be replaced by another Judge of that Chamber, according to the order of the list referred to in Article 28(3). If it is not possible to replace the Judge prevented from acting by a Judge of the same Chamber, the President of that Chamber shall so inform the President of the Court who may designate another Judge to complete the Chamber.

Section 2
Deliberations

Article 32 Procedures concerning deliberations

1. The deliberations of the Court shall be and shall remain secret.

2. When a hearing has taken place, only those Judges who participated in that hearing and, where relevant, the Assistant Rapporteur responsible for the consideration of the case shall take part in the deliberations.

3. Every Judge taking part in the deliberations shall state his opinion and the reasons for it.

4. The conclusions reached by the majority of the Judges after final discussion shall determine the decision of the Court.

Article 33 Number of Judges taking part in the deliberations

Where, by reason of a Judge being prevented from acting, there is an even number of Judges, the most junior Judge for the purposes of Article 7 of these Rules shall abstain from taking part in the deliberations unless he is the Judge-Rapporteur. In that case the Judge immediately senior to him shall abstain from taking part in the deliberations.

Article 34 Quorum of the Grand Chamber

1. If, for a case assigned to the Grand Chamber, it is not possible to attain the quorum referred to in the third paragraph of Article 17 of the Statute, the President of the Court shall designate one or more other Judges according to the order of the list referred to in Article 27(4) of these Rules.
2. If a hearing has taken place before that designation, the Court shall re-hear oral argument from the parties and the Opinion of the Advocate General.

Article 35 Quorum of the Chambers of five and of three Judges

1. If, for a case assigned to a Chamber of five or of three Judges, it is not possible to attain the quorum referred to in the second paragraph of Article 17 of the Statute, the President of the Court shall designate one or more other Judges according to the order of the list referred to in Article 28(2) or (3), respectively, of these Rules. If it is not possible to replace the Judge prevented from acting by a Judge of the same Chamber, the President of that Chamber shall so inform the President of the Court forthwith who shall designate another Judge to complete the Chamber.
2. Article 34(2) shall apply, mutatis mutandis, to the Chambers of five and of three Judges.

Chapter 8
Languages

Article 36 Language of a case

The language of a case shall be Bulgarian, Croatian, Czech, Danish, Dutch, English, Estonian, Finnish, French, German, Greek, Hungarian, Irish, Italian, Latvian, Lithuanian, Maltese, Polish, Portuguese, Romanian, Slovak, Slovenian, Spanish or Swedish.

Article 37 Determination of the language of a case

1. In direct actions, the language of a case shall be chosen by the applicant, except that:
    (a) where the defendant is a Member State, the language of the case shall be the official language of that State; where that State has more than one official language, the applicant may choose between them;

(b) at the joint request of the parties, the use of another of the languages mentioned in Article 36 for all or part of the proceedings may be authorised;

(c) at the request of one of the parties, and after the opposite party and the Advocate General have been heard, the use of another of the languages mentioned in Article 36 may be authorised as the language of the case for all or part of the proceedings by way of derogation from subparagraphs (a) and (b); such a request may not be submitted by one of the institutions of the European Union.

2. Without prejudice to the provisions of paragraph 1(b) and (c), and of Article 38(4) and (5) of these Rules,

(a) in appeals against decisions of the General Court as referred to in Articles 56 and 57 of the Statute, the language of the case shall be the language of the decision of the General Court against which the appeal is brought;

(b) where, in accordance with the second paragraph of Article 62 of the Statute, the Court decides to review a decision of the General Court, the language of the case shall be the language of the decision of the General Court which is the subject of review;

(c) in the case of challenges concerning the costs to be recovered, applications to set aside judgments by default, third-party proceedings and applications for interpretation or revision of a judgment or for the Court to remedy a failure to adjudicate, the language of the case shall be the language of the decision to which those applications or challenges relate.

3. In preliminary ruling proceedings, the language of the case shall be the language of the referring court or tribunal. At the duly substantiated request of one of the parties to the main proceedings, and after the other party to the main proceedings and the Advocate General have been heard, the use of another of the languages mentioned in Article 36 may be authorised for the oral part of the procedure. Where granted, such authorisation shall apply in respect of all the interested persons referred to in Article 23 of the Statute.

4. Requests as above may be decided on by the President; the latter may, and where he wishes to accede to a request without the agreement of all the parties must, refer the request to the Court.

Article 38 Use of the language of the case

1. The language of the case shall in particular be used in the written and oral pleadings of the parties, including the items and documents produced or annexed to them, and also in the minutes and decisions of the Court.

2. Any item or document produced or annexed that is expressed in another language must be accompanied by a translation into the language of the case.

3. However, in the case of substantial items or lengthy documents, translations may be confined to extracts. At any time the Court may, of its own motion or at the request of one of the parties, call for a complete or fuller translation.

4. Notwithstanding the foregoing provisions, a Member State shall be entitled to use its official language when taking part in preliminary ruling proceedings, when intervening in a case before the Court or when bringing a matter before the Court pursuant to Article 259

TFEU. This provision shall apply both to written documents and to oral statements. The Registrar shall arrange in each instance for translation into the language of the case.

5. The States, other than the Member States, which are parties to the EEA Agreement, and also the EFTA Surveillance Authority, may be authorised to use one of the languages mentioned in Article 36, other than the language of the case, when they take part in preliminary ruling proceedings or intervene in a case before the Court. This provision shall apply both to written documents and to oral statements. The Registrar shall arrange in each instance for translation into the language of the case.

6. Non-Member States taking part in preliminary ruling proceedings pursuant to the fourth paragraph of Article 23 of the Statute may be authorised to use one of the languages mentioned in Article 36 other than the language of the case. This provision shall apply both to written documents and to oral statements. The Registrar shall arrange in each instance for translation into the language of the case.

7. Where a witness or expert states that he is unable adequately to express himself in one of the languages referred to in Article 36, the Court may authorise him to give his evidence in another language. The Registrar shall arrange for translation into the language of the case.

8. The President and the Vice-President of the Court and also the Presidents of Chambers in conducting oral proceedings, Judges and Advocates General in putting questions and Advocates General in delivering their Opinions may use one of the languages referred to in Article 36 other than the language of the case. The Registrar shall arrange for translation into the language of the case.

Article 39 Responsibility of the Registrar concerning language arrangements

The Registrar shall, at the request of any Judge, of the Advocate General or of a party, arrange for anything said or written in the course of the proceedings before the Court to be translated into the languages chosen from those referred to in Article 36.

Article 40 Languages of the publications of the Court

Publications of the Court shall be issued in the languages referred to in Article 1 of Council Regulation No 1.

Article 41 Authentic texts

The texts of documents drawn up in the language of the case or, where applicable, in another language authorised pursuant to Articles 37 or 38 of these Rules shall be authentic.

Article 42 Language service of the Court

The Court shall set up a language service staffed by experts with adequate legal training and a thorough knowledge of several official languages of the European Union.

Title II
Common procedural provisions

Chapter 1
Rights and obligations of agents, advisers and lawyers

Article 43 Privileges, immunities and facilities
1. Agents, advisers and lawyers who appear before the Court or before any judicial authority to which the Court has addressed letters rogatory shall enjoy immunity in respect of words spoken or written by them concerning the case or the parties.
2. Agents, advisers and lawyers shall also enjoy the following privileges and facilities:
    (a) any papers and documents relating to the proceedings shall be exempt from both search and seizure. In the event of a dispute, the customs officials or police may seal those papers and documents; they shall then be immediately forwarded to the Court for inspection in the presence of the Registrar and of the person concerned;
    (b) agents, advisers and lawyers shall be entitled to travel in the course of duty without hindrance.

Article 44 Status of the parties' representatives
1. In order to qualify for the privileges, immunities and facilities specified in Article 43, persons entitled to them shall furnish proof of their status as follows:
    (a) agents shall produce an official document issued by the party for whom they act, who shall immediately serve a copy thereof on the Registrar;
    (b) lawyers shall produce a certificate that they are authorised to practise before a court of a Member State or of another State which is a party to the EEA Agreement, and, where the party which they represent is a legal person governed by private law, an authority to act issued by that person;
    (c) advisers shall produce an authority to act issued by the party whom they are assisting.
2. The Registrar of the Court shall issue them with a certificate, as required. The validity of this certificate shall be limited to a specified period, which may be extended or curtailed according to the duration of the proceedings.

Article 45 Waiver of immunity
1. The privileges, immunities and facilities specified in Article 43 of these Rules are granted exclusively in the interests of the proper conduct of proceedings.
2. The Court may waive immunity where it considers that the proper conduct of proceedings will not be hindered thereby.

Article 46 Exclusion from the proceedings
1. If the Court considers that the conduct of an agent, adviser or lawyer before the Court is incompatible with the dignity of the Court or with the requirements of the proper

administration of justice, or that such agent, adviser or lawyer is using his rights for purposes other than those for which they were granted, it shall inform the person concerned. If the Court informs the competent authorities to whom the person concerned is answerable, a copy of the letter sent to those authorities shall be forwarded to the person concerned.

2. On the same grounds, the Court may at any time, having heard the person concerned and the Advocate General, decide to exclude an agent, adviser or lawyer from the proceedings by reasoned order. That order shall have immediate effect.

3. Where an agent, adviser or lawyer is excluded from the proceedings, the proceedings shall be suspended for a period fixed by the President in order to allow the party concerned to appoint another agent, adviser or lawyer.

4. Decisions taken under this Article may be rescinded.

Article 47 University teachers and parties to the main proceedings

1. The provisions of this Chapter shall apply to university teachers who have a right of audience before the Court in accordance with Article 19 of the Statute.

2. They shall also apply, in the context of references for a preliminary ruling, to the parties to the main proceedings where, in accordance with the national rules of procedure applicable, those parties are permitted to bring or defend court proceedings without being represented by a lawyer, and to persons authorised under those rules to represent them.

Chapter 2
Services

Article 48 Methods of service

1. Where these Rules require that a document be served on a person, the Registrar shall ensure that service is effected at that person's address for service either by the dispatch of a copy of the document by registered post with a form for acknowledgement of receipt or by personal delivery of the copy against a receipt. The Registrar shall prepare and certify the copies of documents to be served, save where the parties themselves supply the copies in accordance with Article 57(2) of these Rules.

2. Where the addressee has agreed that service is to be effected on him by telefax or any other technical means of communication, any procedural document, including a judgment or order of the Court, may be served by the transmission of a copy of the document by such means.

3. Where, for technical reasons or on account of the nature or length of the document, such transmission is impossible or impracticable, the document shall be served, if the addressee has not specified an address for service, at his address in accordance with the procedures laid down in paragraph 1 of this Article. The addressee shall be so informed by telefax or any other technical means of communication. Service shall then be deemed to have been effected on the addressee by registered post on the 10th day following the lodging of the registered letter at the post office of the place in which the Court has its seat, unless it is

shown by the acknowledgement of receipt that the letter was received on a different date or the addressee informs the Registrar, within three weeks of being informed by telefax or any other technical means of communication, that the document to be served has not reached him.

4. The Court may, by decision, determine the criteria for a procedural document to be served by electronic means. That decision shall be published in the Official Journal of the European Union.

Chapter 3
Time-limits

Article 49 Calculation of time-limits

1. Any procedural time-limit prescribed by the Treaties, the Statute or these Rules shall be calculated as follows:

(a) where a time-limit expressed in days, weeks, months or years is to be calculated from the moment at which an event occurs or an action takes place, the day during which that event occurs or that action takes place shall not be counted as falling within the time-limit in question;

(b) a time-limit expressed in weeks, months or years shall end with the expiry of whichever day in the last week, month or year is the same day of the week, or falls on the same date, as the day during which the event or action from which the time-limit is to be calculated occurred or took place. If, in a time-limit expressed in months or years, the day on which it should expire does not occur in the last month, the time-limit shall end with the expiry of the last day of that month;

(c) where a time-limit is expressed in months and days, it shall first be calculated in whole months, then in days;

(d) time-limits shall include Saturdays, Sundays and the official holidays referred to in Article 24(6) of these Rules;

(e) time-limits shall not be suspended during the judicial vacations.

2. If the time-limit would otherwise end on a Saturday, Sunday or an official holiday, it shall be extended until the end of the first subsequent working day.

Article 50 Proceedings against a measure adopted by an institution

Where the time-limit allowed for initiating proceedings against a measure adopted by an institution runs from the publication of that measure, that time-limit shall be calculated, for the purposes of Article 49(1)(a), from the end of the 14th day after publication of the measure in the Official Journal of the European Union.

Article 51 Extension on account of distance

The procedural time-limits shall be extended on account of distance by a single period of 10 days.

Article 52 Setting and extension of time-limits
1. Any time-limit prescribed by the Court pursuant to these Rules may be extended.
2. The President and the Presidents of Chambers may delegate to the Registrar power of signature for the purposes of setting certain time-limits which, pursuant to these Rules, it falls to them to prescribe, or of extending such time-limits.

Chapter 4
Different procedures for dealing with cases

Article 53 Procedures for dealing with cases
1. Without prejudice to the special provisions laid down in the Statute or in these Rules, the procedure before the Court shall consist of a written part and an oral part.
2. Where it is clear that the Court has no jurisdiction to hear and determine a case or where a request or an application is manifestly inadmissible, the Court may, after hearing the Advocate General, at any time decide to give a decision by reasoned order without taking further steps in the proceedings.
3. The President may in special circumstances decide that a case be given priority over others.
4. A case may be dealt with under an expedited procedure in accordance with the conditions provided by these Rules.
5. A reference for a preliminary ruling may be dealt with under an urgent procedure in accordance with the conditions provided by these Rules.

Article 54 Joinder
1. Two or more cases of the same type concerning the same subject-matter may at any time be joined, on account of the connection between them, for the purposes of the written or oral part of the procedure or of the judgment which closes the proceedings.
2. A decision on whether cases should be joined shall be taken by the President after hearing the Judge-Rapporteur and the Advocate General, if the cases concerned have already been assigned, and, save in the case of references for a preliminary ruling, after also hearing the parties. The President may refer the decision on this matter to the Court.
3. Joined cases may be disjoined, in accordance with the provisions of paragraph 2.

Article 55 Stay of proceedings
1. The proceedings may be stayed:
    (a) in the circumstances specified in the third paragraph of Article 54 of the Statute, by order of the Court, made after hearing the Advocate General;
    (b) in all other cases, by decision of the President adopted after hearing the Judge-Rapporteur and the Advocate General and, save in the case of references for a preliminary ruling, the parties.
2. The proceedings may be resumed by order or decision, following the same procedure.

3. The orders or decisions referred to in paragraphs 1 and 2 shall be served on the parties or interested persons referred to in Article 23 of the Statute.
4. The stay of proceedings shall take effect on the date indicated in the order or decision of stay or, in the absence of such indication, on the date of that order or decision.
5. While proceedings are stayed time shall cease to run for the parties or interested persons referred to in Article 23 of the Statute for the purposes of procedural time-limits.
6. Where the order or decision of stay does not fix the length of stay, it shall end on the date indicated in the order or decision of resumption or, in the absence of such indication, on the date of the order or decision of resumption.
7. From the date of resumption of proceedings following a stay, the suspended procedural time-limits shall be replaced by new time-limits and time shall begin to run from the date of that resumption.

Article 56 Deferment of the determination of a case

After hearing the Judge-Rapporteur, the Advocate General and the parties, the President may in special circumstances, either of his own motion or at the request of one of the parties, defer a case to be dealt with at a later date.

Chapter 5
Written part of the procedure

Article 57 Lodging of procedural documents

1. The original of every procedural document must bear the handwritten signature of the party's agent or lawyer or, in the case of observations submitted in the context of preliminary ruling proceedings, that of the party to the main proceedings or his representative, if the national rules of procedure applicable to those main proceedings so permit.
2. The original, accompanied by all annexes referred to therein, shall be submitted together with five copies for the Court and, in the case of proceedings other than preliminary ruling proceedings, a copy for every other party to the proceedings. Copies shall be certified by the party lodging them.
3. The institutions shall in addition produce, within time-limits laid down by the Court, translations of any procedural document into the other languages provided for by Article 1 of Council Regulation No 1. The preceding paragraph of this Article shall apply.
4. To every procedural document there shall be annexed a file containing the items and documents relied on in support of it, together with a schedule listing them.
5. Where in view of the length of an item or document only extracts from it are annexed to the procedural document, the whole item or document or a full copy of it shall be lodged at the Registry.
6. All procedural documents shall bear a date. In the calculation of procedural time-limits, only the date and time of lodgment of the original at the Registry shall be taken into account.

7. Without prejudice to the provisions of paragraphs 1 to 6, the date on and time at which a copy of the signed original of a procedural document, including the schedule of items and documents referred to in paragraph 4, is received at the Registry by telefax or any other technical means of communication available to the Court shall be deemed to be the date and time of lodgment for the purposes of compliance with the procedural time-limits, provided that the signed original of the procedural document, accompanied by the annexes and copies referred to in paragraph 2, is lodged at the Registry no later than 10 days thereafter.

8. Without prejudice to paragraphs 3 to 6, the Court may, by decision, determine the criteria for a procedural document sent to the Registry by electronic means to be deemed to be the original of that document. That decision shall be published in the Official Journal of the European Union.

Article 58 Length of procedural documents

Without prejudice to any special provisions laid down in these Rules, the Court may, by decision, set the maximum length of written pleadings or observations lodged before it. That decision shall be published in the Official Journal of the European Union.

Chapter 6
The preliminary report and assignment of cases to formations of the Court

Article 59 Preliminary report

1. When the written part of the procedure is closed, the President shall fix a date on which the Judge-Rapporteur is to present a preliminary report to the general meeting of the Court.

2. The preliminary report shall contain proposals as to whether particular measures of organisation of procedure, measures of inquiry or, if appropriate, requests to the referring court or tribunal for clarification should be undertaken, and as to the formation to which the case should be assigned. It shall also contain the Judge-Rapporteur's proposals, if any, as to whether to dispense with a hearing and as to whether to dispense with an Opinion of the Advocate General pursuant to the fifth paragraph of Article 20 of the Statute.

3. The Court shall decide, after hearing the Advocate General, what action to take on the proposals of the Judge-Rapporteur.

Article 60 Assignment of cases to formations of the Court

1. The Court shall assign to the Chambers of five and of three Judges any case brought before it in so far as the difficulty or importance of the case or particular circumstances are not such as to require that it should be assigned to the Grand Chamber, unless a Member State or an institution of the European Union participating in the proceedings has requested

that the case be assigned to the Grand Chamber, pursuant to the third paragraph of Article 16 of the Statute.

2. The Court shall sit as a full Court where cases are brought before it pursuant to the provisions referred to in the fourth paragraph of Article 16 of the Statute. It may assign a case to the full Court where, in accordance with the fifth paragraph of Article 16 of the Statute, it considers that the case is of exceptional importance.

3. The formation to which a case has been assigned may, at any stage of the proceedings, request the Court to assign the case to a formation composed of a greater number of Judges.

4. Where the oral part of the procedure is opened without an inquiry, the President of the formation determining the case shall fix the opening date.

Chapter 7
Measures of organisation of procedure and measures of inquiry

Section 1
Measures of organisation of procedure

Article 61 Measures of organisation prescribed by the Court

1. In addition to the measures which may be prescribed in accordance with Article 24 of the Statute, the Court may invite the parties or the interested persons referred to in Article 23 of the Statute to answer certain questions in writing, within the time-limit laid down by the Court, or at the hearing. The written replies shall be communicated to the other parties or the interested persons referred to in Article 23 of the Statute.

2. Where a hearing is organised, the Court shall, in so far as possible, invite the participants in that hearing to concentrate in their oral pleadings on one or more specified issues.

Article 62
Measures of organisation prescribed by the Judge-Rapporteur or the Advocate General

1. The Judge-Rapporteur or the Advocate General may request the parties or the interested persons referred to in Article 23 of the Statute to submit within a specified time-limit all such information relating to the facts, and all such documents or other particulars, as they may consider relevant. The replies and documents provided shall be communicated to the other parties or the interested persons referred to in Article 23 of the Statute.

2. The Judge-Rapporteur or the Advocate General may also send to the parties or the interested persons referred to in Article 23 of the Statute questions to be answered at the hearing.

Section 2
Measures of inquiry

Article 63 Decision on measures of inquiry
1. The Court shall decide in its general meeting whether a measure of inquiry is necessary.
2. Where the case has already been assigned to a formation of the Court, the decision shall be taken by that formation.

Article 64 Determination of measures of inquiry
1. The Court, after hearing the Advocate General, shall prescribe the measures of inquiry that it considers appropriate by means of an order setting out the facts to be proved.
2. Without prejudice to Articles 24 and 25 of the Statute, the following measures of inquiry may be adopted:
    (a) the personal appearance of the parties;
    (b) a request for information and production of documents;
    (c) oral testimony;
    (d) the commissioning of an expert's report;
    (e) an inspection of the place or thing in question.
3. Evidence may be submitted in rebuttal and previous evidence may be amplified.

Article 65 Participation in measures of inquiry
1. Where the formation of the Court does not undertake the inquiry itself, it shall entrust the task of so doing to the Judge-Rapporteur.
2. The Advocate General shall take part in the measures of inquiry.
3. The parties shall be entitled to attend the measures of inquiry.

Article 66 Oral testimony
1. The Court may, either of its own motion or at the request of one of the parties, and after hearing the Advocate General, order that certain facts be proved by witnesses.
2. A request by a party for the examination of a witness shall state precisely about what facts and for what reasons the witness should be examined.
3. The Court shall rule by reasoned order on the request referred to in the preceding paragraph. If the request is granted, the order shall set out the facts to be established and state which witnesses are to be heard in respect of each of those facts.
4. Witnesses shall be summoned by the Court, where appropriate after lodgment of the security provided for in Article 73(1) of these Rules.

Article 67 Examination of witnesses
1. After the identity of the witness has been established, the President shall inform him that he will be required to vouch the truth of his evidence in the manner laid down in these Rules.

2. The witness shall give his evidence to the Court, the parties having been given notice to attend. After the witness has given his evidence the President may, at the request of one of the parties or of his own motion, put questions to him.
3. The other Judges and the Advocate General may do likewise.
4. Subject to the control of the President, questions may be put to witnesses by the representatives of the parties.

Article 68 Witnesses' oath
1. After giving his evidence, the witness shall take the following oath:
'I swear that I have spoken the truth, the whole truth and nothing but the truth.'
2. The Court may, after hearing the parties, exempt a witness from taking the oath.

Article 69 Pecuniary penalties
1. Witnesses who have been duly summoned shall obey the summons and attend for examination.
2. If, without good reason, a witness who has been duly summoned fails to appear before the Court, the Court may impose upon him a pecuniary penalty not exceeding EUR 5 000 and may order that a further summons be served on the witness at his own expense.
3. The same penalty may be imposed upon a witness who, without good reason, refuses to give evidence or to take the oath.

Article 70 Expert's report
1. The Court may order that an expert's report be obtained. The order appointing the expert shall define his task and set a time-limit within which he is to submit his report.
2. After the expert has submitted his report and that report has been served on the parties, the Court may order that the expert be examined, the parties having been given notice to attend. At the request of one of the parties or of his own motion, the President may put questions to the expert.
3. The other Judges and the Advocate General may do likewise.
4. Subject to the control of the President, questions may be put to the expert by the representatives of the parties.

Article 71 Expert's oath
1. After making his report, the expert shall take the following oath:
'I swear that I have conscientiously and impartially carried out my task.'
2. The Court may, after hearing the parties, exempt the expert from taking the oath.

Article 72 Objection to a witness or expert
1. If one of the parties objects to a witness or an expert on the ground that he is not a competent or proper person to act as a witness or expert or for any other reason, or if a witness or expert refuses to give evidence or to take the oath, the matter shall be resolved by the Court.

2. An objection to a witness or an expert shall be raised within two weeks after service of the order summoning the witness or appointing the expert; the statement of objection must set out the grounds of objection and indicate the nature of any evidence offered.

Article 73 Witnesses' and experts' costs
1. Where the Court orders the examination of witnesses or an expert's report, it may request the parties or one of them to lodge security for the witnesses' costs or the costs of the expert's report.
2. Witnesses and experts shall be entitled to reimbursement of their travel and subsistence expenses. The cashier of the Court may make an advance payment towards these expenses.
3. Witnesses shall be entitled to compensation for loss of earnings, and experts to fees for their services. The cashier of the Court shall pay witnesses and experts these sums after they have carried out their respective duties or tasks.

Article 74 Minutes of inquiry hearings
1. The Registrar shall draw up minutes of every inquiry hearing. The minutes shall be signed by the President and by the Registrar. They shall constitute an official record.
2. In the case of the examination of witnesses or experts, the minutes shall be signed by the President or by the Judge-Rapporteur responsible for conducting the examination of the witness or expert, and by the Registrar. Before the minutes are thus signed, the witness or expert must be given an opportunity to check the content of the minutes and to sign them.
3. The minutes shall be served on the parties.

Article 75 Opening of the oral part of the procedure after the inquiry
1. Unless the Court decides to prescribe a time-limit within which the parties may submit written observations, the President shall fix the date for the opening of the oral part of the procedure after the measures of inquiry have been completed.
2. Where a time-limit has been prescribed for the submission of written observations, the President shall fix the date for the opening of the oral part of the procedure after that time-limit has expired.

Chapter 8
Oral part of the procedure

Article 76 Hearing
1. Any reasoned requests for a hearing shall be submitted within three weeks after service on the parties or the interested persons referred to in Article 23 of the Statute of notification of the close of the written part of the procedure. That time-limit may be extended by the President.
2. On a proposal from the Judge-Rapporteur and after hearing the Advocate General, the Court may decide not to hold a hearing if it considers, on reading the written pleadings

or observations lodged during the written part of the procedure, that it has sufficient information to give a ruling.

3. The preceding paragraph shall not apply where a request for a hearing, stating reasons, has been submitted by an interested person referred to in Article 23 of the Statute who did not participate in the written part of the procedure.

Article 77 Joint hearing

If the similarities between two or more cases of the same type so permit, the Court may decide to organise a joint hearing of those cases.

Article 78 Conduct of oral proceedings

Oral proceedings shall be opened and directed by the President, who shall be responsible for the proper conduct of the hearing.

Article 79 Cases heard in camera

1. For serious reasons related, in particular, to the security of the Member States or to the protection of minors, the Court may decide to hear a case in camera.
2. The oral proceedings in cases heard in camera shall not be published.

Article 80 Questions

The members of the formation of the Court and the Advocate General may in the course of the hearing put questions to the agents, advisers or lawyers of the parties and, in the circumstances referred to in Article 47(2) of these Rules, to the parties to the main proceedings or to their representatives.

Article 81 Close of the hearing

After the parties or the interested persons referred to in Article 23 of the Statute have presented oral argument, the President shall declare the hearing closed.

Article 82 Delivery of the Opinion of the Advocate General

1. Where a hearing takes place, the Opinion of the Advocate General shall be delivered after the close of that hearing.
2. The President shall declare the oral part of the procedure closed after the Advocate General has delivered his Opinion.

Article 83 Opening or reopening of the oral part of the procedure

The Court may at any time, after hearing the Advocate General, order the opening or reopening of the oral part of the procedure, in particular if it considers that it lacks sufficient information or where a party has, after the close of that part of the procedure, submitted a new fact which is of such a nature as to be a decisive factor for the decision of the Court, or where the case must be decided on the basis of an argument which has not been debated between the parties or the interested persons referred to in Article 23 of the Statute.

Article 84 Minutes of hearings
1. The Registrar shall draw up minutes of every hearing. The minutes shall be signed by the President and by the Registrar. They shall constitute an official record.
2. The parties and interested persons referred to in Article 23 of the Statute may inspect the minutes at the Registry and obtain copies.

Article 85 Recording of the hearing
The President may, on a duly substantiated request, authorise a party or an interested person referred to in Article 23 of the Statute who has participated in the written or oral part of the proceedings to listen, on the Court's premises, to the soundtrack of the hearing in the language used by the speaker during that hearing.

Chapter 9
Judgements and orders

Article 86 Date of delivery of a judgment
The parties or interested persons referred to in Article 23 of the Statute shall be informed of the date of delivery of a judgment.

Article 87 Content of a judgment
A judgment shall contain:
    (a) a statement that it is the judgment of the Court,
    (b) an indication as to the formation of the Court,
    (c) the date of delivery,
    (d) the names of the President and of the Judges who took part in the deliberations, with an indication as to the name of the Judge-Rapporteur,
    (e) the name of the Advocate General,
    (f) the name of the Registrar,
    (g) a description of the parties or of the interested persons referred to in Article 23 of the Statute who participated in the proceedings,
    (h) the names of their representatives,
    (i) in the case of direct actions and appeals, a statement of the forms of order sought by the parties,
    (j) where applicable, the date of the hearing,
    (k) a statement that the Advocate General has been heard and, where applicable, the date of his Opinion,
    (l) a summary of the facts,
    (m) the grounds for the decision,
    (n) the operative part of the judgment, including, where appropriate, the decision as to costs.

Article 88 Delivery and service of the judgment
1. The judgment shall be delivered in open court.
2. The original of the judgment, signed by the President, by the Judges who took part in the deliberations and by the Registrar, shall be sealed and deposited at the Registry; certified copies of the judgment shall be served on the parties and, where applicable, the referring court or tribunal, the interested persons referred to in Article 23 of the Statute and the General Court.

Article 89 Content of an order
1. An order shall contain:
   (a) a statement that it is the order of the Court,
   (b) an indication as to the formation of the Court,
   (c) the date of its adoption,
   (d) an indication as to the legal basis of the order,
   (e) the names of the President and, where applicable, the Judges who took part in the deliberations, with an indication as to the name of the Judge-Rapporteur,
   (f) the name of the Advocate General,
   (g) the name of the Registrar,
   (h) a description of the parties or of the parties to the main proceedings,
   (i) the names of their representatives,
   (j) a statement that the Advocate General has been heard,
   (k) the operative part of the order, including, where appropriate, the decision as to costs.
2. Where, in accordance with these Rules, an order must be reasoned, it shall in addition contain:
   (a) in the case of direct actions and appeals, a statement of the forms of order sought by the parties,
   (b) a summary of the facts,
   (c) the grounds for the decision.

Article 90 Signature and service of the order
The original of the order, signed by the President and by the Registrar, shall be sealed and deposited at the Registry; certified copies of the order shall be served on the parties and, where applicable, the referring court or tribunal, the interested persons referred to in Article 23 of the Statute and the General Court.

Article 91 Binding nature of judgments and orders
1. A judgment shall be binding from the date of its delivery.
2. An order shall be binding from the date of its service.

Article 92 Publication in the Official Journal of the European Union
A notice containing the date and the operative part of the judgment or order of the Court which closes the proceedings shall be published in the Official Journal of the European Union.

Title III
References for a preliminary ruling

Chapter 1
General provisions

Article 93 Scope
The procedure shall be governed by the provisions of this Title:
 (a) in the cases covered by Article 23 of the Statute,
 (b) as regards references for interpretation which may be provided for by agreements to which the European Union or the Member States are parties.

Article 94 Content of the request for a preliminary ruling
In addition to the text of the questions referred to the Court for a preliminary ruling, the request for a preliminary ruling shall contain:
 (a) a summary of the subject-matter of the dispute and the relevant findings of fact as determined by the referring court or tribunal, or, at least, an account of the facts on which the questions are based;
 (b) the tenor of any national provisions applicable in the case and, where appropriate, the relevant national case-law;
 (c) a statement of the reasons which prompted the referring court or tribunal to inquire about the interpretation or validity of certain provisions of European Union law, and the relationship between those provisions and the national legislation applicable to the main proceedings.

Article 95 Anonymity
1. Where anonymity has been granted by the referring court or tribunal, the Court shall respect that anonymity in the proceedings pending before it.
2. At the request of the referring court or tribunal, at the duly reasoned request of a party to the main proceedings or of its own motion, the Court may also, if it considers it necessary, render anonymous one or more persons or entities concerned by the case.

Article 96 Participation in preliminary ruling proceedings
1. Pursuant to Article 23 of the Statute, the following shall be authorised to submit observations to the Court:
 (a) the parties to the main proceedings,

(b) the Member States,

(c) the European Commission,

(d) the institution which adopted the act the validity or interpretation of which is in dispute,

(e) the States, other than the Member States, which are parties to the EEA Agreement, and also the EFTA Surveillance Authority, where a question concerning one of the fields of application of that Agreement is referred to the Court for a preliminary ruling,

(f) non-Member States which are parties to an agreement relating to a specific subject-matter, concluded with the Council, where the agreement so provides and where a court or tribunal of a Member State refers to the Court of Justice for a preliminary ruling a question falling within the scope of that agreement.

2. Non-participation in the written part of the procedure does not preclude participation in the oral part of the procedure.

Article 97 Parties to the main proceedings

1. The parties to the main proceedings are those who are determined as such by the referring court or tribunal in accordance with national rules of procedure.

2. Where the referring court or tribunal informs the Court that a new party has been admitted to the main proceedings, when the proceedings before the Court are already pending, that party must accept the case as he finds it at the time when the Court was so informed. That party shall receive a copy of every procedural document already served on the interested persons referred to in Article 23 of the Statute.

3. As regards the representation and attendance of the parties to the main proceedings, the Court shall take account of the rules of procedure in force before the court or tribunal which made the reference. In the event of any doubt as to whether a person may under national law represent a party to the main proceedings, the Court may obtain information from the referring court or tribunal on the rules of procedure applicable.

Article 98 Translation and service of the request for a preliminary ruling

1. The requests for a preliminary ruling referred to in this Title shall be served on the Member States in the original version, accompanied by a translation into the official language of the State to which they are being addressed. Where appropriate, on account of the length of the request, such translation shall be replaced by the translation into the official language of the State to which it is addressed of a summary of that request, which will serve as a basis for the position to be adopted by that State. The summary shall include the full text of the question or questions referred for a preliminary ruling. That summary shall contain, in particular, in so far as that information appears in the request for a preliminary ruling, the subject-matter of the main proceedings, the essential arguments of the parties to those proceedings, a succinct presentation of the reasons for the reference for a preliminary ruling and the case-law and the provisions of national law and European Union law relied on.

2. In the cases covered by the third paragraph of Article 23 of the Statute, the requests for a preliminary ruling shall be served on the States, other than the Member States, which are

parties to the EEA Agreement and also on the EFTA Surveillance Authority in the original version, accompanied by a translation of the request, or where appropriate of a summary, into one of the languages referred to in Article 36, to be chosen by the addressee.

3. Where a non-Member State has the right to take part in preliminary ruling proceedings pursuant to the fourth paragraph of Article 23 of the Statute, the original version of the request for a preliminary ruling shall be served on it accompanied by a translation of the request, or where appropriate of a summary, into one of the languages referred to in Article 36, to be chosen by the non-Member State concerned.

Article 99 Reply by reasoned order

Where a question referred to the Court for a preliminary ruling is identical to a question on which the Court has already ruled, where the reply to such a question may be clearly deduced from existing case-law or where the answer to the question referred for a preliminary ruling admits of no reasonable doubt, the Court may at any time, on a proposal from the Judge-Rapporteur and after hearing the Advocate General, decide to rule by reasoned order.

Article 100 Circumstances in which the Court remains seised

1. The Court shall remain seised of a request for a preliminary ruling for as long as it is not withdrawn by the court or tribunal which made that request to the Court. The withdrawal of a request may be taken into account until notice of the date of delivery of the judgment has been served on the interested persons referred to in Article 23 of the Statute.

2. However, the Court may at any time declare that the conditions of its jurisdiction are no longer fulfilled.

Article 101 Request for clarification

1. Without prejudice to the measures of organisation of procedure and measures of inquiry provided for in these Rules, the Court may, after hearing the Advocate General, request clarification from the referring court or tribunal within a time-limit prescribed by the Court.

2. The reply of the referring court or tribunal to that request shall be served on the interested persons referred to in Article 23 of the Statute.

Article 102 Costs of the preliminary ruling proceedings

It shall be for the referring court or tribunal to decide as to the costs of the preliminary ruling proceedings.

Article 103 Rectification of judgments and orders

1. Clerical mistakes, errors in calculation and obvious inaccuracies affecting judgments or orders may be rectified by the Court, of its own motion or at the request of an interested person referred to in Article 23 of the Statute made within two weeks after delivery of the judgment or service of the order.

2. The Court shall take its decision after hearing the Advocate General.

3. The original of the rectification order shall be annexed to the original of the rectified decision. A note of this order shall be made in the margin of the original of the rectified decision.

Article 104 Interpretation of preliminary rulings
1. Article 158 of these Rules relating to the interpretation of judgments and orders shall not apply to decisions given in reply to a request for a preliminary ruling.
2. It shall be for the national courts or tribunals to assess whether they consider that sufficient guidance is given by a preliminary ruling, or whether it appears to them that a further reference to the Court is required.

Chapter 2
Expedited preliminary ruling procedure

Article 105 Expedited procedure
1. At the request of the referring court or tribunal or, exceptionally, of his own motion, the President of the Court may, where the nature of the case requires that it be dealt with within a short time, after hearing the Judge-Rapporteur and the Advocate General, decide that a reference for a preliminary ruling is to be determined pursuant to an expedited procedure derogating from the provisions of these Rules.
2. In that event, the President shall immediately fix the date for the hearing, which shall be communicated to the interested persons referred to in Article 23 of the Statute when the request for a preliminary ruling is served.
3. The interested persons referred to in the preceding paragraph may lodge statements of case or written observations within a time-limit prescribed by the President, which shall not be less than 15 days. The President may request those interested persons to restrict the matters addressed in their statement of case or written observations to the essential points of law raised by the request for a preliminary ruling.
4. The statements of case or written observations, if any, shall be communicated to all the interested persons referred to in Article 23 of the Statute prior to the hearing.
5. The Court shall rule after hearing the Advocate General.

Article 106 Transmission of procedural documents
1. The procedural documents referred to in the preceding Article shall be deemed to have been lodged on the trans mission to the Registry, by telefax or any other technical means of communication available to the Court, of a copy of the signed original and the items and documents relied on in support of it, together with the schedule referred to in Article 57(4). The original of the document and the annexes referred to above shall be sent to the Registry immediately.
2. Where the preceding Article requires that a document be served on or communicated to a person, such service or communication may be effected by transmission of a copy of the

document by telefax or any other technical means of communication available to the Court and the addressee.

Chapter 3
Urgent preliminary ruling procedure

Article 107 Scope of the urgent preliminary ruling procedure

1. A reference for a preliminary ruling which raises one or more questions in the areas covered by Title V of Part Three of the Treaty on the Functioning of the European Union may, at the request of the referring court or tribunal or, exceptionally, of the Court's own motion, be dealt with under an urgent procedure derogating from the provisions of these Rules.

2. The referring court or tribunal shall set out the matters of fact and law which establish the urgency and justify the application of that exceptional procedure and shall, in so far as possible, indicate the answer that it proposes to the questions referred.

3. If the referring court or tribunal has not submitted a request for the urgent procedure to be applied, the President of the Court may, if the application of that procedure appears, prima facie, to be required, ask the Chamber referred to in Article 108 to consider whether it is necessary to deal with the reference under that procedure.

Article 108 Decision as to urgency

1. The decision to deal with a reference for a preliminary ruling under the urgent procedure shall be taken by the designated Chamber, acting on a proposal from the Judge-Rapporteur and after hearing the Advocate General. The composition of that Chamber shall be determined in accordance with Article 28(2) on the day on which the case is assigned to the Judge-Rapporteur if the application of the urgent procedure is requested by the referring court or tribunal, or, if the application of that procedure is considered at the request of the President of the Court, on the day on which that request is made.

2. If the case is connected with a pending case assigned to a Judge-Rapporteur who is not a member of the designated Chamber, that Chamber may propose to the President of the Court that the case be assigned to that Judge-Rapporteur. Where the case is reassigned to that Judge-Rapporteur, the Chamber of five Judges which includes him shall carry out the duties of the designated Chamber in respect of that case. Article 29(1) shall apply.

Article 109 Written part of the urgent procedure

1. A request for a preliminary ruling shall, where the referring court or tribunal has requested the application of the urgent procedure or where the President has requested the designated Chamber to consider whether it is necessary to deal with the reference under that procedure, be served forthwith by the Registrar on the parties to the main proceedings, on the Member State from which the reference is made, on the European Commission and on the institution which adopted the act the validity or interpretation of which is in dispute.

2. The decision as to whether or not to deal with the reference for a preliminary ruling under the urgent procedure shall be served immediately on the referring court or tribunal and on the parties, Member State and institutions referred to in the preceding paragraph. The decision to deal with the reference under the urgent procedure shall prescribe the time-limit within which those parties or entities may lodge statements of case or written observations. The decision may specify the matters of law to which such statements of case or written observations must relate and may specify the maximum length of those documents.

3. Where a request for a preliminary ruling refers to an administrative procedure or judicial proceedings conducted in a Member State other than that from which the reference is made, the Court may invite that first Member State to provide all relevant information in writing or at the hearing.

4. As soon as the service referred to in paragraph 1 above has been effected, the request for a preliminary ruling shall also be communicated to the interested persons referred to in Article 23 of the Statute, other than the persons served, and the decision whether or not to deal with the reference for a preliminary ruling under the urgent procedure shall be communicated to those interested persons as soon as the service referred to in paragraph 2 has been effected.

5. The interested persons referred to in Article 23 of the Statute shall be informed as soon as possible of the likely date of the hearing.

6. Where the reference is not to be dealt with under the urgent procedure, the proceedings shall continue in accordance with the provisions of Article 23 of the Statute and the applicable provisions of these Rules.

Article 110
Service and information following the close of the written part of the procedure

1. Where a reference for a preliminary ruling is to be dealt with under the urgent procedure, the request for a preliminary ruling and the statements of case or written observations which have been lodged shall be served on the interested persons referred to in Article 23 of the Statute other than the parties and entities referred to in Article 109(1). The request for a preliminary ruling shall be accompanied by a translation, where appropriate of a summary, in accordance with Article 98.

2. The statements of case or written observations which have been lodged shall also be served on the parties and other interested persons referred to in Article 109(1).

3. The date of the hearing shall be communicated to the interested persons referred to in Article 23 of the Statute at the same time as the documents referred to in the preceding paragraphs are served.

Article 111 Omission of the written part of the procedure

The designated Chamber may, in cases of extreme urgency, decide to omit the written part of the procedure referred to in Article 109(2).

Article 112 Decision on the substance
The designated Chamber shall rule after hearing the Advocate General.

Article 113 Formation of the Court
1. The designated Chamber may decide to sit in a formation of three Judges. In that event, it shall be composed of the President of the designated Chamber, the Judge-Rapporteur and the first Judge or, as the case may be, the first two Judges designated from the list referred to in Article 28(2) on the date on which the composition of the designated Chamber is determined in accordance with Article 108(1).
2. The designated Chamber may also request the Court to assign the case to a formation composed of a greater number of Judges. The urgent procedure shall continue before the new formation of the Court, where necessary after the reopening of the oral part of the procedure.

Article 114 Transmission of procedural documents
Procedural documents shall be transmitted in accordance with Article 106.

Chapter 4
Legal aid

Article 115 Application for legal aid
1. A party to the main proceedings who is wholly or in part unable to meet the costs of the proceedings before the Court may at any time apply for legal aid.
2. The application shall be accompanied by all information and supporting documents making it possible to assess the applicant's financial situation, such as a certificate issued by a competent national authority attesting to his financial situation.
3. If the applicant has already obtained legal aid before the referring court or tribunal, he shall produce the decision of that court or tribunal and specify what is covered by the sums already granted.

Article 116 Decision on the application for legal aid
1. As soon as the application for legal aid has been lodged it shall be assigned by the President to the Judge-Rapporteur responsible for the case in the context of which the application has been made.
2. The decision to grant legal aid, in full or in part, or to refuse it shall be taken, on a proposal from the Judge-Rapporteur and after hearing the Advocate General, by the Chamber of three Judges to which the Judge-Rapporteur is assigned. The formation of the Court shall, in that event, be composed of the President of that Chamber, the Judge-Rapporteur and the first Judge or, as the case may be, the first two Judges designated from the list referred to in Article 28(3) on the date on which the application for legal aid is brought before that Chamber by the Judge-Rapporteur.

3. If the Judge-Rapporteur is not a member of a Chamber of three Judges, the decision shall be taken, under the same conditions, by the Chamber of five Judges to which he is assigned. In addition to the Judge-Rapporteur, the formation of the Court shall be composed of four Judges designated from the list referred to in Article 28(2) on the date on which the application for legal aid is brought before that Chamber by the Judge-Rapporteur.

4. The formation of the Court shall give its decision by way of order. Where the application for legal aid is refused in whole or in part, the order shall state the reasons for that refusal.

Article 117 Sums to be advanced as legal aid

Where legal aid is granted, the cashier of the Court shall be responsible, where applicable within the limits set by the formation of the Court, for costs involved in the assistance and representation of the applicant before the Court. At the request of the applicant or his representative, an advance on those costs may be paid.

Article 118 Withdrawal of legal aid

The formation of the Court which gave a decision on the application for legal aid may at any time, either of its own motion or on request, withdraw that legal aid if the circum stances which led to its being granted alter during the proceedings.

Title IV
Direct actions

Chapter 1
Representation of the parties

Article 119 Obligation to be represented

1. A party may be represented only by his agent or lawyer.
2. Agents and lawyers must lodge at the Registry an official document or an authority to act issued by the party whom they represent.
3. The lawyer acting for a party must also lodge at the Registry a certificate that he is authorised to practise before a court of a Member State or of another State which is a party to the EEA Agreement.
4. If those documents are not lodged, the Registrar shall prescribe a reasonable time-limit within which the party concerned is to produce them. If the applicant fails to produce the required documents within the time-limit prescribed, the Court shall, after hearing the Judge-Rapporteur and the Advocate General, decide whether the non-compliance with that procedural requirement renders the application or written pleading formally inadmissible.

Chapter 2
Written part of the procedure

Article 120 Content of the application
An application of the kind referred to in Article 21 of the Statute shall state:
   (a) the name and address of the applicant;
   (b) the name of the party against whom the application is made;
   (c) the subject-matter of the proceedings, the pleas in law and arguments relied on and a summary of those pleas in law;
   (d) the form of order sought by the applicant;
   (e) where appropriate, any evidence produced or offered.

Article 121 Information relating to service
1. For the purpose of the proceedings, the application shall state an address for service. It shall indicate the name of the person who is authorised and has expressed willingness to accept service.
2. In addition to, or instead of, specifying an address for service as referred to in paragraph 1, the application may state that the lawyer or agent agrees that service is to be effected on him by telefax or any other technical means of communication.
3. If the application does not comply with the requirements referred to in paragraphs 1 or 2, all service on the party concerned for the purpose of the proceedings shall be effected, for so long as the defect has not been cured, by registered letter addressed to the agent or lawyer of that party. By way of derogation from Article 48, service shall then be deemed to be duly effected by the lodging of the registered letter at the post office of the place in which the Court has its seat.

Article 122 Annexes to the application
1. The application shall be accompanied, where appropriate, by the documents specified in the second paragraph of Article 21 of the Statute.
2. An application submitted under Article 273 TFEU shall be accompanied by a copy of the special agreement concluded between the Member States concerned.
3. If an application does not comply with the requirements set out in paragraphs 1 or 2 of this Article, the Registrar shall prescribe a reasonable time-limit within which the applicant is to produce the abovementioned documents. If the applicant fails to put the application in order, the Court shall, after hearing the Judge-Rapporteur and the Advocate General, decide whether the non-compliance with these conditions renders the application formally inadmissible.

Article 123 Service of the application
The application shall be served on the defendant. In cases where Article 119(4) or Article 122(3) applies, service shall be effected as soon as the application has been put in order or

the Court has declared it admissible notwithstanding the failure to observe the requirements set out in those two Articles.

Article 124 Content of the defence

1. Within two months after service on him of the application, the defendant shall lodge a defence, stating:
   (a) the name and address of the defendant;
   (b) the pleas in law and arguments relied on;
   (c) the form of order sought by the defendant;
   (d) where appropriate, any evidence produced or offered.
2. Article 121 shall apply to the defence.
3. The time-limit laid down in paragraph 1 may exceptionally be extended by the President at the duly reasoned request of the defendant.

Article 125 Transmission of documents

Where the European Parliament, the Council or the European Commission is not a party to a case, the Court shall send to them copies of the application and of the defence, without the annexes thereto, to enable them to assess whether the inapplicability of one of their acts is being invoked under Article 277 TFEU.

Article 126 Reply and rejoinder

1. The application initiating proceedings and the defence may be supplemented by a reply from the applicant and by a rejoinder from the defendant.
2. The President shall prescribe the time-limits within which those procedural documents are to be produced. He may specify the matters to which the reply or the rejoinder should relate.

Chapter 3
Pleas in law and evidence

Article 127 New pleas in law

1. No new plea in law may be introduced in the course of proceedings unless it is based on matters of law or of fact which come to light in the course of the procedure.
2. Without prejudice to the decision to be taken on the admissibility of the plea in law, the President may, on a proposal from the Judge-Rapporteur and after hearing the Advocate General, prescribe a time-limit within which the other party may respond to that plea.

Article 128 Evidence produced or offered

1. In reply or rejoinder a party may produce or offer further evidence in support of his arguments. The party must give reasons for the delay in submitting such evidence.

2. The parties may, exceptionally, produce or offer further evidence after the close of the written part of the procedure. They must give reasons for the delay in submitting such evidence. The President may, on a proposal from the Judge-Rapporteur and after hearing the Advocate General, prescribe a time-limit within which the other party may comment on such evidence.

Chapter 4
Intervention

Article 129 Object and effects of the intervention

1. The intervention shall be limited to supporting, in whole or in part, the form of order sought by one of the parties. It shall not confer the same procedural rights as those conferred on the parties and, in particular, shall not give rise to any right to request that a hearing be held.
2. The intervention shall be ancillary to the main proceedings. It shall become devoid of purpose if the case is removed from the register of the Court as a result of a party's discontinuance or withdrawal from the proceedings or of an agreement between the parties, or where the application is declared inadmissible.
3. The intervener must accept the case as he finds it at the time of his intervention.
4. Consideration may be given to an application to intervene which is made after the expiry of the time-limit prescribed in Article 130 but before the decision to open the oral part of the procedure provided for in Article 60(4). In that event, if the President allows the intervention, the intervener may submit his observations during the hearing, if it takes place.

Article 130 Application to intervene

1. An application to intervene must be submitted within six weeks of the publication of the notice referred to in Article 21(4).
2. The application to intervene shall contain:
   (a) a description of the case;
   (b) a description of the main parties;
   (c) the name and address of the intervener;
   (d) the form of order sought, in support of which the intervener is applying for leave to intervene;
   (e) a statement of the circumstances establishing the right to intervene, where the application is submitted pursuant to the second or third paragraph of Article 40 of the Statute.
3. The intervener shall be represented in accordance with Article 19 of the Statute.
4. Articles 119, 121 and 122 of these Rules shall apply.

Article 131 Decision on applications to intervene

1. The application to intervene shall be served on the parties in order to obtain any written or oral observations they may wish to make on that application.
2. Where the application is submitted pursuant to the first or third paragraph of Article 40 of the Statute, the intervention shall be allowed by decision of the President and the intervener shall receive a copy of every procedural document served on the parties, provided that those parties have not, within 10 days after the service referred to in paragraph 1 has been effected, put forward observations on the application to intervene or identified secret or confidential items or documents which, if communicated to the intervener, the parties claim would be prejudicial to them.
3. In any other case, the President shall decide on the application to intervene by order or shall refer the application to the Court.
4. If the application to intervene is granted, the intervener shall receive a copy of every procedural document served on the parties, save, where applicable, for the secret or confidential items or documents excluded from such communication pursuant to paragraph 3.

Article 132 Submission of statements

1. The intervener may submit a statement in intervention within one month after communication of the procedural documents referred to in the preceding Article. That time-limit may be extended by the President at the duly reasoned request of the intervener.
2. The statement in intervention shall contain:
    (a) the form of order sought by the intervener in support, in whole or in part, of the form of order sought by one of the parties;
    (b) the pleas in law and arguments relied on by the intervener;
    (c) where appropriate, any evidence produced or offered.
3. After the statement in intervention has been lodged, the President shall, where necessary, prescribe a time-limit within which the parties may reply to that statement.

Chapter 5
Expedited procedure

Article 133 Decision relating to the expedited procedure

1. At the request of the applicant or the defendant, the President of the Court may, where the nature of the case requires that it be dealt with within a short time, after hearing the other party, the Judge-Rapporteur and the Advocate General, decide that a case is to be determined pursuant to an expedited procedure derogating from the provisions of these Rules.
2. The request for a case to be determined pursuant to an expedited procedure must be made by a separate document submitted at the same time as the application initiating proceedings or the defence, as the case may be, is lodged.
3. Exceptionally the President may also take such a decision of his own motion, after hearing the parties, the Judge-Rapporteur and the Advocate General.

Article 134 Written part of the procedure
1. Under the expedited procedure, the application initiating proceedings and the defence may be supplemented by a reply and a rejoinder only if the President, after hearing the Judge-Rapporteur and the Advocate General, considers this to be necessary.
2. An intervener may submit a statement in intervention only if the President, after hearing the Judge-Rapporteur and the Advocate General, considers this to be necessary.

Article 135 Oral part of the procedure
1. Once the defence has been submitted or, if the decision to determine the case pursuant to an expedited procedure is not made until after that pleading has been lodged, once that decision has been taken, the President shall fix a date for the hearing, which shall be communicated forthwith to the parties. He may postpone the date of the hearing where it is necessary to undertake measures of inquiry or where measures of organisation of procedure so require.
2. Without prejudice to Articles 127 and 128, a party may supplement his arguments and produce or offer evidence during the oral part of the procedure. The party must, however, give reasons for the delay in producing such further arguments or evidence.

Article 136 Decision on the substance
The Court shall give its ruling after hearing the Advocate General.

Chapter 6
Costs

Article 137 Decision as to costs
A decision as to costs shall be given in the judgment or order which closes the proceedings.

Article 138 General rules as to allocation of costs
1. The unsuccessful party shall be ordered to pay the costs if they have been applied for in the successful party's pleadings.
2. Where there is more than one unsuccessful party the Court shall decide how the costs are to be shared.
3. Where each party succeeds on some and fails on other heads, the parties shall bear their own costs. However, if it appears justified in the circumstances of the case, the Court may order that one party, in addition to bearing its own costs, pay a proportion of the costs of the other party.

Article 139 Unreasonable or vexatious costs
The Court may order a party, even if successful, to pay costs which the Court considers that party to have unreasonably or vexatiously caused the opposite party to incur.

Article 140 Costs of interveners

1. The Member States and institutions which have intervened in the proceedings shall bear their own costs.
2. The States, other than the Member States, which are parties to the EEA Agreement, and also the EFTA Surveillance Authority, shall similarly bear their own costs if they have intervened in the proceedings.
3. The Court may order an intervener other than those referred to in the preceding paragraphs to bear his own costs.

Article 141 Costs in the event of discontinuance or withdrawal

1. A party who discontinues or withdraws from proceedings shall be ordered to pay the costs if they have been applied for in the other party's observations on the discontinuance.
2. However, at the request of the party who discontinues or withdraws from proceedings, the costs shall be borne by the other party if this appears justified by the conduct of that party.
3. Where the parties have come to an agreement on costs, the decision as to costs shall be in accordance with that agreement.
4. If costs are not claimed, the parties shall bear their own costs.

Article 142 Costs where a case does not proceed to judgment

Where a case does not proceed to judgment the costs shall be in the discretion of the Court.

Article 143 Costs of proceedings

Proceedings before the Court shall be free of charge, except that:

(a) where a party has caused the Court to incur avoidable costs the Court may, after hearing the Advocate General, order that party to refund them;

(b) where copying or translation work is carried out at the request of a party, the cost shall, in so far as the Registrar considers it excessive, be paid for by that party on the Registry's scale of charges referred to in Article 22.

Article 144 Recoverable costs

Without prejudice to the preceding Article, the following shall be regarded as recoverable costs:

(a) sums payable to witnesses and experts under Article 73 of these Rules;

(b) expenses necessarily incurred by the parties for the purpose of the proceedings, in particular the travel and subsistence expenses and the remuneration of agents, advisers or lawyers.

Article 145 Dispute concerning the costs to be recovered

1. If there is a dispute concerning the costs to be recovered, the Chamber of three Judges to which the Judge-Rapporteur who dealt with the case is assigned shall, on application by

the party concerned and after hearing the opposite party and the Advocate General, make an order. In that event, the formation of the Court shall be composed of the President of that Chamber, the Judge-Rapporteur and the first Judge or, as the case may be, the first two Judges designated from the list referred to in Article 28(3) on the date on which the dispute is brought before that Chamber by the Judge-Rapporteur.

2. If the Judge-Rapporteur is not a member of a Chamber of three Judges, the decision shall be taken, under the same conditions, by the Chamber of five Judges to which he is assigned. In addition to the Judge-Rapporteur, the formation of the Court shall be composed of four Judges designated from the list referred to in Article 28(2) on the date on which the dispute is brought before that Chamber by the Judge-Rapporteur.

3. The parties may, for the purposes of enforcement, apply for an authenticated copy of the order.

Article 146 Procedure for payment

1. Sums due from the cashier of the Court and from its debtors shall be paid in euro.

2. Where costs to be recovered have been incurred in a currency other than the euro or where the steps in respect of which payment is due were taken in a country of which the euro is not the currency, the conversion shall be effected at the European Central Bank's official rates of exchange on the day of payment.

Chapter 7
Amicable settlement, discontinuance, cases that do not proceed to judgment and preliminary issues

Article 147 Amicable settlement

1. If, before the Court has given its decision, the parties reach a settlement of their dispute and inform the Court of the abandonment of their claims, the President shall order the case to be removed from the register and shall give a decision as to costs in accordance with Article 141, having regard to any proposals made by the parties on the matter.

2. This provision shall not apply to proceedings under Articles 263 TFEU and 265 TFEU.

Article 148 Discontinuance

If the applicant informs the Court in writing or at the hearing that he wishes to discontinue the proceedings, the President shall order the case to be removed from the register and shall give a decision as to costs in accordance with Article 141.

Article 149 Cases that do not proceed to judgment

If the Court declares that the action has become devoid of purpose and that there is no longer any need to adjudicate on it, the Court may at any time of its own motion, on a proposal from the Judge-Rapporteur and after hearing the parties and the Advocate General, decide to rule by reasoned order. It shall give a decision as to costs.

Article 150 Absolute bar to proceeding with a case
On a proposal from the Judge-Rapporteur, the Court may at any time of its own motion, after hearing the parties and the Advocate General, decide to rule by reasoned order on whether there exists any absolute bar to proceeding with a case.

Article 151 Preliminary objections and issues
1. A party applying to the Court for a decision on a preliminary objection or issue not going to the substance of the case shall submit the application by a separate document.
2. The application must state the pleas of law and arguments relied on and the form of order sought by the applicant; any supporting items and documents must be annexed to it.
3. As soon as the application has been submitted, the President shall prescribe a time-limit within which the opposite party may submit in writing his pleas in law and the form of order which he seeks.
4. Unless the Court decides otherwise, the remainder of the proceedings on the application shall be oral.
5. The Court shall, after hearing the Advocate General, decide on the application as soon as possible or, where special circumstances so justify, reserve its decision until it rules on the substance of the case.
6. If the Court refuses the application or reserves its decision, the President shall prescribe new time-limits for the further steps in the proceedings.

Chapter 8
Judgments by default

Article 152 Judgments by default
1. If a defendant on whom an application initiating proceedings has been duly served fails to respond to the application in the proper form and within the time-limit prescribed, the applicant may apply to the Court for judgment by default.
2. The application for judgment by default shall be served on the defendant. The Court may decide to open the oral part of the procedure on the application.
3. Before giving judgment by default the Court shall, after hearing the Advocate General, consider whether the application initiating proceedings is admissible, whether the appropriate formalities have been complied with, and whether the applicant's claims appear well founded. The Court may adopt measures of organisation of procedure or order measures of inquiry.
4. A judgment by default shall be enforceable. The Court may, however, grant a stay of execution until the Court has given its decision on any application under Article 156 to set aside the judgment, or it may make execution subject to the provision of security of an amount and nature to be fixed in the light of the circumstances; this security shall be released if no such application is made or if the application fails.

Chapter 9
Requests and applications relating to judgments and orders

Article 153 Competent formation of the Court
1. With the exception of applications referred to in Article 159, the requests and applications referred to in this Chapter shall be assigned to the Judge-Rapporteur who was responsible for the case to which the request or application relates, and shall be assigned to the formation of the Court which gave a decision in that case.
2. If the Judge-Rapporteur is prevented from acting, the President of the Court shall assign the request or application referred to in this Chapter to a Judge who was a member of the formation of the Court which gave a decision in the case to which that request or application relates.
3. If the quorum referred to in Article 17 of the Statute can no longer be attained, the Court shall, on a proposal from the Judge-Rapporteur and after hearing the Advocate General, assign the request or application to a new formation of the Court.

Article 154 Rectification
1. Without prejudice to the provisions relating to the interpretation of judgments and orders, clerical mistakes, errors in calculation and obvious inaccuracies may be rectified by the Court, of its own motion or at the request of a party made within two weeks after delivery of the judgment or service of the order.
2. Where the request for rectification concerns the operative part or one of the grounds constituting the necessary support for the operative part, the parties, whom the Registrar shall duly inform, may submit written observations within a time-limit prescribed by the President.
3. The Court shall take its decision after hearing the Advocate General.
4. The original of the rectification order shall be annexed to the original of the rectified decision. A note of this order shall be made in the margin of the original of the rectified decision.

Article 155 Failure to adjudicate
1. If the Court has failed to adjudicate on a specific head of claim or on costs, any party wishing to rely on that may, within a month after service of the decision, apply to the Court to supplement its decision.
2. The application shall be served on the opposite party and the President shall prescribe a time-limit within which that party may submit written observations.
3. After these observations have been submitted, the Court shall, after hearing the Advocate General, decide both on the admissibility and on the substance of the application.

Article 156 Application to set aside
1. Application may be made pursuant to Article 41 of the Statute to set aside a judgment delivered by default.

2. The application to set aside the judgment must be made within one month from the date of service of the judgment and must be submitted in the form prescribed by Articles 120 to 122 of these Rules.
3. After the application has been served, the President shall prescribe a time-limit within which the other party may submit his written observations.
4. The proceedings shall be conducted in accordance with Articles 59 to 92 of these Rules.
5. The Court shall decide by way of a judgment which may not be set aside.
6. The original of this judgment shall be annexed to the original of the judgment by default. A note of the judgment on the application to set aside shall be made in the margin of the original of the judgment by default.

Article 157 Third-party proceedings

1. Articles 120 to 122 of these Rules shall apply to an application initiating third-party proceedings made pursuant to Article 42 of the Statute. In addition such an application shall:
    (a) specify the judgment or order contested;
    (b) state how the contested decision is prejudicial to the rights of the third party;
    (c) indicate the reasons for which the third party was unable to take part in the original case.
2. The application must be made against all the parties to the original case.
3. The application must be submitted within two months of publication of the decision in the Official Journal of the European Union.
4. The Court may, on application by the third party, order a stay of execution of the contested decision. The provisions of Chapter 10 of this Title shall apply.
5. The contested decision shall be varied on the points on which the submissions of the third party are upheld.
6. The original of the judgment in the third-party proceedings shall be annexed to the original of the contested decision. A note of the judgment in the third-party proceedings shall be made in the margin of the original of the contested decision.

Article 158 Interpretation

1. In accordance with Article 43 of the Statute, if the meaning or scope of a judgment or order is in doubt, the Court shall construe it on application by any party or any institution of the European Union establishing an interest therein.
2. An application for interpretation must be made within two years after the date of delivery of the judgment or service of the order.
3. An application for interpretation shall be made in accordance with Articles 120 to 122 of these Rules. In addition it shall specify:
    (a) the decision in question;
    (b) the passages of which interpretation is sought.
4. The application must be made against all the parties to the case in which the decision of which interpretation is sought was given.

5. The Court shall give its decision after having given the parties an opportunity to submit their observations and after hearing the Advocate General.

6. The original of the interpreting decision shall be annexed to the original of the decision interpreted. A note of the interpreting decision shall be made in the margin of the original of the decision interpreted.

Article 159 Revision

1. In accordance with Article 44 of the Statute, an application for revision of a decision of the Court may be made only on discovery of a fact which is of such a nature as to be a decisive factor and which, when the judgment was delivered or the order served, was unknown to the Court and to the party claiming the revision.

2. Without prejudice to the time-limit of 10 years prescribed in the third paragraph of Article 44 of the Statute, an application for revision shall be made within three months of the date on which the facts on which the application is founded came to the applicant's knowledge.

3. Articles 120 to 122 of these Rules shall apply to an application for revision. In addition such an application shall:

(a) specify the judgment or order contested;
(b) indicate the points on which the decision is contested;
(c) set out the facts on which the application is founded;
(d) indicate the nature of the evidence to show that there are facts justifying revision, and that the time-limits laid down in paragraph 2 have been observed.

4. The application for revision must be made against all parties to the case in which the contested decision was given.

5. Without prejudice to its decision on the substance, the Court shall, after hearing the Advocate General, give in the form of an order its decision on the admissibility of the application, having regard to the written observations of the parties.

6. If the Court declares the application admissible, it shall proceed to consider the substance of the application and shall give its decision in the form of a judgment in accordance with these Rules.

7. The original of the revising judgment shall be annexed to the original of the decision revised. A note of the revising judgment shall be made in the margin of the original of the decision revised.

Chapter 10
Suspension of operation or enforcement and other interim measures

Article 160 Application for suspension or for interim measures

1. An application to suspend the operation of any measure adopted by an institution, made pursuant to Article 278 TFEU or Article 157 TEAEC, shall be admissible only if the applicant has challenged that measure in an action before the Court.

2. An application for the adoption of one of the other interim measures referred to in Article 279 TFEU shall be admissible only if it is made by a party to a case before the Court and relates to that case.

3. An application of a kind referred to in the preceding paragraphs shall state the subject-matter of the proceedings, the circumstances giving rise to urgency and the pleas of fact and law establishing a prima facie case for the interim measure applied for.

4. The application shall be made by a separate document and in accordance with the provisions of Articles 120 to 122 of these Rules.

5. The application shall be served on the opposite party, and the President shall prescribe a short time-limit within which that party may submit written or oral observations.

6. The President may order a preparatory inquiry.

7. The President may grant the application even before the observations of the opposite party have been submitted. This decision may be varied or cancelled even without any application being made by any party.

Article 161 Decision on the application

1. The President shall either decide on the application himself or refer it immediately to the Court.

2. If the President is prevented from acting, Articles 10 and 13 of these Rules shall apply.

3. Where the application is referred to it, the Court shall give a decision immediately, after hearing the Advocate General.

Article 162 Order for suspension of operation or for interim measures

1. The decision on the application shall take the form of a reasoned order, from which no appeal shall lie. The order shall be served on the parties forthwith.

2. The execution of the order may be made conditional on the lodging by the applicant of security, of an amount and nature to be fixed in the light of the circumstances.

3. Unless the order fixes the date on which the interim measure is to lapse, the measure shall lapse when the judgment which closes the proceedings is delivered.

4. The order shall have only an interim effect, and shall be without prejudice to the decision of the Court on the substance of the case.

Article 163 Change in circumstances

On application by a party, the order may at any time be varied or cancelled on account of a change in circumstances.

Article 164 New application

Rejection of an application for an interim measure shall not bar the party who made it from making a further application on the basis of new facts.

Article 165
Applications pursuant to Articles 280 TFEU and 299 TFEU and Article 164 TEAEC

1. The provisions of this Chapter shall apply to applications to suspend the enforcement of a decision of the Court or of any measure adopted by the Council, the European Commission or the European Central Bank, submitted pursuant to Articles 280 TFEU and 299 TFEU or Article 164 TEAEC.

2. The order granting the application shall fix, where appropriate, a date on which the interim measure is to lapse.

Article 166 Application pursuant to Article 81 TEAEC

1. An application of a kind referred to in the third and fourth paragraphs of Article 81 TEAEC shall contain:

 (a) the names and addresses of the persons or undertakings to be inspected;

 (b) an indication of what is to be inspected and of the purpose of the inspection.

2. The President shall give his decision in the form of an order. Article 162 of these Rules shall apply.

3. If the President is prevented from acting, Articles 10 and 13 of these Rules shall apply.

Title V
Appeals against decisions of the General Court

Chapter 1
Form and content of the appeal and form of order sought

Article 167 Lodging of the appeal

1. An appeal shall be brought by lodging an application at the Registry of the Court of Justice or of the General Court.

2. The Registry of the General Court shall forthwith transmit to the Registry of the Court of Justice the file in the case at first instance and, where necessary, the appeal.

Article 168 Content of the appeal

1. An appeal shall contain:

 (a) the name and address of the appellant;

 (b) a reference to the decision of the General Court appealed against;

 (c) the names of the other parties to the relevant case before the General Court;

 (d) the pleas in law and legal arguments relied on, and a summary of those pleas in law;

 (e) the form of order sought by the appellant.

2. Articles 119, 121 and 122(1) of these Rules shall apply to appeals.

3. The appeal shall state the date on which the decision appealed against was served on the appellant.

4. If an appeal does not comply with paragraphs 1 to 3 of this Article, the Registrar shall prescribe a reasonable time-limit within which the appellant is to put the appeal in order. If the appellant fails to put the appeal in order within the time-limit prescribed, the Court of Justice shall, after hearing the Judge-Rapporteur and the Advocate General, decide whether the non-compliance with that formal requirement renders the appeal formally inadmissible.

Article 169 Form of order sought, pleas in law and arguments of the appeal

1. An appeal shall seek to have set aside, in whole or in part, the decision of the General Court as set out in the operative part of that decision.
2. The pleas in law and legal arguments relied on shall identify precisely those points in the grounds of the decision of the General Court which are contested.

Article 170 Form of order sought in the event that the appeal is allowed

1. An appeal shall seek, in the event that it is declared well founded, the same form of order, in whole or in part, as that sought at first instance and shall not seek a different form of order. The subject-matter of the proceedings before the General Court may not be changed in the appeal.
2. Where the appellant requests that the case be referred back to the General Court if the decision appealed against is set aside, he shall set out the reasons why the state of the proceedings does not permit a decision by the Court of Justice.

Chapter 2
Responses, replies and rejoinders

Article 171 Service of the appeal

1. The appeal shall be served on the other parties to the relevant case before the General Court.
2. In a case where Article 168(4) of these Rules applies, service shall be effected as soon as the appeal has been put in order or the Court of Justice has declared it admissible notwithstanding the failure to observe the formal requirements laid down by that Article.

Article 172 Parties authorised to lodge a response

Any party to the relevant case before the General Court having an interest in the appeal being allowed or dismissed may submit a response within two months after service on him of the appeal. The time-limit for submitting a response shall not be extended.

Article 173 Content of the response

1. A response shall contain:
    (a) the name and address of the party submitting it;
    (b) the date on which the appeal was served on him;

(c) the pleas in law and legal arguments relied on;
(d) the form of order sought.
2. Articles 119 and 121 of these Rules shall apply to responses.

Article 174 Form of order sought in the response
A response shall seek to have the appeal allowed or dismissed, in whole or in part.

Article 175 Reply and rejoinder
1. The appeal and the response may be supplemented by a reply and a rejoinder only where the President, on a duly reasoned application submitted by the appellant within seven days of service of the response, considers it necessary, after hearing the Judge-Rapporteur and the Advocate General, in particular to enable the appellant to present his views on a plea of inadmissibility or on new matters relied on in the response.
2. The President shall fix the date by which the reply is to be produced and, upon service of that pleading, the date by which the rejoinder is to be produced. He may limit the number of pages and the subject-matter of those pleadings.

Chapter 3
Form and content of the cross-appeal, and form of order sought

Article 176 Cross-appeal
1. The parties referred to in Article 172 of these Rules may submit a cross-appeal within the same time-limit as that prescribed for the submission of a response.
2. A cross-appeal must be introduced by a document separate from the response.

Article 177 Content of the cross-appeal
1. A cross-appeal shall contain:
   (a) the name and address of the party bringing the cross-appeal;
   (b) the date on which the appeal was served on him;
   (c) the pleas in law and legal arguments relied on;
   (d) the form of order sought.
2. Articles 119, 121 and 122(1) and (3) of these Rules shall apply to cross-appeals.

Article 178
Form of order sought, pleas in law and arguments of the cross-appeal
1. A cross-appeal shall seek to have set aside, in whole or in part, the decision of the General Court.
2. It may also seek to have set aside an express or implied decision relating to the admissibility of the action before the General Court.

3. The pleas in law and legal arguments relied on shall identify precisely those points in the grounds of the decision of the General Court which are contested. The pleas in law and arguments must be separate from those relied on in the response.

Chapter 4
Pleadings consequent on the cross-appeal

Article 179 Response to the cross-appeal
Where a cross-appeal is brought, the applicant at first instance or any other party to the relevant case before the General Court having an interest in the cross-appeal being allowed or dismissed may submit a response, which must be limited to the pleas in law relied on in that cross-appeal, within two months after its being served on him. That time-limit shall not be extended.

Article 180 Reply and rejoinder on a cross-appeal
1. The cross-appeal and the response thereto may be supplemented by a reply and a rejoinder only where the President, on a duly reasoned application submitted by the party who brought the cross-appeal within seven days of service of the response to the cross-appeal, considers it necessary, after hearing the Judge-Rapporteur and the Advocate General, in particular to enable that party to present his views on a plea of inadmissibility or on new matters relied on in the response to the cross-appeal.
2. The President shall fix the date by which that reply is to be produced and, upon service of that pleading, the date by which the rejoinder is to be produced. He may limit the number of pages and the subject-matter of those pleadings.

Chapter 5
Appeals determined by order

Article 181
Manifestly inadmissible or manifestly unfounded appeal or cross-appeal
Where the appeal or cross-appeal is, in whole or in part, manifestly inadmissible or manifestly unfounded, the Court may at any time, acting on a proposal from the Judge-Rapporteur and after hearing the Advocate General, decide by reasoned order to dismiss that appeal or cross-appeal in whole or in part.

Article 182 Manifestly well-founded appeal or cross-appeal
Where the Court has already ruled on one or more questions of law identical to those raised by the pleas in law of the appeal or cross-appeal and considers the appeal or cross-appeal to

be manifestly well founded, it may, acting on a proposal from the Judge-Rapporteur and after hearing the parties and the Advocate General, decide by reasoned order in which reference is made to the relevant case-law to declare the appeal or cross-appeal manifestly well founded.

Chapter 6
Effect on a cross-appeal of the removal of the appeal from the register

Article 183
Effect on a cross-appeal of the discontinuance or manifest inadmissibility of the appeal

A cross-appeal shall be deemed to be devoid of purpose:

(a) if the appellant discontinues his appeal;

(b) if the appeal is declared manifestly inadmissible for non-compliance with the time-limit for lodging an appeal;

(c) if the appeal is declared manifestly inadmissible on the sole ground that it is not directed against a final decision of the General Court or against a decision disposing of the substantive issues in part only or disposing of a procedural issue concerning a plea of lack of competence or inadmissibility within the meaning of the first paragraph of Article 56 of the Statute.

Chapter 7
Costs and legal aid in appeals

Article 184 Costs in appeals

1. Subject to the following provisions, Articles 137 to 146 of these Rules shall apply, mutatis mutandis, to the procedure before the Court of Justice on an appeal against a decision of the General Court.

2. Where the appeal is unfounded or where the appeal is well founded and the Court itself gives final judgment in the case, the Court shall make a decision as to the costs.

3. When an appeal brought by a Member State or an institution of the European Union which did not intervene in the proceedings before the General Court is well founded, the Court of Justice may order that the parties share the costs or that the successful appellant pay the costs which the appeal has caused an unsuccessful party to incur.

4. Where the appeal has not been brought by an intervener at first instance, he may not be ordered to pay costs in the appeal proceedings unless he participated in the written or oral part of the proceedings before the Court of Justice. Where an intervener at first instance takes part in the proceedings, the Court may decide that he shall bear his own costs.

Article 185 Legal aid

1. A party who is wholly or in part unable to meet the costs of the proceedings may at any time apply for legal aid.
2. The application shall be accompanied by all information and supporting documents making it possible to assess the applicant's financial situation, such as a certificate issued by a competent national authority attesting to his financial situation.

Article 186 Prior application for legal aid

1. If the application is made prior to the appeal which the applicant for legal aid intends to commence, it shall briefly state the subject of the appeal.
2. The application for legal aid need not be made through a lawyer.
3. The introduction of an application for legal aid shall, with regard to the person who made that application, suspend the time-limit prescribed for the bringing of the appeal until the date of service of the order making a decision on that application.
4. The President shall assign the application for legal aid, as soon as it is lodged, to a Judge-Rapporteur who shall put forward, promptly, a proposal as to the action to be taken on it.

Article 187 Decision on the application for legal aid

1. The decision to grant legal aid, in whole or in part, or to refuse it shall be taken, on a proposal from the Judge-Rapporteur and after hearing the Advocate General, by the Chamber of three Judges to which the Judge-Rapporteur is assigned. In that event, the formation of the Court shall be composed of the President of that Chamber, the Judge-Rapporteur and the first Judge or, as the case may be, the first two Judges designated from the list referred to in Article 28(3) on the date on which the application for legal aid is brought before that Chamber by the Judge-Rapporteur. It shall consider, if appropriate, whether the appeal is manifestly unfounded.
2. If the Judge-Rapporteur is not a member of a Chamber of three Judges, the decision shall be taken, under the same conditions, by the Chamber of five Judges to which he is assigned. In addition to the Judge-Rapporteur, the formation of the Court shall be composed of four Judges designated from the list referred to in Article 28(2) on the date on which the application for legal aid is brought before that Chamber by the Judge-Rapporteur.
3. The formation of the Court shall give its decision by way of order. Where the application for legal aid is refused in whole or in part, the order shall state the reasons for that refusal.

Article 188 Sums to be advanced as legal aid

1. Where legal aid is granted, the cashier of the Court shall be responsible, where applicable within the limits set by the formation of the Court, for costs involved in the assistance and representation of the applicant before the Court. At the request of the applicant or his representative, an advance on those costs may be paid.

2. In its decision as to costs the Court may order the payment to the cashier of the Court of sums advanced as legal aid.

3. The Registrar shall take steps to obtain the recovery of these sums from the party ordered to pay them.

Article 189 Withdrawal of legal aid

The formation of the Court which gave a decision on the application for legal aid may at any time, either of its own motion or on request, withdraw that legal aid if the circumstances which led to its being granted alter during the proceedings.

Chapter 8
Other provisions applicable to appeals

Article 190 Other provisions applicable to appeals

1. Articles 127, 129 to 136, 147 to 150, 153 to 155 and 157 to 166 of these Rules shall apply to the procedure before the Court of Justice on an appeal against decisions of the General Court.

2. By way of derogation from Article 130(1), an application to intervene shall, however, be made within one month of the publication of the notice referred to in Article 21(4).

3. Article 95 shall apply, mutatis mutandis, to the procedure before the Court of Justice on an appeal against decisions of the General Court.

Title VI
Review of decisions of the General Court

Article 191 Reviewing Chamber

A Chamber of five Judges shall be designated for a period of one year for the purpose of deciding, in accordance with Articles 193 and 194 of these Rules, whether a decision of the General Court is to be reviewed in accordance with Article 62 of the Statute.

Article 192
Information and communication of decisions which may be reviewed

1. As soon as the date for the delivery or signature of a decision to be given under Article 256(2) or (3) TFEU is fixed, the Registry of the General Court shall inform the Registry of the Court of Justice.

2. The decision shall be communicated to the Registry of the Court of Justice immediately upon its delivery or signature, as shall the file in the case, which shall be made available forthwith to the First Advocate General.

Article 193 Review of decisions given on appeal

1. The proposal of the First Advocate General to review a decision of the General Court given under Article 256(2) TFEU shall be forwarded to the President of the Court of Justice and to the President of the reviewing Chamber. Notice of that transmission shall be given to the Registrar at the same time.
2. As soon as he is informed of the existence of a proposal, the Registrar shall communicate the file in the case before the General Court to the members of the reviewing Chamber.
3. As soon as the proposal to review has been received, the President of the Court shall designate the Judge-Rapporteur from among the Judges of the reviewing Chamber on a proposal from the President of that Chamber. The composition of the formation of the Court shall be determined in accordance with Article 28(2) of these Rules on the day on which the case is assigned to the Judge-Rapporteur.
4. That Chamber, acting on a proposal from the Judge-Rapporteur, shall decide whether the decision of the General Court is to be reviewed. The decision to review the decision of the General Court shall indicate only the questions which are to be reviewed.
5. The General Court, the parties to the proceedings before it and the other interested persons referred to in the second paragraph of Article 62a of the Statute shall forthwith be informed by the Registrar of the decision of the Court of Justice to review the decision of the General Court.
6. Notice of the date of the decision to review the decision of the General Court and of the questions which are to be reviewed shall be published in the Official Journal of the European Union.

Article 194 Review of preliminary rulings

1. The proposal of the First Advocate General to review a decision of the General Court given under Article 256(3) TFEU shall be forwarded to the President of the Court of Justice and to the President of the reviewing Chamber. Notice of that transmission shall be given to the Registrar at the same time.
2. As soon as he is informed of the existence of a proposal, the Registrar shall communicate the file in the case before the General Court to the members of the reviewing Chamber.
3. The Registrar shall also inform the General Court, the referring court or tribunal, the parties to the main proceedings and the other interested persons referred to in the second paragraph of Article 62a of the Statute of the existence of a proposal to review.
4. As soon as the proposal to review has been received, the President of the Court shall designate the Judge-Rapporteur from among the Judges of the reviewing Chamber on a proposal from the President of that Chamber. The composition of the formation of the Court shall be determined in accordance with Article 28(2) of these Rules on the day on which the case is assigned to the Judge-Rapporteur.
5. That Chamber, acting on a proposal from the Judge-Rapporteur, shall decide whether the decision of the General Court is to be reviewed. The decision to review the decision of the General Court shall indicate only the questions which are to be reviewed.

6. The General Court, the referring court or tribunal, the parties to the main proceedings and the other interested persons referred to in the second paragraph of Article 62a of the Statute shall forthwith be informed by the Registrar of the decision of the Court of Justice as to whether or not the decision of the General Court is to be reviewed.

7. Notice of the date of the decision to review the decision of the General Court and of the questions which are to be reviewed shall be published in the Official Journal of the European Union.

Article 195 Judgment on the substance of the case after a decision to review

1. The decision to review a decision of the General Court shall be served on the parties and other interested persons referred to in the second paragraph of Article 62a of the Statute. The decision served on the Member States, and the States, other than the Member States, which are parties to the EEA Agreement, as well as the EFTA Surveillance Authority, shall be accompanied by a translation of the decision of the Court of Justice in accordance with the provisions of Article 98 of these Rules. The decision of the Court of Justice shall also be communicated to the General Court and, if applicable, to the referring court or tribunal.

2. Within one month of the date of service referred to in paragraph 1, the parties and other interested persons on whom the decision of the Court of Justice has been served may lodge statements or written observations on the questions which are subject to review.

3. As soon as a decision to review a decision of the General Court has been taken, the First Advocate General shall assign the review to an Advocate General.

4. The reviewing Chamber shall rule on the substance of the case, after hearing the Advocate General.

5. It may, however, request the Court of Justice to assign the case to a formation of the Court composed of a greater number of Judges.

6. Where the decision of the General Court which is subject to review was given under Article 256(2) TFEU, the Court of Justice shall make a decision as to costs.

Title VII
Opinions

Article 196 Written part of the procedure

1. In accordance with Article 218(11) TFEU, a request for an Opinion may be made by a Member State, by the European Parliament, by the Council or by the European Commission.

2. A request for an Opinion may relate both to whether the envisaged agreement is compatible with the provisions of the Treaties and to whether the European Union or any institution of the European Union has the power to enter into that agreement.

3. It shall be served on the Member States and on the institutions referred to in paragraph 1, and the President shall prescribe a time-limit within which they may submit written observations.

Article 197 Designation of the Judge-Rapporteur and of the Advocate General
As soon as the request for an Opinion has been submitted, the President shall designate a Judge-Rapporteur and the First Advocate General shall assign the case to an Advocate General.

Article 198 Hearing
The Court may decide that the procedure before it shall also include a hearing.

Article 199 Time-limit for delivering the Opinion
The Court shall deliver its Opinion as soon as possible, after hearing the Advocate General.

Article 200 Delivery of the Opinion
The Opinion, signed by the President, the Judges who took part in the deliberations and the Registrar, shall be delivered in open court. It shall be served on all the Member States and on the institutions referred to in Article 196(1).

Title VIII
Particular forms of procedure

Article 201 Appeals against decisions of the arbitration committee
1. An application initiating an appeal under the second paragraph of Article 18 TEAEC shall state:
    (a) the name and permanent address of the applicant;
    (b) the description of the signatory;
    (c) a reference to the arbitration committee's decision against which the appeal is made;
    (d) the names of the respondents;
    (e) a summary of the facts;
    (f) the grounds on which the appeal is based and arguments relied on, and a brief statement of those grounds;
    (g) the form of order sought by the applicant.
2. Articles 119 and 121 of these Rules shall apply to the application.
3. A certified copy of the contested decision shall be annexed to the application.
4. As soon as the application has been lodged, the Registrar of the Court shall request the arbitration committee registry to transmit to the Court the file in the case.
5. Articles 123 and 124 of these Rules shall apply to this procedure. The Court may decide that the procedure before it shall also include a hearing.
6. The Court shall give its decision in the form of a judgment. Where the Court sets aside the decision of the arbitration committee it may refer the case back to the committee.

Article 202 Procedure under Article 103 TEAEC

1. Four certified copies shall be lodged of an application under the third paragraph of Article 103 TEAEC. The application shall be accompanied by the draft of the agreement or contract concerned, by the observations of the European Commission addressed to the State concerned and by all other supporting documents.
2. The application and annexes thereto shall be served on the European Commission, which shall have a time-limit of 10 days from such service to submit its written observations. This time-limit may be extended by the President after the State concerned has been heard.
3. Following the lodging of such observations, which shall be served on the State concerned, the Court shall give its decision promptly, after hearing the Advocate General and, if they so request, the State concerned and the European Commission.

Article 203 Procedures under Articles 104 TEAEC and 105 TEAEC

Applications under the third paragraph of Article 104 TEAEC and the second paragraph of Article 105 TEAEC shall be governed by the provisions of Titles II and IV of these Rules. Such applications shall also be served on the State to which the respondent person or undertaking belongs.

Article 204 Procedure provided for by Article 111(3) of the EEA Agreement

1. In the case governed by Article 111(3) of the EEA Agreement, the matter shall be brought before the Court by a request submitted by the Contracting Parties which are parties to the dispute. The request shall be served on the other Contracting Parties, on the European Commission, on the EFTA Surveillance Authority and, where appropriate, on the other interested persons on whom a request for a preliminary ruling raising the same question of interpretation of European Union legislation would be served.
2. The President shall prescribe a time-limit within which the Contracting Parties and the other interested persons on whom the request has been served may submit written observations.
3. The request shall be made in one of the languages referred to in Article 36 of these Rules. Article 38 shall apply. The provisions of Article 98 shall apply mutatis mutandis.
4. As soon as the request referred to in paragraph 1 of this Article has been submitted, the President shall designate a Judge-Rapporteur. The First Advocate General shall, immediately afterwards, assign the request to an Advocate General.
5. The Court shall, after hearing the Advocate General, give a reasoned decision on the request.
6. The decision of the Court, signed by the President, the Judges who took part in the deliberations and the Registrar, shall be served on the Contracting Parties and on the other interested persons referred to in paragraphs 1 and 2.

Article 205
Settlement of the disputes referred to in Article 35 TEU in the version in force before the entry into force of the Treaty of Lisbon

1. In the case of disputes between Member States as referred to in Article 35(7) TEU in the version in force before the entry into force of the Treaty of Lisbon, as maintained in force by Protocol No 36 annexed to the Treaties, the matter shall be brought before the Court by an application by a party to the dispute. The application shall be served on the other Member States and on the European Commission.

2. In the case of disputes between Member States and the European Commission as referred to in Article 35(7) TEU in the version in force before the entry into force of the Treaty of Lisbon, as maintained in force by Protocol No 36 annexed to the Treaties, the matter shall be brought before the Court by an application by a party to the dispute. The application shall be served on the other Member States, the Council and the European Commission if it was submitted by a Member State. The application shall be served on the Member States and on the Council if it was submitted by the European Commission.

3. The President shall prescribe a time-limit within which the institutions and the Member States on which the application has been served may submit written observations.

4. As soon as the application referred to in paragraphs 1 and 2 has been submitted, the President shall designate a Judge-Rapporteur. The First Advocate General shall, immediately afterwards, assign the application to an Advocate General.

5. The Court may decide that the procedure before it shall also include a hearing.

6. The Court shall, after the Advocate General has delivered his Opinion, give its ruling on the dispute by way of judgment.

7. The same procedure as that laid down in the preceding paragraphs shall apply where an agreement concluded between the Member States confers jurisdiction on the Court to rule on a dispute between Member States or between Member States and an institution.

Article 206 Requests under Article 269 TFEU

1. Four certified copies shall be submitted of a request under Article 269 TFEU. The request shall be accompanied by any relevant document and, in particular, any observations and recommendations made pursuant to Article 7 TEU.

2. The request and annexes thereto shall be served on the European Council or on the Council, as appropriate, each of which shall have a time-limit of 10 days from such service to submit its written observations. This time-limit shall not be extended.

3. The request and annexes thereto shall also be communicated to the Member States other than the State in question, to the European Parliament and to the European Commission.

4. Following the lodging of the observations referred to in paragraph 2, which shall be served on the Member State concerned and on the States and institutions referred to in

paragraph 3, the Court shall give its decision within a time-limit of one month from the lodging of the request and after hearing the Advocate General. At the request of the Member State concerned, the European Council or the Council, or of its own motion, the Court may decide that the procedure before it shall also include a hearing, which all the States and institutions referred to in this Article shall be given notice to attend.

Final provisions

Article 207 Supplementary rules

Subject to the provisions of Article 253 TFEU and after consultation with the Governments concerned, the Court shall adopt supplementary rules concerning its practice in relation to:
  (a) letters rogatory;
  (b) applications for legal aid;
  (c) reports by the Court of perjury by witnesses or experts, delivered pursuant to Article 30 of the Statute.

Article 208 Implementing rules

The Court may, by a separate act, adopt practice rules for the implementation of these Rules.

Article 209 Repeal

These Rules replace the Rules of Procedure of the Court of Justice of the European Communities adopted on 19 June 1991, as last amended on 24 May 2011 (Official Journal of the European Union, L 162 of 22 June 2011, p. 17).

Article 210 Publication and entry into force of these Rules

These Rules, which are authentic in the languages referred to in Article 36 of these Rules, shall be published in the Official Journal of the European Union and shall enter into force on the first day of the second month following their publication.

Done at Luxembourg, 25 September 2012.

Charter of Fundamental Rights of the European Union

Date   7 December 2000
In force 1 December 2009
Source   consolidated Version OJ C 326 of 26 October 2012, p. 391

Preamble

The peoples of Europe, in creating an ever closer union among them, are resolved to share a peaceful future based on common values.
Conscious of its spiritual and moral heritage, the Union is founded on the indivisible, universal values of human dignity, freedom, equality and solidarity; it is based on the principles of democracy and the rule of law. It places the individual at the heart of its activities, by establishing the citizenship of the Union and by creating an area of freedom, security and justice.
The Union contributes to the preservation and to the development of these common values while respecting the diversity of the cultures and traditions of the peoples of Europe as well as the national identities of the Member States and the organisation of their public authorities at national, regional and local levels; it seeks to promote balanced and sustainable development and ensures free movement of persons, services, goods and capital, and the freedom of establishment.

© European Union, http://eur-lex.europa.eu/, 1998-2015.

To this end, it is necessary to strengthen the protection of fundamental rights in the light of changes in society, social progress and scientific and technological developments by making those rights more visible in a Charter.

This Charter reaffirms, with due regard for the powers and tasks of the Union and for the principle of subsidiarity, the rights as they result, in particular, from the constitutional traditions and international obligations common to the Member States, the European Convention for the Protection of Human Rights and Fundamental Freedoms, the Social Charters adopted by the Union and by the Council of Europe and the case-law of the Court of Justice of the European Union and of the European Court of Human Rights. In this context the Charter will be interpreted by the courts of the Union and the Member States with due regard to the explanations prepared under the authority of the Praesidium of the Convention which drafted the Charter and updated under the responsibility of the Praesidium of the European Convention.

Enjoyment of these rights entails responsibilities and duties with regard to other persons, to the human community and to future generations.

The Union therefore recognises the rights, freedoms and principles set out hereafter.

Title I
Dignity

Article 1 Human dignity
Human dignity is inviolable. It must be respected and protected.

Article 2 Right to life
1. Everyone has the right to life.
2. No one shall be condemned to the death penalty, or executed.

Article 3 Right to the integrity of the person
1. Everyone has the right to respect for his or her physical and mental integrity.
2. In the fields of medicine and biology, the following must be respected in particular:
    (a) the free and informed consent of the person concerned, according to the procedures laid down by law;
    (b) the prohibition of eugenic practices, in particular those aiming at the selection of persons;
    (c) the prohibition on making the human body and its parts as such a source of financial gain;
    (d) the prohibition of the reproductive cloning of human beings.

Article 4
Prohibition of torture and inhuman or degrading treatment or punishment
No one shall be subjected to torture or to inhuman or degrading treatment or punishment.

Article 5 Prohibition of slavery and forced labour
1. No one shall be held in slavery or servitude.
2. No one shall be required to perform forced or compulsory labour.
3. Trafficking in human beings is prohibited.

Title II
Freedoms

Article 6 Right to liberty and security
Everyone has the right to liberty and security of person.

Article 7 Respect for private and family life
Everyone has the right to respect for his or her private and family life, home and communications.

Article 8 Protection of personal data
1. Everyone has the right to the protection of personal data concerning him or her.
2. Such data must be processed fairly for specified purposes and on the basis of the consent of the person concerned or some other legitimate basis laid down by law. Everyone has the right of access to data which has been collected concerning him or her, and the right to have it rectified.
3. Compliance with these rules shall be subject to control by an independent authority.

Article 9 Right to marry and right to found a family
The right to marry and the right to found a family shall be guaranteed in accordance with the national laws governing the exercise of these rights.

Article 10 Freedom of thought, conscience and religion
1. Everyone has the right to freedom of thought, conscience and religion. This right includes freedom to change religion or belief and freedom, either alone or in community with others and in public or in private, to manifest religion or belief, in worship, teaching, practice and observance.
2. The right to conscientious objection is recognised, in accordance with the national laws governing the exercise of this right.

Article 11 Freedom of expression and information
1. Everyone has the right to freedom of expression. This right shall include freedom to hold opinions and to receive and impart information and ideas without interference by public authority and regardless of frontiers.
2. The freedom and pluralism of the media shall be respected.

Article 12 Freedom of assembly and of association
1. Everyone has the right to freedom of peaceful assembly and to freedom of association at all levels, in particular in political, trade union and civic matters, which implies the right of everyone to form and to join trade unions for the protection of his or her interests.
2. Political parties at Union level contribute to expressing the political will of the citizens of the Union.

Article 13 Freedom of the arts and sciences
The arts and scientific research shall be free of constraint. Academic freedom shall be respected.

Article 14 Right to education
1. Everyone has the right to education and to have access to vocational and continuing training.
2. This right includes the possibility to receive free compulsory education.
3. The freedom to found educational establishments with due respect for democratic principles and the right of parents to ensure the education and teaching of their children in conformity with their religious, philosophical and pedagogical convictions shall be respected, in accordance with the national laws governing the exercise of such freedom and right.

Article 15 Freedom to choose an occupation and right to engage in work
1. Everyone has the right to engage in work and to pursue a freely chosen or accepted occupation.
2. Every citizen of the Union has the freedom to seek employment, to work, to exercise the right of establishment and to provide services in any Member State.
3. Nationals of third countries who are authorised to work in the territories of the Member States are entitled to working conditions equivalent to those of citizens of the Union.

Article 16 Freedom to conduct a business
The freedom to conduct a business in accordance with Union law and national laws and practices is recognised.

Article 17 Right to property
1. Everyone has the right to own, use, dispose of and bequeath his or her lawfully acquired possessions. No one may be deprived of his or her possessions, except in the public interest and in the cases and under the conditions provided for by law, subject to fair compensation being paid in good time for their loss. The use of property may be regulated by law in so far as is necessary for the general interest.
2. Intellectual property shall be protected.

Article 18 Right to asylum
The right to asylum shall be guaranteed with due respect for the rules of the Geneva Convention of 28 July 1951 and the Protocol of 31 January 1967 relating to the status of refugees and in accordance with the Treaty on European Union and the Treaty on the Functioning of the European Union (hereinafter referred to as 'the Treaties').

Article 19 Protection in the event of removal, expulsion or extradition
1. Collective expulsions are prohibited.
2. No one may be removed, expelled or extradited to a State where there is a serious risk that he or she would be subjected to the death penalty, torture or other inhuman or degrading treatment or punishment.

Title III
Equality

Article 20 Equality before the law
Everyone is equal before the law.

Article 21 Non-discrimination
1. Any discrimination based on any ground such as sex, race, colour, ethnic or social origin, genetic features, language, religion or belief, political or any other opinion, membership of a national minority, property, birth, disability, age or sexual orientation shall be prohibited.
2. Within the scope of application of the Treaties and without prejudice to any of their specific provisions, any discrimination on grounds of nationality shall be prohibited.

Article 22 Cultural, religious and linguistic diversity
The Union shall respect cultural, religious and linguistic diversity.

Article 23 Equality between women and men
Equality between women and men must be ensured in all areas, including employment, work and pay.
The principle of equality shall not prevent the maintenance or adoption of measures providing for specific advantages in favour of the under-represented sex.

Article 24 The rights of the child
1. Children shall have the right to such protection and care as is necessary for their well-being. They may express their views freely. Such views shall be taken into consideration on matters which concern them in accordance with their age and maturity.
2. In all actions relating to children, whether taken by public authorities or private institutions, the child's best interests must be a primary consideration.

3. Every child shall have the right to maintain on a regular basis a personal relationship and direct contact with both his or her parents, unless that is contrary to his or her interests.

Article 25 The rights of the elderly
The Union recognises and respects the rights of the elderly to lead a life of dignity and independence and to participate in social and cultural life.

Article 26 Integration of persons with disabilities
The Union recognises and respects the right of persons with disabilities to benefit from measures designed to ensure their independence, social and occupational integration and participation in the life of the community.

Title IV
Solidarity

Article 27
Workers' right to information and consultation within the undertaking
Workers or their representatives must, at the appropriate levels, be guaranteed information and consultation in good time in the cases and under the conditions provided for by Union law and national laws and practices.

Article 28 Right of collective bargaining and action
Workers and employers, or their respective organisations, have, in accordance with Union law and national laws and practices, the right to negotiate and conclude collective agreements at the appropriate levels and, in cases of conflicts of interest, to take collective action to defend their interests, including strike action.

Article 29 Right of access to placement services
Everyone has the right of access to a free placement service.

Article 30 Protection in the event of unjustified dismissal
Every worker has the right to protection against unjustified dismissal, in accordance with Union law and national laws and practices.

Article 31 Fair and just working conditions
1. Every worker has the right to working conditions which respect his or her health, safety and dignity.
2. Every worker has the right to limitation of maximum working hours, to daily and weekly rest periods and to an annual period of paid leave.

Article 32 Prohibition of child labour and protection of young people at work

The employment of children is prohibited. The minimum age of admission to employment may not be lower than the minimum school-leaving age, without prejudice to such rules as may be more favourable to young people and except for limited derogations.

Young people admitted to work must have working conditions appropriate to their age and be protected against economic exploitation and any work likely to harm their safety, health or physical, mental, moral or social development or to interfere with their education.

Article 33 Family and professional life

1. The family shall enjoy legal, economic and social protection.
2. To reconcile family and professional life, everyone shall have the right to protection from dismissal for a reason connected with maternity and the right to paid maternity leave and to parental leave following the birth or adoption of a child.

Article 34 Social security and social assistance

1. The Union recognises and respects the entitlement to social security benefits and social services providing protection in cases such as maternity, illness, industrial accidents, dependency or old age, and in the case of loss of employment, in accordance with the rules laid down by Union law and national laws and practices.
2. Everyone residing and moving legally within the European Union is entitled to social security benefits and social advantages in accordance with Union law and national laws and practices.
3. In order to combat social exclusion and poverty, the Union recognises and respects the right to social and housing assistance so as to ensure a decent existence for all those who lack sufficient resources, in accordance with the rules laid down by Union law and national laws and practices.

Article 35 Health care

Everyone has the right of access to preventive health care and the right to benefit from medical treatment under the conditions established by national laws and practices. A high level of human health protection shall be ensured in the definition and implementation of all the Union's policies and activities.

Article 36 Access to services of general economic interest

The Union recognises and respects access to services of general economic interest as provided for in national laws and practices, in accordance with the Treaties, in order to promote the social and territorial cohesion of the Union.

Article 37 Environmental protection

A high level of environmental protection and the improvement of the quality of the environment must be integrated into the policies of the Union and ensured in accordance with the principle of sustainable development.

Article 38 Consumer protection

Union policies shall ensure a high level of consumer protection.

Title V
Citizens' Rights

Article 39
Right to vote and to stand as a candidate at elections to the European Parliament

1. Every citizen of the Union has the right to vote and to stand as a candidate at elections to the European Parliament in the Member State in which he or she resides, under the same conditions as nationals of that State.
2. Members of the European Parliament shall be elected by direct universal suffrage in a free and secret ballot.

Article 40 Right to vote and to stand as a candidate at municipal elections

Every citizen of the Union has the right to vote and to stand as a candidate at municipal elections in the Member State in which he or she resides under the same conditions as nationals of that State.

Article 41 Right to good administration

1. Every person has the right to have his or her affairs handled impartially, fairly and within a reasonable time by the institutions, bodies, offices and agencies of the Union.
2. This right includes:
   (a) the right of every person to be heard, before any individual measure which would affect him or her adversely is taken;
   (b) the right of every person to have access to his or her file, while respecting the legitimate interests of confidentiality and of professional and business secrecy;
   (c) the obligation of the administration to give reasons for its decisions.
3. Every person has the right to have the Union make good any damage caused by its institutions or by its servants in the performance of their duties, in accordance with the general principles common to the laws of the Member States.
4. Every person may write to the institutions of the Union in one of the languages of the Treaties and must have an answer in the same language.

Article 42 Right of access to documents

Any citizen of the Union, and any natural or legal person residing or having its registered office in a Member State, has a right of access to documents of the institutions, bodies, offices and agencies of the Union, whatever their medium.

Article 43 European Ombudsman

Any citizen of the Union and any natural or legal person residing or having its registered office in a Member State has the right to refer to the European Ombudsman cases of maladministration in the activities of the institutions, bodies, offices or agencies of the Union, with the exception of the Court of Justice of the European Union acting in its judicial role.

Article 44 Right to petition

Any citizen of the Union and any natural or legal person residing or having its registered office in a Member State has the right to petition the European Parliament.

Article 45 Freedom of movement and of residence

1. Every citizen of the Union has the right to move and reside freely within the territory of the Member States.
2. Freedom of movement and residence may be granted, in accordance with the Treaties, to nationals of third countries legally resident in the territory of a Member State.

Article 46 Diplomatic and consular protection

Every citizen of the Union shall, in the territory of a third country in which the Member State of which he or she is a national is not represented, be entitled to protection by the diplomatic or consular authorities of any Member State, on the same conditions as the nationals of that Member State.

Title VI
Justice

Article 47 Right to an effective remedy and to a fair trial

Everyone whose rights and freedoms guaranteed by the law of the Union are violated has the right to an effective remedy before a tribunal in compliance with the conditions laid down in this Article.

Everyone is entitled to a fair and public hearing within a reasonable time by an independent and impartial tribunal previously established by law. Everyone shall have the possibility of being advised, defended and represented.

Legal aid shall be made available to those who lack sufficient resources in so far as such aid is necessary to ensure effective access to justice.

Article 48 Presumption of innocence and right of defence

1. Everyone who has been charged shall be presumed innocent until proved guilty according to law.

2. Respect for the rights of the defence of anyone who has been charged shall be guaranteed.

Article 49
Principles of legality and proportionality of criminal offences and penalties
1. No one shall be held guilty of any criminal offence on account of any act or omission which did not constitute a criminal offence under national law or international law at the time when it was committed. Nor shall a heavier penalty be imposed than the one that was applicable at the time the criminal offence was committed. If, subsequent to the commission of a criminal offence, the law provides for a lighter penalty, that penalty shall be applicable.
2. This Article shall not prejudice the trial and punishment of any person for any act or omission which, at the time when it was committed, was criminal according to the general principles recognised by the community of nations.
3. The severity of penalties must not be disproportionate to the criminal offence.

Article 50
Right not to be tried or punished twice in criminal proceedings for the same criminal offence
No one shall be liable to be tried or punished again in criminal proceedings for an offence for which he or she has already been finally acquitted or convicted within the Union in accordance with the law.

Title VII
General Provisions governing the Interpretation and Application of the Charter

Article 51 Field of application
1. The provisions of this Charter are addressed to the institutions, bodies, offices and agencies of the Union with due regard for the principle of subsidiarity and to the Member States only when they are implementing Union law. They shall therefore respect the rights, observe the principles and promote the application thereof in accordance with their respective powers and respecting the limits of the powers of the Union as conferred on it in the Treaties.
2. The Charter does not extend the field of application of Union law beyond the powers of the Union or establish any new power or task for the Union, or modify powers and tasks as defined in the Treaties.

Article 52 Scope and interpretation of rights and principles
1. Any limitation on the exercise of the rights and freedoms recognised by this Charter must be provided for by law and respect the essence of those rights and freedoms. Subject

to the principle of proportionality, limitations may be made only if they are necessary and genuinely meet objectives of general interest recognised by the Union or the need to protect the rights and freedoms of others.
2. Rights recognised by this Charter for which provision is made in the Treaties shall be exercised under the conditions and within the limits defined by those Treaties.
3. In so far as this Charter contains rights which correspond to rights guaranteed by the Convention for the Protection of Human Rights and Fundamental Freedoms, the meaning and scope of those rights shall be the same as those laid down by the said Convention. This provision shall not prevent Union law providing more extensive protection.
4. In so far as this Charter recognises fundamental rights as they result from the constitutional traditions common to the Member States, those rights shall be interpreted in harmony with those traditions.
5. The provisions of this Charter which contain principles may be implemented by legislative and executive acts taken by institutions, bodies, offices and agencies of the Union, and by acts of Member States when they are implementing Union law, in the exercise of their respective powers. They shall be judicially cognisable only in the interpretation of such acts and in the ruling on their legality.
6. Full account shall be taken of national laws and practices as specified in this Charter.
7. The explanations drawn up as a way of providing guidance in the interpretation of this Charter shall be given due regard by the courts of the Union and of the Member States.

Article 53 Level of protection
Nothing in this Charter shall be interpreted as restricting or adversely affecting human rights and fundamental freedoms as recognised, in their respective fields of application, by Union law and international law and by international agreements to which the Union or all the Member States are party, including the European Convention for the Protection of Human Rights and Fundamental Freedoms, and by the Member States' constitutions.

Article 54 Prohibition of abuse of rights
Nothing in this Charter shall be interpreted as implying any right to engage in any activity or to perform any act aimed at the destruction of any of the rights and freedoms recognised in this Charter or at their limitation to a greater extent than is provided for herein.

The above text adapts the wording of the Charter proclaimed on 7 December 2000, and will replace it as from the date of entry into force of the Treaty of Lisbon.

Explanations* relating to the Charter of Fundamental Rights

Source   OJ C 303 of 14 December 2007, p. 17

These explanations were originally prepared under the authority of the Praesidium of the Convention which drafted the Charter of Fundamental Rights of the European Union. They have been updated under the responsibility of the Praesidium of the European Convention, in the light of the drafting adjustments made to the text of the Charter by that Convention (notably to Articles 51 and 52) and of further developments of Union law. Although they do not as such have the status of law, they are a valuable tool of interpretation intended to clarify the provisions of the Charter.

Title I
Dignity

Explanation on Article 1 Human dignity
The dignity of the human person is not only a fundamental right in itself but constitutes the real basis of fundamental rights. The 1948 Universal Declaration of Human Rights enshrined human dignity in its preamble: 'Whereas recognition of the inherent dignity and of the equal and inalienable rights of all members of the human family is the foundation of freedom, justice and peace in the world.' In its judgment of 9 October 2001 in Case C-377/98 Netherlands v European Parliament and Council [2001] ECR I-7079, at grounds 70-77, the Court of Justice confirmed that a fundamental right to human dignity is part of Union law.

---

*   Editor's note: References to article numbers in the Treaties have been updated and some minor technical errors have been corrected.
©   European Union, http://eur-lex.europa.eu/, 1998-2015.

It results that none of the rights laid down in this Charter may be used to harm the dignity of another person, and that the dignity of the human person is part of the substance of the rights laid down in this Charter. It must therefore be respected, even where a right is restricted.

Explanation on Article 2 Right to life

1. Paragraph 1 of this Article is based on the first sentence of Article 2(1) of the ECHR, which reads as follows:

'1. Everyone's right to life shall be protected by law ....'.

2. The second sentence of the provision, which referred to the death penalty, was superseded by the entry into force of Article 1 of Protocol No 6 to the ECHR, which reads as follows:

'The death penalty shall be abolished. No-one shall be condemned to such penalty or executed.'

Article 2(2) of the Charter is based on that provision.

3. The provisions of Article 2 of the Charter correspond to those of the above Articles of the ECHR and its Protocol. They have the same meaning and the same scope, in accordance with Article 52(3) of the Charter. Therefore, the 'negative' definitions appearing in the ECHR must be regarded as also forming part of the Charter:

(a) Article 2(2) of the ECHR:

'Deprivation of life shall not be regarded as inflicted in contravention of this article when it results from the use of force which is no more than absolutely necessary:

(a) in defence of any person from unlawful violence;

(b) in order to effect a lawful arrest or to prevent the escape of a person lawfully detained;

(c) in action lawfully taken for the purpose of quelling a riot or insurrection.'

(b) Article 2 of Protocol No 6 to the ECHR:

'A State may make provision in its law for the death penalty in respect of acts committed in time of war or of imminent threat of war; such penalty shall be applied only in the instances laid down in the law and in accordance with its provisions...'.

Explanation on Article 3 Right to the integrity of the person

1. In its judgment of 9 October 2001 in Case C-377/98 Netherlands v European Parliament and Council [2001] ECR I-7079, at grounds 70, 78 to 80, the Court of Justice confirmed that a fundamental right to human integrity is part of Union law and encompasses, in the context of medicine and biology, the free and informed consent of the donor and recipient.

2. The principles of Article 3 of the Charter are already included in the Convention on Human Rights and Biomedicine, adopted by the Council of Europe (ETS 164 and additional protocol ETS 168). The Charter does not set out to depart from those principles, and therefore prohibits only reproductive cloning. It neither authorises nor prohibits other forms of cloning. Thus it does not in any way prevent the legislature from prohibiting other forms of cloning.

3. The reference to eugenic practices, in particular those aiming at the selection of persons, relates to possible situations in which selection programmes are organised and implemented, involving campaigns for sterilisation, forced pregnancy, compulsory ethnic marriage among others, all acts deemed to be international crimes in the Statute of the International Criminal Court adopted in Rome on 17 July 1998 (see its Article 7(1)(g)).

Explanation on Article 4 Prohibition of torture and inhuman or degrading treatment or punishment

The right in Article 4 is the right guaranteed by Article 3 of the ECHR, which has the same wording: 'No one shall be subjected to torture or to inhuman or degrading treatment or punishment'. By virtue of Article 52(3) of the Charter, it therefore has the same meaning and the same scope as the ECHR Article.

Explanation on Article 5 Prohibition of slavery and forced labour

1. The right in Article 5(1) and (2) corresponds to Article 4(1) and (2) of the ECHR, which has the same wording. It therefore has the same meaning and scope as the ECHR Article, by virtue of Article 52(3) of the Charter. Consequently:
– no limitation may legitimately affect the right provided for in paragraph 1,
– in paragraph 2, 'forced or compulsory labour' must be understood in the light of the 'negative' definitions contained in Article 4(3) of the ECHR:
'For the purpose of this article the term "forced or compulsory labour" shall not include:
> (a) any work required to be done in the ordinary course of detention imposed according to the provisions of Article 5 of this Convention or during conditional release from such detention;
> (b) any service of a military character or, in case of conscientious objectors in countries where they are recognised, service exacted instead of compulsory military service;
> (c) any service exacted in case of an emergency or calamity threatening the life or well-being of the community;
> (d) any work or service which forms part of normal civic obligations.'.

2. Paragraph 3 stems directly from human dignity and takes account of recent developments in organised crime, such as the organisation of lucrative illegal immigration or sexual exploitation networks. The Annex to the Europol Convention contains the following definition which refers to trafficking for the purpose of sexual exploitation: 'traffic in human beings: means subjection of a person to the real and illegal sway of other persons by using violence or menaces or by abuse of authority or intrigue with a view to the exploitation of prostitution, forms of sexual exploitation and assault of minors or trade in abandoned children'. Chapter VI of the Convention implementing the Schengen Agreement, which has been integrated into the Union's acquis, in which the United Kingdom and Ireland participate, contains the following wording in Article 27(1) which refers to illegal immigration networks: 'The Contracting Parties undertake to impose appropriate penalties on any person who, for financial gain, assists or tries to assist an alien to enter or reside within the

territory of one of the Contracting Parties in breach of that Contracting Party's laws on the entry and residence of aliens.' On 19 July 2002, the Council adopted a framework decision on combating trafficking in human beings (OJ L 203, 1.8.2002, p. 1) whose Article 1 defines in detail the offences concerning trafficking in human beings for the purposes of labour exploitation or sexual exploitation, which the Member States must make punishable by virtue of that framework decision.

Title II
Freedoms

Explanation on Article 6 Right to liberty and security

The rights in Article 6 are the rights guaranteed by Article 5 of the ECHR, and in accordance with Article 52(3) of the Charter, they have the same meaning and scope. Consequently, the limitations which may legitimately be imposed on them may not exceed those permitted by the ECHR, in the wording of Article 5:

'1. Everyone has the right to liberty and security of person. No one shall be deprived of his liberty save in the following cases and in accordance with a procedure prescribed by law:

(a) the lawful detention of a person after conviction by a competent court;

(b) the lawful arrest or detention of a person for non-compliance with the lawful order of a court or in order to secure the fulfilment of any obligation prescribed by law;

(c) the lawful arrest or detention of a person effected for the purpose of bringing him before the competent legal authority on reasonable suspicion of having committed an offence or when it is reasonably considered necessary to prevent his committing an offence or fleeing after having done so;

(d) the detention of a minor by lawful order for the purpose of educational supervision or his lawful detention for the purpose of bringing him before the competent legal authority;

(e) the lawful detention of persons for the prevention of the spreading of infectious diseases, of persons of unsound mind, alcoholics or drug addicts or vagrants;

(f) the lawful arrest or detention of a person to prevent his effecting an unauthorised entry into the country or of a person against whom action is being taken with a view to deportation or extradition.

2. Everyone who is arrested shall be informed promptly, in a language which he understands, of the reasons for his arrest and of any charge against him.

3. Everyone arrested or detained in accordance with the provisions of paragraph 1.c of this Article shall be brought promptly before a judge or other officer authorised by law to exercise judicial power and shall be entitled to trial within a reasonable time or to release pending trial. Release may be conditioned by guarantees to appear for trial.

4. Everyone who is deprived of his liberty by arrest or detention shall be entitled to take proceedings by which the lawfulness of his detention shall be decided speedily by a court and his release ordered if the detention is not lawful.

5. Everyone who has been the victim of arrest or detention in contravention of the provisions of this Article shall have an enforceable right to compensation.'

The rights enshrined in Article 6 must be respected particularly when the European Parliament and the Council adopt legislative acts in the area of judicial cooperation in criminal matters, on the basis of Articles 82, 83 and 85 of the Treaty on the Functioning of the European Union, notably to define common minimum provisions as regards the categorisation of offences and punishments and certain aspects of procedural law.

Explanation on Article 7 Respect for private and family life

The rights guaranteed in Article 7 correspond to those guaranteed by Article 8 of the ECHR. To take account of developments in technology the word 'correspondence' has been replaced by 'communications'.

In accordance with Article 52(3), the meaning and scope of this right are the same as those of the corresponding article of the ECHR. Consequently, the limitations which may legitimately be imposed on this right are the same as those allowed by Article 8 of the ECHR:

'1. Everyone has the right to respect for his private and family life, his home and his correspondence.

2. There shall be no interference by a public authority with the exercise of this right except such as is in accordance with the law and is necessary in a democratic society in the interests of national security, public safety or the economic well-being of the country, for the prevention of disorder or crime, for the protection of health or morals, or for the protection of the rights and freedoms of others.'

Explanation on Article 8 Protection of personal data

This Article has been based on Article 286 of the Treaty establishing the European Community and Directive 95/46/EC of the European Parliament and of the Council on the protection of individuals with regard to the processing of personal data and on the free movement of such data (OJ L 281, 23.11.1995, p. 31) as well as on Article 8 of the ECHR and on the Council of Europe Convention of 28 January 1981 for the Protection of Individuals with regard to Automatic Processing of Personal Data, which has been ratified by all the Member States. Article 286 of the EC Treaty is now replaced by Article 16 of the Treaty on the Functioning of the European Union and Article 39 of the Treaty on European Union. Reference is also made to Regulation (EC) No 45/2001 of the European Parliament and of the Council on the protection of individuals with regard to the processing of personal data by the Community institutions and bodies and on the free movement of such data (OJ L 8, 12.1.2001, p. 1). The above-mentioned Directive and Regulation contain conditions and limitations for the exercise of the right to the protection of personal data.

Explanation on Article 9 Right to marry and right to found a family
This Article is based on Article 12 of the ECHR, which reads as follows: 'Men and women of marriageable age have the right to marry and to found a family according to the national laws governing the exercising of this right.' The wording of the Article has been modernised to cover cases in which national legislation recognises arrangements other than marriage for founding a family. This Article neither prohibits nor imposes the granting of the status of marriage to unions between people of the same sex. This right is thus similar to that afforded by the ECHR, but its scope may be wider when national legislation so provides.

Explanation on Article 10 Freedom of thought, conscience and religion
The right guaranteed in paragraph 1 corresponds to the right guaranteed in Article 9 of the ECHR and, in accordance with Article 52(3) of the Charter, has the same meaning and scope. Limitations must therefore respect Article 9(2) of the Convention, which reads as follows:
> 'Freedom to manifest one's religion or beliefs shall be subject only to such limitations as are prescribed by law and are necessary in a democratic society in the interests of public safety, for the protection of public order, health or morals, or for the protection of the rights and freedoms of others.'

The right guaranteed in paragraph 2 corresponds to national constitutional traditions and to the development of national legislation on this issue.

Explanation on Article 11 Freedom of expression and information
1. Article 11 corresponds to Article 10 of the European Convention on Human Rights, which reads as follows:
> '1. Everyone has the right to freedom of expression. This right shall include freedom to hold opinions and to receive and impart information and ideas without interference by public authority and regardless of frontiers. This Article shall not prevent States from requiring the licensing of broadcasting, television or cinema enterprises.
>
> 2. The exercise of these freedoms, since it carries with it duties and responsibilities, may be subject to such formalities, conditions, restrictions or penalties as are prescribed by law and are necessary in a democratic society, in the interests of national security, territorial integrity or public safety, for the prevention of disorder or crime, for the protection of health or morals, for the protection of the reputation or rights of others, for preventing the disclosure of information received in confidence, or for maintaining the authority and impartiality of the judiciary.'

Pursuant to Article 52(3) of the Charter, the meaning and scope of this right are the same as those guaranteed by the ECHR. The limitations which may be imposed on it may therefore not exceed those provided for in Article 10(2) of the Convention, without prejudice to any restrictions which the competition law of the Union may impose on Member States' right to introduce the licensing arrangements referred to in the third sentence of Article 10(1) of the ECHR.

2. Paragraph 2 of this Article spells out the consequences of paragraph 1 regarding freedom of the media. It is based in particular on Court of Justice case-law regarding television,

particularly in Case C-288/89 (judgment of 25 July 1991, Stichting Collectieve Antennevoorziening Gouda and others [1991] ECR I-4007), and on the Protocol on the system of public broadcasting in the Member States annexed to the EC Treaty and now to the Treaties, and on Council Directive 89/552/EC (particularly its seventeenth recital).

Explanation on Article 12 Freedom of assembly and of association

1. Paragraph 1 of this Article corresponds to Article 11 of the ECHR, which reads as follows:

> '1. Everyone has the right to freedom of peaceful assembly and to freedom of association with others, including the right to form and to join trade unions for the protection of his interests.
>
> 2. No restrictions shall be placed on the exercise of these rights other than such as are prescribed by law and are necessary in a democratic society in the interests of national security or public safety, for the prevention of disorder or crime, for the protection of health or morals or for the protection of the rights and freedoms of others. This article shall not prevent the imposition of lawful restrictions on the exercise of these rights by members of the armed forces, of the police or of the administration of the State.'

The meaning of the provisions of paragraph 1 of this Article 12 is the same as that of the ECHR, but their scope is wider since they apply at all levels including European level. In accordance with Article 52(3) of the Charter, limitations on that right may not exceed those considered legitimate by virtue of Article 11(2) of the ECHR.

2. This right is also based on Article 11 of the Community Charter of the Fundamental Social Rights of Workers.

3. Paragraph 2 of this Article corresponds to Article 10(4) of the Treaty on European Union.

Explanation on Article 13 Freedom of the arts and sciences

This right is deduced primarily from the right to freedom of thought and expression. It is to be exercised having regard to Article 1 and may be subject to the limitations authorised by Article 10 of the ECHR.

Explanation on Article 14 Right to education

1. This Article is based on the common constitutional traditions of Member States and on Article 2 of the Protocol to the ECHR, which reads as follows:

> 'No person shall be denied the right to education. In the exercise of any functions which it assumes in relation to education and to teaching, the State shall respect the right of parents to ensure such education and teaching in conformity with their own religious and philosophical convictions.'

It was considered useful to extend this Article to access to vocational and continuing training (see point 15 of the Community Charter of the Fundamental Social Rights of Workers and Article 10 of the Social Charter) and to add the principle of free compulsory education. As it is worded, the latter principle merely implies that as regards compulsory education, each child has the possibility of attending an establishment which offers free education. It does not require all establishments which provide education or vocational and continuing training, in particular private ones, to be free of charge. Nor does it exclude certain specific forms of education having to be paid for, if the State takes measures to grant financial compensation. In so far as the Charter applies to the Union, this means that in its training policies the Union must respect free compulsory education, but this does not, of course, create new powers. Regarding the right of parents, it must be interpreted in conjunction with the provisions of Article 24.

2. Freedom to found public or private educational establishments is guaranteed as one of the aspects of freedom to conduct a business but it is limited by respect for democratic principles and is exercised in accordance with the arrangements defined by national legislation.

Explanation on Article 15 Freedom to choose an occupation and right to engage in work

Freedom to choose an occupation, as enshrined in Article 15(1), is recognised in Court of Justice case-law (see inter alia judgment of 14 May 1974, Case 4/73 Nold [1974] ECR 491, paragraphs 12 to 14 of the grounds; judgment of 13 December 1979, Case 44/79 Hauer [1979] ECR 3727; judgment of 8 October 1986, Case 234/85 Keller [1986] ECR 2897, paragraph 8 of the grounds).

This paragraph also draws upon Article 1(2) of the European Social Charter, which was signed on 18 October 1961 and has been ratified by all the Member States, and on point 4 of the Community Charter of the Fundamental Social Rights of Workers of 9 December 1989. The expression 'working conditions' is to be understood in the sense of Article 156 of the Treaty on the Functioning of the European Union.

Paragraph 2 deals with the three freedoms guaranteed by Articles 26, 45, 49 and 56 of the Treaty on the Functioning of the European Union, namely freedom of movement for workers, freedom of establishment and freedom to provide services.

Paragraph 3 has been based on Article 153(1)(g) of the Treaty on the Functioning of the European Union, and on Article 19(4) of the European Social Charter signed on 18 October 1961 and ratified by all the Member States. Article 52(2) of the Charter is therefore applicable. The question of recruitment of seamen having the nationality of third States for the crews of vessels flying the flag of a Member State of the Union is governed by Union law and national legislation and practice.

Explanation on Article 16 Freedom to conduct a business

This Article is based on Court of Justice case-law which has recognised freedom to exercise an economic or commercial activity (see judgments of 14 May 1974, Case 4/73 Nold [1974] ECR 491, paragraph 14 of the grounds, and of 27 September 1979, Case 230-78 SpA Eridiana and others [1979] ECR 2749, paragraphs 20 and 31 of the grounds) and freedom of contract (see inter alia Sukkerfabriken Nykøbing judgment, Case 151/78 [1979] ECR 1, paragraph 19 of the grounds, and judgment of 5 October 1999, C-240/97 Spain v Commission [1999]

ECR I-6571, paragraph 99 of the grounds) and Article 119(1) and (3) of the Treaty on the Functioning of the European Union, which recognises free competition. Of course, this right is to be exercised with respect for Union law and national legislation. It may be subject to the limitations provided for in Article 52(1) of the Charter.

Explanation on Article 17 Right to property
This Article is based on Article 1 of the Protocol to the ECHR:
> 'Every natural or legal person is entitled to the peaceful enjoyment of his possessions. No one shall be deprived of his possessions except in the public interest and subject to the conditions provided for by law and by the general principles of international law.
> The preceding provisions shall not, however, in any way impair the right of a State to enforce such laws as it deems necessary to control the use of property in accordance with the general interest or to secure the payment of taxes or other contributions or penalties.'

This is a fundamental right common to all national constitutions. It has been recognised on numerous occasions by the case-law of the Court of Justice, initially in the Hauer judgment (13 December 1979, [1979] ECR 3727). The wording has been updated but, in accordance with Article 52(3), the meaning and scope of the right are the same as those of the right guaranteed by the ECHR and the limitations may not exceed those provided for there.

Protection of intellectual property, one aspect of the right of property, is explicitly mentioned in paragraph 2 because of its growing importance and Community secondary legislation. Intellectual property covers not only literary and artistic property but also inter alia patent and trademark rights and associated rights. The guarantees laid down in paragraph 1 shall apply as appropriate to intellectual property.

Explanation on Article 18 Right to asylum
The text of the Article has been based on TEC Article 63, now replaced by Article 78 of the Treaty on the Functioning of the European Union, which requires the Union to respect the Geneva Convention on refugees. Reference should be made to the Protocols relating to the United Kingdom and Ireland, annexed to the Treaties, and to Denmark, to determine the extent to which those Member States implement Union law in this area and the extent to which this Article is applicable to them. This Article is in line with the Protocol on Asylum annexed to the Treaties.

Explanation on Article 19 Protection in the event of removal, expulsion or extradition
Paragraph 1 of this Article has the same meaning and scope as Article 4 of Protocol No 4 to the ECHR concerning collective expulsion. Its purpose is to guarantee that every decision is based on a specific examination and that no single measure can be taken to expel all persons having the nationality of a particular State (see also Article 13 of the Covenant on Civil and Political Rights).

Paragraph 2 incorporates the relevant case-law from the European Court of Human Rights regarding Article 3 of the ECHR (see Ahmed v. Austria, judgment of 17 December 1996, 1996-VI, p. 2206, and Soering, judgment of 7 July 1989).

Title III
Equality

Explanation on Article 20 Equality before the law
This Article corresponds to a general principle of law which is included in all European constitutions and has also been recognised by the Court of Justice as a basic principle of Community law (judgment of 13 November 1984, Case 283/83 Racke [1984] ECR 3791, judgment of 17 April 1997, Case C-15/95 EARL [1997] ECR I-1961, and judgment of 13 April 2000, Case C-292/97 Karlsson [2000] ECR 2737).

Explanation on Article 21 Non-discrimination
Paragraph 1 draws on Article 13 of the EC Treaty, now replaced by Article 19 of the Treaty on the Functioning of the European Union, Article 14 of the ECHR and Article 11 of the Convention on Human Rights and Biomedicine as regards genetic heritage. In so far as this corresponds to Article 14 of the ECHR, it applies in compliance with it.

There is no contradiction or incompatibility between paragraph 1 and Article 19 of the Treaty on the Functioning of the European Union which has a different scope and purpose: Article 19 confers power on the Union to adopt legislative acts, including harmonisation of the Member States' laws and regulations, to combat certain forms of discrimination, listed exhaustively in that Article. Such legislation may cover action of Member State authorities (as well as relations between private individuals) in any area within the limits of the Union's powers. In contrast, the provision in Article 21(1) does not create any power to enact anti-discrimination laws in these areas of Member State or private action, nor does it lay down a sweeping ban of discrimination in such wide-ranging areas. Instead, it only addresses discriminations by the institutions and bodies of the Union themselves, when exercising powers conferred under the Treaties, and by Member States only when they are implementing Union law. Paragraph 1 therefore does not alter the extent of powers granted under Article 19 nor the interpretation given to that Article.

Paragraph 2 corresponds to the first paragraph of Article 18 of the Treaty on the Functioning of the European Union and must be applied in compliance with that Article.

Explanation on Article 22 Cultural, religious and linguistic diversity
This Article has been based on Article 6 of the Treaty on European Union and on Article 151(1) and (4) of the EC Treaty, now replaced by Article 167(1) and (4) of the Treaty on the Functioning of the European Union, concerning culture. Respect for cultural and linguistic diversity is now also laid down in Article 3(3) of the Treaty on European Union. The Article is also

inspired by Declaration No 11 to the Final Act of the Amsterdam Treaty on the status of churches and non-confessional organisations, now taken over in Article 17 of the Treaty on the Functioning of the European Union.

Explanation on Article 23 Equality between women and men

The first paragraph has been based on Articles 2 and 3(2) of the EC Treaty, now replaced by Article 3 of the Treaty on European Union and Article 8 of the Treaty on the Functioning of the European Union which impose the objective of promoting equality between men and women on the Union, and on Article 157(1) of the Treaty on the Functioning of the European Union. It draws on Article 20 of the revised European Social Charter of 3 May 1996 and on point 16 of the Community Charter on the rights of workers.

It is also based on Article 157(3) of the Treaty on the Functioning of the European Union and Article 2(4) of Council Directive 76/207/EEC on the implementation of the principle of equal treatment for men and women as regards access to employment, vocational training and promotion, and working conditions.

The second paragraph takes over in shorter form Article 157(4) of the Treaty on the Functioning of the European Union which provides that the principle of equal treatment does not prevent the maintenance or adoption of measures providing for specific advantages in order to make it easier for the under-represented sex to pursue a vocational activity or to prevent or compensate for disadvantages in professional careers. In accordance with Article 52(2), the present paragraph does not amend Article 157(4).

Explanation on Article 24 The rights of the child

This Article is based on the New York Convention on the Rights of the Child signed on 20 November 1989 and ratified by all the Member States, particularly Articles 3, 9, 12 and 13 thereof.

Paragraph 3 takes account of the fact that, as part of the establishment of an area of freedom, security and justice, the legislation of the Union on civil matters having cross-border implications, for which Article 81 of the Treaty on the Functioning of the European Union confers power, may include notably visiting rights ensuring that children can maintain on a regular basis a personal and direct contact with both of their parents.

Explanation on Article 25 The rights of the elderly

This Article draws on Article 23 of the revised European Social Charter and Articles 24 and 25 of the Community Charter of the Fundamental Social Rights of Workers. Of course, participation in social and cultural life also covers participation in political life.

Explanation on Article 26 Integration of persons with disabilities

The principle set out in this Article is based on Article 15 of the European Social Charter and also draws on point 26 of the Community Charter of the Fundamental Social Rights of Workers.

Title IV
Solidarity

Explanation on Article 27 Workers' right to information and consultation within the undertaking

This Article appears in the revised European Social Charter (Article 21) and in the Community Charter on the rights of workers (points 17 and 18). It applies under the conditions laid down by Union law and by national laws. The reference to appropriate levels refers to the levels laid down by Union law or by national laws and practices, which might include the European level when Union legislation so provides. There is a considerable Union acquis in this field: Articles 154 and 155 of the Treaty on the Functioning of the European Union, and Directives 2002/14/EC (general framework for informing and consulting employees in the European Community), 98/59/EC (collective redundancies), 2001/23/EC (transfers of undertakings) and 94/45/EC (European works councils).

Explanation on Article 28 Right of collective bargaining and action

This Article is based on Article 6 of the European Social Charter and on the Community Charter of the Fundamental Social Rights of Workers (points 12 to 14). The right of collective action was recognised by the European Court of Human Rights as one of the elements of trade union rights laid down by Article 11 of the ECHR. As regards the appropriate levels at which collective negotiation might take place, see the explanation given for the above Article. The modalities and limits for the exercise of collective action, including strike action, come under national laws and practices, including the question of whether it may be carried out in parallel in several Member States.

Explanation on Article 29 Right of access to placement services

This Article is based on Article 1(3) of the European Social Charter and point 13 of the Community Charter of the Fundamental Social Rights of Workers.

Explanation on Article 30 Protection in the event of unjustified dismissal

This Article draws on Article 24 of the revised Social Charter. See also Directive 2001/23/EC on the safeguarding of employees' rights in the event of transfers of undertakings, and Directive 80/987/EEC on the protection of employees in the event of the insolvency of their employer, as amended by Directive 2002/74/EC.

Explanation on Article 31 Fair and just working conditions

1. Paragraph 1 of this Article is based on Directive 89/391/EEC on the introduction of measures to encourage improvements in the safety and health of workers at work. It also draws on Article 3 of the Social Charter and point 19 of the Community Charter on the rights of workers, and, as regards dignity at work, on Article 26 of the revised Social Charter. The

expression 'working conditions' is to be understood in the sense of Article 156 of the Treaty on the Functioning of the European Union.

2. Paragraph 2 is based on Directive 93/104/EC concerning certain aspects of the organisation of working time, Article 2 of the European Social Charter and point 8 of the Community Charter on the rights of workers.

Explanation on Article 32 Prohibition of child labour and protection of young people at work

This Article is based on Directive 94/33/EC on the protection of young people at work, Article 7 of the European Social Charter and points 20 to 23 of the Community Charter of the Fundamental Social Rights of Workers.

Explanation on Article 33 Family and professional life

Article 33(1) is based on Article 16 of the European Social Charter.

Paragraph 2 draws on Council Directive 92/85/EEC on the introduction of measures to encourage improvements in the safety and health at work of pregnant workers and workers who have recently given birth or are breastfeeding and Directive 96/34/EC on the framework agreement on parental leave concluded by UNICE, CEEP and the ETUC. It is also based on Article 8 (protection of maternity) of the European Social Charter and draws on Article 27 (right of workers with family responsibilities to equal opportunities and equal treatment) of the revised Social Charter. 'Maternity' covers the period from conception to weaning.

Explanation on Article 34 Social security and social assistance

The principle set out in Article 34(1) is based on Articles 153 and 156 of the Treaty on the Functioning of the European Union, Article 12 of the European Social Charter and point 10 of the Community Charter on the rights of workers. The Union must respect it when exercising the powers conferred on it by Articles 153 and 156 of the Treaty on the Functioning of the European Union. The reference to social services relates to cases in which such services have been introduced to provide certain advantages but does not imply that such services must be created where they do not exist. 'Maternity' must be understood in the same sense as in the preceding Article.

Paragraph 2 is based on Articles 12(4) and 13(4) of the European Social Charter and point 2 of the Community Charter of the Fundamental Social Rights of Workers and reflects the rules arising from Regulation (EEC) No 1408/71 and Regulation (EEC) No 1612/68.

Paragraph 3 draws on Article 13 of the European Social Charter and Articles 30 and 31 of the revised Social Charter and point 10 of the Community Charter. The Union must respect it in the context of policies based on Article 153 of the Treaty on the Functioning of the European Union.

Explanation on Article 35 Health care

The principles set out in this Article are based on Article 152 of the EC Treaty, now replaced by Article 168 of the Treaty on the Functioning of the European Union, and on Articles 11 and 13 of the European Social Charter. The second sentence of the Article takes over Article 168(1).

Explanation on Article 36 Access to services of general economic interest
This Article is fully in line with Article 14 of the Treaty on the Functioning of the European Union and does not create any new right. It merely sets out the principle of respect by the Union for the access to services of general economic interest as provided for by national provisions, when those provisions are compatible with Union law.

Explanation on Article 37 Environmental protection
The principles set out in this Article have been based on Articles 2, 6 and 174 of the EC Treaty, which have now been replaced by Article 3(3) of the Treaty on European Union and Articles 11 and 191 of the Treaty on the Functioning of the European Union.
It also draws on the provisions of some national constitutions.

Explanation on Article 38 Consumer protection
The principles set out in this Article have been based on Article 169 of the Treaty on the Functioning of the European Union.

Title V
Citizen's rights

Explanation on Article 39 Right to vote and to stand as a candidate at elections to the European Parliament
Article 39 applies under the conditions laid down in the Treaties, in accordance with Article 52(2) of the Charter. Article 39(1) corresponds to the right guaranteed in Article 20(2) of the Treaty on the Functioning of the European Union (cf. also the legal base in Article 22 of the Treaty on the Functioning of the European Union for the adoption of detailed arrangements for the exercise of that right) and Article 39(2) corresponds to Article 14(3) of the Treaty on European Union. Article 39(2) takes over the basic principles of the electoral system in a democratic State.

Explanation on Article 40 Right to vote and to stand as a candidate at municipal elections
This Article corresponds to the right guaranteed by Article 20(2) of the Treaty on the Functioning of the European Union (cf. also the legal base in Article 22 of the Treaty on the Functioning of the European Union for the adoption of detailed arrangements for the exercise of that right). In accordance with Article 52(2) of the Charter, it applies under the conditions defined in these Articles in the Treaties.

Explanation on Article 41 Right to good administration

Article 41 is based on the existence of the Union as subject to the rule of law whose characteristics were developed in the case-law which enshrined inter alia good administration as a general principle of law (see inter alia Court of Justice judgment of 31 March 1992 in Case C-255/90 P Burban [1992] ECR I-2253, and Court of First Instance judgments of 18 September 1995 in Case T-167/94 Nölle [1995] ECR II-2589, and 9 July 1999 in Case T-231/97 New Europe Consulting and others [1999] ECR II-2403). The wording for that right in the first two paragraphs results from the case-law (Court of Justice judgment of 15 October 1987 in Case 222/86 Heylens [1987] ECR 4097, paragraph 15 of the grounds, judgment of 18 October 1989 in Case 374/87 Orkem [1989] ECR 3283, judgment of 21 November 1991 in Case C-269/90 TU München [1991] ECR I-5469, and Court of First Instance judgments of 6 December 1994 in Case T-450/93 Lisrestal [1994] ECR II-1177, 18 September 1995 in Case T-167/94 Nölle [1995] ECR II-2589) and the wording regarding the obligation to give reasons comes from Article 296 of the Treaty on the Functioning of the European Union (cf. also the legal base in Article 298 of the Treaty on the Functioning of the European Union for the adoption of legislation in the interest of an open, efficient and independent European administration).

Paragraph 3 reproduces the right now guaranteed by Article 340 of the Treaty on the Functioning of the European Union. Paragraph 4 reproduces the right now guaranteed by Article 20(2)(d) and Article 25 of the Treaty on the Functioning of the European Union. In accordance with Article 52(2) of the Charter, those rights are to be applied under the conditions and within the limits defined by the Treaties.

The right to an effective remedy, which is an important aspect of this question, is guaranteed in Article 47 of this Charter.

Explanation on Article 42 Right of access to documents

The right guaranteed in this Article has been taken over from Article 255 of the EC Treaty, on the basis of which Regulation (EC) No 1049/2001 has subsequently been adopted. The European Convention has extended this right to documents of institutions, bodies and agencies generally, regardless of their form (see Article 15(3) of the Treaty on the Functioning of the European Union). In accordance with Article 52(2) of the Charter, the right of access to documents is exercised under the conditions and within the limits for which provision is made in Article 15(3) of the Treaty on the Functioning of the European Union.

Explanation on Article 43 European Ombudsman

The right guaranteed in this Article is the right guaranteed by Articles 20 and 228 of the Treaty on the Functioning of the European Union. In accordance with Article 52(2) of the Charter, it applies under the conditions defined in these two Articles.

Explanation on Article 44 Right to petition

The right guaranteed in this Article is the right guaranteed by Articles 20 and 227 of the Treaty on the Functioning of the European Union. In accordance with Article 52(2) of the Charter, it applies under the conditions defined in these two Articles.

Explanation on Article 45 Freedom of movement and of residence

The right guaranteed by paragraph 1 is the right guaranteed by Article 20(2)(a) of the Treaty on the Functioning of the European Union (cf. also the legal base in Article 21; and the judgment of the Court of Justice of 17 September 2002, Case C-413/99 Baumbast [2002] ECR I-7091). In accordance with Article 52(2) of the Charter, those rights are to be applied under the conditions and within the limits defined by the Treaties.

Paragraph 2 refers to the power granted to the Union by Articles 77, 78 and 79 of the Treaty on the Functioning of the European Union. Consequently, the granting of this right depends on the institutions exercising that power.

Explanation on Article 46 Diplomatic and consular protection

The right guaranteed in this Article is the right guaranteed by Article 20 of the Treaty on the Functioning of the European Union (cf. also the legal base in Article 23). In accordance with Article 52(2) of the Charter, it applies under the conditions defined in these two Articles.

Title VI
Justice

Explanation on Article 47 Right to an effective remedy and to a fair trial

The first paragraph is based on Article 13 of the ECHR:

> 'Everyone whose rights and freedoms as set forth in this Convention are violated shall have an effective remedy before a national authority notwithstanding that the violation has been committed by persons acting in an official capacity.'

However, in Union law the protection is more extensive since it guarantees the right to an effective remedy before a court. The Court of Justice enshrined that right in its judgment of 15 May 1986 as a general principle of Union law (Case 222/84 Johnston [1986] ECR 1651; see also judgment of 15 October 1987, Case 222/86 Heylens [1987] ECR 4097 and judgment of 3 December 1992, Case C-97/91 Borelli [1992] ECR I-6313). According to the Court, that general principle of Union law also applies to the Member States when they are implementing Union law. The inclusion of this precedent in the Charter has not been intended to change the system of judicial review laid down by the Treaties, and particularly the rules relating to admissibility for direct actions before the Court of Justice of the European Union. The European Convention has considered the Union's system of judicial review including the rules on admissibility, and confirmed them while amending them as to certain aspects, as reflected in Articles 251 to 281 of the Treaty on the Functioning of the European Union, and in particular in the fourth paragraph of Article 263. Article 47 applies to the institutions of the Union and of Member States when they are implementing Union law and does so for all rights guaranteed by Union law.

The second paragraph corresponds to Article 6(1) of the ECHR which reads as follows:

'In the determination of his civil rights and obligations or of any criminal charge against him, everyone is entitled to a fair and public hearing within a reasonable time by an independent and impartial tribunal established by law. Judgment shall be pronounced publicly but the press and public may be excluded from all or part of the trial in the interests of morals, public order or national security in a democratic society, where the interests of juveniles or the protection of the private life of the parties so require, or to the extent strictly necessary in the opinion of the court in special circumstances where publicity would prejudice the interests of justice.'

In Union law, the right to a fair hearing is not confined to disputes relating to civil law rights and obligations. That is one of the consequences of the fact that the Union is a community based on the rule of law as stated by the Court in Case 294/83, 'Les Verts' v European Parliament (judgment of 23 April 1986, [1986] ECR 1339). Nevertheless, in all respects other than their scope, the guarantees afforded by the ECHR apply in a similar way to the Union.

With regard to the third paragraph, it should be noted that in accordance with the case-law of the European Court of Human Rights, provision should be made for legal aid where the absence of such aid would make it impossible to ensure an effective remedy (ECHR judgment of 9 October 1979, Airey, Series A, Volume 32, p. 11). There is also a system of legal assistance for cases before the Court of Justice of the European Union.

Explanation on Article 48 Presumption of innocence and right of defence

Article 48 is the same as Article 6(2) and (3) of the ECHR, which reads as follows:

'2. Everyone charged with a criminal offence shall be presumed innocent until proved guilty according to law.

3. Everyone charged with a criminal offence has the following minimum rights:

(a) to be informed promptly, in a language which he understands and in detail, of the nature and cause of the accusation against him;

(b) to have adequate time and facilities for the preparation of his defence;

(c) to defend himself in person or through legal assistance of his own choosing or, if he has not sufficient means to pay for legal assistance, to be given it free when the interests of justice so require;

(d) to examine or have examined witnesses against him and to obtain the attendance and examination of witnesses on his behalf under the same conditions as witnesses against him;

(e) to have the free assistance of an interpreter if he cannot understand or speak the language used in court.'

In accordance with Article 52(3), this right has the same meaning and scope as the right guaranteed by the ECHR.

Explanation on Article 49 Principles of legality and proportionality of criminal offences and penalties

This Article follows the traditional rule of the non-retroactivity of laws and criminal sanctions. There has been added the rule of the retroactivity of a more lenient penal law, which exists in a number of Member States and which features in Article 15 of the Covenant on Civil and Political Rights.
Article 7 of the ECHR is worded as follows:

'1. No one shall be held guilty of any criminal offence on account of any act or omission which did not constitute a criminal offence under national or international law at the time when it was committed. Nor shall a heavier penalty be imposed than the one that was applicable at the time the criminal offence was committed.

2. This Article shall not prejudice the trial and punishment of any person for any act or omission which, at the time when it was committed, was criminal according to the general principles of law recognised by civilised nations.'

In paragraph 2, the reference to 'civilised' nations has been deleted; this does not change the meaning of this paragraph, which refers to crimes against humanity in particular. In accordance with Article 52(3), the right guaranteed here therefore has the same meaning and scope as the right guaranteed by the ECHR.

Paragraph 3 states the general principle of proportionality between penalties and criminal offences which is enshrined in the common constitutional traditions of the Member States and in the case-law of the Court of Justice of the Communities.

Explanation on Article 50 Right not to be tried or punished twice in criminal proceedings for the same criminal offence

Article 4 of Protocol No 7 to the ECHR reads as follows:

'1. No one shall be liable to be tried or punished again in criminal proceedings under the jurisdiction of the same State for an offence for which he has already been finally acquitted or convicted in accordance with the law and penal procedure of that State.

2. The provisions of the preceding paragraph shall not prevent the reopening of the case in accordance with the law and the penal procedure of the State concerned, if there is evidence of new or newly discovered facts, or if there has been a fundamental defect in the previous proceedings, which could affect the outcome of the case.

3. No derogation from this Article shall be made under Article 15 of the Convention.'

The 'non bis in idem' rule applies in Union law (see, among the many precedents, the judgment of 5 May 1966, Joined Cases 18/65 and 35/65 Gutmann v Commission [1966] ECR 149 and a recent case, the decision of the Court of First Instance of 20 April 1999, Joined Cases T-305/94 and others Limburgse Vinyl Maatschappij NV v Commission [1999] ECR II-931). The rule prohibiting cumulation refers to cumulation of two penalties of the same kind, that is to say criminal-law penalties.

In accordance with Article 50, the 'non bis in idem' rule applies not only within the jurisdiction of one State but also between the jurisdictions of several Member States. That corresponds to the acquis in Union law; see Articles 54 to 58 of the Schengen Convention and the judgment of the Court of Justice of 11 February 2003, C-187/01 Gözütok [2003] ECR I-1345, Article 7 of the Convention on the Protection of the European Communities' Financial Interests and Article 10 of the Convention on the fight against corruption. The very limited exceptions in those Conventions permitting the Member States to derogate from the 'non bis in idem' rule are covered by the horizontal clause in Article 52(1) of the Charter concerning limitations. As regards the situations referred to by Article 4 of Protocol No 7, namely the application of the principle within the same Member State, the guaranteed right has the same meaning and the same scope as the corresponding right in the ECHR.

Title VII
General provisions governing the interpretation and application of the Charter

Explanation on Article 51 Field of application

The aim of Article 51 is to determine the scope of the Charter. It seeks to establish clearly that the Charter applies primarily to the institutions and bodies of the Union, in compliance with the principle of subsidiarity. This provision was drafted in keeping with Article 6(2) of the Treaty on European Union, which required the Union to respect fundamental rights, and with the mandate issued by the Cologne European Council. The term 'institutions' is enshrined in the Treaties. The expression 'bodies, offices and agencies' is commonly used in the Treaties to refer to all the authorities set up by the Treaties or by secondary legislation (see, e.g., Articles 15 or 16 of the Treaty on the Functioning of the European Union).

As regards the Member States, it follows unambiguously from the case-law of the Court of Justice that the requirement to respect fundamental rights defined in the context of the Union is only binding on the Member States when they act in the scope of Union law (judgment of 13 July 1989, Case 5/88 Wachauf [1989] ECR 2609; judgment of 18 June 1991, Case C-260/89 ERT [1991] ECR I-2925; judgment of 18 December 1997, Case C-309/96 Annibaldi [1997] ECR I-7493). The Court of Justice confirmed this case-law in the following terms: 'In addition, it should be remembered that the requirements flowing from the protection of fundamental rights in the Community legal order are also binding on Member States when they implement Community rules ...' (judgment of 13 April 2000, Case C-292/97 [2000] ECR I-2737, paragraph 37 of the grounds). Of course this rule, as enshrined in this Charter, applies to the central authorities as well as to regional or local bodies, and to public organisations, when they are implementing Union law.

Paragraph 2, together with the second sentence of paragraph 1, confirms that the Charter may not have the effect of extending the competences and tasks which the Treaties confer on the Union. Explicit mention is made here of the logical consequences of the principle of subsidiarity and of the fact that the Union only has those powers which have been conferred upon it. The fundamental rights as guaranteed in the Union do not have any effect other than in the context of the powers determined by the Treaties. Consequently, an obligation, pursuant to the second sentence of paragraph 1, for the Union's institutions to promote principles laid down in the Charter may arise only within the limits of these same powers. Paragraph 2 also confirms that the Charter may not have the effect of extending the field of application of Union law beyond the powers of the Union as established in the Treaties. The Court of Justice has already established this rule with respect to the fundamental rights recognised as part of Union law (judgment of 17 February 1998, C-249/96 Grant [1998] ECR I-621, paragraph 45 of the grounds). In accordance with this rule, it goes without saying that the reference to the Charter in Article 6 of the Treaty on European Union cannot be understood as extending by itself the range of Member State action considered to be 'implementation of Union law' (within the meaning of paragraph 1 and the above-mentioned case-law).

Explanation on Article 52 Scope and interpretation of rights and principles

The purpose of Article 52 is to set the scope of the rights and principles of the Charter, and to lay down rules for their interpretation. Paragraph 1 deals with the arrangements for the limitation of rights. The wording is based on the case-law of the Court of Justice: '... it is well established in the case-law of the Court that restrictions may be imposed on the exercise of fundamental rights, in particular in the context of a common organisation of the market, provided that those restrictions in fact correspond to objectives of general interest pursued by the Community and do not constitute, with regard to the aim pursued, disproportionate and unreasonable interference undermining the very substance of those rights' (judgment of 13 April 2000, Case C-292/97, paragraph 45 of the grounds). The reference to general interests recognised by the Union covers both the objectives mentioned in Article 3 of the Treaty on European Union and other interests protected by specific provisions of the Treaties such as Article 4(1) of the Treaty on European Union and Articles 35(3), 36 and 346 of the Treaty on the Functioning of the European Union.

Paragraph 2 refers to rights which were already expressly guaranteed in the Treaty establishing the European Community and have been recognised in the Charter, and which are now found in the Treaties (notably the rights derived from Union citizenship). It clarifies that such rights remain subject to the conditions and limits applicable to the Union law on which they are based, and for which provision is made in the Treaties. The Charter does not alter the system of rights conferred by the EC Treaty and taken over by the Treaties.

Paragraph 3 is intended to ensure the necessary consistency between the Charter and the ECHR by establishing the rule that, in so far as the rights in the present Charter also correspond to rights guaranteed by the ECHR, the meaning and scope of those rights, including authorised limitations, are the same as those laid down by the ECHR. This means in particular that the legislator, in laying down limitations to those rights, must comply with the same standards as are fixed by the detailed limitation arrangements laid down in the ECHR, which are thus made applicable for the rights covered by this paragraph, without thereby adversely affecting the autonomy of Union law and of that of the Court of Justice of the European Union.

The reference to the ECHR covers both the Convention and the Protocols to it. The meaning and the scope of the guaranteed rights are determined not only by the text of those instruments, but also by the case-law of the European Court of Human Rights and by the Court of Justice of the European Union. The last sentence of the paragraph is designed to allow the Union to guarantee more extensive protection. In any event, the level of protection afforded by the Charter may never be lower than that guaranteed by the ECHR.

The Charter does not affect the possibilities of Member States to avail themselves of Article 15 ECHR, allowing derogations from ECHR rights in the event of war or of other public dangers threatening the life of the nation, when they take action in the areas of national defence in the event of war and of the maintenance of law and order, in accordance with their responsibilities recognised in Article 4(1) of the Treaty on European Union and in Articles 72 and 347 of the Treaty on the Functioning of the European Union.

The list of rights which may at the present stage, without precluding developments in the law, legislation and the Treaties, be regarded as corresponding to rights in the ECHR within the meaning of the present paragraph is given hereafter. It does not include rights additional to those in the ECHR.

1. Articles of the Charter where both the meaning and the scope are the same as the corresponding Articles of the ECHR:

- Article 2 corresponds to Article 2 of the ECHR,
- Article 4 corresponds to Article 3 of the ECHR,
- Article 5(1) and (2) corresponds to Article 4 of the ECHR,
- Article 6 corresponds to Article 5 of the ECHR,
- Article 7 corresponds to Article 8 of the ECHR,
- Article 10(1) corresponds to Article 9 of the ECHR,
- Article 11 corresponds to Article 10 of the ECHR without prejudice to any restrictions which Union law may impose on Member States' right to introduce the licensing arrangements referred to in the third sentence of Article 10(1) of the ECHR,
- Article 17 corresponds to Article 1 of the Protocol to the ECHR,
- Article 19(1) corresponds to Article 4 of Protocol No 4,
- Article 19(2) corresponds to Article 3 of the ECHR as interpreted by the European Court of Human Rights,
- Article 48 corresponds to Article 6(2) and (3) of the ECHR,
- Article 49(1) (with the exception of the last sentence) and (2) correspond to Article 7 of the ECHR.

2. Articles where the meaning is the same as the corresponding Articles of the ECHR, but where the scope is wider:

- Article 9 covers the same field as Article 12 of the ECHR, but its scope may be extended to other forms of marriage if these are established by national legislation,
- Article 12(1) corresponds to Article 11 of the ECHR, but its scope is extended to European Union level,
- Article 14(1) corresponds to Article 2 of the Protocol to the ECHR, but its scope is extended to cover access to vocational and continuing training,

– Article 14(3) corresponds to Article 2 of the Protocol to the ECHR as regards the rights of parents,
– Article 47(2) and (3) corresponds to Article 6(1) of the ECHR, but the limitation to the determination of civil rights and obligations or criminal charges does not apply as regards Union law and its implementation,
– Article 50 corresponds to Article 4 of Protocol No 7 to the ECHR, but its scope is extended to European Union level between the Courts of the Member States,
– Finally, citizens of the European Union may not be considered as aliens in the scope of the application of Union law, because of the prohibition of any discrimination on grounds of nationality. The limitations provided for by Article 16 of the ECHR as regards the rights of aliens therefore do not apply to them in this context.

The rule of interpretation contained in paragraph 4 has been based on the wording of Article 6(3) of the Treaty on European Union and takes due account of the approach to common constitutional traditions followed by the Court of Justice (e.g., judgment of 13 December 1979, Case 44/79 Hauer [1979] ECR 3727; judgment of 18 May 1982, Case 155/79 AM&S [1982] ECR 1575). Under that rule, rather than following a rigid approach of 'a lowest common denominator', the Charter rights concerned should be interpreted in a way offering a high standard of protection which is adequate for the law of the Union and in harmony with the common constitutional traditions.

Paragraph 5 clarifies the distinction between 'rights' and 'principles' set out in the Charter. According to that distinction, subjective rights shall be respected, whereas principles shall be observed (Article 51(1)). Principles may be implemented through legislative or executive acts (adopted by the Union in accordance with its powers, and by the Member States only when they implement Union law); accordingly, they become significant for the Courts only when such acts are interpreted or reviewed. They do not however give rise to direct claims for positive action by the Union's institutions or Member States authorities. This is consistent both with case-law of the Court of Justice (cf. notably case-law on the 'precautionary principle' in Article 191(2) of the Treaty on the Functioning of the European Union: judgment of the CFI of 11 September 2002, Case T-13/99 Pfizer v Council, with numerous references to earlier case-law; and a series of judgments on Article 33 (ex-39) on the principles of agricultural law, e.g. judgment of the Court of Justice in Case 265/85 Van den Berg [1987] ECR 1155: scrutiny of the principle of market stabilisation and of reasonable expectations) and with the approach of the Member States' constitutional systems to 'principles', particularly in the field of social law. For illustration, examples for principles, recognised in the Charter include e.g. Articles 25, 26 and 37. In some cases, an Article of the Charter may contain both elements of a right and of a principle, e.g. Articles 23, 33 and 34.

Paragraph 6 refers to the various Articles in the Charter which, in the spirit of subsidiarity, make reference to national laws and practices.

Explanation on Article 53 Level of protection

This provision is intended to maintain the level of protection currently afforded within their respective scope by Union law, national law and international law. Owing to its importance, mention is made of the ECHR.

Explanation on Article 54 Prohibition of abuse of rights

This Article corresponds to Article 17 of the ECHR:

'Nothing in this Convention may be interpreted as implying for any State, group or person any right to engage in any activity or perform any act aimed at the destruction of any of the rights and freedoms set forth herein or at their limitation to a greater extent than is provided for in the Convention.'.

Convention for the Protection of Human Rights and Fundamental Freedoms*

Date 4 November 1950
In force 3 September 1953
Source CETS No. 005

The Governments signatory hereto, being members of the Council of Europe,
Considering the Universal Declaration of Human Rights proclaimed by the General Assembly of the United Nations on 10th December 1948;
Considering that this Declaration aims at securing the universal and effective recognition and observance of the Rights therein declared;
Considering that the aim of the Council of Europe is the achievement of greater unity between its members and that one of the methods by which that aim is to be pursued is the maintenance and further realisation of human rights and fundamental freedoms;
Reaffirming their profound belief in those fundamental freedoms which are the foundation of justice and peace in the world and are best maintained on the one hand by an effective political democracy and on the other by a common understanding and observance of the human rights upon which they depend;
Being resolved, as the governments of European countries which are like-minded and have a common heritage of political traditions, ideals, freedom and the rule of law, to take the first steps for the collective enforcement of certain of the rights stated in the Universal Declaration,
Have agreed as follows:

---

*   The text of the Convention is presented as amended by the provisions of Protocol No. 14 (CETS No. 194) as from its entry into force on 1 June 2010.
©   Council of Europe.

Article 1 Obligation to respect human rights
The High Contracting Parties shall secure to everyone within their jurisdiction the rights and freedoms defined in Section I of this Convention.

Section I
Rights and Freedoms

Article 2 Right to life
1. Everyone's right to life shall be protected by law. No one shall be deprived of his life intentionally save in the execution of a sentence of a court following his conviction of a crime for which this penalty is provided by law.
2. Deprivation of life shall not be regarded as inflicted in contravention of this Article when it results from the use of force which is no more than absolutely necessary:
   (a) in defence of any person from unlawful violence;
   (b) in order to effect a lawful arrest or to prevent the escape of a person lawfully detained;
   (c) in action lawfully taken for the purpose of quelling a riot or insurrection.

Article 3 Prohibition of torture
No one shall be subjected to torture or to inhuman or degrading treatment or punishment.

Article 4 Prohibition of slavery and forced labour
1. No one shall be held in slavery or servitude.
2. No one shall be required to perform forced or compulsory labour.
3. For the purpose of this Article the term "forced or compulsory labour" shall not include:
   (a) any work required to be done in the ordinary course of detention imposed according to the provisions of Article 5 of this Convention or during conditional release from such detention;
   (b) any service of a military character or, in case of conscientious objectors in countries where they are recognised, service exacted instead of compulsory military service;
   (c) any service exacted in case of an emergency or calamity threatening the life or well-being of the community;
   (d) any work or service which forms part of normal civic obligations.

Article 5 Right to liberty and security
1. Everyone has the right to liberty and security of person. No one shall be deprived of his liberty save in the following cases and in accordance with a procedure prescribed by law:
   (a) the lawful detention of a person after conviction by a competent court;
   (b) the lawful arrest or detention of a person for non-compliance with the lawful order of a court or in order to secure the fulfilment of any obligation prescribed by law;

(c) the lawful arrest or detention of a person effected for the purpose of bringing him before the competent legal authority on reasonable suspicion of having committed an offence or when it is reasonably considered necessary to prevent his committing an offence or fleeing after having done so;

(d) the detention of a minor by lawful order for the purpose of educational supervision or his lawful detention for the purpose of bringing him before the competent legal authority;

(e) the lawful detention of persons for the prevention of the spreading of infectious diseases, of persons of unsound mind, alcoholics or drug addicts or vagrants;

(f) the lawful arrest or detention of a person to prevent his effecting an unauthorised entry into the country or of a person against whom action is being taken with a view to deportation or extradition.

2. Everyone who is arrested shall be informed promptly, in a language which he understands, of the reasons for his arrest and of any charge against him.

3. Everyone arrested or detained in accordance with the provisions of paragraph 1 (c) of this Article shall be brought promptly before a judge or other officer authorised by law to exercise judicial power and shall be entitled to trial within a reasonable time or to release pending trial. Release may be conditioned by guarantees to appear for trial.

4. Everyone who is deprived of his liberty by arrest or detention shall be entitled to take proceedings by which the lawfulness of his detention shall be decided speedily by a court and his release ordered if the detention is not lawful.

5. Everyone who has been the victim of arrest or detention in contravention of the provisions of this Article shall have an enforceable right to compensation.

Article 6 Right to a fair trial

1. In the determination of his civil rights and obligations or of any criminal charge against him, everyone is entitled to a fair and public hearing within a reasonable time by an independent and impartial tribunal established by law. Judgment shall be pronounced publicly but the press and public may be excluded from all or part of the trial in the interests of morals, public order or national security in a democratic society, where the interests of juveniles or the protection of the private life of the parties so require, or to the extent strictly necessary in the opinion of the court in special circumstances where publicity would prejudice the interests of justice.

2. Everyone charged with a criminal offence shall be presumed innocent until proved guilty according to law.

3. Everyone charged with a criminal offence has the following minimum rights:

(a) to be informed promptly, in a language which he understands and in detail, of the nature and cause of the accusation against him;

(b) to have adequate time and facilities for the preparation of his defence;

(c) to defend himself in person or through legal assistance of his own choosing or, if he has not sufficient means to pay for legal assistance, to be given it free when the interests of justice so require;

(d) to examine or have examined witnesses against him and to obtain the attendance and examination of witnesses on his behalf under the same conditions as witnesses against him;
(e) to have the free assistance of an interpreter if he cannot understand or speak the language used in court.

Article 7 No punishment without law
1. No one shall be held guilty of any criminal offence on account of any act or omission which did not constitute a criminal offence under national or international law at the time when it was committed. Nor shall a heavier penalty be imposed than the one that was applicable at the time the criminal offence was committed.
2. This Article shall not prejudice the trial and punishment of any person for any act or omission which, at the time when it was committed, was criminal according to the general principles of law recognised by civilised nations.

Article 8 Right to respect for private and family life
1. Everyone has the right to respect for his private and family life, his home and his correspondence.
2. There shall be no interference by a public authority with the exercise of this right except such as is in accordance with the law and is necessary in a democratic society in the interests of national security, public safety or the economic well-being of the country, for the prevention of disorder or crime, for the protection of health or morals, or for the protection of the rights and freedoms of others.

Article 9 Freedom of thought, conscience and religion
1. Everyone has the right to freedom of thought, conscience and religion; this right includes freedom to change his religion or belief and freedom, either alone or in community with others and in public or private, to manifest his religion or belief, in worship, teaching, practice and observance.
2. Freedom to manifest one's religion or beliefs shall be subject only to such limitations as are prescribed by law and are necessary in a democratic society in the interests of public safety, for the protection of public order, health or morals, or for the protection of the rights and freedoms of others.

Article 10 Freedom of expression
1. Everyone has the right to freedom of expression. This right shall include freedom to hold opinions and to receive and impart information and ideas without interference by public authority and regardless of frontiers. This Article shall not prevent States from requiring the licensing of broadcasting, television or cinema enterprises.
2. The exercise of these freedoms, since it carries with it duties and responsibilities, may be subject to such formalities, conditions, restrictions or penalties as are prescribed by law and are necessary in a democratic society, in the interests of national security, territorial

integrity or public safety, for the prevention of disorder or crime, for the protection of health or morals, for the protection of the reputation or rights of others, for preventing the disclosure of information received in confidence, or for maintaining the authority and impartiality of the judiciary.

Article 11 Freedom of assembly and association
1. Everyone has the right to freedom of peaceful assembly and to freedom of association with others, including the right to form and to join trade unions for the protection of his interests.
2. No restrictions shall be placed on the exercise of these rights other than such as are prescribed by law and are necessary in a democratic society in the interests of national security or public safety, for the prevention of disorder or crime, for the protection of health or morals or for the protection of the rights and freedoms of others. This Article shall not prevent the imposition of lawful restrictions on the exercise of these rights by members of the armed forces, of the police or of the administration of the State.

Article 12 Right to marry
Men and women of marriageable age have the right to marry and to found a family, according to the national laws governing the exercise of this right.

Article 13 Right to an effective remedy
Everyone whose rights and freedoms as set forth in this Convention are violated shall have an effective remedy before a national authority notwithstanding that the violation has been committed by persons acting in an official capacity.

Article 14 Prohibition of discrimination
The enjoyment of the rights and freedoms set forth in this Convention shall be secured without discrimination on any ground such as sex, race, colour, language, religion, political or other opinion, national or social origin, association with a national minority, property, birth or other status.

Article 15 Derogation in time of emergency
1. In time of war or other public emergency threatening the life of the nation any High Contracting Party may take measures derogating from its obligations under this Convention to the extent strictly required by the exigencies of the situation, provided that such measures are not inconsistent with its other obligations under international law.
2. No derogation from Article 2, except in respect of deaths resulting from lawful acts of war, or from Articles 3, 4 (paragraph 1) and 7 shall be made under this provision.
3. Any High Contracting Party availing itself of this right of derogation shall keep the Secretary General of the Council of Europe fully informed of the measures which it has taken and the reasons therefor. It shall also inform the Secretary General of the Council of Europe

when such measures have ceased to operate and the provisions of the Convention are again being fully executed.

Article 16 Restrictions on political activity of aliens
Nothing in Articles 10, 11 and 14 shall be regarded as preventing the High Contracting Parties from imposing restrictions on the political activity of aliens.

Article 17 Prohibition of abuse of rights
Nothing in this Convention may be interpreted as implying for any State, group or person any right to engage in any activity or perform any act aimed at the destruction of any of the rights and freedoms set forth herein or at their limitation to a greater extent than is provided for in the Convention.

Article 18 Limitation on use of restrictions on rights
The restrictions permitted under this Convention to the said rights and freedoms shall not be applied for any purpose other than those for which they have been prescribed.

Section II
European Court of Human Rights

Article 19 Establishment of the Court
To ensure the observance of the engagements undertaken by the High Contracting Parties in the Convention and the Protocols thereto, there shall be set up a European Court of Human Rights, hereinafter referred to as "the Court". It shall function on a permanent basis.

Article 20 Number of judges
The Court shall consist of a number of judges equal to that of the High Contracting Parties.

Article 21 Criteria for office
1. The judges shall be of high moral character and must either possess the qualifications required for appointment to high judicial office or be jurisconsults of recognised competence.
2. The judges shall sit on the Court in their individual capacity.
3. During their term of office the judges shall not engage in any activity which is incompatible with their independence, impartiality or with the demands of a full-time office; all questions arising from the application of this paragraph shall be decided by the Court.

Article 22 Election of judges
The judges shall be elected by the Parliamentary Assembly with respect to each High Contracting Party by a majority of votes cast from a list of three candidates nominated by the High Contracting Party.

Article 23 Terms of office and dismissal
1. The judges shall be elected for a period of nine years. They may not be re-elected.
2. The terms of office of judges shall expire when they reach the age of 70.
3. The judges shall hold office until replaced. They shall, however, continue to deal with such cases as they already have under consideration.
4. No judge may be dismissed from office unless the other judges decide by a majority of two-thirds that that judge has ceased to fulfil the required conditions.

Article 24 Registry and rapporteurs
1. The Court shall have a Registry, the functions and organisation of which shall be laid down in the rules of the Court.
2. When sitting in a single-judge formation, the Court shall be assisted by rapporteurs who shall function under the authority of the President of the Court. They shall form part of the Court's Registry.

Article 25 Plenary Court
The plenary Court shall
(a) elect its President and one or two Vice-Presidents for a period of three years; they may be re-elected;
(b) set up Chambers, constituted for a fixed period of time;
(c) elect the Presidents of the Chambers of the Court; they may be re-elected;
(d) adopt the rules of the Court;
(e) elect the Registrar and one or more Deputy Registrars;
(f) make any request under Article 26, paragraph 2.

Article 26 Single-judge formation, Committees, Chambers and Grand Chamber
1. To consider cases brought before it, the Court shall sit in a single-judge formation, in committees of three judges, in Chambers of seven judges and in a Grand Chamber of seventeen judges. The Court's Chambers shall set up committees for a fixed period of time.
2. At the request of the plenary Court, the Committee of Ministers may, by a unanimous decision and for a fixed period, reduce to five the number of judges of the Chambers.
3. When sitting as a single judge, a judge shall not examine any application against the High Contracting Party in respect of which that judge has been elected.
4. There shall sit as an ex-officio member of the Chamber and the Grand Chamber the judge elected in respect of the High Contracting Party concerned. If there is none or if that judge is unable to sit, a person chosen by the President of the Court from a list submitted in advance by that Party shall sit in the capacity of judge.
5. The Grand Chamber shall also include the President of the Court, the Vice-Presidents, the Presidents of the Chambers and other judges chosen in accordance with the rules of the Court. When a case is referred to the Grand Chamber under Article 43, no judge from the Chamber which rendered the judgment shall sit in the Grand Chamber, with the exception

of the President of the Chamber and the judge who sat in respect of the High Contracting Party concerned.

Article 27 Competence of single judges

1. A single judge may declare inadmissible or strike out of the Court's list of cases an application submitted under Article 34, where such a decision can be taken without further examination.
2. The decision shall be final.
3. If the single judge does not declare an application inadmissible or strike it out, that judge shall forward it to a committee or to a Chamber for further examination.

Article 28 Competence of Committees

1. In respect of an application submitted under Article 34, a committee may, by a unanimous vote,
   (a) declare it inadmissible or strike it out of its list of cases, where such decision can be taken without further examination; or
   (b) declare it admissible and render at the same time a judgment on the merits, if the underlying question in the case, concerning the interpretation or the application of the Convention or the Protocols thereto, is already the subject of well-established case-law of the Court.
2. Decisions and judgments under paragraph 1 shall be final.
3. If the judge elected in respect of the High Contracting Party concerned is not a member of the committee, the committee may at any stage of the proceedings invite that judge to take the place of one of the members of the committee, having regard to all relevant factors, including whether that Party has contested the application of the procedure under paragraph 1.b.

Article 29 Decisions by Chambers on admissibility and merits

1. If no decision is taken under Article 27 or 28, or no judgment rendered under Article 28, a Chamber shall decide on the admissibility and merits of individual applications submitted under Article 34. The decision on admissibility may be taken separately.
2. A Chamber shall decide on the admissibility and merits of inter-State applications submitted under Article 33. The decision on admissibility shall be taken separately unless the Court, in exceptional cases, decides otherwise.

Article 30 Relinquishment of jurisdiction to the Grand Chamber

Where a case pending before a Chamber raises a serious question affecting the interpretation of the Convention or the Protocols thereto, or where the resolution of a question before the Chamber might have a result inconsistent with a judgment previously delivered by the Court, the Chamber may, at any time before it has rendered its judgment, relinquish jurisdiction in favour of the Grand Chamber, unless one of the parties to the case objects.

Article 31 Powers of the Grand Chamber
The Grand Chamber shall
(a) determine applications submitted either under Article 33 or Article 34 when a Chamber has relinquished jurisdiction under Article 30 or when the case has been referred to it under Article 43;
(b) decide on issues referred to the Court by the Committee of Ministers in accordance with Article 46, paragraph 4; and
(c) consider requests for advisory opinions submitted under Article 47.

Article 32 Jurisdiction of the Court
1. The jurisdiction of the Court shall extend to all matters concerning the interpretation and application of the Convention and the Protocols thereto which are referred to it as provided in Articles 33, 34, 46 and 47.
2. In the event of dispute as to whether the Court has jurisdiction, the Court shall decide.

Article 33 Inter-State cases
Any High Contracting Party may refer to the Court any alleged breach of the provisions of the Convention and the Protocols thereto by another High Contracting Party.

Article 34 Individual applications
The Court may receive applications from any person, non-governmental organisation or group of individuals claiming to be the victim of a violation by one of the High Contracting Parties of the rights set forth in the Convention or the Protocols thereto. The High Contracting Parties undertake not to hinder in any way the effective exercise of this right.

Article 35 Admissibility criteria
1. The Court may only deal with the matter after all domestic remedies have been exhausted, according to the generally recognized rules of international law, and within a period of six months from the date on which the final decision was taken.
2. The Court shall not deal with any application submitted under Article 34 that
(a) is anonymous; or
(b) is substantially the same as a matter that has already been examined by the Court or has already been submitted to another procedure of international investigation or settlement and contains no relevant new information.
3. The Court shall declare inadmissible any individual application submitted under Article 34 if it considers that:
(a) the application is incompatible with the provisions of the Convention or the Protocols thereto, manifestly ill-founded, or an abuse of the right of individual application; or
(b) the applicant has not suffered a significant disadvantage, unless respect for human rights as defined in the Convention and the Protocols thereto requires an examination

of the application on the merits and provided that no case may be rejected on this ground which has not been duly considered by a domestic tribunal.

4. The Court shall reject any application which it considers inadmissible under this Article. It may do so at any stage of the proceedings.

Article 36 Third party intervention

1. In all cases before a Chamber or the Grand Chamber, a High Contracting Party one of whose nationals is an applicant shall have the right to submit written comments and to take part in hearings.

2. The President of the Court may, in the interest of the proper administration of justice, invite any High Contracting Party which is not a party to the proceedings or any person concerned who is not the applicant to submit written comments or take part in hearings.

3. In all cases before a Chamber or the Grand Chamber, the Council of Europe Commissioner for Human Rights may submit written comments and take part in hearings.

Article 37 Striking out applications

1. The Court may at any stage of the proceedings decide to strike an application out of its list of cases where the circumstances lead to the conclusion that

   (a) the applicant does not intend to pursue his application; or

   (b) the matter has been resolved; or

   (c) for any other reason established by the Court, it is no longer justified to continue the examination of the application.

However, the Court shall continue the examination of the application if respect for human rights as defined in the Convention and the Protocols thereto so requires.

2. The Court may decide to restore an application to its list of cases if it considers that the circumstances justify such a course.

Article 38 Examination of the case

The Court shall examine the case together with the representatives of the parties and, if need be, undertake an investigation, for the effective conduct of which the High Contracting Parties concerned shall furnish all necessary facilities.

Article 39 Friendly settlements

1. At any stage of the proceedings, the Court may place itself at the disposal of the parties concerned with a view to securing a friendly settlement of the matter on the basis of respect for human rights as defined in the Convention and the Protocols thereto.

2. Proceedings conducted under paragraph 1 shall be confidential.

3. If a friendly settlement is effected, the Court shall strike the case out of its list by means of a decision which shall be confined to a brief statement of the facts and of the solution reached.

4. This decision shall be transmitted to the Committee of Ministers, which shall supervise the execution of the terms of the friendly settlement as set out in the decision.

Article 40 Public hearings and access to documents
1. Hearings shall be in public unless the Court in exceptional circumstances decides otherwise.
2. Documents deposited with the Registrar shall be accessible to the public unless the President of the Court decides otherwise.

Article 41 Just satisfaction
If the Court finds that there has been a violation of the Convention or the Protocols thereto, and if the internal law of the High Contracting Party concerned allows only partial reparation to be made, the Court shall, if necessary, afford just satisfaction to the injured party.

Article 42 Judgments of Chambers
Judgments of Chambers shall become final in accordance with the provisions of Article 44, paragraph 2.

Article 43 Referral to the Grand Chamber
1. Within a period of three months from the date of the judgment of the Chamber, any party to the case may, in exceptional cases, request that the case be referred to the Grand Chamber.
2. A panel of five judges of the Grand Chamber shall accept the request if the case raises a serious question affecting the interpretation or application of the Convention or the Protocols thereto, or a serious issue of general importance.
3. If the panel accepts the request, the Grand Chamber shall decide the case by means of a judgment.

Article 44 Final judgments
1. The judgment of the Grand Chamber shall be final.
2. The judgment of a Chamber shall become final
   (a) when the parties declare that they will not request that the case be referred to the Grand Chamber; or
   (b) three months after the date of the judgment, if reference of the case to the Grand Chamber has not been requested; or
   (c) when the panel of the Grand Chamber rejects the request to refer under Article 43.
3. The final judgment shall be published.

Article 45 Reasons for judgments and decisions
1. Reasons shall be given for judgments as well as for decisions declaring applications admissible or inadmissible.
2. If a judgment does not represent, in whole or in part, the unanimous opinion of the judges, any judge shall be entitled to deliver a separate opinion.

Article 46 Binding force and execution of judgments

1. The High Contracting Parties undertake to abide by the final judgment of the Court in any case to which they are parties.
2. The final judgment of the Court shall be transmitted to the Committee of Ministers, which shall supervise its execution.
3. If the Committee of Ministers considers that the supervision of the execution of a final judgment is hindered by a problem of interpretation of the judgment, it may refer the matter to the Court for a ruling on the question of interpretation. A referral decision shall require a majority vote of two thirds of the representatives entitled to sit on the committee.
4. If the Committee of Ministers considers that a High Contracting Party refuses to abide by a final judgment in a case to which it is a party, it may, after serving formal notice on that Party and by decision adopted by a majority vote of two thirds of the representatives entitled to sit on the committee, refer to the Court the question whether that Party has failed to fulfil its obligation under paragraph 1.
5. If the Court finds a violation of paragraph 1, it shall refer the case to the Committee of Ministers for consideration of the measures to be taken. If the Court finds no violation of paragraph 1, it shall refer the case to the Committee of Ministers, which shall close its examination of the case.

Article 47 Advisory opinions

1. The Court may, at the request of the Committee of Ministers, give advisory opinions on legal questions concerning the interpretation of the Convention and the Protocols thereto.
2. Such opinions shall not deal with any question relating to the content or scope of the rights or freedoms defined in Section I of the Convention and the Protocols thereto, or with any other question which the Court or the Committee of Ministers might have to consider in consequence of any such proceedings as could be instituted in accordance with the Convention.
3. Decisions of the Committee of Ministers to request an advisory opinion of the Court shall require a majority vote of the representatives entitled to sit on the committee.

Article 48 Advisory jurisdiction of the Court

The Court shall decide whether a request for an advisory opinion submitted by the Committee of Ministers is within its competence as defined in Article 47.

Article 49 Reasons for advisory opinions

1. Reasons shall be given for advisory opinions of the Court.
2. If the advisory opinion does not represent, in whole or in part, the unanimous opinion of the judges, any judge shall be entitled to deliver a separate opinion.
3. Advisory opinions of the Court shall be communicated to the Committee of Ministers.

Article 50 Expenditure on the Court

The expenditure on the Court shall be borne by the Council of Europe.

Article 51 Privileges and immunities of judges
The judges shall be entitled, during the exercise of their functions, to the privileges and immunities provided for in Article 40 of the Statute of the Council of Europe and in the agreements made thereunder.

Section III
Miscellaneous Provisions

Article 52 Inquiries by the Secretary General
On receipt of a request from the Secretary General of the Council of Europe any High Contracting Party shall furnish an explanation of the manner in which its internal law ensures the effective implementation of any of the provisions of the Convention.

Article 53 Safeguard for existing human rights
Nothing in this Convention shall be construed as limiting or derogating from any of the human rights and fundamental freedoms which may be ensured under the laws of any High Contracting Party or under any other agreement to which it is a party.

Article 54 Powers of the Committee of Ministers
Nothing in this Convention shall prejudice the powers conferred on the Committee of Ministers by the Statute of the Council of Europe.

Article 55 Exclusion of other means of dispute settlement
The High Contracting Parties agree that, except by special agreement, they will not avail themselves of treaties, conventions or declarations in force between them for the purpose of submitting, by way of petition, a dispute arising out of the interpretation or application of this Convention to a means of settlement other than those provided for in this Convention.

Article 56 Territorial application
1. Any State may at the time of its ratification or at any time thereafter declare by notification addressed to the Secretary General of the Council of Europe that the present Convention shall, subject to paragraph 4 of this Article, extend to all or any of the territories for whose international relations it is responsible.
2. The Convention shall extend to the territory or territories named in the notification as from the thirtieth day after the receipt of this notification by the Secretary General of the Council of Europe.
3. The provisions of this Convention shall be applied in such territories with due regard, however, to local requirements.
4. Any State which has made a declaration in accordance with paragraph 1 of this Article may at any time thereafter declare on behalf of one or more of the territories to which the

declaration relates that it accepts the competence of the Court to receive applications from individuals, non-governmental organisations or groups of individuals as provided by Article 34 of the Convention.

Article 57 Reservations

1. Any State may, when signing this Convention or when depositing its instrument of ratification, make a reservation in respect of any particular provision of the Convention to the extent that any law then in force in its territory is not in conformity with the provision. Reservations of a general character shall not be permitted under this Article.

2. Any reservation made under this Article shall contain a brief statement of the law concerned.

Article 58 Denunciation

1. A High Contracting Party may denounce the present Convention only after the expiry of five years from the date on which it became a party to it and after six months' notice contained in a notification addressed to the Secretary General of the Council of Europe, who shall inform the other High Contracting Parties.

2. Such a denunciation shall not have the effect of releasing the High Contracting Party concerned from its obligations under this Convention in respect of any act which, being capable of constituting a violation of such obligations, may have been performed by it before the date at which the denunciation became effective.

3. Any High Contracting Party which shall cease to be a member of the Council of Europe shall cease to be a Party to this Convention under the same conditions.

4. The Convention may be denounced in accordance with the provisions of the preceding paragraphs in respect of any territory to which it has been declared to extend under the terms of Article 56.

Article 59 Signature and ratification

1. This Convention shall be open to the signature of the members of the Council of Europe. It shall be ratified. Ratifications shall be deposited with the Secretary General of the Council of Europe.

2. The European Union may accede to this Convention.

3. The present Convention shall come into force after the deposit of ten instruments of ratification.

4. As regards any signatory ratifying subsequently, the Convention shall come into force at the date of the deposit of its instrument of ratification.

5. The Secretary General of the Council of Europe shall notify all the members of the Council of Europe of the entry into force of the Convention, the names of the High Contracting Parties who have ratified it, and the de-posit of all instruments of ratification which may be effected subsequently.

Done at Rome this 4th day of November 1950, in English and French, both texts being equally authentic, in a single copy which shall remain deposited in the archives of the Council of Europe. The Secretary General shall transmit certified copies to each of the signatories.

Protocol
to the Convention for the Protection of Human Rights and Fundamental Freedoms

Date   20 March 1952
In force 18 May 1954
Source   CETS No. 009

The Governments signatory hereto, being members of the Council of Europe,
Being resolved to take steps to ensure the collective enforcement of certain rights and freedoms other than those already included in Section I of the Convention for the Protection of Human Rights and Fundamental Freedoms signed at Rome on 4 November 1950 (hereinafter referred to as "the Convention"),
Have agreed as follows:

Article 1 Protection of property
Every natural or legal person is entitled to the peaceful enjoyment of his possessions. No one shall be deprived of his possessions except in the public interest and subject to the conditions provided for by law and by the general principles of international law.
The preceding provisions shall not, however, in any way impair the right of a State to enforce such laws as it deems necessary to control the use of property in accordance with the general interest or to secure the payment of taxes or other contributions or penalties.

Article 2 Right to education
No person shall be denied the right to education. In the exercise of any functions which it assumes in relation to education and to teaching, the State shall respect the right of parents to ensure such education and teaching in conformity with their own religious and philosophical convictions.

Article 3 Right to free elections
The High Contracting Parties undertake to hold free elections at reasonable intervals by secret ballot, under conditions which will ensure the free expression of the opinion of the people in the choice of the legislature.

Article 4 Territorial application
Any High Contracting Party may at the time of signature or ratification or at any time thereafter communicate to the Secretary General of the Council of Europe a declaration stating the extent to which it undertakes that the provisions of the present Protocol shall apply to such of the territories for the international relations of which it is responsible as are named therein.
Any High Contracting Party which has communicated a declaration in virtue of the preceding paragraph may from time to time communicate a further declaration modifying the terms of any former declaration or terminating the application of the provisions of this Protocol in respect of any territory.
A declaration made in accordance with this Article shall be deemed to have been made in accordance with paragraph 1 of Article 56 of the Convention.

Article 5 Relationship to the Convention
As between the High Contracting Parties the provisions of Articles 1, 2, 3 and 4 of this Protocol shall be regarded as additional Articles to the Convention and all the provisions of the Convention shall apply accordingly.

Article 6 Signature and ratification
This Protocol shall be open for signature by the members of the Council of Europe, who are the signatories of the Convention; it shall be ratified at the same time as or after the ratification of the Convention. It shall enter into force after the deposit of ten instruments of ratification. As regards any signatory ratifying subsequently, the Protocol shall enter into force at the date of the deposit of its instrument of ratification.
The instruments of ratification shall be deposited with the Secretary General of the Council of Europe, who will notify all members of the names of those who have ratified.

Done at Paris on the 20th day of March 1952, in English and French, both texts being equally authentic, in a single copy which shall remain deposited in the archives of the Council of Europe. The Secretary General shall transmit certified copies to each of the signatory governments.

Protocol No. 4 to the Convention for the Protection of Human Rights and Fundamental Freedoms securing certain rights and freedoms other than those already included in the Convention and in the First Protocol thereto

Date 16 September 1963
In force 2 May 1968
Source CETS No. 046

The Governments signatory hereto, being members of the Council of Europe,
Being resolved to take steps to ensure the collective enforcement of certain rights and freedoms other than those already included in Section I of the Convention for the Protection of Human Rights and Fundamental Freedoms signed at Rome on 4th November 1950 (hereinafter referred to as the "Convention") and in Articles 1 to 3 of the First Protocol to the Convention, signed at Paris on 20th March 1952,
Have agreed as follows:

Article 1 Prohibition of imprisonment for debt
No one shall be deprived of his liberty merely on the ground of inability to fulfill a contractual obligation.

Article 2 Freedom of movement

1. Everyone lawfully within the territory of a State shall, within that territory, have the right to liberty of movement and freedom to choose his residence.
2. Everyone shall be free to leave any country, including his own.
3. No restrictions shall be placed on the exercise of these rights other than such as are in accordance with law and are necessary in a democratic society in the interests of national security or public safety, for the maintenance of ordre public, for the prevention of crime, for the protection of health or morals, or for the protection of the rights and freedoms of others.
4. The rights set forth in paragraph 1 may also be subject, in particular areas, to restrictions imposed in accordance with law and justified by the public interest in a democratic society.

Article 3 Prohibition of expulsion of nationals

1. No one shall be expelled, by means either of an individual or of a collective measure, from the territory of the State of which he is a national.
2. No one shall be deprived of the right to enter the territory of the state of which he is a national.

Article 4 Prohibition of collective expulsion of aliens

Collective expulsion of aliens is prohibited.

Article 5 Territorial application

1. Any High Contracting Party may, at the time of signature or ratification of this Protocol, or at any time thereafter, communicate to the Secretary General of the Council of Europe a declaration stating the extent to which it undertakes that the provisions of this Protocol shall apply to such of the territories for the international relations of which it is responsible as are named therein.
2. Any High Contracting Party which has communicated a declaration in virtue of the preceding paragraph may, from time to time, communicate a further declaration modifying the terms of any former declaration or terminating the application of the provisions of this Protocol in respect of any territory.
3. A declaration made in accordance with this Article shall be deemed to have been made in accordance with paragraph 1 of Article 56 of the Convention.
4. The territory of any State to which this Protocol applies by virtue of ratification or acceptance by that State, and each territory to which this Protocol is applied by virtue of a declaration by that State under this Article, shall be treated as separate territories for the purpose of the references in Articles 2 and 3 to the territory of a State.
5. Any State which has made a declaration in accordance with paragraph 1 or 2 of this Article may at any time thereafter declare on behalf of one or more of the territories to which the declaration relates that it accepts the competence of the Court to receive applications from individuals, non-governmental organisations or groups of individuals as provided in Article 34 of the Convention in respect of all or any of Article 1 to 4 of this Protocol.

Article 6 Relationship to the Convention

As between the High Contracting Parties the provisions of Articles 1 to 5 of this Protocol shall be regarded as additional Articles to the Convention, and all the provisions of the Convention shall apply accordingly.

Article 7 Signature and ratification

1. This Protocol shall be open for signature by the members of the Council of Europe who are the signatories of the Convention; it shall be ratified at the same time as or after the ratification of the Convention. It shall enter into force after the deposit of five instruments of ratification. As regards any signatory ratifying subsequently, the Protocol shall enter into force at the date of the deposit of its instrument of ratification.
2. The instruments of ratification shall be deposited with the Secretary General of the Council of Europe, who will notify all members of the names of those who have ratified.

In witness whereof the undersigned, being duly authorised thereto, have signed this Protocol.

Done at Strasbourg, this 16th day of September 1963, in English and in French, both texts being equally authoritative, in a single copy which shall remain deposited in the archives of the Council of Europe. The Secretary General shall transmit certified copies to each of the signatory states.

Protocol No. 6
to the Convention for the Protection of Human Rights and Fundamental Freedoms concerning the Abolition of the Death Penalty

Date   28 April 1983
In force 1 March 1985
Source   CETS No. 114

The member States of the Council of Europe, signatory to this Protocol to the Convention for the Protection of Human Rights and Fundamental Freedoms, signed at Rome on 4 November 1950 (hereinafter referred to as "the Convention"),
Considering that the evolution that has occurred in several member States of the Council of Europe expresses a general tendency in favour of abolition of the death penalty;
Have agreed as follows:

Article 1 Abolition of the death penalty
The death penalty shall be abolished. No one shall be condemned to such penalty or executed.

Article 2 Death penalty in time of war
A State may make provision in its law for the death penalty in respect of acts committed in time of war or of imminent threat of war; such penalty shall be applied only in the instances laid down in the law and in accordance with its provisions. The State shall communicate to the Secretary General of the Council of Europe the relevant provisions of that law.

Article 3 Prohibition of derogations
No derogation from the provisions of this Protocol shall be made under Article 15 of the Convention.

Article 4 Prohibition of reservations
No reservation may be made under Article 57 of the Convention in respect of the provisions of this Protocol.

Article 5 Territorial application
1. Any State may at the time of signature or when depositing its instrument of ratification, acceptance or approval, specify the territory or territories to which this Protocol shall apply.
2. Any State may at any later date, by a declaration addressed to the Secretary General of the Council of Europe, extend the application of this Protocol to any other territory specified in the declaration. In respect of such territory the Protocol shall enter into force on the first day of the month following the date of receipt of such declaration by the Secretary General.
3. Any declaration made under the two preceding paragraphs may, in respect of any territory specified in such declaration, be withdrawn by a notification addressed to the Secretary General. The withdrawal shall become effective on the first day of the month following the date of receipt of such notification by the Secretary General.

Article 6 Relationship to the Convention
As between the States Parties the provisions of Articles 1 to 5 of this Protocol shall be regarded as additional Articles to the Convention and all the provisions of the Convention shall apply accordingly.

Article 7 Signature and ratification
The Protocol shall be open for signature by the member States of the Council of Europe, signatories to the Convention. It shall be subject to ratification, acceptance or approval. A member State of the Council of Europe may not ratify, accept or approve this Protocol unless it has, simultaneously or previously, ratified the Convention. Instruments of ratification, acceptance or approval shall be deposited with the Secretary General of the Council of Europe.

Article 8 Entry into force
1. This Protocol shall enter into force on the first day of the month following the date on which five member States of the Council of Europe have expressed their consent to be bound by the Protocol in accordance with the provisions of Article 7.
2. In respect of any member State which subsequently expresses its consent to be bound by it, the Protocol shall enter into force on the first day of the month following the date of the deposit of the instrument of ratification, acceptance or approval.

Article 9 Depositary functions

The Secretary General of the Council of Europe shall notify the member States of the Council of:

    (a) any signature;
    (b) the deposit of any instrument of ratification, acceptance or approval;
    (c) any date of entry into force of this Protocol in accordance with Articles 5 and 8;
    (d) any other act, notification or communication relating to this Protocol.

In witness whereof the undersigned, being duly authorised thereto, have signed this Protocol.

Done at Strasbourg, this 28th day of April 1983, in English and in French, both texts being equally authentic, in a single copy which shall be deposited in the archives of the Council of Europe. The Secretary General of the Council of Europe shall transmit certified copies to each member State of the Council of Europe.

Protocol No. 7
to the Convention for the Protection of Human Rights and Fundamental Freedoms

Date 22 November 1984
In force 1 November 1988
Source CETS No. 117

The member States of the Council of Europe, signatory hereto,
Being resolved to take further steps to ensure the collective enforcement of certain rights and freedoms by means of the Convention for the Protection of Human Rights and Fundamental Freedoms signed at Rome on 4 November 1950 (hereinafter referred to as "the Convention"),
Have agreed as follows:

Article 1 Procedural safeguards relating to expulsion of aliens

1. An alien lawfully resident in the territory of a State shall not be expelled therefrom except in pursuance of a decision reached in accordance with law and shall be allowed:
    (a) to submit reasons against his expulsion,
    (b) to have his case reviewed, and
    (c) to be represented for these purposes before the competent authority or a person or persons designated by that authority.
2. An alien may be expelled before the exercise of his rights under paragraph 1.a, b and c of this Article, when such expulsion is necessary in the interests of public order or is grounded on reasons of national security.

Article 2 Right of appeal in criminal matters

1. Everyone convicted of a criminal offence by a tribunal shall have the right to have his conviction or sentence reviewed by a higher tribunal. The exercise of this right, including the grounds on which it may be exercised, shall be governed by law.
2. This right may be subject to exceptions in regard to offences of a minor character, as prescribed by law, or in cases in which the person concerned was tried in the first instance by the highest tribunal or was convicted following an appeal against acquittal.

Article 3 Compensation for wrongful conviction

When a person has by a final decision been convicted of a criminal offence and when subsequently his conviction has been reversed, or he has been pardoned, on the ground that a new or newly discovered fact shows conclusively that there has been a miscarriage of justice, the person who has suffered punishment as a result of such conviction shall be compensated according to the law or the practice of the State concerned, unless it is proved that the non-disclosure of the unknown fact in time is wholly or partly attributable to him.

Article 4 Right not to be tried or punished twice

1. No one shall be liable to be tried or punished again in criminal proceedings under the jurisdiction of the same State for an offence for which he has already been finally acquitted or convicted in accordance with the law and penal procedure of that State.
2. The provisions of the preceding paragraph shall not prevent the reopening of the case in accordance with the law and penal procedure of the State concerned, if there is evidence of new or newly discovered facts, or if there has been a fundamental defect in the previous proceedings, which could affect the outcome of the case.
3. No derogation from this Article shall be made under Article 15 of the Convention.

Article 5 Equality between spouses

Spouses shall enjoy equality of rights and responsibilities of a private law character between them, and in their relations with their children, as to marriage, during marriage and in the event of its dissolution. This Article shall not prevent States from taking such measures as are necessary in the interests of the children.

Article 6 Territorial application

1. Any State may at the time of signature or when depositing its instrument of ratification, acceptance or approval, specify the territory or territories to which the Protocol shall apply and state the extent to which it undertakes that the provisions of this Protocol shall apply to such territory or territories.
2. Any State may at any later date, by a declaration addressed to the Secretary General of the Council of Europe, extend the application of this Protocol to any other territory specified in the declaration. In respect of such territory the Protocol shall enter into force on the first day of the month following the expiration of a period of two months after the date of receipt by the Secretary General of such declaration.

3. Any declaration made under the two preceding paragraphs may, in respect of any territory specified in such declaration, be withdrawn or modified by a notification addressed to the Secretary General. The withdrawal or modification shall become effective on the first day of the month following the expiration of a period of two months after the date of receipt of such notification by the Secretary General.

4. A declaration made in accordance with this Article shall be deemed to have been made in accordance with paragraph 1 of Article 56 of the Convention.

5. The territory of any State to which this Protocol applies by virtue of ratification, acceptance or approval by that State, and each territory to which this Protocol is applied by virtue of a declaration by that State under this Article, may be treated as separate territories for the purpose of the reference in Article 1 to the territory of a State.

6. Any State which has made a declaration in accordance with paragraph 1 or 2 of this Article may at any time thereafter declare on behalf of one or more of the territories to which the declaration relates that it accepts the competence of the Court to receive applications from individuals, non-governmental organisations or groups of individuals as provided in Article 34 of the Convention in respect of Articles 1 to 5 of this Protocol.

Article 7 Relationship to the Convention

As between the States Parties, the provisions of Article 1 to 6 of this Protocol shall be regarded as additional Articles to the Convention, and all the provisions of the Convention shall apply accordingly.

Article 8 Signature and ratification

This Protocol shall be open for signature by member States of the Council of Europe which have signed the Convention. It is subject to ratification, acceptance or approval. A member State of the Council of Europe may not ratify, accept or approve this Protocol without previously or simultaneously ratifying the Convention. Instruments of ratification, acceptance or approval shall be deposited with the Secretary General of the Council of Europe.

Article 9 Entry into force

1. This Protocol shall enter into force on the first day of the month following the expiration of a period of two months after the date on which seven member States of the Council of Europe have expressed their consent to be bound by the Protocol in accordance with the provisions of Article 8.

2. In respect of any member State which subsequently expresses its consent to be bound by it, the Protocol shall enter into force on the first day of the month following the expiration of a period of two months after the date of the deposit of the instrument of ratification, acceptance or approval.

Article 10 Depositary functions

The Secretary General of the Council of Europe shall notify all the member States of the Council of Europe of:

(a) any signature;
(b) the deposit of any instrument of ratification, acceptance or approval;
(c) any date of entry into force of this Protocol in accordance with Articles 6 and 9;
(d) any other act, notification or declaration relating to this Protocol.

In witness whereof the undersigned, being duly authorised thereto, have signed this Protocol.

Done at Strasbourg, this 22nd day of November 1984, in English and French, both texts being equally authentic, in a single copy which shall be deposited in the archives of the Council of Europe. The Secretary General of the Council of Europe shall transmit certified copies to each member State of the Council of Europe.

Protocol No. 12
to the Convention for the Protection of Human Rights and Fundamental Freedoms

Date   4 November 2000
In force   1 April 2005
Source   CETS No. 177

The member States of the Council of Europe, signatory hereto,
Having regard to the fundamental principle according to which all persons are equal before the law and are entitled to the equal protection of the law;
Being resolved to take further steps to promote the equality of all persons through the collective enforcement of a general prohibition of discrimination by means of the Convention for the Protection of Human Rights and Fundamental Freedoms signed at Rome on 4 November 1950 (hereinafter referred to as "the Convention");
Reaffirming that the principle of non-discrimination does not prevent States Parties from taking measures in order to promote full and effective equality, provided that there is an objective and reasonable justification for those measures,
Have agreed as follows:

Article 1 General prohibition of discrimination

1. The enjoyment of any right set forth by law shall be secured without discrimination on any ground such as sex, race, colour, language, religion, political or other opinion, national or social origin, association with a national minority, property, birth or other status.

2. No one shall be discriminated against by any public authority on any ground such as those mentioned in paragraph 1.

Article 2 Territorial application

1. Any State may, at the time of signature or when depositing its instrument of ratification, acceptance or approval, specify the territory or territories to which this Protocol shall apply.
2. Any State may at any later date, by a declaration addressed to the Secretary General of the Council of Europe, extend the application of this Protocol to any other territory specified in the declaration. In respect of such territory the Protocol shall enter into force on the first day of the month following the expiration of a period of three months after the date of receipt by the Secretary General of such declaration.
3. Any declaration made under the two preceding paragraphs may, in respect of any territory specified in such declaration, be withdrawn or modified by a notification addressed to the Secretary General of the Council of Europe. The withdrawal or modification shall become effective on the first day of the month following the expiration of a period of three months after the date of receipt of such notification by the Secretary General.
4. A declaration made in accordance with this Article shall be deemed to have been made in accordance with paragraph 1 of Article 56 of the Convention.
5. Any State which has made a declaration in accordance with paragraph 1 or 2 of this Article may at any time thereafter declare on behalf of one or more of the territories to which the declaration relates that it accepts the competence of the Court to receive applications from individuals, non-governmental organisations or groups of individuals as provided by Article 34 of the Convention in respect of Article 1 of this Protocol.

Article 3 Relationship to the Convention

As between the States Parties, the provisions of Articles 1 and 2 of this Protocol shall be regarded as additional Articles to the Convention, and all the provisions of the Convention shall apply accordingly.

Article 4 Signature and ratification

This Protocol shall be open for signature by member States of the Council of Europe which have signed the Convention. It is subject to ratification, acceptance or approval. A member State of the Council of Europe may not ratify, accept or approve this Protocol without previously or simultaneously ratifying the Convention. Instruments of ratification, acceptance or approval shall be deposited with the Secretary General of the Council of Europe.

Article 5 Entry into force

1. This Protocol shall enter into force on the first day of the month following the expiration of a period of three months after the date on which ten member States of the Council of Europe have expressed their consent to be bound by the Protocol in accordance with the provisions of Article 4.
2. In respect of any member State which subsequently expresses its consent to be bound by it, the Protocol shall enter into force on the first day of the month following the expiration of a period of three months after the date of the deposit of the instrument of ratification, acceptance or approval.

Article 6 Depositary functions

The Secretary General of the Council of Europe shall notify all the member States of the Council of Europe of:

(a) any signature;

(b) the deposit of any instrument of ratification, acceptance or approval;

(c) any date of entry into force of this Protocol in accordance with Articles 2 and 5;

(d) any other act, notification or communication relating to this Protocol.

In witness whereof the undersigned, being duly authorised thereto, have signed this Protocol.

Done at Rome, this 4th day of November 2000, in English and in French, both texts being equally authentic, in a single copy which shall be deposited in the archives of the Council of Europe. The Secretary General of the Council of Europe shall transmit certified copies to each member State of the Council of Europe.

Protocol No. 13
to the Convention for the Protection of Human Rights and Fundamental Freedoms concerning the Abolition of the Death Penalty in all circumstances

Date   3 May 2002
In force 1 July 2003
Source CETS No. 187

The member States of the Council of Europe, signatory hereto,
Convinced that everyone's right to life is a basic value in a democratic society and that the abolition of the death penalty is essential for the protection of this right and for the full recognition of the inherent dignity of all human beings;
Wishing to strengthen the protection of the right to life guaranteed by the Convention for the Protection of Human Rights and Fundamental Freedoms signed at Rome on 4 November 1950 (hereinafter referred to as "the Convention");
Noting that Protocol No. 6 to the Convention, concerning the Abolition of the Death Penalty, signed at Strasbourg on 28 April 1983, does not exclude the death penalty in respect of acts committed in time of war or of imminent threat of war;
Being resolved to take the final step in order to abolish the death penalty in all circumstances,
Have agreed as follows:

Article 1 Abolition of the death penalty
The death penalty shall be abolished. No one shall be condemned to such penalty or executed.

Article 2 Prohibition of derogations
No derogation from the provisions of this Protocol shall be made under Article 15 of the Convention.

Article 3 Prohibition of reservations
No reservation may be made under Article 57 of the Convention in respect of the provisions of this Protocol.

Article 4 Territorial application
1. Any state may, at the time of signature or when depositing its instrument of ratification, acceptance or approval, specify the territory or territories to which this Protocol shall apply.
2. Any state may at any later date, by a declaration addressed to the Secretary General of the Council of Europe, extend the application of this Protocol to any other territory specified in the declaration. In respect of such territory the Protocol shall enter into force on the first day of the month following the expiration of a period of three months after the date of receipt by the Secretary General of such declaration.
3. Any declaration made under the two preceding paragraphs may, in respect of any territory specified in such declaration, be withdrawn or modified by a notification addressed to the Secretary General. The withdrawal or modification shall become effective on the first day of the month following the expiration of a period of three months after the date of receipt of such notification by the Secretary General.

Article 5 Relationship to the Convention
As between the states Parties the provisions of Articles 1 to 4 of this Protocol shall be regarded as additional Articles to the Convention, and all the provisions of the Convention shall apply accordingly.

Article 6 Signature and ratification
This Protocol shall be open for signature by member states of the Council of Europe which have signed the Convention. It is subject to ratification, acceptance or approval. A member state of the Council of Europe may not ratify, accept or approve this Protocol without previously or simultaneously ratifying the Convention. Instruments of ratification, acceptance or approval shall be deposited with the Secretary General of the Council of Europe.

Article 7 Entry into force
1. This Protocol shall enter into force on the first day of the month following the expiration of a period of three months after the date on which ten member states of the Council of Europe have expressed their consent to be bound by the Protocol in accordance with the provisions of Article 6.
2. In respect of any member state which subsequently expresses its consent to be bound by it, the Protocol shall enter into force on the first day of the month following the expiration

of a period of three months after the date of the deposit of the instrument of ratification, acceptance or approval.

Article 8 Depositary functions
The Secretary General of the Council of Europe shall notify all the member states of the Council of Europe of:
- (a) any signature;
- (b) the deposit of any instrument of ratification, acceptance or approval;
- (c) any date of entry into force of this Protocol in accordance with Articles 4 and 7;
- (d) any other act, notification or communication relating to this Protocol.

In witness whereof the undersigned, being duly authorised thereto, have signed this Protocol.

Done at Vilnius, this 3rd day of May 2002, in English and in French, both texts being equally authentic, in a single copy which shall be deposited in the archives of the Council of Europe. The Secretary General of the Council of Europe shall transmit certified copies to each member State of the Council of Europe.

Protocol No. 15
amending the Convention for the Protection of Human Rights and Fundamental Freedoms

Date 24 June 2013
In force Not yet in force
Source CETS No. 213

Preamble

The member States of the Council of Europe and the other High Contracting Parties to the Convention for the Protection of Human Rights and Fundamental Freedoms, signed at Rome on 4 November 1950 (hereinafter referred to as "the Convention"), signatory hereto,
Having regard to the declaration adopted at the High Level Conference on the Future of the European Court of Human Rights, held in Brighton on 19 and 20 April 2012, as well as the declarations adopted at the conferences held in Interlaken on 18 and 19 February 2010 and zmir on 26 and 27 April 2011;
Having regard to Opinion No. 283 (2013) adopted by the Parliamentary Assembly of the Council of Europe on 26 April 2013;
Considering the need to ensure that the European Court of Human Rights (hereinafter referred to as "the Court") can continue to play its pre-eminent role in protecting human rights in Europe,
Have agreed as follows:

Article 1
At the end of the preamble to the Convention, a new recital shall be added, which shall read as follows:
"Affirming that the High Contracting Parties, in accordance with the principle of subsidiarity, have the primary responsibility to secure the rights and freedoms defined in this Convention and the Protocols thereto, and that in doing so they enjoy a margin of appreciation, subject to the supervisory jurisdiction of the European Court of Human Rights established by this Convention".

Article 2
1. In Article 21 of the Convention, a new paragraph 2 shall be inserted, which shall read as follows:
"Candidates shall be less than 65 years of age at the date by which the list of three candidates has been requested by the Parliamentary Assembly, further to Article 22."
2. Paragraphs 2 and 3 of Article 21 of the Convention shall become paragraphs 3 and 4 of Article 21 respectively.
3. Paragraph 2 of Article 23 of the Convention shall be deleted. Paragraphs 3 and 4 of Article 23 shall become paragraphs 2 and 3 of Article 23 respectively.

Article 3
In Article 30 of the Convention, the words "unless one of the parties to the case objects" shall be deleted.

Article 4
In Article 35, paragraph 1 of the Convention, the words "within a period of six months" shall be replaced by the words "within a period of four months".

Article 5
In Article 35, paragraph 3, sub-paragraph b of the Convention, the words "and provided that no case may be rejected on this ground which has not been duly considered by a domestic tribunal" shall be deleted.

Final and transitional provisions

Article 6
1. This Protocol shall be open for signature by the High Contracting Parties to the Convention, which may express their consent to be bound by:
   (a) signature without reservation as to ratification, acceptance or approval; or
   (b) signature subject to ratification, acceptance or approval, followed by ratification, acceptance or approval.

2. The instruments of ratification, acceptance or approval shall be deposited with the Secretary General of the Council of Europe.

Article 7
This Protocol shall enter into force on the first day of the month following the expiration of a period of three months after the date on which all High Contracting Parties to the Convention have expressed their consent to be bound by the Protocol, in accordance with the provisions of Article 6.

Article 8
1. The amendments introduced by Article 2 of this Protocol shall apply only to candidates on lists submitted to the Parliamentary Assembly by the High Contracting Parties under Article 22 of the Convention after the entry into force of this Protocol.
2. The amendment introduced by Article 3 of this Protocol shall not apply to any pending case in which one of the parties has objected, prior to the date of entry into force of this Protocol, to a proposal by a Chamber of the Court to relinquish jurisdiction in favour of the Grand Chamber.
3. Article 4 of this Protocol shall enter into force following the expiration of a period of six months after the date of entry into force of this Protocol. Article 4 of this Protocol shall not apply to applications in respect of which the final decision within the meaning of Article 35, paragraph 1 of the Convention was taken prior to the date of entry into force of Article 4 of this Protocol.
4. All other provisions of this Protocol shall apply from its date of entry into force, in accordance with the provisions of Article 7.

Article 9
The Secretary General of the Council of Europe shall notify the member States of the Council of Europe and the other High Contracting Parties to the Convention of:
   (a) any signature;
   (b) the deposit of any instrument of ratification, acceptance or approval;
   (c) the date of entry into force of this Protocol in accordance with Article 7; and
   (d) any other act, notification or communication relating to this Protocol.

In witness whereof, the undersigned, being duly authorised thereto, have signed this Protocol.

Done at Strasbourg, this 24th day of June 2013, in English and in French, both texts being equally authentic, in a single copy which shall be deposited in the archives of the Council of Europe. The Secretary General of the Council of Europe shall transmit certified copies to each member State of the Council of Europe and to the other High Contracting Parties to the Convention.

Protocol No. 16
to the Convention for the Protection of Human Rights and Fundamental Freedoms

Date   2 October 2013
In force Not yet in force
Source   CETS No. 214

Preamble

The member States of the Council of Europe and other High Contracting Parties to the Convention for the Protection of Human Rights and Fundamental Freedoms, signed at Rome on 4 November 1950 (hereinafter referred to as "the Convention"), signatories hereto,
Having regard to the provisions of the Convention and, in particular, Article 19 establishing the European Court of Human Rights (hereinafter referred to as "the Court");
Considering that the extension of the Court's competence to give advisory opinions will further enhance the interaction between the Court and national authorities and thereby reinforce implementation of the Convention, in accordance with the principle of subsidiarity;
Having regard to Opinion No. 285 (2013) adopted by the Parliamentary Assembly of the Council of Europe on 28 June 2013,
Have agreed as follows:

Article 1
1. Highest courts and tribunals of a High Contracting Party, as specified in accordance with Article 10, may request the Court to give advisory opinions on questions of principle relating to the interpretation or application of the rights and freedoms defined in the Convention or the protocols thereto.
2. The requesting court or tribunal may seek an advisory opinion only in the context of a case pending before it.
3. The requesting court or tribunal shall give reasons for its request and shall provide the relevant legal and factual background of the pending case.

Article 2

1. A panel of five judges of the Grand Chamber shall decide whether to accept the request for an advisory opinion, having regard to Article 1. The panel shall give reasons for any refusal to accept the request.
2. If the panel accepts the request, the Grand Chamber shall deliver the advisory opinion.
3. The panel and the Grand Chamber, as referred to in the preceding paragraphs, shall include ex officio the judge elected in respect of the High Contracting Party to which the requesting court or tribunal pertains. If there is none or if that judge is unable to sit, a person chosen by the President of the Court from a list submitted in advance by that Party shall sit in the capacity of judge.

Article 3

The Council of Europe Commissioner for Human Rights and the High Contracting Party to which the requesting court or tribunal pertains shall have the right to submit written comments and take part in any hearing. The President of the Court may, in the interest of the proper administration of justice, invite any other High Contracting Party or person also to submit written comments or take part in any hearing.

Article 4

1. Reasons shall be given for advisory opinions.
2. If the advisory opinion does not represent, in whole or in part, the unanimous opinion of the judges, any judge shall be entitled to deliver a separate opinion.
3. Advisory opinions shall be communicated to the requesting court or tribunal and to the High Contracting Party to which that court or tribunal pertains.
4. Advisory opinions shall be published.

Article 5

Advisory opinions shall not be binding.

Article 6

As between the High Contracting Parties the provisions of Articles 1 to 5 of this Protocol shall be regarded as additional articles to the Convention, and all the provisions of the Convention shall apply accordingly.

Article 7

1. This Protocol shall be open for signature by the High Contracting Parties to the Convention, which may express their consent to be bound by:
   (a) signature without reservation as to ratification, acceptance or approval; or
   (b) signature subject to ratification, acceptance or approval, followed by ratification, acceptance or approval.
2. The instruments of ratification, acceptance or approval shall be deposited with the Secretary General of the Council of Europe.

Article 8

1. This Protocol shall enter into force on the first day of the month following the expiration of a period of three months after the date on which ten High Contracting Parties to the Convention have expressed their consent to be bound by the Protocol in accordance with the provisions of Article 7.

2. In respect of any High Contracting Party to the Convention which subsequently expresses its consent to be bound by it, the Protocol shall enter into force on the first day of the month following the expiration of a period of three months after the date of the expression of its consent to be bound by the Protocol in accordance with the provisions of Article 7.

Article 9

No reservation may be made under Article 57 of the Convention in respect of the provisions of this Protocol.

Article 10

Each High Contracting Party to the Convention shall, at the time of signature or when depositing its instrument of ratification, acceptance or approval, by means of a declaration addressed to the Secretary General of the Council of Europe, indicate the courts or tribunals that it designates for the purposes of Article 1, paragraph 1, of this Protocol. This declaration may be modified at any later date and in the same manner.

Article 11

The Secretary General of the Council of Europe shall notify the member States of the Council of Europe and the other High Contracting Parties to the Convention of:

(a) any signature;

(b) the deposit of any instrument of ratification, acceptance or approval;

(c) any date of entry into force of this Protocol in accordance with Article 8;

(d) any declaration made in accordance with Article 10; and

(e) any other act, notification or communication relating to this Protocol.

In witness whereof the undersigned, being duly authorised thereto, have signed this Protocol.

Done at Strasbourg, this 2nd day of October 2013, in English and French, both texts being equally authentic, in a single copy which shall be deposited in the archives of the Council of Europe. The Secretary General of the Council of Europe shall transmit certified copies to each member State of the Council of Europe and to the other High Contracting Parties to the Convention.

Act concerning the Elections of the Members of the European Parliament by Direct Universal Suffrage

Source OJ L 278 of 8 October 1976, p. 5
last amended by Council Decision 2002/772/EC, Euratom of 25 June and 23 September 2002, OJ L 283 of 21 October 2002, p. 1

Article 1
1. In each Member State, members of the European Parliament shall be elected on the basis of proportional representation, using the list system or the single transferable vote.
2. Member States may authorise voting based on a preferential list system in accordance with the procedure they adopt.
3. Elections shall be by direct universal suffrage and shall be free and secret.

Article 2
In accordance with its specific national situation, each Member State may establish constituencies for elections to the European Parliament or subdivide its electoral area in a different manner, without generally affecting the proportional nature of the voting system.

Article 3
Member States may set a minimum threshold for the allocation of seats. At national level this threshold may not exceed 5 per cent of votes cast.

Article 4
Each Member State may set a ceiling for candidates' campaign expenses.

© European Union, http://eur-lex.europa.eu/, 1998-2015.

Article 5

1. The five-year term for which members of the European Parliament are elected shall begin at the opening of the first session following each election.
It may be extended or curtailed pursuant to the second subparagraph of Article 10(2).
2. The term of office of each member of the European Parliament shall begin and end at the same time as the period referred to in paragraph 1.

Article 6

1. Members of the European Parliament shall vote on an individual and personal basis. They shall not be bound by any instructions and shall not receive a binding mandate.
2. Members of the European Parliament shall enjoy the privileges and immunities applicable to them by virtue of the Protocol of 8 April 1965 on the privileges and immunities of the European Communities.

Article 7

1. The office of member of the European Parliament shall be incompatible with that of:
   - member of the Government of a Member State,
   - member of the Commission of the European Communities,
   - Judge, Advocate-General or Registrar of the Court of Justice of the European Communities or of the Court of First Instance,
   - member of the Board of Directors of the European Central Bank,
   - member of the Court of Auditors of the European Communities,
   - Ombudsman of the European Communities,
   - member of the Economic and Social Committee of the European Economic Community and of the European Atomic Energy Community,
   - member of committees or other bodies set up pursuant to the Treaties establishing the European Economic Community and the European Atomic Energy Community for the purpose of managing the Communities' funds or carrying out a permanent direct administrative task,
   - member of the Board of Directors, Management Committee or staff of the European Investment Bank,
   - active official or servant of the institutions of the European Communities or of the specialised bodies attached to them or of the European Central Bank.
2. From the European Parliament elections in 2004, the office of member of the European Parliament shall be incompatible with that of member of a national parliament.
By way of derogation from that rule and without prejudice to paragraph 3:
   - members of the Irish National Parliament who are elected to the European Parliament at a subsequent poll may have a dual mandate until the next election to the Irish National Parliament, at which juncture the first subparagraph of this paragraph shall apply;
   - members of the United Kingdom Parliament who are also members of the European Parliament during the five-year term preceding election to the European Parliament in

2004 may have a dual mandate until the 2009 European Parliament elections, when the first subparagraph of this paragraph shall apply.

3. In addition, each Member State may, in the circumstances provided for in Article 7, extend rules at national level relating to incompatibility.

4. Members of the European Parliament to whom paragraphs 1, 2 and 3 become applicable in the course of the five-year period referred to in Article 3 shall be replaced in accordance with Article 12.

Article 8

Subject to the provisions of this Act, the electoral procedure shall be governed in each Member State by its national provisions.

These national provisions, which may if appropriate take account of the specific situation in the Member States, shall not affect the essentially proportional nature of the voting system.

Article 9

No one may vote more than once in any election of members of the European Parliament.

Article 10

1. Elections to the European Parliament shall be held on the date and at the times fixed by each Member State; for all Member States this date shall fall within the same period starting on a Thursday morning and ending on the following Sunday.

2. Member States may not officially make public the results of their count until after the close of polling in the Member State whose electors are the last to vote within the period referred to in paragraph 1.

Article 11

1. The Council, acting unanimously after consulting the European Parliament, shall determine the electoral period for the first elections.

2. Subsequent elections shall take place in the corresponding period in the last year of the five-year period referred to in Article 3.

Should it prove impossible to hold the elections in the Community during that period, the Council acting unanimously shall, after consulting the European Parliament, determine, at least one year before the end of the five-year term referred to in Article 3, another electoral period which shall not be more than two months before or one month after the period fixed pursuant to the preceding subparagraph.

3. Without prejudice to Article 139 of the Treaty establishing the European Community and Article 109 of the Treaty establishing the European Atomic Energy Community, the European Parliament shall meet, without requiring to be convened, on the first Tuesday after expiry of an interval of one month from the end of the electoral period.

4. The powers of the outgoing European Parliament shall cease upon the opening of the first sitting of the new European Parliament.

Article 12

The European Parliament shall verify the credentials of members of the European Parliament. For this purpose it shall take note of the results declared officially by the Member States and shall rule on any disputes which may arise out of the provisions of this Act other than those arising out of the national provisions to which the Act refers.

Article 13

1. A seat shall fall vacant when the mandate of a member of the European Parliament ends as a result of resignation, death or withdrawal of the mandate.
2. Subject to the other provisions of this Act, each Member State shall lay down appropriate procedures for filling any seat which falls vacant during the five-year term of office referred to in Article 3 for the remainder of that period.
3. Where the law of a Member State makes explicit provision for the withdrawal of the mandate of a member of the European Parliament, that mandate shall end pursuant to those legal provisions. The competent national authorities shall inform the European Parliament thereof.
4. Where a seat falls vacant as a result of resignation or death, the President of the European Parliament shall immediately inform the competent authorities of the Member State concerned thereof.

Article 14

Should it appear necessary to adopt measures to implement this Act, the Council, acting unanimously on a proposal from the Assembly after consulting the Commission, shall adopt such measures after endeavouring to reach agreement with the Assembly in a conciliation committee consisting of the Council and representatives of the Assembly.

Article 15

This Act is drawn up in the Danish, Dutch, English, Finnish, French, German, Greek, Irish, Italian, Portuguese, Spanish and Swedish languages, all the texts being equally authentic. Annexes II and III shall form an integral part of this Act.

Article 16

The provisions of this Act shall enter into force on the first day of the month following that during which the last of the notifications referred to in the Decision is received.

Done at Brussels on the twentieth day of September in the year one thousand nine hundred and seventy-six.

Annex I

The United Kingdom will apply the provisions of this Act only in respect of the United Kingdom.

Annex II

Declaration on Article 14

As regards the procedure to be followed by the Conciliation Committee, it is agreed to have recourse to the provisions of paragraphs 5, 6 and 7 of the procedure laid down in the joint declaration of the European Parliament, the Council and the Commission of 4 March 1975.[1]

---

1 OJ No C 89, 22.4.1975, p. 1.

Council Decision of 13 December 2007 relating to the Implementation of Article 9c(4) of the Treaty on European Union and Article 205(2) of the Treaty on the Functioning of the European Union between 1 November 2014 and 31 March 2017 on the one hand, and as from 1 April 2017 on the other (2009/857/EC)

Source OJ L 314 of 1 December 2009, p. 73

The Council of the European Union,

Whereas:

(1) Provisions should be adopted allowing for a smooth transition from the system for decision-making in the Council by a qualified majority as defined in Article 3(3) of the Protocol on the transitional provisions, which will continue to apply until 31 October 2014, to the voting system provided for in Article 9c(4) of the Treaty on European Union and Article 205(2) of the Treaty on the Functioning of the European Union, which will apply with effect from 1 November 2014, including, during a transitional period until 31 March 2017, specific provisions laid down in Article 3(2) of that Protocol.

(2) It is recalled that it is the practice of the Council to devote every effort to strengthening the democratic legitimacy of decisions taken by a qualified majority,

Has decided as follows:

© European Union, http://eur-lex.europa.eu/, 1998-2015.

Section 1
Provisions to be applied from 1 November 2014 to 31 March 2017

Article 1
From 1 November 2014 to 31 March 2017, if members of the Council, representing:
- (a) at least three quarters of the population; or
- (b) at least three quarters of the number of Member States;

necessary to constitute a blocking minority resulting from the application of Article 9c(4), first subparagraph, of the Treaty on European Union or Article 205(2) of the Treaty on the Functioning of the European Union, indicate their opposition to the Council adopting an act by a qualified majority, the Council shall discuss the issue.

Article 2
The Council shall, in the course of these discussions, do all in its power to reach, within a reasonable time and without prejudicing obligatory time limits laid down by Union law, a satisfactory solution to address concerns raised by the members of the Council referred to in Article 1.

Article 3
To this end, the President of the Council, with the assistance of the Commission and in compliance with the Rules of Procedure of the Council, shall undertake any initiative necessary to facilitate a wider basis of agreement in the Council. The members of the Council shall lend him or her their assistance.

Section 2
Provisions to be applied as from 1 April 2017

Article 4
As from 1 April 2017, if members of the Council, representing:
- (a) at least 55 % of the population; or
- (b) at least 55 % of the number of Member States;

necessary to constitute a blocking minority resulting from the application of Article 9c(4), first subparagraph, of the Treaty on European Union or Article 205(2) of the Treaty on the Functioning of the European Union, indicate their opposition to the Council adopting an act by a qualified majority, the Council shall discuss the issue.

Article 5
The Council shall, in the course of these discussions, do all in its power to reach, within a reasonable time and without prejudicing obligatory time limits laid down by Union law, a satisfactory solution to address concerns raised by the members of the Council referred to in Article 4.

Article 6
To this end, the President of the Council, with the assistance of the Commission and in compliance with the Rules of Procedure of the Council, shall undertake any initiative necessary to facilitate a wider basis of agreement in the Council. The members of the Council shall lend him or her their assistance.

Section 3
Entry into force

Article 7
This Decision shall enter into force on the date of the entry into force of the Treaty of Lisbon.

Done at Brussels, 13 December 2007.

Framework Agreement on Relations between the European Parliament and the European Commission

Date   20 October 2010
Source OJ L 304 of 20 November 2010, p. 47

The European Parliament and the European Commission (hereinafter referred to as 'the two Institutions'),
- having regard to the Treaty on European Union (TEU), the Treaty on the Functioning of the European Union (TFEU), in particular Article 295 thereof, and the Treaty establishing the European Atomic Energy Community (hereinafter referred to as 'the Treaties'),
- having regard to the Interinstitutional Agreements and texts governing relations between the two Institutions,
- having regard to Parliament's Rules of Procedure[1], and in particular Rules 105, 106 and 127 thereof and Annexes VIII and XIV thereto,
- having regard to the political guidelines issued, and the relevant statements made, by the President-elect of the Commission on 15 September 2009 and 9 February 2010 and the statements made by each of the candidate Members of the Commission in the course of their hearings by parliamentary committees,
A. whereas the Lisbon Treaty strengthens the democratic legitimacy of the Union's decision-making process,
B. whereas the two Institutions attach the utmost importance to the effective transposition and implementation of Union law,
C. whereas this Framework Agreement does not affect the powers and prerogatives of Parliament, the Commission or any other institution or organ of the Union but seeks to ensure that those powers and prerogatives are exercised as effectively and transparently as possible,

1   OJ L 44, 15.2.2005, p. 1.
©   European Union, http://eur-lex.europa.eu/, 1998-2015.

D. whereas this Framework Agreement should be interpreted in conformity with the institutional framework as organised by the Treaties,

E. whereas the Commission will take due account of the respective roles conferred by the Treaties on Parliament and the Council, in particular with reference to the basic principle of equal treatment laid down under point 9,

F. whereas it is appropriate to update the Framework Agreement concluded in May 2005[2] and to replace it by the following text,

Agree as follows:

I. Scope

1. To better reflect the new 'special partnership' between Parliament and the Commission, the two Institutions agree on the following measures to strengthen the political responsibility and legitimacy of the Commission, extend constructive dialogue, improve the flow of information between the two Institutions and improve cooperation on procedures and planning. They also agree on specific provisions:

    – on Commission meetings with national experts, as set out in Annex I,
    – on the forwarding of confidential information to Parliament, as set out in Annex II,
    – on the negotiation and conclusion of international agreements, as set out in Annex III, and
    – on the timetable for the Commission Work Programme, as set out in Annex IV.

II. Political responsibility

2. After being nominated by the European Council, the President-designate of the Commission will submit to Parliament political guidelines for his/her term of office in order to enable an informed exchange of views to take place with Parliament before its election vote.

3. In conformity with Rule 106 of its Rules of Procedure, Parliament shall communicate with the President-elect of the Commission in good time before the opening of the procedures relating to giving its consent to the new Commission. Parliament shall take into account the remarks expressed by the President-elect.

The designated Members of the Commission shall ensure full disclosure of all relevant information, in conformity with the obligation of independence laid down in Article 245 TFEU.

---

2 OJ C 117 E, 18.5.2006, p. 125.

The procedures shall be designed in such a way as to ensure that the entire Commission-designate is assessed in an open, fair and consistent manner.

4. Each Member of the Commission shall take political responsibility for action in the field of which he/she is in charge, without prejudice to the principle of Commission collegiality. The President of the Commission shall be fully responsible for identifying any conflict of interest which renders a Member of the Commission unable to perform his/her duties.

The President of the Commission shall likewise be responsible for any subsequent action taken in such circumstances and shall inform the President of Parliament thereof immediately and in writing.

The participation of Members of the Commission in electoral campaigns is governed by the Code of Conduct for Commissioners.

Members of the Commission participating actively in electoral campaigns as candidates in elections to the Parliament should take unpaid electoral leave with effect from the end of the last part-session before the elections.

The President of the Commission shall inform Parliament in due time of his/her decision to grant such leave, indicating which Member of the Commission will take over the relevant responsibilities for that period of leave.

5. If Parliament asks the President of the Commission to withdraw confidence in an individual Member of the Commission, he/she will seriously consider whether to request that Member to resign, in accordance with Article 17(6) TEU. The President shall either require the resignation of that Member or explain his/her refusal to do so before Parliament in the following part-session.

6. Where it becomes necessary to arrange for the replacement of a Member of the Commission during his/her term of office pursuant to the second paragraph of Article 246 TFEU, the President of the Commission will seriously consider the result of Parliament's consultation before giving accord to the decision of the Council.

Parliament shall ensure that its procedures are conducted with the utmost dispatch, in order to enable the President of the Commission to seriously consider Parliament's opinion before the new Member is appointed.

Similarly, pursuant to the third paragraph of Article 246 TFEU, when the remainder of the Commission's term of office is short, the President of the Commission will seriously consider Parliament's position.

7. If the President of the Commission intends to reshuffle the allocation of responsibilities amongst the Members of the Commission during its term of office, pursuant to Article 248 TFEU, he/she shall inform Parliament in due time for the relevant parliamentary consultation with regard to those changes. The President's decision to reshuffle the portfolios can take effect immediately.

8. When the Commission comes forward with a revision of the Code of Conduct for Commissioners relating to conflict of interest or ethical behaviour, it will seek Parliament's opinion.

III. Constructive dialogue and flow of information

(i) General provisions

9. The Commission guarantees that it will apply the basic principle of equal treatment for Parliament and the Council, especially as regards access to meetings and the provision of contributions or other information, in particular on legislative and budgetary matters.
10. Within its competences, the Commission shall take measures to better involve Parliament in such a way as to take Parliament's views into account as far as possible in the area of the Common Foreign and Security Policy.
11. A number of arrangements are made to implement the 'special partnership' between Parliament and the Commission, as follows:
    – the President of the Commission will at Parliament's request meet the Conference of Presidents at least twice a year to discuss issues of common interest,
    – the President of the Commission will have a regular dialogue with the President of Parliament on key horizontal issues and major legislative proposals. This dialogue should also include invitations to the President of Parliament to attend meetings of the College of Commissioners,
    – the President of the Commission or the Vice-President responsible for interinstitutional relations is to be invited to attend meetings of the Conference of Presidents and the Conference of Committee Chairs when specific issues relating to plenary agenda-setting, interinstitutional relations between Parliament and the Commission and legislative and budgetary matters are to be discussed,
    – meetings shall take place annually between the Conference of Presidents and the Conference of Committee Chairs and the College of Commissioners, to discuss relevant issues including the preparation and implementation of the Commission Work Programme,
    – the Conference of Presidents and the Conference of Committee Chairs shall inform the Commission in due time of the results of their discussions having an interinstitutional dimension. Parliament shall also keep the Commission fully and regularly informed of the outcome of its meetings dealing with the preparation of the part-sessions, taking into account the Commission's views. This is without prejudice to point 45,
    – to ensure a regular flow of relevant information between the two Institutions, the Secretaries-General of Parliament and of the Commission shall meet on a regular basis.
12. Each Member of the Commission shall make sure that there is a regular and direct flow of information between the Member of the Commission and the chair of the relevant parliamentary committee.
13. The Commission shall not make public any legislative proposal or any significant initiative or decision before notifying Parliament thereof in writing.
On the basis of the Commission Work Programme, the two Institutions shall identify in advance, by common agreement, key initiatives to be presented in plenary. In principle, the

Commission will present these initiatives first in plenary and only afterwards to the public. Similarly, they shall identify those proposals and initiatives for which information is to be provided before the Conference of Presidents or conveyed, in an appropriate manner, to the relevant parliamentary committee or its chair.

These decisions shall be taken within the framework of the regular dialogue between the two Institutions, as provided for in point 11, and shall be updated on a regular basis, taking due account of any political developments.

14. If an internal Commission document – of which Parliament has not been informed pursuant to this Framework Agreement – is circulated outside the Institutions, the President of Parliament may request that the document concerned be forwarded to Parliament without delay, in order to communicate it to any Member of Parliament who may request it.

15. The Commission will provide full information and documentation on its meetings with national experts within the framework of its work on the preparation and implementation of Union legislation, including soft law and delegated acts. If so requested by Parliament, the Commission may also invite Parliament's experts to attend those meetings.

The relevant provisions are laid down in Annex I.

16. Within 3 months after the adoption of a parliamentary resolution, the Commission shall provide information to Parliament in writing on action taken in response to specific requests addressed to it in Parliament's resolutions, including in cases where it has not been able to follow Parliament's views. That period may be shortened where a request is urgent. It may be extended by 1 month where a request calls for more exhaustive work and this is duly substantiated. Parliament will make sure that this information is widely distributed within the institution.

Parliament will endeavour to avoid asking oral or written questions concerning issues in respect of which the Commission has already informed Parliament of its position through a written follow-up communication.

The Commission shall commit itself to report on the concrete follow-up of any request to submit a proposal pursuant to Article 225 TFEU (legislative initiative report) within 3 months following adoption of the corresponding resolution in plenary. The Commission shall come forward with a legislative proposal at the latest after 1 year or shall include the proposal in its next year's Work Programme. If the Commission does not submit a proposal, it shall give Parliament detailed explanations of the reasons.

The Commission shall also commit itself to a close and early cooperation with Parliament on any legislative initiative requests emanating from citizens' initiatives.

As regards the discharge procedure, the specific provisions laid down in point 31 shall apply.

17. Where initiatives, recommendations or requests for legislative acts are made pursuant to Article 289(4) TFEU, the Commission shall inform Parliament, if so requested, of its position on those proposals before the relevant parliamentary committee.

18. The two Institutions agree to cooperate in the area of relations with national Parliaments.

Parliament and the Commission shall cooperate on the implementation of TFEU Protocol No 2 on the application of the principles of subsidiarity and proportionality. Such cooperation shall include arrangements related to any necessary translation of reasoned opinions presented by national Parliaments.

When the thresholds mentioned in Article 7 of TFEU Protocol No 2 are met, the Commission shall provide the translations of all the reasoned opinions presented by national Parliaments together with its position thereon.

19. The Commission shall inform Parliament of the list of its expert groups set up in order to assist the Commission in the exercise of its right of initiative. That list shall be updated on a regular basis and made public.

Within this framework, the Commission shall, in an appropriate manner, inform the competent parliamentary committee, at the specific and reasoned request of its chair, on the activities and composition of such groups.

20. The two Institutions shall hold, through the appropriate mechanisms, a constructive dialogue on questions concerning important administrative matters, notably on issues having direct implications for Parliament's own administration.

21. Parliament will seek the opinion of the Commission when it comes forward with a revision of its Rules of Procedures concerning relations with the Commission.

22. Where confidentiality is invoked as regards any of the information forwarded pursuant to this Framework Agreement, the provisions laid down in Annex II shall be applied.

(ii) International agreements and enlargement

23. Parliament shall be immediately and fully informed at all stages of the negotiation and conclusion of international agreements, including the definition of negotiating directives. The Commission shall act in a manner to give full effect to its obligations pursuant to Article 218 TFEU, while respecting each Institution's role in accordance with Article 13(2) TEU.

The Commission shall apply the arrangements set out in Annex III.

24. The information referred to in point 23 shall be provided to Parliament in sufficient time for it to be able to express its point of view if appropriate, and for the Commission to be able to take Parliament's views as far as possible into account. This information shall, as a general rule, be provided to Parliament through the responsible parliamentary committee and, where appropriate, at a plenary sitting. In duly justified cases, it shall be provided to more than one parliamentary committee.

Parliament and the Commission undertake to establish appropriate procedures and safeguards for the forwarding of confidential information from the Commission to Parliament, in accordance with the provisions of Annex II.

25. The two Institutions acknowledge that, due to their different institutional roles, the Commission is to represent the European Union in international negotiations, with the

exception of those concerning the Common Foreign and Security Policy and other cases as provided for in the Treaties.

Where the Commission represents the Union in international conferences, it shall, at Parliament's request, facilitate the inclusion of a delegation of Members of the European Parliament as observers in Union delegations, so that it may be immediately and fully informed about the conference proceedings. The Commission undertakes, where applicable, to systematically inform the Parliament delegation about the outcome of negotiations.

Members of the European Parliament may not participate directly in these negotiations. Subject to the legal, technical and diplomatic possibilities, they may be granted observer status by the Commission. In the event of refusal, the Commission will inform Parliament of the reasons therefor.

In addition, the Commission shall facilitate the participation of Members of the European Parliament as observers in all relevant meetings under its responsibility before and after negotiation sessions.

26. Under the same conditions, the Commission shall keep Parliament systematically informed about, and facilitate access as observers for Members of the European Parliament forming part of Union delegations to, meetings of bodies set up by multilateral international agreements involving the Union, whenever such bodies are called upon to take decisions which require the consent of Parliament or the implementation of which may require the adoption of legal acts in accordance with the ordinary legislative procedure.

27. The Commission shall also give Parliament's delegation included in Union delegations to international conferences access to use all Union delegation facilities on these occasions, in line with the general principle of good cooperation between the institutions and taking into account the available logistics.

The President of Parliament shall send to the President of the Commission a proposal for the inclusion of a Parliament delegation in the Union delegation no later than 4 weeks before the start of the conference, specifying the head of the Parliament delegation and the number of Members of the European Parliament to be included. In duly justified cases, this deadline can exceptionally be shortened.

The number of Members of the European Parliament included in the Parliament delegation and of supporting staff shall be proportionate to the overall size of the Union delegation.

28. The Commission shall keep Parliament fully informed of the progress of accession negotiations and in particular on major aspects and developments, so as to enable it to express its views in good time through the appropriate parliamentary procedures.

29. When Parliament adopts a recommendation on matters referred to in point 28, pursuant to Rule 90(4) of its Rules of Procedure, and when, for important reasons, the Commission decides that it cannot support such a recommendation, it shall explain the reasons before Parliament, at a plenary sitting or at the next meeting of the relevant parliamentary committee.

(iii) Budgetary implementation

30. Before making, at donors' conferences, financial pledges which involve new financial undertakings and require the agreement of the budgetary authority, the Commission shall inform the budgetary authority and examine its remarks.
31. In connection with the annual discharge governed by Article 319 TFEU, the Commission shall forward all information necessary for supervising the implementation of the budget for the year in question, which the chair of the parliamentary committee responsible for the discharge procedure pursuant to Annex VII to Parliament's Rules of Procedure requests from it for that purpose.
If new aspects come to light concerning previous years for which discharge has already been given, the Commission shall forward all the necessary information on the matter with a view to arriving at a solution acceptable to both sides.

(iv) Relationship with regulatory agencies

32. Nominees for the post of Executive Director of regulatory agencies should come to parliamentary committee hearings.
In addition, in the context of the discussions of the interinstitutional Working Group on Agencies set up in March 2009, the Commission and Parliament will aim at a common approach on the role and position of decentralised agencies in the Union's institutional landscape, accompanied by common guidelines for the creation, structure and operation of those agencies, together with funding, budgetary, supervision and management issues.

IV. Cooperation as regards legislative procedures and planning

(i) Commission Work Programme and the European Union's programming

33. The Commission shall initiate the Union's annual and multiannual programming, with a view to achieving interinstitutional agreements.
34. Every year the Commission shall present its Work Programme.
35. The two Institutions shall cooperate in accordance with the timetable set out in Annex IV. The Commission shall take into account the priorities expressed by Parliament.
The Commission shall provide sufficient detail as to what is envisaged under each point in its Work Programme.
36. The Commission shall explain when it cannot deliver individual proposals in its Work Programme for the year in question or when it departs from it. The Vice-President of the Commission responsible for interinstitutional relations undertakes to report to the

Conference of Committee Chairs regularly, outlining the political implementation of the Commission Work Programme for the year in question.

(ii) Procedures for the adoption of acts

37. The Commission undertakes to carefully examine amendments to its legislative proposals adopted by Parliament, with a view to taking them into account in any amended proposal.

When delivering its opinion on Parliament's amendments pursuant to Article 294 TFEU, the Commission undertakes to take the utmost account of amendments adopted at second reading; should it decide, for important reasons and after consideration by the College, not to adopt or support such amendments, it shall explain its decision before Parliament, and in any event in its opinion on Parliament's amendments by virtue of point (c) of Article 294(7) TFEU.

38. Parliament undertakes, when dealing with an initiative submitted by at least a quarter of Member States, in conformity with Article 76 TFEU, not to adopt any report in the relevant committee before receiving the Commission's opinion on the initiative.

The Commission undertakes to issue its opinion on such an initiative no later than 10 weeks after it has been submitted.

39. The Commission shall provide a detailed explanation in due time before withdrawing any proposals on which Parliament has already expressed a position at first reading.

The Commission shall proceed with a review of all pending proposals at the beginning of the new Commission's term of office, in order to politically confirm or withdraw them, taking due account of the views expressed by Parliament.

40. For special legislative procedures on which Parliament is to be consulted, including other procedures such as that laid down in Article 148 TFEU, the Commission:

    (i) shall take measures to better involve Parliament in such a way as to take Parliament's views into account as far as possible, in particular to ensure that Parliament has the necessary time to consider the Commission's proposal;

    (ii) shall ensure that Council bodies are reminded in good time not to reach a political agreement on its proposals before Parliament has adopted its opinion. It shall ask for discussion to be concluded at ministerial level after a reasonable period has been given to the members of the Council to examine Parliament's opinion;

    (iii) shall ensure that the Council adheres to the rules developed by the Court of Justice of the European Union requiring Parliament to be reconsulted if the Council substantially amends a Commission proposal. The Commission shall inform Parliament of any reminder to the Council of the need for reconsultation;

    (iv) undertakes, if appropriate, to withdraw a legislative proposal that Parliament has rejected. If, for important reasons and after consideration by the College, the Commission decides to maintain its proposal, it shall explain the reasons for that decision in a statement before Parliament.

41. For its part, in order to improve legislative planning, Parliament undertakes:
   (i) to plan the legislative sections of its agendas, bringing them into line with the current Commission Work Programme and with the resolutions it has adopted on that programme, in particular with a view to the improved planning of the priority debates;
   (ii) to meet reasonable deadlines, in so far as is useful for the procedure, when adopting its position at first reading under the ordinary legislative procedure or its opinion under the consultation procedure;
   (iii) as far as possible to appoint rapporteurs on future proposals as soon as the Commission Work Programme is adopted;
   (iv) to consider requests for reconsultation as a matter of absolute priority provided that all the necessary information has been forwarded to it.

(iii) Issues linked to better lawmaking

42. The Commission shall ensure that its impact assessments are conducted under its responsibility by means of a transparent procedure which guarantees an independent assessment. Impact assessments shall be published in due time, taking into consideration a number of different scenarios, including a 'do nothing' option, and shall in principle be presented to the relevant parliamentary committee during the phase of the provision of information to national Parliaments under TFEU Protocols Nos 1 and 2.

43. In areas where Parliament is usually involved in the legislative process, the Commission shall use soft law, where appropriate and on a duly justified basis after having given Parliament the opportunity to express its views. The Commission shall provide a detailed explanation to Parliament on how its views have been taken into account when it adopts its proposal.

44. In order to ensure better monitoring of the transposition and application of Union law, the Commission and Parliament shall endeavour to include compulsory correlation tables and a binding time limit for transposition, which in directives should not normally exceed a period of 2 years.

In addition to specific reports and the annual report on the application of Union law, the Commission shall make available to Parliament summary information concerning all infringement procedures from the letter of formal notice, including, if so requested by Parliament, on a case-by-case basis and respecting the confidentiality rules, in particular those acknowledged by the Court of Justice of the European Union, on the issues to which the infringement procedure relates.

V. The Commission's participation in parliamentary proceedings

45. The Commission shall give priority to its presence, if requested, at the plenary sittings or meetings of other bodies of Parliament, as compared to other competing events or invitations.
In particular, the Commission shall ensure that, as a general rule, Members of the Commission are present at plenary sittings for agenda items falling under their responsibility, whenever Parliament so requests. This is applicable to the preliminary draft agendas approved by the Conference of Presidents during the previous part-session.
Parliament shall seek to ensure that, as a general rule, agenda items of the part-sessions falling under the responsibility of a Member of the Commission are grouped together.
46. At the request of Parliament, provision will be made for a regular Question Hour with the President of the Commission. This Question Hour will comprise two parts: the first with leaders of political groups or their representatives, conducted on an entirely spontaneous basis; the second devoted to a policy theme agreed upon in advance, at the latest on the Thursday before the relevant part-session, but without prepared questions.
Furthermore, a Question Hour with Members of the Commission, including the Vice-President for External Relations/High Representative of the Union for Foreign Affairs and Security Policy shall be introduced, following the model of the Question Hour with the President of the Commission, with the aim of reforming the existing Question Time. This Question Hour shall relate to the portfolio of the respective Members of the Commission.
47. Members of the Commission shall be heard at their request.
Without prejudice to Article 230 TFEU, the two Institutions shall agree on general rules relating to the allocation of speaking time between the Institutions.
The two Institutions agree that their indicative allocation of speaking time should be respected.
48. With a view to ensuring the presence of Members of the Commission, Parliament undertakes to do its best to maintain its final draft agendas.
Where Parliament amends its final draft agenda, or where it moves items within the agenda within a part-session, Parliament shall immediately inform the Commission. The Commission shall use its best endeavours to ensure the presence of the Member of the Commission responsible.
49. The Commission may propose the inclusion of items on the agenda not later than the meeting of the Conference of Presidents that decides on the final draft agenda of a part-session. Parliament shall take the fullest account of such proposals.
50. Parliamentary committees shall seek to maintain their draft agendas and agendas.
Whenever a parliamentary committee amends its draft agenda or its agenda, the Commission shall be immediately informed thereof. In particular, parliamentary committees shall endeavour to respect a reasonable deadline so as to allow for the presence of Members of the Commission at their meetings.

Where the presence of a Member of the Commission is not explicitly required at a parliamentary committee meeting, the Commission shall ensure that it is represented by a competent official at an appropriate level.

Parliamentary committees will endeavour to coordinate their work, including avoiding parallel meetings on the same issue, and will endeavour not to deviate from the draft agenda, so that the Commission can ensure an appropriate level of representation.

If the presence of a high-level official (Director-General or Director) has been requested at a committee meeting dealing with a Commission proposal, the representative of the Commission shall be allowed to intervene.

VI. Final provisions

51. The Commission confirms its commitment to examine as soon as possible the legislative acts which were not adapted to the regulatory procedure with scrutiny before the entry into force of the Lisbon Treaty, in order to assess whether those instruments need to be adapted to the regime of delegated acts introduced by Article 290 TFEU.

As a final goal, a coherent system of delegated and implementing acts, fully consistent with the Treaty, should be achieved through a progressive assessment of the nature and contents of measures currently subject to the regulatory procedure with scrutiny, in order to adapt them in due course to the regime laid down by Article 290 TFEU.

52. The provisions of this Framework Agreement complement the Interinstitutional Agreement on better lawmaking[3] without affecting it and do not prejudice any further revision thereof. Without prejudice to forthcoming negotiations between Parliament, the Commission and the Council, the two Institutions commit to agree on key changes in preparation of future negotiations on adaptation of the Interinstitutional Agreement on better lawmaking to the new provisions introduced by the Lisbon Treaty, taking into account current practices and this Framework Agreement.

They also agree on the need to reinforce the existing interinstitutional contact mechanism, at political and at technical level, in relation to better lawmaking, so as to ensure effective interinstitutional cooperation between Parliament, the Commission and the Council.

53. The Commission commits to initiate rapidly the Union's annual and multiannual programming with a view to achieving interinstitutional agreements, in accordance with Article 17 TEU.

The Commission Work Programme is the Commission's contribution to the Union's annual and multiannual programming. Following its adoption by the Commission, a trialogue between Parliament, the Council and the Commission should take place with a view to reaching an agreement on the Union's programming.

---

3   OJ C 321, 31.12.2003, p. 1.

In this context and as soon as Parliament, the Council and the Commission have reached a common understanding on the Union's programming, the two Institutions shall review the provisions of this Framework Agreement related to programming.

Parliament and the Commission call on the Council to engage as soon as possible in discussions on the Union's programming as provided for in Article 17 TEU.

54. The practical implementation of this Framework Agreement and its Annexes shall be assessed periodically by the two Institutions. A review shall be carried out by the end of 2011, in the light of practical experience.

Done at Strasbourg, 20 October 2010.

Annex I
Commission meetings with national experts

This Annex lays down the modalities for implementation of point 15 of the Framework Agreement.

1. Scope
The provisions of point 15 of the Framework Agreement concern the following meetings:
(1) Commission meetings taking place within the framework of expert groups established by the Commission to which national authorities from all Member States are invited, where they concern the preparation and implementation of Union legislation, including soft law and delegated acts;
(2) ad hoc Commission meetings to which national experts from all Member States are invited, where they concern the preparation and implementation of Union legislation, including soft law and delegated acts.
Meetings of comitology committees are excluded, without prejudice to existing and future specific arrangements concerning the provision to Parliament of information concerning the exercise of the Commission's implementing powers[1].

2. Information to be transmitted to Parliament
The Commission commits to send Parliament the same documentation it sends to national authorities in relation to the abovementioned meetings. The Commission will transmit those documents, including agendas, to a functional Parliament mailbox at the same time as they are sent to the national experts.

3. Invitation of Parliament's experts
Upon being requested by Parliament, the Commission may decide to invite Parliament to send Parliament experts to attend Commission meetings with national experts as identified in point 1.

---

[1] The information to be provided to Parliament on the work of comitology committees and Parliament's prerogatives in the operation of comitology procedures are clearly defined in other instruments: (1) Council Decision 1999/468/EC of 28 June 1999 laying down the procedures for the exercise of implementing powers (OJ L 184, 17.7.1999, p. 23); (2) the interinstitutional agreement of 3 June 2008 between Parliament and the Commission on comitology procedures; and (3) instruments necessary for the implementation of Article 291 TFEU.

Annex II
Forwarding of confidential information to Parliament

1. Scope

1.1. This Annex shall govern the forwarding to Parliament and the handling of confidential information, as defined in point 1.2, from the Commission in connection with the exercise of Parliament's prerogatives and competences. The two Institutions shall act in accordance with their mutual duties of sincere cooperation, in a spirit of complete mutual trust and in the strictest conformity with the relevant Treaty provisions.

1.2. 'Information' shall mean any written or oral information, whatever the medium and whoever the author may be.

    1.2.1. 'Confidential information' shall mean 'EU classified information' (EUCI) and non-classified 'other confidential information'.

    1.2.2. 'EU classified information' (EUCI) shall mean any information and material, classified as 'TRÈS SECRET UE/EU TOP SECRET', 'SECRET UE', 'CONFIDENTIEL UE' or 'RESTREINT UE' or bearing equivalent national or international classification markings, an unauthorised disclosure of which could cause varying degrees of prejudice to Union interests, or to one or more Member States, whether such information originates within the Union or is received from Member States, third States or international organisations.

        (a) TRÈS SECRET UE/EU TOP SECRET: this classification shall be applied only to information and material the unauthorised disclosure of which could cause exceptionally grave prejudice to the essential interests of the Union or of one or more of its Member States.

        (b) SECRET UE: this classification shall be applied only to information and material the unauthorised disclosure of which could seriously harm the essential interests of the Union or of one or more of its Member States.

        (c) CONFIDENTIEL UE: this classification shall be applied to information and material the unauthorised disclosure of which could harm the essential interests of the Union or of one or more of its Member States.

        (d) RESTREINT UE: this classification shall be applied to information and material the unauthorised disclosure of which could be disadvantageous to the interests of the Union or of one or more of its Member States.

    1.2.3. 'Other confidential information' shall mean any other confidential information, including information covered by the obligation of professional secrecy, requested by Parliament and/or forwarded by the Commission.

1.3. The Commission shall ensure that Parliament is given access to confidential information, in accordance with the provisions of this Annex, whenever it receives from one of the parliamentary bodies or office-holders mentioned in point 1.4 a request relating to the forwarding of confidential information. Moreover, the Commission may forward any confidential information on its own initiative to Parliament in accordance with the provisions of this Annex.

1.4. In the context of this Annex, the following may request confidential information from the Commission:
- the President of Parliament,
- the chairs of the parliamentary committees concerned,
- the Bureau and the Conference of Presidents, and
- the head of Parliament's delegation included in the Union delegation at an international conference.

1.5. Information on infringement procedures and procedures relating to competition, in so far as they are not covered by a final Commission decision or by a judgment of the Court of Justice of the European Union on the date when the request from one of the parliamentary bodies/office-holders mentioned in point 1.4 is received, and information relating to the protection of the Union's financial interests, shall be excluded from the scope of this Annex. This is without prejudice to point 44 of the Framework Agreement and to the budgetary control rights of Parliament.

1.6. These provisions shall apply without prejudice to Decision 95/167/EC, Euratom, ECSC of the European Parliament, of the Council and of the Commission of 19 April 1995 on the detailed provisions governing the exercise of the European Parliament's right of inquiry[1] and the relevant provisions of Commission Decision 1999/352/EC, ECSC, Euratom of 28 April 1999 establishing the European Anti-fraud Office (OLAF)[2].

2. General rules

2.1. At the request of one of the parliamentary bodies/office-holders referred to in point 1.4, the Commission shall forward to that parliamentary body/office-holder with all due despatch any confidential information required for the exercise of Parliament's prerogatives and competences. In accordance with their respective powers and responsibilities, the two Institutions shall respect:
- fundamental human rights, including the right to a fair trial and the right to protection of privacy,
- provisions governing judicial and disciplinary procedures,
- protection of business secrecy and commercial relations,
- protection of the interests of the Union, in particular those relating to public safety, defence, international relations, monetary stability and financial interests.

In the event of a disagreement, the matter shall be referred to the Presidents of the two Institutions so that they may resolve the dispute.

---

1 OJ L 113, 19.5.1995, p. 1.
2 OJ L 136, 31.5.1999, p. 20.

Confidential information from a State, an institution or an international organisation shall be forwarded only with its consent.

2.2. EUCI shall be forwarded to, and handled and protected by, Parliament in compliance with the common minimum standards of security applied by other Union Institutions, in particular the Commission.

When classifying information for which it is the originator, the Commission will ensure that it applies appropriate levels of classification in line with the international standards and definitions and its internal rules, whilst taking due account of the need for Parliament to be able to access classified documents for the effective exercise of its competences and prerogatives.

2.3. In the event of any doubt as to the confidential nature of an item of information or its appropriate level of classification, or where it is necessary to lay down the appropriate arrangements for it to be forwarded in accordance with one of the options set out in point 3.2, the two Institutions shall consult each other without delay and before transmission of the document. In these consultations, Parliament shall be represented by the chair of the parliamentary body concerned, accompanied, where necessary, by the rapporteur, or the office-holder who submitted the request. The Commission shall be represented by the Member of the Commission with responsibility for that area, after consultation of the Member of the Commission responsible for security matters. In the event of a disagreement, the matter shall be referred to the Presidents of the two Institutions so that they may resolve the dispute.

2.4. If, at the end of the procedure referred to in point 2.3, no agreement has been reached, the President of Parliament, in response to a reasoned request from the parliamentary body/office-holder who submitted the request, shall call on the Commission to forward, within the appropriate deadline duly indicated, the confidential information in question, selecting the arrangements from among the options laid down in point 3.2 of this Annex. Before the expiry of that deadline, the Commission shall inform Parliament in writing of its final position, in respect of which Parliament reserves the right, if appropriate, to exercise its right to seek redress.

2.5. Access to EUCI shall be granted in accordance with applicable rules for personal security clearance.

    2.5.1. Access to information classified as 'TRÈS SECRET UE /EU TOP SECRET', 'SECRET UE' and 'CONFIDENTIEL UE' may only be granted to Parliament officials and those employees of Parliament working for political groups to whom it is strictly necessary, who have been designated in advance by the parliamentary body/office-holder as having a need to know and who have been given an appropriate security clearance.

    2.5.2. In light of Parliament's prerogatives and competences, those Members who have not been given a personal security clearance shall be granted access to 'CONFIDENTIEL UE' documents under practical arrangements defined by common accord, including signature of a solemn declaration that they will not disclose the contents of those documents to any third person.

Access to 'SECRET UE' documents shall be granted to Members who have been given an appropriate personal security clearance.

2.5.3. Arrangements shall be made with the support of the Commission to ensure that the necessary contribution of national authorities within the framework of the clearance procedure can be obtained by Parliament as quickly as possible.

Details of the category or categories of persons who are to have access to the confidential information shall be communicated simultaneously with the request.

Prior to being granted access to such information each person shall be briefed on its confidentiality level and the resulting security obligations.

In the context of the review of this Annex and future security arrangements, as referred to in points 4.1 and 4.2, the issue of security clearances will be re-examined.

3. Arrangements for access to and the handling of confidential information

3.1. Confidential information forwarded in accordance with the procedures set out in point 2.3 and, where appropriate, point 2.4 shall be made available, on the responsibility of the President or of a Member of the Commission, to the parliamentary body/office-holder who submitted the request, in accordance with the following conditions:

Parliament and the Commission will ensure the registration and the traceability of confidential information.

More specifically, EUCI classified as 'CONFIDENTIEL UE' and 'SECRET UE' shall be forwarded from the Commission's Secretariat General central registry to the equivalent competent Parliament service who will be responsible for making it available under the agreed arrangements to the parliamentary body/office-holder who submitted the request.

The forwarding of EUCI classified as 'TRÈS SECRET UE/EU TOP SECRET' shall be subject to further arrangements, agreed between the Commission and the parliamentary body/office-holder who submitted the request, aimed at ensuring a level of protection commensurate with that classification.

3.2. Without prejudice to the provisions of points 2.2 and 2.4 and the future security arrangements referred to in point 4.1, access and the arrangements designed to preserve the confidentiality of the information shall be laid down by common accord before the information is forwarded. That accord between the Member of the Commission with responsibility for the policy area involved and the parliamentary body (represented by its chair)/office-holder who submitted the request, shall provide for the selection of one of the options set out in points 3.2.1 and 3.2.2 in order to ensure the appropriate level of confidentiality.

3.2.1. Regarding the addressees of confidential information, provision should be made for one of the following options:

– information intended for the President of Parliament alone, in instances justified on absolutely exceptional grounds,

- the Bureau and/or the Conference of Presidents,
- the chair and rapporteur of the relevant parliamentary committee,
- all members (full and substitute) of the relevant parliamentary committee,
- all Members of the European Parliament.

The confidential information in question may not be published or forwarded to any other addressee without the consent of the Commission.

3.2.2. Regarding the arrangements for the handling of confidential information, provision should be made for the following options:

(a) examination of documents in a secure reading room if the information is classified as 'CONFIDENTIEL UE' and above;

(b) holding the meeting in camera, attended only by the members of the Bureau, the members of the Conference of Presidents or full members and substitute members of the competent parliamentary committee as well as by Parliament officials and those Parliament employees working for political groups who have been designated in advance by the chair as having a need to know and whose presence is strictly necessary, provided they have been given the required level of security clearance, taking into account the following conditions:

- any documents may be numbered, distributed at the beginning of the meeting and collected again at the end. No notes of those documents and no photocopies thereof may be taken,

- the minutes of the meeting shall make no mention of the discussion of the item taken under the confidential procedure.

Before transmission, all personal data may be expunged from the documents.

Confidential information provided orally to recipients in Parliament shall be subject to the equivalent level of protection as that accorded to confidential information provided in written form. This may include a solemn declaration by recipients of that information not to divulge its contents to any third person.

3.2.3. When written information is to be examined in a secure reading room, Parliament shall ensure that the following arrangements are in place:

- a secure storage system for confidential information,

- a secure reading room without photocopying machines, telephones, fax facilities, scanners or any other technical equipment for the reproduction and transmission of documents etc.,

- security provisions governing access to the reading room, including the requirements of signature in an access register and a solemn declaration not to disseminate the confidential information examined.

3.2.4. The above does not preclude other equivalent arrangements agreed between the Institutions.

3.3. In the event of non-compliance with these arrangements, the provisions relating to sanctions of Members set out in Annex VIII to Parliament's Rules of Procedure and, in respect of Parliament officials and other employees, the applicable provisions of Article 86 of the

Staff Regulations[3] or Article 49 of the Conditions of employment of other servants of the European Communities shall apply.

4. Final provisions

4.1. The Commission and Parliament shall take all the measures required for the implementation of the provisions of this Annex.
To that end, the competent services of the Commission and of Parliament shall closely coordinate the implementation of this Annex. This shall include the verification of traceability of confidential information and periodic joint monitoring of security arrangements and standards applied.
Parliament undertakes to adapt, where necessary, its internal provisions so as to implement the security rules for confidential information laid down in this Annex.
Parliament undertakes to adopt as soon as possible its future security arrangements and to verify those arrangements by common accord with the Commission, with a view to establishing equivalence of security standards. This will give effect to this Annex with regard to:
– technical security provisions and standards regarding the handling and storage of confidential information, including security measures in the field of physical, personnel, document and IT security,
– the establishment of a specially established oversight committee, composed of appropriately cleared Members for the handling of EUCI classified as 'TRÈS SECRET UE/ EU TOP SECRET'.
4.2. Parliament and the Commission will review this Annex and, where necessary, adapt it, no later than at the time of the review referred to in point 54 of the Framework Agreement, in light of developments concerning:
– future security arrangements involving Parliament and the Commission,
– other agreements or legal acts relevant for the forwarding of information between the Institutions.

---

3   Regulation (EEC, Euratom, ECSC) No 259/68 of the Council of 29 February 1968 laying down the Staff Regulations of Officials and the Conditions of employment of other servants of the European Communities and instituting special measures temporarily applicable to officials of the Commission.

Annex III
Negotiation and conclusion of international agreements

This Annex lays down detailed arrangements for the provision of information to Parliament concerning the negotiation and conclusion of international agreements as referred to in points 23, 24 and 25 of the Framework Agreement.

1. The Commission shall inform Parliament about its intention to propose the start of negotiations at the same time as it informs the Council.
2. In line with the provisions of point 24 of the Framework Agreement, when the Commission proposes draft negotiating directives with a view to their adoption by the Council, it shall at the same time present them to Parliament.
3. The Commission shall take due account of Parliament's comments throughout the negotiations.
4. In line with the provisions of point 23 of the Framework Agreement, the Commission shall keep Parliament regularly and promptly informed about the conduct of negotiations until the agreement is initialled, and explain whether and how Parliament's comments were incorporated in the texts under negotiation and if not why.
5. In the case of international agreements the conclusion of which requires Parliament's consent, the Commission shall provide to Parliament during the negotiation process all relevant information that it also provides to the Council (or to the special committee appointed by the Council). This shall include draft amendments to adopted negotiating directives, draft negotiating texts, agreed articles, the agreed date for initialling the agreement and the text of the agreement to be initialled. The Commission shall also transmit to Parliament, as it does to the Council (or to the special committee appointed by the Council), any relevant documents received from third parties, subject to the originator's consent. The Commission shall keep the responsible parliamentary committee informed about developments in the negotiations and, in particular, explain how Parliament's views have been taken into account.
6. In the case of international agreements the conclusion of which does not require Parliament's consent, the Commission shall ensure that Parliament is immediately and fully informed, by providing information covering at least the draft negotiating directives, the adopted negotiating directives, the subsequent conduct of negotiations and the conclusion of the negotiations.
7. In line with the provisions of point 24 of the Framework Agreement, the Commission shall give thorough information to Parliament in due time when an international agreement is initialled, and shall inform Parliament as early as possible when it intends to propose its provisional application to the Council and of the reasons therefor, unless reasons of urgency preclude it from doing so.
8. The Commission shall inform the Council and Parliament simultaneously and in due time of its intention to propose to the Council the suspension of an international agreement and of the reasons therefor.

9. For international agreements which would fall under the consent procedure provided for by the TFEU, the Commission shall also keep Parliament fully informed before approving modifications to an agreement which are authorised by the Council, by way of derogation, in accordance with Article 218(7) TFEU.

Annex IV
Timetable for the Commission Work Programme

The Commission Work Programme shall be accompanied by a list of legislative and non-legislative proposals for the following years. The Commission Work Programme covers the next year in question, and provides a detailed indication of the Commission's priorities for the subsequent years. The Commission Work Programme can thus be the basis for a structured dialogue with Parliament, with a view to seeking a common understanding.
The Commission Work Programme shall also include planned initiatives on soft law, withdrawals and simplification.
1. In the first semester of a given year, Members of the Commission shall undertake an ongoing regular dialogue with the corresponding parliamentary committees on the implementation of the Commission Work Programme for that year and on the preparation of the future Commission Work Programme. On the basis of that dialogue each parliamentary committee shall report on the outcome thereof to the Conference of Committee Chairs.
2. In parallel the Conference of Committee Chairs shall hold a regular exchange of views with the Vice-President of the Commission responsible for interinstitutional relations, in order to assess the state of implementation of the current Commission Work Programme, discuss the preparation of the future Commission Work Programme and take stock of the results of the ongoing bilateral dialogue between the parliamentary committees concerned and relevant Members of the Commission.
3. In June, the Conference of Committees Chairs shall submit a summary report to the Conference of Presidents, which should include results of the screening of the implementation of the Commission Work Programme as well as Parliament's priorities for the forthcoming Commission Work Programme, and Parliament shall inform the Commission thereof.
4. On the basis of that summary report, Parliament shall adopt a resolution at the July part-session, outlining its position and including in particular requests based on legislative initiative reports.
5. Each year in the first part-session of September, a State of the Union debate will be held in which the President of the Commission shall deliver an address, taking stock of the current year and looking ahead to priorities for the following years. To that end, the President of the Commission will in parallel set out in writing to Parliament the main elements guiding the preparation of the Commission Work Programme for the following year.

6. From the start of September, the competent parliamentary committees and the relevant Members of the Commission may meet for a more detailed exchange of views on future priorities in each policy area. These meetings shall be rounded off by a meeting between the Conference of Committee Chairs and the College of Commissioners and by a meeting between the Conference of Presidents and the President of the Commission, as appropriate.

7. In October, the Commission shall adopt its Work Programme for the following year. Subsequently, the President of the Commission shall present that Work Programme to Parliament at an appropriate level.

8. Parliament may hold a debate and adopt a resolution at the December part-session.

9. This timetable shall be applied to each regular programming cycle, except for Parliament election years coinciding with the end of the Commission's term of office.

10. This timetable shall not prejudice any future agreement on interinstitutional programming.

Council Statement – Framework Agreement on Relations between the European Parliament and the Commission

Source OJ C 287 of 23 October 2010, p. 1

The Council has taken note of the Framework Agreement on relations between the European Parliament and the Commission signed by the two Institutions on 20 October 2010.

The Council, which was not party to the negotiating of the Framework Agreement, points out that compliance with the founding Treaties of the Union, in the terms in which they have been ratified by the Member States, is the fundamental principle governing the existence and the functioning of the Union. The Treaties define exhaustively the respective powers conferred on the Institutions (Article 13(2) TEU). Those powers may not be modified or supplemented by the Institutions themselves either unilaterally or by agreement between them.

The Council notes that several provisions of the Framework Agreement have the effect of modifying the institutional balance set out in the Treaties in force, according the European Parliament prerogatives that are not provided for in the Treaties and limiting the autonomy of the Commission and its President. The Council is particularly concerned by the provisions on international agreements, infringement proceedings against Member States and transmission of classified information to the European Parliament.

The Framework Agreement cannot be applied to the Council. The Council will submit to the Court of Justice any act or action of the European Parliament or of the Commission performed in application of the provisions of the Framework Agreement that would have an effect contrary to the interests of the Council and the prerogatives conferred upon it by the Treaties.

European Council Decision of 22 May 2013 concerning the Number of Members of the European Commission (2013/272/EU)

Date 22 May 2013
Source OJ L 165 of 18 June 2013, p. 98

The European Council,
Having regard to the Treaty on European Union, and in particular Article 17(5) thereof,
Whereas:
(1) At its meetings of 11-12 December 2008 and 18-19 June 2009, the European Council noted the concerns of the Irish people with respect to the Treaty of Lisbon and therefore agreed that, provided the Treaty of Lisbon entered into force, a decision would be taken, in accordance with the necessary legal procedures, to the effect that the Commission continue to include one national of each Member State.
(2) The decision on the number of members of the Commission should be adopted in due time before the appointment of the Commission due to take up its duties on 1 November 2014.
(3) The implications of this Decision should be kept under review,
Has adopted this Decision:

Article 1
The Commission shall consist of a number of members, including its President and the High Representative of the Union for Foreign Affairs and Security Policy, equal to the number of Member States.

© European Union, http://eur-lex.europa.eu/, 1998-2015.

Article 2
The European Council shall review this Decision, in view of its effect on the functioning of the Commission, in sufficient time in advance of either the appointment of the first Commission following the date of accession of the 30th Member State or the appointment of the Commission succeeding that due to take up its duties on 1 November 2014, whichever is earlier.

Article 3
This Decision shall enter into force on the day following that of its publication in the Official Journal of the European Union.
It shall apply from 1 November 2014.

Done at Brussels, 22 May 2013.

European Council Decision of 28 June 2013 establishing the Composition of the European Parliament (2013/312/EU)

Date   28 June 2013
Source OJ L 181 of 29 June 2013, p. 57

The European Council,
Having regard to the Treaty on European Union, and in particular Article 14(2) thereof,
Having regard to Article 2(3) of Protocol 36 on transitional provisions,
Having regard to the initiative of the European Parliament,[1]
Having regard to the consent of the European Parliament,[2]
Whereas:
(1) Article 2(1) and (2) of Protocol 36 on transitional provisions will expire at the end of the 2009-2014 parliamentary term.
(2) Article 19(1) of the Act concerning the conditions of accession of the Republic of Croatia and the adjustments to the Treaty on European Union, the Treaty on the Functioning of the European Union and the Treaty establishing the European Atomic Energy Community will expire at the end of the 2009-2014 parliamentary term.
(3) It is necessary to comply without delay with the provisions of Article 2(3) of Protocol 36 and therefore to adopt the decision provided for in the second subparagraph of Article 14(2) of the Treaty on European Union, in order to enable Member States to enact in good time the necessary domestic measures for organising the elections to the European Parliament for the 2014-2019 parliamentary term.
(4) The first subparagraph of Article 14(2) of the Treaty on European Union lays down the criteria for the composition of the European Parliament, namely that representatives of the Union's citizens are not to exceed 750 in number, plus the President, that representation is to be degressively proportional, with a minimum threshold of six members per Member State, and that no Member State is to be allocated more than 96 seats.

---

1   Initiative adopted on 13 March 2013 (not yet published in the Official Journal).
2   Consent of 12 June 2013 (not yet published in the Official Journal).
©   European Union, http://eur-lex.europa.eu/, 1998-2015.

(5) Article 10 of the Treaty on European Union provides, inter alia, that the functioning of the Union shall be founded on representative democracy with citizens being directly represented at Union level in the European Parliament and Member States being represented by their governments, themselves being democratically accountable to their national Parliaments or citizens, in the Council. Article 14(2) of the Treaty on European Union on the composition of the European Parliament therefore applies within the context of the wider institutional arrangements set out in the Treaties, which also include the provisions on decision making in the Council,
Has adopted this Decision:

Article 1
In the application of the principle of degressive proportionality provided for in the first subparagraph of Article 14(2) of the Treaty on European Union, the following principles shall apply:
– the allocation of seats in the European Parliament shall fully utilise the minimum and maximum numbers set by the Treaty on European Union in order to reflect as closely as possible the sizes of the respective populations of Member States,
– the ratio between the population and the number of seats of each Member State before rounding to whole numbers shall vary in relation to their respective populations in such a way that each Member of the European Parliament from a more populous Member State represents more citizens than each Member from a less populous Member State and, conversely, that the larger the population of a Member State, the greater its entitlement to a large number of seats.

Article 2
The total population of the Member States shall be calculated by the Commission (Eurostat) on the basis of data provided by the Member States, in accordance with a method established by means of a regulation of the European Parliament and of the Council.

Article 3
Pursuant to Article 1, the number of representatives in the European Parliament elected in each Member State is hereby set as follows for the 2014-2019 parliamentary term:

Belgium	21
Bulgaria	17
Czech Republic	21
Denmark	13
Germany	96
Estonia	6
Ireland	11
Greece	21
Spain	54

France	74
Croatia	11
Italy	73
Cyprus	6
Latvia	8
Lithuania	11
Luxembourg	6
Hungary	21
Malta	6
Netherlands	26
Austria	18
Poland	51
Portugal	21
Romania	32
Slovenia	8
Slovakia	13
Finland	13
Sweden	20
United Kingdom	73

Article 4

This Decision shall be revised sufficiently far in advance of the beginning of the 2019-2024 parliamentary term on the basis of an initiative of the European Parliament presented before the end of 2016 with the aim of establishing a system which in future will make it possible, before each fresh election to the European Parliament, to allocate the seats between Member States in an objective, fair, durable and transparent way, translating the principle of degressive proportionality as laid down in Article 1, taking account of any change in their number and demographic trends in their population, as duly ascertained thus respecting the overall balance of the institutional system as laid down in the Treaties.

Article 5

This Decision shall enter into force on the day following that of its publication in the Official Journal of the European Union.

Done at Brussels, 28 June 2013.

Regulation (EU) No 182/2011 of the European Parliament and of the Council of 16 February 2011 laying down the Rules and General Principles concerning Mechanisms for Control by Member States of the Commission's Exercise of Implementing Powers

Source OJ L 55 of 28 February 2011, p. 13

The European Parliament and the Council of the European Union,
Having regard to the Treaty on the Functioning of the European Union, and in particular Article 291(3) thereof,
Having regard to the proposal from the Commission,
After transmission of the draft legislative act to the national parliaments,
Acting in accordance with the ordinary legislative procedure[1],
Whereas:

(1) Where uniform conditions for the implementation of legally binding Union acts are needed, those acts (hereinafter 'basic acts') are to confer implementing powers on the Commission, or, in duly justified specific cases and in the cases provided for in Articles 24 and 26 of the Treaty on European Union, on the Council.

(2) It is for the legislator, fully respecting the criteria laid down in the Treaty on the Functioning of the European Union ('TFEU'), to decide in respect of each basic act whether to confer implementing powers on the Commission in accordance with Article 291(2) of that Treaty.

(3) Hitherto, the exercise of implementing powers by the Commission has been governed by Council Decision 1999/468/EC[2].

(4) The TFEU now requires the European Parliament and the Council to lay down the rules and general principles concerning mechanisms for control by Member States of the Commission's exercise of implementing powers.

1   Position of the European Parliament of 16 December 2010 (not yet published in the Official Journal) and decision of the Council of 14 February 2011.
2   OJ L 184, 17.7.1999, p. 23.
©   European Union, http://eur-lex.europa.eu/, 1998-2015.

(5) It is necessary to ensure that the procedures for such control are clear, effective and proportionate to the nature of the implementing acts and that they reflect the institutional requirements of the TFEU as well as the experience gained and the common practice followed in the implementation of Decision 1999/468/EC.

(6) In those basic acts which require the control of the Member States for the adoption by the Commission of implementing acts, it is appropriate, for the purposes of such control, that committees composed of the representatives of the Member States and chaired by the Commission be set up.

(7) Where appropriate, the control mechanism should include referral to an appeal committee which should meet at the appropriate level.

(8) In the interests of simplification, the Commission should exercise implementing powers in accordance with one of only two procedures, namely the advisory procedure or the examination procedure.

(9) In order to simplify further, common procedural rules should apply to the committees, including the key provisions relating to their functioning and the possibility of delivering an opinion by written procedure.

(10) Criteria should be laid down to determine the procedure to be used for the adoption of implementing acts by the Commission. In order to achieve greater consistency, the procedural requirements should be proportionate to the nature and impact of the implementing acts to be adopted.

(11) The examination procedure should in particular apply for the adoption of acts of general scope designed to implement basic acts and specific implementing acts with a potentially important impact. That procedure should ensure that implementing acts cannot be adopted by the Commission if they are not in accordance with the opinion of the committee, except in very exceptional circumstances, where they may apply for a limited period of time. The procedure should also ensure that the Commission is able to review the draft implementing acts where no opinion is delivered by the committee, taking into account the views expressed within the committee.

(12) Provided that the basic act confers implementing powers on the Commission relating to programmes with substantial budgetary implications or directed to third countries, the examination procedure should apply.

(13) The chair of a committee should endeavour to find solutions which command the widest possible support within the committee or the appeal committee and should explain the manner in which the discussions and suggestions for amendments have been taken into account. For that purpose, the Commission should pay particular attention to the views expressed within the committee or the appeal committee as regards draft definitive anti-dumping or countervailing measures.

(14) When considering the adoption of other draft implementing acts concerning particularly sensitive sectors, notably taxation, consumer health, food safety and protection of the environment, the Commission, in order to find a balanced solution, will, as far as possible, act in such a way as to avoid going against any predominant position which might emerge within the appeal committee against the appropriateness of an implementing act.

(15) The advisory procedure should, as a general rule, apply in all other cases or where it is considered more appropriate.

(16) It should be possible, where this is provided for in a basic act, to adopt implementing acts which are to apply immediately on imperative grounds of urgency.

(17) The European Parliament and the Council should be promptly informed of committee proceedings on a regular basis.

(18) Either the European Parliament or the Council should be able at any time to indicate to the Commission that, in its view, a draft implementing act exceeds the implementing powers provided for in the basic act, taking into account their rights relating to the review of the legality of Union acts.

(19) Public access to information on committee proceedings should be ensured in accordance with Regulation (EC) No 1049/2001 of the European Parliament and of the Council of 30 May 2001 regarding public access to European Parliament, Council and Commission documents[3].

(20) A register containing information on committee proceedings should be kept by the Commission. Consequently, rules relating to the protection of classified documents applicable to the Commission should also apply to the use of the register.

(21) Decision 1999/468/EC should be repealed. In order to ensure the transition between the regime provided for in Decision 1999/468/EC and this Regulation, any reference in existing legislation to the procedures provided for in that Decision should, with the exception of the regulatory procedure with scrutiny provided for in Article 5a thereof, be understood as a reference to the corresponding procedures provided for in this Regulation. The effects of Article 5a of Decision 1999/468/EC should be provisionally maintained for the purposes of existing basic acts which refer to that Article.

(22) The Commission's powers, as laid down by the TFEU, concerning the implementation of the competition rules are not affected by this Regulation,

Have adopted this regulation:

Article 1 Subject-matter

This Regulation lays down the rules and general principles governing the mechanisms which apply where a legally binding Union act (hereinafter a 'basic act') identifies the need for uniform conditions of implementation and requires that the adoption of implementing acts by the Commission be subject to the control of Member States.

Article 2 Selection of procedures

1. A basic act may provide for the application of the advisory procedure or the examination procedure, taking into account the nature or the impact of the implementing act required.

---

[3] OJ L 145, 31.5.2001, p. 43.

2. The examination procedure applies, in particular, for the adoption of:
   (a) implementing acts of general scope;
   (b) other implementing acts relating to:
      (i) programmes with substantial implications;
      (ii) the common agricultural and common fisheries policies;
      (iii) the environment, security and safety, or protection of the health or safety, of humans, animals or plants;
      (iv) the common commercial policy;
      (v) taxation.
3. The advisory procedure applies, as a general rule, for the adoption of implementing acts not falling within the ambit of paragraph 2. However, the advisory procedure may apply for the adoption of the implementing acts referred to in paragraph 2 in duly justified cases.

Article 3 Common provisions

1. The common provisions set out in this Article shall apply to all the procedures referred to in Articles 4 to 8.
2. The Commission shall be assisted by a committee composed of representatives of the Member States. The committee shall be chaired by a representative of the Commission. The chair shall not take part in the committee vote.
3. The chair shall submit to the committee the draft implementing act to be adopted by the Commission.
Except in duly justified cases, the chair shall convene a meeting not less than 14 days from submission of the draft implementing act and of the draft agenda to the committee. The committee shall deliver its opinion on the draft implementing act within a time limit which the chair may lay down according to the urgency of the matter. Time limits shall be proportionate and shall afford committee members early and effective opportunities to examine the draft implementing act and express their views.
4. Until the committee delivers an opinion, any committee member may suggest amendments and the chair may present amended versions of the draft implementing act.
The chair shall endeavour to find solutions which command the widest possible support within the committee. The chair shall inform the committee of the manner in which the discussions and suggestions for amendments have been taken into account, in particular as regards those suggestions which have been largely supported within the committee.
5. In duly justified cases, the chair may obtain the committee's opinion by written procedure. The chair shall send the committee members the draft implementing act and shall lay down a time limit for delivery of an opinion according to the urgency of the matter. Any committee member who does not oppose the draft implementing act or who does not explicitly abstain from voting thereon before the expiry of that time limit shall be regarded as having tacitly agreed to the draft implementing act.
Unless otherwise provided in the basic act, the written procedure shall be terminated without result where, within the time limit referred to in the first subparagraph, the chair

so decides or a committee member so requests. In such a case, the chair shall convene a committee meeting within a reasonable time.

6. The committee's opinion shall be recorded in the minutes. Committee members shall have the right to ask for their position to be recorded in the minutes. The chair shall send the minutes to the committee members without delay.

7. Where applicable, the control mechanism shall include referral to an appeal committee. The appeal committee shall adopt its own rules of procedure by a simple majority of its component members, on a proposal from the Commission.

Where the appeal committee is seised, it shall meet at the earliest 14 days, except in duly justified cases, and at the latest 6 weeks, after the date of referral. Without prejudice to paragraph 3, the appeal committee shall deliver its opinion within 2 months of the date of referral.

A representative of the Commission shall chair the appeal committee.

The chair shall set the date of the appeal committee meeting in close cooperation with the members of the committee, in order to enable Member States and the Commission to ensure an appropriate level of representation. By 1 April 2011, the Commission shall convene the first meeting of the appeal committee in order to adopt its rules of procedure.

Article 4 Advisory procedure

1. Where the advisory procedure applies, the committee shall deliver its opinion, if necessary by taking a vote. If the committee takes a vote, the opinion shall be delivered by a simple majority of its component members.

2. The Commission shall decide on the draft implementing act to be adopted, taking the utmost account of the conclusions drawn from the discussions within the committee and of the opinion delivered.

Article 5 Examination procedure

1. Where the examination procedure applies, the committee shall deliver its opinion by the majority laid down in Article 16(4) and (5) of the Treaty on European Union and, where applicable, Article 238(3) TFEU, for acts to be adopted on a proposal from the Commission. The votes of the representatives of the Member States within the committee shall be weighted in the manner set out in those Articles.

2. Where the committee delivers a positive opinion, the Commission shall adopt the draft implementing act.

3. Without prejudice to Article 7, if the committee delivers a negative opinion, the Commission shall not adopt the draft implementing act. Where an implementing act is deemed to be necessary, the chair may either submit an amended version of the draft implementing act to the same committee within 2 months of delivery of the negative opinion, or submit the draft implementing act within 1 month of such delivery to the appeal committee for further deliberation.

4. Where no opinion is delivered, the Commission may adopt the draft implementing act, except in the cases provided for in the second subparagraph. Where the Commission does

not adopt the draft implementing act, the chair may submit to the committee an amended version thereof.

Without prejudice to Article 7, the Commission shall not adopt the draft implementing act where:

(a) that act concerns taxation, financial services, the protection of the health or safety of humans, animals or plants, or definitive multilateral safeguard measures;

(b) the basic act provides that the draft implementing act may not be adopted where no opinion is delivered; or

(c) a simple majority of the component members of the committee opposes it.

In any of the cases referred to in the second subparagraph, where an implementing act is deemed to be necessary, the chair may either submit an amended version of that act to the same committee within 2 months of the vote, or submit the draft implementing act within 1 month of the vote to the appeal committee for further deliberation.

5. By way of derogation from paragraph 4, the following procedure shall apply for the adoption of draft definitive anti-dumping or countervailing measures, where no opinion is delivered by the committee and a simple majority of its component members opposes the draft implementing act.

The Commission shall conduct consultations with the Member States. 14 days at the earliest and 1 month at the latest after the committee meeting, the Commission shall inform the committee members of the results of those consultations and submit a draft implementing act to the appeal committee. By way of derogation from Article 3(7), the appeal committee shall meet 14 days at the earliest and 1 month at the latest after the submission of the draft implementing act. The appeal committee shall deliver its opinion in accordance with Article 6. The time limits laid down in this paragraph shall be without prejudice to the need to respect the deadlines laid down in the relevant basic acts.

Article 6 Referral to the appeal committee

1. The appeal committee shall deliver its opinion by the majority provided for in Article 5(1).

2. Until an opinion is delivered, any member of the appeal committee may suggest amendments to the draft implementing act and the chair may decide whether or not to modify it.

The chair shall endeavour to find solutions which command the widest possible support within the appeal committee.

The chair shall inform the appeal committee of the manner in which the discussions and suggestions for amendments have been taken into account, in particular as regards suggestions for amendments which have been largely supported within the appeal committee.

3. Where the appeal committee delivers a positive opinion, the Commission shall adopt the draft implementing act.

Where no opinion is delivered, the Commission may adopt the draft implementing act.

Where the appeal committee delivers a negative opinion, the Commission shall not adopt the draft implementing act.

4. By way of derogation from paragraph 3, for the adoption of definitive multilateral safeguard measures, in the absence of a positive opinion voted by the majority provided for in Article 5(1), the Commission shall not adopt the draft measures.

5. By way of derogation from paragraph 1, until 1 September 2012, the appeal committee shall deliver its opinion on draft definitive anti-dumping or countervailing measures by a simple majority of its component members.

Article 7 Adoption of implementing acts in exceptional cases

By way of derogation from Article 5(3) and the second subparagraph of Article 5(4), the Commission may adopt a draft implementing act where it needs to be adopted without delay in order to avoid creating a significant disruption of the markets in the area of agriculture or a risk for the financial interests of the Union within the meaning of Article 325 TFEU.

In such a case, the Commission shall immediately submit the adopted implementing act to the appeal committee. Where the appeal committee delivers a negative opinion on the adopted implementing act, the Commission shall repeal that act immediately. Where the appeal committee delivers a positive opinion or no opinion is delivered, the implementing act shall remain in force.

Article 8 Immediately applicable implementing acts

1. By way of derogation from Articles 4 and 5, a basic act may provide that, on duly justified imperative grounds of urgency, this Article is to apply.

2. The Commission shall adopt an implementing act which shall apply immediately, without its prior submission to a committee, and shall remain in force for a period not exceeding 6 months unless the basic act provides otherwise.

3. At the latest 14 days after its adoption, the chair shall submit the act referred to in paragraph 2 to the relevant committee in order to obtain its opinion.

4. Where the examination procedure applies, in the event of the committee delivering a negative opinion, the Commission shall immediately repeal the implementing act adopted in accordance with paragraph 2.

5. Where the Commission adopts provisional anti-dumping or countervailing measures, the procedure provided for in this Article shall apply. The Commission shall adopt such measures after consulting or, in cases of extreme urgency, after informing the Member States. In the latter case, consultations shall take place 10
days at the latest after notification to the Member States of the measures adopted by the Commission.

Article 9 Rules of procedure

1. Each committee shall adopt by a simple majority of its component members its own rules of procedure on the proposal of its chair, on the basis of standard rules to be drawn up by the Commission following consultation with Member States. Such standard rules shall be published by the Commission in the Official Journal of the European Union.

In so far as may be necessary, existing committees shall adapt their rules of procedure to the standard rules.

2. The principles and conditions on public access to documents and the rules on data protection applicable to the Commission shall apply to the committees.

Article 10 Information on committee proceedings

1. The Commission shall keep a register of committee proceedings which shall contain:
   (a) a list of committees;
   (b) the agendas of committee meetings;
   (c) the summary records, together with the lists of the authorities and organisations to which the persons designated by the Member States to represent them belong;
   (d) the draft implementing acts on which the committees are asked to deliver an opinion;
   (e) the voting results;
   (f) the final draft implementing acts following delivery of the opinion of the committees;
   (g) information concerning the adoption of the final draft implementing acts by the Commission; and
   (h) statistical data on the work of the committees.
2. The Commission shall also publish an annual report on the work of the committees.
3. The European Parliament and the Council shall have access to the information referred to in paragraph 1 in accordance with the applicable rules.
4. At the same time as they are sent to the committee members, the Commission shall make available to the European Parliament and the Council the documents referred to in points (b), (d) and (f) of paragraph 1 whilst also informing them of the availability of such documents.
5. The references of all documents referred to in points (a) to (g) of paragraph 1 as well as the information referred to in paragraph 1(h) shall be made public in the register.

Article 11 Right of scrutiny for the European Parliament and the Council

Where a basic act is adopted under the ordinary legislative procedure, either the European Parliament or the Council may at any time indicate to the Commission that, in its view, a draft implementing act exceeds the implementing powers provided for in the basic act. In such a case, the Commission shall review the draft implementing act, taking account of the positions expressed, and shall inform the European Parliament and the Council whether it intends to maintain, amend or withdraw the draft implementing act.

Article 12 Repeal of Decision 1999/468/EC

Decision 1999/468/EC is hereby repealed.
The effects of Article 5a of Decision 1999/468/EC shall be maintained for the purposes of existing basic acts making reference thereto.

Article 13 Transitional provisions: adaptation of existing basic acts

1. Where basic acts adopted before the entry into force of this Regulation provide for the exercise of implementing powers by the Commission in accordance with Decision 1999/468/EC, the following rules shall apply:

(a) where the basic act makes reference to Article 3 of Decision 1999/468/EC, the advisory procedure referred to in Article 4 of this Regulation shall apply;

(b) where the basic act makes reference to Article 4 of Decision 1999/468/EC, the examination procedure referred to in Article 5 of this Regulation shall apply, with the exception of the second and third subparagraphs of Article 5(4);

(c) where the basic act makes reference to Article 5 of Decision 1999/468/EC, the examination procedure referred to in Article 5 of this Regulation shall apply and the basic act shall be deemed to provide that, in the absence of an opinion, the Commission may not adopt the draft implementing act, as envisaged in point (b) of the second subparagraph of Article 5(4);

(d) where the basic act makes reference to Article 6 of Decision 1999/468/EC, Article 8 of this Regulation shall apply;

(e) where the basic act makes reference to Articles 7 and 8 of Decision 1999/468/EC, Articles 10 and 11 of this Regulation shall apply.

2. Articles 3 and 9 of this Regulation shall apply to all existing committees for the purposes of paragraph 1.

3. Article 7 of this Regulation shall apply only to existing procedures which make reference to Article 4 of Decision 1999/468/EC.

4. The transitional provisions laid down in this Article shall not prejudge the nature of the acts concerned.

Article 14 Transitional arrangement

This Regulation shall not affect pending procedures in which a committee has already delivered its opinion in accordance with Decision 1999/468/EC.

Article 15 Review

By 1 March 2016, the Commission shall present a report to the European Parliament and the Council on the implementation of this Regulation, accompanied, if necessary, by appropriate legislative proposals.

Article 16 Entry into force

This Regulation shall enter into force on 1 March 2011.

This Regulation is binding in its entirety and directly applicable in all Member States.
Done at Strasbourg, 16 February 2011.

Statement by the European Parliament, the Council and the Commission

Article 5(2) of this Regulation requires the Commission to adopt a draft implementing act where the committee delivers a positive opinion. This provision does not preclude that Commission may, as is the current practice, in very exceptional cases, take into consideration new circumstances that have arisen after the vote and decide not to adopt a draft implementing act, after having duly informed the committee and the legislator.

Statement by the Commission

The Commission will proceed to an examination of all legislative acts in force which were not adapted to the regulatory procedure with scrutiny before the entry into force of the Lisbon Treaty, in order to assess if those instruments need to be adapted to the regime of delegated acts introduced by Article 290 of the Treaty on the Functioning of the European Union. The Commission will make the appropriate proposals as soon as possible and no later than at the dates mentioned in the indicative calendar annexed to this declaration.

While this alignment exercise is underway, the Commission will keep the European Parliament regularly informed on draft implementing measures related to these instruments which should become, in the future, delegated acts.

As regards legislative acts in force which currently contain references to the regulatory procedure with scrutiny, the Commission will review the provisions attached to this procedure in each instrument it intends to modify, in order to adapt them in due course according to the criteria laid down in the Treaty. In addition, the European Parliament and the Council will be entitled to signal basic acts they consider important to adapt as a matter of priority.

The Commission will assess the results of this process by the end of 2012 in order to estimate how many legislative acts containing references to the regulatory procedure with scrutiny remain in force. The Commission will then prepare the appropriate legislative initiatives to complete the adaptation. The overall objective of the Commission is that, by the end of the 7th term of the Parliament, all provisions referring to the regulatory procedure with scrutiny would have been removed from all legislative instruments.

The Commission notes that it has recently launched a study which will provide a complete and objective review of all aspects of the EU's trade defence policy and practice, including an evaluation of the performance, methods, utilisation and effectiveness of the present TDI scheme in achieving its trade policy objectives, an evaluation of the effectiveness of the existing and potential policy decisions of the European Union (e.g., the Union interest test, the lesser duty rule, the duty collection system) in comparison with the policy decisions made by certain trading partners and an examination of the basic anti-dumping and anti-subsidy regulations in light of the administrative practice of the EU institutions, the judgments of the Court of Justice of the European Union and the recommendations and rulings of the WTO Dispute Settlement Body.

The Commission intends, in the light of the results of the study and of developments in the Doha Development Agenda negotiations to explore whether and how to further update and modernize the EU's trade defence instruments

The Commission also recalls the recent initiatives it has taken to improve the transparency of the operation of trade defence instruments (such as the appointment of a Hearing Officer) and its work with Member States to clarify key elements of trade defence practice. The Commission attaches substantial importance to this work, and will seek to identify, in consultation with the Member States, other initiatives which could be taken in this respect. Under the comitology rules based on Council Decision 1999/468/EC, where a Common Agricultural Policy (CAP) management committee has delivered an unfavourable opinion, the Commission must submit the draft measure in question to the Council which may take a different decision within a month. However, the Commission is not barred from acting but has the choice to either put the measure in place or defer its application. Hence, the Commission may take the measure where it considers on balance that suspending its application would for instance provoke irreversible negative market effects. When afterwards the Council decides otherwise the measure put in effect by the Commission becomes of course redundant. Thus the current rules equip the Commission with an instrument that allows protecting the common interest of the whole Union by adopting a measure at least on an interim basis.

Article 7 of this Regulation pursues the objective of maintaining this approach within the new comitology arrangements but limited to exceptional situations and on the basis of clearly defined and restrictive criteria. It would allow the Commission to adopt a draft measure despite the unfavourable opinion of the examination committee provided that its 'non adoption within an imperative deadline would create a significant disruption of the markets (...) or for the financial interests of the Union.' The provision refers to situations where it is not possible to wait until the committee votes again on the same or another draft measure because in the meantime the market would be significantly disrupted e.g. due to the speculative behaviour of operators. To ensure the Union's ability to act it would give Member States and the Commission the opportunity to have another informed discussion on the draft measure without leaving things undecided and open to speculation with the negative consequences for the markets and the budget.

Such situations may namely arise in the context of the day-to-day management of the CAP (e.g. fixing of export refunds, management of licences, special safeguard clause) where decisions need often to be taken quickly and can have significant economic consequences for the markets and thus farmers and operators but also for the budget of the Union.

In cases where the European Parliament or the Council indicate to the Commission that they consider a draft implementing act to exceed the implementing powers provided for in the basic act, the Commission will immediately review the draft implementing act taking into account the positions expressed by the European Parliament or the Council.

The Commission will act in a manner which takes duly into account the urgency of the matter.

Before deciding whether the draft implementing act shall be adopted, amended or withdrawn, the Commission will inform the European Parliament or the Council of the action it intends to take and of its reasons for doing so.

Regulation (EU) No 211/2011 of the European Parliament and of the Council of 16 February 2011 on the Citizens' Initiative

Source   OJ L 65 of 11 March 2011, p. 1
   last amended by Commission Delegated Regulation (EU) No 531/2014 of 12 March 2014,
   OJ L 148 of 20 May 2014, p. 52

The European parliament and the Council of the European Union,
Having regard to the Treaty on the Functioning of the European Union, and in particular the first paragraph of Article 24 thereof,
Having regard to the proposal from the European Commission,
After transmission of the draft legislative act to the national parliaments,
Having regard to the opinion of the European Economic and Social Committee[1],
Having regard to the opinion of the Committee of the Regions[2],
Acting in accordance with the ordinary legislative procedure[3],
Whereas:

(1) The Treaty on European Union (TEU) reinforces citizenship of the Union and enhances further the democratic functioning of the Union by providing, inter alia, that every citizen is to have the right to participate in the democratic life of the Union by way of a European citizens' initiative. That procedure affords citizens the possibility of directly approaching the Commission with a request inviting it to submit a proposal for a legal act of the Union for the purpose of implementing the Treaties similar to the right conferred on the European Parliament under Article 225 of the Treaty on the Functioning of the European Union (TFEU) and on the Council under Article 241 TFEU.

1   OJ C 44, 11.2.2011, p. 182.
2   OJ C 267, 1.10.2010, p. 57.
3   Position of the European Parliament of 15 December 2010 (not yet published in the Official Journal) and decision of the Council of 14 February 2011.
©   European Union, http://eur-lex.europa.eu/, 1998-2015.

(2) The procedures and conditions required for the citizens' initiative should be clear, simple, user-friendly and proportionate to the nature of the citizens' initiative so as to encourage participation by citizens and to make the Union more accessible. They should strike a judicious balance between rights and obligations.

(3) They should also ensure that citizens of the Union are subject to similar conditions for supporting a citizens' initiative regardless of the Member State from which they come.

(4) The Commission should, upon request, provide citizens with information and informal advice about citizens' initiatives, notably as regards the registration criteria.

(5) It is necessary to establish the minimum number of Member States from which citizens must come. In order to ensure that a citizens' initiative is representative of a Union interest, while ensuring that the instrument remains easy to use, that number should be set at one quarter of Member States.

(6) For that purpose, it is also appropriate to establish the minimum number of signatories coming from each of those Member States. In order to ensure similar conditions for citizens to support a citizens' initiative, those minimum numbers should be degressively proportional. For the purpose of clarity, those minimum numbers should be set out for each Member State in an annex to this Regulation. The minimum number of signatories required in each Member State should correspond to the number of Members of the European Parliament elected in each Member State, multiplied by 750. The Commission should be empowered to amend that annex in order to reflect any modification in the composition of the European Parliament.

(7) It is appropriate to fix a minimum age for supporting a citizens' initiative. That should be set as the age at which citizens are entitled to vote in elections to the European Parliament.

(8) A minimum organised structure is needed in order to successfully carry through a citizens' initiative. That should take the form of a citizens' committee, composed of natural persons (organisers) coming from at least seven different Member States, in order to encourage the emergence of European-wide issues and to foster reflection on those issues. For the sake of transparency and smooth and efficient communication, the citizens' committee should designate representatives to liaise between the citizens' committee and the institutions of the Union throughout the procedure.

(9) Entities, notably organisations which under the Treaties contribute to forming European political awareness and to expressing the will of citizens of the Union, should be able to promote a citizens' initiative, provided that they do so with full transparency.

(10) In order to ensure coherence and transparency in relation to proposed citizens' initiatives and to avoid a situation where signatures are being collected for a proposed citizens' initiative which does not comply with the conditions laid down in this Regulation, it should be mandatory to register such initiatives on a website made available by the Commission prior to collecting the necessary statements of support from citizens. All proposed citizens' initiatives that comply with the conditions laid down in this Regulation should be registered by the Commission. The Commission should deal with registration in accordance with the general principles of good administration.

(11) Once a proposed citizens' initiative is registered, statements of support from citizens may be collected by the organisers.

(12) It is appropriate to set out the form for the statement of support in an annex to this Regulation, specifying the data required for the purposes of verification by the Member States. The Commission should be empowered to amend that annex in accordance with Article 290 TFEU, taking into account information forwarded to it by Member States.

(13) With due respect for the principle that personal data must be adequate, relevant and not excessive in relation to the purposes for which they are collected, the provision of personal data, including, where applicable, a personal identification number or a personal identification document number by signatories of a proposed citizens' initiative is required as far as may be necessary in order to allow for the verification of statements of support by Member States, in accordance with national law and practice.

(14) In order to put modern technology to good use as a tool of participatory democracy, it is appropriate to provide for statements of support to be collected online as well as in paper form. Online collection systems should have adequate security features in place in order to ensure, inter alia, that the data are securely collected and stored. For that purpose, the Commission should set out detailed technical specifications for online collection systems.

(15) It is appropriate for Member States to verify the conformity of online collection systems with the requirements of this Regulation before statements of support are collected.

(16) The Commission should make available an open-source software incorporating the relevant technical and security features necessary in order to comply with the provisions of this Regulation as regards online collection systems.

(17) It is appropriate to ensure that statements of support for a citizens' initiative are collected within a specific time limit. In order to ensure that proposed citizens' initiatives remain relevant, whilst taking account of the complexity of collecting statements of support across the Union, that time limit should not be longer than 12 months from the date of registration of the proposed citizens' initiative.

(18) It is appropriate to provide that, where a citizens' initiative has received the necessary statements of support from signatories, each Member State should be responsible for the verification and certification of statements of support collected from signatories coming from that Member State. Taking account of the need to limit the administrative burden for Member States, they should, within a period of three months from receipt of a request for certification, carry out such verifications on the basis of appropriate checks, which may be based on random sampling, and should issue a document certifying the number of valid statements of support received.

(19) Organisers should ensure that all the relevant conditions set out in this Regulation are met prior to submitting a citizens' initiative to the Commission.

(20) The Commission should examine a citizens' initiative and set out its legal and political conclusions separately. It should also set out the action it intends to take in response to it, within a period of three months. In order to demonstrate that a citizens' initiative supported by at least one million Union citizens and its possible follow-up are carefully examined, the Commission should explain in a clear, comprehensible and detailed manner the reasons for

its intended action, and should likewise give its reasons if it does not intend to take any action. When the Commission has received a citizens' initiative supported by the requisite number of signatories which fulfils the other requirements of this Regulation, the organisers should be entitled to present that initiative at a public hearing at Union level.

(21) Directive 95/46/EC of the European Parliament and of the Council of 24 October 1995 on the protection of individuals with regard to the processing of personal data and on the free movement of such data[4] is fully applicable to the processing of personal data carried out in application of this Regulation. In this respect, for the sake of legal certainty, it is appropriate to clarify that the organisers of a citizens' initiative and the competent authorities of the Member States are the data controllers within the meaning of Directive 95/46/EC and to specify the maximum period within which the personal data collected for the purposes of a citizens' initiative may be retained. In their capacity as data controllers, organisers need to take all the appropriate measures to comply with the obligations imposed by Directive 95/46/EC, in particular those relating to the lawfulness of the processing, the security of the processing activities, the provision of information and the rights of data subjects to have access to their personal data, as well as to procure the correction and erasure of their personal data.

(22) The provisions of Chapter III of Directive 95/46/EC on judicial remedies, liability and sanctions are fully applicable as regards the data processing carried out in application of this Regulation. Organisers of a citizens' initiative should be liable in accordance with applicable national law for any damage that they cause. In addition, Member States should ensure that organisers are subject to appropriate penalties for infringements of this Regulation.

(23) Regulation (EC) No 45/2001 of the European Parliament and of the Council of 18 December 2000 on the protection of individuals with regard to the processing of personal data by the Community institutions and bodies and on the free movement of such data[5] is fully applicable to the processing of personal data carried out by the Commission in application of this Regulation.

(24) In order to address future adaptation needs, the Commission should be empowered to adopt delegated acts in accordance with Article 290 TFEU for the purpose of amending the Annexes to this Regulation. It is of particular importance that the Commission carry out appropriate consultations during its preparatory work, including at expert level.

(25) The measures necessary for the implementation of this Regulation should be adopted in accordance with Council Decision 1999/468/EC of 28 June 1999 laying down the procedures for the exercise of implementing powers conferred on the Commission[6].

(26) This Regulation respects fundamental rights and observes the principles enshrined in the Charter of Fundamental Rights of the European Union, in particular Article 8 thereof,

---

4   OJ L 281, 23.11.1995, p. 31.
5   OJ L 8, 12.1.2001, p. 1.
6   OJ L 184, 17.7.1999, p. 23.

which states that everyone has the right to the protection of personal data concerning him or her.

(27) The European Data Protection Supervisor was consulted and adopted an opinion[7],

Have adopted this regulation:

Article 1 Subject matter

This Regulation establishes the procedures and conditions required for a citizens' initiative as provided for in Article 11 TEU and Article 24 TFEU.

Article 2 Definitions

For the purpose of this Regulation the following definitions shall apply:

1. 'citizens' initiative' means an initiative submitted to the Commission in accordance with this Regulation, inviting the Commission, within the framework of its powers, to submit any appropriate proposal on matters where citizens consider that a legal act of the Union is required for the purpose of implementing the Treaties, which has received the support of at least one million eligible signatories coming from at least one quarter of all Member States;

2. 'signatories' means citizens of the Union who have supported a given citizens' initiative by completing a statement of support form for that initiative;

3. 'organisers' means natural persons forming a citizens' committee responsible for the preparation of a citizens' initiative and its submission to the Commission.

Article 3 Requirements for organisers and for signatories

1. The organisers shall be citizens of the Union and be of the age to be entitled to vote in elections to the European Parliament.

2. The organisers shall form a citizens' committee of at least seven persons who are residents of at least seven different Member States.

The organisers shall designate one representative and one substitute ('the contact persons'), who shall liaise between the citizens' committee and the institutions of the Union throughout the procedure and who shall be mandated to speak and act on behalf of the citizens' committee.

Organisers who are Members of the European Parliament shall not be counted for the purposes of reaching the minimum number required to form a citizens' committee.

For the purpose of registering a proposed citizens' initiative in accordance with Article 4, only the information concerning the seven members of the citizens' committee who are needed in order to comply with the requirements laid down in paragraph 1 of this Article and in this paragraph shall be considered by the Commission.

3. The Commission may request the organisers to provide appropriate proof that the requirements laid down in paragraphs 1 and 2 are fulfilled.

7 OJ C 323, 30.11.2010, p. 1.

4. In order to be eligible to support a proposed citizens' initiative, signatories shall be citizens of the Union and shall be of the age to be entitled to vote in elections to the European Parliament.

Article 4 Registration of a proposed citizens' initiative

1. Prior to initiating the collection of statements of support from signatories for a proposed citizens' initiative, the organisers shall be required to register it with the Commission, providing the information set out in Annex II, in particular on the subject matter and objectives of the proposed citizens' initiative.

That information shall be provided in one of the official languages of the Union, in an online register made available for that purpose by the Commission ('the register').

The organisers shall provide, for the register and where appropriate on their website, regularly updated information on the sources of support and funding for the proposed citizens' initiative.

After the registration is confirmed in accordance with paragraph 2, the organisers may provide the proposed citizens' initiative in other official languages of the Union for inclusion in the register. The translation of the proposed citizens' initiative into other official languages of the Union shall be the responsibility of the organisers.

The Commission shall establish a point of contact which provides information and assistance.

2. Within two months from the receipt of the information set out in Annex II, the Commission shall register a proposed citizens' initiative under a unique registration number and send a confirmation to the organisers, provided that the following conditions are fulfilled:

(a) the citizens' committee has been formed and the contact persons have been designated in accordance with Article 3(2);

(b) the proposed citizens' initiative does not manifestly fall outside the framework of the Commission's powers to submit a proposal for a legal act of the Union for the purpose of implementing the Treaties;

(c) the proposed citizens' initiative is not manifestly abusive, frivolous or vexatious; and

(d) the proposed citizens' initiative is not manifestly contrary to the values of the Union as set out in Article 2 TEU.

3. The Commission shall refuse the registration if the conditions laid down in paragraph 2 are not met.

Where it refuses to register a proposed citizens' initiative, the Commission shall inform the organisers of the reasons for such refusal and of all possible judicial and extrajudicial remedies available to them.

4. A proposed citizens' initiative that has been registered shall be made public in the register. Without prejudice to their rights under Regulation (EC) No 45/2001, data subjects shall be entitled to request the removal of their personal data from the register after the expiry of a period of two years from the date of registration of a proposed citizens' initiative.

5. At any time before the submission of statements of support in accordance with Article 8, the organisers may withdraw a proposed citizens' initiative that has been registered. In that case, an indication to that effect shall be entered in the register.

Article 5 Procedures and conditions for the collection of statements of support

1. The organisers shall be responsible for the collection of the statements of support from signatories for a proposed citizens' initiative which has been registered in accordance with Article 4.

Only forms which comply with the models set out in Annex III and which are in one of the language versions included in the register for that proposed citizens' initiative may be used for the collection of statements of support. The organisers shall complete the forms as indicated in Annex III prior to initiating the collection of statements of support from signatories. The information given in the forms shall correspond to the information contained in the register.

2. The organisers may collect statements of support in paper form or electronically. Where statements of support are collected online, Article 6 shall apply.

For the purpose of this Regulation, statements of support which are electronically signed using an advanced electronic signature, within the meaning of Directive 1999/93/EC of the European Parliament and of the Council of 13 December 1999 on a Community framework for electronic signatures[8], shall be treated in the same way as statements of support in paper form.

3. Signatories shall be required to complete statement of support forms made available by the organisers. They shall indicate only the personal data that are required for the purposes of verification by the Member States, as set out in Annex III.

Signatories may only support a given proposed citizens' initiative once.

4. Member States shall forward to the Commission any changes to the information set out in Annex III. Taking into account those changes, the Commission may adopt, by means of delegated acts, in accordance with Article 17 and subject to the conditions of Articles 18 and 19, amendments to Annex III.

5. All statements of support shall be collected after the date of registration of the proposed citizens' initiative and within a period not exceeding 12 months.

At the end of that period, the register shall indicate that the period has expired and, where appropriate, that the required number of statements of support was not collected.

Article 6 Online collection systems

1. Where statements of support are collected online, the data obtained through the online collection system shall be stored in the territory of a Member State.

The online collection system shall be certified in accordance with paragraph 3 in the Member State in which the data collected through the online collection system will be stored. The

---

8 OJ L 13, 19.1.2000, p. 12.

organisers may use one online collection system for the purpose of collecting statements of support in several or all Member States.

The models for the statement of support forms may be adapted for the purpose of the online collection.

2. The organisers shall ensure that the online collection system used for the collection of statements of support complies with paragraph 4.

Prior to initiating the collection of statements of support, the organisers shall request the competent authority of the relevant Member State to certify that the online collection system used for that purpose complies with paragraph 4.

The organisers may only start collecting statements of support through the online collection system once they have obtained the certificate referred to in paragraph 3. The organisers shall make a copy of that certificate publicly available on the website used for the online collection system.

By 1 January 2012, the Commission shall set up and thereafter shall maintain open-source software incorporating the relevant technical and security features necessary for compliance with the provisions of this Regulation regarding the online collection systems. The software shall be made available free of charge.

3. Where the online collection system complies with paragraph 4, the relevant competent authority shall within one month issue a certificate to that effect in accordance with the model set out in Annex IV.

Member States shall recognise the certificates issued by the competent authorities of other Member States.

4. Online collection systems shall have adequate security and technical features in place in order to ensure that:

(a) only natural persons may submit a statement of support form online;

(b) the data provided online are securely collected and stored, in order to ensure, inter alia, that they may not be modified or used for any purpose other than their indicated support of the given citizens' initiative and to protect personal data against accidental or unlawful destruction or accidental loss, alteration or unauthorised disclosure or access;

(c) the system can generate statements of support in a form complying with the models set out in Annex III, in order to allow for the verification by the Member States in accordance with Article 8(2).

5. By 1 January 2012, the Commission shall adopt technical specifications for the implementation of paragraph 4, in accordance with the regulatory procedure referred to in Article 20(2).

Article 7 Minimum number of signatories per Member State

1. The signatories of a citizens' initiative shall come from at least one quarter of Member States.

2. In at least one quarter of Member States, signatories shall comprise at least the minimum number of citizens set out, at the time of registration of the proposed citizens' initiative, in

Annex I. Those minimum numbers shall correspond to the number of the Members of the European Parliament elected in each Member State, multiplied by 750.

3. The Commission shall adopt, by means of delegated acts, in accordance with Article 17 and subject to the conditions of Articles 18 and 19, appropriate adjustments to Annex I in order to reflect any modification in the composition of the European Parliament.

4. Signatories shall be considered as coming from the Member State which is responsible for the verification of their statement of support in accordance with the second subparagraph of Article 8(1).

Article 8
Verification and certification by Member States of statements of support

1. After collecting the necessary statements of support from signatories in accordance with Articles 5 and 7, the organisers shall submit the statements of support, in paper or electronic form, to the relevant competent authorities referred to in Article 15 for verification and certification. For that purpose the organisers shall use the form set out in Annex V and shall separate those statements of support collected in paper form, those which were electronically signed using an advanced electronic signature and those collected through an online collection system.

The organisers shall submit statements of support to the relevant Member State as follows:
  (a) to the Member State of residence or of nationality of the signatory, as specified in point 1 of Part C of Annex III, or
  (b) to the Member State that issued the personal identification number or the personal identification document indicated in the statement of support, as specified in point 2 of Part C of Annex III.

2. The competent authorities shall, within a period not exceeding three months from receipt of the request, verify the statements of support submitted on the basis of appropriate checks, in accordance with national law and practice, as appropriate. On that basis they shall deliver to the organisers a certificate in accordance with the model set out in Annex VI, certifying the number of valid statements of support for the Member State concerned.

For the purpose of the verification of statements of support, the authentication of signatures shall not be required.

3. The certificate provided for in paragraph 2 shall be issued free of charge.

Article 9 Submission of a citizens' initiative to the Commission

After obtaining the certificates provided for in Article 8(2), and provided that all relevant procedures and conditions set out in this Regulation have been complied with, the organisers may submit the citizens' initiative to the Commission, accompanied by information regarding any support and funding received for that initiative. That information shall be published in the register.

The amount of support and funding received from any source in excess of which information is to be provided shall be identical to that set out in Regulation (EC) No 2004/2003 of the

European Parliament and of the Council of 4 November 2003 on the regulations governing political parties at European level and the rules regarding their funding[9].

For the purpose of this Article, the organisers shall make use of the form set out in Annex VII and shall submit the completed form together with copies, in paper or electronic form, of the certificates provided for in Article 8(2).

Article 10
Procedure for the examination of a citizens' initiative by the Commission

1. Where the Commission receives a citizens' initiative in accordance with Article 9 it shall:
   (a) publish the citizens' initiative without delay in the register;
   (b) receive the organisers at an appropriate level to allow them to explain in detail the matters raised by the citizens' initiative;
   (c) within three months, set out in a communication its legal and political conclusions on the citizens' initiative, the action it intends to take, if any, and its reasons for taking or not taking that action.
2. The communication referred to in paragraph 1(c) shall be notified to the organisers as well as to the European Parliament and the Council and shall be made public.

Article 11 Public hearing

Where the conditions of Article 10(1)(a) and (b) are fulfilled, and within the deadline laid down in Article 10(1)(c), the organisers shall be given the opportunity to present the citizens' initiative at a public hearing. The Commission and the European Parliament shall ensure that this hearing is organised at the European Parliament, if appropriate together with such other institutions and bodies of the Union as may wish to participate, and that the Commission is represented at an appropriate level.

Article 12 Protection of personal data

1. In processing personal data pursuant to this Regulation, the organisers of a citizens' initiative and the competent authorities of the Member State shall comply with Directive 95/46/EC and the national provisions adopted pursuant thereto.
2. For the purposes of their respective processing of personal data, the organisers of a citizens' initiative and the competent authorities designated in accordance with Article 15(2) shall be considered as data controllers in accordance with Article 2(d) of Directive 95/46/EC.
3. The organisers shall ensure that personal data collected for a given citizen's initiative are not used for any purpose other than their indicated support for that initiative, and shall destroy all statements of support received for that initiative and any copies thereof at the latest one month after submitting that initiative to the Commission in accordance with Article 9 or 18 months after the date of registration of the proposed citizens' initiative, whichever is the earlier.

---

9   OJ L 297, 15.11.2003, p. 1.

4. The competent authority shall use the personal data it receives for a given citizens' initiative only for the purpose of verifying the statements of support in accordance with Article 8(2), and shall destroy all statements of support and copies thereof at the latest one month after issuing the certificate referred to in that Article.

5. Statements of support for a given citizens' initiative and copies thereof may be retained beyond the time limits laid down in paragraphs 3 and 4 if necessary for the purpose of legal or administrative proceedings relating to a proposed citizen's initiative. The organisers and the competent authority shall destroy all statements of support and copies thereof at the latest one week after the date of conclusion of the said proceedings by a final decision.

6. The organisers shall implement appropriate technical and organisational measures to protect personal data against accidental or unlawful destruction or accidental loss, alteration, unauthorised disclosure or access, in particular where the processing involves the transmission of data over a network, and against all other unlawful forms of processing.

Article 13 Liability

Organisers shall be liable for any damage they cause in the organisation of a citizens' initiative in accordance with applicable national law.

Article 14 Penalties

1. Member States shall ensure that organisers are subject to appropriate penalties for infringements of this Regulation and in particular for:
    (a) false declarations made by organisers;
    (b) the fraudulent use of data.
2. The penalties referred to in paragraph 1 shall be effective, proportionate and dissuasive.

Article 15 Competent authorities within the Member States

1. For the purpose of the implementation of Article 6(3), Member States shall designate competent authorities responsible for issuing the certificate provided for therein.

2. For the purpose of the implementation of Article 8(2), each Member State shall designate one competent authority responsible for coordinating the process of verification of statements of support and for delivering the certificates provided for therein.

3. Not later than 1 March 2012, Member States shall forward the names and addresses of the competent authorities to the Commission.

4. The Commission shall make the list of competent authorities publicly available.

Article 16 Amendment of the Annexes

The Commission may adopt, by means of delegated acts in accordance with Article 17 and subject to the conditions of Articles 18 and 19, amendments to the Annexes to this Regulation within the scope of the relevant provisions of this Regulation.

Article 17 Exercise of the delegation
1. The power to adopt the delegated acts referred to in Article 16 shall be conferred on the Commission for an indeterminate period of time.
2. As soon as it adopts a delegated act, the Commission shall notify it simultaneously to the European Parliament and to the Council.
3. The power to adopt delegated acts is conferred on the Commission subject to the conditions laid down in Articles 18 and 19.

Article 18 Revocation of the delegation
1. The delegation of power referred to in Article 16 may be revoked at any time by the European Parliament or by the Council.
2. The institution which has commenced an internal procedure for deciding whether to revoke the delegation of power shall endeavour to inform the other institution and the Commission within a reasonable time before the final decision is taken, indicating the delegated powers which could be subject to revocation and possible reasons for a revocation.
3. The decision of revocation shall put an end to the delegation of the powers specified in that decision. It shall take effect immediately or at a later date specified therein. It shall not affect the validity of the delegated acts already in force. It shall be published in the Official Journal of the European Union.

Article 19 Objections to delegated acts
1. The European Parliament or the Council may object to the delegated act within a period of two months from the date of notification. At the initiative of the European Parliament or the Council this period shall be extended by two months.
2. If, on expiry of the period referred to in paragraph 1, neither the European Parliament nor the Council has objected to the delegated act it shall be published in the Official Journal of the European Union and shall enter into force on the date stated therein.
The delegated act may be published in the Official Journal of the European Union and enter into force before the expiry of that period if the European Parliament and the Council have both informed the Commission of their intention not to raise objections.
3. If either the European Parliament or the Council objects to a delegated act within the period referred to in paragraph 1, it shall not enter into force. The institution which objects shall state the reasons for objecting to the delegated act.

Article 20 Committee
1. For the purpose of the implementation of Article 6(5), the Commission shall be assisted by a committee.
2. Where reference is made to this paragraph, Articles 5 and 7 of Decision 1999/468/EC shall apply, having regard to the provisions of Article 8 thereof.
The period laid down in Article 5(6) of Decision 1999/468/EC shall be set at three months.

Article 21 Notification of national provisions

Each Member State shall notify to the Commission the specific provisions it adopts in order to implement this Regulation.

The Commission shall inform the other Member States thereof.

Article 22 Review

By 1 April 2015, and every three years thereafter, the Commission shall present a report to the European Parliament and the Council on the application of this Regulation.

Article 23 Entry into force and application

This Regulation shall enter into force on the 20th day following its publication in the Official Journal of the European Union.

It shall apply from 1 April 2012.

This Regulation shall be binding in its entirety and directly applicable in all Member States.

Annex I
Minimum Number of Signatories per Member State

Belgium	15 750	Lithuania	8 250
Bulgaria	12 750	Luxembourg	4 500
Czech Republic	15 750	Hungary	15 750
Denmark	9 750	Malta	4 500
Germany	72 000	Netherlands	19 500
Estonia	4 500	Austria	13 500
Ireland	8 250	Poland	38 250
Greece	15 750	Portugal	15 750
Spain	40 500	Romania	24 000
France	55 500	Slovenia	6 000
Croatia	8 250	Slovakia	9 750
Italy	54 750	Finland	9 750
Cyprus	4 500	Sweden	15 000
Latvia	6 000	United Kingdom	54 750

Annex II
Required Information for Registering a Proposed Citizens' Initiative

1. The title of the proposed citizens' initiative, in no more than 100 characters;
2. The subject matter, in no more than 200 characters;
3. A description of the objectives of the proposed citizens' initiative on which the Commission is invited to act, in no more than 500 characters;
4. The provisions of the Treaties considered relevant by the organisers for the proposed action;
5. The full names, postal addresses, nationalities and dates of birth of the seven members of the citizens' committee, indicating specifically the representative and the substitute as well as their e-mail addresses and telephone numbers[10];
6. Documents that prove the full names, postal addresses, nationalities and dates of birth of each of the seven members of the citizens' committee;
7. All sources of support and funding for the proposed citizens' initiative at the time of registration[10].

Organisers may provide more detailed information on the subject, objectives and background to the proposed citizens' initiative in an annex. They may also, if they wish, submit a draft legal act.

[Annexes III-VII not reproduced.]

---

10 Privacy statement: in accordance with Article 11 of Regulation (EC) No 45/2001 of the European Parliament and of the Council of 18 December 2000 on the protection of individuals with regard to the processing of personal data by the Community institutions and bodies and on the free movement of such data, data subjects are informed that these personal data are compiled by the Commission for the purpose of the procedure in respect of the proposed citizens' initiative. Only the full names of the organisers, the e-mail addresses of the contact persons and information relating to the sources of support and funding will be made available to the public in the Commission's online register. Data subjects are entitled to object to the publication of their personal data on compelling legitimate grounds relating to their particular situation, and to request the rectification of that data at any time and its removal from the Commission's online register after the expiry of a period of two years from the date of registration of the proposed citizens' initiative.

Treaty establishing the European Stability Mechanism

Date   2 February 2012
In force   27 September 2012
Link   http://www.efsf.europa.eu/attachments/ESM%20Treaty%20consolidated
        %2003-02-2015.pdf

The Contracting Parties, the Kingdom of Belgium, the Federal Republic of Germany, the Republic of Estonia, Ireland, the Hellenic Republic, the Kingdom of Spain, the French Republic, the Italian Republic, the Republic of Cyprus, the Republic of Latvia, the Republic of Lithuania, the Grand Duchy of Luxembourg, Malta, the Kingdom of the Netherlands, the Republic of Austria, the Portuguese Republic, the Republic of Slovenia, the Slovak Republic and the Republic of Finland (the "euro area Member States" or "ESM Members");
Committed to ensuring the financial stability of the euro area;
Recalling the Conclusions of the European Council adopted on 25 March 2011 on the establishment of a European stability mechanism;

Whereas:
(1) The European Council agreed on 17 December 2010 on the need for euro area Member States to establish a permanent stability mechanism. This European Stability Mechanism ("ESM") will assume the tasks currently fulfilled by the European Financial Stability Facility ("EFSF") and the European Financial Stabilisation Mechanism ("EFSM") in providing, where needed, financial assistance to euro area Member States.
(2) On 25 March 2011, the European Council adopted Decision 2011/199/EU amending Article 136 of the Treaty on the Functioning of the European Union with regard to a stability mechanism for Member States whose currency is the euro[1] adding the following paragraph to Article 136: "The Member States whose currency is the euro may establish a stability mechanism to be activated if indispensable to safeguard the stability of the euro area as a whole. The granting of any required financial assistance under the mechanism will be made subject to strict conditionality".

1   OJ L 91, 6.4.2011, p. 1.
©   European Union, http://eur-lex.europa.eu/, 1998-2015.

(3) With a view to increasing the effectiveness of the financial assistance and to prevent the risk of financial contagion, the Heads of State or Government of the Member States whose currency is the euro agreed on 21 July 2011 to "increase [the] flexibility [of the ESM] linked to appropriate conditionality".

(4) Strict observance of the European Union framework, the integrated macro-economic surveillance, in particular the Stability and Growth Pact, the macroeconomic imbalances framework and the economic governance rules of the European Union, should remain the first line of defence against confidence crises affecting the stability of the euro area.

(5) On 9 December 2011 the Heads of State or Government of the Member States whose currency is the euro agreed to move towards a stronger economic union including a new fiscal compact and strengthened economic policy coordination to be implemented through an international agreement, the Treaty on Stability, Coordination and Governance in the Economic and Monetary Union ("TSCG"). The TSCG will help develop a closer coordination within the euro area with a view to ensuring a lasting, sound and robust management of public finances and thus addresses one of the main sources of financial instability. This Treaty and the TSCG are complementary in fostering fiscal responsibility and solidarity within the economic and monetary union. It is acknowledged and agreed that the granting of financial assistance in the framework of new programmes under the ESM will be conditional, as of 1 March 2013, on the ratification of the TSCG by the ESM Member concerned and, upon expiration of the transposition period referred to in Article 3(2) TSCG on compliance with the requirements of that article.

(6) Given the strong interrelation within the euro area, severe risks to the financial stability of Member States whose currency is the euro may put at risk the financial stability of the euro area as a whole. The ESM may therefore provide stability support on the basis of a strict conditionality, appropriate to the financial assistance instrument chosen if indispensable to safeguard the financial stability of the euro area as a whole and of its Member States. The initial maximum lending volume of the ESM is set at EUR 500 000 million, including the outstanding EFSF stability support. The adequacy of the consolidated ESM and EFSF maximum lending volume will, however, be reassessed prior to the entry into force of this Treaty. If appropriate, it will be increased by the Board of Governors of the ESM, in accordance with Article 10, upon entry into force of this Treaty.

(7) All euro area Member States will become ESM Members. As a consequence of joining the euro area, a Member State of the European Union should become an ESM Member with full rights and obligations, in line with those of the Contracting Parties.

(8) The ESM will cooperate very closely with the International Monetary Fund ("IMF") in providing stability support. The active participation of the IMF will be sought, both at technical and financial level. A euro area Member State requesting financial assistance from the ESM is expected to address, wherever possible, a similar request to the IMF.

(9) Member States of the European Union whose currency is not the euro ("non euro area Member States") participating on an ad hoc basis alongside the ESM in a stability support operation for euro area Member States will be invited to participate, as observers, in the

ESM meetings when this stability support and its monitoring will be discussed. They will have access to all information in a timely manner and be properly consulted.

(10) On 20 June 2011, the representatives of the Governments of the Member States of the European Union authorised the Contracting Parties of this Treaty to request the European Commission and the European Central Bank ("ECB") to perform the tasks provided for in this Treaty.

(11) In its statement of 28 November 2010, the Euro Group stated that standardised and identical Collective Action Clauses ("CACs") will be included, in such a way as to preserve market liquidity, in the terms and conditions of all new euro area government bonds. As requested by the European Council on 25 March 2011, the detailed legal arrangements for including CACs in euro area government securities were finalised by the Economic and Financial Committee.

(12) In accordance with IMF practice, in exceptional cases an adequate and proportionate form of private sector involvement shall be considered in cases where stability support is provided accompanied by conditionality in the form of a macro-economic adjustment programme.

(13) Like the IMF, the ESM will provide stability support to an ESM Member when its regular access to market financing is impaired or is at risk of being impaired. Reflecting this, Heads of State or Government have stated that the ESM loans will enjoy preferred creditor status in a similar fashion to those of the IMF, while accepting preferred creditor status of the IMF over the ESM. This status will be effective as of the date of entry into force of this Treaty. In the event of ESM financial assistance in the form of ESM loans following a European financial assistance programme existing at the time of the signature of this Treaty, the ESM will enjoy the same seniority as all other loans and obligations of the beneficiary ESM Member, with the exception of the IMF loans.

(14) The euro area Member States will support equivalent creditor status of the ESM and that of other States lending bilaterally in coordination with the ESM.

(15) ESM lending conditions for Member States subject to a macroeconomic adjustment programme, including those referred to in Article 40 of this Treaty, shall cover the financing and operating costs of the ESM and should be consistent with the lending conditions of the Financial Assistance Facility Agreements signed between the EFSF, Ireland and the Central Bank of Ireland on the one hand and the EFSF, the Portuguese Republic and Banco de Portugal on the other.

(16) Disputes concerning the interpretation and application of this Treaty arising between the Contracting Parties or between the Contracting Parties and the ESM should be submitted to the jurisdiction of the Court of Justice of the European Union, in accordance with Article 273 of the Treaty on the Functioning of the European Union ("TFEU").

(17) Post-programme surveillance will be carried out by the European Commission and by the Council of the European Union within the framework laid down in Articles 121 and 136 TFEU,

Have agreed as follows:

Chapter 1
Membership and Purpose

Article 1 Establishment and members
1. By this Treaty, the Contracting Parties establish among themselves an international financial institution, to be named the „European Stability Mechanism" ("ESM").
2. The Contracting Parties are ESM Members.

Article 2 New members
1. Membership in the ESM shall be open to the other Member States of the European Union as from the entry into force of the decision of the Council of the European Union taken in accordance with Article 140(2) TFEU to abrogate their derogation from adopting the euro.
2. New ESM Members shall be admitted on the same terms and conditions as existing ESM Members, in accordance with Article 44.
3. A new member acceding to the ESM after its establishment shall receive shares in the ESM in exchange for its capital contribution, calculated in accordance with the contribution key provided for in Article 11.

Article 3 Purpose
The purpose of the ESM shall be to mobilise funding and provide stability support under strict conditionality, appropriate to the financial assistance instrument chosen, to the benefit of ESM Members which are experiencing, or are threatened by, severe financing problems, if indispensable to safeguard the financial stability of the euro area as a whole and of its Member States. For this purpose, the ESM shall be entitled to raise funds by issuing financial instruments or by entering into financial or other agreements or arrangements with ESM Members, financial institutions or other third parties.

Chapter 2
Governance

Article 4 Structure and voting rules
1. The ESM shall have a Board of Governors and a Board of Directors, as well as a Managing Director and other dedicated staff as may be considered necessary.
2. The decisions of the Board of Governors and the Board of Directors shall be taken by mutual agreement, qualified majority or simple majority as specified in this Treaty. In respect of all decisions, a quorum of 2/3 of the members with voting rights representing at least 2/3 of the voting rights must be present.
3. The adoption of a decision by mutual agreement requires the unanimity of the members participating in the vote. Abstentions do not prevent the adoption of a decision by mutual agreement.

4. By way of derogation from paragraph 3, an emergency voting procedure shall be used where the Commission and the ECB both conclude that a failure to urgently adopt a decision to grant or implement financial assistance, as defined in Articles 13 to 18, would threaten the economic and financial sustainability of the euro area. The adoption of a decision by mutual agreement by the Board of Governors referred to in points (f) and (g) of Article 5(6) and the Board of Directors under that emergency procedure requires a qualified majority of 85 % of the votes cast.

Where the emergency procedure referred to in the first subparagraph is used, a transfer from the reserve fund and/or the paid-in capital to an emergency reserve fund is made in order to constitute a dedicated buffer to cover the risks arising from the financial support granted under that emergency procedure. The Board of Governors may decide to cancel the emergency reserve fund and transfer its content back to the reserve fund and/or paid-in capital.

5. The adoption of a decision by qualified majority requires 80 % of the votes cast.
6. The adoption of a decision by simple majority requires a majority of the votes cast.
7. The voting rights of each ESM Member, as exercised by its appointee or by the latter's representative on the Board of Governors or Board of Directors, shall be equal to the number of shares allocated to it in the authorised capital stock of the ESM as set out in Annex II.
8. If any ESM Member fails to pay any part of the amount due in respect of its obligations in relation to paid-in shares or calls of capital under Articles 8, 9 and 10, or in relation to the reimbursement of the financial assistance under Article 16 or 17, such ESM Member shall be unable, for so long as such failure continues, to exercise any of its voting rights. The voting thresholds shall be recalculated accordingly.

Article 5 Board of Governors

1. Each ESM Member shall appoint a Governor and an alternate Governor. Such appointments are revocable at any time. The Governor shall be a member of the government of that ESM Member who has responsibility for finance. The alternate Governor shall have full power to act on behalf of the Governor when the latter is not present.
2. The Board of Governors shall decide either to be chaired by the President of the Euro Group, as referred to in Protocol (No 14) on the Euro Group annexed to the Treaty on the European Union and to the TFEU or to elect a Chairperson and a Vice-Chairperson from among its members for a term of two years. The Chairperson and the Vice-Chairperson may be re-elected. A new election shall be organised without delay if the incumbent no longer holds the function needed for being designated Governor.
3. The Member of the European Commission in charge of economic and monetary affairs and the President of the ECB, as well as the President of the Euro Group (if he or she is not the Chairperson or a Governor) may participate in the meetings of the Board of Governors as observers.
4. Representatives of non-euro area Member States participating on an ad hoc basis alongside the ESM in a stability support operation for a euro area Member State shall also

be invited to participate, as observers, in the meetings of the Board of Governors when this stability support and its monitoring will be discussed.

5. Other persons, including representatives of institutions or organisations, such as the IMF, may be invited by the Board of Governors to attend meetings as observers on an ad hoc basis.

6. The Board of Governors shall take the following decisions by mutual agreement:

(a) to cancel the emergency reserve fund and transfer its content back to the reserve fund and/or paid-in capital, in accordance with Article 4(4);

(b) to issue new shares on terms other than at par, in accordance with Article 8(2);

(c) to make the capital calls, in accordance with Article 9(1);

(d) to change the authorised capital stock and adapt the maximum lending volume of the ESM, in accordance with Article 10(1);

(e) to take into account a possible update of the key for the subscription of the ECB capital, in accordance with Article 11(3), and the changes to be made to Annex I in accordance with Article 11(6);

(f) to provide stability support by the ESM, including the economic policy conditionality as stated in the memorandum of understanding referred to in Article 13(3), and to establish the choice of instruments and the financial terms and conditions, in accordance with Articles 12 to 18;

(g) to give a mandate to the European Commission to negotiate, in liaison with the ECB, the economic policy conditionality attached to each financial assistance, in accordance with Article 13(3);

(h) to change the pricing policy and pricing guideline for financial assistance, in accordance with Article 20;

(i) to change the list of financial assistance instruments that may be used by the ESM, in accordance with Article 19;

(j) to establish the modalities of the transfer of EFSF support to the ESM, in accordance with Article 40;

(k) to approve the application for membership of the ESM by new members, referred to in Article 44;

(l) to make adaptations to this Treaty as a direct consequence of the accession of new members, including changes to be made to the distribution of capital among ESM Members and the calculation of such a distribution as a direct consequence of the accession of a new member to the ESM, in accordance with Article 44; and

(m) to delegate to the Board of Directors the tasks listed in this Article.

7. The Board of Governors shall take the following decisions by qualified majority:

(a) to set out the detailed technical terms of accession of a new member to the ESM, in accordance with Article 44;

(b) whether to be chaired by the President of the Euro Group or to elect, by qualified majority, the Chairperson and Vice-Chairperson of the Board of Governors, in accordance with paragraph 2;

(c) to set out by-laws of the ESM and the rules of procedure applicable to the Board of Governors and Board of Directors (including the right to establish committees and subsidiary bodies), in accordance with paragraph 9;
(d) to determine the list of activities incompatible with the duties of a Director or an alternate Director, in accordance with Article 6(8);
(e) to appoint and to end the term of office of the Managing Director, in accordance with Article 7;
(f) to establish other funds, in accordance with Article 24;
(g) on the actions to be taken for recovering a debt from an ESM Member, in accordance with Article 25(2) and (3);
(h) to approve the annual accounts of the ESM, in accordance with Article 27(1);
(i) to appoint the members of the Board of Auditors, in accordance with Article 30(1);
(j) to approve the external auditors, in accordance with Article 29;
(k) to waive the immunity of the Chairperson of the Board of Governors, a Governor, alternate Governor, Director, alternate Director or the Managing Director, in accordance with Article 35(2);
(l) to determine the taxation regime applicable to the ESM staff, in accordance with Article 36(5);
(m) on a dispute, in accordance with Article 37(2); and
(n) any other necessary decision not explicitly provided for by this Treaty.
8. The Chairperson shall convene and preside over the meetings of the Board of Governors. The Vice-Chairperson shall preside over these meetings when the Chairperson is unable to participate.
9. The Board of Governors shall adopt their rules of procedure and the by-laws of the ESM.

Article 6 Board of Directors

1. Each Governor shall appoint one Director and one alternate Director from among people of high competence in economic and financial matters. Such appointments shall be revocable at any time. The alternate Directors shall have full power to act on behalf of the Director when the latter is not present.
2. The Member of the European Commission in charge of economic and monetary affairs and the President of the ECB may appoint one observer each.
3. Representatives of non-euro area Member States participating on an ad hoc basis alongside the ESM in a financial assistance operation for a euro area Member State shall also be invited to participate, as observers, in the meetings of the Board of Directors when this financial assistance and its monitoring will be discussed.
4. Other persons, including representatives of institutions or organisations, may be invited by the Board of Governors to attend meetings as observers on an ad hoc basis.
5. The Board of Directors shall take decisions by qualified majority, unless otherwise stated in this Treaty. Decisions to be taken on the basis of powers delegated by the Board of Governors shall be adopted in accordance with the relevant voting rules set in Article 5(6) and (7).

6. Without prejudice to the powers of the Board of Governors as set out in Article 5, the Board of Directors shall ensure that the ESM is run in accordance with this Treaty and the by-laws of the ESM adopted by the Board of Governors. It shall take decisions as provided for in this Treaty or which are delegated to it by the Board of Governors.

7. Any vacancy in the Board of Directors shall be immediately filled in accordance with paragraph 1.

8. The Board of Governors shall lay down what activities are incompatible with the duties of a Director or an alternate Director, the by-laws of the ESM and rules of procedure of the Board of Directors.

Article 7 Managing Director

1. The Managing Director shall be appointed by the Board of Governors from among candidates having the nationality of an ESM Member, relevant international experience and a high level of competence in economic and financial matters. Whilst holding office, the Managing Director may not be a Governor or Director or an alternate of either.

2. The term of office of the Managing Director shall be five years. He or she may be re-appointed once. The Managing Director shall, however, cease to hold office when the Board of Governors so decides.

3. The Managing Director shall chair the meetings of the Board of Directors and shall participate in the meetings of the Board of Governors.

4. The Managing Director shall be chief of the staff of the ESM. He or she shall be responsible for organising, appointing and dismissing staff in accordance with staff rules to be adopted by the Board of Directors.

5. The Managing Director shall be the legal representative of the ESM and shall conduct, under the direction of the Board of Directors, the current business of the ESM.

Chapter 3
Capital

Article 8 Authorised capital stock

1. The authorised capital stock shall be EUR 704 798.7 million. It shall be divided into seven million forty-seven thousand nine hundred and eighty-seven shares, having a nominal value of EUR 100 000 each, which shall be available for subscription according to the initial contribution key provided for in Article 11 and calculated in Annex I.

2. The authorised capital stock shall be divided into paid-in shares and callable shares. The initial total aggregate nominal value of paid-in shares shall be EUR 80 000 million. Shares of authorised capital stock initially subscribed shall be issued at par. Other shares shall be issued at par, unless the Board of Governors decides to issue them in special circumstances on other terms.

3. Shares of authorised capital stock shall not be encumbered or pledged in any manner whatsoever and they shall not be transferable, with the exception of transfers for the

purposes of implementing adjustments of the contribution key provided for in Article 11 to the extent necessary to ensure that the distribution of shares corresponds to the adjusted key.

4. ESM Members hereby irrevocably and unconditionally undertake to provide their contribution to the authorised capital stock, in accordance with their contribution key in Annex I. They shall meet all capital calls on a timely basis in accordance with the terms set out in this Treaty.

5. The liability of each ESM Member shall be limited, in all circumstances, to its portion of the authorised capital stock at its issue price. No ESM Member shall be liable, by reason of its membership, for obligations of the ESM. The obligations of ESM Members to contribute to the authorised capital stock in accordance with this Treaty are not affected if any such ESM Member becomes eligible for, or is receiving, financial assistance from the ESM.

Article 9 Capital calls

1. The Board of Governors may call in authorised unpaid capital at any time and set an appropriate period of time for its payment by the ESM Members.

2. The Board of Directors may call in authorised unpaid capital by simple majority decision to restore the level of paid-in capital if the amount of the latter is reduced by the absorption of losses below the level established in Article 8(2), as may be amended by the Board of Governors following the procedure provided for in Article 10, and set an appropriate period of time for its payment by the ESM Members.

3. The Managing Director shall call authorised unpaid capital in a timely manner if needed to avoid the ESM being in default of any scheduled or other payment obligation due to ESM creditors. The Managing Director shall inform the Board of Directors and the Board of Governors of any such call. When a potential shortfall in ESM funds is detected, the Managing Director shall make such capital call(s) as soon as possible with a view to ensuring that the ESM shall have sufficient funds to meet payments due to creditors in full on their due date. ESM Members hereby irrevocably and unconditionally undertake to pay on demand any capital call made on them by the Managing Director pursuant to this paragraph, such demand to be paid within seven days of receipt.

4. The Board of Directors shall adopt the detailed terms and conditions which shall apply to calls on capital pursuant to this Article.

Article 10 Changes in authorised capital stock

1. The Board of Governors shall review regularly and at least every five years the maximum lending volume and the adequacy of the authorised capital stock of the ESM. It may decide to change the authorised capital stock and amend Article 8 and Annex II accordingly. Such decision shall enter into force after the ESM Members have notified the Depositary of the completion of their applicable national procedures. The new shares shall be allocated to the ESM Members according to the contribution key provided for in Article 11 and in Annex I.

2. The Board of Directors shall adopt the detailed terms and conditions which shall apply to all or any capital changes made under paragraph 1.

3. Upon a Member State of the European Union becoming a new ESM Member, the authorised capital stock of the ESM shall be automatically increased by multiplying the respective amounts then prevailing by the ratio, within the adjusted contribution key provided for in Article 11, between the weighting of the new ESM Member and the weighting of the existing ESM Members.

Article 11 Contribution key

1. The contribution key for subscribing to ESM authorised capital stock shall, subject to paragraphs 2 and 3, be based on the key for subscription, by the national central banks of ESM Members, of the ECB's capital pursuant to Article 29 of Protocol (No 4) on the Statute of the European System of Central Banks and of the European Central Bank (the "ESCB Statute") annexed to the Treaty on European Union and to the TFEU.
2. The contribution key for the subscription of the ESM authorised capital stock is specified in Annex I.
3. The contribution key for the subscription of the ESM authorised capital stock shall be adjusted when:

>   (a) a Member State of the European Union becomes a new ESM Member and the ESM's authorised capital stock automatically increases, as specified in Article 10(3); or

>   (b) the twelve year temporary correction applicable to an ESM Member established in accordance with Article 42 ends.

4. The Board of Governors may decide to take into account possible updates to the key for the subscription of the ECB's capital referred to in paragraph 1 when the contribution key is adjusted in accordance with paragraph 3 or when there is a change in the authorised capital stock, as specified in Article 10(1).
5. When the contribution key for the subscription of the ESM authorised capital stock is adjusted, the ESM Members shall transfer among themselves authorised capital stock to the extent necessary to ensure that the distribution of authorised capital stock corresponds to the adjusted key.
6. Annex I shall be amended upon decision by the Board of Governors upon any adjustment referred to in this Article.
7. The Board of Directors shall take all other measures necessary for the application of this Article.

Chapter 4
Operations

Article 12 Principles

1. If indispensable to safeguard the financial stability of the euro area as a whole and of its Member States, the ESM may provide stability support to an ESM Member subject to strict conditionality, appropriate to the financial assistance instrument chosen. Such conditionality may range from a macro-economic adjustment programme to continuous respect of pre-established eligibility conditions.
2. Without prejudice to Article 19, ESM stability support may be granted through the instruments provided for in Articles 14 to 18.
3. Collective action clauses shall be included, as of 1 January 2013, in all new euro area government securities, with maturity above one year, in a way which ensures that their legal impact is identical.

Article 13 Procedure for granting stability support

1. An ESM Member may address a request for stability support to the Chairperson of the Board of Governors. Such a request shall indicate the financial assistance instrument(s) to be considered. On receipt of such a request, the Chairperson of the Board of Governors shall entrust the European Commission, in liaison with the ECB, with the following tasks:

    (a) to assess the existence of a risk to the financial stability of the euro area as a whole or of its Member States, unless the ECB has already submitted an analysis under Article 18(2);

    (b) to assess whether public debt is sustainable. Wherever appropriate and possible, such an assessment is expected to be conducted together with the IMF;

    (c) to assess the actual or potential financing needs of the ESM Member concerned.

2. On the basis of the request of the ESM Member and the assessment referred to in paragraph 1, the Board of Governors may decide to grant, in principle, stability support to the ESM Member concerned in the form of a financial assistance facility.
3. If a decision pursuant to paragraph 2 is adopted, the Board of Governors shall entrust the European Commission – in liaison with the ECB and, wherever possible, together with the IMF – with the task of negotiating, with the ESM Member concerned, a memorandum of understanding (an "MoU") detailing the conditionality attached to the financial assistance facility. The content of the MoU shall reflect the severity of the weaknesses to be addressed and the financial assistance instrument chosen. In parallel, the Managing Director of the ESM shall prepare a proposal for a financial assistance facility agreement, including the financial terms and conditions and the choice of instruments, to be adopted by the Board of Governors.

The MoU shall be fully consistent with the measures of economic policy coordination provided for in the TFEU, in particular with any act of European Union law, including any opinion, warning, recommendation or decision addressed to the ESM Member concerned.

4. The European Commission shall sign the MoU on behalf of the ESM, subject to prior compliance with the conditions set out in paragraph 3 and approval by the Board of Governors.
5. The Board of Directors shall approve the financial assistance facility agreement detailing the financial aspects of the stability support to be granted and, where applicable, the disbursement of the first tranche of the assistance.
6. The ESM shall establish an appropriate warning system to ensure that it receives any repayments due by the ESM Member under the stability support in a timely manner.
7. The European Commission – in liaison with the ECB and, wherever possible, together with the IMF – shall be entrusted with monitoring compliance with the conditionality attached to the financial assistance facility.

Article 14 ESM precautionary financial assistance

1. The Board of Governors may decide to grant precautionary financial assistance in the form of a precautionary conditioned credit line or in the form of an enhanced conditions credit line in accordance with Article 12(1).
2. The conditionality attached to the ESM precautionary financial assistance shall be detailed in the MoU, in accordance with Article 13(3).
3. The financial terms and conditions of the ESM precautionary financial assistance shall be specified in a precautionary financial assistance facility agreement, to be signed by the Managing Director.
4. The Board of Directors shall adopt the detailed guidelines on the modalities for implementing the ESM precautionary financial assistance.
5. The Board of Directors shall decide by mutual agreement on a proposal from the Managing Director and after having received a report from the European Commission in accordance with Article 13(7), whether the credit line should be maintained.
6. After the ESM Member has drawn funds for the first time (via a loan or a primary market purchase), the Board of Directors shall decide by mutual agreement on a proposal from the Managing Director and based on an assessment conducted by the European Commission, in liaison with the ECB, whether the credit line continues to be adequate or whether another form of financial assistance is needed.

Article 15
Financial assistance for the re-capitalisation of financial institutions of an ESM Member

1. The Board of Governors may decide to grant financial assistance through loans to an ESM Member for the specific purpose of re-capitalising the financial institutions of that ESM Member.
2. The conditionality attached to financial assistance for the re-capitalisation of an ESM Member's financial institutions shall be detailed in the MoU, in accordance with Article 13(3).
3. Without prejudice to Articles 107 and 108 TFEU, the financial terms and conditions of financial assistance for the re-capitalisation of an ESM Member's financial institutions shall

be specified in a financial assistance facility agreement, to be signed by the Managing Director.

4. The Board of Directors shall adopt the detailed guidelines on the modalities for implementing financial assistance for the re-capitalisation of an ESM Member's financial institutions.

5. Where applicable, the Board of Directors shall decide by mutual agreement, on a proposal from the Managing Director and after having received a report from the European Commission in accordance with Article 13(7), the disbursement of the tranches of the financial assistance subsequent to the first tranche.

Article 16 ESM loans

1. The Board of Governors may decide to grant financial assistance in the form of a loan to an ESM Member, in accordance with Article 12.

2. The conditionality attached to the ESM loans shall be contained in a macro-economic adjustment programme detailed in the MoU, in accordance with Article 13(3).

3. The financial terms and conditions of each ESM loan shall be specified in a financial assistance facility agreement, to be signed by the Managing Director.

4. The Board of Directors shall adopt the detailed guidelines on the modalities for implementing ESM loans.

5. The Board of Directors shall decide by mutual agreement, on a proposal from the Managing Director and after having received a report from the European Commission in accordance with Article 13(7), the disbursement of the tranches of the financial assistance subsequent to the first tranche.

Article 17 Primary market support facility

1. The Board of Governors may decide to arrange for the purchase of bonds of an ESM Member on the primary market, in accordance with Article 12 and with the objective of maximising the cost efficiency of the financial assistance.

2. The conditionality attached to the primary market support facility shall be detailed in the MoU, in accordance with Article 13(3).

3. The financial terms and conditions under which the bond purchase is conducted shall be specified in a financial assistance facility agreement, to be signed by the Managing Director.

4. The Board of Directors shall adopt the detailed guidelines on the modalities for implementing the primary market support facility.

5. The Board of Directors shall decide by mutual agreement, on a proposal from the Managing Director and after having received a report from the European Commission in accordance with Article 13(7), the disbursement of financial assistance to a beneficiary Member State through operations on the primary market.

Article 18 Secondary market support facility

1. The Board of Governors may decide to arrange for operations on the secondary market in relation to the bonds of an ESM Member in accordance with Article 12(1).
2. Decisions on interventions on the secondary market to address contagion shall be taken on the basis of an analysis of the ECB recognising the existence of exceptional financial market circumstances and risks to financial stability.
3. The conditionality attached to the secondary market support facility shall be detailed in the MoU, in accordance with Article 13(3).
4. The financial terms and conditions under which the secondary market operations are to be conducted shall be specified in a financial assistance facility agreement, to be signed by the Managing Director.
5. The Board of Directors shall adopt the detailed guidelines on the modalities for implementing the secondary market support facility.
6. The Board of Directors shall decide by mutual agreement, on a proposal from the Managing Director, to initiate operations on the secondary market.

Article 19 Review of the list of financial assistance instruments

The Board of Governors may review the list of financial assistance instruments provided for in Articles 14 to 18 and decide to make changes to it.

Article 20 Pricing policy

1. When granting stability support, the ESM shall aim to fully cover its financing and operating costs and shall include an appropriate margin.
2. For all financial assistance instruments, pricing shall be detailed in a pricing guideline, which shall be adopted by the Board of Governors.
3. The pricing policy may be reviewed by the Board of Governors.

Article 21 Borrowing operations

1. The ESM shall be empowered to borrow on the capital markets from banks, financial institutions or other persons or institutions for the performance of its purpose.
2. The modalities of the borrowing operations shall be determined by the Managing Director, in accordance with detailed guidelines to be adopted by the Board of Directors.
3. The ESM shall use appropriate risk management tools, which shall be reviewed regularly by the Board of Directors.

Chapter 5
Financial Management

Article 22 Investment policy
1. The Managing Director shall implement a prudent investment policy for the ESM, so as to ensure its highest creditworthiness, in accordance with guidelines to be adopted and reviewed regularly by the Board of Directors. The ESM shall be entitled to use part of the return on its investment portfolio to cover its operating and administrative costs.
2. The operations of the ESM shall comply with the principles of sound financial and risk management.

Article 23 Dividend policy
1. The Board of Directors may decide, by simple majority, to distribute a dividend to the ESM Members where the amount of paid-in capital and the reserve fund exceed the level required for the ESM to maintain its lending capacity and where proceeds from the investment are not required to avoid a payment shortfall to creditors. Dividends are distributed pro rata to the contributions to the paid-in capital, taking into account the possible acceleration referred to in Article 41(3).
2. As long as the ESM has not provided financial assistance to one of its members, the proceeds from the investment of the ESM paid-in capital shall be returned to the ESM Members according to their respective contributions to the paid-in capital, after deductions for operational costs, provided that the targeted effective lending capacity is fully available.
3. The Managing Director shall implement the dividend policy for the ESM in accordance with guidelines to be adopted by the Board of Directors.

Article 24 Reserve and other funds
1. The Board of Governors shall establish a reserve fund and, where appropriate, other funds.
2. Without prejudice to Article 23, the net income generated by the ESM operations and the proceeds of the financial sanctions received from the ESM Members under the multilateral surveillance procedure, the excessive deficit procedure and the macro-economic imbalances procedure established under the TFEU shall be put aside in a reserve fund.
3. The resources of the reserve fund shall be invested in accordance with guidelines to be adopted by the Board of Directors.
4. The Board of Directors shall adopt such rules as may be required for the establishment, administration and use of other funds.

Article 25 Coverage of losses
1. Losses arising in the ESM operations shall be charged:
   (a) firstly, against the reserve fund;
   (b) secondly, against the paid-in capital; and

(c) lastly, against an appropriate amount of the authorised unpaid capital, which shall be called in accordance with Article 9(3).

2. If an ESM Member fails to meet the required payment under a capital call made pursuant to Article 9(2) or (3), a revised increased capital call shall be made to all ESM Members with a view to ensuring that the ESM receives the total amount of paid-in capital needed. The Board of Governors shall decide an appropriate course of action for ensuring that the ESM Member concerned settles its debt to the ESM within a reasonable period of time. The Board of Governors shall be entitled to require the payment of default interest on the overdue amount.

3. When an ESM Member settles its debt to the ESM, as referred to in paragraph 2, the excess capital shall be returned to the other ESM Members in accordance with rules to be adopted by the Board of Governors.

Article 26 Budget
The Board of Directors shall approve the ESM budget annually.

Article 27 Annual accounts
1. The Board of Governors shall approve the annual accounts of the ESM.
2. The ESM shall publish an annual report containing an audited statement of its accounts and shall circulate to ESM Members a quarterly summary statement of its financial position and a profit and loss statement showing the results of its operations.

Article 28 Internal Audit
An internal audit function shall be established according to international standards.

Article 29 External audit
The accounts of the ESM shall be audited by independent external auditors approved by the Board of Governors and responsible for certifying the annual financial statements. The external auditors shall have full power to examine all books and accounts of the ESM and obtain full information about its transactions.

Article 30 Board of Auditors
1. The Board of Auditors shall consist of five members appointed by the Board of Governors for their competence in auditing and financial matters and shall include two members from the supreme audit institutions of the ESM Members – with a rotation between the latter – and one from the European Court of Auditors.
2. The members of the Board of Auditors shall be independent. They shall neither seek nor take instructions from the ESM governing bodies, the ESM Members or any other public or private body.
3. The Board of Auditors shall draw up independent audits. It shall inspect the ESM accounts and verify that the operational accounts and balance sheet are in order. It shall have full access to any document of the ESM needed for the implementation of its tasks.

4. The Board of Auditors may inform the Board of Directors at any time of its findings. It shall, on an annual basis, draw up a report to be submitted to the Board of Governors.
5. The Board of Governors shall make the annual report accessible to the national parliaments and supreme audit institutions of the ESM Members and to the European Court of Auditors.
6. Any matter relating to this Article shall be detailed in the by-laws of the ESM.

Chapter 6
General Provisions

Article 31 Location
1. The ESM shall have its seat and principal office in Luxembourg.
2. The ESM may establish a liaison office in Brussels.

Article 32 Legal status, privileges and immunities
1. To enable the ESM to fulfil its purpose, the legal status and the privileges and immunities set out in this Article shall be accorded to the ESM in the territory of each ESM Member. The ESM shall endeavour to obtain recognition of its legal status and of its privileges and immunities in other territories in which it performs functions or holds assets.
2. The ESM shall have full legal personality; it shall have full legal capacity to:
    (a) acquire and dispose of movable and immovable property;
    (b) contract;
    (c) be a party to legal proceedings; and
    (d) enter into a headquarter agreement and/or protocols as necessary for ensuring that its legal status and its privileges and immunities are recognised and enforced.
3. The ESM, its property, funding and assets, wherever located and by whomsoever held, shall enjoy immunity from every form of judicial process except to the extent that the ESM expressly waives its immunity for the purpose of any proceedings or by the terms of any contract, including the documentation of the funding instruments.
4. The property, funding and assets of the ESM shall, wherever located and by whomsoever held, be immune from search, requisition, confiscation, expropriation or any other form of seizure, taking or foreclosure by executive, judicial, administrative or legislative action.
5. The archives of the ESM and all documents belonging to the ESM or held by it, shall be inviolable.
6. The premises of the ESM shall be inviolable.
7. The official communications of the ESM shall be accorded by each ESM Member and by each state which has recognised the legal status and the privileges and immunities of the ESM, the same treatment as it accords to the official communications of an ESM Member.
8. To the extent necessary to carry out the activities provided for in this Treaty, all property, funding and assets of the ESM shall be free from restrictions, regulations, controls and moratoria of any nature.

9. The ESM shall be exempted from any requirement to be authorised or licensed as a credit institution, investment services provider or other authorised licensed or regulated entity under the laws of each ESM Member.

Article 33 Staff of the ESM

The Board of Directors shall lay down the conditions of employment of the Managing Director and other staff of the ESM.

Article 34 Professional secrecy

The Members or former Members of the Board of Governors and of the Board of Directors and any other persons who work or have worked for or in connection with the ESM shall not disclose information that is subject to professional secrecy. They shall be required, even after their duties have ceased, not to disclose information of the kind covered by the obligation of professional secrecy.

Article 35 Immunities of persons

1. In the interest of the ESM, the Chairperson of the Board of Governors, Governors, alternate Governors, Directors, alternate Directors, as well as the Managing Director and other staff members shall be immune from legal proceedings with respect to acts performed by them in their official capacity and shall enjoy inviolability in respect of their official papers and documents.
2. The Board of Governors may waive to such extent and upon such conditions as it determines any of the immunities conferred under this Article in respect of the Chairperson of the Board of Governors, a Governor, an alternate Governor, a Director, an alternate Director or the Managing Director.
3. The Managing Director may waive any such immunity in respect of any member of the staff of the ESM other than himself or herself.
4. Each ESM Member shall promptly take the action necessary for the purposes of giving effect to this Article in the terms of its own law and shall inform the ESM accordingly.

Article 36 Exemption from taxation

1. Within the scope of its official activities, the ESM, its assets, income, property and its operations and transactions authorised by this Treaty shall be exempt from all direct taxes.
2. The ESM Members shall, wherever possible, take the appropriate measures to remit or refund the amount of indirect taxes or sales taxes included in the price of movable or immovable property where the ESM makes, for its official use, substantial purchases, the price of which includes taxes of this kind.
3. No exemption shall be granted in respect of taxes and dues which amount merely to charges for public utility services.
4. Goods imported by the ESM and necessary for the exercise of its official activities shall be exempt from all import duties and taxes and from all import prohibitions and restrictions.

5. Staff of the ESM shall be subject to an internal tax for the benefit of the ESM on salaries and emoluments paid by the ESM, subject to rules to be adopted by the Board of Governors. From the date on which this tax is applied, such salaries and emoluments shall be exempt from national income tax.

6. No taxation of any kind shall be levied on any obligation or security issued by the ESM including any interest or dividend thereon by whomsoever held:

(a) which discriminates against such obligation or security solely because of its origin; or

(b) if the sole jurisdictional basis for such taxation is the place or currency in which it is issued, made payable or paid, or the location of any office or place of business maintained by the ESM.

Article 37 Interpretation and dispute settlement

1. Any question of interpretation or application of the provisions of this Treaty and the by-laws of the ESM arising between any ESM Member and the ESM, or between ESM Members, shall be submitted to the Board of Directors for its decision.

2. The Board of Governors shall decide on any dispute arising between an ESM Member and the ESM, or between ESM Members, in connection with the interpretation and application of this Treaty, including any dispute about the compatibility of the decisions adopted by the ESM with this Treaty. The votes of the member(s) of the Board of Governors of the ESM Member(s) concerned shall be suspended when the Board of Governors votes on such decision and the voting threshold needed for the adoption of that decision shall be recalculated accordingly.

3. If an ESM Member contests the decision referred to in paragraph 2, the dispute shall be submitted to the Court of Justice of the European Union. The judgement of the Court of Justice of the European Union shall be binding on the parties in the procedure, which shall take the necessary measures to comply with the judgment within a period to be decided by said Court.

Article 38 International cooperation

The ESM shall be entitled, for the furtherance of its purposes, to cooperate, within the terms of this Treaty, with the IMF, any State which provides financial assistance to an ESM Member on an ad hoc basis and any international organisation or entity having specialised responsibilities in related fields.

Chapter 7
Transitional Arrangements

Article 39 Relation with EFSF lending
During the transitional phase spanning the period from the entry into force of this Treaty until the complete run-down of the EFSF, the consolidated ESM and EFSF lending shall not exceed EUR 500 000 million, without prejudice to the regular review of the adequacy of the maximum lending volume in accordance with Article 10. The Board of Directors shall adopt detailed guidelines on the calculation of the forward commitment capacity to ensure that the consolidated lending ceiling is not breached.

Article 40 Transfer of EFSF supports
1. By way of derogation from Article 13, the Board of Governors may decide that the EFSF commitments to provide financial assistance to an ESM Member under its agreement with that member shall be assumed by the ESM as far as such commitments relate to undisbursed and unfunded parts of loan facilities.
2. The ESM may, if authorised by its Board of Governors, acquire the rights and assume the obligations of the EFSF, in particular in respect of all or part of its outstanding rights and obligations under, and related to, its existing loan facilities.
3. The Board of Governors shall adopt the detailed modalities necessary to give effect to the transfer of the obligations from the EFSF to the ESM, as referred to in paragraph 1 and any transfer of rights and obligations as described in paragraph 2.

Article 41 Payment of the initial capital
1. Without prejudice to paragraph 2, payment of paid-in shares of the amount initially subscribed by each ESM Member shall be made in five annual instalments of 20 % each of the total amount. The first instalment shall be paid by each ESM Member within fifteen days of the date of entry into force of this Treaty. The remaining four instalments shall each be payable on the first, second, third and fourth anniversary of the payment date of the first instalment.
2. During the five-year period of capital payment by instalments, ESM Members shall accelerate the payment of paid-in shares, in a timely manner prior to the issuance date, in order to maintain a minimum 15 % ratio between paid-in capital and the outstanding amount of ESM issuances and guarantee a minimum combined lending capacity of the ESM and of the EFSF of EUR 500 000 million.
3. An ESM Member may decide to accelerate the payment of its share of paid-in capital.

Article 42 Temporary correction of the contribution key
1. At inception, the ESM Members shall subscribe the authorised capital stock on the basis of the initial contribution key as specified in Annex I. The temporary correction included in this initial contribution key shall apply for a period of twelve years after the date of adoption of the euro by the ESM Member concerned.

2. If a new ESM Member's gross domestic product (GDP) per capita at market prices in euro in the year immediately preceding its accession to the ESM is less than 75 % of the European Union average GDP per capita at market prices, then its contribution key for subscribing to ESM authorised capital stock, determined in accordance with Article 10, shall benefit from a temporary correction and equal the sum of:
   (a) 25 % of the percentage share in the ECB capital of the national central bank of that ESM Member, determined in accordance with Article 29 of the ESCB Statute; and
   (b) 75 % of that ESM Member's percentage share in the gross national income (GNI) at market prices in euro of the euro area in the year immediately preceding its accession to the ESM.
The percentages referred to in points (a) and (b) shall be rounded up or down to the nearest multiple of 0,0001 percentage points. The statistical terms shall be those published by Eurostat.
3. The temporary correction referred to in paragraph 2 shall apply for a period of twelve years from the date of adoption of the euro by the ESM Member concerned.
4. As a result of the temporary correction of the key, the relevant proportion of shares allocated to an ESM Member pursuant to paragraph 2 shall be reallocated amongst the ESM Members not benefiting from a temporary correction on the basis of their shareholding in the ECB, determined in accordance with Article 29 of the ESCB Statute, subsisting immediately prior to the issue of shares to the acceding ESM Member.

Article 43 First appointments
1. Each ESM Member shall designate its Governor and alternate Governor within the two weeks of the entry into force of this Treaty.
2. The Board of Governors shall appoint the Managing Director and each Governor shall appoint a Director and an alternate Director within the two months of the entry into force of this Treaty.

Chapter 8
Final Provisions

Article 44 Accession
This Treaty shall be open for accession by other Member States of the European Union in accordance with Article 2 upon application for membership that any such Member State of the European Union shall file with the ESM after the adoption by the Council of the European Union of the decision to abrogate its derogation from adopting the euro in accordance with Article 140(2) TFEU. The Board of Governors shall approve the application for accession of the new ESM Member and the detailed technical terms related thereto, as well as the adaptations to be made to this Treaty as a direct consequence of the accession. Following the approval of the application for membership by the Board of Governors, new ESM Members shall accede upon the deposit of the instruments of accession with the Depositary, who shall notify other ESM Members thereof.

Article 45 Annexes
The following Annexes to this Treaty shall constitute an integral part thereof:
1) Annex I: Contribution key of the ESM; and
2) Annex II: Subscriptions to the authorised capital stock.

Article 46 Deposit
This Treaty shall be deposited with the General Secretariat of the Council of the European Union ("the Depositary"), which shall communicate certified copies to all the signatories.

Article 47 Ratification, approval or acceptance
1. This Treaty shall be subject to ratification, approval or acceptance by the signatories. Instruments of ratification, approval or acceptance shall be deposited with the Depositary.
2. The Depositary shall notify the other signatories of each deposit and the date thereof.

Article 48 Entry into force
1. This Treaty shall enter into force on the date when instruments of ratification, approval or acceptance have been deposited by signatories whose initial subscriptions represent no less than 90 % of the total subscriptions set forth in Annex II. Where appropriate, the list of ESM Members shall be adjusted; the key in Annex I shall then be recalculated and the total authorised capital stock in Article 8(1) and Annex II and the initial total aggregated nominal value of paid-in shares in Article 8(2) shall be reduced accordingly.
2. For each signatory which thereafter deposits its instrument of ratification, approval or acceptance, this Treaty shall enter into force on the day following the date of deposit.
3. For each State which accedes to this Treaty in accordance with Article 44, this Treaty shall enter into force on the twentieth day following the deposit of its instrument of accession.

Done at Brussels on the second day of February in the year two thousand and twelve in a single original, whose Dutch, English, Estonian, Finnish, French, German, Greek, Irish, Italian, Maltese, Portuguese, Slovak, Slovenian, Spanish and Swedish texts are equally authentic, which shall be deposited in the archives of the Depositary which shall transmit a duly certified copy to each of the Contracting Parties.

Upon accession of the Republic of Latvia, the Latvian text shall be equally authentic, which shall be deposited in the archives of the Depositary which shall transmit a duly certified copy to each of the Contracting Parties.

Upon accession of the Republic of Lithuania, the Lithuanian text shall be equally authentic, which shall be deposited in the archives of the Depositary which shall transmit a duly certified copy to each of the Contracting Parties.

Annex I
Contribution Key of the ESM

ESM Member	ESM key (%)
Kingdom of Belgium	3.4534
Federal Republic of Germany	26.9616
Republic of Estonia	0.1847
Ireland	1.5814
Hellenic Republic	2.7975
Kingdom of Spain	11.8227
French Republic	20.2471
Italian Republic	17.7917
Republic of Cyprus	0.1949
Republic of Latvia	0.2746
Republic of Lithuania	0.4063
Grand Duchy of Luxembourg	0.2487
Malta	0.0726
Kingdom of the Netherlands	5.6781
Republic of Austria	2.7644
Portuguese Republic	2.4921
Republic of Slovenia	0.4247
Slovak Republic	0.8184
Republic of Finland	1.7852
Total	**100,0**

The above figures are rounded to four decimals.

Annex II
Subscriptions to the authorised capital stock

ESM Member	Number of shares	Capital subscription (EUR)
Kingdom of Belgium	243 397	24 339 700 000
Federal Republic of Germany	1 900 248	190 024 800 000
Republic of Estonia	13 020	1 302 000 000
Ireland	111 454	11 145 400 000
Hellenic Republic	197 169	19 716 900 000
Kingdom of Spain	833 259	83 325 900 000
French Republic	1 427 013	142 701 300 000
Italian Republic	1 253 959	125 395 900 000
Republic of Cyprus	13 734	1 373 400 000
Republic of Latvia	19 353	1 935 300 000
Republic of Lithuania	28 634	2 863 400 000
Grand Duchy of Luxembourg	17 528	1 752 800 000
Malta	5 117	511 700 000
Kingdom of the Netherlands	400 190	40 019 000 000
Republic of Austria	194 838	19 483 800 000
Portuguese Republic	175 644	17 564 400 000
Republic of Slovenia	29 932	2 993 200 000
Slovak Republic	57 680	5 768 000 000
Republic of Finland	125 818	12 581 800 000
Total	**7 047 987**	**704 798 700 000**

Treaty on Stability, Coordination and Governance in the Economic and Monetary Union

Date 2 March 2012
In force 1 January 2013
Link http://www.eurozone.europa.eu/media/304649/st00tscg26_en12.pdf

The Kingdom of Belgium, the Republic of Bulgaria, the Kingdom of Denmark, the Federal Republic Germany, the Republic of Estonia, Ireland, the Hellenic Republic, the Kingdom of Spain, the French Republic, the Italian Republic, the Republic of Cyprus, the Republic of Latvia, the Republic of Lithuania, the Grand Duchy of Luxembourg, Hungary, Malta, the Kingdom of the Netherlands, the Republic of Austria, the Republic of Poland, the Portuguese Republic, Romania, the Republic of Slovenia, the Slovak Republic, the Republic of Finland and the Kingdom of Sweden,
hereinafter referred to as "the Contracting Parties";
Conscious of their obligation, as Member States of the European Union, to regard their economic policies as a matter of common concern;
Desiring to promote conditions for stronger economic growth in the European Union and, to that end, to develop ever-closer coordination of economic policies within the euro area;
Bearing in mind that the need for governments to maintain sound and sustainable public finances and to prevent a general government deficit becoming excessive is of essential importance to safeguard the stability of the euro area as a whole, and accordingly, requires the introduction of specific rules, including a "balanced budget rule" and an automatic mechanism to take corrective action;

© European Union, http://eur-lex.europa.eu/, 1998-2015.

Conscious of the need to ensure that their general government deficit does not exceed 3 % of their gross domestic product at market prices and that their general government debt does not exceed, or is sufficiently declining towards, 60 % of their gross domestic product at market prices;

Recalling that the Contracting Parties, as Member States of the European Union, are to refrain from any measure which could jeopardise the attainment of the Union's objectives in the framework of the economic union, particularly the practice of accumulating debt outside the general government accounts;

Bearing in mind that the Heads of State or Government of the euro area Member States agreed on 9 December 2011 on a reinforced architecture for economic and monetary union, building upon the Treaties on which the European Union is founded and facilitating the implementation of measures taken on the basis of Articles 121, 126 and 136 of the Treaty on the Functioning of the European Union;

Bearing in mind that the objective of the Heads of State or Government of the euro area Member States and of other Member States of the European Union is to incorporate the provisions of this Treaty as soon as possible into the Treaties on which the European Union is founded;

Welcoming the legislative proposals made by the European Commission for the euro area, within the framework of the Treaties on which the European Union is founded, on 23 November 2011, on the strengthening of economic and budgetary surveillance of Member States experiencing or threatened with serious difficulties with respect to their financial stability, and on common provisions for monitoring and assessing draft budgetary plans and ensuring the correction of excessive deficit of the Member States, and **taking note** of the European Commission's intention to present further legislative proposals for the euro area concerning, in particular, ex ante reporting of debt issuance plans, economic partnership programmes detailing structural reforms for Member States under an excessive deficit procedure as well as the coordination of major economic policy reform plans of Member States;

Expressing their readiness to support proposals which the European Commission might present to further strengthen the Stability and Growth Pact by introducing, for Member States whose currency is the euro, a new range for medium-term objectives in line with the limits established in this Treaty;

Taking note that, when reviewing and monitoring the budgetary commitments under this Treaty, the European Commission will act within the framework of its powers, as provided by the Treaty on the Functioning of the European Union, in particular Articles 121, 126 and 136 thereof;

Noting in particular that, in respect of the application of the "balanced budget rule" set out in Article 3 of this Treaty, that monitoring will be carried out through the setting up, for each Contracting Party, of country-specific medium-term objectives and of calendars of convergence, as appropriate;

Noting that the medium-term objectives should be updated regularly on the basis of a commonly agreed method, the main parameters of which are also to be reviewed regularly, reflecting appropriately the risks of explicit and implicit liabilities for public finance, as embodied in the aims of the Stability and Growth Pact;

Noting that sufficient progress towards the medium-term objectives should be evaluated on the basis of an overall assessment with the structural balance as a reference, including an analysis of expenditure net of discretionary revenue measures, in line with the provisions specified under European Union law, in particular Council Regulation (EC) No 1466/97 of 7 July 1997 on the strengthening of the surveillance of budgetary positions and the surveillance and coordination of economic policies, as amended by Regulation (EU) No 1175/2011 of the European Parliament and of the Council of 16 November 2011 ("the revised Stability and Growth Pact");

Noting that the correction mechanism to be introduced by the Contracting Parties should aim at correcting deviations from the medium-term objective or the adjustment path, including their cumulated impact on government debt dynamics;

Noting that compliance with the Contracting Parties' obligation to transpose the "balanced budget rule" into their national legal systems, through binding, permanent and preferably constitutional provisions, should be subject to the jurisdiction of the Court of Justice of the European Union, in accordance with Article 273 of the Treaty on the Functioning of the European Union;

Recalling that Article 260 of the Treaty on the Functioning of the European Union empowers the Court of Justice of the European Union to impose a lump sum or penalty payment on a Member State of the European Union which has failed to comply with one of its judgments and

Recalling that the European Commission has established criteria for determining the lump sum or penalty payment to be imposed in the framework of that Article;

Recalling the need to facilitate the adoption of measures under the excessive deficit procedure of the European Union in respect of Member States whose currency is the euro and whose planned or actual ratio of general government deficit to gross domestic product exceeds 3 %, whilst strongly reinforcing the objective of that procedure, namely to encourage and, if necessary, compel a Member State to reduce a deficit which might be identified;

Recalling the obligation for those Contracting Parties whose general government debt exceeds the 60 % reference value to reduce it at an average rate of one twentieth per year as a benchmark;

Bearing in mind the need to respect, in the implementation of this Treaty, the specific role of the social partners, as it is recognised in the laws or national systems of each of the Contracting Parties;

Stressing that no provision of this Treaty is to be interpreted as altering in any way the economic policy conditions under which financial assistance has been granted to a Contracting Party in a stabilisation programme involving the European Union, its Member States or the International Monetary Fund;

Noting that the proper functioning of the economic and monetary union requires the Contracting Parties to work jointly towards an economic policy where, whilst building upon the mechanisms of economic policy coordination, as defined in the Treaties on which the

European Union is founded, they take the necessary actions and measures in all the areas which are essential to the proper functioning of the euro area;

Noting, in particular, the wish of the Contracting Parties to make a more active use of enhanced cooperation, as provided for in Article 20 of the Treaty on European Union and Articles 326 to 334 of the Treaty on the Functioning of the European Union, without undermining the internal market, and their wish to have full recourse to measures specific to the Member States whose currency is the euro pursuant to Article 136 of the Treaty on the Functioning of the European Union, and to a procedure for the ex ante discussion and coordination among the Contracting Parties whose currency is the euro of all major economic policy reforms planned by them, with a view to benchmarking best practices;

Recalling the agreement of the Heads of State or Government of the euro area Member States, of 26 October 2011, to improve the governance of the euro area, including the holding of at least two Euro Summit meetings per year, to be convened, unless justified by exceptional circumstances, immediately after meetings of the European Council or meetings with the participation of all Contracting Parties having ratified this Treaty;

Recalling also the endorsement by the Heads of State or Government of the euro area Member States and of other Member States of the European Union, on 25 March 2011, of the Euro Plus Pact, which identifies the issues that are essential to fostering competitiveness in the euro area;

Stressing the importance of the Treaty establishing the European Stability Mechanism as an element of the global strategy to strengthen the economic and monetary union and pointing out that the granting of financial assistance in the framework of new programmes under the European Stability Mechanism will be conditional, as of 1 March 2013, on the ratification of this Treaty by the Contracting Party concerned and, as soon as the transposition period referred to in Article 3(2) of this Treaty has expired, on compliance with the requirements of that Article;

Noting that the Kingdom of Belgium, the Federal Republic of Germany, the Republic of Estonia, Ireland, the Hellenic Republic, the Kingdom of Spain, the French Republic, the Italian Republic, the Republic of Cyprus, the Grand Duchy of Luxembourg, Malta, the Kingdom of the Netherlands, the Republic of Austria, the Portuguese Republic, the Republic of Slovenia, the Slovak Republic and the Republic of Finland are Contracting Parties whose currency is the euro and that, as such, they will be bound by this Treaty from the first day of the month following the deposit of their instrument of ratification if the Treaty is in force at that date; Noting also that the Republic of Bulgaria, the Kingdom of Denmark, the Republic of Latvia, the Republic of Lithuania, Hungary, the Republic of Poland, Romania and the Kingdom of Sweden are Contracting Parties which, as Member States of the European Union, have, at the date of signature of this Treaty, a derogation or an exemption from participation in the single currency and may be bound, as long as such derogation or exemption is not abrogated, only by those provisions of Titles III and IV of this Treaty by which they declare, on depositing their instrument of ratification or at a later date, that they intend to be bound;

Have agreed upon the following provisions:

Title I
Purpose and Scope

Article 1
1. By this Treaty, the Contracting Parties agree, as Member States of the European Union, to strengthen the economic pillar of the economic and monetary union by adopting a set of rules intended to foster budgetary discipline through a fiscal compact, to strengthen the coordination of their economic policies and to improve the governance of the euro area, thereby supporting the achievement of the European Union's objectives for sustainable growth, employment, competitiveness and social cohesion.
2. This Treaty shall apply in full to the Contracting Parties whose currency is the euro. It shall also apply to the other Contracting Parties to the extent and under the conditions set out in Article 14.

Title II
Consistency and relationship with the law of the Union

Article 2
1. This Treaty shall be applied and interpreted by the Contracting Parties in conformity with the Treaties on which the European Union is founded, in particular Article 4(3) of the Treaty on European Union, and with European Union law, including procedural law whenever the adoption of secondary legislation is required.
2. This Treaty shall apply insofar as it is compatible with the Treaties on which the European Union is founded and with European Union law. It shall not encroach upon the competence of the Union to act in the area of the economic union.

Title III
Fiscal Compact

Article 3
1. The Contracting Parties shall apply the rules set out in this paragraph in addition and without prejudice to their obligations under European Union law:
  (a) the budgetary position of the general government of a Contracting Party shall be balanced or in surplus;
  (b) the rule under point (a) shall be deemed to be respected if the annual structural balance of the general government is at its country-specific medium-term objective, as defined in the revised Stability and Growth Pact, with a lower limit of a structural deficit of 0,5 % of the gross domestic product at market prices. The Contracting Parties shall ensure rapid convergence towards their respective medium-term objective. The time-frame for such convergence will be proposed by the European Commission taking into

consideration country-specific sustainability risks. Progress towards, and respect of, the medium-term objective shall be evaluated on the basis of an overall assessment with the structural balance as a reference, including an analysis of expenditure net of discretionary revenue measures, in line with the revised Stability and Growth Pact;

(c) the Contracting Parties may temporarily deviate from their respective medium-term objective or the adjustment path towards it only in exceptional circumstances, as defined in point (b) of paragraph 3;

(d) where the ratio of the general government debt to gross domestic product at market prices is significantly below 60 % and where risks in terms of long-term sustainability of public finances are low, the lower limit of the medium-term objective specified under point (b) can reach a structural deficit of at most 1,0 % of the gross domestic product at market prices;

(e) in the event of significant observed deviations from the medium-term objective or the adjustment path towards it, a correction mechanism shall be triggered automatically. The mechanism shall include the obligation of the Contracting Party concerned to implement measures to correct the deviations over a defined period of time.

2. The rules set out in paragraph 1 shall take effect in the national law of the Contracting Parties at the latest one year after the entry into force of this Treaty through provisions of binding force and permanent character, preferably constitutional, or otherwise guaranteed to be fully respected and adhered to throughout the national budgetary processes. The Contracting Parties shall put in place at national level the correction mechanism referred to in paragraph 1(e) on the basis of common principles to be proposed by the European Commission, concerning in particular the nature, size and time-frame of the corrective action to be undertaken, also in the case of exceptional circumstances, and the role and independence of the institutions responsible at national level for monitoring compliance with the rules set out in paragraph 1. Such correction mechanism shall fully respect the prerogatives of national Parliaments.

3. For the purposes of this Article, the definitions set out in Article 2 of the Protocol (No 12) on the excessive deficit procedure, annexed to the European Union Treaties, shall apply.

The following definitions shall also apply for the purposes of this Article:

(a) "annual structural balance of the general government" refers to the annual cyclically-adjusted balance net of one-off and temporary measures;

(b) "exceptional circumstances" refers to the case of an unusual event outside the control of the Contracting Party concerned which has a major impact on the financial position of the general government or to periods of severe economic downturn as set out in the revised Stability and Growth Pact, provided that the temporary deviation of the Contracting Party concerned does not endanger fiscal sustainability in the medium-term.

Article 4

When the ratio of a Contracting Party's general government debt to gross domestic product exceeds the 60 % reference value referred to in Article 1 of the Protocol (No 12) on the excessive deficit procedure, annexed to the European Union Treaties, that Contracting Party shall reduce it at an average rate of one twentieth per year as a benchmark, as provided for in Article 2 of Council Regulation (EC) No 1467/97 of 7 July 1997 on speeding up and clarifying the implementation of the excessive deficit procedure, as amended by Council Regulation (EU) No 1177/2011 of 8 November 2011. The existence of an excessive deficit due to the breach of the debt criterion will be decided in accordance with the procedure set out in Article 126 of the Treaty on the Functioning of the European Union.

Article 5
1. A Contracting Party that is subject to an excessive deficit procedure under the Treaties on which the European Union is founded shall put in place a budgetary and economic partnership programme including a detailed description of the structural reforms which must be put in place and implemented to ensure an effective and durable correction of its excessive deficit. The content and format of such programmes shall be defined in European Union law. Their submission to the Council of the European Union and to the European Commission for endorsement and their monitoring will take place within the context of the existing surveillance procedures under the Stability and Growth Pact.
2. The implementation of the budgetary and economic partnership programme, and the yearly budgetary plans consistent with it, will be monitored by the Council of the European Union and by the European Commission.

Article 6
With a view to better coordinating the planning of their national debt issuance, the Contracting Parties shall report ex-ante on their public debt issuance plans to the Council of the European Union and to the European Commission.

Article 7
While fully respecting the procedural requirements of the Treaties on which the European Union is founded, the Contracting Parties whose currency is the euro commit to supporting the proposals or recommendations submitted by the European Commission where it considers that a Member State of the European Union whose currency is the euro is in breach of the deficit criterion in the framework of an excessive deficit procedure. This obligation shall not apply where it is established among the Contracting Parties whose currency is the euro that a qualified majority of them, calculated by analogy with the relevant provisions of the Treaties on which the European Union is founded, without taking into account the position of the Contracting Party concerned, is opposed to the decision proposed or recommended.

Article 8
1. The European Commission is invited to present in due time to the Contracting Parties a report on the provisions adopted by each of them in compliance with Article 3(2). If the European Commission, after having given the Contracting Party concerned the opportunity

to submit its observations, concludes in its report that such Contracting Party has failed to comply with Article 3(2), the matter will be brought to the Court of Justice of the European Union by one or more Contracting Parties. Where a Contracting Party considers, independently of the Commission's report, that another Contracting Party has failed to comply with Article 3(2), it may also bring the matter to the Court of Justice. In both cases, the judgment of the Court of Justice shall be binding on the parties to the proceedings, which shall take the necessary measures to comply with the judgment within a period to be decided by the Court of Justice.

2. Where, on the basis of its own assessment or that of the European Commission, a Contracting Party considers that another Contracting Party has not taken the necessary measures to comply with the judgment of the Court of Justice referred to in paragraph 1, it may bring the case before the Court of Justice and request the imposition of financial sanctions following criteria established by the European Commission in the framework of Article 260 of the Treaty on the Functioning of the European Union. If the Court of Justice finds that the Contracting Party concerned has not complied with its judgment, it may impose on it a lump sum or a penalty payment appropriate in the circumstances and that shall not exceed 0,1 % of its gross domestic product. The amounts imposed on a Contracting Party whose currency is the euro shall be payable to the European Stability Mechanism. In other cases, payments shall be made to the general budget of the European Union.

3. This Article constitutes a special agreement between the Contracting Parties within the meaning of Article 273 of the Treaty on the Functioning of the European Union.

Title IV
Economic policy coordination and convergence

Article 9
Building upon economic policy coordination, as defined in the Treaty on the Functioning of the European Union, the Contracting Parties undertake to work jointly towards an economic policy that fosters the proper functioning of the economic and monetary union and economic growth through enhanced convergence and competitiveness. To that end, the Contracting Parties shall take the necessary actions and measures in all the areas which are essential to the proper functioning of the euro area in pursuit of the objectives of fostering competitiveness, promoting employment, contributing further to the sustainability of public finances and reinforcing financial stability.

Article 10
In accordance with the requirements of the Treaties on which the European Union is founded, the Contracting Parties stand ready to make active use, whenever appropriate and necessary, of measures specific to those Member States whose currency is the euro, as provided for in Article 136 of the Treaty on the Functioning of the European Union, and of enhanced cooperation, as provided for in Article 20 of the Treaty on European Union and

in Articles 326 to 334 of the Treaty on the Functioning of the European Union on matters that are essential for the proper functioning of the euro area, without undermining the internal market.

Article 11
With a view to benchmarking best practices and working towards a more closely coordinated economic policy, the Contracting Parties ensure that all major economic policy reforms that they plan to undertake will be discussed ex-ante and, where appropriate, coordinated among themselves. Such coordination shall involve the institutions of the European Union as required by European Union law.

Title V
Governance of the Euro Area

Article 12
1. The Heads of State or Government of the Contracting Parties whose currency is the euro shall meet informally in Euro Summit meetings, together with the President of the European Commission. The President of the European Central Bank shall be invited to take part in such meetings.
The President of the Euro Summit shall be appointed by the Heads of State or Government of the Contracting Parties whose currency is the euro by simple majority at the same time as the European Council elects its President and for the same term of office.
2. Euro Summit meetings shall take place when necessary, and at least twice a year, to discuss questions relating to the specific responsibilities which the Contracting Parties whose currency is the euro share with regard to the single currency, other issues concerning the governance of the euro area and the rules that apply to it, and strategic orientations for the conduct of economic policies to increase convergence in the euro area.
3. The Heads of State or Government of the Contracting Parties other than those whose currency is the euro, which have ratified this Treaty, shall participate in discussions of Euro Summit meetings concerning competitiveness for the Contracting Parties, the modification of the global architecture of the euro area and the fundamental rules that will apply to it in the future, as well as, when appropriate and at least once a year, in discussions on specific issues of implementation of this Treaty on Stability, Coordination and Governance in the Economic and Monetary Union.
4. The President of the Euro Summit shall ensure the preparation and continuity of Euro Summit meetings, in close cooperation with the President of the European Commission. The body charged with the preparation of and follow up to the Euro Summit meetings shall be the Euro Group and its President may be invited to attend such meetings for that purpose.
5. The President of the European Parliament may be invited to be heard. The President of the Euro Summit shall present a report to the European Parliament after each Euro Summit meeting.

6. The President of the Euro Summit shall keep the Contracting Parties other than those whose currency is the euro and the other Member States of the European Union closely informed of the preparation and outcome of the Euro Summit meetings.

Article 13
As provided for in Title II of Protocol (No 1) on the role of national Parliaments in the European Union annexed to the European Union Treaties, the European Parliament and the national Parliaments of the Contracting Parties will together determine the organisation and promotion of a conference of representatives of the relevant committees of the European Parliament and representatives of the relevant committees of national Parliaments in order to discuss budgetary policies and other issues covered by this Treaty.

Title VI
General and final provisions

Article 14
1. This Treaty shall be ratified by the Contracting Parties in accordance with their respective constitutional requirements. The instruments of ratification shall be deposited with the General Secretariat of the Council of the European Union ("the Depositary").
2. This Treaty shall enter into force on 1 January 2013, provided that twelve Contracting Parties whose currency is the euro have deposited their instrument of ratification, or on the first day of the month following the deposit of the twelfth instrument of ratification by a Contracting Party whose currency is the euro, whichever is the earlier.
3. This Treaty shall apply as from the date of entry into force amongst the Contracting Parties whose currency is the euro which have ratified it. It shall apply to the other Contracting Parties whose currency is the euro as from the first day of the month following the deposit of their respective instrument of ratification.
4. By derogation from paragraphs 3 and 5, Title V shall apply to all Contracting Parties concerned as from the date of entry into force of this Treaty.
5. This Treaty shall apply to the Contracting Parties with a derogation, as defined in Article 139(1) of the Treaty on the Functioning of the European Union, or with an exemption, as referred to in Protocol (No 16) on certain provisions related to Denmark annexed to the European Union Treaties, which have ratified this Treaty, as from the date when the decision abrogating that derogation or exemption takes effect, unless the Contracting Party concerned declares its intention to be bound at an earlier date by all or part of the provisions in Titles III and IV of this Treaty.

Article 15
This Treaty shall be open to accession by Member States of the European Union other than the Contracting Parties. Accession shall be effective upon depositing the instrument of accession with the Depositary, which shall notify the other Contracting Parties thereof.

Following authentication by the Contracting Parties, the text of this Treaty in the official language of the acceding Member State that is also an official language and a working language of the institutions of the Union, shall be deposited in the archives of the Depositary as an authentic text of this Treaty.

Article 16
Within five years, at most, of the date of entry into force of this Treaty, on the basis of an assessment of the experience with its implementation, the necessary steps shall be taken, in accordance with the Treaty on the European Union and the Treaty on the Functioning of the European Union, with the aim of incorporating the substance of this Treaty into the legal framework of the European Union.

Done at Brussels this second day of March in the year two thousand and twelve.

This Treaty, drawn up in a single original in the Bulgarian, Danish, Dutch, English, Estonian, Finnish, French, German, Greek, Hungarian, Irish, Italian, Latvian, Lithuanian, Maltese, Polish, Portuguese, Romanian, Slovak, Slovenian, Spanish and Swedish languages, each text being equally authentic, shall be deposited in the archives of the Depositary, which shall transmit a certified copy to each of the Contracting Parties.

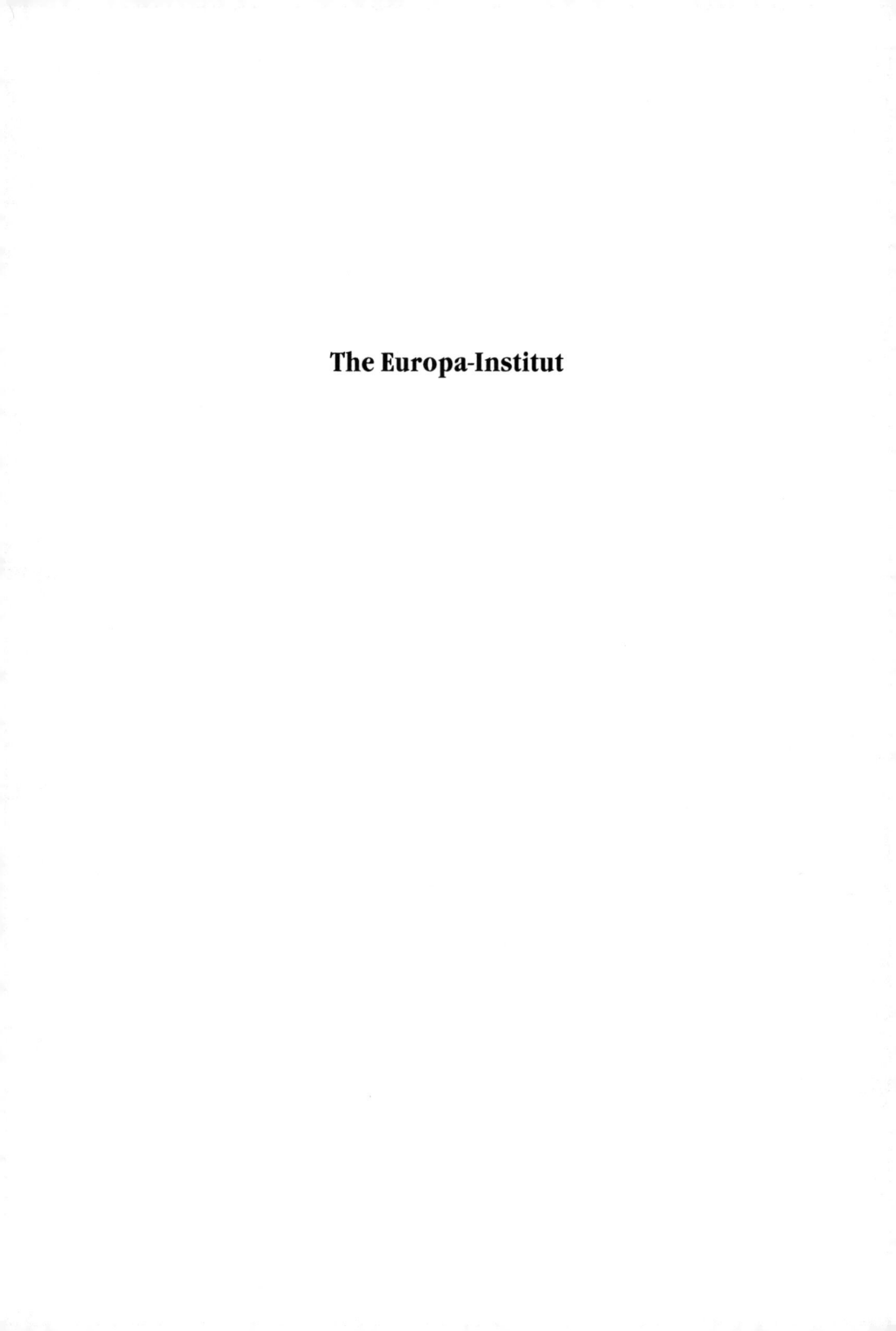

The Europa-Institut

LL.M. at the Europa-Institut

We invite you to apply for our one-year Master's program "European and International Law", awarding the title Master of Laws (LL.M.) to its successful participants. The postgraduate study program focuses on European and International Law. There are five modules – Module 1 European Integration and Modules 2 to 5 with the Study Units European Economic Law, Foreign Trade and Investment, International Dispute Resolution and European Protection of Human Rights.

We are looking forward to meeting and greeting 75 students from all over the world, ready to start studying in an exceptional and interesting international atmosphere, each academic year. The mixture of nationalities allows for a polyglot and a unique cross-cultural environment.

We offer highly qualified lecturers who prepare our students for the specific demands of the European and international job market. In addition to professors teaching at Saarland University, the Europa-Institut hosts international guest professors and lecturers. Amongst them are top EU civil servants from the Commission, the Council, the European Parliament and the European Courts as well as inspiring personalities holding top positions in the judiciary sector, the business world as well as in the administrative and political sector.

We enable you to complete the Master's program entirely in English, entirely in German or in a combination of these. The Master's program consists of a unique mixture of lectures, seminars, interactive exercises, moot courts, language courses, communication skills training and discussions, and allows us to offer an optimal combination of theoretic knowledge and practical application.

We make sure that we support our students in all matters, not only within the frame of the academic program, but also in the organization of their daily life in Saarbrücken. Dedicated and experienced staff members provide specialized study advice as well as counseling and guidance with regard to the visa application process and later on with matters such as finding an accommodation, health insurance, matriculation, fees and financing.

Last but not least regular excursions to various European institutions form a natural and important part of the study program. Our widely ramified network – established in cooperation with our alumni organization EVER e.V. – enables students to interact directly with the "makers" of Europe.

Admission requirements

University degree: The most important requirement for admission is a university degree in law or a comparable subject from a German or foreign university and proof of sound knowledge of German and/or English.

Terms of admission: The program starts each winter term. Deadline for applications each year is 15 July. Optional deadline for applicants having obtained their university degree by spring is 1 April. Late applications are accepted until 30 September. The number of available places is limited. Candidates are selected on the basis of academic record and grade average, plus criteria applied to their specialized field of study and suitability according thereto.

Tuition fees: The Europa-Institut charges fees with the sole aim of covering costs. The amount is in line with the official schedule of fees for postgraduate study programs issued by Saarland University. The current fee is stated on the application form. Additionally, an administrative fee is payable to Saarland University each semester. Costs for accommodation and food are not included in those fees.

Grants: The Europa-Institut itself does not award grants. Numerous institutions offer grants to students. Further information can be obtained on our website.

Further information and application forms: www.europainstitut.de/application

Contact
Saarland University
Europa-Institut, Law Department
Head of Program
P.O. Box 15 11 50
D-66041 Saarbrücken

Telephone: + 49 (0)681 302 3653
Fax: + 49 (0)681 302 4369
E-mail: LLM@europainstitut.de

Brussels office:
Europa-Institut
Boulevard Louis Schmidt 26
B-1040 Brussels

Telephone: +32 (0)2 234 1168

EVER e.V.
The Alumni Association of the Europa-Institut

One goal of EVER, the alumni association of the Europa-Institut (Law Department), is to increase and intensify the contact with former students of the postgraduate program at the Europa-Institut of Saarland University. Numerous activities foster the development of an extensive network of graduates of the Institute and thereby enable mutual exchange after graduation among alumni, but also between current students and alumni.

EVER was founded in 1996 by 15 current and former students of the Europa-Institut and has been an incorporated association since 2002. The association can show a continuously increasing number of members: today, we count more than 650 members, approximately half of them living in Germany, the other half living abroad, within and outside European borders, from Argentina to Greece, Japan, and New Zealand, from Romania, Russia, Slovenia, Turkey, Ukraine to the United States, just to name a few. Thus, EVER is connected to almost the entire world.

EVER offers its members a variety of activities, some of which help members to get in touch, whilst others facilitate professional networking and academic discourse. In this regard EVER established the **job and internship pool** which enables the association to act as intermediary for students who want to get in touch with companies and law firms. Moreover, EVER established a new series of events called "Job opportunities in ..." where alumni talk about their way from the Europa-Institut to their current work position. EVER manages an **address database and a regularly updated register of all members**. Furthermore, EVER grants scholarships to give students the opportunity to finish their postgraduate studies once they encounter financial hardship and as a private **sponsor**, it supports the so-called "Deutschland-Stipendium". Finally, EVER also **supports** the Europa-Institut on a regular basis on the occasion of events, e.g. scientific or certain cultural events of the Europa-Institut. Last but not least, EVER organizes convivial get-togethers which allow for professional **networking**! On top of that, EVER members meet at so called regulars' tables ("Stammtische") in different European cities to support exchange between new students and EVER alumni.

Further information: www.europainstitut.de/ever

Contact
EVER e.V.
Saarland University
Europa-Institut, Law Department
P.O. Box 15 11 50
D-66041 Saarbrücken

Telephone: + 49 (0)681 302 3653
Fax: + 49 (0)681 302 4369
E-mail: ever@europainstitut.de